The Developmental Psychopathology of Eating Disorders

Implications for Research, Prevention, and Treatment

The Developmental Psychopathology of Eating Disorders

Implications for Research, Prevention, and Treatment

edited by

Linda Smolak
Michael P. Levine
Kenyon College
Ruth Striegel-Moore
Wesleyan University

LEA LAWRENCE ERLBAUM ASSOCIATES, PUBLISHERS
1996   Mahwah, New Jersey

Lawrence Erlbaum Associates, Inc., Publishers
10 Industrial Avenue
Mahwah, New Jersey 07430

Cover design by Gail Silverman
Cover illustration by Sean McWilliams

Library of Congress Cataloging-in-Publication Data

The developmental psychopathology of eating disorders : implications for research, prevention, and treatment / edited by Linda Smolak, Michael P. Levine, Ruth Striegel-Moore.
     p.   cm.
    Includes bibliographical references and index.
    ISBN 0-8058-1746-8 (c : alk. paper). — ISBN 0-8058-1747-6 (p : alk. paper)
    1. Eating disorders. 2. Developmental psychology. 3. Eating disorders—Etiology. I. Smolak, Linda, 1951– . II Levine, Michael P. III. Striegel-Moore, Ruth.
    [DNLM: 1. Eating Disorders—etiology. 2. Psychopathology—methods. 3. Personality Development. WM 175 D489 1996]
    RC552.E18D48 1996
    616.85'26—dc20
    DNLM/DLC
    for Library of Congress   **95-43187**
                                 CIP

Books published by Lawrence Erlbaum Associates are printed on acid-free paper, and their bindings are chosen for strength and durability.

Printed in the United States of America
10 9 8 7 6 5 4 3 2

To our daughters

Marlyce Tryon Lagalo

Meghan Claire Keeler

Zeva Rae Levine

Stefanie Elizabeth Neale

Contents

Acknowledgments

Finishing a book requires a combination of good ideas, amazing cooperation, and excellent luck. We have had the good fortune to receive the support and assistance of many people as we worked our way through this project.

This book was born at a conference sponsored by the National Anorexic Aid Society (later National Eating Disorders Organization). We would like to thank Amy Baker Dennis and Laura Hill for providing a conference at which researchers, clinicians, and educators could gather to share ideas and to revitalize their interests. Amy and Laura have been inspirational examples of an unwavering commitment to develop solutions for the problems faced by American women.

This book represents the work of a variety of talented contributors. We are, of course, grateful for their willingness to share their ideas and we will always be impressed by their commitment to the project. This book was never more than a few weeks off deadline because the contributors were willing to be prompt and thorough in their work.

The secretary of the Science Division at Kenyon, Sonja Gallagher, kept things organized for us. We appreciate her work.

As always, the publishing firm's personnel were keys to the organization and execution of this project. We especially want to thank Judith Amsel and Teresa Horton for their support, assistance, and overall effort in making this book a reality.

Finally, any project of this magnitude means someone else had to do extra housework, childcare, household shopping, and so on. That same person was simultaneously asked to enthusiastically provide support and concern. Part of our excellent luck is that we have spouses who will do all of that. We thank James P. Keeler, Mary A. Suydam, and Michael S. Neale for everything.

Linda Smolak
Michael P. Levine
Ruth Striegel-Moore

Contributors

Thomas J. Berndt, PhD   Professor of Psychology, Purdue University, West Lafayette, IN 47907

Marjorie Crago, PhD   College of Medicine, Department of Family and Community Medicine, University of Arizona, 2231 E. Speedway, Tucson, AZ 85719

Mary E. Connors, PhD, ABPP   Professor of Psychology, Illinois School of Professional Psychology, Chicago, IL 60603

Linda S. Estes, PhD   College of Medicine, Department of Family and Community Medicine, University of Arizona, 2231 E. Speedway, Tucson, AZ 85719

Fontaine Ewell   Department of Psychology, Catholic University of America, Washington, DC 20064

Norma Gray, PhD   College of Medicine, Department of Family and Community Medicine, University of Arizona, 2231 E. Speedway, Tucson, AZ 85719

Daniel Hart, PhD   Professor of Psychology, Rutgers University, Camden, NJ 08102

Stephen L. Hestenes, MS   Psychological Sciences, Purdue University, West Lafayette, IN 47907

Russell A. Isabella, PhD   Family and Consumer Studies, 228 Alfred Emery Building, University of Utah, Salt Lake City, UT 84112

Mary Pat Karmel   Illinois Institute of Technology, Department of Psychology, Chicago, IL 60616

Joel D. Killen, PhD Associate Professor, Department of Medicine, Stanford University, School of Medicine, 1000 Welch Road, Palo Alto, CA 94304

Michael P. Levine, PhD Professor of Psychology, Kenyon College, Gambier, OH 43022

Kathleen M. Pike, PhD Assistant Professor of Clinical Psychology, Columbia Presbyterian Medical Center, 722 W. 168th Street, New York, NY 10032

Richard Rende, PhD Department of Psychology, Rutgers University, Busch Campus, New Brunswick, NJ 08903

Karen Rosen, PhD Professor of Psychology, Boston College, Chestnut Hill, MA 02167

Catherine M. Shisslak, PhD College of Medicine, Department of Family and Community Medicine, University of Arizona, 2231 E. Speedway, Tucson, AZ 85719

Susan Smith Department of Psychology, Catholic University of America, Washington, DC 20064

Linda Smolak, PhD Professor of Psychology, Kenyon College, Gambier, OH 43022

Janet Todd 1967 Lyndale Avenue, Memphis, TN 38107

Ruth Striegel-Moore, PhD Professor of Psychology, Wesleyan University, Middletown, CT 06459

Denise E. Wilfley, PhD Associate Research Scientist/Lecturer in Psychology and Co-Director, The Yale Center for Eating and Weight Disorders, Yale University, Department of Psychology, P.O. Box 208205, New Haven, CT 06520

Judith Worell, PhD Educational and Counseling Psychology, University of Kentucky, 235 Dickey Hall, Lexington, KY 40506

Introduction

This book was born out of a transaction between frustration and optimism. The frustrations reflected the limitations of current knowledge
about eating problems and disorders. Etiological "causes" that are
sensitive and specific to eating disorders have been elusive. Although
there is some understanding of risk factors, very little is known about
protective factors. This has made prevention (among other things)
difficult. Furthermore, the mechanisms underlying the association between risk factors and disordered eating are poorly understood. So, for
example, it is known that women are at greater risk than men are, but
experts in the field remain hard-pressed to move beyond gender-based
speculations and to demonstrate why this is true.

The optimism grows from familiarity with the field of developmental
psychopathology. It seems evident to us that this approach has much to
offer the field of eating disorders. We hope that this book is an early step
in the integration of developmental psychopathology into theorizing,
research, treatment, and prevention of eating disorders.

THE EATING DISORDERS

Before we can effectively discuss how developmental psychopathology
and psychology might be particularly valuable in examining eating
disorders, it is important to define the field. Eating disorders include
anorexia nervosa (AN) and bulimia nervosa (BN). Table 1 shows the
definitions provided in the *Diagnostic and Statistical Manual of Mental
Disorders, 4th edition* (*DSM–IV;* American Psychiatric Association,
1994). These definitions are more stringent (i.e., will probably lead to
fewer diagnoses of the disorders) than the earlier *DSM–III* and
DSM–III–R versions that have been used in most of the existing research. Probably about 0.5% of women meet the diagnostic criteria for
AN (Walters & Kendler, 1995) and 1% to 2% of adult women meet BN
diagnostic criteria (Fairburn & Beglin, 1990). The rate may be higher
among adolescents (Striegel-Moore & Marcus, 1995).

TABLE 1
Eating Disorders Definitions

Diagnostic criteria for 307.1 Anorexia Nervosa

A. Refusal to maintain body weight at or above a minimally normal weight for age and height (e.g., weight loss leading to maintenance of body weight less than 85% of that expected; or failure to make expected weight gain during period of growth, leading to body weight less than 85% of that expected).
B. Intense fear of gaining weight or becoming fat. even though underweight.
C. Disturbance in the way in which one's body weight or shape is experienced, undue influence of body weight or shape on self-evaluation, or denial of the seriousness of the current low body weight.
D. In postmenarcheal females, amenorrhea, i.e., the absence of at least three consecutive menstrual cycles. (A woman is considered to have amenorrhea if her periods occur only following hormone, e.g., estrogen, administration.)

Specify type:

Restricting Type: during the current episode of Anorexia Nervosa, the person has not regularly engaged in binge-eating or purging behavior (i.e., self-induced vomiting or the misuse of laxatives, diuretics, or enemas)
Binge-Eating/Purging Type: during the current episode of Anorexia Nervosa, the person has regularly engaged in binge-eating or purging behavior (i.e., self-induced vomiting or the misuse of laxatives, diuretics, or enemas)

Diagnostic criteria for 307.51 Bulimia Nervosa

A. Recurrent episodes of binge eating. An episode of binge eating is characterized by both of the following:
   (1) eating, in a discrete period of time (e.g., within any 2-hour period), an amount of food that is definitely larger than most people would eat during a similar period of time and under similar circumstances
   (2) a sense of lack of control over eating during the episode (e.g., a feeling that one cannot stop eating or control what or how much one is eating)
B. Recurrent inappropriate compensatory behavior in order to prevent weight gain, such as self-induced vomiting; misuse of laxatives, diuretics, enemas, or other medications; fasting; or excessive exercise.
C. The binge eating and inappropriate compensatory behaviors both occur, on average, at least twice a week for 3 months.
D. Self-evaluation is unduly influenced by body shape and weight.
E. The disturbance does not occur exclusively during episodes of Anorexia Nervosa.

Specify type:

Purging Type: during the current episode of Bulimia Nervosa, the person has regularly engaged in self-induced vomiting or the misuse of laxatives, diuretics, or enemas
Nonpurging Type: during the current episode of Bulimia Nervosa, the person has used other inappropriate compensatory behaviors, such as fasting or excessive exercise, but has not regularly engaged in self-induced vomiting or the misuse of laxatives, diuretics, or enemas

307.50 Eating Disorder Not Otherwise Specified

The Eating Disorder Not Otherwise Specified category is for disorders of eating that do not meet the criteria for any specific Eating Disorder. Examples include:

1. For females, all of the criteria for Anorexia Nervosa are met except that the individual has regular menses.
2. All of the criteria for Anorexia Nervosa are met except that, despite significant weight loss, the individual's current weight is in the normal range.
3. All of the criteria for Bulimia Nervosa are met except that the binge eating and inappropriate compensatory mechanisms occur at a frequency of less than twice a week or for a duration of less than 3 months.
4. The regular use of inappropriate compensatory behavior by an individual of normal body weight after eating small amounts of food (e.g., self-induced vomiting after the consumption of two cookies).
5. Repeatedly chewing and spitting out, but not swallowing, large amounts of food.
6. Binge-eating disorder: recurrent episodes of binge eating in the absence of the regular use of inappropriate compensatory behaviors characteristic of Bulimia Nervosa (see p. 729 for suggested criteria).

Research criteria for binge-eating disorder

A. Recurrent episodes of binge eating. An episode of binge eating is characterized by both of the following:
   (1) eating, in a discrete period of time (e.g., within any 2-hour period), an amount of food that is definitely larger than most people would eat in a similar period of time under similar circumstances
   (2) a sense of lack of control over eating during the episode (e.g., a feeling that one cannot stop eating or control what or how much one is eating)
B. The binge-eating episodes are associated with three (or more) of the following:
   (1) eating much more rapidly than normal
   (2) eating until feeling uncomfortably full
   (3) eating large amounts of food when not feeling physically hungry
   (4) eating alone because of being embarrassed by how much one is eating
   (5) feeling disgusted with oneself, depressed, or very guilty after overeating
C. Marked distress regarding binge eating is present.
D. The binge eating occurs, on average, at least 2 days a week for 6 months.
Note: The method of determining frequency differs from that used for Bulimia Nervosa; future research should address whether the preferred method of setting a frequency threshold is counting the number of days on which binges occur or counting the number of episodes of binge eating.
E. The binge eating is not associated with the regular use of inappropriate compensatory behaviors (e.g., purging, fasting, excessive exercise) and does not occur exclusively during the course of Anorexia Nervosa or Bulimia Nervosa.

Note: From American Psychiatric Association (1994), pp. 544–545, 549–550, 731.

Subthreshold eating disorders are discussed in several of the chapters in this book. People with subthreshold disorders are "missing" one or more of the diagnostic criteria. For example, there are women who have not missed three consecutive menstrual periods or have not fallen below 85% of their expected body weight; they cannot be diagnosed with AN even though they may display other symptoms, may have lost substantial weight, and may not be menstruating regularly. These subthreshold women may be diagnosed as having "Eating Disorders–Not Otherwise

Specified" (EDNOS; see Table 1). Estimates suggest that women with such partial (or subthreshold) syndromes constitute 3% to 5% of the general population. They may represent 40% or more of those women presenting at clinics for evaluations for eating disturbances (Shisslak, Crago, & Estes, 1995).

Individuals with EDNOS represent a very heterogeneous group. Members can be expected to have not only followed differing paths to EDNOS, but to find varying paths out of it. Some will develop full-blown AN or BN, others will continue at subthreshold levels, and still others will recover. Their symptoms, comorbid conditions or characteristics, and sequelae may eventually lead researchers to redefine eating disorders categories (Striegel-Moore & Marcus, 1995). In any case, they present a fascinating group from a developmental psychopathology perspective because they represent yet another set of paths, potentially different from those already identified for BN and AN, that the development of eating attitudes and behaviors can take. Given that some of these women will not develop BN or AN, the EDNOS women may also provide some special insight into "last-line-of-defense" protective factors, an area of great importance to developmental psychopathologists (e.g., Garmezy & Masten, 1991; Rosen, chapter 1, this volume) but relatively neglected in the eating disorders literature.

Some of the chapters in the book also deal with binge-eating disorder (BED; see Table 1). Initial prevalence studies suggest that BED occurs in 2% to 3% of adults (Spitzer et al., 1992; Spitzer et al., 1993). It has been included in *DSM–IV* as a provisional diagnostic category in need of further study (American Psychiatric Association, 1994), and is often considered to be a specific example of EDNOS. Bingeing is defined the same way for both BN and BED. There is also some evidence that restrictive dieting may lead to bingeing in both disorders, although it is not the only pathway (Striegel-Moore, 1993). On the other hand, there is virually no empirical research on the connection (or lack thereof) between BN and BED (Striegel-Moore & Marcus, 1995). Furthermore, BED is not marked by purging or by an undue investment in weight and shape in the way BN is. It would, therefore, be premature to assume that etiological models of BN are also applicable to BED. Thus, BED may provide yet another set of pathways, related to but perhaps separate from those for BN, in the development of eating problems.

Like earlier *DSM* editions, *DSM–IV* treats AN, BN, EDNOS, and BED as separate disorders, albeit with some shared personality dimensions. Researchers have, however, found it difficult to distinguish between the etiologies of even AN and BN (but see, e.g., Higgins, Vookles, & Tykocinski, 1992; Smolak & Levine, 1993), much less the more poorly understood EDNOS and BED. Similarly, theorists do not always carefully delineate among them (but see, e.g., Johnson & Connors, 1987). Not surprisingly, then, in several of the chapters in this book, the discussion is of eating disorders in general rather than of AN, BN, EDNOS, or BED specifically.

Finally, this volume does not address obesity. Obesity is, of course, a significant health risk in its own right and is sometimes considered to be (or to reflect) an eating problem (Rand, 1994). Furthermore, BED is probably 2 to 4 times more common among obese people than in the general population, although that still means that approximately 90% of all obese people do not have BED (Striegel-Moore & Marcus, 1995). In addition, obesity shows several important differences from AN, BN, EDNOS, and BED. Obesity is not necessarily associated with psychopathology; it also has a strong genetic component, demonstrates a moderately steady developmental course, and is somewhat more common among men than women (Guo, Roche, Chumlea, Gardner, & Siervogel, 1994; Meyer & Stunkard, 1993; Yuker & Allison, 1994). Obesity is routinely considered to be a medical problem more than a psychological one. Indeed, it does not appear in *DSM–IV.* Clearly, etiological models of obesity are considerably different from those of BN, AN, BED, and EDNOS.

ASSUMPTIONS OF THE BOOK

The argument that application of developmental psychopathology models will bring new insights to the understanding of eating disorders is predicated on two fundamental assumptions. The first is as old as Freudian theory: There is an important relationship between normal and pathological development. In the field of eating disorders, this relationship is represented by the partial continuum between the "normative discontents" (Rodin, Silberstein, & Striegel-Moore, 1985) of weight and shape dissatisfaction and weight control techniques at one end and the extreme attitudes and behaviors symptomatic of eating disorders at the other. A number of chapters in this volume, including those by Rosen (chapter 1); Smolak and Levine (chapter 9); Striegel-Moore and Smolak (chapter 11); Connors (chapter 12); and Shisslak, Crago, Estes, and Gray (chapter 14) describe this continuum and its implications.

Our second assumption is that eating problems and disorders represent transactions among sociocultural, personality, social, and biological factors. In other words, they are developmental phenomena. As such, models, theory, and data from developmental research should be helpful in elucidating the etiology and course of eating problems. Indeed, from the beginning of modern writing about the problem, eating disorders theorists, including Bruch (1973) and Crisp (1980), have cited developmental factors. Unfortunately, limited attention to developmental process has hampered a full understanding of the impact of these factors.

GOALS OF THE BOOK

The lack of attention to developmental processes was one of the concerns that led us to put this book together. This problem has several corollaries and implications, all of which influenced the design of this volume. More specifically, we believed that many of the extant models of the etiology of eating disorders overlooked the developmental mediators and moderators that influenced the nature of eating disorder symptoms during different developmental periods, intervened between a particular risk factor (such as child sexual abuse, inadequate infant–mother attachment, or early puberty) and the appearance of eating symptomatology, and created the interpretive context for such events. In other words, too much emphasis was being placed on particular events. The literature concerning child sexual abuse and eating disorders has dramatically portrayed the problems created by such an approach (Connors & Morse, 1993; Kearney-Cooke & Striegel-Moore, 1994; Waller, Everill, & Calam, 1994; Wooley, 1994).

We also believed that developmental data and methods had not been exploited to their greatest advantage. From our perspective, just keeping up with the eating disorders literature is time-consuming and demanding. Because most eating disorders theorists and researchers have not been trained in developmental psychology, trying to learn that literature on top of the eating disorders and general clinical literature represents an immense (and infinite) task. Therefore, we thought that it would be helpful to assemble up-to-date information on several aspects of developmental psychology that frequently appear in multidimensional models of eating disorders.

Finally, developmental principles and data have implications for treatment and prevention. For example, understanding the developmental demands of the period of maximal risk (e.g., late adolescence) may make it possible to more appropriately target issues for inclusion in prevention programs. We were interested in exploring such implications.

All of these goals, of course, arise from our assumption that developmental psychopathology can provide a helpful approach in health and mental health professionals' endeavors to understand, treat, and prevent eating disorders and symptoms. In summary, then, the book has four specific goals:

1. To introduce the principles and methodologies of developmental psychopathology.
2. To review the work of developmental psychologists in several major areas of behavior relevant to understanding the causes, treatment, and prevention of eating disorders.

3. To apply developmental psychopathology principles to the area of eating problems, both in the form of theoretical models and in specific areas and issues raised by developmental psychopathology.
4. To discuss the implications of developmental approaches for prevention programs and treatment.

STRUCTURE OF THE BOOK

This volume is divided into four sections. Although these sections are interrelated, they are also fairly autonomous. Each one is intended to address one of the primary goals of this book.

Part I constitutes an introduction to the field of developmental psychopathology. Rosen (chapter 1) lays out the fundamental principles of developmental psychopathology, and Smolak (chapter 2) considers their implications for research design and statistics. These chapters form the foundation for later applications (in Part III and IV) of developmental psychopathology to eating disorders.

Part II is arguably the most unusual one. Its first five chapters are overviews of several core areas of developmental psychology that have been repeatedly postulated to be influential in the development of eating disorders. As previously noted, theories referring to these factors have often overlooked key elements of developmental theory and data. The chapters cover the areas of genetics (Rende, chapter 3), social support systems (Berndt & Hestenes, chapter 4), self-development (Ewell, Smith, Karmel, & Hart, chapter 5), gender roles (Worell & Todd, chapter 6), and attachment (Isabella, chapter 7). The focus in these chapters is much more on normal development than on eating disorders (or any other pathology) per se; this may highlight potential sources of protection as well as vulnerability. The final chapter of this section develops specific links between the core areas of developmental psychology and eating disorders (Smolak & Striegel-Moore, chapter 8).

In the chapters in Part III, the principles of developmental process and context have been applied to areas related to eating disorders. These chapters are more the sort one expects to find in a book concerning the developmental psychopathology of a particular disorder. They cover adolescent transitions (Smolak & Levine, chapter 9), media influences (Levine & Smolak, chapter 10), race (Striegel-Moore & Smolak, chapter 11), and developmental vulnerabilities (Connors, chapter 12).

Finally, in Part IV, two chapters examine the implications of developmental models for prevention programs. Killen (chapter 13) looks at what information can be gleaned from other types of prevention programs (e.g., smoking prevention) and presents a comprehensive, school-based prevention program. Shisslak, Crago, Estes, and Gray (chapter

14) consider how prevention programs might be geared to audiences of different ages. In the final chapter of this section, Pike and Wilfley (chapter 15) explore the developmental issues inherent in treating clients of different ages with the different forms of eating disorders. The book closes with a final chapter in which we reflect on the implications of the various contributions in this book for research, treatment, and prevention of eating disorders (Levine, Smolak, & Striegel-Moore, chapter 16).

Overall, we think that we have assembled information important in taking some of the first steps toward employing developmental psychopathology in understanding eating disorders. As always, the chapters often raise as many questions as they answer. This is part of what made us optimistic about the approach's value in the first place. Developmental psychopathology raises new questions for us; we hope that it will provide new answers.

REFERENCES

American Psychiatric Association. (1994). *Diagnostic and statistical manual of mental disorders* (4th ed.). Washington, DC: Author.

Bruch, H. (1973). *Eating disorders: Obesity, anorexia nervosa, and the person within*. New York: Basic Books.

Connors, M., & Morse, W. (1993). Sexual abuse and eating disorders: A review. *International Journal of Eating Disorders, 13*, 1–11.

Crisp, A. (1980). *Anorexia nervosa: Let me be*. Orlando, FL: Grune & Stratton.

Fairburn, C., & Beglin, S. (1990). Studies of the epidemiology of bulimia nervosa. *American Journal of Psychiatry, 147*, 401–408.

Garmezy, N., & Masten, A. (1991). The protective role of competence indicators in children at risk. In E. M. Cummings, A. Greene, & K. Karraker (Eds.), *Life-span developmental psychology: Perspectives on stress and coping* (pp. 151–174). Hillsdale, NJ: Lawrence Erlbaum Associates.

Guo, S., Roche, A., Chumlea, W., Gardner, J., & Siervogel, R. (1994). The predictive value of childhood body mass index values for overweight at age 35 y. *American Journal od Clinical Nutrition, 59*, 810–819.

Higgins, E., Vookles, J., & Tykocinski, O. (1992). Self and health: How "patterns" of self-beliefs predict types of emotional and physical problems. *Social Cognition, 10*, 125–150.

Johnson, C., & Connors, M. (1987). *The etiology and treatment of bulimia nervosa: A biopsychosocial perspective*. New York: Basic Books.

Kearney-Cooke, A., & Striegel-Moore, R. (1994). Treatment of child sexual abuse in anorexia nervosa and bulimia nervosa: A feminist psychodynamic approach. *International Journal of Eating Disorders, 15*, 305–319.

Meyer, J., & Stunkard, A. (1993). Genetics and human obesity. In A. Stunkard & T. Wadden (Eds.), *Obesity: Theory and therapy* (2nd ed., pp. 137–150). New York: Raven.

Rand, C. (1994). Obesity: Definition, diagnostic criteria, and associated health problems. In L. Alexander-Mott & D. Lumsden (Eds.), *Understanding eating disorders: Anorexia nervosa, bulimia nervosa, and obesity* (pp. 221–242). Washington, DC: Taylor & Francis.

Rodin, J., Silberstein, L., & Striegel-Moore, R. (1985). Women and weight: A normative discontent. In T. Sonderegger (Ed.), *Nebraska Symposium on Motivation: Vol. 32. Psychology and gender* (pp. 267–307). Lincoln: University of Nebraska Press.

Shisslak, C., Crago, M., & Estes, L. (1995). The spectrum of eating disturbances. *International Journal of Eating Disorders, 18,* 209–219.

Smolak, L., & Levine, M. (1993). Separation–individuation difficulties and the distinction between bulimia nervosa and anorexia nervosa in college women. *International Journal of Eating Disorders, 14,* 33–41.

Spitzer, R. L., Devlin, M., Walsh, B. T., Hasin, D., Wing, R., Marcus, M., Stunkard, A., Wadden, T., Yanovski, S., Agras, S., Mitchell, J., & Nonas, C. (1992). Binge eating disorder: A multisite field trial of the diagnostic criteria. *International Journal of Eating Disorders, 11,* 191–204.

Spitzer, R. L., Yanovski, S., Wadden, T., Wing, R., Marcus, M. D., Stunkard, A., Devlin, M., Mitchell, J., & Hasin, D. (1993). Binge eating disorder: Its further validation in a multisite study. *International Journal of Eating Disorders, 13,* 137–154.

Striegel-Moore, R. (1993). Etiology of binge eating: A developmental perspective. In C. Fairburn & G. Wilson (Eds.), *Binge eating: Nature, assessment, and treatment* (pp. 144–172). New York: Guilford.

Striegel-Moore, R., & Marcus, M. (1995). Eating disorders in women: Current issues and debates. In A. Stanton & S. Gallant (Eds.), *Women's health* (pp. 445–487). Washington, DC: American Psychological Association.

Waller, G., Everill, J., & Calam, R. (1994). Sexual abuse and eating disorders. In L. Alexander-Mott & D. B. Lumsden (Eds.), *Understanding eating disorders: Anorexia nervosa, bulimia nervosa, and obesity* (pp. 243–270). Washington, DC: Taylor & Francis.

Walters, E., & Kendler, K. (1995). Anorexia nervosa and anorexic-like syndromes in a population-based female twin sample. *American Journal of Psychiatry, 152,* 64–71.

Wooley, S. (1994). Sexual abuse and eating disorders: The concealed debate. In P. Fallon, M. Katzman, & S. Wooley (Eds.), *Feminist perspectives on eating disorders* (pp. 171–211). New York: Guilford.

Yuker, H., & Allison, D. (1994). Obesity: Sociocultural perspective. In L. Alexander-Mott & D. B. Lumsden (Eds.), *Understanding eating disorders: Anorexia nervosa, bulimia nervosa, and obesity* (pp. 243–270). Washington, DC: Taylor & Francis.

I

INTRODUCTION TO DEVELOPMENTAL PSYCHOPATHOLOGY

1

The Principles of Developmental Psychopathology: Illustration From the Study of Eating Disorders

Karen Rosen

The current literature on eating disorders is replete with theoretical explanations for the causes of anorexia nervosa (AN) and bulimia nervosa (BN) and with recommendations for the treatment of these disorders (e.g., Alexander & Lumsden, 1994; Brownell & Foreyt, 1986; Bruch, 1973; Crowther, Tennenbaum, Hobfoll, & Stephens, 1992; Johnson, 1991; Johnson & Connors, 1987; Root, Fallon, & Friedrich, 1986). The approaches to understanding eating disorders range from psychodynamic (Bruch, 1973, 1985; Goodsitt, 1985) to cognitive–behavioral (Fairburn, 1985; Garner, 1986) to a consideration of family systems (Minuchin, Rosman, & Baker, 1978; Sargent, Liebman, & Silver, 1985). Within each of these theoretical orientations, inferences have been made with regard to the primary etiology of the disorder, and an assumption has been made that there is a direct association between predisposing factors and the onset of illness (see, e.g., Becker, Bell, & Billington, 1987; Friedlander & Siegel, 1990). Where the effects of multiple etiological variables have been considered simultaneously (Garfinkel & Garner, 1982; Johnson & Connors, 1987), there is still an implicit assumption that when an eating disorder occurs, these determinants necessarily predispose to illness; what is neglected is a consideration of the actual paths and processes by which, in certain individuals, these diverse factors are transformed over time into disorder.

What appears to be missing from current theoretical perspectives on eating disorders is a consideration of the numerous familial, personality, biological, and sociocultural factors that may contribute to a particular vulnerability to the development of an eating disorder and that may, in combination with certain biophysical, psychological, or environmental stressors, lead to the onset of illness, particularly at especially vulnerable transition periods (cf. Smolak & Levine, 1994; Strober, 1991). This approach to the study of eating disorders requires a more complex framework for conceptualizing etiology, treatment, and prognosis. It also requires the development of diagnostic criteria that consider the age and level of functioning of the individuals being studied, as well as the use of multidimensional research models that incorporate longitudinal prospective studies of adaptation and maladaptation. Developmental psychopathology offers a conceptual paradigm within which to begin addressing these critical issues.

In this chapter the principles of developmental psychopathology are discussed. The historical antecedents to this orientation are identified, and several core concepts of a developmental approach to psychopathology are then presented. The organizational approach to development is described as the framework for developmental psychopathology, along with the central ideas of holism or the understanding of behavior in context, the organization within and between behavioral systems, and the coherence of development. The transactional model is then presented. Finally, the implications of the developmental approach for the study of eating disorders are introduced, particularly in terms of the advantages this approach offers with regard to the conceptualization of eating difficulties, the diagnosis and treatment of eating disorders, and the understanding of the etiological determinants and long-term adaptation of individuals with eating disorders. Several key issues are addressed, including the continuities and discontinuities between normal growth and the development of psychopathologies; the relation between eating problems (e.g., binge eating, dieting) and eating disorders (AN, BN); developmental changes in modes of adaptation and symptom expression; behavioral reorganizations occurring with each salient developmental transition; and compensatory and potentiating mechanisms that may mediate the multiple pathways to the development of eating disorders over time.

THE HISTORICAL CONTEXT WITHIN WHICH THE DEVELOPMENTAL APPROACH TO PSYCHOPATHOLOGY EVOLVED

Prior to the 1970s there were three major developmental theories that figured prominently within the behavioral sciences: psychoanalytic developmental theory, Wernerian organismic–developmental theory, and Piagetian structural developmental theory. These theories were all rooted in the organismic conceptualization of development (Overton, 1984; Overton & Reese, 1973). Implicit in this model was a focus on the dynamic role of the individual, who was seen as playing an active part in the developmental process. This dynamic relationship between the individual and the environment was of primary importance and changed over time. Developmental advances occurred in multiple behavioral domains, and these advances were continually reorganized both within and across behavioral systems. Developmental change was therefore qualitative. This view stood in contrast to the mechanistic model of development, in which the individual was viewed as a passive, reactive organism whose development occurred as a result of external forces; this process resulted only in quantitative change (Overton, 1976; Santostefano, 1978).

Although the developmental theories of Freud, Werner, and Piaget all stemmed from a common organismic tradition (Cicchetti, 1990), there were many important differences between them (see, e.g., Baldwin, 1980). One difference that contributed to an already existing schism between clinicians and researchers was that psychoanalytic theory focused primarily on emotions, whereas the developmental theories of Werner and Piaget emphasized cognition (Cicchetti & Hesse, 1983; Cicchetti & Pogge-Hesse, 1981). As a consequence, psychoanalytic theory was influential among clinicians, and the Wernerian and Piagetian structural developmental theories had a profound influence on researchers (Cicchetti, 1990). Conversely, the developmental theories that so heavily influenced the work of researchers and academicians had minimal impact on clinicians (Anthony, 1956; Santostefano, 1978). Very few academics were conducting clinical research, which further perpetuated the division between the academic and clinical worlds. This distinction also led to an artificial separation between psychoanalysts and developmental researchers: The former were seen as concerned primarily with dysfunction and patterns of disturbed behavior, whereas the latter were viewed as focused on expanding the knowledge base in normal developmental processes.

However, with the evolution of the developmental approach to psychopathology in the 1970s, the distinctions between the clinical and academic worlds began to disappear. Researchers began to recognize the value of clinical inferences, methods, theories, and models; clinicians began to acknowledge that empirical research could help create a solid knowledge base for the assessment of competence, vulnerability, and developmental deviations, and for the testing and validation of theories and models. As the schism became less pronounced, both clinicians and researchers began to appreciate an implicit working assumption inherent in their work: namely, that there was an important interrelation between normal and abnormal functioning. An understanding of pathology could be informed by knowledge of what was normal; alternatively, greater insight into normal processes of development could be achieved by illuminating the causes and consequences of psychopathology. Neither clinicians nor researchers needed to view their work as focused exclusively only on normal or atypical patterns of development; rather, the study of both normal developmental sequences and of alternative pathways of development could provide much-needed information for understanding the roots of adaptation and maladaptation.

Historical precedence for this position was established both by structural developmental researchers and by psychoanalysts. For example, Werner (1948) believed that the study of psychopathology had much value for the understanding of mental development, just as the study of normal development enriched the understanding of psychopathology and facilitated further research. The interconnections between abnormal and normal functioning were also seen in the work of S. Freud (1927/1955b, 1937/1955c, 1940/1955d, 1940/1955e), who viewed normality and abnormality as existing on a continuum and drew no sharp distinctions between the two. In addition, both psychoanalytic theory and the developmental theories of Werner and Piaget provided other important ideas that were integrated into the principles of developmental psychopathology.

The Contributions of Psychoanalytic Theory to Developmental Psychopathology

Psychoanalytic theorists had a significant impact on the principles of developmental psychopathology. In addition to S. Freud's emphasis on the continuity between normality and pathology, the work of Bowlby, Mahler, and A. Freud provided key ideas that were later integrated into the framework of developmental psychopathology. Bowlby's (1944, 1979) efforts to connect the work of ethologists such as Lorenz (1950) with that of experimental psychologists such as Harlow and Zimmerman (1959) foreshadowed the multidisciplinary emphasis found in modern developmental psychopathology. Bowlby also made important contributions to the understanding of the developmental roots of psychopathology in his search for early factors (e.g., maternal deprivation) that led to the later onset of psychopathology (e.g., juvenile delinquency). He maintained that maternal deprivation and other problems in the early mother–child relationship lay at the root of many forms of psychopathology (Bowlby, 1951, 1961, 1969/1982, 1979) and described the process of protest, despair, and detachment as the response to object loss (Bowlby, 1961). He also introduced the concept of *representational models* as the developmental mechanism for explaining the connection between early life events and later behavior. Thus, Bowlby's work had a profound impact on the defining principles of developmental psychopathology (Sroufe, 1986).

Mahler's work on psychopathology was derived directly from analytic developmental theory. Especially noteworthy was her formulation regarding the development of infantile autism. Mahler (1952) attributed infantile autism to a developmental arrest in ego functioning. For example, symbiotic infantile psychosis was characterized by a failure of the early mother–infant symbiotic relationship to progress to the stage of object–libidinal cathexis of the mother. The mental representation of the mother remained regressively fused with the self, leading to the delusion of omnipotence on the part of the child. The developmental transition in the third and fourth years from dependence on the mother toward ego differentiation and psychosexual development could lead to this developmental arrest. According to Mahler, this represented a fearful response on the part of the young child.

Mahler argued that when separation anxiety overwhelmed the fragile ego, the child created the delusion of oneness with the primary care-taker. This could be further accompanied by somatic delusions and hallucinations of reunion, characteristic of symbiotic infantile psychosis (Mahler, 1952). Thus, Mahler's ideas provided developmental psycho-pathologists with a model for viewing pathological outcomes as the result of a disruption in the developmental process, one that was rooted in an early disturbance in the mother–child relationship. Moreover, like Bowlby, Mahler integrated the concept of mental representations into her work, arguing for their importance in both normal and atypical development.

A. Freud (1965) suggested that children's development was normally expected to proceed along "developmental lines." Within her model, children progressed from emotional dependency to emotional self-reli-ance and from egocentricity to companionship. This progress resulted from the mastering of tasks within the realm of object relations (e.g., the internalization of norms). Whatever developmental level was achieved was seen as a result of interactions between the child and the environment, between maturation and adaptation. When problems arose, they needed to be viewed in the context of the expected develop-mental level of functioning. For example, stealing or lying would not be viewed in young children as symptoms of a clinical disorder because young children are not capable of distinguishing cognitively between lying and fantasy. Thus, knowledge of normal development was critical in allowing distinctions to be made between normal, age-appropriate behavior and abnormal behavior.

However, children's development within different domains of func-tioning (e.g., emotional, cognitive, and motor) could progress at different rates. Transitions from one developmental level to the next constituted points of potential vulnerability where arrests, fixations, or regressions could occur; these could undermine movement into the next level and account for developmental delays that might result in temporary or permanent deviations. A. Freud (1965) argued that no sharp line could be drawn between normal and pathological development (cf. S. Freud, 1909/1955a). The demarcation was even more difficult to draw in children, given their constant and often uneven growth toward maturity. Moreover, there was not necessarily a continuity between early and later psychopathology, because a particular early symptom pattern (e.g., aggression, school failure, anxiety, antisocial behavior, and poor peer relations) could result in a different pathological solution in adolescence or adulthood (e.g., depression). Thus, even when symptoms were assumed to reflect the same underlying drive component (e.g., aggression), the overt manifestation of the drive (e.g., in the form of overcontrol, undercontrol, or poorly modulated control of aggression) could be altered with maturation and development.

The Contributions of Organismic Developmental Theory to Developmental Psychopathology

The contributions of both Werner and Kaplan had a profound influence on the understanding of developmental organization in atypical populations; moreover, research with clinical populations has continued to provide support for their developmental framework (see, e.g., Cicchetti & Beeghly, 1987). Werner, who studied a variety of cultures and patient populations, illustrated the significance of developmental psychology for understanding, treating, and preventing abnormal behavior (Werner, 1948, 1957; Werner & Kaplan, 1963). Kaplan (1966), in his studies of psychiatric patients, used the organismic developmental model for examining language and symbolic functioning and elucidated parallels between developmentally early levels of symbolic functioning and those found in psychiatric patients. Although normal development was characterized by increasing differentiation and hierarchical integration of functioning, Kaplan argued that typical patterns of linguistic and symbolic functioning in different forms of pathology could be explained by the principles of disintegration and dedifferentiation.

A number of psychiatric researchers and clinicians have adopted an organismic developmental perspective, relying on the phenomena of dedifferentiation and disintegration to account for the symptoms characteristic of psychopathology (e.g., Arieti, 1955, 1967; Goldstein, 1939, 1948; McGhie & Chapman, 1961; Rapaport, 1951; Shakow, 1946, 1962). Arieti (1967) argued, for example, that primitive forms of cognitions and emotions become hierarchically integrated into more advanced cognitive and affective forms in the process of normal development. With the development of psychopathology, however, these primitive forms may again become available and may be used to reduce anxiety. Because the individual originally operated on a higher level of functioning, this is considered to be a maladaptive or pathological alternative to which the patient would have difficulty adjusting.

The Contributions of Piagetian Developmental Theory to Developmental Psychopathology

Piaget's theory of cognitive development provided a valuable framework for conceptualizing and understanding psychopathology. Although Piaget's framework offered relatively little in its ability to account for emotional functioning (Anthony, 1956), it did elucidate the underlying mental processes that could lead to pathological symptoms (Cicchetti & Hesse, 1983). Individuals could manifest disturbances that reflected a lack of synchronization between chronological age and developmental level. For example, the psychotic child shows evidence of disturbance in both the development of object permanence and in space–time development (Anthony, 1956). This might lead to certain characteristic cognitive or affective symptoms. Moreover, the examination of interrelations between affective and cognitive processes in psychopathology could be essential to understanding developmental retardations or fixations that occur either within or across domains of functioning (Cicchetti & Schneider-Rosen, 1984a). This emphasis on the multidomain approach is reflected in research by developmental psychopathologists (e.g., Cicchetti & Sroufe, 1978).

Piaget's collaborator, Inhelder (1943/1968, 1966, 1976), used developmental theory to diagnose the reasoning abilities of retarded children. She found that mentally retarded children often revealed traces of previous levels of thinking, which reflected a difficulty in integrating one developmental level with the next. Inhelder's developmental perspective added to the understanding of the nature of mental retardation. She identified the ways in which the mentally retarded child failed to demonstrate a movement toward increasing integration, differentiation, and hierarchical organization, as postulated by Piaget and Werner in their developmental models. Even more important, however, she described the nature of the stage transitions and went beyond the simple description of behavior to a consideration of the underlying mechanisms. This, too, reflects a concern that developmental psychopathologists maintain in their work, that is, to elucidate the processes underlying the overt manifestation of behavior, whether adaptive or maladaptive, so as to better understand the multiple factors that may lead to continuity or discontinuity in functioning.

THE PRINCIPLES OF DEVELOPMENTAL PSYCHOPATHOLOGY

Developmental psychopathology provides both researchers and clinicians with a framework for conceptualizing normal and pathological development. It also prescribes a model for considering the multiple transactions among child and familial characteristics and environmental forces that contribute in a dynamic and reciprocal manner to the events and outcomes of the developmental process. The framework that is most useful is the organizational approach to development; the model that is most suitable for understanding psychopathology is the transactional model.

The Organizational Approach to Development

The organizational approach to development offers a set of principles that serve as heuristic tools. These tools are intended to guide the process of identifying meaningful patterns in the diverse and growing body of data that has accumulated in the study of normal and atypical patterns of development (Cicchetti & Schneider-Rosen, 1986; Sroufe & Rutter, 1984). According to this organizational approach, development is viewed as a series of qualitative reorganizations within and across the social, emotional, and cognitive domains. These reorganizations occur as a result of differentiation and hierarchical integration (Kaplan, 1967; Werner, 1957; Werner & Kaplan, 1963), which consists of the articulation and integration of earlier competencies into later modes of functioning within and across behavioral domains. Many variables influence the nature of these reorganizations over time, including biological, behavioral, psychological, environmental, and sociocultural, and these variables exist in a dynamic relation with one another. Thus, adaptation is defined as the integration of early competencies into later modes of functioning, whereas maladaptation is conceived of as a lack of integration of the social, emotional, and cognitive competencies that are important to a particular developmental level (Cicchetti & Schneider-Rosen, 1984a; Kaplan, 1966; Sroufe, 1979; Sroufe & Rutter, 1984).

Early patterns of adaptation tend to promote later adaptation, just as early patterns of maladaptation tend to lead to later maladaptation. Yet this isomorphism in functioning is not the only expectable outcome, particularly as multiple factors may influence the nature of reorganizations over time. Thus, there are many different pathways by which the same developmental outcomes may be achieved, whether these outcomes are adaptive or maladaptive. What is needed in order to map out these different pathways is a framework for conceptualizing "normal development," one that considers the emergence of competencies across the social, emotional, and cognitive domains (e.g., Sroufe, 1979, 1989; Sroufe & Rutter, 1984).

As the individual develops and earlier forms of behavior are hierarchically integrated within more complex forms, there is a concomitant change in the relationship between the individual and the environment. For example, although physiological processes (e.g., temperament) largely influence the individual's initial reactions to external stimuli and guide behavior, cognitive factors play a more important role with development, as children come to interpret, filter, and actively "construct" their experiences. Behavior and thought are therefore no longer distinct; the individual's reactions to the external environment reflect an integration of temperamental responses and cognitive processes. Changes in the relationship between the individual and the environment also occur as children become more psychologically differentiated from their caregivers and develop a conception of themselves and their emotions; this results in transformations in their social relationships, which in turn have an effect on the opportunities that are created for further social, emotional, and cognitive growth (Schneider-Rosen, 1990).

Although early structures are incorporated into later ones by means of hierarchical integration, they still remain accessible to the individual and can be activated during periods of crisis, transition, stress, novelty, and creativity. This notion of hierarchic motility accounts for the apparent regression to a less mature level of functioning within a relevant domain, followed by renewed differentiation, integration, and organization (e.g., in problem-solving; Werner, 1957). Thus, a 4-year-old who is presented with a challenging shape-sorting problem to solve may initially become distressed and may attempt methods that were appropriate at a younger age (e.g., putting pieces into his or her mouth, turning them over, building a tower with them). However, these methods may then be replaced by more developmentally appropriate behaviors (e.g., sorting the pieces into differently colored piles and then turning over the shape sorter and working on the other side). The flexible use of earlier structures facilitates the negotiation of the stressful task; this capacity to substitute relatively immature behaviors with those that are more suitable for the child's age represents the mobility of functioning that promotes adaptation to the environment.

Alternatively, however, the 4-year-old may pick up the puzzle pieces, attempt unsuccessfully to put them into different holes in the puzzle, put them into his or her mouth, try to open the top of the shape sorter, become frustrated when he or she cannot open the locked lid, stack the pieces on top of each other, knock them down, throw them on the floor, start to cry, and run around the room looking for something else to do. The inflexible use of early structures with regard to the current adaptational task (i.e., solving the problem) may indicate a maladaptive behavioral pattern. The increased frustration and intensification of distress and the inability to develop a more appropriate solution to the problem signify a regression to an earlier mode of functioning that prevents adaptation to the current situation. Therefore, it is not the use of early, less differentiated behaviors that is atypical; rather, it is the inability to negotiate a stressful situation by modulating one's responses and integrating earlier modes with more recently developed patterns of functioning that signifies an atypical pattern of responding.

More recently integrated patterns of behavior are most susceptible to disruption during periods of stress, yielding to earlier, less differentiated forms (Sroufe & Rutter, 1984). However, earlier forms are always still available to the individual and are part of the person's ongoing adaptation, being used at times to promote adaptation to the environment. Hierarchic motility does not necessarily demand a going back in time, as does the psychoanalytic concept of regression. Individuals who are able to exploit this capacity for hierarchic motility are presumably best able to cope with stressors and to deal with transitions, change, and novelty. Psychopathology may in part result from a lack of motility, from an inability to redifferentiate following periods of regression in response to stressors, or from the inflexible use of less differentiated modes despite the demands of the ongoing adaptational task (Cicchetti & Schneider-Rosen, 1986).

Holism: The Evaluation of Behavior in Context.   The frequency or duration of particular behaviors is not as critical as the organization of these behaviors in development. This is because any behavior can serve a variety of different functions depending on the context in which it is evaluated; the same function within one context may be served by many different behaviors (Santostefano, 1978; Sroufe & Waters, 1977; Werner & Kaplan, 1963). Interrelationships between behaviors are only meaningful to the extent that those behaviors play the same or related functions. These principles of organization have several implications. First, it is necessary to consider context in order to understand the meaning and significance of any behavior or group of behaviors that have been integrated into a distinct pattern within that context. Second, the biological, emotional, and motivational needs of the individual often have to be inferred from the ongoing situation so as to further define the context in which the individual is operating; observable behaviors reflect these needs and influence them in a reciprocal manner (see Rothbaum & Rosen, 1991). Third, context may also include the psychologically significant relationships that the individual develops; these relationships often provide further information for understanding individual behavior (Schneider-Rosen, 1990). For example, a 2-year-old may display gaze aversion upon reunion with a caregiver from whom he or she has been separated for several minutes. However, the gaze aversion alone is not a sufficient index of an avoidant attachment pattern: It may be accompanied by a movement away from and subsequent ignoring of the caregiver, in which case it may signify avoidance, or it may enable the child to redirect attention back to an ongoing activity in which the caregiver is then invited to participate, thereby suggesting a secure attachment pattern (Schneider-Rosen, 1990). Thus, the interpretation of the gaze aversion can only be made by considering the behaviors in context.

Behavioral Systems. The organizational approach conceptualizes development in terms of emerging competencies in three general behavioral systems or domains: social, emotional, and cognitive. Specific developmental advances may be identified within each of these domains, reflecting the increased differentiation of early competencies and the integration within and between behavioral systems. Moreover, these emerging competencies influence the resolution of developmental tasks or issues that may be identified at each stage of development (e.g., Sroufe, 1979, 1989).

As an example, learning to explore and to modulate affect in the first year are two early competencies that emerge in the cognitive and emotional domains, respectively, although they also reflect the reciprocal influence of each domain on the other (for instance, modulating affect requires the cognitive capacity to identify and discriminate between different affective states). The increased differentiation of these abilities within each domain, the integration of these abilities with additional emerging competencies across domains (e.g., object permanence, prelinguistic skills, affective signaling), and the development of these competencies in the context of the early caregiving relationship all lay the groundwork for the negotiation of an early developmental task, that of developing an attachment relationship.

Similarly, the resolution of subsequent developmental tasks is influenced by emerging competencies within and across these behavioral domains. Examples of such tasks include exploration and mastery between 12 and 18 months, the development of autonomy and a sense of self between 18 and 30 months, and impulse management, gender role identification, and the development of peer relations between 30 months and 5 years. The manner in which previous issues have been resolved influences the negotiation of each of these new issues; moreover, the previous issues continue to be important to the individual, although they will become less salient relative to the new developmental task (Schneider-Rosen, 1990).

The organization of the social, emotional, and cognitive behavioral systems in normal development, and the lack of organization in psychopathology, are two central concerns of developmental psychopathologists. The development of competencies in one behavioral system may be a necessary condition for the development of competencies in another. Advances or lags in one behavioral system, when compared to the others, may help to account for developmental deviations or delays. These system lags may result in the development of compensatory mechanisms or may leave the individual vulnerable to pathology (see Cicchetti

& Schneider-Rosen, 1984a; Schneider-Rosen, Braunwald, Carlson, & Cicchetti, 1985).

The Coherence of Development. Evaluating the organization of developing competencies in the child at different periods of development requires an analysis of process, which is as important as the study of outcome (see Werner, 1957). Development is seen as following a lawful pattern whereby there is a coherence to each individual's development across periods of discontinuous growth and despite transformations in overt behavior (Rutter, 1983; Sroufe & Rutter, 1984). Consistency is expected in the general adaptive or maladaptive pattern achieved while the individual is organizing experiences and interacting with the environment (Block & Block, 1980; Rutter, 1977). Thus, a particular organization of behavior displayed in one context at a given developmental level is not necessarily expected to recur in the same pattern or in similar contexts at a later point in development. Nevertheless, there is coherence in the manner in which experiences are integrated and organized. This continuity is especially important to maintaining integrity of function, although there may be multiple pathways to achieving adaptation or maladaptation (Rutter, 1990).

Continuity is preserved by an orderly development in the organization of behaviors. The expression of adaptation and maladaptation will be characterized by continuities in underlying cognitive and personality structures, which Cicchetti and Schneider-Rosen (1986) termed *molar continuities*. At the molecular level, however, the behaviors that are exhibited at different developmental periods may vary (Block & Block, 1980; Kagan, 1980; Kohlberg, LaCrosse, & Ricks, 1972), resulting in molecular discontinuities and change. Thus, despite behavioral change and homotypic discontinuity, there is an underlying organization and continuity of functioning in adaptation and maladaptation (Schneider-Rosen, 1990).

The Transactional Model

The developmental approach suggests a more complex transactional model, in which the individual and the environment exert a dynamic, reciprocal influence on each other over time (Sameroff & Chandler, 1975; Smolak, 1986). This transactional model extends beyond the consideration of simple, linear main effects or static interactional determinants of outcome. It recognizes the importance of the dynamic transactions between genetic, constitutional, biochemical, neurobiological, psychological, and sociocultural factors as they influence behavior. If pathology occurs, it is considered to result from a longstanding maladaptive response pattern that the individual has developed over time. The continued manifestation of maladaptation depends on support from the environment, which both determines the child's characteristics and is determined by them. Continuity of experience, continuity in individual reactions to the environment, and continuity in coping methods and family interactions are more likely to predict the development and maintenance of disordered behavior than any single event in an individual's early experiences.

The multiple factors that operate in a pathological process of development do so through a hierarchy of dispositions (see Cicchetti & Schneider-Rosen, 1986). For example, a genetic diathesis to the early onset of pubertal changes may create a predisposition to control food intake through the emergence of dieting behavior, but only given the action of certain psychological mechanisms such as perfectionist strivings, depressive symptoms, feelings of ineffectiveness, or self-regulatory deficits (Johnson & Maddi, 1986). The dieting behavior may in turn lead to the development of body image disturbances and other problems in self-representations and self-esteem, but only given a particular pattern of socialization such as that found in families with high achievement standards, blurred interpersonal boundaries, and little support for autonomy. The relative importance of each of these potential factors may vary over time, as well as with regard to the onset or maintenance of a pathological process.

The transactional model also suggests that certain factors may operate as potentiating or risk factors that increase the likelihood that psychopathology may occur, whereas other compensatory factors may decrease vulnerability and enhance resilience. The potentiating factors may create an enduring vulnerability to disorder or reflect a more transient challenger to the individual; similarly, the compensatory factors may be relatively enduring protective factors or more transient buffers. The relation between development and these potentiating and compensatory factors is important to study. It may be that both the enduring vulnerability to disorder and the protective factors that compensate against disorder are dependent on certain developmental changes necessary for their operation. In contrast, the more transient challengers and buffers may be age specific and may vary with developmental level. Moreover, there may be a coordination among potentiating and compensatory factors such that for every potentiating factor that develops there may be a corresponding compensatory one, accounting for the "self-righting" characteristic of development (Sameroff & Chandler, 1975; Waddington, 1966).

Finally, according to the transactional model, no one period of development is central in determining the course of development, and difficulties in the early years are not inevitably predictive of later psychopathology (Sroufe, 1989). However, an early adaptational solution that may be critical to the child at one point in development (e.g., developing an avoidant attachment relationship to an abusive parent) may compromise development at a later point (because avoidance in infant attachment relationships is associated with problems in toddler peer relations; see Schneider-Rosen et al., 1985). Moreover, although childhood disorders are not directly linked to the same disorders in adulthood (with a few possible exceptions, such as antisocial behavior; Robins, 1978), childhood adaptations may leave the individual differentially vulnerable to particular adult disorders.

THE IMPLICATIONS OF DEVELOPMENTAL PSYCHOPATHOLOGY FOR THE STUDY OF EATING DISORDERS

The developmental perspective views normal processes of development with reference to what they may contribute to an understanding of psychopathology. Recent advances in the understanding of social, emotional, and cognitive development have been significant in providing a frame of reference for identifying particular deviations relevant to AN and BN; these include the study of self-development (Cassidy, 1990; Damon & Hart, 1982; Harter, 1983; Lewis & Brooks-Gunn, 1979), emotional regulation (Greenberg, Kusche, & Speltz, 1991), social development (Bretherton & Waters, 1985; Greenberg, Cicchetti, & Cummings, 1990; Sroufe, 1989), sociocognitive development (Selman, 1980), and sex-role development (Jacklin & Maccoby, 1983). It is within this context that significant progress may be made in the classification and categorization of eating disorders; researchers and clinicians need to rely on this expanding knowledge base to determine deviations from the normal course of development that are unique to AN and BN.

A developmental approach to psychopathology necessitates a consideration of the age-appropriate experience and expression of symptomatic behavior for the particular disorder under study. Age-appropriate advances in the child's social, emotional, or cognitive development influence the patterning, duration, and temporal course of symptomatology. Thus, what appears to be disordered behavior at one age may look very different at another. The childhood precursors of eating disorders may take a different form from that which is seen in adolescence or adulthood; thus, the symptoms of AN and BN need to be viewed in terms of the age and developmental level of the individual.

The links between these disorders in childhood, in adolescence, and in adulthood need to be better understood. It would be erroneous to assume that adult forms of the disorders are equivalent to childhood versions, as if children were miniature adults; it would be equally problematic to assume that the childhood manifestations of AN or BN necessarily portend the same adult syndromes. Some childhood disorders may be transient reactions to developmental or situational stressors, whereas others may well be early signs of certain adult disorders (Achenbach, 1990). However, there is not enough research to date that confirms that eating disorders in childhood lead to eating disorders in adulthood. The developmental periods that may be most critical for determining later patterns of adaptation or maladaptation have not been identified. Also, it is not clear whether early clinical problems are the result of some continuous maladaptive process, whether they will interfere with subsequent development, or whether they are early manifestations of disorders that will become apparent at later developmental periods.

The possibility arises that certain characteristics identified as central to true eating disorders may not be present in young children and that developmental limitations may prevent their appearance until some later point. This is the case, for example, with lack of interoceptive awareness, considered to be one of the critical components of eating disorders (Bruch, 1973; Garfinkel & Garner, 1982). Questions have been raised concerning whether prepubertal children who are diagnosed as anorexic (e.g., Gowers, Crisp, Joughin, & Bhat, 1991) can truly possess this characteristic, which is thought to underlie the "nervosa" component of the disorder (Smolak & Levine, 1994). Developmental limitations may make children incapable of identifying and distinguishing internal emotions and needs and of integrating iinguistic and cognitive information such that this information can both mediate impulse control and contribute to self-awareness. Thus, although the inability to integrate these components may be a central deficit in older individuals with eating disorders (Greenberg et al., 1991), it may not be appropriate to include this characteristic as central to the identification of eating disorders in children.

It is interesting to note that two of the major eating disorders, AN and BN, were included in earlier versions of the *Diagnostic and Statistical Manual of Mental Disorders* (3rd ed. [*DSM–III*]; American Psychiatric Association, 1980; 3rd ed., rev. [*DSM–III–R*]; American Psychiatric Association, 1987), in the section of disorders of infancy, childhood, and adolescence. Whereas clinicians and researchers working with other childhood disorders, for example, childhood depression, were required to extrapolate from the adult criteria in order to accurately diagnose the disorder in children (Cicchetti & Schneider-Rosen, 1984b, 1986), the diagnostic criteria for eating disorders were considered with regard to the specific manifestation of symptoms in children and adolescents.

What was missing from *DSM–III* and *DSM–III–R,* however, was a description of earlier problem behaviors that may not have comprised a clear eating disorder but that may have reflected early precursors to AN or BN. The developmental approach provides a reminder that there may be early signs of a developing eating disorder that may not reflect a fully developed and diagnosable syndrome but that include some of the affective and cognitive aspects of an eating disorder; for example, intense fears of gaining weight or a disturbance in the way in which body weight is experienced. When a child makes the transition to adolescence, the manner in which these fears or concerns are expressed may vary at the molecular level owing to cognitive or affective advances that influence the experience and expression of certain symptoms. Thus, one may not expect to find behavioral isomorphism in the way in which symptoms manifest themselves in childhood versus in adolescence, although at the molar level there is a continuity or isomorphism.

In the most recent edition of the *Diagnostic and Statistical Manual of Mental Disorders* (4th ed. [*DSM–IV*]; American Psychiatric Association, 1994), the eating disorders have been placed in a separate category from the disorders of infancy, childhood, and adolescence. Perhaps this shift was intended to reflect the finding that eating disorders more commonly appear in adolescence or young adulthood (Attie & Brooks-Gunn, 1989). The unfortunate consequence is that now clinicians working with children once again need to apply the same criteria appropriate for older patients. Thus, clinicians and researchers must intuitively adjust the criteria in a manner appropriate to the particular developmental levels of children and adolescents, being sensitive to the behavioral differences at the molecular level.

Some of the criteria that were introduced to provide greater clarity in the conception of BN or AN in older patients (e.g., "undue influence of body weight or shape on self-evaluation," APA, 1994, p. 545) may still be appropriate for younger children, who often include conceptions of possessions or of their bodies in self-descriptions (what Damon & Hart, 1982, called *material characteristics*). Nevertheless, the self-evaluations in younger children may be more transient, less well articulated, and less available to them in their spontaneous self-descriptions (see Cicchetti & Schneider-Rosen, 1986). Thus, the introduction of these criteria, although potentially useful in working with older patients, may once again complicate the diagnostic classification of children or adolescents. If the developmental approach is to be integrated into current diagnostic formulations for eating disorders, then more precise criteria need to be delineated by referring to the normal sequence of development. Only then will it be possible to specify the ways in which the expression of the molar symptoms of an eating disorder remain stable, even when there is substantial variation at the molecular level (see Cicchetti & Schneider-Rosen, 1986). This will contribute to greater reliability in the diagnosis of eating disorders.

A developmental approach is also important for understanding the etiology and sequelae of eating disorders. A variety of etiological factors have been implicated in eating disorders (see, e..g, Bruch, 1973; Johnson & Connors, 1987; Levine & Smolak, 1992; Wonderlich, 1992). In most cases, the model of causality that is advocated is a main effects model, where the eating disorder is seen to be the direct and inevitable result of some specific early pathogenic experience or of some more general process that affects development over time. Thus, for example, a failure to negotiate successfully the separation–individuation process (Mahler, Pine, & Bergman, 1975) during the first 3 years of life is viewed as critical to developing an eating disorder in later life (Johnson & Connors, 1987). Researchers who study eating disorders using this model focus on uncovering these early separation–individuation difficulties to substantiate their etiological view.

However, this main-effects model posits a determinism that is rarely seen so unequivocally in clinical practice and is not supported consistently by experimental work (see, e.g., Finn, Hartman, Leon, & Lawson, 1986). The individual is not viewed as being capable of actively responding to the presumed factor that causes the pathology; thus, the individual is seen as a passive victim of early influences. This simplistic model cannot address the question of why the eating disorder may not appear until years after the pathological experience, or of the role of individual or environmental factors that might influence the form, content, or severity of the eating disorder. Related to this concern is the fact that a failure to examine experiences that occur throughout the life span ignores the possibility that these experiences may either interact with the early pathological experience and mitigate against their potentially negative impact or create new vulnerabilities that may result in more severe pathology (e.g., as when an eating disorder develops concomitant to a character disorder such as the borderline or narcissistic personality disorder; Johnson & Connors, 1987).

Future longitudinal research will be important in articulating the relevance of the transactional model for the study of AN and BN. The beginning point for developing this model specifically for the study of eating disorders comes from a consideration of the multiple factors that have been implicated in the etiology of AN and BN. It has been found, for example, that adolescence, a period associated with extensive biological and physical changes and psychological challenges, creates particular problems for girls (Attie & Brooks-Gunn, 1989; Crisp, 1984). The increase in body fat that occurs during the pubertal years is one of the most dramatic physical changes associated with puberty (Brooks-Gunn & Warren, 1985) and has been found to be associated with desires to be thinner (Dornbusch et al., 1984). Other pubertal changes such as breast development may also lead to efforts to control food intake, particularly in girls from higher social status backgrounds (Dornbusch et al., 1984). The process of integrating these physical changes with feelings about the self requires a reorganization of the adolescent's body image and self-representations (Blos, 1962).

A variety of socialization agents instill in girls the message that they should be concerned with physical appearance; these agents include families, peers, schools, the mass media, children's books, and television. Evidence of an inverse relationship between social class and weight (Stunkard, D'Aquili, Fox, & Filion, 1972) and the correlations of weight problems with gender and affluence (Striegel-Moore, McAvay, & Rodin, 1986), considered together with the gender-related pressures to aspire to a thin body ideal, reflect the importance of sociocultural influences in mediating concerns about weight (Garfinkel & Garner, 1982) and place women at greater risk for eating disorders than men (see Striegel-Moore, Silberstein, & Rodin, 1986, for a review).

There are certain family characteristics that may increase the likelihood that an eating disorder will develop. Specifically, the enmeshment, rigidity, parental overprotectiveness, and lack of conflict resolution that characterize the "psychosomatic family" (Minuchin et al., 1978) have been identified as a general risk factor for the development of psychopathology; the combination of this pattern with more specific risk factors inherent in the sociocultural milieu, the family context, and the individual may lead to the development of an eating disorder (Rodin, Striegel-Moore, & Silberstein, 1990).

For example, the families of women with eating disorders have been found to advocate high standards for achievement, provide little support for autonomy, and maintain blurred interpersonal boundaries (Kog, Vandereycken, & Vertommen, 1985; Minuchin et al., 1978). Individual personality characteristics such as perfectionistic strivings, self-regulatory deficits (e.g., the inability to appropriately modulate affect and impulse), feelings of ineffectiveness, and depressive symptoms have been frequently observed in patients with eating disorders (Johnson & Maddi, 1986). The combination of these individual and familial variables may heighten vulnerability to developing an eating disorder; this is particularly true in the adolescent period, when there are salient developmental tasks that need to be negotiated and increased sociocultural pressures that mediate the resolution of these tasks. Three primary psychological tasks that both male and female adolescents need to master include achieving a new and cohesive sense of self that allows for the regulation of mood and control of impulses; establishing peer relationships, and heterosexual relationships in particular; and developing greater psychological and physical autonomy while concomitantly loosening the childhood ties to parents (Attie & Brooks-Gunn, 1989; Blyth & Traeger, 1983; Erikson, 1968; Gunnar & Collins, 1988; Lerner & Foch, 1987; Simmons, Blyth, & McKinney, 1983; Tobin-Richards, Boxer, & Petersen, 1983; Wittig, 1983). The negotiation and resolution of these stage-salient tasks depends on the emergence of certain social, emotional, and cognitive competencies that result in increased differentiation and hierarchical integration of previously developed abilities. For example, the entrance into formal operational thought allows for greater modulation and control of a broader range of affective reactions and of more differentiated impulses. It also results in newly organized conceptions of the self and of the self in relation to others.

The manner in which these developmental tasks of adolescence are negotiated differs for males and females. It is commonly believed that women define themselves primarily with reference to relationships, through connections to others, whereas men view individuation and a sense of agency as central in forming a sense of self (Chodorow, 1978; Gilligan, 1982; Miller, 1976; but see Berndt & Hestenes, chapter 4, this volume). Thus, these gender differences are likely to influence the ways in which these tasks are resolved (Striegel-Moore, Silberstein, & Rodin, 1986). For example, because the self-image of adolescent girls seems to be more interpersonally oriented than that of boys, girls seem to worry more about what people think of them, try to avoid negative reactions from others, are more self-conscious and insecure, and care more about being liked (McGuire & McGuire, 1982; Simmons & Rosenberg, 1975). These qualities make the adolescent girl, in an effort to avoid negative evaluations by others and to reduce feelings of insecurity, more sensitive to and compliant with sociocultural standards and gender-role expectations. Therefore, it is not a surprise to find the adolescent girl more concerned with and unhappy about her pubertal increase in fat (Striegel-Moore, McAvay, & Rodin, 1986). However, it is then necessary to ask why some adolescents, given all of these relevant etiological factors, never develop eating disorders. What individual characteristics (e.g., self-regulatory deficits) interact with what particular biological risk factors (e.g., the early onset of puberty), family variables (e.g., early and repeated occurrences of sexual abuse), and sociocultural factors (e.g., demands for achievement) to lead to the development of a clearly defined eating disorder (as opposed to an obsession with dieting or compulsive eating, which may be less severe manifestations of maladaptation)? And how do these multiple influences shift in importance during different stages of development?

The transactional model provides a means of organizing existing data on the etiology of eating disorders; moreover, it identifies certain questions that still need to be addressed if the development of AN and BN is to be fully understood. For example, the model could be further elaborated as future research identifies the salient potentiating and compensatory factors relevant to eating disorders and determines which of these factors are transient and which are enduring. The potentiating factors that are relatively enduring characteristics of the individual, the family, or the social environment and that have been identified as playing a significant role in the etiology of eating disorders may then be viewed as vulnerability factors, whereas more transient individual, familial, or environmental factors that could trigger the onset of an episode of illness may be viewed as challengers. Distinguishing between these vulnerability factors and challengers could have important implications for the treatment and prevention of eating disorders.

Similarly, an understanding of the compensatory factors that enhance resilience and protect individuals from developing an eating disorder even when the risk factors are present could help in prevention efforts as well (Rutter, 1985, 1990). These include both the transient buffers, which protect the individual during periods of unexpected stress, and the enduring protective factors, which include relatively stable psychological, biological, and sociocultural influences. It is also possible that the potentiating and compensatory factors for AN and BN are quite separate; the question of common versus distinct factors for these two eating disorders requires further attention and research to resolve the current controversy over the relationship between them (see Fairburn & Garner, 1986).

CONCLUSIONS AND DIRECTIONS FOR FUTURE RESEARCH

The developmental perspective reminds us that disordered behavior is not different in kind from that of normal individuals; rather, behavior disturbances may be seen as falling along a continuum of severity. With regard to the eating disorders, this continuum may be thought of as beginning on one end with dieting as a response to the physical changes and psychosocial challenges of puberty. Further along the continuum are the persistent patterns of compulsive eating associated with certain personality characteristics; these characteristics reflect a failure to resolve salient development tasks (e.g., enhanced autonomy, modulation of impulses and of expressions of mood states, and integration of changing images of the body and self). At the far end of the continuum are the more serious psychosocial impairments and eating disturbances seen in adolescents with eating disorders (Attie & Brooks-Gunn, 1989). Viewing eating disorders within the context of this developmental perspective raises questions with regard to the individual, familial, or sociocultural factors that move an individual along this continuum to developing AN or BN.

Longitudinal prospective research could identify a population of young women at risk for eating disorders owing to their familial or sociocultural environment and focus on the group's transition from childhood to adolescence. An important component of the research would be the identification and isolation of the multiple potentiating and compensatory factors that may influence the developmental process. This will help to illuminate those variables that are differentially or commonly associated with the onset of AN and BN, as well as those that lead to resilience. In particular, those women who appear to be resilient in spite of the presence of potentiating factors are an important group to study in an effort to better understand the causes of eating disorders. The little that is known about the development of eating disorders during childhood and adolescence comes from a few retrospective reports and longitudinal investigations (e.g., Attie & Brooks-Gunn, 1989, 1992; Smolak, Levine, & Gralen, 1993). The adoption of an organizational developmental approach in future prospective studies is especially appropriate because it is likely that individual vulnerability, established in the process of development, is likely to interact with the stressors of adolescence and lead to disorder only in a relatively small sample of adolescent girls.

Use of the transactional model would be helpful for addressing questions concerning, for example, the aspects of female development that make women more vulnerable than men to developing eating disorders or the reasons that some women are more vulnerable than other women. Additional questions that this model would help to illuminate relate to the various pathways toward the development of an eating disorder, the kinds of potentiating factors that heighten vulnerability at different ages to different forms of eating disorders, the maintenance of adaptive functioning despite the presence of early potentiating factors, and the potential for identifying different pathways that lead to the two major types of eating disorders.

More research that is conducted within the framework of the developmental perspective would provide much-needed information that could refine our understanding of the etiology, course, and sequelae of AN and BN. This could, in turn, facilitate the development of more sophisticated diagnostic schemes and treatment plans, thereby influencing clinical intervention. Thus, the principles of developmental psychopathology provide important guidelines for the direction in which future work needs to proceed in order to formulate a more comprehensive model of the development of eating disorders that would have implications for researchers and clinicians.

REFERENCES

Achenbach, T. M. (1990). What is "developmental" about developmental psychopathology? In J. Rolf, A. S. Masten, D. Cicchetti, K. H. Nuechterlein, & S. Weintraub (Eds.), *Risk and protective factors in the development of psychopathology* (pp. 29–48). New York: Cambridge University Press.

Alexander, L., & Lumsden, D. B. (Eds.). (1994). *Understanding eating disorders.* Washington, DC: Taylor & Francis.

American Psychiatric Association. (1980). *Diagnostic and statistical manual of mental disorders* (3rd ed.). Washington, DC: Author.

American Psychiatric Association. (1987). *Diagnostic and statistical manual of mental disorders* (3rd ed., rev.). Washington, DC: Author.

American Psychiatric Association. (1994). *Diagnostic and statistical manual of mental disorders* (4th ed.). Washington, DC: Author.

Anthony, E. J. (1956). The significance of Jean Piaget for child psychiatry. *British Journal of Medical Psychology, 29,* 20–34.

Arieti, S. (1955). *Interpretation of schizophrenia.* New York: Brunner/Mazel.

Arieti, S. (1967). *The intrapsychic self: Feeling, cognition, and creativity in health and mental illness.* New York: Basic Books.

Attie, I., & Brooks-Gunn, J. (1989). Development of eating problems in adolescent girls: A longitudinal study. *Developmental Psychology, 25,* 70–79.

Attie, I., & Brooks-Gunn, J. (1992). Developmental issues in the study of eating problems. In J. H. Crowther, D. L. Tennenbaum, S. E. Hobfoll, & M. A. P. Stephens (Eds.), *The etiology of bulimia nervosa: The individual and familial context* (pp. 35–58). Washington, DC: Hemisphere.

Baldwin, A. (1980). *Theories of child development.* New York: Wiley.

Becker, B., Bell, M., & Billington, R. (1987). Object relations ego deficits in bulimic college women. *Journal of Consulting and Clinical Psychology, 43,* 92–95.

Block, J. H., & Block, J. (1980). The role of ego-control and ego-resiliency in the organization of behavior. In W. A. Collins (Ed.), *Minnesota symposia on child psychology, Vol. 13: Development of cognition, affect, and social relations* (pp. 39–101). Hillsdale, NJ: Lawrence Erlbaum Associates.

Blos, P. (1962). *On adolescence: A psychoanalytic interpretation.* New York: The Free Press.

Blyth, D. A., & Traeger, C. M. (1983). The self-concept and self-esteem of early adolescents. *Theory Into Practice, 22,* 91–97.

Bowlby, J. (1944). *Forty-four juvenile thieves.* London: Bailliere, Tindall, & Cox.

Bowlby, J. (1951). *Maternal care and mental health* (WHO Monograph No. 2). Geneva: World Health Organization.

Bowlby, J. (1961). Childhood mourning and its implications for psychiatry. *American Journal of Psychiatry, 118,* 481–498.

Bowlby, J. (1979). *The making and breaking of affectional bonds.* London: Tavistock.

Bowlby, J. (1982). *Attachment and loss: Vol. 1. Attachment.* New York: Basic Books. (Original work published 1969)

Bretherton, I., & Waters, E. (Eds.). (1985). Growing points in attachment theory and research. *Monographs of the Society for Research in Child Development, 50* (1–2, Serial No. 209).

Brooks-Gunn, J., & Warren, M. P. (1985). Measuring physical status and timing in early adolescence: A developmental perspective. *Journal of Youth and Adolescence, 14,* 163–184.

Brownell, K. D., & Foreyt, J. P. (1986). *Handbook of eating disorders.* New York: Basic Books.

Bruch, H. (1973). *Eating disorders: Obesity, anorexia nervosa and the person within.* New York: Basic Books.

Bruch, H. (1985). Four decades of eating disorders. In D. M. Garner & P. E. Garfinkel (Eds.), *Handbook of psychotherapy for anorexia and bulimia* (pp. 7–18). New York: Guilford.

Cassidy, J. (1990). Theoretical and methodological considerations in the study of attachment and the self in young children. In M. T. Greenberg, D. Cicchetti, & E. M. Cummings (Eds.), *Attachment in the preschool years: Theory, research, and intervention* (pp. 87–119). Chicago: University of Chicago Press.

Chodorow, N. (1978). *The reproduction of mothering: Psychoanalysis and the sociology of gender.* Berkeley: University of California Press.

Cicchetti, D. (1990). A historical perspective on the discipline of developmental psychopathology. In J. Rolf, A. S. Masten, D. Cicchetti, K. H. Nuechterlein, & S. Weintraub (Eds.),

Risk and protective factors in the development of psychopathology (pp. 2–28). New York: Cambridge University Press.

Cicchetti, D., & Beeghly, M. (Eds.). (1987). *Atypical symbolic development*. San Francisco: Jossey-Bass.

Cicchetti, D., & Hesse, P. (1983). Affect and intellect: Piaget's contributions to the study of infant emotional development. In R. Plutchik & H. Kellerman (Eds.), *Emotion: Research and theory* (Vol. 2, pp. 115–169). New York: Academic Press.

Cicchetti, D., & Pogge-Hesse, P. (1981). The relation between emotion and cognition in infant development: Past, present, and future perspectives. In M. Lamb & L. Sherrod (Eds.), *Infant social cognition: Empirical and theoretical considerations* (pp. 205–272). Hillsdale, NJ: Lawrence Erlbaum Associates.

Cicchetti, D., & Schneider-Rosen, K. (1984a). Theoretical and empirical considerations in the investigation of the relationship between affect and cognition in atypical populations of infants: Contributions to the formulation of an integrative theory of development. In C. Izard, J. Kagan, & R. Zajonc (Eds.), *Emotions, cognition, and behavior* (pp. 366–406). New York: Cambridge University Press.

Cicchetti, D., & Schneider-Rosen, K. (1984b). Toward a developmental model of the depressive disorders. *New Directions for Child Development, 26,* 5–27.

Cicchetti, D., & Schneider-Rosen, K. (1986). An organizational approach to childhood depression. In M. Rutter, C. E. Izard, & P. B. Read (Eds.), *Depression in young people: Developmental and clinical perspectives* (pp. 71–134). New York: Guilford.

Cicchetti, D., & Sroufe, L. A. (1978). An organizational view of affect: Illustration from the study of Down's syndrome infants. In M. Lewis & L. Rosenblum (Eds.), *The development of affect* (pp. 309–350). New York: Plenum.

Crisp, A. H. (1984). The psychopathology of anorexia nervosa: Getting the "heat" out of the system. In A. J. Stunkard & E. Stellar (Eds.), *Eating and its disorders* (pp. 209–234). New York: Raven.

Crowther, J. H., Tennenbaum, D. L., Hobfoll, S. E., & Stephens, M. A. P. (Eds.). (1992). *The etiology of bulimia nervosa: The individual and familial context.* Washington, DC: Hemisphere.

Damon, W., & Hart, D. (1982). The development of self-understanding from infancy through adolescence. *Child Development, 53,* 841–864.

Dornbusch, S. M., Carlsmith, J. M., Duncan, P. D., Gross, R. T., Martin, J. A., Ritter, P. L., & Siegel-Gorelick, B. (1984). Sexual maturation, social class, and the desire to be thinner among adolescent females. *Developmental and Behavioral Pediatrics, 5,* 308–314.

Erikson, E. H. (1968). *Identity: Youth and crisis.* New York: Norton.

Fairburn, C. G. (1985). Cognitive-behavioral treatment for bulimia. In D. M. Garner & P. E. Garfinkel (Eds.), *Handbook of psychotherapy for anorexia and bulimia* (pp. 147–159). New York: Guilford.

Fairburn, C. G., & Garner, D. M. (1986). The diagnosis of bulimia nervosa. *International Journal of Eating Disorders, 5,* 403–419.

Finn, S., Hartman, M., Leon, G., & Lawson, L. (1986). Eating disorders and sexual abuse: Lack of confirmation for a clinical hypothesis. *International Journal of Eating Disorders, 5,* 1051–1060.

Freud, A. (1965). *Normality and pathology in childhood.* New York: International Universities Press.

Freud, S. (1955a). Analysis of a phobia in a five-year-old boy. In J. Strachey (Ed. and Trans.), *The standard edition of the complete psychological works of Sigmund Freud* (Vol. 10). London: Hogarth. (Original work published 1909)

Freud, S. (1955b). Fetishism. In J. Strachey (Ed. and Trans.), *The standard edition of the complete psychological works of Sigmund Freud* (Vol. 21). London: Hogarth. (Original work published 1927)

Freud, S. (1955c). Analysis terminable and interminable. In J. Strachey (Ed. and Trans.), *The standard edition of the complete psychological works of Sigmund Freud* (Vol. 23). London: Hogarth. (Original work published 1937)

Freud, S. (1955d). An outline of psycho-analysis. In J. Strachey (Ed. and Trans.), *The standard edition of the complete psychological works of Sigmund Freud* (Vol. 23). London: Hogarth. (Original work published 1940)

Freud, S. (1955e). Splitting of the ego in the process of defense. In J. Strachey (Ed. and Trans.), *The standard edition of the complete psychological works of Sigmund Freud* (Vol. 23). London: Hogarth. (Original work published 1940)

Friedlander, M. L., & Siegel, S. M. (1990). Separation-individuation difficulties and cognitive-behavior indicators of eating disorders among college women. *Journal of Counseling Psychology, 37,* 74–78.

Garfinkel, P. E., & Garner, D. M. (1982). *Anorexia nervosa: A multidimensional perspective.* New York: Brunner/Mazel.

Garner, D. M. (1986). Cognitive therapy for anorexia nervosa. In K. Brownell & J. P. Foreyt (Eds.), *Handbook of eating disorders* (pp. 301–327). New York: Basic Books.

Gilligan, C. (1982). *In a different voice: Psychological theory and women's development.* Cambridge, MA: Harvard University Press.

Goldstein, K. (1939). *The organism.* New York: American Book Company.

Goldstein, K. (1948). *Language and language disturbances.* New York: Grune & Stratton.

Goodsitt, A. (1985). Self psychology and the treatment of bulimia. In D. M. Garner & P. E. Garfinkel (Eds.), *Handbook of psychotherapy for anorexia and bulimia* (pp. 55–82). New York: Guilford.

Gowers, S., Crisp, A., Joughin, N., & Bhat, A. (1991). Premenarcheal anorexia nervosa. *Journal of Child Psychology and Psychiatry, 32,* 515–524.

Greenberg, M. T., Cicchetti, D., & Cummings, E. M. (Eds.). (1990). *Attachment in the preschool years: Theory, research, and intervention.* Chicago: University of Chicago Press.

Greenberg, M., Kusche, C., & Speltz, M. (1991). Emotional regulation, self-control, and psychopathology: The role of relationships in early childhood. In D. Cicchetti & S. Toth (Eds.), *Internalizing and externalizing expressions of dysfunction: Rochester symposium on developmental psychopathology* (Vol. 2, pp. 21–56). Hillsdale, NJ: Lawrence Erlbaum Associates.

Gunnar, M., & Collins, A. (Eds.). (1988). *Minnesota Symposia on Child Psychology, Vol. 21: Development during transition to adolescence.* Hillsdale, NJ: Lawrence Erlbaum Associates.

Harlow, H., & Zimmerman, R. (1959). Affectional response in the infant monkey. *Science, 130,* 421–432.

Harter, S. (1983). Developmental perspectives on the self-system. In E. M. Hetherington (Ed.), *Handbook of child psychology* (pp. 275–385). New York: Wiley.

Inhelder, B. (1966). Cognitive development and its contribution to the diagnosis of some phenomena of mental deficiency. *Merrill-Palmer Quarterly, 22,* 299–319.

Inhelder, B. (1968). *The diagnosis of reasoning in the mentally retarded.* New York: John Day. (Original work published 1943)

Inhelder, B. (1976). Some pathological phenomena analyzed in the perspective of developmental psychology. In B. Inhelder & H. Chipman (Eds.), *Piaget and his school* (pp. 221–227). New York: Springer.

Jacklin, C., & Maccoby, E. (1983). Issues of gender differentiation in normal development. In M. Levine, W. Carey, A. Crocker, & R. Gross (Eds.), *Developmental-behavioral pediatrics* (pp. 175–184). Philadelphia: Saunders.

Johnson, C. L. (1991). Treatment of eating-disordered patients with borderline and false-self/narcisstic disorders. In C. L. Johnson (Ed.), *Psychodynamic treatment of anorexia nervosa and bulimia* (pp. 165–193). New York: Guilford.

Johnson, C. L., & Connors, M. E. (1987). *The etiology and treatment of bulimia nervosa: A biopsychosocial perspective.* New York: Basic Books.

Johnson, C. L., & Maddi, K. L. (1986). The etiology of bulimia: Biopsychosocial perspectives. *Adolescent Psychiatry, 13,* 253–274.

Kagan, J. (1980). Perspectives on continuity. In O. G. Brim & J. Kagan (Eds.), *Constancy and change in human development* (pp. 26–74). Cambridge, MA: Harvard University Press.

Kaplan, B. (1966). The study of language in psychiatry: The comparative developmental approach and its application to symbolization and language in psychopathology. In S. Arieti (Ed.), *American handbook of psychiatry* (pp. 659–688). New York: Basic Books.

Kaplan, B. (1967). Meditations on genesis. *Human Development, 10,* 65–87.

Kog, E., Vandereycken, W., & Vertommen, H. (1985). Towards a verification of the psychosomatic family model: A pilot study of ten families with an anorexia/bulimia patient. *International Journal of Eating Disorders, 4,* 525–538.

Kohlberg, L., LaCrosse, J., & Ricks, D. (1972). The predictability of adult mental health from childhood behavior. In B. Wolman (Ed.), *Manual of child psychopathology* (pp. 1217–1284). New York: McGraw-Hill.

Lerner, R. M., & Foch, T. T. (Eds.). (1987). *Biological-psychosocial interactions in early adolescence: A life-span perspective.* Hillsdale, NJ: Lawrence Erlbaum Associates.

Levine, M. P., & Smolak, L. (1992). Toward a model of the developmental psychopathology of eating disorders: The example of early adolescence. In J. H. Crowther, D. L. Tennenbaum, S. E. Hobfoll, & M. A. P. Stephens (Eds.), *The etiology of bulimia nervosa: The individual and familial context* (pp. 59–80). Washington, DC: Hemisphere.

Lewis, M., & Brooks-Gunn, J. (1979). *Social cognition and the acquisition of self.* New York: Plenum.

Lorenz, K. (1950). The comparative method in studying innate behaviour patterns. In J. F. Danielli & R. Brown (Eds.), *Physiological mechanisms in animal behavior* (pp. 221–268). New York: Cambridge University Press.

Mahler, M. (1952). On childhood psychosis and schizophrenia: Autistic and symbiotic infantile psychoses. In R. S. Eissler, A. Freud, H. Hartmann, & E. Kris (Eds.), *The psychoanalytic study of the child* (Vol. 7, pp. 286–305). New York: International Universities Press.

Mahler, M., Pine, F., & Bergman, A. (1975). *The psychological birth of the human infant.* New York: Basic Books.

McGhie, A., & Chapman, J. (1961). Disorders of attention and perception in early schizophrenia. *British Journal of Medical Psychology, 34,* 103–115.

McGuire, W. J., & McGuire, C. V. (1982). Significant others in self-space: Sex differences and developmental trends in the social self. In J. Suls (Ed.), *Social psychological perspectives on the self* (pp. 71–96). Hillsdale, NJ: Lawrence Erlbaum Associates.

Miller, J. B. (1976). *Toward a new psychology of women.* Boston, MA: Beacon Press.

Minuchin, S., Rosman, B. L., & Baker, L. (1978). *Psychosomatic families: Anorexia nervosa in context.* Cambridge, MA: Harvard University Press.

Overton, W. (1976). The active organism in structuralism. *Human Development, 19,* 71–86.

Overton, W. (1984). World views and their influence on psychological theory and research: Kuhn-Lakatos-Laudan. In H. Reese (Ed.), *Advances in child development and behvaior* (Vol. 18, pp. 191–226). New York: Academic Press.

Overton, W., & Reese, H. (1973). Models of development: Methodological implications. In J. R. Nesselroade & H. Reese (Ed.), *Life-span developmental psychology: Methodological issues.* New York: Academic Press.

Rapaport, D. (1951). *Organization and pathology of thought.* New York: Columbia University Press.

Robins, L. N. (1978). Study of childhood predictors of adult antisocial behavior: Replications from longitudinal studies. *Psychological Medicine, 8,* 611–622.

Rodin, J., Striegel-Moore, R. H., & Silberstein, L. R. (1990). Vulnerability and resilience in the age of eating disorders: Risk and protective factors for bulimia nervosa. In J. Rolf, A. S. Masten, D. Cicchetti, K. H. Nuechterlein, & S. Weintraub (Eds.), *Risk and protective factors in the development of psychopathology* (pp. 361–383). New York: Cambridge University Press.

Root, M. P. P., Fallon, P., & Friedrich, W. N. (1986). *Bulimia: A systems approach to treatment.* New York: Norton.

Rothbaum, F., & Rosen, K. S. (1991). *Parental acceptance scoring manual: A system for assessing interactions between parents and their young children* (3rd Version). Unpublished manuscript, Tufts University and Boston College, Boston.

Rutter, M. (1977). Individual differences. In M. Rutter & L. Hersov (Eds.), *Child psychiatry: Modern approaches* (pp. 3–21). Oxford, England: Blackwell.

Rutter, M. (1983). Continuities and discontinuities in socio-emotional development: Empirical and conceptual perspectives. In R. Emde & R. Harmon (Eds.), *Continuities and discontinuities in development* (pp. 41–68). New York: Plenum.

Rutter, M. (1985). Resilience in the face of adversity: Protective factors and resistance to psychiatric disorder. *British Journal of Psychiatry, 147,* 598–611.

Rutter, M. (1990). Psychosocial resilience and protective mechanisms. In J. Rolf, A. S. Masten, D. Cicchetti, K. H. Nuechterlein, & S. Weintraub (Eds.), *Risk and protective factors in the development of psychopathology* (pp. 181–214). New York: Cambridge University Press.

Sameroff, A., & Chandler, M. (1975). Reproductive risk and the continuum of caretaking casualty. In F. Horowitz (Ed.), *Review of child development research* (Vol. 4, pp. 197–244). Chicago: University of Chicago Press.

Santostefano, S. (1978). *A bio-developmental approach to clinical child psychology.* New York: Wiley.

Sargent, J., Liebman, R., & Silver, M. (1985). Family therapy for anorexia nervosa. In D. M. Garner & P. E. Garfinkel (Eds.), *Handbook of psychotherapy for anorexia and bulimia* (pp. 257–279). New York: Guilford.

Schneider-Rosen, K. (1990). The developmental reorganization of attachment relationships: Guidelines for classification beyond infancy. In M. T. Greenberg, D. Cicchetti, & E. M. Cummings (Eds.), *Attachment in the preschool years: Theory, research, and intervention* (pp. 185–220). Chicago: University of Chicago Press.

Schneider-Rosen, K., Braunwald, K., Carlson, V., & Cicchetti, D. (1985). Current perspectives in attachment theory: Illustrations from the study of maltreated infants. In I. Bretherton & E. Waters (Eds.), Growing points in attachment theory and research, *Monographs of the Society for Research in Child Development, 50* (1–2, Serial No. 209).

Selman, R. (1980). *The growth of interpersonal understanding.* New York: Academic Press.

Shakow, D. (1946). The nature of deterioration in schizphrenic conditions. *Journal of Nervous and Mental Diseases Monographs, 70,* 1–88.

Shakow, D. (1962). Segmental set: A theory of the formal psychological deficit in schizophrenia. *Archives of General Psychiatry, 6,* 1–17.

Simmons, R. G., Blyth, D. A., & McKinney, K. L. (1983). The social and psychological effects of puberty on white females. In J. Brooks-Gunn & A. C. Petersen (Eds.), *Girls at puberty* (pp. 229–278). New York: Plenum.

Simmons, R. G., & Rosenberg, F. (1975). Sex, sex roles, and self-image. *Journal of Youth and Adolescence, 4,* 229–258.

Smolak, L. (1986). *Infancy.* Englewood Cliffs, NJ: Prentice-Hall.

Smolak, L., & Levine, M. P. (1994). Critical issues in the developmental psychopathology of eating disorders. In L. Alexander & D. B. Lumsden (Eds.), *Understanding eating disorders* (pp. 37–60). Washington, DC: Taylor & Francis.

Smolak, L., Levine, M. P., & Gralen, S. J. (1993). The impact of puberty and dating on eating problems among middle school girls. *Journal of Youth and Adolescence, 22,* 355–368.

Sroufe, L. A. (1979). The coherence of individual development: Early care, attachment, and subsequent developmental issues. *American Psychologist, 43,* 834–841.

Sroufe, L. A. (1986). Appraisal: Bowlby's contribution to analytic theory and developmental psychopathology. *Journal of Child Psychology and Psychiatry, 27,* 841–849.

Sroufe, L. A. (1989). Pathways to adaptation and maladaptation: Psychopathology as developmental deviation. In D. Cicchetti (Ed.), *The emergence of a discipline: Rochester symposium on developmental psychopathology* (Vol. 1, pp. 13–40). Hillsdale, NJ: Lawrence Erlbaum Associates.

Sroufe, L. A., & Rutter. M. (1984). The domain of developmental psychopathology. *Child Development, 83,* 173–189.

Sroufe, L. A., & Waters, E. (1977). Attachment as an organizational construct. *Child Development, 48,* 1184–1199.

Striegel-Moore, R. H., McAvay, G., & Rodin, J. (1986). Psychological and behavioral correlates of feeling fat in women. *International Journal of Eating Disorders, 5,* 935–949.

Striegel-Moore, R. H., Silberstein, L. H., & Rodin, J. (1986). Toward an understanding of risk factors for bulimia. *American Psychologist, 41,* 246–263.

Strober, M. (1991). Disorders of the self in anorexia nervosa: An organismic-developmental paradigm. In C. L. Johnson (Ed.), *Psychodynamic treatment of anorexia nervosa and bulimia* (pp. 354–373). New York: Guilford.

Stunkard, A. J., D'Aquili, E., Fox, S., & Filion, R. D. L. (1972). The influence of social class on obesity and thinness in children. *Journal of the American Medical Association, 22,* 579–584.

Tobin-Richards, M. H., Boxer, A. M., & Petersen, A. C. (1983). The psychological significance of pubertal change: Sex differences in perceptions of self during early adolescence. In J. Brooks-Gunn & A. C. Petersen (Eds.), *Girls at puberty* (pp. 127–154). New York: Plenum.

Waddington, C. H. (1966). *Principles of development and differentiation.* New York: Macmillan.

Werner, H. (1948). *Comparative psychology of mental development.* New York: International Universities Press.

Werner, H. (1957). The concept of development from a comparative and organismic point of view. In D. B. Harris (Ed.), *The concept of development* (pp. 125–148). Minneapolis: University of Minnesota Press.

Werner, H., & Kaplan, B. (1963). *Symbol formation: An organismic-developmental approach to language and the expression of thought.* New York: Wiley.

Wittig, M. A. (1983). Sex role development in early adolescence. *Theory Into Practice, 22,* 105–111.

Wonderlich, S. (1992). Relationship of family and personality factors in bulimia. In J. H. Crowther, D. L. Tennenbaum, S. E. Hobfoll, & M. A. P. Stephens (Eds.), *The etiology of bulimia nervosa: the individual and familial context* (pp. 103–126). Washington, DC: Hemisphere.

2

Methodological Implications of a Developmental Psychopathology Approach to the Study of Eating Problems

Linda Smolak

A developmental perspective on the study of psychopathology takes into account the continuities and discontinuities between normal growth and psychopathology, age-related changes in modes of adaptation and symptom expression, behavioral reorganizations that occur around salient developmental transitions, internal and external sources of competence and vulnerability, and the effects of development on pathology and of pathology on development.

—Attie and Brooks-Gunn (1992, p. 35)

Attie and Brooks-Gunn thus succinctly summarized the major points of a developmental psychopathology approach. One crucial component of their definition is the relation between normal growth and psychopathology. This relation is analogous to a highway with branching roads, some of which return to the highway, some of which go only to one place, several of which may lead to various places depending on where one turns off, and some of which share a common destination (Sroufe, 1989). In other words, there are multiple pathways from each point and multiple pathways to each point.

This concept helps to explain why multidimensional models of eating disorders have flourished. Although these models sometimes appear to be straining to include every possible factor implicated in the etiology of eating disorders, they do acknowledge that different factors may play different roles for different girls at different times. Untangling the combination and timing of factors that facilitate or impede the development of eating disorders generally requires longitudinal data. Thus, one implication of a developmental psychopathology model is the need to collect and analyze longitudinal data. This chapter accordingly begins with a discussion of the costs and benefits of longitudinal designs and data analysis techniques.

Attie and Brooks-Gunn's (1992) definition also points out the need for qualitative data analysis. In both normal and pathological development, underlying cognitive and personality structures, sometimes referred to as molar structures (Cicchetti & Schneider-Rosen, 1986), may undergo organizational changes (see, e.g., Ewell, Smith, Karmel, & Hart, chapter 5, this volume, for a description of changes in self-structures). Surface similarity does not necessarily imply deep structure similarity. Thus, although both children and adults may diet, the relation between dieting and ideas of attractiveness, success, self-worth, and self-control (i.e., the underlying *thinness schema*) may not be the same for children and adults (Smolak & Levine, 1994a, 1994c). Perhaps children have not yet developed a consolidated thinness schema; if so, this may be one reason that eating problems are so rare among elementary school children, even among those who diet.

In addition to qualitative independent variables (e.g., "schema" vs. "no schema"), eating disorders research often focuses on qualitative outcomes. The dependent variable may be the presence of eating disorders symptoms (e.g., Killen et al., 1994; Striegel-Moore, Silberstein, Frensch, & Rodin, 1989), the risk level for developing eating problems (e.g., Leon, Fulkerson, Perry, & Early-Zald, 1995), or dieting status (e.g., Levine, Smolak, Moodey, Shuman, & Hessen, 1994). Techniques such as analysis of variance (ANOVA) and multiple regression are not designed to handle categorical dependent variables. Therefore, a second topic addressed in this chapter concerns the techniques that can be used with qualitative variables.

Developmental psychopathology also emphasizes the role of developmental transitions in the pathways toward psychological disorder. In some cases this means looking at normal transitions (e.g., early adolescence; see Smolak & Levine, chapter 9, this volume). Other times it means looking at developmental turning points (i.e., life or behavioral decisions that increase the likelihood of a particular outcome; Pickles & Rutter, 1989). The decision to diet at an early age (e.g., in elementary school) might represent such a turning point in the development of eating problems (Smolak & Levine, 1994c). Again, longitudinal data are required to address these issues and data analysis methods must make it possible to identify various outcomes from the different turning point decisions. Thus, there may be both a qualitative precursor (e.g., the decision to diet) and a qualitative dependent variable (the presence of an eating problem), and possibly one or more mediating variables (Pickles & Rutter, 1989). Furthermore, the existence of a turning point or structural change implies a nonlinear relation. Thus, the third section of this chapter is devoted to a discussion of techniques for analyzing turning points and nonlinear relations.

Finally, inasmuch as developmental psychopathology models include elements borrowed from the related field of developmental psychology, there is a substantial emphasis on reciprocal relationships (Rosen, chapter 1, this volume; Smolak & Levine, 1994a). For example, parents are not seen as merely influencing child behavior; rather, parental behavior is shaped not only by parental beliefs and characteristics but also by parental reaction to child behaviors and characteristics. For example, some mothers make frequent weight- and shape-related comments to their daughters, and these comments may be related to the daughters' dieting and body satisfaction (Levine, Smolak, & Hayden, 1994; Pike & Rodin, 1991); however, researchers may eventually find that not only are these comments more likely to be made to girls than to boys, but also, perhaps, to girls of a certain age and body shape, or to girls who exhibit preferences for sweet food, or to girls who tend to be strongly influenced by their parents. Data analysis therefore needs to distinguish between predominant (unidirectional) causality and reciprocal causality (Menard, 1991). This in turn implies the need for sufficient points of measurement as well as for adequate space between measurements. Thus, assumptions and definitions underlying various longitudinal techniques are also discussed in this chapter.

Over and over, then, it is evident that longitudinal data play an important role in addressing the key components of a developmental psychopathology model. It is also apparent that specific types of data analysis are needed to process time-lagged data, qualitative data, mediating variables, individual differences, and various forms of causality. In addition, researchers should be prepared to analyze the discontinuity in development associated with normal transitions and turning points. The model also raises the probability that we will increasingly be working with young children; this raises both measurement and ethical issues. Thus, in the final section of this chapter some of the special demands of doing research with children are discussed.

THE IMPORTANCE AND NATURE OF LONGITUDINAL DATA

Longitudinal designs have two major advantages over cross-sectional research. First, longitudinal data allow researchers to examine age-related changes, whereas cross-sectional data can only provide information concerning age differences. Differences between age groups may be caused by factors other than age. Consider, for example, a hypothetical cross-sectional study indicating that 50-year-old women exhibit significantly less body dissatisfaction than do 20-year-old women. It cannot be

determined whether this reflects an age-related decrease in body dissatisfaction or whether the 50-year-olds had lower body dissatisfaction
even when they were 20 years old themselves. Given changes in the
societal definition of an attractive female body (Attie & Brooks-Gunn,
1987), it would not be surprising to find that this is a cohort effect
(related to shared experiences of the age group) rather than a developmental (age-related) effect (Smolak, 1993). If the data were longitudinal,
on the other hand, it would be clear that the women's body dissatisfaction had decreased as they got older. Although it would still be necessary
to identify factors causing changes in body dissatisfaction (because age
per se would be considered a marker rather than a causal factor), we
would have a more accurate description of the dynamic developmental
process.

The second advantage of longitudinal data is that they can be used
to examine individual differences in patterns of development. Particularly for developmental psychopathology, with its argument of multiple
pathways to or away from pathology (Smolak & Levine, 1994a), the
ability to map the natural history of individuals and of their eating
problems is crucial.

For most developmentalists, these two advantages are so great as to
virtually outweigh the disadvantages of longitudinal research. However,
there are at least two disadvantages that researchers in the field of
eating disorders need to consider as they design studies. First, attrition
is a problem in longitudinal studies. In recent prospective research on
eating problems, the subject loss has ranged from about 12% to about
35% (Killen et al., 1994; Leon et al., 1995; Rosen, Compas, & Tacy, 1993;
Smolak, Levine, & Gralen, 1993; Striegel-Moore et al., 1989). None of
these studies lasted more than 3 years. Both the choice of subject pool
and the availability of staff to track down participants who have moved
affect attrition rate. Nonetheless, the longer a longitudinal study continues, the more selective the subject pool becomes. For example, research concerning intelligence in old age has documented that
longitudinal samples tend to underestimate general population declines
because the participants who stay in the studies are the healthiest, best
educated, and most integrated into society (Smolak, 1993). Thus, it may
be difficult to maintain a subsample with psychological problems.

In fact, for researchers interested in eating disorders per se, the initial
sample size needed for studying etiological issues may be prohibitively
large. Consider, as a hypothetical example, a study in which the desired
final sample includes at least 30 diagnosed patients. Assuming that the
combined rates of anorexia nervosa (AN) and bulimia nervosa (BN) are
somewhere between 5% and 10% of all the women in the sample and
that overall attrition rate maybe 20% over a decade, the initial sample
will need to include at least 700 individuals to ensure sufficient numbers

for data analysis. Even then, not all forms of data analysis will be possible.

Although this scenario is a discouraging one, it does apply only to the most common form of longitudinal study, the *prospective panel study* (Menard, 1991). In this type of study, the same people are tested repeatedly, typically on the same set of variables, although it is possible to add or delete measures (Pickles & Rutter, 1989). However, an alternative design is the *retrospective panel study* (Menard, 1991), in which the so-called repeated testings are really examinations of earlier points in development. Psychologists are often reluctant to rely on retrospective reports because of the very real possibility of memory distortion. However, cognitive schemata (e.g., thinness or depressive schemata) may result in comparable distortions in self-reports of current circumstances.

Researchers using self-reports must either provide corroborating evidence or temper their interpretations. Similar caveats apply to retrospective data. Often corroborating evidence does exist; it is just difficult to find and integrate. For example, childhood weight records may be obtained from pediatricians; elementary school report cards (which include ratings of conduct as well as parent and teacher comments) may provide useful information about achievement orientation; high school yearbooks may provide information about activities, thereby giving an indication of the number of areas in which the student tried to achieve. Retrospective data are not inherently inferior to prospective data; rather, the use of retrospective report requires careful planning in order to ensure accuracy of (or at least support for) subjects' recollections (Menard, 1991).

A second pitfall of longitudinal research, in addition to ther problem of attrition, is that the measures often become outdated. There may also be a problem in finding measures that are comparable across age periods. These measurement problems may be particularly severe in eating disorders research involving children. Children's measures do exist of some components of eating problems: For example, there is the Children's Eating Attitudes Test (ChEAT; Maloney, McGuire, & Daniels, 1988), a Body Esteem Scale (BES; Mendelson & White, 1985, 1993), and a visual measure of body dissatisfaction (Collins, 1991). Although these scales address some components of eating problems, as might be expected they do not cover all eating issues for all ages. As new measures are developed and existing ones are refined, researchers conducting longitudinal research may find themselves with discredited measures. Again, such risks must be evaluated against the information to be gained. Multiple measures of a behavior or attitude, which can sometimes be treated statistically as latent variables, may also help to ameliorate this problem. A researcher might, for example, use three measures of body satisfaction, such as the BES, a question asking how satisfied you are with your body, and Collins' (1991) body figures task. Assuming that these measures indeed prove to be redundant in a particular sample (i.e., that they share substantial amounts of variance), they could be entered into a regression in a single block (see Attie & Brooks-Gunn, 1989, for an example) or collapsed into a single scale (see Leon et al., 1995, for an example).

Despite the expense and difficulties of longitudinal research, developmental psychopathology models of eating disorders virtually require it. The question then becomes how to make the best use of the data.

Statistical Analysis of Longitudinal Data: General Considerations

Longitudinal data can effectively describe patterns of development that may form the basis for theories. Case studies, for example, may provide rich detail about the course of development of an illness. Group data analysis can indicate the generalizability of such patterns. When causality becomes the issue, however, longitudinal data are only as good as the theories on which they are based. In other words, causality is always rooted in theory and design, not in a statistical test per se. Whereas a theory can direct us toward appropriate variables, reasonable operational definitions, and meaningful causal paths, statistics cannot.

This basic point needs to be reiterated here because although all researchers "know" that causality arises from theory rather than from statistics, they do not always proceed accordingly (Biddle & Marlin, 1987; Martin, 1987). When using structural equation modeling (SEM), and especially the variants of path analysis and linear structural relations (LISREL; Burchinal & Appelbaum, 1991; Martin, 1987), the tendency is to discuss results as if they yielded causal information independently of the theory. It is not uncommon, for example, for a researcher to start out with a theoretical model and then to "revise" it using multiple runs through LISREL; the end product is then discussed as a causal model. This is inappropriate because it is no longer a test of the theoretical model (Biddle & Marlin, 1987).

The temptation to treat descriptive relationships as causal is especially great when longitudinal data are available. Although many definitions of causality can be applied to the research endeavor (see, e.g., Muliak, 1987), researchers often assume that if one event or characteristic (which may be called A) temporally precedes another (B), then A has caused B. It may be that A initiates B, increases (or decreases) the strength of B, or is ended by B (Menard, 1991) but there is, in any event, a tendency to see them as causally related. Nonetheless, the temporal precedence of one variable does not define it as causal (although failure to establish temporal precedence of A probably does eliminate the possibility that A causes B; Menard, 1991). There remain the possibilities of reciprocal causality, third variables, or mismeasured variables. Given the nature of developmental processes, the probability of at least some form of reciprocal causality is very high. For example, stress contributes to the intensification of eating problems, but eating problems also increase the likelihood of stress (Rosen et al., 1993). Reciprocity in relationships is one reason that cross-lagged correlations (CLC), in which a variable from one time of measurement is correlated with a variable from a later time of measurement, are not a particularly effective technique for the analysis of longitudinal data (Rogosa, 1980). Again, then, it can be argued that it is the theory or model, rather than the data per se, that provides the foundation for causal arguments.

A second caveat concerns the sophistication of data analysis techniques. It is, of course, true that some techniques may be too simple to capture the complexity of the models or issues. CLC, although frequently used, seem to be an example (Rogosa, 1980). On the other hand, ordinary least squares (OLS) multiple regression is able not only to consider multiple predictors of a dependent variable but also to take into account the correlations among the predictors. As such it is clearly a major improvement over CLC. However, unlike LISREL (or EQS [Bentler, 1989] or other path analysis programs), OLS cannot generate latent variables (variables based on multiple measures of a construct, similar to a factor score), and it cannot accommodate nonrecursive models (models with reciprocal paths) without using specialized, cumbersome techniques (Biddle & Marlin, 1987).

Why not always choose LISREL over OLS? First, for LISREL analysis (or other causal or structural modeling techniques) to be meaningful, the investigator must specify a causal model in advance. Among other things, this means indicating a priori which variables are exogenous (treated as givens for which no causal explanation is offered) and which are endogenous (explained within the model); which pathways are direct and which are indirect; which relationships are recursive (characterized by unidirectional causality) and which are nonrecursive (characterized by bidirectional or reciprocal causality); and whether the postulated relationships will be positive or negative. One cannot leave such decisions to the statistics generated for the sample.

A recent, cross-sectional study by Stice, Schupak-Neuberg, Shaw, and Stein (1994) exemplifies the a priori modeling specificity needed to use SEM (in this case, with EQS). Figure 2.1 shows the model that was tested. In this model, media exposure is an exogenous variable (i.e., there are no variables hypothesized to explain media exposure levels). All other variables are endogenous. The relationship between media exposure and eating disorder symptoms shown by the bottom line in Fig. 2.1 (marked with a coefficient of .30) represents a direct relationship. Two indirect paths between media exposure and eating disorder symptoms are also postulated. The one supported by the data has media

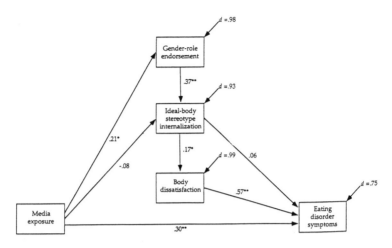

FIG. 2.1. An example of a structural equations (EQS) model used to example eating disorder symptoms. From Stice et al. (1994, p. 838).

exposure affecting gender-role endorsement, which in turn predicts ideal-body stereotype internalization, which is then related to body dissatisfaction, a significant predictor of eating disorder symptoms. All hypothesized relationships are positive and recursive.

With any statistical technique, of course, it is preferable to specify a theoretical model a priori. However, failure to do so does not typically make the analysis meaningless, as it does with LISREL or path analysis. Causal modeling techniques such as LISREL or path analysis cannot be used effectively to discover causal relationships. Rather, their purpose is to test hypothesized causal relations (Muliak, 1987). The level of model specificity required by these techniques is frequently beyond that which can be provided by theorizing about eating problems. It should also be kept in mind that all of these relationships must be adequately measured.

A second disadvantage of LISREL compared to OLS is that the former makes many more assumptions about the data, some of which may be impossible for psychologists to meet most of the time (Martin, 1987; Muliak, 1987; Pedhazur, 1982). For example, structural relationships must be properly identified. Each path in a path analysis can be represented by a regression equation (Pedhazur, 1982); thus, a path analysis actually represents a system of equations. *Identification* means that each of these equations must have its own unique solution; that is, one equation cannot be algebraically transformed to represent another equation. In other words, each equation must contain at least one exogenous variable that does not appear in any other equation. In fully recursive models, this identification requirement is fairly easy to meet (see Pedhazur, 1982, for restrictions). However, in nonrecursive models, which are likely to be the norm in eating problems research, identification is much more problematic. Eating disorders models tend to suggest that various endogenous variables are multiply determined and that each determinant influences several different endogenous variables. One might imagine, for example, a model including parental attitudes, child's dieting, and body dissatisfaction as endogenous variables, and media influences and child's weight as exogenous variables. It is easy to argue for nonrecursive relationships among several of these variables (e.g., dieting and body dissatisfaction). Furthermore, one can argue that media influences and child weight affect all of the endogenous variables. This would represent an identification problem and, hence, a problem in using LISREL.

In such cases, OLS may well be a better choice, although one may have to execute multiple passes before arriving at the information that LISREL can provide (Biddle & Marlin, 1987). These different equations will be generated as if they were independent of one another, when in fact they are not. This creates a potential source of bias in the system. In addition, OLS cannot provide the goodness-of-fit and latent variable information that LISREL can, although a factor analysis prior to OLS can provide somewhat similar, albeit more error-prone, information. Nonetheless, given the problems of meeting LISREL's assumptions and the limitations on LISREL's goodness-of-fit and latent variable estimates, OLS is often preferable (Biddle & Marlin, 1987; Tanaka, 1987). Simpler is frequently better.

Finally, there is the question of sample size. This is one reason that LISREL is so difficult to use with longitudinal data. Statisticians typically argue that a minimum of 200 subjects is needed to effectively use LISREL's goodness-of-fit tests (Tanaka, 1987). Goodness-of-fit tests are particularly negatively affected in studies with non-normal distributions, a situation likely to be fairly common in research concerning eating disorders and other forms of psychopathology. Furthermore, there is often an important trade-off between data quality and sample size in a longitudinal study. Although a researcher might be able to interview (rather than survey) 50 subjects in annual 1-hour sessions for 5 years, it would be much more difficult to do so for 200 or more subjects. This trade-off of poorer quality data for more sophisticated analytic techniques may not be justifiable (Martin, 1987).

A fair number of subjects is also required in order for OLS to yield stable coefficient estimates. Although there is some disagreement as to a minimum number, estimates of at least 10 to 15 subjects per variable seem common. Thus, in a study with six predictor variables, a minimum of 60 to 90 subjects is needed. It is noteworthy how quickly a researcher can accumulate six or more predictor variables in longitudinal research, particularly when consideration is given to temporal precursors, previous levels of the dependent variable, concurrent relationships, and interaction effects. For example, Attie and Brooks-Gunn (1989) generated 34 variables in a longitudinal study using just two times of measurement. They did not include concurrent, interaction, or nonlinear (e.g., quadratic) predictor variables in their longitudinal analysis, but they nonetheless had six predictor variables.

Attie and Brooks-Gunn's (1989) work does point out one solution to the problem of too many predictors. They did two concurrent analyses, one for Time 1 data and one for Time 2 data. These were then interpreted along with the longitudinal analysis to assess whether effects were likely to be reciprocal rather than directional. Although a path analysis may have answered this question more directly, their sample size of 193 was questionable for use in LISREL but was adequate for OLS hierarchical regressions.

Tanaka (1987) developed a procedure for estimating latent-variable (LISREL, EQS) models with small samples. This new ME2 estimator holds promise for developmentally oriented research. However, theoretical constraints make it only useful for exploratory, as opposed to inferential, efforts. In addition, because it has not been widely used, problems may yet be found.

Noncorrelational techniques such as multivariate analysis of varience (MANOVA) also require attention to sample size. There should be at least 10 to 15 subjects per variable. Like multivariate correlational techniques, MANOVA relies on generating the inverse of the covariance matrix. If the sample size is insufficient a singular matrix may result. Because it is impossible to generate an inverse for a singular matrix, the analysis becomes meaningless; that is, the solution is not stable.

Analytic Techniques and Longitudinal Data

It is impossible to consider all of the possible ways to analyze longitudinal data within the confines of this chapter. It also seems of limited value to select one or two methods and spend considerable time describing them, as they may not be of use to many readers. Instead, the focus here is on selecting appropriate techniques (see Table 2.1) and on defining variables.

Table 2.1 is arranged in terms of whether the variables (both dependent and independent) are qualitative or quantitative; both types are used in eating disorders research. When the outcome variable is categorical, such as presence or absence of eating disorders symptoms (e.g., Killen et al., 1994; Striegel-Moore et al., 1989), a logit (or probit), log-linear, or logistic regression analysis is probably most appropriate. A logistic analysis make it possible to estimate the probability of an event, (e.g., diagnosis of BN). This can be done even if there is more than

TABLE 2.1
Methods of Analyzing Longitudinal Data

Dependent Variable	Independent Variable	Methods of Analysis
Quantitative/continuous	Quantitative/continuous	Differential equations; Regression; Multivariate ARIMA time-series analysis; Latent variable structural equation models
	Mixed continuous and categorical	ANOVA with ANCOVA; Regression with dummy variables
	Qualitative/categorical	ANOVA; Nonparametric ANOVA; Dummy variable regression
Qualitative/categorical	Quantitative/continuous	Discriminant analysis; Logit or probit analysis; Logistic regression; Hazard/survival/event history analysis
	Mixed continuous and categorical	Log-linear analysis; Logistic regression; Hazard/survival/event history analysis
	Qualitative/categorical	Log-linear analysis; Multistate life table models; Hazard/survival/event history analysis

Note. From Menard (1991, p. 63).

one independent variable (Norusis, 1990). Similarly, a survival or hazard analysis can estimate how long it will take for groups of people to enter a particular category (Norusis, 1990; Willett & Singer, 1991). Killen et al. (1994) used such an analysis to assess how long girls with varying levels of weight concerns "survived" before showing eating disorders symptoms. A log-linear model uses natural log transformations to analyze cross-tabulation data, including interaction effects (in a hierarchical log-linear analysis). Log-linear analysis can also test quadratic models (as discussed later). A logit or probit analysis is particularly useful in detecting a threshold effect. For example, one might be interested in whether there is a particular level of caloric restriction at which subthreshold and clinical eating disorders become much more of a risk (but above which the risk does not substantially increase).

It is assumed that the case of a quantitative, continuous dependent variable is more familiar to most readers and that ANOVA, analysis of covarience (ANCOVA), and OLS regression analyses are also well-known. The major issue to be considered here is how to use these techniques with longitudinal (repeated-measures) data, and, more specifically, how to represent change. Researchers sometimes opt to use change scores as dependent variables (e.g., Striegel-Moore et al., 1989). This process often seems convenient to researchers who only have two points of measurement and who are trying to avoid a repeated-measures ANOVA. Using change scores may be preferable in order to maximize available degrees of freedom (e.g., in a between-groups vs. correlated t test). There are also OLS situations in which change scores might be preferred. A researcher might, for example, want to reduce the predictors by omitting Y_1 from the equation predicting Y_2. Another concern might be that Y_1 will be a dominant variable in the equation predicting Y_2, thereby statistically eliminating any other predictor variable as a significant contributor to the equation.

There are three common ways to calculate change scores. One can calculate a *raw change score,* in which Y_1 is subtracted from the Y_2 score. A second possibility is the *residual gain score.* Here Y_2 is regressed on Y_1 and the difference is calculated between the expected value of Y_2, denoted as $E(Y_2)$, and the actual value: $(Y_2 - E(Y_2)$. (The expected value is derived from the equation.) Finally, if the scale of measurement is a ratio, a *percent change* can be calculated (Menard, 1991).

Change scores can be very helpful for descriptive purposes. However, they may not always be appropriate in explanatory models (Menard, 1991). For example, raw change scores are influenced by measurement error and may actually be less reliable than the originally measured variables. Residual gain scores have a similar problem and are arguably best used to identify people with a unusual amount of change in their scores. An alternative might be to use lagged endogenous variables. In this case, Y_1 is first regressed on the independent variables (IVs) measured at Time 1. Then a separate equation regresses Y_2 on all of the Time 1 and Time 2 variables of interest (including Y_1). The two equations provide information about the stability of Y scores as well as indicating which factors originally predicted Y (i.e., Y_1); which of those still predict Y at a later time; and whether concurrent measures (at Time 2) add any information not available from the Time 1 measures. Of course, one is still left with the possibility of the dominant variable effect, but many researchers may find it important to know that Y_1 is a better predictor than all other Time 1 and Time 2 X variables, individually or combined. Indeed, prospective eating disorders research has commonly found this to be the case (Attie & Brooks-Gunn, 1989; Leon et al., 1995; Rosen et al., 1993).

Change scores may also be problematic if the measurement scale being used has a maximum score. In such cases, the change scores will have a truncated range and a non-normal distribution. This creates problems for correlation-based techniques, including OLS. The F test associated with OLS is quite robust in the face of such non-normality. In more severe cases, data transformations (e.g., the log transformation) may be attempted to correct for the non-normal distribution (Norusis, 1990). Another way to address change is to use earlier measures of the dependent variable as a covariate. To accomplish this, Y_1 can be forced into a hierarchical regression as the first variable, as for example, in Attie and Brooks-Gunn's (1989) study. Alternatively, Y_1 can be the covariate in an analysis of covariance, as, for example, in Smolak, Levine, and Gralen's (1993) study. These procedures have the effect of equating the participants at Time 1. This means that any additional independent variables related to Y_2 are explaining change over time in the dependent variable.

Change may also be captured in more qualitative ways. For example, Graber, Brooks-Gunn, Paikoff, and Warren (1994) categorized women as exceeding high-risk scores at none, one, or two times of measurement using the Eating Attitudes Test (EAT; Garfinkel & Garner, 1982). These categories were then treated as an independent variable (indicating chronicity of eating problems) in examining Time 3 behaviors and attitudes. In this case, the relative lack of stability of EAT scores led to the decision to examine trajectories for different types of change rather than to look at overall sample change (as in a regression analysis) in EAT scores from Time 1 to Time 3.

Special Issues in Analyzing Developmental Psychopathology Data

Interaction Effects. It is, of course, important to examine the interaction effects before interpreting the main effects in a two-way (or more) ANOVA. When OLS is used, there are virtually always two or more predictor variables that are conceptually comparable to the independent variables in the ANOVA. Nevertheless, it is unusual to see interaction terms represented in the equations.

Interaction terms can be created by multiplying the two variables (Cassidy, 1981). This term is then entered into the equation and treated like other predictors. Because an interaction term is not a linear combination of the two original variables, it does not necessarily create multicollinearity. Interaction terms can be created even if one of the variables in question is a categorical variable. Interpretation is often made easier by actually graphing or tabling values for the interaction.

There are many situations in eating disorders research in which interaction terms are appropriate. In chapter 9 of this volume, for example, Levine and I propose a model that suggests that personality predispositions interact with simultaneity of developmental tasks to increase risk of eating problems. Specifically, we hypothesize that girls with rigid thinness schemata who face multiple and simultaneous developmental tasks are at greater risk for developing eating problems than are girls with less rigid thinness schemata. This might be best captured by a term representing the interaction between thinness schema and simultaneity of tasks (see also Levine & Smolak, 1992).

Nonlinear Effects.   Strict linearity is fairly rare in developmental relationships. Even physical growth, often thought of as linear, actually has at least two postnatal periods of rapid growth (infancy and adolescence) separated by a period of slower, more gradual growth. Thus, a curve depicting human growth looks more like the one in Fig. 2.2 than a true straight line.

It is also possible that there are "turning points" in developmental processes (Pickles & Rutter, 1989). These are points at which an important decision or choice is made that tends to narrow the options as to which developmental path will be followed. Thus, the risk (or likelihood) of a particular outcome is increased. The event does not necessarily have the same meaning at every point in development, nor is there only one turning point for a particular outcome. For example, the decision to diet in elementary school might substantially increase a girl's chances of developing an adolescent eating problem, but it is possible that girls who

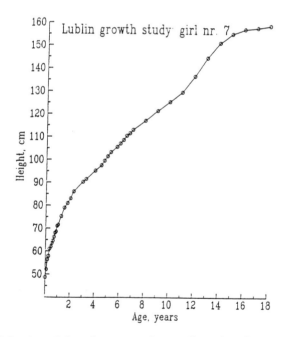

FIG. 2.2.   Actual data demonstrating nonlinearity of a growth curve (from Hauspie et al., 1989, p. 29). Note, for example, the rapid increase in height at about age 11.

do not enter the high-risk pool at this point make a later decision that is also a turning point toward eating problems. This provides an additional reminder that a hallmark of the developmental psychopathology model is the argument that there are multiple paths coming off from normal development that may lead to or away from psychopathology. Such turning points cannot be adequately captured in a linear model.

Finally, it may be common to see threshold effects, especially in the study of developmental psychopathology. Eating problems can be conceptualized as occurring on a partial continuum with nonpathological dieting and body dissatisfaction (Heatherton & Polivy, 1992; Levine & Smolak, 1992). It may be that dieting or body dissatisfaction must reach a certain level before the risk of eating disorders becomes serious. A graph of the relation between body dissatisfaction and the risk of BN, for example, might show a flat or slowly accelerating curve that then rapidly accelerates after the threshold is reached.

All of these examples are situations in which a straight line does not fully capture the relation between predictor and outcome variables. How might these be handled? In the simplest cases, when all data involved are quantitative, a quadratic (or even cubic) term can be added to the regression equation. If a quadratic term (calculated as X^2) is significant, then the line turns once. The direction of the turn can be determined by the signs of the linear and quadratic terms' coefficients. If, for example, both terms are positive, this suggests a rapidly accelerating curve. If the linear coefficient is negative and the quadratic is positive, this suggests that the line initially moves downward but turns up at some point. Often, the turning point and the shape of the curve can best be conceptualized by actually graphing the function using the linear and quadratic terms' coefficients to identify the turning point.

Pickles and Rutter (1989) provided an example of analysis of turning points in qualitative data. They suggested several possible approaches. First, one can arrange the data into cross-tabulation tables or graphs to describe the relationships. These data can then be subjected to logit or log-linear analyses, depending on whether all predictor variables are categorical or not. However, Pickles and Rutter noted that this often leads to a piecemeal approach. In a study analagous to one that eating disorders researchers might design, Pickles and Rutter examined successful adult psychosocial functioning. In their analyses, for example, they first used a logit analysis to eliminate artifactual explanations and identified a major determining event (marriage to a deviant spouse). In the next phase (a second logit), they examined whether planfulness (forethought concerning life-choice decisions) was a mediator of the relationship between spousal choice and adult social functioning. Finally, in a third analysis, they looked at factors contributing to planfulness. The biggest problem with this approach is that each equation is treated as if it were independent of the others when, in fact, the equations have potentially correlated error variances. In addition, without a causal modeling approach it is difficult to discern whether some paths to successful adult functioning are direct and others are indirect. Pickles and Rutter (1989) then suggested using one of two causal modeling types of analysis. If the events have what they called a "natural" ordering, they suggested a latent-class Markov transition model. In their data, for example, there was some natural ordering in that childhood conduct disorder was assumed to predict adult functioning. If there is no natural ordering of events, then multistate event history models, which are related to survival and hazard analyses, might be employed (see Blossfeld, Hamerle, & Mayer, 1989, for a description). These actually might be preferable even if some natural ordering is assumed because issues of timing of events can more adequately be addressed. In either case, the parameters of the model must be carefully specified (see the earlier discussion of model specification for causal modeling techniques). Thus, Pickles and Rutter needed a strong theoretical model of how childhood and adult measures might combine to form the adult outcome states. These types of analyses are not appropriate for "fishing expeditions."

Individual Differences. First, it is possible to examine individuals or cases as the focus of analysis rather than adopting the more traditional focus on variables (Bergman, Eklund, & Magnusson, 1989). Cluster analysis groups together similar individuals based on scores on several variables. Thus, with the use of longitudinal data it is possible to examine, in cross-tabulations or in graphs, whether individuals remain in the same clusters over time. Prototypic growth curves can be generated using the cluster definitions at each time (Burchinal & Appelbaum, 1991). Factors contributing to movement from one cluster to another can also be examined (Bergman et al., 1989). Definition of time intervals between measures is critical to an understanding of the timing and dynamics of change. In data sets with many points of measurement, this approach may be unwieldy.

An alternative is to analyze the entire set of longitudinal data in one cluster analysis. The disadvantage of this approach is that individuals are placed in the cluster that is most appropriate across the entire data set. Thus, it is possible that two people could be placed in the same cluster because they were similar for 8 of the 10 points of measurement. However, this type of analysis would miss the point at which they diverged developmentally (Bergman et al., 1989).

Growth curve analysis may also prove useful in analyzing individual differences because its goal is to describe time-related patterns of change in a particular behavior or attribute of an individual. Once these patterns have been described, a second stage of analysis allows examination of influences on or outcomes of the growth processes (Burchinal &

Appelbaum, 1991). This is a powerful type of analysis because it makes it possible to abandon the assumption that one growth curve applies to the entire sample. Instead, researchers can describe either a variety of types of individual patterns of development or different patterns for different groups (Burchinal & Appelbaum, 1991).

There are some important restrictions on the use of growth curve analysis. First, it is virtually imperative that more than two observations be made (Burchinal & Appelbaum, 1991; Rogosa, Brandt, & Zimowski, 1982). The use of only two longitudinal points provides only a mediocre identification of developmental patterns. Furthermore, in a growth curve analysis, individual curves are generated by estimating the parameters of a regression function. These typically are better defined with the use of polynomial or logistic terms than by assuming a simple linear function (Burchinal & Appelbaum, 1991; Hauspie, Lindgren, Tanner, & Chrzastek-Spruch, 1989). A minimum number of observations is needed to generate a stable estimate, just as is true of regression using entire samples (see previous discussion). In the case of growth curve analysis, however, the term *observations* refers to the number of repeated measures per individual (rather than to the sample size). Two to five times as many observations as parameters are needed to estimate a stable individual function (Burchinal & Appelbaum, 1991). Thus, a two-point longitudinal study allows nothing more than a simple linear estimate, and even that is of questionable stability.

Second, the data used in a growth curve analysis must be quantitative. Furthermore, the characteristic being measured must be assumed to be structurally constant over time (Burchinal & Appelbaum, 1991). Phrased differently, there is no assumption of qualitative (or molar) shifts in the attribute over time. This may present a substantial problem for eating disorders researchers tracing pathways from childhood to adolescence or adulthood. There is some reason to believe that both personality dimensions (such as self-organization) and eating attitudes and behaviors (such as thinness schemata) undergo structural changes between childhood and adulthood (Smolak & Levine, 1994a, 1994c), although there is also some evidence for stability of eating disorder constructs throughout adolescence (Brooks-Gunn, Rock, & Warren, 1989). In general, it is currently not known whether there are normative qualitative shifts in the structures that eventually define eating problems. It should be emphasized that qualitative shifts in structures are not synonomous with different forms of a questionnaire or other measure given at different ages.

Measurement Issues With Children

As has been noted, researchers studying adolescents have commonly found earlier scores on eating problems measures (such as weight concerns or the EAT) to be the best predictor of later measures of eating problems (e.g., Attie & Brooks-Gunn, 1989; Killen et al., 1994; Leon et al., 1995). This suggests that research with younger children is needed to identify the root causes of disordered eating attitudes and behavior (Smolak & Levine, 1994c). This will require the development of new instruments to use with child samples. Although several measures have already been developed (see, e.g., Collins, 1991; Maloney et al., 1988; Mendelson & White, 1985, 1993), it is beyond the scope of this chapter to examine each of these measures. However, as the development of children's measures is in its infancy, there are a few general points worth noting.

The most common approach in developing measures for children has been to adapt an adult measure. For example, the body figures used to assess body ideal, perceived body shape, and body dissatisfaction with adults (Stunkard, Sorensen, & Schulsinger, 1983) have been redrawn for use with children (Collins, 1991) and adolescents (Cohn et al., 1987). Similarly, the ChEAT (Maloney et al., 1988) represents a rewording of the EAT for use with children and young adolescents.

The risk of this approach is that the construct underlying the measure changes across development. As has been noted already, it is not at all clear that children's attitudes and beliefs about body shape are associated with dieting in the way that adults' attitudes are. For example, elementary school children who diet do not necessarily see slimness as important to attractiveness, although there is an association between body dissatisfaction and dieting (Smolak & Levine, 1994c). Furthermore, it is not clear that dieting means the same thing to children, adolescents, and adults (Nichter & Nichter, 1991). Similarly, ChEAT data provided by Maloney et al. (1988) and by Maloney, McGuire, Daniels, and Specker (1989) suggest that young boys may have more eating problems than do elementary school girls. However, these findings are not consistent with other data (see, e.g., Gustafson-Larson & Terry, 1992; Smolak & Levine, 1994c), which suggests that there may be problems with the ChEAT itself.

There have been only limited attempts to demonstrate that the adapted measures assess the same constructs with children and adolescents as with adults. Smolak and Levine (1994b) have shown that the factor structure of the ChEAT given to middle school girls is similar to that of the EAT taken by adults. Similar analyses have not been attempted when children are the subjects, however. Existing psychometric data are not always strong and may raise more questions than they answer (see, e.g., Collins, 1991).

There is also the issue of how children comprehend certain questions. When working with middle school girls, for example, it has frequently been found that they interpret the ChEAT question concerning vomiting after eating to mean that they have the flu or some other illness. The problem here is not simply the use of the word *vomit* which could easily be replaced with a phrase that even preschoolers understand (such as *throw up*). The issue is that children interpret the question within the framework that they know. This may be a problem for younger children who may define frequency ratings (e.g., "sometimes") in terms of recent experience and so, for example, might answer "yes" if they have recently had the flu.

Reading difficulties may also interfere with accuracy of assessments. This is particularly likely if group testing techniques are used. Given practical issues, including both school and experimenter time, group testing can be very tempting. However, studies using this methodology are often marked by missing data (e.g., Killen et al., 1994; Levine et al., 1994), in part because some children have difficulty completing the questions within the appointed time or do not understand the instructions. The younger the children, the more imperative it is that they be interviewed individually, even if this simply means reading the questionnaire to them. This is probably particularly important with children who are under 10 years of age (approximately third grade and younger).

Finally, there is some information that young children simply do not provide reliably. For example, children under about 14 years of age do not supply reliable data concerning their parents' occupations (Hauser, 1994). In addition, children and adolescents (and perhaps even college students) often do not accurately report family income. Thus, information concerning socioeconomic status must be obtained from parents (Entwisle & Astone, 1994). Similarly, children may not know their height and weight. Obtaining information from parents presents additional challenges to the researcher, however. Questions may be asked on permission slips, on questionnaires sent home to the parents (preferably via the postal service, not the children themselves), or during brief telephone interviews.

Ethical Issues in Research With Children

Working with children raises special ethical concerns, especially in the area of informed consent. Of course, parental consent for children's research participation must always be obtained. In addition, however, children should have the right to refuse to participate in any procedure once they are old enough to understand (simple) explanations of the procedure and their rights. What types of problems does this requirement raise? When do children understand their rights as research participants? And how can researchers help them to better understand those rights?

Informed consent actually involves several components. First, the participants must be told about the relevant aspects of the procedure, for example, what they will be asked to do and what risks are involved.

Second, participants should be assured of the confidentiality of their responses and behaviors. Finally, participants should understand that they are able to withdraw or limit (e.g., by refusing to answer certain questions) their participation at any point without penalty. For children, the second and third components are intimately intertwined; in order to really believe that they can ask to stop the procedure, they must be convinced that their parents and teachers will not be told about their decision.

Abramovitch, Freedman, Thoden, and Nikolich (1991) described the purposes and procedures of their research to children in two different studies. They found that about one third of the 5- to 6-year-olds could not repeat the procedure for the experiment after it had been described to them. By age 9, however, all of the children understood what was going to happen during the experiment.

Why the experiment was being done was less clear to the children. Only 5% to 10% of the 5- to 7-year-old children could repeat the explanation of the goals and purposes of the research. Even among the 9- to 11-year-olds a third or more did not understand the purposes of the experiment well enough to explain them to the interviewer (Abramovitch et al., 1991).

Clearly, children's limited ability to understand the "what" and "why" of a project raises several problems. Some children might mistakenly believe that it is a school project or test and react with anxiety or answer the questions as they believe their teacher would want them to answer. Lack of clarity about procedures may result in an increased number of errors, a problem that may be particularly pronounced among children who are too shy to ask for assistance.

Children's performance in research projects may also be affected by their understanding of the confidentiality requirement. After being assured that their answers to questions would be confidential, 8- to 12-year-olds were asked whether they thought the experimenter would tell anyone (Abramovitch et al., 1991). "Yes" answers were given by 41% to 56% of the children. Interestingly, the oldest children tested, who had been identified by the school as gifted, were the most likely to believe that the experimenter would not maintain confidentiality.

Children typically believe that parents will be told of their performance. For studies dealing with sensitive family issues such as parental pressures to diet or family fighting, this could introduce substantial bias. The children may answer questions falsely in order to protect their families. Similarly, if children think that the teacher might be told if they complain about classroom ambience, they may not accurately report peer or teacher teasing about weight and shape.

The American Psychological Association's (1982) ethical guidelines require that all research participants be permitted to withdraw at any time. Although a majority of children over about 8 years of age understand that they may tell the experimenter that they wish to stop, about one fifth of them think that the experimenter or their parents will be angry if they do so (Abramovitch et al., 1991). This may make them particularly reluctant to refuse to continue.

Researchers must find ways to ensure children's rights as research participants. They can, for example, periodically ask children whether they wish to stop and return to the classroom. Parents should be told that their children can refuse to participate and should be encouraged to discuss this with their children. Researchers need to explicitly state to children that no one, including parents and teachers, will be told about their performance. It is also necessary to find ways to present more clearly the whys and whats of research to children. This might involve demonstrating how to do things, in person or on video, or asking the children to explain or repeat back what is being done. Such changes are important both out of respect to the children and to reduce error in data.

CONCLUSIONS

The application of developmental psychopathology models to the study of eating problems raises at least three broad concerns. First, there will be a substantial increase in the prevalence of longitudinal designs because only longitudinal data can identify the pathways to and away from eating problems. Such designs raise numerous practical problems, including attrition and instrument decay. They also raise a variety of statistical questions ranging from what constitutes a sufficient sample size and sufficient number of observations to how one disentangles interindividual from intraindividual differences.

Second, there is a need for more techniques that can deal with qualitative data. Dependent variables are sometimes best defined categorically (e.g., eating-disordered vs. not eating-disordered). Nevertheless, researchers have tended to rely substantially on continuous variables such as on the Eating Disorders Inventory scores as outcomes. In part, this reflects a common training bias in favor of ANOVA and regression techniques.

Researchers also need to be prepared to analyze qualitative structural change. This is a trickier issue because many analytic techniques in common use assume no such change. Nevertheless, many theories of cognitive and personality development, including those of Piaget and Erikson, are built on such changes. There is currently little reason to believe in a direct structural (molar) continuity from childhood to adulthood in the personality, behavioral, and attitudinal components of eating problems.

These issues are related to the third concern. Developmental psychopathology models will demand more work with children. This in turn requires that researchers develop psychometrically and theoretically sound measures. It also requires special attention to the ethical concerns involved in working with children, even those who do not have an eating problem.

Some tentative solutions to these problems have been offered in this chapter. However, only experience will indicate which research designs and statistical methods are most effective for eating disorders research. Similarly, only research can answer questions about molar change and about how later outcomes can be predicted from structurally distinct precursors. Despite such challenges, the promise of the developmental psychopathology model is great and may well be the only approach that will ultimately yield understanding of the multiple pathways to eating problems.

REFERENCES

Abramovitch, R., Freedman, J., Thoden, K., & Nikolich, C. (1991). Children's capacity to consent to participation in psychological research: Empirical findings. *Child Development, 62,* 1100–1109.

American Psychological Association. (1982). *Ethical principles in the conduct of research with human participants.* Washington, DC: Author.

Attie, I., & Brooks-Gunn, J. (1987). Weight-related concerns in women: A response to a cause of stress. In R. Barnett, L. Biener, & G. Baruch (Eds.), *Gender and stress* (pp. 218–254). New York: The Free Press.

Attie, I., & Brooks-Gunn, J. (1989). Development of eating problems in adolescent girls: A longitudinal study. *Developmental Psychology, 25,* 70–79.

Attie, I., & Brooks-Gunn, J. (1992). Developmental issues in the study of eating problems and disorders. In J. Crowther, D. Tennenbaum, S. Hobfoll, & M. Stephens (Eds.), *The etiology of bulimia nervosa: The individual and familial context* (pp. 35–58). Washington, DC: Hemisphere.

Bentler, P. (1989). *EQS: Structural equations program manual.* Los Angeles: BMDP Software.

Bergman, L., Eklund, G., & Magnusson, D. (1989). Studying individual development: Problems and methods. In D. Magnusson, L. Bergman, G. Rudinger, & B. Torestad (Eds.), *Problems and methods in longitudinal research: Stability and change* (pp. 1–27). Cambridge, England: Cambridge University Press.

Biddle, B., & Marlin, M. (1987). Causality, confirmation, credulity, and structural equation modeling. *Child Development, 58,* 4–17.

Blossfeld, H., Hamerle, A., & Mayer, K. (1989). Event-history models in social mobility research. In D. Magnusson, L. Bergman, G. Rudinger, & B. Torestad (Eds.), *Problems and methods in longitudinal research: Stability and change* (pp. 236–249). Cambridge, England: Cambridge University Press.

Brooks-Gunn, J., Rock, D., & Warren, M. (1989). Comparability of constructs across the adolescent years. *Developmental Psychology, 25,* 51–60.

Burchinal, M., & Appelbaum, M. (1991). Estimating individual developmental functions: Methods and their assumptions. *Child Development, 62,* 23–43.

Cassidy, H. (1981). *Using econometrics: A beginner's guide.* Reston, VA: Reston.

Cicchetti, D., & Schneider-Rosen, K. (1986). An organizational approach to childhood depression. In M. Rutter, C. Izard, & P. Read (Eds.), *Depression in young people: Developmental and clinical perspectives* (pp. 71–134). New York: Guilford.

Cohn, L., Adler, N., Irwin, C., Millstein, S., Kegeles, S., & Stone, G. (1987). Body-figure preferences in male and female adolescents. *Journal of Abnormal Psychology, 96,* 276–279.

Collins, M. (1991). Body figure perceptions and preferences among preadolescent children. *International Journal of Eating Disorders, 10,* 100–108.

Entwisle, D., & Astone, N. (1994). Some practical guidelines for measuring youth's race/ethnicity and socieconomic status. *Child Development, 65,* 1521–1540.

Garfinkel, P., & Garner, D. (1982). *Anorexia nervosa: A multidimensional approach.* New York: Brunner/Mazel.

Graber, J., Brooks-Gunn, J., Paikoff, R., & Warren, M. (1994). Prediction of eating problems: An eight year study of adolescent girls. *Developmental Psychology, 30,* 823–834.

Gustafson-Larson, A. M., & Terry, R. D. (1992). Weight-related behaviors and concerns of fourth-grade children. *Journal of the American Dietetic Association, 92,* 818–822.

Hauser, R. (1994). Measuring socioeconomic status in studies of child development. *Child Development, 65,* 1541–1545.

Hauspie, R., Lindgren, G., Tanner, J., & Chrzastek-Spruch, H. (1989). Modeling individual and average human growth data from childhood to adulthood. In D. Magnusson, L. Bergman, G. Rudinger, & B. Törestad (Eds.), *Problems and methods in longitudinal research: Stability and change* (pp. 28–46). Cambridge, England: Cambridge University Press.

Heatherton, T., & Polivy, J. (1992). Chronic dieting and eating disorders: A spiral model. In J. Crowther, D. Tennenbaum, S. Hobfoll, & M. Stephens (Eds.), *The etiology of bulimia nervosa: The individual and familial context* (pp. 133–156). Washington, DC: Hemisphere.

Killen, J., Taylor, C., Hayward, C., Wilson, D., Haydel, K., Hammer, L., Simmonds, B., Robinson, T., Litt, I., Varady, A., & Kraemer, H. (1994). Pursuit of thinness and onset of eating disorder symptoms in a community sample of adolescent girls: A three year prospective analysis. *International Journal of Eating Disorders, 16,* 227–238.

Leon, G., Fulkerson, J., Perry, C., & Early-Zald, M. (1995). Prospective analysis of personality and behavioral vulnerabilities and gender influences in the later development of disordered eating. *Journal of Abnormal Psychology, 104,* 140–149.

Levine, M. P., & Smolak, L. (1992). Toward a model of the developmental psychopathology of eating disorders: The example of early adolescence. In J. Crowther, D. Tennenbaum, S. Hobfoll, & M. Stephens (Eds.), *The etiology of bulimia nervosa: The individual and familial context* (pp. 59–80). Washington, DC: Hemisphere.

Levine, M. P., Smolak, L., & Hayden, H. (1994). The relation of sociocultural factors to eating attitudes and behaviors among middle school girls. *Journal of Early Adolescence, 14,* 471–490.

Levine, M. P., Smolak, L., Moodey, A., Shuman, M., & Hessen, L. (1994). Normative developmental challenges and dieting and eating disturbances in middle school girls. *International Journal of Eating Disorders, 15,* 11–20.

Maloney, M., McGuire, J., & Daniels, S. (1988). Reliability testing of a children's version of the Eating Attitudes Test. *Journal of the American Academy of Child and Adolescent Psychiatry, 5,* 541–543.

Maloney, M., McGuire, J., Daniels, S., & Specker, B. (1989). Dieting behavior and eating attitudes in children. *Pediatrics, 84,* 482–489.

Martin, J. (1987). Structural equation modeling: A guide for the perplexed. *Child Development, 58,* 33–37.

Menard, S. (1991). *Longitudinal data.* Newbury Park, CA: Sage.

Mendelson, B., & White, D. (1985). Development of self-body-esteem in overweight children. *Developmental Psychology, 21,* 90–96.

Mendelson, B., & White, D. (1993). *Manual for the Body-Esteem Scale—Children.* (Available from Donna White, Concordia University, Center for Research in Human Development, Montreal, Quebec, Canada H4B 1R6.)

Muliak, S. (1987). Toward a conception of causality applicable to experimentation and causal modeling. *Child Development, 58,* 18–32.

Nichter, M., & Nichter, M. (1991). Hype and weight. *Medical Anthropology, 13,* 249–284.

Norusis, M. (1990). *SPSS advanced statistics user's guide.* Chicago: SPSS, Inc.

Pedhazur, E. (1982). *Multiple regression in behavioral research.* New York: CBS College Publishing.

Pickles, A., & Rutter, M. (1989). Statistical and conceptual models of "turning points" in developmental processes. In D. Magnusson, L. Bergman, G. Rudinger, & B. Torestad (Eds.), *Problems and methods in longitudinal research: Stability and change* (pp. 133–165). Cambridge, England: Cambridge University Press.

Pike, K., & Rodin, J. (1991). Mothers, daughters, and disordered eating. *Journal of Abnormal Psychology, 100,* 198–204.

Rogosa, D. (1980). A critique of cross-lagged correlation. *Psychological Bulletin, 88,* 245–258.

Rogosa, D., Brandt, D., & Zimowski, M. (1982). A growth curve approach to the measurement of change. *Psychological Bulletin, 92,* 726–748.

Rosen, J., Compas, B., & Tacy, B. (1993). The relation among stress, psychological symptoms, and eating disorder symptoms: A prospective analysis. *International Journal of Eating Disorders, 14,* 153–162.

Smolak, L. (1993). *Adult development.* Englewood Cliffs, NJ: Prentice-Hall.

Smolak, L., & Levine, M. (1994a). Critical issues in the developmental psychopathology of eating disorders. In L. Alexander-Mott & D. Lumsden (Eds.), *Understanding eating disorders: Anorexia nervosa, bulimia nervosa, and obesity* (pp. 37–60). Washington, DC: Taylor & Francis.

Smolak, L., & Levine, M. (1994b). Psychometric properties of the Children's Eating Attitudes Test. *International Journal of Eating Disorders, 16,* 275–282.

Smolak, L., & Levine, M. (1994c). Toward an empirical basis for primary prevention of eating problems with elementary school children. *Eating Disorders: The Journal of Treatment & Prevention, 2,* 293–307.

Smolak, L., Levine, M. P., & Gralen, S. (1993). The impact of puberty and dating on eating problems among middle school girls. *Journal of Youth and Adolescence, 22,* 355–368.

Sroufe, A. (1989). Pathways to adaptation and maladaptation: Psychopathology as developmental deviation. In D. Cicchetti (Ed.), *Rochester Symposium on Developmental Psychopathology: Vol. 1. The emergence of a discipline* (pp. 13–40). Hillsdale, NJ: Lawrence Erlbaum Associates.

Stice, E., Schupak-Neuberg, E., Shaw, H., & Stein, R. (1994). Relation of media exposure to eating disorder symptomatology: An examination of mediating mechanisms. *Journal of Abnormal Psychology, 103,* 836–840.

Striegel-Moore, R., Silberstein, L., Frensch, P., & Rodin, J. (1989). A prospective study of disordered eating among college students. *International Journal of Eating Disorders, 8,* 499–509.

Stunkard, A., Sorensen, T., & Schulsinger, F. (1983). Use of the Danish adoption register for the study of obesity and thinness. In S. Kety (Ed.), *The genetics of neurological and psychiatric disorders* (pp. 115–120). New York: Raven.

Tanaka, J. S. (1987). "How big is big enough?": Sample size and goodness of fit in structural equation models with latent variables. *Child Development, 58,* 134–146.

Willett, J., & Singer, J. (1991). How long did it take? Using survival analysis in educational and psychological research. In L. Collins & J. Horn (Eds.), *Best methods for the analysis of change* (pp. 310–328). Washington, DC: American Psychological Association.

II

CONTRIBUTIONS FROM DEVELOPMENTAL PSYCHOLOGY

3

Liability to Psychopathology: A Quantitative Genetic Perspective

Richard Rende

The rapid progress in molecular genetics over the past few decades has led to many assumptions and assertions concerning the role that genes play in the development of psychopathology. The classic nature–nurture debate has been replaced in some publications by debates over the precise mode by which genes cause particular forms of psychopathology. It has been suggested that the classification of psychiatric disorders may in the future be revamped in terms of genetic etiology.

Although there is no question that genetic strategies represent an essential research tool for studying the etiology of most forms of psychopathology (e.g., Plomin, Rende, & Rutter, 1991; Rende & Plomin, 1994; Rutter et al., 1990), the case may be made that the pendulum in the nature–nurture debate has swung too far in the direction of biological causes (Plomin & Rende, 1991). There are numerous ways in which genes and environments may play a role in the development of psychopathology, and it is essential that researchers who are not specialists in quantitative genetics or related disciplines become acquainted with their fundamental etiological models, research strategies, and statistical approaches in order to make reasonable inferences from the research literature.

This chapter consists of an explicit introduction, in language accessible to nongeneticists, of some of the key issues in the study of nature and nurture, especially as applied to developmental psychopathology. A brief overview of the purpose and methods of family studies is provided in the first section because family studies represent a first step in genetic approaches to psychopathology. The second section contains a simple outline of the various etiological models that specify how genes and environments contribute to psychopathological conditions and indicates the typical research strategies that correspond to the different models. The focus of the third section is the concept of genetic liability, which appears to be a plausible construct for many forms of psychopathology including eating disorders. In the fourth and final section is a discussion of the developmental principles involved in investigating the genetic liability to psychopathology.

DO SPECIFIC FORMS OF PSYCHOPATHOLOGY RUN IN FAMILIES?

The current interest in genetic bases of psychopathology stems in part from a large body of family studies. Family studies are used for the straightforward purpose of indicating whether a given trait or condition "runs in families." If a condition does not run in families, it then seems that familial—including genetic—mechansims are not implicated in the etiology of the disorder. Similarly, if a disorder is shown to be highly familial, it is then worthwhile to consider additional research strategies to determine whether the familial aggregation is due to common genes, common environment, or some combination of these factors.

The current methodologies used in family studies are more complicated than might be assumed, given the straightforward purpose of conducting a family study (Rende & Weissman, in press; Weissman et al., 1986). Hence, before considering what familial aggregation means, it is necessary to review the most important principles in designing and conducting family studies. One consideration is the source of information in a family design. A traditional method for collecting family data in clinical research has been to ask the patient, or proband, about psychopathology in the family. This approach, referred to as the family history method, has been standardized so that the questions included are precise (Andreasen, Endicott, Spitzer, & Winokur, 1977). Although this is an important method of assessing the family history of psychiatric disorders, a better and more powerful method is to interview the family members directly, as direct interviews have been found to be a more complete source of diagnostic information on individuals within the family (Weissman et al., 1986). One difficulty with this latter approach, however, is the pragmatic problem of being able to conduct direct interviews with all family members, for reasons including refusal by relatives to participate in the study, unavailability caused by geographic distance, and death. For this reason, the family history method has a place alongside the family study method in the assessment of the family history of psychiatric disorder, although it must be emphasized that family history approaches tend to underestimate rates of disorders in relatives (Weissman et al., 1986).

Another important consideration in the conducting of family studies is the selection of probands and controls. In most family studies the probands or index cases are patients receiving treatment for the disorder of interest. This situation represents a potential bias in family studies, as the majority of individuals with psychiatric disorders never receive treatment (Weissman et al., 1986). Hence, questions may be raised about the generalizability of findings to the population as a whole if the sampling procedure involves recruitment from a specialty clinic. A preferable sampling strategy for selecting probands is to secure a representative sample from the general population (Kendler, 1993); however, this method poses practical limitations, especially for psychiatric disorders that have low prevalence rates.

Similarly, it is essential to use appropriately matched control groups. The purpose here is to select individuals without the disorder of interest and to determine rates of disorders in their family members; this information is then compared to the rates of disorders in family members of probands. Hence, probands and controls should be matched on confounding factors likely to affect the rates of disorders in relatives, such as age, gender, and social class. The types of control groups used in family studies vary according to the purpose of the study. Many family studies have used a normal control group consisting of individuals recruited from the community who have never had a psychiatric disorder. Other control groups, however, may be considered in order to examine questions about the specificity of familial aggregation. For example, in a family study of eating disorders, a control group of individuals who have a disorder other than that of interest (e.g., depression) provides a test of the hypothesis that rates of disorders in relatives of probands "breed true" (e.g., siblings of probands with eating disorders are more likely to develop eating disorders, whereas siblings of probands with depression are more likely to develop depression). Because there is no consensus to date as to the best type of control group for family studies (e.g., normal vs. psychiatric controls), it is imperative that the type of control group used is specified in order to determine the implications of a given family study (e.g., whether it shows familial aggregation as compared to normal control groups or specificity of aggregation as compared to psychiatric control groups).

Once probands and controls are selected, family studies generally make use of a retrospective cohort design in which family members are asked to recall their lifetime course of psychiatric disorders. As already discussed, all living and willing first-degree relatives are assessed to determine their lifetime course of disorders, and family history information is obtained on deceased relatives or on relatives who are unable to be interviewed directly. Variations of this design include the high-risk paradigm, in which the focus is specific to offspring of affected probands (and matched controls), and bottom-up studies, in which the focus is on the family members of child or adolescent probands (see Rende & Weissman, in press). Whichever design is used, family studies profit from the use of reliable and valid diagnostic instruments to determine the lifetime course of disorders (Rende & Weissman, in press; Weissman et al., 1986).

The final step is to determine statistically whether a given disorder runs in families. The prevalence of the disorder under study in first-degree relatives of probands is compared with the prevalence among relatives of controls. If the prevalence is statistically greater in the relatives of affected probands, then the disorder under investigation is considered to aggregate within families. As with other issues in family studies, this straightforward process is complicated by analytic complexities, and many sophisticated methods are used in state-of-the-art family studies (Rende & Weissman, in press; Weissman et al., 1986). Although probands and controls are matched as closely as possible on potential confounding factors such as age and gender, it is likely that perfect matching is not attained. For this reason potential confounding factors must be controlled for statistically and prevalence rates must be estimated for relatives of probands and controls. A standard method is to use a multivariate regression model for survival data, such as Cox's (1972) proportional-hazards model, with the potential confounding factors included as independent variables (Weissman et al., 1986).

A fundamental concern in the calculation of prevalence rates in family studies is the age of onset of the disorder under study. In a family study, lifetime risk refers to the risk of onset of a particular disorder between birth and a particular age, such as the age of the individual when an interview is conducted. However, because age of onset varies for given disorders and usually encompasses a rather wide range, studies must take into account the ages of subjects under investigation because some or many may not have passed through the age of risk. A number of statistical methods have been developed to adjust for variable age of onset in relatives (see Weissman et al., 1986), and these are regarded as essential in conducting or interpreting family studies, especially when children and adolescents are assessed (Rende & Weissman, in press).

This brief overview of key methodological issues demonstrates that determining whether a given form of psychopathology runs in families is a laborious and technical proposition. This point is important because many family studies have been published that do not meet the most rigorous standards. For example, Kendler et al. (1991) suggested that some studies that examine whether bulimia nervosa (BN) aggregates in families have suffered from several methodological limitations including an exclusive reliance on family history information. A review of studies that have met minimum standards of methodological rigor has suggested that eating disorders do run in families, or, more specifically, that "rates of anorexia nervosa and bulimia nervosa in families of anorexia nervosa and bulimia nervosa probands are elevated compared to control populations" (Woodside, 1993, p. 201). This conclusion is well worded because it literally states what may be inferred from properly conducted family studies: that a given form of psychopathology occurs at an increased rate in family members of individuals with the condition of interest as compared to appropriate control groups. What family studies do not indicate, however, is the reason for this phenomenon. Hence, for forms of psychopathology such as eating disorders, which do seem to show evidence of familial aggregation (Woodside, 1993), the next question to consider is which factors are responsible for the tendency of these conditions to run in families.

WHY DO FORMS OF PSYCHOPATHOLOGY AGGREGATE IN FAMILIES?

The proliferation and success of molecular genetic techniques (sometimes referred to as the *new genetics*) has led to an expectation that all forms of psychopathology that have a familial basis will be shown eventually to be genetic conditions. Although it is possible that a familial disorder may be entirely genetic, familial aggregation can clearly be caused by genetic effects, environmental effects, or a combination of genes and environments. Because family studies confound genetic and environmental influences (i.e., first-degree relatives who live together share common genes as well as common environmental influences), specialized methods are necessary to attempt to decompose familial aggregation into genetic and environmental sources.

Perhaps the most important point is that it is incorrect to assume that familial aggregation proves (or disproves) either genetic or environmental transmission. Rather, familial aggregation implies only that there are factors common to family members that result in a disorder aggregating in the family. The next task is to determine the most feasible model to explain familial aggregation. As shown in Table 3.1, there are a number of plausible models to be considered.

Over the past decade there has been much interest in the promise of the first model shown in Table 3.1, the *single gene* model (e.g., Mullan & Murray, 1989). This interest stems from the spectacular success of genetic linkage studies that have isolated the specific regions of the genomes responsible for a number of genetic conditions such as Huntington's Disease (Gusella et al., 1983). The hope of similar breakthroughs in the study of psychopathology were bolstered by reports of the isolation of the genomic regions underlying schizophrenia (Sherrington et al., 1988) and bipolar illness (Egeland, Gerhard, Pauls, Sussex, & Kidd, 1987). However, the excitement generated by these

TABLE 3.1
Etiological Models Specifying the Number of Genetic and Environmental
Influences on Psychopathology

	Number of Factors	
Model	Genetic	Environmental
Mendelian ("single gene")	One	None
Oligogenic	Few	None
Polygenic	Many	None
Multifactorial	Many	Many
Polyenvironmental	None	Many
Oligoenvironmental	None	Few
Single environmental	None	One

reports was soon tempered by the lack of replicated results and the retraction of findings (Plomin & Rende, 1991). To date, molecular genetic strategies have not had a major impact on the understanding of psychopathology, with the exception of rare disorders such as the Fragile-X syndrome (Rende & Plomin, 1994).

This somewhat pessimistic conclusion is not intended to imply that the genetic basis of different forms of psychopathology will not be uncovered. Rather, it is presented to demonstrate that the isolation of genomic regions underlying well-defined psychiatric disorders that are assumed to have a genetic origin may be a time-consuming and complex process. For example, although autism is considered to be a highly genetic disorder, the molecular basis of this condition remains a mystery (e.g., Rutter et al., 1990). Perhaps more important, it must be appreciated that the new genetics works only for disorders that are caused by single genes and that breakthroughs should therefore not be expected for forms of psychopathology that are not single-gene conditions (Plomin, 1990).

This caveat is especially important because it appears that many forms of psychopathology are not single-gene disorders (Rende & Plomin, 1994). Sophisticated statistical strategies (such as segregation analysis) are available and can determine whether patterns of familial aggregation follow specific laws of genetics that govern single-gene conditions (see Rutter et al., 1990). It is appropriate to conclude that at this point many psychopathological disorders, as currently defined, do not present clear patterns of inheritance consistent with single-gene models (Rende & Plomin, 1995). Hence, it is necessary to use research strategies that are not geared toward single-gene conditions, but that rather invoke models that allow for the possibility of multiple genetic and environmental influences.

An especially influential approach to the etiology of psychopathology has been the multifactorial model used by quantitative geneticists (for an overview see Plomin, DeFries, & McClearn, 1990). This model focuses on variation in traits in the population, that is, on the ubiquitous individual differences that are routinely studied by developmentalists. Quantitative genetic theory attempts to decompose this phenotypic variation into different components of variance, namely, variation caused by genetic differences among individuals, variation caused by differences in environment, and the possible interaction and correlation of genetic and environmental factors. In quantitative genetic theory the emphasis is on estimating the total impact of a number of genes rather than on searching for a single gene that completely explains variation in a trait. This approach, which has historical roots in the early 1900s, is based on the realization that a continuous distribution (or individual differences) will emerge for a trait if several genes affect the trait (Plomin et al., 1990). In addition, it is possible within the quantitative genetic approach to allow for and model statistically the overall amount of variance in a trait that is accounted for by genetic differences among individuals; this subject is addressed in greater detail subsequently.

Before discussing the fundamental research designs used in quantitative genetic studies, it is important to emphasize that environmental effects are also examined in this approach. Quantitative genetic research may actually provide the best evidence for environmental influence because the possibility of genetic influence is also evaluated. Hence, the point of quantitative genetic research is not to determine that a trait is genetic but to determine the extent to which genetic and environmental factors influence behavioral variation.

As pointed out earlier, family studies assess the extent of resemblance for genetically related individuals, although they cannot disentangle possible environmental sources of resemblance. Hence, quantitative geneticists use two classic methods, adoption studies and twin studies, to sort out the effects of nature and nurture on a trait (see Plomin et al., 1990; Rende & Plomin, 1994; Rutter et al., 1990). In adoption paradigms, genetically related individuals adopted apart provide evidence of the degree to which familial resemblance is caused by hereditary resemblance. This is like a natural experiment in which family members share heredity but not environment. The other side of the adoption design tests the influence of nature by studying the resemblance of genetically unrelated individuals living together in adoptive families. The concern with this research design is that nature and nurture are not clearly separated if selective placement occurs in which children are placed with adoptive parents who resemble the birth parents. However, the extent of selective placement can and should be assessed empirically when reporting results of an adoption study. Research to date suggests that selective placement has not confounded the results of major adoption studies such as the Colorado Adoption Project (Plomin, DeFries, & Fulker, 1988).

Twin studies are also like natural experiments in which the resemblance of identical twins, whose genetic identity can be expressed as a genetic relatedness of 1.0, is compared to the resemblance of fraternal twins, first-degree relatives whose coefficient of genetic relatedness is 0.50. If heredity affects a behavioral trait, identical twins will resemble each other on the trait to a greater extent than will fraternal twins. The concern with the twin experiment is the possibility that identical twins experience more similar environments than fraternal twins and thus that the greater similarity of identical twins as compared to fraternal twins may be mediated in part by environmental factors. This issue, referred to as the equal environments assumption of the twin method, may also be tested empirically. To date, empirical tests of the equal environments assumption have shown it to be valid (Kendler, Neale, Kessler, Heath, & Eaves, 1993).

Genetic designs exist other than the classical adoption and twin designs. For example, a variant of the adoption methodology is the cross-fostering design, in which adopted children are reared by parents with the disorder under study. Variations of the classical twin design include the families-of-identical-twins design, co-twin control studies in which members of identical twin pairs are treated differently, and studies of discordant identical twin pairs. Combinations of designs are particularly important for triangulating estimates of quantitative genetic parameters. For example, twin and adoption designs can be combined by studying twins reared apart as well as control twins reared together. The combination of designs helps to ensure that estimates of genetic and environmental influence are not specific to a particular methodology (Rutter et al., 1990).

Quantitative genetic methods can assess the statistical significance and the magnitude of the genetic effect (Rende & Plomin, 1994). Heritability is a descriptive statistic that assigns an effect size to genetic influence. For example, the correlation for identical twins reared apart in uncorrelated environments directly estimates heritability. This correlation represents the proportion of variance that covaries for identical twins who share all of their heredity but not their rearing environments. If hereditary influence were unimportant the correlation would be low; conversely, the correlation would be high if heredity were primarily responsible for phenotypic variance. Although behavioral scientists reflexively square correlations to estimate variance (this is an appropriate way to estimate the amount of variance in one trait that can be predicted by another trait), correlations for family members such as that for identical twins reared apart represent components of variance and are not squared. Thus, a correlation of .40 for reared-apart identical twins implies a heritability of 40%. That is, genetic variance accounts for 40% of the observed variance in the population.

Model-fitting techniques are routinely used in quantitative genetic analyses to estimate heritability because they make assumptions explicit, provide a test of the model, and make it possible to analyze data from multiple groups simultaneously, provide standard errors of estimate, and compare the fit of alternative models (Kendler, 1993). Model fitting essentially involves solving a series of simultaneous equations. For example, the twin method consists of two equations that express the observed correlations for identical and fraternal twins in terms of two unknowns that represent expected components of variance ($1.0\ G + E$ for identical twins and $0.5\ G + E$ for fraternal twins). The solution to these two equations with two unknowns merely involves doubling the difference between the identical and fraternal twin correlations to estimate G; E is estimated as the residual twin similarity not explained by G. As data for other family groups are added, more equations are available that make it possible to solve for more parameters and to compare alternative models.

The standard approach to model fitting is to apply what has been termed an ACE model (Kendler, 1993; Neale & Cardon, 1992). This model specifies the three latent variables of interest to quantitative geneticists: A, or additive genetic variance (the variance term used to estimate heritability); C, the common or shared environments (environmental influences that produce similarities in family members independently of genetic influence); and E, the individual specific or nonshared environment (environment that is specific to an individual and hence not correlated or shared with a family member; more technically, variance that is not explained by common genetic or environmental factors). In the ACE approach, a series of models are fitted to the observed data to determine statistically the most parsimonious model. Hence, a full ACE model can be compared to a reduced model (e.g., AC or AE) to determine which parameters must be included in a best-fitting model; that is, if a reduced model achieves as good a fit as the full model, then the reduced model is accepted.

In interpreting the results of a quantitative genetic analysis, it is crucial to bear in mind that the ACE parameters are descriptive statistics. They are no different from any other statistical parameters calculated in a model-fitting approach. This means that the results of a quantitative genetic analysis are specific to the particular population assessed, and that the parameter estimates have the usual statistical properties of descriptive statistics, including error of measurement. The descriptive nature of the analytic approach leads to best estimates of the relative contributions of genetics and environments on a trait, and conclusions are best drawn when there are a number of studies, using a number of quantitative genetic designs, that converge on similar parameters.

A final consideration is that the sampling scheme used in a quantitative genetic study should be considered when evaluating the results. Because findings are technically limited to the populations studied, it is important to know whether there are potential biases in recruiting the samples. For example, the point made previously about the possible limitations of selecting probands from treatment facilities in family studies also applies to twin and adoption paradigms. Although no sampling procedure is without problems, quantitative genetic studies that use an epidemiological framework in selecting samples may be preferable to those that recruit referred samples (see Kendler, 1993).

WHAT IS LIABILITY TO PSYCHOPATHOLOGY IN QUANTITATIVE GENETIC TERMS?

Over the past two decades a large number of quantitative genetic studies have implied that genetic factors play a substantial role in individual differences in the core traits studied by developmentalists, especially cognitive and personality traits, as well as in most forms of psychopathology (Rende & Plomin, 1995). Overall, the pattern of results for most traits has been similar and may be described by two principles. First, familial resemblance appears to be caused primarily by genes shared by family members rather than by shared environmental factors. Second, genetic factors only partially explain variation in traits, and a substantial portion of variance remains unexplained by shared genes or shared environment and has been labeled nonshared environment.

A key consideration in interpreting the core findings from quantitative genetic studies is that these portions of variance are "anonymous" in the sense that their sources are ascribed to latent variables. That is, the informative research designs and statistical models only indicate statistical effect sizes of the latent constructs "heritability," "shared environment," and "nonshared environment." It is wrong to assume, then, that if a trait has been demonstrated through quantitative genetic studies to have a significant heritability, that researchers understand what it is that is inherited. Rather, substantial heritability estimates may be viewed as an impetus to search for the genes that affect variation in a trait as well as for the biological and psychosocial pathways through which genetic factors affect phenotypic expression.

The recognition that heritability estimates do not indicate what is inherited was formalized in a liability model of disease proposed by Falconer (1965). In the prototypical liability model, a disorder that is defined categorically (i.e., as a diagnosed condition) may be attributable to a varying combination of genetic and environmental risk factors, or to the same latent traits used in quantitative genetic research discussed earlier. The key contribution in the liability approach is the suggestion that a hypothetical distribution of risk or liability to categorical disorders may be assumed. The normal distribution of liability (sometimes referred to as vulnerability) may then have a threshold that determines whether an individual develops the disorder. Estimates of genetic and environmental influences on the liability to disorders may be made from statistical transformations of concordance rates for a given disorder into the more typical components of variance utilized in quantitative genetic research (see Kendler, 1993).

Although the statistical basis of the liability approach is complex, the crucial point is that quantitative geneticists studying diagnosed forms of psychopathology attempt to estimate the genetic and environmental influences on a hypothetical construct of liability or risk to a disorder. This approach rejects the notion that the disorder under study is caused by a single gene that has a sledgehammer effect on development, as is the case with numerous medical conditions such as Huntington's disease. Rather, the emphasis is on studying genetic influences that may make only a partial and probabilistic contribution to phenotypic variation. More simply, the idea is, in genetic terms, that what is inherited is not a genetic disorder but genes that convey risk for developing the disorder.

For example, it is estimated that an individual with a schizophrenic genotype has only a 50% chance of eventually developing schizophrenia (Gottesman, 1991). It is also believed that for most individuals at risk for schizophrenia, the pathway from genotype to phenotype is probabilistic and reflective of both genetic and environmental influences (e.g., Goldsmith & Gottesman, in press). Such a probabilistic influence of genes on phenotypic variation has been described as setting a "reaction range" or "reaction surface" of behavior rather than deterministically producing a phenotype (Turkheimer & Gottesman, 1991).

A good example of the probabilistic effect of genes on psychopathology is a recent twin study of BN (Kendler et al., 1991). A genetic epidemiological approach was used, such that twins were recruited from the general population rather than through a specialty clinic. Two basic findings highlight the probabilistic nature of genetic influence inferred from the biometrical model fitting conducted in this study. First, the authors concluded that about 50% of the variance in liability to BN could be ascribed to genes, with the remaining variance due to nonshared (or individual-specific) environments. Second, the genetic influence detected by model-fitting procedures was captured best by a multiple threshold model, in which genes could contribute to either classic BN or subsyndromal cases. Hence, the current available evidence on genetic contributions to BN suggests that genes can explain only half of the phenotypic variance in liability and that the impact of genes may lead to a range of eating dysfunctions rather than to a tightly defined clinical condition.

WHAT ARE THE DEVELOPMENTAL
IMPLICATIONS OF THE LIABILITY APPROACH TO
PSYCHOPATHOLOGY?

The implication of the liability approach to psychopathology is that the estimation of parameters in quantitative genetic studies is a first step in the lengthy process of understanding the etiology of a given disorder. Quantitative genetic research is essential in first identifying the most important sources of phenotypic variation. For example, if a number of twin and adoption studies consistently demonstrated very low estimates of heritability for a given disorder, then it would seem unreasonable to search intensively for a genetic basis. In contrast, significant and substantial heritability estimates may highlight the need to examine further the mechanisms by which genes contribute to the trait or disorder of interest.

Ideally, quantitative genetic studies that demonstrated a significant contribution of genetic variation to a trait would be followed by molecular genetic strategies that would isolate the specific region (or regions) on the genome. Although there is much hope that quantitative genetics will be enriched by a merger with molecular genetics (e.g., Plomin et al., 1991; Rende & Plomin, 1994), such a merger is still a long-term proposition for the study of most forms of psychopathology. A more feasible approach may be to use quantitative and behaviorally based research to help identify in more concrete terms the specific phenotypic domain in which the hypothetical genetic liability to a given form of psychopathology manifests itself.

One notable example of such an approach is the search for biological markers of psychopathology; these markers may be more heritable than the diagnosed conditions they underlie (Rende & Plomin, 1995). Current research on schizophrenia has highlighted the possible utility of this strategy (Moldin & Erlenmeyer-Kimling, 1994). For example, one focus has been to examine eye movement abnormalities as a potential biological marker for the genetic liability to schizophrenia (Holzman & Matthysse, 1990). Other potential markers that are under investigation include structural brain abnormalities, biochemical markers, and attentional and cognitive disturbances (Moldin & Erlenmeyer-Kimling, 1994). This work is notable in that attempts are made to specify which biobehavioral pathways may represent the genetic liability to the complex phenotype of clinically defined schizophrenia.

The search for genetic liability does not have to focus specifically on biological markers. For example, a number of studies have identified a particular aspect of temperament that may be a risk factor for the development of anxiety disorders (see Rosenbaum et al., 1993). This work suggests that behavioral inhibition to the unfamiliar is a genetically influenced trait that may be a marker of risk for anxiety disorders and that it may be observed in early childhood and perhaps infancy. What is important here is the idea that the genetically influenced trait may emerge at an earlier point in time than the clinical condition that it underlies.

The example of behavioral inhibition to the unfamiliar highlights the importance of adopting a developmental perspective on the timing of the expression of genetic liability. A crucial theme in current thinking about genetic liability for psychopathology is that genetic effects may "turn on" at different points in the life span (Rende & Plomin, 1995). In some psychopathological conditions the manifestation of genetic liability occurs very early in the life span, two such conditions include the Fragile X syndrome and autism. In contrast, schizophrenia, which as discussed earlier is believed to have a substantial genetic component, typically emerges in late adolescence (Weinberger, 1987) and in many cases does so without any obvious phenotypic warnings prior to the first onset. Moreover, the clinical symptomatology that characterizes Huntington's disease does not emerge until adulthood, even though this disorder is known to be attributable to a single gene locus. Hence, genetic effects on psychopathology should not automatically be assumed to occur early in development, as the impact of genes on behavior is dynamic throughout the life span.

The challenge for researchers interested in uncovering the genetic liability for psychopathology is to search for biobehavioral pathways that represent a diathesis to a disorder but that may be present before the emergence of the clinical syndrome. In this regard both clinical and developmental approaches may be essential in detecting potential biobehavioral and phenotypic markers that predate the onset of clinical conditions. For example, numerous studies have suggested that impaired attention—as measured using the Continuous Performance Test (CPT)—may be a useful marker of liability to schizophrenia because it is detectable before the onset of the disorder and predictive of later behavioral disturbances (Cornblatt & Kelip, 1994). The importance of this work is twofold: Not only does it suggest that the study of attentional impairment may provide clues about the pathophysiology of schizophrenia, it also suggests that the CPT would be a useful sceening instrument to identify vulnerable individuals for preventive intervention programs (Cornblatt & Kelip, 1994).

In addition to examining appropriate markers of a disorder from both a clinical and developmental perspective, it is important to consider that a given clinical condition may in fact reflect a set of conditions with different etiologies (Rende & Plomin, 1995). Such thinking has characterized research on severe forms of psychopathology, including schizophrenia (Gottesman, 1991). Conversely, it is also possible that different forms of psychopathology may share common genetic roots, which may not be surprising given that comorbidity may be the rule rather than the exception for many forms of developmental psychopathology (Caron & Rutter, 1991).

The search for either genetic heterogeneity within a disorder or genetic homogeneity across disorders may be aided by recent developments in multivariate genetic strategies (Neale & Cardon, 1992). Although the methods are complex, the gist of the approach may be understood as an extension of the basic designs discussed earlier, such as the twin design (Plomin et al., 1990; Rende & Plomin, 1994). In the case of twins, rather than comparing the prevalence in monozygotic versus dizygotic twins of a single Trait X, the basis for multivariate genetic analysis is the "cross-twin" resemblance for one twin on Trait X and the co-twin on Trait Y. The phenotypic correlation between X and Y is assumed to be mediated genetically to the extent that monozygotic cross-twin resemblance exceeds dizygotic cross-twin resemblance. For example, such a bivariate approach has been used recently to demonstrate that the notable comorbidity between depression and BN may reflect some genetic influences that are common to both disorders (Walters et al., 1992).

The general multivariate model already described may also be used to examine genetic correlations over time if longitudinal data are available (see Plomin, 1986). The basis for estimating age-to-age genetic correlations, in the case of the twin design, is the twin cross-correlation across ages rather than the usual twin correlation at each age. The developmental approach may be combined with multivariate strategies to determine whether a trait at a particular point in time has genetic influences in common with a different trait observed at a later point in time (Neale & Cardon, 1992). This method may represent a feasible way of examining from a quantitative genetic perspective whether a putative marker of liability to a disorder is genetically correlated to the manifestation of the disorder at a later point in the life span.

HOW SHOULD RESEARCHERS APPROACH THE STUDY OF LIABILITY IN DEVELOPMENTAL PSYCHOPATHOLOGY?

The availability of multivariate genetic techniques may prove to be very valuable in the study of liability in developmental psychopathology. The best studies will result from a sophisticated merger of these strategies with informative measures derived from developmental psychopathology research and theory (Plomin et al., 1991). Developmental psychopathologists may identify the typical longitudinal course of disorders, including the salient risk factors that may predate the onset of symptomatology. Such information would be essential to quantitative geneticists interested in identifying potential phenotypic or biobehavioral markers that may reflect the underlying genetic liability to a disorder. Consider, as an example, current research on eating disorders. As discussed earlier, the twin study conducted by Kendler et al. (1991) has suggested that BN has a substantial genetic component that is estimated to account for about half of the variance in liability to this disorder. This study also suggested that the genetic liability contributes to a broad spectrum of eating problems rather than to a tightly defined clinical disorder. Hence, an important issue from a developmental psychopathology perspective is to identify potential biobehavioral or phenotypic markers of the genetic liability to BN that may emerge earlier in the life span than the onset of the clinical condition.

Woodside (1993) suggested that binge eating in the presence of dietary restraint may represent, in part, a genetic liability to develop BN. To test this hypothesis the sophisticated methodology used in developmental multivariate genetic studies may be exploited. Although the techniques are complex, the basic strategy can be outlined in relatively simple terms in order to convey the most fundamental concepts.

To begin, a longitudinal design would be used to measure the candidate trait (binge eating in the presence of dietary restraint) at one point in time, and the clinical condition (a spectrum of bulimialike symptomatology) at a later point in time. In this longitudinal design an informed developmental perspective is crucial to ensure that the traits of interest are measured at salient points in the life span. For example, it would be necessary to assess the candidate trait during a developmental period in which variance in this trait may be observed: If there were no variance (e.g., if an age were selected in which this trait had yet to emerge), then the trait would have no prognostic value. Similarly, when sampling for a diagnostic condition it would be important to select an age past the typical age of first onset to help ensure that some cases of the disorder begin to emerge in the sample.

In choosing the sample the decision might be made to focus exclusively on females because of the noted gender difference in BN (i.e., many more females than males are affected). Although there are quantitative genetic methods that can test for gender differences in patterns of heritability (Neale & Cardon, 1992), it must be appreciated that quantitative genetics takes as a starting point phenotypic variation, which may be divided into genetic and environmental components. Without notable variation within a gender (e.g., if very few males in the population are affected), such genetic methods cannot be applied. Simply put, researchers can analyze only the phenotypes that emerge in quantitative genetic studies, without making claims about which phenotypes are present in subpopulations.

Thus far, then, the hypothetical longitudinal study outlined here tests whether a candidate trait measured at one point in time is predictive of the onset of a clinical condition measured at a later point in time. To make this design informative in terms of genetic liability, it would be necessary to ensure that the sample includes at least two types of paired individuals that represent different degrees of genetic relatedness, such as monozygotic and dizygotic twins. To enhance confidence in the generalizability of the sample, an epidemiological sampling frame would also be beneficial in selecting a pool of twins to be recruited.

If such a sample of twins were secured it would then be possible, at the conclusion of measurement, to consider whether the candidate trait showed evidence of genetic influence, whether the clinical condition showed evidence of genetic influence, and whether there was considerable overlap in the genetic influences on the candidate trait and the clinical condition. If these three conditions were satisfied empirically then the possibility would exist that the candidate trait was indeed a manifestation of genetic liability to the disorder.

This simplified outline of a very complicated research undertaking is not presented as a recipe for conducting a multivariate, longitudinal quantitative genetic study. Rather, the intention is to map out conceptually the fundamental ideas that should be considered when thinking about the genetic liability for developmental psychopathology. To offer a concluding comment, I believe that identifying genetic liability is an essential step in formulating more definitive etiological models that include the effects of the environment. That is, identifying the genetic liability in biobehavioral or phenotypic terms may inform the design of studies that examine the interplay between this liability and salient environmental influences. Until the liability is identified, however, it will be an extremely difficult task to examine possible ways in which nature and nurture intersect, including genotype–environment interaction and correlation (see Rende & Plomin, 1992), simply because the "genotype" is a latent construct. It is very much the case that genetic strategies provide especially useful ways of understanding how the environment works (Plomin & Rende, 1991; Plomin et al., 1991; Rende & Plomin, 1994). However, in terms of developmental psychopathology such work may require the initial specification of genetic liability in order to feasibly study how this vulnerability intersects with environmental effects in contributing to the expression of complex phenotypes such as the eating disorders.

ACKNOWLEDGMENTS

The support of an Aaron Diamond Postdoctoral Research Fellowship in the Biomedical and Social Sciences and a NARSAD Young Investigator Award are gratefully acknowledged.

REFERENCES

Andreasen, N., Endicott, J., Spitzer, R., & Winokur, G. (1977). The family history method using diagnostic criteria: Reliability and validity. *Archives of General Psychiatry, 34,* 1229–1235.

Caron, C., & Rutter, M. (1991). Comorbidity in child psychopathology: Concepts, issues, and research strategies. *Journal of Child Psychology and Psychiatry, 32,* 1063–1080.

Cornblatt, B., & Kelip, J. (1994). Impaired attention, genetics, and the pathophysiology of schizophrenia. *Schizophrenia Bulletin, 20,* 31–46.

Cox, D. R. (1972). Regression models and life tables. *Journal of the Royal Statistical Society, 34,* 187–220.

Egeland, J., Gerhard, D., Pauls, D., Sussex, J., & Kidd, K. (1987). Bipolar affective disorders linked to DNA markers on chromosome 11. *Nature, 325,* 783–787.

Falconer, D.S. (1965). The inheritance of liability to certain diseases, estimated from the incidence among relatives. *Annals of Human Genetics, 29,* 51–76.

Goldsmith, H., & Gottesman, I. (in press). Heritable variability and variable heritability in developmental psychopathology. In M. Lenzenweger & J. Haugaard (Eds.), *Frontiers of developmental psychopathology.* New York: Oxford University Press.

Gottesman, I. I. (1991). *Schizophrenia genesis: The origins of madness.* New York: Freeman.

Gusella, J., Wexler, N., Conneally, P., Naylor, S., Anderson, M., & Tanzi, R. (1983). A polymorphic DNA marker genetically linked to Huntington's Disease. *Nature, 306,* 234–238.

Holzman, P., & Matthysse, S. (1990). The genetics of schizophrenia: A review. *Psychological Science, 1,* 279–286.

Kendler, K. (1993). Twin studies of psychiatric illness. *Archives of General Psychiatry, 50,* 905–915.

Kendler, K., MacLean, C., Neale, M., Kessler, R., Heath, A., & Eaves, L. (1991). The genetic epidemiology of bulimia nervosa. *American Journal of Psychiatry, 148,* 1627–1637.

Kendler, K., Neale, M., Kessler, R., Heath, A., & Eaves, L. (1993). A test of the equal environment assumption in twin studies of psychiatric illness. *Behavior Genetics, 23,* 21–27.

Moldin, S., & Erlenmeyer-Kimling, L. (1994). Measuring liability to schizophrenia: Progress report 1994: Editors' introduction. *Schizophrenia Bulletin, 20,* 25–29.

Mullan, M., & Murray, R. (1989). The impact of molecular genetics on our understanding of the psychoses. *British Journal of Psychiatry, 154,* 591–595.

Neale, M., & Cardon, L. (1992). *Methodology for genetic studies of twins and families.* Norwell, MA: Kluwer Academic.

Plomin, R. (1986). *Development, genetics, and psychology.* Hillsdale, NJ: Lawrence Erlbaum Associates.

Plomin, R. (1990). The role of inheritance in behavior. *Science, 248,* 183–188.

Plomin, R., DeFries, J. C., & Fulker, D. (1988). *Nature and nurture in infancy and early childhood.* New York: Cambridge University Press.

Plomin, R., DeFries, J. C., & McClearn, G. (1990). *Behavioral genetics: A primer* (2nd ed.). New York: Freeman.

Plomin, R., & Rende, R. (1991). Human behavioral genetics. *Annual Review of Psychology, 42,* 161–190.

Plomin, R., Rende, R., & Rutter, M. (1991). Quantitative genetics and developmental psychopathology. In D. Cicchetti & S. Toth (Eds.), *Rochester Symposium on Developmental Psychopathology: Vol. 2. Internalizing and externalizing expressions of dysfunction* (pp. 155–202). Hillsdale, NJ: Lawrence Erlbaum Associates.

Rende, R., & Plomin, R. (1992). Diathesis-stress models of psychopathology: A quantitative genetic perspective. *Applied and Preventive Psychology, 1,* 177–182.

Rende, R., & Plomin, R. (1994). Genetic influences on behavioural development. In M. Rutter & D. Hay (Eds.), *Developmental principles and clinical issues in psychology and psychiatry* (pp. 23–46). Oxford, England: Blackwell.

Rende, R., & Plomin, R. (1995). Nature, nurture, and the development of psychopathology. In D. Cicchetti & D. Cohen (Eds.), *Developmental psychopathology: Vol. 1. Theory and method* (pp. 291–314). New York: Wiley.

Rende, R., & Weissman, M. M. (in press). Assessment of family history of psychiatric disorder. In D. Shaffer & J. Richters (Eds.), *Assessment in child psychopathology.* New York: Guilford.

Rosenbaum, J., Biederman, J., Bolduc-Murphy, E., Faraone, S., Chaloff, J., Hirshfeld, D., & Kagan, J. (1993). Behavioral inhibition in childhood: A risk factor for anxiety disorders. *Harvard Review of Psychiatry, 1,* 2–16.

Rutter, M., Bolton, P., Harrington, R., Le Couteur, A., MacDonald, H., & Simonoff, E. (1990). Genetic factors in childhood psychiatric disorders: I. A review of research strategies. *Journal of Child Psychology and Psychiatry, 31,* 3–37.

Sherrington, R., Brynjolfsson, J., Petursson, H., Potter, M., Dudleston, K., Barraclough, B., Wasmuth, J., Dodds, M., & Gurling, H. (1988). Localization of a susceptibility locus for schizophrenia on chromosome 5. *Nature, 336,* 164–167.

Turkheimer, E., & Gottesman, I. I. (1991). Individual differences and the canalization of behavior. *Developmental Psychology, 27,* 18–22.

Walters, E., Neale, M., Eaves, L., Heath, A., Kessler, R., & Kendler, K. (1992). Bulimia nervosa and major depression: A study of common genetic and environmental factors. *Psychological Medicine, 22,* 617–622.

Weinberger, D. R. (1987). Implications of normal brain development for the pathogenesis of schizophrenia. *Archives of General Psychiatry, 44,* 660–669.

Weissman, M. M., Merikangas, K., John, K., Wickramaratne, P., Prusoff, B., & Kidd, K. K. (1986). Family-genetic studies of psychiatric disorders: Developing technologies. *Archives of General Psychiatry, 43,* 1104–1116.

Woodside, D. (1993). Genetic contributions to eating disorders. In A. Kaplan & P. Garfinkel (Eds.), *Medical issues and the eating disorders* (pp. 193–212). New York: Brunner/Mazel.

4

The Developmental Course of
Social Support: Family and Peers

Thomas J. Berndt
Stephen L. Hestenes

At all ages human beings benefit from having relationships with other people who spend time with them, help them, give them advice, and affirm their self-worth. This simple fact is the basis for current theories and research on supportive relationships (Belle, 1989; Sarason, Sarason, & Pierce, 1990; Veiel & Baumann, 1992). The construct of social support first gained prominence in the fields of psychiatry and psychosocial epidemiology (e.g., Cobb, 1976). Then sociologists, clinical psychologists, and other researchers interested in physical and mental health adopted the construct (see Cohen & Wills, 1985; Sarason et al., 1990). During the 1980s, the idea of supportive relationships also sparked research in the field of social development (e.g., Berndt & Perry, 1986; Reid, Landesman, Treder, & Jaccard, 1989). Developmental psychologists have, in particular, examined the nature and effects of support from two sources: family members, especially parents; and peers, especially best friends.

This chapter consists of a review of theories and research on social support in childhood and adolescence. We range beyond the traditional domain of social support, however, to draw connections to other theoretical perspectives on parent–child and peer relationships. In drawing these connections our purpose is to build bridges between researchers who have so far worked independently. We believe that building these bridges may not only prevent duplication of research efforts but may also suggest directions for future research on the development of social relationships.

The chapter is divided into three major sections. The first section is devoted to the definition and measurement of supportive social relationships. One theme of this section is that social support refers essentially to the positive features of social relationships. Therefore, the recently developed measures of parental and peer support overlap with older measures of parent–child relationships and friendships. This overlap should be considered when interpreting the relations among measures and drawing conclusions about the effects of social support.

The second section of the chapter focuses on developmental changes in the support that children receive from parents and peers. One theme of this section is that support from parents and peers reflects children's involvement in the family and in other social worlds. Therefore, decreases in parent–child interaction and increases in peer interaction as children move toward adulthood bring changes in social support from parents and peers.

The central topic of the third section is the effect of supportive relationships on children's development. We examine not only the effects of social support as narrowly defined but also the effects of relationship quality as interpreted more broadly. One theme of this section is that social-support theorists have often emphasized the effects of supportive relationships on children's characteristics without acknowledging the effects of children's characteristics on their relationships. We present evidence that children's characteristics influence their social support as well as vice versa. As a corollary, we argue that hypotheses about the effects of supportive relationships must be stated more precisely and tested more rigorously than has been customary in the past.

Before turning to our major topics we should state one caveat explicitly. This chapter provides only an overview of issues and findings on the development of social support. Discussing this subject fully would call for an exposition of the nature and effects of family and peer relationships from birth to adulthood, and we have neither the space nor the expertise for such an exposition. Our goal is instead to highlight issues that are central to current thinking about social support and that will move social-support research in promising new directions.

DEFINING AND MEASURING CHILDREN'S
SOCIAL SUPPORT

Writers on social support have offered many different definitions of this construct. Cobb (1976) viewed social support as information that makes people believe that they are cared for, loved, or esteemed, or that they belong to a network of communication and mutual obligations. Newcomb and Bentler (1987) defined social support in terms of the networks of personal relationships that give people companionship, assistance, attachment, and emotional nourishment. Other writers have defined social support by actions such as giving advice, teaching, cooperating on tasks, and helping people to master emotional distress (Barrera, Sandler, & Ramsey, 1981).

These various definitions imply that social support currently refers not to a single construct but to multiple constructs. These multiple constructs encompass a broad research area (Vaux, 1988; Wolchik, Beals, & Sandler, 1989). Explorations of this area have proceeded in two directions. One is a specification of the types of support that can come from participation in social relationships; the other is a classification of different indicators of an individual's social support. We look first at types of support. When we turn to the discussion of various indicators, we also examine the measures of support most often used in research with children and adolescents.

Four Types of Social Support

Various systems for classifying types of support have been proposed. We will focus on a system with four major categories that has been discussed by both clinical and developmental researchers (Berndt, 1989; Cohen & Wills, 1985; Reid et al., 1989). The first category, called *esteem support,* includes support that bolsters or enhances a person's self-esteem. People provide esteem support when they affirm an individual's worth. Specific behaviors that fall into this category include compliments and social recognition for achievement. Esteem support can be linked to the dimension of warmth in parent–child relationships (Maccoby & Martin, 1983). One facet of parental warmth is the praise or positive reinforcement that a parent gives when a child has succeeded in a task or shown other desirable behaviors. Esteem support is also part of peer relationships. Sullivan (1953) suggested that intimate friendships among preadolescents and adolescents contribute to the validation of personal worth. As friends interact, they show that they respect one another and value one another's ideas. According to Sullivan, friends' validation of one another is a primary reason for the positive effects of friendships on adolescent development.

A second type of social support refers to advice or guidance that is helpful in coping with problems. This kind of help has been labeled *informational support* (Cohen & Wills, 1985), but it is not as strictly cognitive and practical as that label might imply. A typical example of informational support is that of giving a person suggestions for dealing with serious personal problems. When faced with problems, people want a sensitive listener who will not only give them advice but will also encourage and reassure them. That is, people want to receive a combination of informational and esteem support. Probably most conversations about personal problems involve a mix of bolstering another's confidence and giving practical advice.

Informational support can also be linked to the dimension of warmth in parent–child relationships. A key facet of parental warmth is responsiveness to a child's needs (Berndt, 1992). One way that parents are responsive is by giving their children advice and guidance in solving problems and facing challenges. Sometimes children may not want their parents' advice, particularly as they move into adolescence. However, even adolescents expect their parents to give them information about a wide range of issues from religion to their future occupations (Hunter, 1985). That is, informational support remains important in parent–child relationships as children grow up.

Friends also provide informational support, although not in exactly the same ways as parents do (Hunter, 1985; Sullivan, 1953). Friends give advice, and their advice is valued, not because they are older and wiser but because they may have faced similar situations themselves. One major function of friendship, according to Sullivan (1953), is to help children understand their social world. Friends often have conversations in which they discuss their beliefs and opinions about other people's behavior, events at school, and broader issues. These conversations are likely to give children new perspectives about themselves and their world. Gaining such new perspectives can correct children's misconceptions and thus make them better able to adapt to social life and its challenges.

Informational support is closely related to intimacy in friendships. Sullivan (1953) stated that intimacy refers generally to closeness in a friendship, but most later writers have defined this construct more narrowly. Intimacy refers most often to friends' disclosure of personal and private information to each other (Berndt & Perry, 1986; Hartup, 1992). When friends tell each other virtually everything because they trust each other to respond positively and keep the information confidential, they have an intimate relationship.

A third type of social support refers to the sharing of material resources and to help with practical problems. Labeled *instrumental support* by some writers (e.g., Cohen & Wills, 1985), this category includes such things as loaning money or helping someone with a school assignment. Many writers have suggested that this type of support is less critical to psychological adjustment than the two types mentioned earlier, but the evidence on this point is debatable. Several theorists have suggested that instrumental support may under certain conditions be the only type of support that is beneficial. For example, if a child has a problem with a school assignment, then instrumental support may be more effective than anything else (see Berndt, 1989).

Responsive parents give all sorts of instrumental support to their children (Maccoby & Martin, 1983). At the most basic level, parents provide nutritious food to their children. Parents also help their children in more specific ways, ranging from teaching preschoolers how to tie their shoes to teaching adolescents how to drive a car. Friends do less direct teaching than parents, but they also provide many kinds of instrumental support (Berndt, 1989; Furman & Buhrmester, 1992).

Young children share toys with friends. Older children and adolescents cooperate on school projects. For adolescents, the instrumental support that friends provide is less critical than the intimacy of these friendships, but it is nevertheless important (Berndt & Savin-Williams, 1993). The final type of social support in this classification system is labeled *companionship*. People who have supportive relationships often spend time in enjoyable activities together (Rook, 1987). Applied to parent–child relationships, this type of support is often called involvement (Berndt, 1992; Maccoby & Martin, 1983). More involved parents spend more time with their children. Applied to friendship, this type of support can be judged from friends' frequency of interaction. However, most researchers assume that the assurance of companionship is more important than its frequency (Davies, 1982). That is, children have supportive friendships when their friends are usually willing and able to accept their invitations to do things with them.

Measuring Children's Support: Three Options

The measurement of social support is controversial because researchers have proposed strikingly different approaches. These approaches differ because researchers disagree about which indicators of a child's social support are most important. The three most common options for measuring children's support can be linked to the three definitions of social support given earlier (see Sarason et al., 1990; Wolchik et al., 1989).

First, Cobb's (1976) definition refers to people's beliefs that they are involved in caring, loving relationships. These beliefs are assessed by researchers who use measures of *perceived support*. These measures assess children's perceptions of the characteristics and quality of their relationships.

Second, Newcomb and Bentler's (1987) definition refers to people's involvement in *social networks* with supportive others. Thus, another strand of current research is based on measures of these networks. This research focuses on children's social embeddedness (Barrera, 1986). Researchers typically assess the size of children's networks, how many members of their networks know one another, and other facets of the networks' structure.

The third definition (Barrera et al., 1981) refers not to people's perceptions or to the structure of their social networks but to their interactions with other people. Many writers have suggested a focus on *enacted support,* or how much support people actually receive from other people (e.g., Thoits, 1985). These writers also suggest a need for direct assessments of the nature of supportive interactions.

More research has been done with measures of perceived support than with the other two types of measures. In addition, perceived-support measures exist in greater number and variety than measures of the other types. Therefore, this type of measure is reviewed first.

Perceived Support. In its purest form, a measure of perceived support would include no information about support providers. Such a measure might include items that paraphrase Cobb's (1976) definition of social support. For example, one item might be, "I believe other people care for and love me." This item focuses exclusively on the existence of supportive relationships, not on the identity of those supporters.

In actuality, most perceived-support measures for children and adolescents include some information about support providers. Often, these measures specifically assess children's perceived support from parents and peers. For example, Procidano and Heller (1983) created a Perceived Social Support Scale (PSSS) that includes subscales for family support and friends' support. A sample item for family support is, "Members of my family are good at helping me solve problems." Most items for friends' support are worded similarly, except that the phrase "my friends" replaces the phrase "members of my family." People respond by answering "yes," "no," or "don't know" to each item.

Although Procidano and Heller (1983) created the PSSS for use with college students, it has also been used with adolescents (e.g., Licitra-Kleckler & Waas, 1993). Scores on the two subscales are high in internal consistency, with alpha coefficients above .85 (Windle, 1992). The validity of the scale is suggested by evidence that adolescents reporting more social support also report less anxiety and fewer depressive feelings (DuBois, Felner, Brand, Adan, & Evans, 1992).

Dubow and Ullman (1989) created a Social Support Appraisals Scale for third graders and older children. Items on the scale assess perceived support from family, peers, and teachers. The items are stated as questions. For example, one item on all three subscales is, "Do you think your family (or friends, or teachers) care about you?" Students respond on a 5-point scale. The internal consistency of these measures is slightly lower than for the PSSS (alpha coefficients = .78–.83). Scores on the measures are significantly correlated with children's self-esteem and with other measures of psychological adjustment. Neither this scale nor the PSSS, however, attempts to distinguish among the different types of social support described earlier.

Types of support are distinguished in the My Family and Friends measure (Reid et al., 1989). Because this measure is intended for children as young as age 5, it is administered as an individual interview rather than as a questionnaire. Moreover, the measure assesses children's social networks as thoroughly as it does their perceptions of support. The interviewer first asks children to name the important people in their network. These people normally include parents, siblings, friends, relatives, and teachers. Then children are asked to say to whom they go most often when they need a specific type of support. Reid et al. (1989) did not define types of support in exactly the same way as we did earlier in the chapter. They distinguished between emotional, informational, instrumental, and companionship support, but their category of informational support was concerned only with learning about things. Their category of emotional support includes both self-esteem enhancement (e.g., "someone else does or says things that help make you feel good about yourself") and advice on personal problems (e.g., "someone you go to when you want to share your feelings"). The resulting measures of emotional support from different people have adequate reliability (alpha coefficients of .78–.92). However, Reid et al. reported alpha coefficients of less than .70 for some measures of the other types of support.

Furman and Buhrmester (1992) did not set out to create a measure of social support when they devised their Network of Relationships Inventory (NRI). Instead, they wanted to measure the seven provisions that, according to Weiss (1974), people obtain from social relationships. These provisions include reliable alliance, enhancement of worth, affection, companionship, instrumental help, intimacy, and nurturance. To obtain a fuller picture of social relationships, Furman and Buhrmester included items to assess conflict, punishment, relative power, and satisfaction with a relationship. On the inventory children rate these qualities of relationships with their mother, father, closest other adult relative, most important teacher, best same-sex friend, best opposite-sex friend, boyfriend or girlfriend, and up to four siblings.

The NRI has been used with college students and with children as young as age 10 (Clark-Lempers, Lempers, & Ho, 1991; East, 1991; Furman & Buhrmester, 1992). Furman and Buhrmester combined scores on all seven of Weiss' (1974) provisions into a single measure because they were strongly correlated and yielded measures high in internal consistency (alpha coefficients > .80). Strong correlations among subscales intended to assess different types of perceived support have also been found in research with adults (e.g., Cohen, Mermelstein, Kamarck, & Hoberman, 1985). Moreover, strong intercorrelations of subscales for various positive aspects of best friendships have been consistently found in research with children and adolescents (Berndt & Keefe, 1995; Furman, in press). Researchers who have studied parenting have also found that praise, responsiveness, and other positive behaviors comprise a broad dimension of warmth in parent–child relationships (Maccoby & Martin, 1983).

In sum, many studies indicate that neither children nor adults differentiate greatly among the types of support provided by a specific person (Cauce, Reid, Landesman, & Gonzales, 1990; Cohen et al., 1985; Wolchik et al., 1989). These studies imply that measures of total support are more desirable than measures that claim to distinguish among types of support. However, this conclusion is controversial (cf. Parker & Asher, 1993). More research is needed to show whether measures of specific types of support reveal important information about the development or effects of supportive relationships.

More research is also needed on the validity of perceived-support measures. Most researchers have assumed that correlations of these measures with measures of children's adjustment can be treated as evidence of validity. Better evidence of validity could be obtained by correlating children's reports of parents' and friends' support with the parents' and friends' reports on the same relationships. In other words, researchers should try to assess the views of support providers instead of focusing entirely on the children receiving support.

Support Networks.   As already noted, perceived-support measures usually include some information about an individual's social network because researchers want to know who is providing the individual with support. Conversely, measures of support networks usually include some information about the types of support that network members are perceived to supply (but see Feiring & Lewis, 1991). Nevertheless, the two kinds of measures differ in administration and in the variables derived from children's responses.

When assessing support networks, researchers often begin with open-ended questions about the people who are important in a child's social world. For example, some researchers have used the model of a *social convoy* as a basis for mapping children's social networks (Levitt, Guacci-Franco, & Levitt, 1993). Children are shown a diagram with three concentric circles. They are asked to name for the innermost circle the people who are closest and most important to them. For the next circle they name people who are not quite as close but who are still important. For the outer circle they name people who are still less close but whom the children still really love or like. Then children are asked which people in the network provide them with specific kinds of support, for example, helping them with homework. Whether these people are parents, other relatives, friends, or fall into another relationship category is also determined.

The procedure for Coates' (1981) Social Network Record is somewhat more structured than that of social convoy mapping. In one study (Coates, 1987), adolescents were first presented with a specific target group: family, friends, or other people. They were asked to list all the people whom they knew in each target group (e.g., all family members with whom they had had contact in the past 5 years). Then the size of each group and the average frequency of contact with members of the group were determined. The adolescents were also asked to estimate the density of their entire network, that is the number of people who knew each other. Additional questions were asked about which people in the network provided support. For example, adolescents were asked to whom they would go if they needed money desperately, and to whom they would go if they had a falling-out with a best friend. Most adolescents named a parent as the person they would ask if they needed money. Most adolescents said that they would talk to a peer if they had a falling-out with a best friend. Very few adolescents named an adult outside the family as the person they would go to for help with either of these problems. These data suggest that family and friends are the most important people in the social networks of children and adolescents (see also Fischer, Sollie, & Morrow, 1986; Levitt et al., 1993; Wolchik et al., 1989).

For some purposes, however, going beyond family and friends when examining children's social networks may be necessary. For example, researchers interested in educational issues need to consider students' perceptions of their teachers' support (e.g., Eccles et al., 1993). However, most students view teachers as much less supportive than their parents and friends, although elementary school children perceive teachers as more supportive than adolescents do (Furman & Buhrmester, 1992). Therefore, researchers interested in capturing the most important variations in social support during childhood and adolescence can legitimately limit themselves to family support and friends' support.

Enacted Support.   How much support do children actually receive from the people with whom they have close relationships? What are the characteristics of supportive interactions? Interpreted narrowly, these questions are extremely difficult to answer. Previous reviewers of the literature concluded that few researchers had assessed enacted support among children (e.g., Wolchik et al., 1989). Moreover, some measures that the previous reviewers placed in the category of enacted support are ones that we would consider to be perceived-support measures.

The NRI (Furman, in press; Furman & Buhrmester, 1992) includes some items that refer to supportive interactions (e.g., "How much does this person help you figure out or fix things?"). Other items, however, refer to feelings or attitudes rather than to specific interactions (e.g., "How much does this person really care about you?"). Also, the items that refer to precise interactions are rated on a general scale that does not yield specific measures of interaction frequency. Children, for example, rate the help given by a particular person on a scale ranging from *little or none* to *the most.*

By contrast, the Inventory of Socially Supportive Behavior (Barrera et al., 1981) includes items about the frequency of practical assistance or of other types of support received during the past month. However, this measure has been used primarily with college students. A few researchers have used the scale with adolescents (Barrera et al., 1981), but apparently it has not been used with children. Moreover, scores on the scale often correlate positively with measures of psychological distress (Sarason et al., 1990; Wolchik et al., 1989). That is, individuals who report having received more support show more severe emotional or behavioral problems. These findings may show that people under stress call more often for support, but they are not easy to reconcile with hypotheses about the benefits of social support. In other words, the findings raise questions about the validity of this measure.

Whether people can accurately report on the frequency of their supportive interactions has been questioned (cf. Dohrenwend & Shrout, 1985). When people are under stress they are not especially good at remembering and evaluating what other people have done to help them. Moreover, when people are not under stress they may not notice the small ways in which other people bolster their self-esteem, give practical help, or provide other kinds of support (Berndt, 1989). In sum, people's perceptions of supportive interactions may not correspond closely to the support that they have actually received.

These issues suggest a need for direct observations of supportive interactions. Readers who focus narrowly on the social-support literature might assume that few observations of this kind have been done. Yet if social support is defined more broadly and linked to the related constructs discussed earlier, a wealth of observational data can be assembled. We have space here to mention only a few examples.

Many researchers have assessed the support that parents provide for their infants and young children. In this research, support provided by parents has been given labels such as sensitivity (Isabella, 1993), responsiveness (Ainsworth, Blehar, Waters, & Wall, 1978), and interactional synchrony (Isabella & Belsky, 1991). Other researchers have assessed the support that parents provide for older children and adolescents. In this research, supportive interactions have been defined in terms of enabling communication (Hauser et al., 1984), mutuality and permeability (Grotevant & Cooper, 1985), and cognitive responsiveness (Baumrind, 1989). All these constructs can be linked to the broad dimension of warmth in childrearing and, therefore, to support in parent–child relationships.

Friendships have also been examined in observational research (Newcomb & Bagwell, in press). Researchers have explored the expression of positive affect in friendships (Newcomb & Brady, 1982), friends' sharing and helping (Berndt, 1986), the intimacy of friends' self-disclosures (Gottman & Parker, 1986), and the sheer frequency of agreements during friends' conversations (Gottman, 1983). These attributes of friends' interactions can all be linked to various types of friends' support (e.g., Berndt & Perry, 1986; Furman, in press; Furman & Buhrmester, 1992).

Our examples show that supportive interactions can and have been assessed directly, both in families and in friendships. Although, we do not believe that observational measures should replace other measures of social support, it can be argued that researchers should devote more effort to studying support as it is given and received during social interactions in naturalistic settings. Observations of supportive interactions should then be compared with existing social-support measures. Attempts should also be made to integrate evidence from existing measures with evidence from future observational studies.

Of course, research done with different measures may yield different results. This outcome would not be surprising because, as noted earlier, social support refers not to a single construct but to multiple constructs. Understanding of the social-support domain will increase most rapidly if researchers explicitly define the aspect of social support that they are investigating. Researchers should also discuss the relations of their social-support measures to other measures.

THE DEVELOPMENTAL COURSE OF
SOCIAL SUPPORT

For virtually all children, social life begins in the family. Relationships with parents, especially, are critical for young children's physical survival and psychological growth. As children grow older they move into a wider social world that includes other adults and peers, and as they move into adolescence peer interactions become more important. Research on the developmental course of social support partly documents these changes in children's social relationships. Social-support research is also helpful in understanding individual differences in development.

Developments in Family Support

During the first year of life infants form attachments to their parents. Theories of infant–parent attachment emphasize the protection, nurturance, and responsive care that most parents give their infants (Ainsworth et al., 1978; Bowlby, 1969; Isabella, chapter 7, this volume). By emphasizing parents' responsiveness these theories draw on a longer tradition of research on parental warmth (Maccoby & Martin, 1983). As noted earlier, the dimension of parental warmth is closely linked to definitions of supportive parent–child relationships.

Despite this link, few researchers have compared assumptions and hypotheses about attachment and about family support. The reason for this state of affairs is simple. Until recently, attachment researchers focused on parent–child relationships in infancy and early childhood (cf. Ainsworth, 1989). By contrast, developmental researchers interested in social support have focused on parent–child relationships in middle childhood and adolescence. They have probably done so because the standard measures of social support cannot be used with infants and preschoolers.

Our focus, therefore, is on developments in family support between school entry and adulthood. Information on the lower portion of this age range comes from a study with the My Family and Friends measure discussed earlier (Cauce et al., 1990). In this study, children between 5 and 12 years of age rated their mothers and fathers separately on several types of social support. Overall ratings of mothers' support were very high and changed little across this age range. However, a modest increase with age was found in ratings of mothers' information and help. Ratings of all types of support from fathers increased with age, but even the oldest children rated most types of support from fathers less positively than that from mothers.

With older children and adolescents, the NRI has been used to examine age changes in perceived parental support. In one study (Furman & Buhrmester, 1992), seventh graders rated their mothers' and fathers' support less positively than did fourth graders. Ratings of parents' support dropped still further by 10th grade but recovered slightly by college age. Other researchers have also reported decreases in parents' perceived support during adolescence (Clark-Lempers et al., 1991; Lamborn & Steinberg, 1993; Slavin, 1991; but see Blyth & Foster-Clark, 1987).

The age changes in ratings of fathers' support are similar for the two sexes, but ratings of mothers' support may decrease with age more among boys than among girls (Clark-Lempers et al., 1991; Furman & Buhrmester, 1992). This conclusion must be stated cautiously because the evidence comes mainly from studies using the NRI. Some studies with other measures have yielded comparable age trends for both sexes (e.g., Slavin, 1991).

Data from observational studies also suggest a decrease in positive interactions between parents and their children during adolescence (Paikoff & Brooks-Gunn, 1991). These data imply that direct measures of enacted support from parents would show age trends similar to those found for perceived-support measures. However, this hypothesis has not yet been tested adequately.

Scattered findings suggest that many adolescents perceive their same-sex parent as more supportive than their opposite-sex parent. In one study (Blyth & Foster-Clark, 1987), 7th- to 10th-grade girls reported less intimacy in their relationships with their fathers than boys did. In another study, sixth-grade girls rated their mothers' support more positively than did sixth-grade boys (East, 1991). In a third study (Clark-Lempers et al., 1991), boys between 11 and 19 years of age rated their fathers as more supportive than did girls. Unfortunately, this issue could not be addressed in many studies because many perceived-support measures do not differentiate between mothers and fathers (e.g., Lamborn & Steinberg, 1993; Slavin, 1991).

The evidence for decreases in parental support during adolescence is controversial. On one hand, the decreases might be seen as normal and even desirable (Lamborn & Steinberg, 1993). Adolescents need to develop greater autonomy as they move toward adulthood. Adolescents also have a larger social world than do young children, so parents naturally become just one of several sources of social support. From this perspective, the decrease with age in parents' support is not only understandable but is a sign of healthy development.

On the other hand, adolescents benefit when they continue to have close relationships with their parents. Although adolescents become more independent they still need to rely on parents for advice and guidance (Youniss & Smollar, 1985). From this perspective, decreases in parents' support during adolescence are alarming. They suggest some emotional detachment of adolescents from parents (Ryan & Lynch, 1989) that may result from a decrease in parental warmth. Such changes in parent–adolescent relationships could conceivably reduce adolescents' psychological adjustment and increase their risk of psychopathology. Given the practical importance of this possibility, more research on the age changes in parents' support would be worthwhile.

Finally, the magnitude of the age changes in parent–child relationships should not be exaggerated. Most adolescents continue to have positive relationships with their parents (Paikoff & Brooks-Gunn, 1991). Stated differently, parents may become less important as support providers during adolescence, but they rarely become unimportant.

Developments in Peer Support

The development of peer relationships is greatly affected by children's social and cultural context. Some children are placed in groups with peers during infancy. Other children do not have regular contacts with peers until they enter elementary school. For almost all children, however, peer relationships become more important when formal schooling begins. For the first time, children spend many hours each day with groups of peers who are engaged in the same activities and against whom their achievement is carefully measured. These peers become their coworkers, competitors, and playmates. A few of these peers become their best friends.

The features of friendship and, therefore, the types of support provided by friends change with age (Berndt & Savin-Williams, 1993). Sullivan (1953) proposed that friendships first become intimate relationships in the preadolescent years. That is, Sullivan assumed that most children find a "chum" with whom they share all their thoughts and feelings when they are 9 or 10 years of age. According to Sullivan, children show special sensitivity to the needs of their chums and try to promote the happiness and self-esteem of the chum. That is, friendships develop into relationships of informational and esteem support.

Later research has qualified some of Sullivan's (1953) assumptions. Contrary to Sullivan's belief, intimacy does not normally become an important feature of friendships until early adolescence. By 12 to 15 years of age, most adolescents say that their friendships are based on sharing personal thoughts and feelings with one another. Before that age, references to intimate self-disclosure in friendship are virtually absent. After that age, the intimacy of friendships increases still further (Berndt & Savin-Williams, 1993; Rawlins, 1992). Intimacy remains the most important feature of friendship in adulthood (Clark & Reis, 1988).

Loyalty also becomes important in friendships during adolescence (Berndt & Perry, 1990). Adolescents increasingly insist that their friends support them when they are around other people. Adolescents say that a best friend will "stick up for you in a fight" and "won't talk about you behind your back." Another facet of loyalty is faithfulness: A best friend would never "leave you for somebody else." Such comments are rarely made by elementary school children, probably because they do not think of best friendships in connection with other peer relationships.

Nevertheless, even before intimacy and loyalty emerge, support from friends is important to children. In one study (Cauce et al., 1990), 5- to 7-year-olds rated their friends' companionship about as positively as parents' companionship. Other research suggests that instrumental support (or prosocial behavior) and self-esteem support are as common in children's friendships as in adolescents' friendships (Berndt & Perry, 1986; but see Berndt, Hawkins, & Hoyle, 1986). Other research with perceived-support measures also suggests that friendships are signifi-cant sources of support during childhood (Furman & Buhrmester, 1992; Levitt et al., 1993).

Friendships also differ significantly for boys and girls. During child-hood, boys and girls rate their friendships similarly, but adolescent girls typically describe their friendships as more supportive than do adoles-cent boys (Berndt & Savin-Williams, 1993; Furman & Buhrmester, 1992; Jones & Dembo, 1989). Some researchers have suggested that as many as one third of adolescent boys lack intimate friendships (Youniss & Smollar, 1985). This conclusion is contradicted by reports of nonsig-nificant sex differences on some measures of the intimacy of best friendships (e.g., Berndt et al., 1986). A more accurate conclusion is that both boys' and girls' friendships increase in their intimacy during ado-lescence, but that girls have friendships that are somewhat more inti-mate than those of boys. Moreover, this difference has been found not only in the United States but in other countries as diverse as Costa Rica (DeRosier & Kupersmidt, 1991) and Russia (Kon, 1981).

In summary, recent studies confirm that friendships become more supportive relationships during adolescence. Intimacy and loyalty emerge as important features of friendships in early adolescence. Friends interact more frequently, thus giving more companionship to each other (Larson & Richards, 1991). Friends provide support even to young children, but they take a more central position in support networks after the transition to adolescence.

EFFECTS OF SOCIAL SUPPORT

Two contrasting hypotheses about the effects of social support have been debated in the literature (e.g., Cohen & Wills, 1985; Vaux, 1988). Perhaps the most popular hypothesis is that supportive relationships provide a buffer against negative effects of life stress. In other words, social support helps people to cope more successfully with failures, disappointments, accidents, and other unpleasant events. This hypothesis implies that social support is especially beneficial to people under stress. It implies that supportive relationships have little effect on the psychological or physical health of people not in stressful conditions.

The alternative hypothesis is that supportive relationships play a role in psychological and physical health regardless of a person's level of stress. Certainly, social support helps people to cope with highly stressful events, but it also helps people to maintain a positive outlook and function adequately when their lives are going fairly well. Stated in statistical terminology, this hypothesis implies that social support has a main effect on people's well-being rather than an effect only in interaction with levels of stress.

Research with adults has yielded some evidence consistent with both the stress-buffering and main-effect hypotheses (Vaux, 1988). The same is true in research with children and adolescents. Some investigators have reported data consistent with the idea of stress buffering (Cauce, Hannan, & Sargeant, 1992; Wills, Vaccaro, & McNamara, 1992). Others have found main effects of social support but no significant interactions of social support with stress (Hoffman, Ushpiz, & Levy-Shiff, 1988; Lustig, Wolchik, & Braver, 1992).

A few researchers have argued that attempts to decide between these two hypotheses should be abandoned because a clear distinction between them cannot be made (see Thoits, 1982; Vaux, 1988). One problem is that some stressful events (e.g., the death of a loved one) also represent, or are confounded with, changes in levels of social support. A second problem is that people's levels of stress are difficult to estimate because stressors differ in kind as well as in intensity.

We are most concerned about a third problem, which concerns the research design of social-support studies. In most studies correlational designs have been used; however, an old saying that bears repeating is that correlation does not imply causation. When researchers assess people's levels of social support, of stress, and of psychological or physical health at a single time, they cannot show whether these variables affect one another. If people's level of social support is related to their health, this could be because health affects social support rather than vice versa. Alternatively, some third variable (e.g., genetic differences in personality) could affect both health and support without these two affecting one another.

Longitudinal studies allow stronger inferences about causality. Therefore, we explicitly contrast the findings of correlational and longitudinal studies, concentrating on studies in which children's and adolescents' perceptions of their social support were assessed. Many writers have argued that perceived support is more important to people's psychological health than are the other constructs in the social support domain (e.g., Lazarus & Folkman, 1984). These writers propose that people cope more successfully with stressful events when they assume that supporters are available to them if needed.

In past research, measures of perceived support have been more strongly related to measures of psychological health than have measures of social networks (Sarason et al., 1990). Moreover, true measures of enacted support have, as noted earlier, been difficult to create and so have seldom been used. For this reason we focus mainly on the effects of perceived support from parents and from friends.

Effects of Parents' Support

That parents have a powerful impact on their children's development is rarely questioned (but see Baumrind, 1993; Scarr, 1992). There also seems little question that the amount of support parents give to their children should strongly affect the children's development. Correlational studies have yielded findings entirely consistent with this assumption.

A Partial Review of Correlational Data.   Children and adolescents who perceive their parents as more supportive receive higher scores on many measures of cognitive, social, and emotional adjustment. In one study (Cauce et al., 1990), first graders who reported more support from parents were judged by their mothers as more self-confident and higher in social adjustment. In another study (East, 1991), sixth-grade boys who viewed their fathers as less supportive were more aggressive toward peers. Sixth-grade girls who viewed their fathers as less supportive were more withdrawn in peer groups. Boys and girls were more withdrawn or aggressive toward peers when their mothers reported being less supportive to them. Other research has shown that third through fifth graders' perceptions of family support are related to behavioral problems as reported by parents, to teachers' ratings of their competence, and to their academic achievement (Dubow & Tisak, 1989). Evidence concerning the correlates of parental support is even more abundant for adolescents. Adolescents who receive more support from parents are higher in self-esteem and view their relationships with peers more positively (Barrera, Chassin, & Rogosch, 1993; Cauce et al., 1992; Hoffman et al., 1988). Adolescents with more supportive parents are less often depressed or psychologically distressed (Dubois et al., 1992; Licitra-Kleckler & Waas, 1993) and receive higher grades (Lamborn & Steinberg, 1993). Not surprisingly, they are less likely to attempt suicide than other adolescents (Morano, Cisler, & Lemerond, 1993).

Drug use and delinquent behavior are less common in adolescents with more supportive parents (Barrera et al., 1993; Licitra-Kleckler & Waas, 1993; Wills et al., 1992). In one study (Licitra-Kleckler & Waas, 1993) a measure of family support was more strongly correlated with the delinquent behavior of males than of females. The researchers suggested that parental support might have greater effects on males than on females. However, the gender difference might be attributed to a floor effect for girls, who rarely reported any delinquent behavior regardless of their level of parental support.

A Review of Longitudinal Studies.   Conclusions from correlational studies about the effects of parental support must be interpreted cautiously until they have been confirmed by longitudinal studies. Caution is necessary partly because of the discrepancies already apparent between correlational and longitudinal data on parental support. In four recent longitudinal studies, strong effects of parental support on adolescents' psychological adjustment were not found.

Students were recruited for one study (Dubow, Tisak, Causey, Hryshko, & Reid, 1991) when they were in the third grade. The students were assessed again when they were fifth graders. Measures of family support were not related to the changes in students' grades or to behavioral problems as reported by parents and teachers. However, students with more supportive parents did show improvements over time in teacher ratings for competent behavior (e.g., frustration tolerance).

The other three studies yielded even weaker effects. In the second study (DuBois et al., 1992), seventh through ninth graders reported their social support and their level of psychological distress (i.e., depression and anxiety). The students' grades were obtained from school records. These assessments were repeated 2 years later. Changes across the 2-year interval in adolescents' psychological distress and grades were not significantly related to their initial levels of parental support.

For the third study (Newcomb, 1990), students in the 10th, 11th, and 12th grades reported their self-esteem, personality traits, and parental support on two occasions a year apart. Girls' perceptions of their parents' support were unrelated to the changes over time in their self-esteem. Boys' perceptions of their parents' support were related to the changes over time on a specific measure, self-derogation. They were not related to boys' scores on a more comprehensive measure of self-esteem.

In the fourth study (Windle, 1992), 10th and 11th graders reported on their support from their families, their level of depression, and their delinquent behavior on two occasions 6 months apart. The longitudinal analyses showed significant effects of family support on the changes in a few measures of girls' adjustment. Girls who reported less support from the family increased in depressive symptoms, alcohol problems, and delinquent activity over time. The comparable effects for boys were nonsignificant.

Windle (1992) speculated that adolescent boys may be less dependent on family support than are adolescent girls. He noted the common belief that girls are socialized to focus on interpersonal relationships, whereas boys are socialized to explore the world independently (Block, 1983; see also Rosen, chapter 1, this volume). Windle's hypothesis can also be linked to Gilligan's (1982) assertions that girls develop an ethical orientation toward responsibility to others whereas boys develop an orientation toward individual rights. These hypotheses about sex differences are controversial. Sex differences in moral reasoning have been difficult to document (Walker, 1986); so have sex differences in socialization (Lytton & Romney, 1991). The idea that parents' support matters more to girls than to boys seems especially doubtful because Windle's findings have not been confirmed by other researchers (DuBois et al., 1992; Newcomb, 1990).

Viewed more generally, the longitudinal studies suggest that parent support can indeed affect the psychological adjustment of children and adolescents. However, these effects are more difficult to document in longitudinal studies with a long interval between assessments. Effects of parental support are more obvious with a 6-month interval between assessments (e.g., Windle, 1992) than with an interval of 1 or 2 years (e.g., Newcomb, 1990). Parental support may change considerably—and somewhat unpredictably—during adolescence. Therefore, its effects may be difficult to show when the interval between assessments is long.

Other findings from the longitudinal studies imply that adolescents' psychological adjustment affects their perceptions of parental support as much or more than vice versa. In one study (DuBois et al., 1992), students who initially were higher in psychological distress perceived their parents' support as decreasing over time. In another study (Newcomb, 1990), boys who initially were more self-confident and had more traditional attitudes about obeying the law perceived their parents' support as increasing over time. Girls who were lower in perseverance and higher in depression perceived their parents' support as decreasing. These findings and those from other studies with adults (Sarason et al., 1990) indicate that people's personalities can affect the formation or quality of their relationships. For example, adolescent boys with more antisocial attitudes may behave in ways that anger their parents and so reduce their parents' support. Adolescent girls who are depressed may become so withdrawn or uncommunicative that their parents exert less effort to interact positively with them. Social development researchers have discussed these kinds of influences of children on their parents for decades (e.g., Lytton, 1990; Maccoby & Martin, 1983). Such influences should be considered and assessed directly in future research on the effects of parental support.

Effects of Peer Support

More than 40 years ago, Sullivan (1953) proposed that intimate friendships in childhood and adolescence enhance self-esteem, contribute to accurate judgments of self and other people, and prepare adolescents for romantic relationships with opposite-sex peers. Other writers have proposed that supportive friendships can improve children's social skills (Hartup, 1992) and psychological health (Goodyear, Wright, & Altham, 1989; Youniss & Smollar, 1985).

A Partial Review of Correlational Data. Almost without exception, correlational studies have yielded data consistent with hypotheses about the benefits of friendships. The relations of friendships to socioemotional adjustment have been examined in many studies. Children and adolescents with more supportive friendships also have higher self-esteem (Barrera et al., 1993; Berndt & Savin-Williams, 1993; Hoffman, Levy-Schiff, & Ushpiz, 1993; Moran & Eckenrode, 1991). In addition, they are less likely to report symptoms of loneliness and depression (Licitra-Kleckler & Waas, 1993; Moran & Eckenrode, 1991; Parker & Asher, 1993; Slavin & Rainer, 1990). They also receive lower scores on composite measures of psychological distress (DuBois et al., 1992).

Moran and Eckenrode (1991) found that a measure of friends' support was correlated with the self-esteem of adolescent males but not of females. However, the differences between the correlations for males and females appear to be too small to reach the conventional level of statistical significance ($p < .05$). In addition, the correlation of friends' support with a measure of depression was similar for males and females. The weight of the evidence from this study and other studies suggests that friends' support is as strongly related to boys' self-esteem as to girls' self-esteem.

Not surprisingly, children and adolescents with supportive friendships have more positive relationships with the rest of their peers. Children with more supportive friendships are less likely to be disliked or rejected by their classmates (Parker & Asher, 1993). Early adolescents who perceive their friends and classmates as more supportive are less often socially isolated from their peer group (East & Rook, 1992).

In addition, high levels of support from friends are correlated with higher academic achievement and better social adjustment (Berndt & Keefe, 1995; DuBois et al., 1992; Dubow & Tisak, 1989). Children and adolescents with more supportive friendships have higher grades in school and report more positive involvement in classroom activities. Parents and teachers rate students with more supportive friendships as higher in behavioral competence (e.g., frustration tolerance) and lower in problem behaviors (e.g., acting out). These data are consistent with, but do not prove, the hypotheses of Sullivan (1953) and of other writers about the effects of friendships.

A few researchers have questioned the hypothesis that supportive friendships have uniformly positive effects on children's behavior and development. In a small sample of first graders, Cauce et al. (1990) found that children with more peer support were rated by their mothers as higher in adjustment on the first day of school but as lower in cognitive competence. Cauce et al. (1992) found that adolescents who reported more peer support were less anxious but perceived their scholastic competence as lower than that of other adolescents. Partly to explain these data, Cauce and Srebnik (1989) argued that supportive friendships may have negative effects on academic achievement if friends provide encouragement for social activities that are incompatible with school work. On the other hand, Cauce's studies have not included measures of academic achievement itself. Evidence from several studies cited earlier indicates that having supportive friendships is usually associated with higher academic achievement and a better adjustment to school.

Some researchers have examined another issue, possible age changes in the correlates of friends' support. Buhrmester (1990) suggested that the effects of supportive friendships are greater in middle adolescence (age 14–16) than in early adolescence (age 10–13). In a correlational study with adolescents of these ages, Buhrmester found that reports of friends' support were significantly correlated with self-reported sociability, hostility, and anxiety or depression during middle adolescence. The comparable correlations for early adolescents were significantly weaker.

More recently, Lustig et al. (1992) examined the relations of friends' support to a composite measure of psychological adjustment based on self-reports of depression, anxiety, and aggressiveness. The correlation between the support and adjustment measures was stronger for adolescents from 13 to 15 years of age than for younger children. The same effect was not found, however, when the measure of friends' support was correlated with a measure of adjustment based on parents' reports. These mixed findings leave open the question of whether friends' support affects psychological adjustment of adolescence more than of younger children.

A Review of Longitudinal Studies. More longitudinal studies have been done on friends' support than on parental support. Most researchers who have assessed children's perceptions of parental support have also assessed their perceptions of friends' support. However, several researchers have examined the effects of supportive (or high-quality) friendships without also examining the effects of parental support. As has been true for parental support, the longitudinal studies of friends' support have often shown either nonsignificant or weak results.

One team of researchers (Dubow et al., 1991) used a 2-year longitudinal design with students who initially were in the third grade. The researchers found no evidence that friends' support was related to the changes over time in students' adjustment to school or their academic achievement. In other words, the researchers could not show that students with more supportive friendships improved in their behavior or grades over time. These null results might be attributed to the limited importance of friends' support during middle childhood. If this explanation is correct, significant effects of friends' support would be expected in longitudinal studies with adolescents.

The available data are only partly consistent with this speculation. Several researchers have examined whether junior high school students with more supportive friendships show increases over time in their psychological or school adjustment. These studies have yielded mostly nonsignificant results. In one study, sixth-graders' reports of their friends' support were not related to the changes in their general self-esteem after they moved from elementary school to junior high school (Hirsch & DuBois, 1991). In another, seventh and eighth graders' reports on the positive features of their friendships were not related to the changes over a 6-month period in their perceptions of their peer acceptance and their feelings of depression (Vernberg, 1990). Likewise, seventh through ninth graders' reports on their friends' support were not related to the changes over 2 years in their psychological distress or their academic achievement (DuBois et al., 1992).

By contrast, significant effects of friends' support were found in a study of junior high school students followed for 6 months during a school year (Berndt & Keefe, 1995; Keefe & Berndt, 1994). Students who described their very best friendship more positively in the fall of the school year reported more positive involvement in classroom activities by the end of the year. Students' descriptions of their friendships were not related to changes during the year in their general self-esteem, perceived social acceptance, or most other facets of self-evaluation. However, students who initially had more supportive friendships and whose friendships were more stable during the year improved in their perceived physical appearance.

Longitudinal studies with still older adolescents have also yielded mixed results. On the one hand, 10th and 11th graders' reports concerning their friends' support were not related to changes over 6 months in depression, alcohol use, or delinquency (Windle, 1992). On the other hand, ninth- through 11th-grade girls who reported more support from friends decreased in depressive symptoms over the course of 7 months; this was not true of boys (Slavin & Rainer, 1990). In another study (Newcomb, 1990), senior high school girls who had more supportive friendships improved over 1 year in their self-acceptance, but the comparable effect for boys was nonsignificant.

The sex differences in the latter two studies are intriguing but difficult to interpret. In each study the sex differences in the effects of friends' support were not tested directly. Instead, the researchers simply analyzed the data for boys and girls separately. If the variances in the boys' and girls' scores differed, the separate analyses could have exaggerated the magnitude of the sex differences (Finney, Mitchell, Cronkite, & Moos, 1984).

In a study described earlier (Berndt & Keefe, 1995; Keefe & Berndt, 1994), sex differences were evaluated by doing regression analyses with terms for the interaction of friends' support and sex (see Finney et al., 1984). The interaction terms were nonsignificant, which suggests that friends' support is equally beneficial for boys and for girls. Because this study had an early adolescent sample, however, it does not settle the question of sex differences entirely. By middle or late adolescence, the benefits of supportive friendships might be greater for girls than for boys.

Longitudinal studies have also suggested some effects of adolescents' adjustment on their participation in supportive friendships. In one study (DuBois et al., 1992), seventh through ninth graders who were high in academic achievement increased their perceptions of friends' support over a 2-year period. One possible explanation is that high-achieving adolescents have greater social understanding, which helps them to form and maintain good friendships. In another study (Newcomb, 1990), 10th through 12th graders with high self-esteem increased over 1 year in their perceptions of friends' support. When linked with previous findings that friends' support may affect self-esteem, this finding suggests that friends' support and self-esteem may reciprocally influence each other.

Not all researchers have found that adolescents' self-esteem and school adjustment are related to changes in their friendships (Berndt & Keefe, 1995; Keefe & Berndt, 1994; Slavin & Rainer, 1990). The question remains open because the available data are extremely limited. Even researchers who have done longitudinal studies have not always reported the relevant analyses of their data. To better understand the reciprocal influences of supportive friendships and psychological adjustment, these analyses should be reported routinely in the future.

In summary, longitudinal studies have suggested that supportive friendships may enhance some aspects of self-evaluation, foster positive involvement in school activities, and reduce depressive feelings. However, these effects have not been found consistently. In some cases, the null results may reflect the use of an inappropriate interval between assessments (Berndt, in press). Friendships among adolescents normally last several months but less than a full year (Berndt & Savin-Williams, 1993). Therefore, researchers who try to determine the effects of supportive friendships assessed 1 or 2 years earlier may be trying to find the effects of friendships that ended long ago. To avoid this problem, information about the stability of students' friendships should be obtained when assessing the effects of friendship (see Berndt & Keefe, 1995; Keefe & Berndt, 1994).

In other cases, null results may be due to the use of brief and potentially unreliable measures of friends' support. More evidence on the reliability and validity of these measures should be supplied. Without this evidence, readers of the literature are likely to underestimate the effects of friends' support on children and adolescents.

Finally, the results of previous studies suggest that researchers need to generate hypotheses about more specific effects of friends' support. Having supportive friendships seems not to affect all facets of children's and adolescents' adjustment and development. The task for researchers is to identify which facets of adjustment and development are most affected by friends' support, and why. Researchers also need to consider the effects of children's and adolescents' adjustment on their friendships. The processes underlying such reciprocal influences need to be explored.

CONCLUSIONS

Relationships with parents and friends are crucial to children's lives. Several issues concerning these relationships have been clarified by recent theories and research on social support. One issue deals with the types of support that children receive. Both parents and friends provide children with esteem support, informational support, instrumental support, and companionship.

To assess supportive relationships, researchers have usually asked children about the amount of support that their parents and friends can or do provide. Although specific items on these measures may focus on different types of support, children's responses to all items are usually averaged to form a single score. This procedure is appropriate because strong correlations exist among the items on most measures. That is, neither children nor adults differentiate greatly among support types when reporting the amount of support that they receive from specific other people.

Besides measures of perceived support, researchers have used measures of the size and structure of children's support networks. Often, network measures are supplemented by questions about the types of support provided by network members. Research with these measures confirms that parents and friends are the most significant support providers for most children.

Occasionally, researchers have tried to assess enacted support, or the amount of support children actually receive and the characteristics of supportive interactions. These measures are usually indirect, based on children's reports rather than on direct observations of their social interactions. However, researchers working outside the narrow domain of social support have often observed parent–child interactions and friends' interactions in laboratory or naturalistic settings. Linking studies of social support to this larger literature would be mutually beneficial.

A second issue in the social-support literature concerns the changes in parents' and friends' support during childhood and adolescence. Because measures of social support have been used only with school-age children and adolescents, evidence is available only for that age range. Young children perceive their parents as highly supportive, but perceptions of fathers' support may increase during middle childhood. Between childhood and adolescence, perceptions of mothers' and fathers' support become less positive. During the same period, however, perceptions of friends' support become more positive. Although these age changes might be seen as a normal consequence of adolescents' movement out of the family circle into the wider world of peer relationships, some writers have argued that decreases in perceptions of parents' support are symptomatic of emotional detachment in parent–adolescent relationships. More research is needed to resolve this controversy.

A third issue is whether age changes in social support differ for boys and girls. The decrease in mothers' support during adolescence may be greater for boys than for girls. The increase in friends' support during adolescence is typically greater for girls than for boys. Some writers have suggested that these changes leave adolescent boys more bereft of support than they do adolescent girls (Youniss & Smollar, 1985). Other writers have suggested that the changes reflect gender-role socialization, with boys moving toward greater independence, whereas girls continue to remain heavily involved in interpersonal relationships (Gilligan, 1982; Windle, 1992). Because relevant data are scarce, the question remains open.

A final issue that underlies much of the research in this area concerns the effects of social support. Correlational studies have shown that children and adolescents who perceive their parents and friends as more supportive show better psychological and school adjustment. However, several longitudinal studies designed to examine the effects of supportive relationships have yielded nonsignificant results. Sometimes the apparent effects of social support differ for boys and girls, but no consistent pattern of sex differences has emerged.

In our view, the current evidence does not show that parents' and friends' support contributes little to children's development. Instead, the evidence shows that researchers must devise better research designs for examining the effects of social support. For example, researchers must choose an interval for longitudinal assessments that is appropriate given the stability of support measures. In addition, researchers must formulate more specific hypotheses about the facets of development that are affected by support from specific people. Finally, researchers must acknowledge that having supportive relationships is not entirely a matter of good fortune. Children's own characteristics partly determine whether they develop good relationships with their parents and friends. Therefore, models of the influence of supportive relationships on children's adjustment must be expanded to recognize the influence of children's adjustment on their relationships.

REFERENCES

Ainsworth, M. D. (1989). Attachments beyond infancy. *American Psychologist, 44,* 709–716.

Ainsworth, M., Blehar, M., Waters, E., & Wall, S. (1978). *Patterns of attachment.* Hillsdale, NJ: Lawrence Erlbaum Associates.

Barrera, M. (1986). Distinctions between social support concepts, measures, and models. *American Journal of Community Psychology, 14,* 413–446.

Barrera, M., Chassin, L., & Rogosch, F. (1993). Effects of social support and conflict on adolescent children of alcoholic and nonalcoholic fathers. *Journal of Personality and Social Psychology, 64,* 602–612.

Barrera, M., Sandler, I. N., & Ramsey, T. B. (1981). Preliminary development of a scale of social support: Studies on college students. *American Journal of Community Psychology, 9,* 435–447.

Baumrind, D. (1989). Rearing competent children. In W. Damon (Ed.), *Child development today and tomorrow* (pp. 349–378). San Francisco: Jossey-Bass.

Baumrind, D. (1993). The average expectable environment is not good enough: A response to Scarr. *Child Development, 64,* 1299–1317.

Belle, D. (Ed.). (1989). *Children's social networks and social supports.* New York: Wiley.

Berndt, T. J. (1986). Sharing between friends: Contexts and consequences. In E. C. Mueller & C. Cooper (Eds.), *Process and outcome in peer relationships* (pp. 129–160). New York: Academic Press.

Berndt, T. J. (1989). Obtaining support from friends in childhood and adolescence. In D. Belle (Ed.), *Children's social networks and social supports* (pp. 308–331). New York: Wiley.

Berndt, T. J. (1992). *Child development*. Fort Worth, TX: Harcourt Brace Jovanovich.

Berndt, T. J. (in press). Exploring the effects of friendship quality on social development. In W. M. Bukowski, A. F. Newcomb, & W. W. Hartup (Eds.), *The company they keep: Friendship in childhood and adolescence*. Cambridge, England: Cambridge University Press.

Berndt, T. J., Hawkins, J. A., & Hoyle, S. G. (1986). Changes in friendship during a school year: Effects on children's and adolescents' impressions of friendship and sharing with friends. *Child Development, 57,* 1284–1297.

Berndt, T. J., & Keefe, K. (1995). Friends' influence on adolescents' adjustment to school. *Child Development, 66,* 1312–1329.

Berndt, T. J., & Perry, T. B. (1986). Children's perceptions of friendship as supportive relationships. *Developmental Psychology, 22,* 640–648.

Berndt, T. J., & Perry, T. B. (1990). Distinctive features and effects of early adolescent friendships. In R. Montemayor, G. R. Adams, & T. P. Gullotta (Eds.), *From childhood to adolescence: A transitional period?* (pp. 269–287). Newbury Park, CA: Sage.

Berndt, T. J., & Savin-Williams, R. C. (1993). Variations in friendships and peer-group relationships in adolescence. In P. Tolan & B. Cohler (Eds.), *Handbook of clinical research and practice with adolescents* (pp. 203–219). New York: Wiley.

Block, J. H. (1983). Differential premises arising from differential socialization of the sexes: Some conjectures. *Child Development, 54,* 1335–1354.

Blyth, D. A., & Foster-Clark, F. S. (1987). Gender differences in perceived intimacy with different members of adolescents' social networks. *Sex Roles, 17,* 689–718.

Bowlby, J. (1969). *Attachment and loss: Vol. 1. Attachment.* New York: Basic Books.

Buhrmester, D. (1990). Intimacy of friendship, interpersonal competence, and adjustment during preadolescence and adolescence. *Child Development, 61,* 1101–1111.

Cauce, A. M., Hannan, K., & Sargeant, M. (1992). Life stress, social support, and locus of control during early adolescence: Interactive effects. *American Journal of Community Psychology, 20,* 787–798.

Cauce, A. M., Reid, M., Landesman, S., & Gonzales, N. (1990). Social support in young children: Measurement, structure, and behavioral impact. In B. R. Sarason, I. G. Sarason, & G. R. Pierce (Eds.), *Social support: An interactional view* (pp. 64–94). New York: Wiley.

Cauce, A. M., & Srebnik, D. S. (1989). Peer networks and social support: A focus for preventive effects with youth. In L. A. Bond & B. E. Compas (Eds.), *Primary prevention and promotion in the schools* (pp. 235–254). Newbury Park, CA: Sage.

Clark, M. S., & Reis, H. T. (1988). Interpersonal processes in close relationships. *Annual Review of Psychology, 39,* 609–672.

Clark-Lempers, D. S., Lempers, J. D., & Ho, C. (1991). Early, middle, and late adolescents' perceptions of their relationships with significant others. *Journal of Adolescent Research, 6,* 296–315.

Coates, D. L. (1981). *The social network record.* Washington, DC: Catholic University, Center for the Study of Youth Development.

Coates, D. L. (1987). Gender differences in the structure and support characteristics of Black adolescents' social networks. *Sex Roles, 17,* 667–687.

Cobb, S. (1976). Social support as a moderator of life stress. *Psychosomatic Medicine, 38,* 300–314.

Cohen, S., Mermelstein, R. J., Kamarck, T., & Hoberman, H. M. (1985). Measuring the functional components of social support. In I. G. Sarason & B. R. Sarason (Eds.), *Social support: Theory, research, and applications* (pp. 349–370). Dordrecht, Netherlands: Martinus Nijhoff.

Cohen, S., & Wills, T. A. (1985). Stress, social support, and the buffering hypotheses. *Psychological Bulletin, 98*, 310–357.

Davies, B. (1982). *Life in the classroom and playground.* London: Routledge & Kegan Paul.

DeRosier, M. E., & Kupersmidt, J. B. (1991). Costa Rican children's perceptions of their social networks. *Developmental Psychology, 27*, 656–662.

Dohrenwend, B. P., & Shrout, P. E. (1985). "Hassles" in the conceptualization and measurement of life stress variables. *American Psychologist, 40*, 780–785.

DuBois, D. L., Felner, R. D., Brand, S., Adan, A. M., & Evans, E. G. (1992). A prospective study of life stress, social support, and adaptation in early adolescence. *Child Development, 63*, 542–557.

Dubow, E. F., & Tisak, J. (1989). The relation between stressful life events and adjustment in elementary school children: The role of social support and social problem-solving skills. *Child Development, 60*, 1412–1423.

Dubow, E. F., Tisak, J., Causey, D., Hryshko, A., & Reid, G. (1991). A two-year longitudinal study of stressful life events, social support, and social problem-solving skills: Contributions to children's behavioral and academic adjustment. *Child Development, 62*, 583–599.

Dubow, E. F., & Ullman, D. G. (1989). Assessing social support in elementary school children: The survey of children's social support. *Journal of Clinical Child Psychology, 18*, 52–64.

East, P. L. (1991). The parent–child relationships of withdrawn, aggressive, and sociable children: Child and parent perspectives. *Merrill-Palmer Quarterly, 37*, 425–444.

East, P. L., & Rook, K. S. (1992). Compensatory patterns of support among children's peer relationships: A test using school friends, non-school friends, and siblings. *Developmental Psychology, 28*, 163–172.

Eccles, J. S., Midgley, C., Wigfield, A., Buchanan, C. M., Reuman, D., Flanagan, C., & MacIver, D. (1993). Development during adolescence: The impact of stage-environment fit on young adolescents' experiences in schools and in families. *American Psychologist, 48*, 90–101.

Feiring, C., & Lewis, M. (1991). The development of social networks from early to middle childhood: Gender differences and the relation to school competence. *Sex Roles, 25*, 237–253.

Finney, J. W., Mitchell, R. E., Cronkite, R. C., & Moos, R. H. (1984). Methodological issues in estimating main and interactive effects: Examples from coping/social support and stress field. *Journal of Health and Social Behavior, 25*, 85–98.

Fischer, J. L., Sollie, D. L., & Morrow, K. B. (1986). Social networks in male and female adolescents. *Journal of Adolescent Research, 6*, 1–14.

Furman, W. (in press). The measurement of children's and adolescents' perceptions of friendships: Conceptual and methodological issues. In W. M. Bukowski, A. F. Newcomb, & W. W. Hartup (Eds.), *The company they keep: Friendship in childhood and adolescence.* Cambridge, England: Cambridge University Press.

Furman, W., & Buhrmester, D. (1992). Age and sex differences in perceptions of networks of personal relationships. *Child Development, 63*, 103–115.

Gilligan, C. (1982). *In a different voice.* Cambridge, MA: Harvard University Press.

Goodyear, I. M., Wright, C., & Altham, P. M. (1989). Recent friendships in anxious and depressed school age children. *Psychological Medicine, 19*, 165–174.

Gottman, J. M. (1983). How children become friends. *Monographs of the Society for Research in Child Development, 48* (3, Serial No. 201).

Gottman, J. M. & Parker, J. G. (Eds.). (1986). *Conversations of friends.* Cambridge, England: Cambridge University Press.
Grotevant, H. D., & Cooper, C. R. (1985). Patterns of interaction in family relationships and the development of identity exploration in adolescence. *Child Development, 56,* 415–428.
Hartup, W. W. (1992). Friendships and their developmental significance. In H. McGurk (Ed.), *Contemporary issues in childhood social development* (pp. 175–205). Hove, UK: Lawrence Erlbaum Associates.
Hauser, S. T., Powers, S. I., Noam, G. G., Jacobson, A. M., Weiss, B., & Follansbee, D. J. (1984). Familial contexts of adolescent ego development. *Child Development, 55,* 195–213.
Hirsch, B. J., & DuBois, D. L. (1991). Self esteem in early adolescence: The identification and prediction of contrasting longitudinal trajectories. *Journal of Youth and Adolescence, 20,* 53–72.
Hoffman, M. A., Levy-Schiff, R., & Ushpiz, V. (1993). Moderating effects of adolescent social orientation on the relation between social support and self-esteem. *Journal of Youth and Adolescence, 22,* 23–31.
Hoffman, M. A., Ushpiz, V., & Levy-Shiff, R. (1988). Social support and self-esteem in adolescence. *Journal of Youth and Adolescence, 17,* 307–316.
Hunter, F. T. (1985). Adolescents' perception of discussions with parents and friends. *Developmental Psychology, 21,* 433–440.
Isabella, R. A. (1993). Origins of attachment: Maternal interactive behavior across the first year. *Child Development, 64,* 605–621.
Isabella, R., & Belsky, J. (1991). Interactional synchrony and the origins of infant-mother attachment: A replication study. *Child Development, 62,* 373–384.
Jones, G. P., & Dembo, M. H. (1989). Age and sex role differences in intimate friendships during childhood and adolescence. *Merrill-Palmer Quarterly, 35,* 445–462.
Keefe, K., & Berndt, T. J. (1994). *Effects of friendship quality on self-esteem in early adolescence.* Unpublished manuscript, University of California at Los Angeles, Department of Psychology.
Kon, I. (1981). Adolescent friendship: Some unanswered questions for future research. In S. Duck & R. Gilmour (Eds.), *Personal relationships 2: Developing personal relationships* (pp. 187–203). New York: Academic Press.
Lamborn, S., & Steinberg, L. (1993). Emotional autonomy redux: Revisiting Ryan and Lynch. *Child Development, 64,* 483–499.
Larson, R., & Richards, M. H. (1991). Daily companionship in late childhood and early adolescence: Changing developmental contexts. *Child Development, 62,* 284–300.
Lazarus, R. S., & Folkman, S. (1984). *Stress, appraisal, and coping.* New York: Springer.
Levitt, M. J., Guacci-Franco, N., & Levitt, J. L. (1993). Convoys of social support in childhood and early adolescence: Structure and function. *Developmental Psychology, 29,* 811–818.
Licitra-Kleckler, D. M., & Waas, G. A. (1993). Perceived social support among high-stress adolescents: The role of family and peers. *Journal of Adolescent Research, 8,* 381–402.
Lustig, J. L., Wolchik, S. A., & Braver, S. L. (1992). Social support in chumships and adjustment in children of divorce. *American Journal of Community Psychology, 20,* 393–399.
Lytton, H. (1990). Child and parent effects in boys' conduct disorder: A reinterpretation. *Developmental Psychology, 26,* 683–697.
Lytton, H., & Romney, D. M. (1991). Parents' differential socialization of boys and girls: A meta-analysis. *Psychological Bulletin, 109,* 267–296.

Maccoby, E. E., & Martin, J. A. (1983). Socialization in the context of the family: Parent–child interaction. In E. M. Hetherington (Ed.), *Socialization, personality, and social development: Vol. 4. Handbook of child psychology* (pp. 1–101). New York: Wiley.

Moran, P. B., & Eckenrode, J. (1991). Gender differences in the costs and benefits of peer relationships during adolescence. *Journal of Adolescent Research, 6,* 396–409.

Morano, C. D., Cisler, R. A., & Lemerond, J. (1993). Risk factors for adolescent suicidal behavior: Loss, insufficient familial support, and hopelessness. *Adolescence, 28,* 851–865.

Newcomb, A. F., & Bagwell, C. L. (in press). Children's friendship relations: Developmental necessity, advantage, or hindrance? In W. M. Bukowski, A. F. Newcomb, & W. W. Hartup (Eds.), *The company they keep: Friendship in childhood and adolescence.* Cambridge, England: Cambridge University Press.

Newcomb, A. F., & Brady, J. E. (1982). Mutuality in boys' friendship relations. *Child Development, 53,* 392–395.

Newcomb, M. D. (1990). Social support and personal characteristics: A developmental and interactional perspective. *Journal of Social and Clinical Psychology, 9,* 54–68.

Newcomb, M. D., & Bentler, P. M. (1987). Loneliness and social support: A confirmatory hierarchical analysis. *Personality and Social Psychology Bulletin, 12,* 520–535.

Paikoff, R. L., & Brooks-Gunn, J. (1991). Do parent–child relationships change during puberty? *Psychological Bulletin, 110,* 47–66.

Parker, J. G., & Asher, S. R. (1993). Friendship and friendship quality in middle childhood: Links with peer group acceptance and loneliness. *Developmental Psychology, 29,* 611–621.

Procidano, M. E., & Heller, K. (1983). Measures of perceived social support from friends and from family: Three validation studies. *American Journal of Community Psychology, 11,* 1–24.

Rawlins, W. K. (1992). *Friendship matters.* New York: Aldine De Gruyter.

Reid, M., Landesman, S., Treder, R., & Jaccard, J. (1989). "My Family and Friends": Six- to twelve-year-old children's perceptions of social support. *Child Development, 60,* 896–910.

Rook, K. S. (1987). Social support versus companionship: Effects on life stress, loneliness, and evaluations by others. *Journal of Personality and Social Psychology, 52,* 1132–1147.

Ryan, R. M., & Lynch, J. H. (1989). Emotional autonomy versus detachment: Revisiting the vicissitudes of adolescence and young adulthood. *Child Development, 60,* 340–356.

Sarason, B. R., Sarason, I. G., & Pierce, G. R. (Eds.). (1990). *Social support: An interactional view.* New York: Wiley.

Scarr, S. (1992). Developmental theories for the 1990s: Development and individual differences. *Child Development, 63,* 1–19.

Slavin, L. A. (1991). Validation studies of the PEPSS, a measure of perceived emotional support for use with adolescents. *Journal of Adolescent Research, 6,* 316–335.

Slavin, L. A., & Rainer, K. L. (1990). Gender differences in emotional support and depressive symptoms among adolescents: A prospective analysis. *American Journal of Community Psychology, 18,* 407–421.

Sullivan, H. S. (1953). *The interpersonal theory of psychiatry.* New York: Norton.

Thoits, P. A. (1982). Conceptual, methodological, and theoretical problems in studying social support as a buffer against life stress. *Journal of Health and Social Behavior, 23,* 145–159.

Thoits, P. A. (1985). Social support and psychological well-being: Theoretical possibilities. In I. G. Sarason & B. R. Sarason (Eds.), *Social support: Theory, research, and applications* (pp. 51–72). Dordrecht, Netherlands: Martinus Nijhoff.

Vaux, A. (1988). *Social support: Theory, research, and intervention.* New York: Praeger.

Veiel, H. O. F., & Baumann, U. (Eds.). (1992). *The meaning and measurement of social support.* New York: Hemisphere.

Vernberg, E. M. (1990). Psychological adjustment and experiences with peers during early adolescence: Reciprocal, incidental, or unidirectional relationships? *Journal of Abnormal Child Psychology, 18,* 187–198.

Walker, L. J. (1986). Sex differences in the development of moral reasoning: A rejoinder to Baumrind. *Child Development, 57,* 522–526.

Weiss, R. S. (1974). The provisions of social relationships. In Z. Rubin (Ed.), *Doing unto others* (pp. 17–26). Englewood Cliffs, NJ: Prentice-Hall.

Wills, T. H., Vaccaro, D., & McNamara, G. (1992). The role of life events, family support, and competence in adolescent substance use: A test of vulnerability and protective factors. *American Journal of Community Psychology, 20,* 349–374.

Windle, M. (1992). A longitudinal study of stress buffering for adolescent problem behaviors. *Developmental Psychology, 28,* 522–530.

Wolchik, S. A., Beals, J., & Sandler, I. N. (1989). Mapping children's support networks: Conceptual and methodological issues. In D. Belle (Ed.), *Children's social networks and social supports* (pp. 191–220). New York: Wiley.

Youniss, J., & Smollar, J. (1985). *Adolescent relations with mothers, fathers, and friends.* Chicago: University of Chicago Press.

5

The Sense of Self and Its Development: A Framework for Understanding Eating Disorders

Fontaine Ewell
Susan Smith
Mary Pat Karmel
Daniel Hart

Disruptions in the sense of self are essential components of nearly all descriptions of the phenomenology of adolescents and young adults with eating disorders. Indeed, those with eating disorders frequently invoke perceptions of self in their explanations for the obsessive focus on weight management that permeates every facet of their lives: The perception of the self as fat or obese in individuals with anorexia nervosa (AN) is seen as terribly discrepant with the ideal or desired self, which is slim. This in turn requires dieting in order to reduce the discrepancy. Consider an excerpt from an interview with a young woman diagnosed as having AN, who participated in one of our studies. What becomes apparent in her comments is her narrow definition of herself in terms of her body and the dominating importance of keeping her body as similar as possible to her slim ideal.

Interviewer: What are you especially proud of about yourself?
Respondent: My body. Sometimes I think I'm thin and really good-looking; sometimes I think I'm really ugly. When I feel I look good I feel really together. . . .
Interviewer: Why are you proud of your body?
Respondent: A lot of people tell me I'm too skinny. I was worried for a while, but now I don't care what they think. People tell me they're jealous of how thin I am. I'm the thinnest in my family. My mother thinks I'm anorexic [in fact she has been diagnosed as having AN and was in outpatient

treatment at the time of this interview]. I don't think I'm fat but I still have some problems around eating. I don't always eat enough . . . but I like the way I look. Sometimes I put my body ahead of everything else. When my self-confidence is down, sometimes I try to impress people with the way I look instead of the way I act. (Levitt & Hart, 1991)

Our goal in this chapter is to explore the ways in which the sense of self becomes a part of eating disorder syndromes. As the preceding example suggests, views of self are deeply integrated into these problems of adaptation. The chapter begins with a discussion of the components of the sense of self; this prepares the ground for later discussions by making clear which sorts of experiences contribute to the sense of self and which do not. The chapter continues with an explication of the ways in which these components to the sense of self develop from infancy through late adolescence. A developmental approach is particularly appropriate for a discussion of eating disorders, because the emergence of these disorders in adolescence suggests that the physical and psychological changes that accompany the transition from childhood to adolescence make girls susceptible to AN and bulimia nervosa (BN). Certainly transformations in the sense of self may be one source of vulnerability to these syndromes. These connections are discussed further in the final sections of the chapter.

THE COMPONENTS OF THE SENSE OF SELF

How should the sense of self be demarcated? What distinctions are useful to make among types of experiences that contribute to the sense of self? Efforts to answer these questions have characterized not only U.S. psychology since its founding by James (1890) and Baldwin (1902) but contemporary and ancient philosophy as well. The definition of the self adopted in this chapter is that of James, who proposed that a person's self is "the sum total of all that he can call his" (p. 291). Several important postulates follow from this definition. The first is that the discussion is necessarily of conscious experiences: To label a sensation or perception or idea as "one's own," one must direct attention to it. By this definition, then, it makes no sense to talk of an unconscious self or a repressed self. Moreover, definitions that use the word *self* interchangeably with the word *personality* (as is often done in the sociological literature) are incompatible with that offered by James. The Jamesian definition also implies substantial individual control over what is and is not considered part of the self. For instance, an individual may agree with an observer that an amputation has caused him or her to lose a foot, but whatever the observer judges to be true of the individual's limitations, the individual may rightfully assert a sense of self that does not include the label "handicapped." This is because persons are ordinarily granted autonomy in the decision of what the constituents of the self are to be.

How should the components of the sense of self be characterized? James (1890) offered considerable insight into this issue as well. James noted—as have theorists of a variety of persuasions before and since—that the sense of self is constituted of both awareness and concept. We believe that it is useful to further distinguish among types self-awareness and types of self-concepts.

Self-Awareness

Self-awareness is a fundamental quality of the reflexive self described by James (1890). Each neurologically intact individual is presumed capable of reflecting on, focusing attention toward, or becoming aware of the self. Two interwoven strands of this self-awareness are discussed here: objective self-awareness and subjective self-awareness.

Objective Self-Awareness. Objective self-awareness refers simply to the focusing of attention onto oneself. Clearly, such a property is only instantiated in an organism capable both of focusing attention and of distinguishing the self from other classes of stimuli. As we have suggested elsewhere (Hart & Karmel, in press; Hart & Whitlow, 1995), it is likely that the capacity for self-awareness is distributed across the different anthropoid species, and perhaps other species as well. Although the capacity for objective self-awareness may not serve as a useful yardstick against which to make inter- or intraspecies comparisons, the disposition to focus on the self may be a more sensitive measure. Some species, particularly humans, may be more likely than others to focus attention on the self. Among humans, moreover, the tendency to focus on the self varies considerably from individual to individual. Indeed, in the developmental review that follows, evidence is presented that suggests that the tendency to focus awareness on the self varies from age to age and among persons within age cohorts.

Subjective Self-Awareness. Self-awareness, as James (1890) described it, is qualitatively different from awareness of other sets of stimuli. This is because reflection on oneself is usually accompanied by identification with and emotional involvement in the stimuli composing the self. Indeed, James (p. 333) suggested that there is a characteristic "warmth and intimacy" that accompanies the consideration of the self's characteristics. This quality is labeled *subjective self-awareness.* Although the identification with and emotional involvement in the self that constitute subjective self-awareness usually accompany objective self-awareness, there are important exceptions. In multiple personality disorder, for instance, one personality in the afflicted individual may be aware of other personalities that share the same body (i.e., objective self-awareness is present), but may deny a connection with the thoughts and actions of that other personality (in which case subjective self-awareness as it is discussed here is absent).

Self-Understanding

There is also a conceptual element to the sense of self that can be called *self-understanding* (see, e.g., Damon & Hart, 1988). In our own work we have found it useful to distinguish among three types of elements: personal memories, representations, and theories of self. Personal memories refer to autobiographical episodes available to conscious recall that are seen by the individual as constitutive of the self. For instance, for some adolescents a particularly defiant act of rebellion may serve to demarcate a "new" self that is at least partially free of parental control.

At an intermediate level of abstraction the individual understands the self as an organization of representations. These representations include images of what the current self is like (e.g., "I am smart, tall, and friendly"), of what the ideal or desired self might be (e.g., "I want to be thin and popular"), and of the kind of person that one is with specific others (e.g., the social selves described by James, 1890: "with my mother I am quiet, but with my friends I'm crazy and wild"), to name just a few of the configurations that these representations might assume. James was the first to suggest how these different representations might interact; thus, for instance, a large discrepancy between the view of what the self is currently like and what the self should ideally be would result in low self-esteem.

Finally, there is a theoretical element to the sense of self. As Taylor (1989) pointed out, the self is in part an answer to questions that orient life, such as "What is good?" and "What is worth pursuing?" The stance that persons assume toward these questions affects the ways in which the self is understood. Individuals with eating disorders, for instance, apparently have theories of self according to which what is good is "to be thin"; the pursuit of this becomes the dominating goal of life. Theories, then, infuse representations and personal memories with meaning.

A Note on Measurement

The complexity of the sense of self makes it exceedingly difficult to assess the different components in developmentally appropriate ways. No single measure, and not even a single measurement approach, can do justice to the richness of the experience of self. In the research reviewed in what follows concerning adolescence (the age range of greatest concern for researchers and clinicians interested in eating disorders), measurement strategies can be arrayed along several dimensions, the most important being the extent to which a measure structures the responses that can be given by the subject. On highly structured questionnaires, including many self-esteem inventories (e.g., Harter, 1985; Rosenberg, 1979), subjects are limited to choosing one multiple-choice response for a particular item. The advantages of structured questionnaires for research are many: They are inexpensive to administer and code, they ensure that all subjects respond in similar ways, and all issues of interest to the experimenter can be tapped.

At the other end of the scale are measures that allow subjects to respond in their own words to open-ended questions about the self (e.g., Damon & Hart, 1988). Asking subjects to describe themselves has the important advantage of allowing subjects' own constructs of self to emerge. Research by Higgins, King, and Mavin (1982) has demonstrated that self-generated traits are more likely to reflect the ways in which subjects actually process social information than are self-ratings on structured questionnaires. Unfortunately, interviewing subjects about themselves or eliciting written self-descriptions demands a major commitment from researchers and subjects. Moreover, coding such self-descriptions is difficult and time-consuming. The seemingly unavoidable conclusion, then, is that the best research approach is to employ both methods. We particularly recommend that researchers begin by interviewing persons in the groups that are to be studied. Interviews allow researchers to gain some grasp on the complexity of the sense of self in the selected groups and help prevent mistaken assumptions about what persons in these groups think about themselves.

DEVELOPMENT OF SELF-AWARENESS AND SELF-UNDERSTANDING

Each of the five components of the sense of self undergoes change during the various transitions between infancy and adolescence (see Table 5.1), with each component assuming different levels of salience in defining the self at different points in time (Damon & Hart, 1988). In the sections that follow, these changes, their sources, and their implications for emotional functioning are briefly considered.

Infancy

Largely because infants cannot describe their experiences of themselves, it has proven difficult for researchers to characterize the sense of self in this age group. A number of experimental and observational

TABLE 5.1
Summary of Developmental Transformations in the Sense of Self and Their Relations to Eating Disorders

	Subjective Self-Awareness	Objective Self-Awareness	Personal Memories	Representations	Theories
Infancy	Identification with and investment in the self is certainly present by approximately 18–24 months of age, when shame, guilt, pride, and embarrassment emerge	Evident in the early differentiation of the self's body from other stimuli; emerges as a consequence of the body's achitecture and is prerequisite for emotional experience	Little evidence to suggest that personal memories form important parts of the infant's sense of self	Representations of the self's physical appearance and capabilities emerge at approximately 18 months of age; development may be fostered by imitation, social interaction	Little evidence that theories of self are salient
Childhood	Little known	Objective self-awareness increases slightly, and is accompanied by increasingly accurate self-attributions	Memories are identified and revisited in early narrative exchanges between toddler and caregiver; later in childhood, salient personal memories can be identified	A range of representations concerning the self are evident; these include attributions about the self's physical, active, social, and psychological characteristics, as well as the formation of views of what the self would ideally be and the self that is expected by others	Social comparison organizes theories of self; talent and ability are elevated, and motivation and acts of will shape the self

TABLE 5.1 (continued)

	Subjective Self-Awareness	Objective Self-Awareness	Personal Memories	Representations	Theories
Adolescence	Generally increases, although it may be withdrawn from some qualities of self, resulting in conscious sense of false self and inauthenticity	Objective self-awareness increases from levels observed in childhood	Particular memories become increasingly drawn upon in the understanding of self	Discrepancies among representations of the actual, ideal, and ought selves become more salient	Social integration becomes the dominant organizing principle; features of self are important to the extent that they contribute to social acceptance; the self is believed to be formed through social interaction
Eating Disorders	Splits and ruptures in subjective self-awareness; frequently a sense that important parts of one's life (i.e., one's body) no longer are part of the self	Chronically high objective self-awareness (self-consciousness); escape from focus on the self may motivate some eating disorders	Sharp memories of weight problems and problems with autonomy within the family	Distorted representations of the body; conflicts among images of what the self is like, what the ideal self would be, and what others expect of the self	Centrality of weight and weight control in achieving life satisfaction

113

studies suggest, however, that infants do posess at least some of the component experiences of self; the evidence is particularly compelling for objective self-awareness.

Objective Self-Awareness.   Within the first few months of life infants are clearly able to distinguish between stimuli that correspond to the self and those that do not, which suggests the presence of at least a rudimentary form of objective self-awareness. The differentiation of the self's vocalizations from those of other infants is evident in the first days of life. For example, Martin and Clark (1982) presented both crying and calm newborns with tape-recorded sounds of their own cries and the cries of other newborns. Those who were calm cried in response to hearing the cries of other newborns, yet gave virtually no response to hearing their own tape-recorded cries. Conversely, infants who were crying when presented with the tape-recordings continued to cry only when the recording was that of the crying of another newborn; when presented with their own cries, this group stopped crying. Thus, both groups of infants responded one way to their own cries and another way to the cries of other infants. Visually, infants distinguish between televised images of their own body parts (legs) and those of other infants (Watson, 1994) in the first months of life and by 9 months of age are able to distinguish between live television images of their entire bodies and the recorded images of other infants (Lewis & Brooks-Gunn, 1979).

How does objective self-awareness develop? There are reasons to suppose that both the evolutionary benefits of the ability to focus attention on the self (see Dennett, 1991) and the structure of the body (Humphrey, 1992) predispose humans toward developing objective self-awareness. However, social experiences are also important. Meltzoff (1990), for example, examined the ways in which social imitation is fundamental for the developing experience of self. Meltzoff pointed to the role of imitation as a social mirror, in which the caregiver's behavior is reflected back to the infant, causing the infant to attend to his or her own actions. Similarly, when the infant attempts to match the actions or emotional expressions of others, the self's actions must be monitored and corrected for close replication. In general, then, the process of imitation fosters objective awareness of self (see Hart & Fegley, 1994a, 1994b, for further discussions).

Subjective Self-Awareness.   What is the infant's stance toward the self? Is there a sense of special investment and emotional responsiveness that is attached to a focus on the self in the fashion that James (1890) described as characteristic of self-reflection? Or is focusing attention on the self essentially similar to focusing attention on any other object in the world? Again, the young infant's inability to communicate makes it nearly impossible to ascertain the answers to these questions.

However, there is considerable evidence to suggest that subjective self-awareness is clearly present in older infants. The most revealing phenomena involve emotions, particularly those of shame, guilt, pride, and embarrassment. Lewis (1992) argued that all of these emotions require that one feel a special attachment to oneself. Shame, for example, requires that one perceive that the self has failed to live up to important standards; this results in the judgment that the self—from the perspective of the individual—is bad. Because the self is of special importance in experience, this results in a disturbingly negative affective response. Although Lewis' work demonstrates that subjective self-awareness is present by late infancy, further research is needed to identify its developmental course.

Self-Understanding. To our knowledge there is little evidence to indicate that personal memories or theories of self are salient components of the infant's sense of self. However, there appears to be a broad consensus that infants develop representations of self at approximately 18 months of age (see Hart & Fegley, 1994a, for a review). Three lines of research support this conclusion. First, between 18 and 24 months of age infants develop the capacity to recognize themselves in mirrors (e.g., Lewis & Brooks-Gunn, 1979). Second, at approximately the same age infants become aware of their capacities to imitate the actions of others and refuse to attempt to emulate modeled actions that excede their abilities, whereas infants of younger ages attempt to imitate the same difficult actions (Kagan, 1981). Finally, infants of this age begin to refer to themselves ("I," "me," "mine"), which presumably requires some representation of self (Zazzo, 1982).

Childhood

During childhood, numerous transformations occur in the ways in which individuals think about themselves; because of space restrictions these changes are only outlined here (for a lengthier treatment see Damon & Hart, 1992).

Objective Self-Awareness. One of the products of focusing attention on the self is increased knowledge about its characteristics. There is some evidence to indicate that over the course of childhood self-focused attention results in greater accuracy in self-evaluation, just as it does in adulthood (e.g., Nasby, 1989). For example, Lerner and Korn (1972) asked boys aged 5 and 15 to select their own body type and their preferred body build from a group of presented possibilities. Over one half of the 5-year-old "chubby" boys misidentified their own body type as "average," whereas only approximately one third of the 15-year-old "chubby" boys did so. Two inferences can be drawn from this finding.

First, over the course of childhood and into adolescence, self-reflection results in increasingly accurate self-appraisals. Second, self-appraisals are frequently wrong (one third of the boys continued to misidentify their body type, even in adolescence); objective self-awareness, therefore, does not guarantee self-knowledge.

Individual differences in the tendency to focus attention on the self also seem to have their roots in childhood. Much of the research relevant to this issue has been based on a measure developed by Fenigstein, Scheier, and Buss (1975) that assesses public and private self-consciousness (two subtypes of objective self-awareness). Nasby (1989) defined private self-consciousness as "habitual attentiveness to covert aspects of the self that the individual but not others can observe (e.g., subjective feelings and thoughts, goals, intentions, motives, plans and values)" (p. 117) and public self-consciousness as "habitual attentiveness to overt aspects of the self (e.g., physical appearance and overt behaviors and expressions of affect) that others can observe as well as evaluate" (p. 117). Public and private self-consciousness are modestly correlated (Fenigstein et al., 1975).

Klonsky, Dutton, and Liebel (1990) identified several personal history and familial variables that are important in the development of self-consciousness. In their study, college students completed questionnaires measuring self-consciousness, self-image, and recollections of their family life; parents also filled out questionnaires concerning childrearing practices. The results suggested that high self-consciousness in adulthood was related to a childhood during which parents were both active disciplinarians and highly concerned with their children's achievement. Not surprisingly, those high in public self-consciousness were found to be less satisfied with their bodies, personalities, and scholastic achievement, with this dissatisfaction being higher for girls than for boys.

Finally, it should be noted that high self-consciousness is related to negative affect; those children who are highest in self-consciousness are more likely than those low in self-consciousness to report low self-esteem and high levels of depressive affect (Rosenberg, 1979).

Subjective Self-Awareness.   Relatively little is known about the development of subjective self-awareness in childhood. It is likely to increase slightly as children identify an increasing range of objects, performances, and thoughts with their selves.

Personal Memories.   It is during childhood that personal memories first become a significant part of one's understanding of self. The connecting of personal memories to the self happens for many reasons, one of the most important of which is the social interaction between caretaker and child. Nelson (1993), for example, explored the narrative exchanges occurring between toddler and mother and found that discussion of specific events happening to the child is quite frequent. Moreover, the mother not only refers to the "who," "what," and "where" of a given event but also explores its meaning with the child. Through this elaboration of the meaning of specific events, the mother communicates both the cultural models of how the self is related to the events that occur in the world and her own specific interpretation of this cultural model. This interpretation, discussion, and rehearsal of memories in intimate personal contexts results in a collection of memories that assume some salience in defining the self. Whereas few memories of events occurring before age 5 or 6 are sufficiently elaborated as to be remembered in adulthood, by middle childhood personal memories are salient constituents of the sense of self and become increasingly so through adolescence.

Representations.   During childhood the individual forms a wide range of representations concerning the self. Much of the early research in which children were asked simply to describe themselves (e.g., Secord & Peevers, 1974; Montemayor & Eisen, 1977) suggested that development over the course of childhood and adolescence was mainly a process of moving from concrete representations (e.g., age, physical characteristics, name) to abstract characterizations (e.g., personality, beliefs, feelings). This shift was believed to result from improvements in cognitive abilities, which allowed older children to infer or identify covert psychological properties of themselves.

Over the last 10 years, however, it has become clear that this simple and appealing description of development is largely incorrect. Observations of the spontaneous speech of young children interacting with each other reveal references to the psychological characteristics and personality traits of which they were presumably ignorant (Bretherton, McNew, & Beeghly-Smith, 1981). Hart, Fegley, Chan, Fisher, and Mulvey (1993) demonstrated that even though a large proportion of 7-year-olds' self-ascriptions in response to open-ended questions asking for self-descriptions (e.g., "What kind of person are you?") were indeed concerned with physical characteristics, the same children, when asked to judge the relative importance of physical and psychological characteristics to the sense of self, judged the latter to be more important. Finally, it is worth noting that the extent to which children respond in terms of psychological traits is in part a consequence of maternal socialization in early childhood (Dunn, Brown, Slomkowski, Tesla, & Youngblade, 1991) and in part a reflection of broad social–structural factors such as social class (Hart & Edelstein, 1992).

In our judgment, important developmental changes over the course of childhood are not to be found in the characteristics that children use to describe themselves but in their understanding of these characteristics and the ways in which these characteristics are related to each other. There is considerable evidence to indicate that as children get older, they increasingly believe that characteristics have traitlike qualities. For instance, Rholes and Ruble (1984) demonstrated that older children are more likely than younger children to believe that behavior in one context is a good predictor of behavior in another: Being smart in school, for instance, is more likely to be viewed as a reflection of a general context-independent trait by older children than by younger children.

Developmental change is likely to occur among representations as well. One of the most productive lines of research on the sense of self in adults has focused on the relation between the representation of the actual self (e.g., "the person I really am now") and representations of other selves: the *ideal self* ("the self I would ideally be"), the *undesired self* ("the self I fear becoming"; Ogilvie, 1987), the *ought self* ("the self others feel I ought to be"; Higgins, 1990), and *future* or *possible selves* (e.g., "The person I believe I will be in the future"; Markus & Nurius, 1986). These other representations are presumed to serve as standards against which the person judges the actual self: One wishes to be successful (the actual self should resemble the ideal self), avoid failure (the actual self should be quite dissimilar from the undesired self), fulfill the expectations of others (the actual self should be similar to the ought self), and so on. Research with adults supports the conclusion that the relation of the representation of the actual self to the representations of these other selves mediates mood and emotion. For instance, persons for whom the actual self is close to the ideal self (as assessed by the similarity between descriptions of the two representations) are likely to have lower levels of depressive affect than persons for whom the actual self is quite distant from the ideal self (Strauman & Higgins, 1987).

There is increasing interest among developmental psychologists in the study of the relations among specific self-representations in childhood. Hart, Fegley, and Brengelman (1993) asked children to describe their actual selves, what they were like 2 and 4 years in the past, and what they would be like in 2 and 4 years in the future. The descriptions of the actual self resembled more closely descriptions of the future selves than they did of past selves; apparently, children and adolescents see more continuity in the self from the present into the future than between the present and past. As in adulthood, the connections among representations appear to influence mood and emotion. For instance, Bybee and Zigler (1991) demonstrated that guilt feelings are more common among children and adolescents for whom the actual self is quite dissimilar to the ideal self than they are among children and adolescents who see the actual self and ideal self as being quite similar.

Theories of Self.   During childhood there is considerable transformation in the theories individuals hold about themselves. Typically, these theories are fairly complex and are concerned with a number of facets of the self; only the broad outlines of these theories can be presented here (for detailed treatments see Damon & Hart, 1988; Hart, 1992). The earliest theories about the self tend to be relatively unorganized; children assert that the meaning of various traits and characteristics of the self resides in the constructs themselves, with few systematic bridges among characteristics. The self and its various characteristics are viewed as a collection of features that comes into existence through the confluence of biological and social pressures. For instance, when young children are asked, "How did you get to be the kind of person you are right now?" they frequently respond with answers such as "My parents made me this way," or "I just grew."

Grade school children typically have a different theory of self, according to which the various characteristics of self draw their meaning from their value as assessed by comparing the self to relevant others. For instance, physical, psychological, social, personality characteristics, as well as activities, are all seen in light of social comparisons: "I'm tall, which is important because I'm the biggest in my class"; "I'm the best kickball player in my class"; "I'm in the highest reading group." These are typical self-attributions for this age range and reflect clearly the idea that the importance of a characteristic derives from its contribution to successful social evaluation. Children of this age typically believe that the origins of the self's characteristics can be traced to the wishes, motivations, and talents of the self (e.g., "I got to be a good kickball player because I tried really hard, and I really like to play it.").

Adolescence

Objective Self-Awareness.   The transition to adolescence brings with it a greater focus on the self. This observation is the basis for much of the Piagetian-based imaginary audience research (e.g., Elkind & Bowen, 1979; Lapsley & Rice, 1988) and emerges in studies of other orientations as well (e.g., Rosenberg, 1979), all of which suggest that early adolescence brings with it heightened self-awareness. As we noted earlier, chronically elevated levels of self-awareness are frequently associated with negative affect in adulthood, and this relation obtains in adolescence as well: There is a sharp increase in depressive affect accompanying the transition from childhood into adolescence (Rosenberg, 1979).

Subjective Self-Awareness.   Beginning in early adolescence, persons begin to make distinctions between characteristics and actions with which the self identifies and characteristics and actions that are seen as "not really" a part of the self. This is reflected most clearly in the emergence of concerns with authenticity, phoniness, and false-self behavior. There is a notion that some of what the self does is not representative of what the self really is; these unrepresentative actions are disowned and considered to be not part of the self. Broughton (1980) argued that many adolescents feel that the roles they enact are "phony" and that consequently the adolescents feel no emotional investment in these roles. In a sense there is a dissociation between the role and the self; in the terms used in this chapter, subjective self-awareness does not extend to the person's behavior in the inauthentic role. This experience, in which a person's actions are experienced in consciousness as not really belonging to the self, is not frequently found in childhood; Harter and Lee (1989) reported that children have a difficult time even understanding the idea of inauthentic or false-self behavior.

Personal Memories.   Little empirical work has been conducted that investigates the developmental transformation of personal memories. Some research has grown out of Marcia's (1966) paradigm of the four different identity statuses, labeled *diffuse, foreclosed, moratorium,* and *achieved.* Each of these statuses falls along a continuum reflecting the presence or absence of exploration and of commitment to one's identity: Persons with a diffuse identity status have not yet negotiated the tasks of identity development because they lack a stable system of commitments and any active process of exploration to achieve them, whereas persons with achieved identity status have decided on a stable system of commitments following an active period of exploration and crisis. More developmentally advanced concerns have been found in the early memories of persons with achieved and moratorium identity status (Orlofsky & Frank, 1986). The achieved and the foreclosed statuses have been associated with a greater number of personal memories in general (Neimeyer & Rareshide, 1991).

Representations.   During adolescence the understanding of characteristics that can be ascribed to the self changes, as do the relations among the various representations of self-descriptions. We begin by considering the changes in the understanding of characteristics. Just as it is inaccurate to characterize young children's sense of self as physicalistic (although, as already discussed, children do have an awareness of and concern for psychological characteristics), it is wrong to imagine that adolescents are concerned only with their social and psychological characteristics. It is true that adolescents are more likely than children to describe themselves in terms of personality and psychological functioning (Damon & Hart, 1988), but adolescents are also very much concerned with their physical characteristics (Hart & Damon, 1986). Typically, adolescents find the changes that occur in their bodies during puberty desirable; however, adolescent females, in comparison with adolescent males, are more ashamed of their bodies and feel less attractive (Koff, Rierdan, & Stubbs, 1990; Offer, Ostrow, & Howard, 1984).

This dissatisfaction appears focused particularly on weight. In a study of college males and females and their parents, Rozin and Fallon (1988) found that both mothers and daughters were generally more dissatisfied with their body images and with their weight than were the males. These researchers (Fallon & Rozin, 1985) also reported that in college-aged adolescent samples, nearly 70% of women reported that they were heavier than their ideal weights.

Relations among representations continue to be quite important in adolescence, although relatively little work has been done on this topic. In one of the few studies explicitly concerned with relations among representations, Hart and Fegley (1995) were able to demonstrate that the relation of the adolescent's actual self to the ideal self and to the selves expected by parents and peers was predictive of committed prosocial behavior. In particular, those adolescents who described their actual selves in ways that incorporated their descriptions of their ideal selves and their conceptions of what parents expected of them were more likely to be involved in prosocial activities; those adolescents whose descriptions of their actual selves incorporated the selves expected by their peers were less likely to be involved in prosocial action. It appears, then, that the relation of the actual self to other self-representations is of considerable importance in adolescence. There is some evidence to indicate that the relation of a specific characteristic of the actual self—one's weight—and the corresponding characteristic of the ideal self (i.e., one's desired weight) may be related to self-criticism, particularly in women (see Rodin, Silberstein, & Striegel-Moore, 1985).

Theories of Self. Young adolescents' theories of themselves are centrally concerned with social acceptance. For instance, when asked why characteristics offered in self-description are important to them, young teenagers frequently explain by reference to networks of friends and family (e.g., "Tall is important about me, because boys don't like tall girls"; "If I didn't play basketball I'd have to make all new friends"; "If I were less shy, I'd have more friends"; "If I weren't smart in school, my parents would be very dissatisfied"; see Damon & Hart, 1988, for several studies). This organizing concern with acceptance into a social network was clearly demonstrated in studies by Hart (1988), and by Hart, Fegley, Chan, et al. (1993). In these studies, children and adolescents were asked to imagine that a hypothetical "person machine" made copies of them. Each of the copies received one subset of the self's characteristics: One body received the self's physical characteristics ("this person has your body and looks exactly like you, but it doesn't have your thoughts and feelings, your capabilities and activities, or your friends and family, only your body"); another body received the self's capabilities and activities ("this person does all the things you do and has all your abilities, but it doesn't have . . . "); the third body received the self's social relationships ("this person has all your friends and family"); the last body received the self's psychological qualities ("this person has your thoughts and feelings"). The participants were then asked to choose (through a paired-comparison procedure) which person was closest to being the self. Young adolescents were most likely to claim that the hypothetical person with the self's friends and family was most nearly the self, even though this hypothetical person lacked the self's body, the self's activities, and the self's thoughts and feelings (older adolescents, and many children, selected the person with the self's psychological qualities as most resembling the self). This research demonstrates the slavish concern with social acceptance that dominates the adolescent's understanding of self. Because females of all ages are slightly more likely to be concerned with interpersonal concordance (Feingold, 1994), it seems reasonable to assume that adolescent girls may be more oriented toward thinking of themselves in terms of social relationships than are boys.

COMPONENTS TO THE SENSE OF SELF IN EATING DISORDERS AND OTHER CLINICAL DISORDERS

Distortions in the sense of self are frequently linked to eating disorders by researchers, by clinicians, and by the persons suffering from these disorders. In the sections that follow, the perturbations in the sense of self that characterize eating disorders are reviewed within the developmental framework outlined in the previous pages.

Objective Self-Awareness

The typical transition from childhood to adolescence brings with it a heightened focus on the self. For some, the entry into adolescence results only in modest increases in self-focus; for others, however, self-consciousness becomes elevated to very high levels. It is difficult to determine when levels of objective self-awareness become so high that poor adaptation results. To some degree, a focusing of attention on oneself may provide useful information that can be used to guide future behavior. Erikson (1950), for instance, suggested that it is important for adolescents to identify goals and ideologies that are consistent with their own views, a process that clearly requires some self-reflection. However, as suggested earlier, too much attention focused on the self is associated with depressive tendencies and other disorders. Moreover, abnormally high levels of self-consciousness may lay the groundwork for eating disorders. One route to eating disorders is through dieting that gets out of control. An interest in dieting has been shown to be related to self-consciousness (Hamilton, Falconer, & Greenberg, 1992), and for eating-disordered adolescents and adults, objective self-awareness increases beyond even the already high levels characteristic of those with an interest in dieting. In one of the first cases of AN to be reported in the clinical literature (reported first by Binswanger), a patient's diary records her fierce desire to be thin and at the same time her rejection of the constant self-focus that the dieting requires: "I want to grow thinner and thinner, but I do not want to have to watch myself constantly (cited in Colman, 1987, p. 142). Heightened self-focus is characteristic of other eating disorders as well: For instance, Striegel-Moore, Silberstein, and Rodin (1993) found that individuals with BN were higher in self-consciousness (objective self-awareness) than were controls.

Why is a chronically high focus on the self associated with eating disorders? Baumeister (1991; Heatherton & Baumeister, 1991) proposed a theory according to which one symptom of eating disorders, binge eating, functions to help the individual to escape from self-awareness. Baumeister argued that people engage in a range of destructive behaviors such as binge eating and drinking to excess, not with the intention of harming or thwarting the self, but instead to escape from the negative affect that accompanies chronic self-focused attention. In particular, Baumeister suggested that directing attention onto the self may reveal that one has not lived up to the expectations for the self held by others (the expectations that form the ought self discussed earlier); this results in a painfully negative self-evaluation, to escape from which some persons may resort to binge eating. By attending to food—an external, powerful stimulus—the individual can shift attention away from the self and its distressing flaws.

Both theory and research suggest that heightened objective self-awareness is characteristic of eating disorders. However, a number of important questions remain to be answered, particularly from within the developmental framework outlined in this chapter. For instance, it is unclear whether those who will develop eating disorders in adolescence have higher levels of self-consciousness in childhood (prior to the onset of the eating disorders) than do other children. Second, more research is needed to understand the sources of heightened self-consciousness. As was noted earlier, retrospective studies suggest that parents who are demanding (in terms of both behavior and achievement) may elicit high self-consciousness in their offspring. Such an explanation is certainly consistent with clinical observations of eating-disordered adolescents, which often report that the parents of these teenagers have extremely high expectations for them. Unfortunately, neither retrospective reports nor clinical anecdotes can replace solid prospective longitudinal research.

Subjective Self-Awareness

One of the most striking features of eating disorders is the disconnection that appears among features of the self: It is as if parts of the self no longer "belong" to the individual. Eating, which ordinarily is partially controlled by a host of physiological cues, becomes regulated entirely by psychological processes. Persons with eating disorders apparently lose contact with their internal sensations, such that they lack the ability to distinguish between true hunger and other physical, social, or emotional states (see Bruch, 1973). The understanding of self in eating-disordered adolescents is often characterized by a withdrawal of emotional involvement in, and identification with, parts of the self. Whereas this is somewhat typical of adolescence in general (as described earlier), it appears exaggerated in adolescents suffering from eating disorders. For instance, a 17-year-old patient with AN describes this split in her sense of self:

> My body could do anything—it could walk forever and ever and not get tired. I separated my mind and my body. My mind was tricky but my body was honest. It knew exactly what to do and I knew exactly what I could do. I felt very powerful on account of my body—my only weakness was my mind. (Bruch, 1973, p. 95)

For this young woman, the mind is seen as deceitful and dishonest; she identifies with her body, which has unlimited power and strength. The refusal to invest concern in certain facets of the self results in conflicts that may sustain maladaptive patterns. In the example just given, the rejection of the psychological characteristics and the identification with the body means that hunger pains and the obsession with eating that permeate her consciousness are disavowed: These sensations do not belong to the real self and should thus be ignored. The adolescent experiences conflict and shame over the division of the phenomenologically real and false facets of self and may consequently feel a sense of "fraudulence and inadequacy" (Johnson, 1991, p. 188).

Why is subjective self-awareness withdrawn from some facets of the self? How can the individual come to regard some features as not really part of the self? In the section on adolescence we reviewed some literature that suggests that this is, in part, a normal phenomenon of adolescence. Entry into the teen years is often accompanied by the identification of parts of the self as false or inauthentic and which are accordingly judged as not belonging to the self. It remains for future research to determine whether this age-typical phenomenon is amplified for some reason in some adolescents, which in turn makes this group vulnerable to the development of eating disorders.

It is also possible that the disruptions in subjective self-awareness just described are *caused* by the eating disorder. For instance, the starvation characteristic of AN may produce dissociative tendencies within the individual (Keys, Brozek, Henschel, Mickelson, & Taylor, 1950). Whether disturbances of subjective self-awareness are a cause or a consequence of eating disorders cannot be determined without additional research; from a treatment perspective, however, this disruption in the sense of self needs to be healed.

Personal Memories

Unfortunately, there is no systematic research on the kinds of personal memories that are particularly salient in those with eating disorders. Anecdotal evidence suggests that personal memories related to body type and autonomy—issues generally judged important in eating disorders—are particularly prominent. Bruch (1973) discussed the case of Gail, who changed her name after years of being taunted as "Two Ton Tilly." Another patient with AN spoke of her childhood, saying, "As far back as I can remember I was too fat and my mother always harped on it. . . . That's why I hate myself and my body. Fat people just disgust me" (p. 99). In one of our studies (Levitt & Hart, 1991) an adolescent recalled this episode concerning autonomy, which she believed led to her anorexic disorder:

> My parents wouldn't let me date, but all these guys were asking me out. Then my parents found out that at a school dance I drank some wine. They found out by reading a letter on the table that my mother read; I can't forgive her for that. And they grounded me. I felt like I had no control; the only thing I could control was the food in my mouth.

In the absence of systematic research it is difficult to know how characteristic these types of personal memories really are of adolescents with AN. Moreover, as the long debate concerning the archaeological facets of Freud's theory demonstrates (Ross, 1991), it is enormously difficult to determine the extent to which memories produce symptomatic behavior, or whether they are merely reconstructions brought on by this behavior itself.

Representations

As was noted in the developmental review, the relation among different sorts of self-representations becomes a salient concern in adolescence. There is some evidence to suggest that problematic relations among representations are characteristic of eating disorders, with the best of this research being done by Higgins and his colleagues (e.g., Higgins, Vookles, & Tykocinski, 1992). Higgins (1990) proposed that distress is generated when there is a discrepancy between the actual self and the ideal self or between the actual self and the ought self, and that different feeling complexes are experienced depending on the type of discrepancy. Discrepancies between the actual and ideal selves are associated with dejection-related syndromes such as depression (i.e., sadness, discouragement, psychomotor retardation); this discrepancy represents the absence of positive outcomes or the nonobtainment or loss of hopes and wishes. When an actual–ought discrepancy is more salient the individual experiences an agitation-related syndrome such as an anxiety disorder (i.e., worry, nervousness, psychomotor agitation); this discrepancy represents the presence of negative outcomes or the expectation of punishment for having violated duties and responsibilities.

In one study by Higgins et al. (1992) that examined eating disorders (among other problems), undergraduate students completed a series of questionnaires. These included the Selves Questionnaire (Higgins, 1987; Higgins, Bond, Klein, & Strauman, 1986), which measures the types of self-discrepancies described previously; the Eating Attitudes Test (Garner & Garfinkel, 1979), which measures the symptoms of AN; and the Binge Eating Scale (Hawkins & Clement, 1980), which measures the severity of binge eating. The Selves Questionnaire is a free-response, idiographic measure that asks subjects to list attributes (up to 10) for each of the following self-representations: actual–own, can–own, future–own, ideal–own, ought–own, ideal–mother (i.e., the respondents' beliefs about whom their mothers would ideally like them to be), ought–mother, ideal–father and ought–father. After listing the attributes the subject is asked to rate the extent to which each attribute applies, using a scale ranging from 1 (*slightly*) to 4 (*extremely*). Self-discrepancy scores are calculated by comparing the attributes listed for the actual–own self with those listed for other self-states. A comparison of two self-states on a particular attribute may yield any of the following relationships: a match, where the two attributes are synonymous (according to a thesaurus) and differ by no more than 1 according to the extent ratings; a synonymous mismatch, where the two attributes are synonymous but differ by 2 or more in extent; an antonymous mismatch, where the two attributes are antonyms; and a nonmatch, where the two attributes are neither synonyms nor antonyms. When computing a discrepancy score matches are counted as –1, nonmatches as 0, synonymous mismatches as +1, and antonymous mismatches as +2. The procedure used in this study to measure the self-states relevant to eating disorders involved first specifying the attributes of the standard self (i.e., the "can" self) and comparing this to the ideal or the ought self. Then the attributes of the standard self were compared to the attributes specified in the actual self.

Higgins et al. (1992) found specific associations between the eating disorders of AN and BN and patterns of self. Specifically, it was found that symptoms associated with BN, but not with AN, were positively related to a self-belief pattern that suggested a "chronic failure to meet one's positive potential" (p. 135). In other words, individuals with BN see themselves as not reaching the type of self that they could be, with the type of self that they could be being defined by an ideal self, or what they hope or wish to be. Higgins et al. also found that symptoms associated with AN, but not with BN, were positively correlated with a self-belief pattern that they described as "chronic deviation from one's prescribed capabilities" (p. 135). In other words, individuals with AN see themselves as not reaching the type of self that they could be, with the type of self that they could be being defined in terms of an ought self, or what they have a duty or obligation to be. Thus, the basic difference between persons with BN and persons with AN, according to this research, is that the former are comparing themselves against an ideal standard whereas the latter are comparing themselves against an ought standard.

This research is very promising; rarely are subtypes of eating disorders distinguished so clearly from each other. Certainly one goal for future research is to replicate these findings using genuine clinical samples. If similar findings are obtained, then the case for the involvement of representations of self in eating disorders will be quite strong. What would remain unanswered even after replication, however, is the ways in which the discrepancies arise. Also unclear is the direction of causality: For example, does the exaggeration of the actual–ought discrepancy result in BN, or does the presence of BN exaggerate the discrepancy? Certainly both paths are possible, and future research is needed to determine which is the accurate characterization.

Theories of Self

Adolescence, as we have suggested, is characterized by a theory according to which features of self have meaning primarily for their value in achieving social acceptance and integration. Adolescents may follow any number of routes to integration into the social fabric of life: academic success, participation in sports, or school activities, to name just a few. Indeed, many adolescents form social networks within these contexts and achieve a measure of satisfaction with themselves.

It is clear, however, that for many adolescents with eating disorders the only route they see to acceptance (by themselves and by others) is through achieving the proper physical appearance. As the adolescent quoted earlier said [in response to the question, "What are you especially proud of about yourself?"]:

> My body. Sometimes I think I'm thin and really good-looking; sometimes I think I'm really ugly. When I feel I look good I feel really together. . . . I like the way I look. Sometimes I put my body ahead of everything else.

When my self-confidence is down, sometimes I try to impress people with the way I look instead of the way I act. (Levitt & Hart, 1991)

This quote reveals the domination of physical appearance in the anorexic individual's theory of what is important about the self. From where is this theory derived? In many ways it is surprising that more adolescents do not have the same theory. Western society places an unusually strong emphasis on the weight and physical appearance of women. Women who are depicted in media images as being successful and socially and romantically desirable are almost always exceedingly thin and have a body weight that is far below the national average (see Levine & Smolak, chapter 10, this volume, for a discussion). This societal emphasis on the desirability of extremely low body weight has resulted in a chronic concern with diet and weight. For instance, in one study in which 854 girls and women between the ages of 12 and 23 were surveyed, 67% of the respondents were dissatisfied with their weight and one third had fasted in order to control their weight (Moore, 1988).

The saturation of U.S. culture with the importance of weight management among women directly affects the ways in which women are perceived. In one particularly compelling study, Basow and Kobrynowicz (1993) asked college students to watch videos of a woman eating four different meals ranging from a small salad to a meatball sub. Afterward, the participants were asked to complete the Bem Sex Role Inventory, the Social Appeal Scale, and the Attractiveness Scale. The authors found that a woman who eats a small amount of food is considered to be more expressive, kind, empathic, concerned about her appearance, better looking, and ultimately more feminine than the woman who eats a large meal. The obvious implication is that a failure to monitor one's food intake puts a woman's reputation at risk. Certainly this is a message that is learned well by all too many women.

It is not surprising, then, that many adolescent girls hold theories about themselves in which social acceptance is achieved through low body weight. Unfortunately, such a theory puts many young adolescents at great risk for self-dissatisfaction. This is because on average females gain about 24 pounds of fat as a direct consequence of the physiological changes that constitute puberty (Warren & Peterson, 1983; see Smolak & Levine, chapter 9, this volume, for further details). From a biological perspective this weight gain is the normal accompaniment of sexual maturation; from the perspective of many adolescents, however, this weight gain is contrary to the goal of achieving social success through weight management.

One consequence of this conflict between biological realities and the theory of self is the reversion to strikingly immature conceptions of self-formation. Levitt and Hart (1991) interviewed adolescents with AN, adolescents with scoliosis (who, like the first group, are largely female and require extended treatment), and adolescents without any diagnosed problems. As part of the interview each girl was asked, "How did you get to be the person you are today?" and related probe questions. These questions were then coded using a scoring manual validated in other studies (Hart & Damon, 1986; Damon & Hart, 1988). As we noted earlier (and in Table 5.1), most children and adolescents assert that they became the persons they are either through hard work or through social interaction with others. This finding was replicated in the present study: Both the adolescents with scoliosis and the adolescents without problems responded with these sorts of theories concerning self-formation. However, the adolescents with AN offered many responses that emphasized the determining influence of biological and social influences; these sorts of responses are characteristic of children. For example, an individual with AN might state, "I got to be the way I am just by growing." This can be understood as the result of the inevitable conflict between a theory of self according to which social success can be achieved only through the control of one's weight, on the one hand, and the weight gain which normally accompanies the transition into adolescence on the other. If the whole of one's self is defined in terms of weight control and if this control is made nearly impossible by the hormonal changes in one's body, then the conclusion that one is essentially controlled by biological factors may be quite reasonable.

CONCLUSIONS

Considerable progress has been made in describing the ways in which distortions of the sense of self are related to eating disorders. In this chapter some of the most promising lines of investigation in this area have been outlined from the perspective of a framework that distinguishes among types of experiences that constitute the sense of self and the ways in which these experiences develop. As the review presented here indicates, there is substantial evidence that disturbances can be detected in each facet of the sense of self: subjective and objective self-awareness, personal memories, representations, and theories. Many of the disturbances, moreover, can be framed within a developmental model. Eating-disordered adolescents frequently experience exaggerations of age-typical transitions in the sense of self (e.g., heightened objective self-awareness, splits in subjective self-awareness, and conflicts among representations), but may evidence relative immaturities as well (i.e., in their theories of self-formation).

Although progress is being made in delineating the relation of the sense of self to eating disorders, it is obvious that much hard work lies ahead. Certainly a developmental framework of the sort outlined here (see also Smolak, chapter 2, this volume) can best be examined in the context of longitudinal studies in which the causal role of disturbances to the sense of self in the ontogeny of eating disorders can be partially assessed. For theoretical and treatment reasons it is important to determine whether the variety of perturbations in the sense of self described in this chapter lead to, or follow from, eating disorders. Longitudinal studies might also illuminate the process of change in therapy for eating disorders. For instance, do reductions in conflicts among representations lead to a reduction in objective self-awareness? Must theories of self be changed before representations become less discrepant with each other? Careful clinical studies can measure these sorts of changes, and it is our belief that the field is now ready to embark on these sorts of studies.

REFERENCES

Baldwin, J. M. (1902). *Social and ethical interpretations in mental development* (3rd ed.). New York: MacMillan.

Basow, S. A., & Kobrynowicz, D. (1993). What is she eating? The effects of meal size on impressions of a female eater. *Sex Roles, 28,* 335–344.

Baumeister, R. F. (1991). The self against itself: Escape or defeat? In R. C. Curtis (Ed.), *The relational self: Theoretical convergences in psychoanalysis and social psychology* (pp. 238–256). New York: Guilford.

Bretherton, I., McNew, S., & Beeghly-Smith, M. (1981). Early person knowledge as expressed in gestural and verbal communication: When do infants acquire a "theory of mind?" In M. E. Lamb & L. R. Sherrod (Eds.), *Infant social cognition* (pp. 333–373). Hillsdale, NJ: Lawrence Erlbaum Associates.

Broughton, J. (1980). The divided self in adolescence. *Human Development, 24,* 13–32.

Bruch, H. (1973). *Eating Disorders: Obesity, anorexia nervosa, and the person within.* New York: Basic Books.

Bybee, J., & Zigler, E. (1991). Self-image and guilt: A further test of the cognitive-developmental formulation. *Journal of Personality, 59,* 733–745.

Colman, A. M. (1987). *Facts, fallacies, and frauds in psychology.* London: Hutchinson.

Damon, W., & Hart, D. (1988). *Self-understanding in childhood and adolescence.* New York: Cambridge University Press.

Damon, W., & Hart, D. (1992). Social understanding, self-understanding, and morality. In M. Bornstein & M. E. Lamb (Eds.), *Developmental psychology: An advanced textbook* (3rd ed., pp. 421–464). Hillsdale, NJ: Lawrence Erlbaum Associates.

Dennett, D. C. (1991). *Consciousness explained.* Boston: Little, Brown.

Dunn, J., Brown, J., Slomkowski, C., Tesla, C., & Youngblade, L. (1991). Young children's understanding of other people's feelings and beliefs: Individual differences and their antecedents. *Child Development, 62,* 1352–1366.

Elkind, D., & Bowen, R. (1979). Imaginary audience behavior in children and adolescents. *Developmental Psychology, 15,* 33–44.

Erikson, E. (1950). *Childhood and society.* New York: Norton.

Fallon, A. E., & Rozin, P. (1985). Sex differences in perceptions of desirable body shape. *Journal of Abnormal Psychology, 94,* 102–105.

Feingold, A. (1994). Gender differences in personality: A meta-analysis. *Psychological Bulletin, 116,* 429–456.

Fenigstein, A., Scheier, M. F., & Buss, A. H. (1975). Public and private self-consciousness: Assessment and theory. *Journal of Consulting and Clinical Psychology, 43,* 522–527.

Garner, D. M., & Garfinkel, P. E. (1979). The Eating Attitudes Test: An index of the symptoms of anorexia nervosa. *Psychological Medicine, 9,* 273–279.

Hamilton, J. C., Falconer, J. J., & Greenberg, M. D. (1992). The relationship between self-consciousness and dietary restraint. *Journal of Social and Clinical Psychology, 11,* 158–166.

Hart, D. (1988). Self-concept in the social context of the adolescent. In D. Lapsley & F. Power (Eds.), *Self, ego, and identity: Integrative approaches* (pp. 71–90). New York: Springer-Verlag.

Hart, D. (1992). *Becoming men: The development of aspirations, values, and adaptational styles.* New York: Plenum.

Hart, D., & Damon, W. (1986). Developmental trends in self-understanding. *Social Cognition, 4,* 388–407.

Hart, D., & Edelstein, D. (1992). The relationship of self-understanding to community type, social class, and teacher-rated intellectual and social competence. *Journal of Cross-Cultural Psychology, 23,* 353–365.

Hart, D., & Fegley, S. (1994a). Social imitation and the emergence of a mental model of self. In S. T. Parker, R. W. Mitchell, & M. L. Boccia (Eds.), *Self-awareness in animals and humans: Developmental perspectives* (pp. 149–165). New York: Cambridge University Press.

Hart, D., & Fegley, S. (1994b). Social imitation and the sense of self. In J. J. Roeder, B. Thierry, J. R. Anderson, & N. Herrenschmidt (Eds.) *Current primatology: Vol. II, Social development, learning and behavior* (pp. 389–396). Strasbourg, France: Université Louis Pasteur.

Hart, D., & Fegley, S. (1995). Altruism and caring in adolescence: Relations to moral judgment and self-understanding. *Child Development, 66,* 1346–1359.

Hart, D., Fegley, S., & Brengelman, D. (1993). Perceptions of past, present, and future selves among children and adolescents. *British Journal of Developmental Psychology, 11,* 265–282.

Hart, D., Fegley, S., Chan, Y., Fisher, L., & Mulvey, D. (1993). Judgments about personal identity in childhood and adolescence. *Social Development, 2,* 66–81.

Hart, D., & Karmel, M. P. (in press). Self-awareness and self-knowledge in humans, great apes, and monkeys. In A. Russon, K. Bard, & S. Parker (Eds.), *Reaching into thought.* New York: Cambridge University Press.

Hart, D., & Whitlow, J. W. (1995). The experience of self in the bottlenose dolphin. *Cognition and Consciousness, 4,* 244–247.

Harter, S. (1985). *The self-perception profile for adolescents.* Unpublished manuscript, University of Denver, Colorado.

Harter, S., & Lee, L. (1989, April). *Manifestations of true and not true selves in adolescence.* Paper presented at the biennial meeting of the Society for Research in Child Development, Kansas City, MO.

Hawkins, R. C., II, & Clement, P. F. (1980). Development and construct validation of a self-report measure of binge eating tendencies. *Addictive Behaviors, 5,* 219–226.

Heatherton, T. F., & Baumeister, R. F. (1991). Binge eating as an escape from self-awareness. *Psychological Bulletin, 110,* 86–108.

Higgins, E. T. (1987). Self-discrepancy: A theory relating self and affect. *Psychological Review, 94,* 319–340.

Higgins, E. T. (1990). Self-state representations: Patterns of interconnected beliefs with specific holistic meanings and importance. *Bulletin of the Psychonomics Society, 28,* 248–253.

Higgins, E. T., Bond, R. N., Klein, R., & Strauman, T. (1986). Self-descrepancies and emotional vulnerability: How magnitude, accessibility, and type of discrepancy influence affect. *Journal of Personality and Social Psychology, 51,* 5–15.

Higgins, E. T., King, G. A., & Mavin, G. H. (1982). Individual construct accessibility and subjective impressions and recall. *Journal of Personality and Social Psychology, 51,* 5–15.

Higgins, E. T., Vookles, J., & Tykocinski, O. (1992). Self and health: How "patterns" of self-beliefs predict types of emotional and physical problems. *Social Cognition, 10,* 125–150.

Humphrey, N. (1992). *A history of the mind.* New York: HarperCollins.

James, W. (1890). *The principles of psychology.* New York: Holt.

Johnson, C. L. (1991). Treatment of eating-disordered patients with borderline and false-self/narcissistic disorders. In C. L. Johnson (Ed.), *Psychodynamic treatment of anorexia nervosa and bulimia* (pp. 165–193). New York: Guilford.

Kagan, J. (1981). *The second year: The emergence of self-awareness.* Cambridge, MA: Harvard University Press.

Keys, A., Brozek, J., Henschel, A., Mickelson, D., & Taylor, H. L. (1950). *The biology of human starvation* (Vol. 1.). Minneapolis: University of Minnesota Press.

Klonsky, B. G., Dutton, D. L., & Liebel, C. N. (1990). Developmental antecedents of private self-consciousness, public self-consciousness and social anxiety. *Genetic, Social, and General Psychology Monographs, 116*(3), 273–297.

Koff, E., Rierdan, J., & Stubbs, M. L. (1990). Gender, body image, and self-concept in early adolescence. *Journal of Early Adolescence, 10,* 56–68.

Lapsley, D., & Rice, K. (1988). The "new look" at the imaginary audience and personal fable: Toward a general model of adolescent ego development. In D. K. Lapsley & F. C. Clark (Eds.), *Self, ego, and identity: Integrative approaches* (pp. 109–129). New York: Springer-Verlag.

Lerner, R. M., & Korn, S. J. (1972). The development of body-build stereotypes in males. *Child Development, 43,* 908–920.

Levitt, M. Z., & Hart, D. (1991). Development of self-understanding in anorectic and nonanorectic adolescent girls. *Journal of Applied Developmental Psychology, 12,* 269–288.

Lewis, M. (1992). *Shame: The exposed self.* New York: The Free Press.

Lewis, M., & Brooks-Gunn, J. (1979). *Social cognition and the acquisition of self.* New York: Plenum.

Marcia, J. E. (1966). Development and validation of ego identity status. *Journal of Personality and Social Psychology, 3,* 551–558.

Markus, H., & Nurius, P. P. (1986). Possible selves. *American Psychologist, 4,* 954–969.

Martin, G. B., & Clark, R. D. (1982). Distress crying in neonates: Species and peer specificity. *Developmental Psychology, 18,* 3–9.

Meltzoff, A. N. (1990). Foundations for developing a concept of self: The role of imitation in relating self to other and the value of social mirroring, social modeling, and self practice in infancy. In D. Cicchetti & M. Beeghly (Eds.), *The self in transition: Infancy to childhood* (pp. 139–164). Chicago: University of Chicago Press.

Montemayor, R., & Eisen, M. (1977). The development of self-conceptions from childhood to adolescence. *Developmental Psychology, 13,* 314–319.

Moore, D. C. (1988). Body image and eating behavior in adolescent girls. *American Journal of the Disturbed Child, 142,* 1114–1118.

Nasby, W. (1989). Private and public self-consciousness and articulation of the self-schema. *Journal of Personality and Social Psychology, 56,* 117–123.

Neimeyer, G. J., & Rareshide, M. B. (1991). Personal memories and personal identity: The impact of ego identity development on autobiographical memory recall. *Journal of Personality and Social Psychology, 60,* 562–569.

Nelson, K. (1993). The psychological and social origins of autobiographical memory. *Psychological Science, 4,* 7–13.

Offer, D., Ostrow, E., & Howard, K. I. (1984). *Patterns of adolescent self-image.* San Francisco: Jossey-Bass.

Ogilvie, D. (1987). The undesired self: A neglected variable in personality research. *Journal of Personality and Social Psychology, 52,* 379–385.

Orlofsky, J., & Frank, W. (1986). Personality structure as viewed through early memories and identity status in college men and women. *Journal of Personality and Social Psychology, 50,* 580–586.

Rholes, W., & Ruble, D. (1984). Children's understanding of dispositional characteristics of others. *Child Development, 55,* 550–560.

Rodin, J., Silberstein, L. R., & Striegel-Moore, R. H. (1985). Women and weight: A normative discontent. In T. B. Sonderegger (Ed.), *Nebraska Symposium on Motivation: Vol. 32. Psychology and gender* (pp. 267–307). Lincoln: University of Nebraska Press.

Rosenberg, M. (1979). *Conceiving the self.* New York: Basic Books.

Ross, B. M. (1991). *Remembering the personal past.* New York: Oxford University Press.

Rozin, P., & Fallon, A. (1988). Body image, attitudes to weight, and misperceptions of figure preferences of the opposite sex: A comparison of men and women in two generations. *Journal of Abnormal Psychology, 97,* 342–345.

Secord, P. F., & Peevers, B. H. (1974). The development and attribution of person concepts. In T. Mischel (Ed.), *Understanding other persons* (pp. 117–142). Totowa, NJ: Rowman & Littlefield.

Strauman, T., & Higgins, E. T. (1987). Automatic activation of self-discrepancies and emotional syndromes: When cognitive structures influence affect. *Journal of Personality and Social Psychology, 53,* 1004–1014.

Striegel-Moore, R. H., Silberstein, L. R., & Rodin, J. (1993). The social self in bulimia nervosa: Public self-consciousness, social anxiety, and perceived fraudulence. *Journal of Abnormal Psychology, 102,* 297–303.

Taylor, C. (1989). *Sources of the self: The making of the modern identity.* Cambridge, MA: Harvard University Press.

Warren, M. P., & Peterson, A. (1983). Physical and biological aspects of puberty. In J. Brooks-Gunn (Ed.), *Girls at puberty: Biological and psychosocial perspectives* (pp. 3–28). New York: Plenum.

Watson, J. (1994). Detection of self: The perfect algorithm. In S. T. Parker, R. W. Mitchell, & M. L. Boccia (Eds.), *Self-awareness in animals and humans: Developmental perspectives* (pp. 131–148). New York: Cambridge University Press.

Zazzo, R. (1982). The person: Objective approaches. In W. W. Hartup (Ed.), *Review of child development research* (Vol. 6, pp. 247–290). Chicago: University of Chicago Press.

6

Development of the Gendered Self

Judith Worell
Janet Todd

When a new child arrives in the family, everyone knows the first question to be asked: "Is it a girl or a boy?" Social scientists can also ask "Why is the sex of the child so important? What use do people make of this information, and how does it affect that child's life story?" From birth onward, the identification of each newborn as female or male has lifelong implications. In all societies, females and males are exposed to differing life circumstances. These differences include sociocultural expectations for gendered behavior from birth through adulthood; socialization patterns experienced via parents, peers, and teachers; opportunities and limitations with respect to life–career choices; experiences of trauma and stress; and access to political, legal, economic, and social resources. Social scientists speak of the process of *gendering* to refer to the sum of all influences on developing persons that channel females and males into divergent life situations. In turn, these gendered expectations become internalized by individuals as aspects of the self, inclining them toward culturally sex-linked characteristics, cognitions, and interpersonal transactions.

In this chapter we discuss how the process of gendering promotes the differential development of girls and boys and encourages individuals toward a gendered identity as a personally and culturally acceptable female or male. To the extent that individuals mature within gendered learning environments, their constructed identity, or who they are as a female or male, will tend to match sociocultural expectations for their sex. These sociocultural expectations are not entirely stable, however, and tend to change over time. In turn, gendered identities tend to be molded in the direction of revised images. The advantages and limitations of gendering are debatable (Bem, 1993). For many individuals, gendering creates a developmental disadvantage with respect to self and other relationships and increases the risk of certain psychological disorders.

To understand the implications of gendered identities, we explore theories of gender development and research related to the appearance of sex-typed cognitions, emotional responses, and behavior patterns. We focus on developmental issues surrounding adolescent and early adult periods, as these are the phases during which disordered eating patterns are most likely to appear. Further, because concerns about self-esteem, self-efficacy, sense of agency, physical attractiveness, and eating patterns are more prevalent in girls and women than in boys and men, we center on issues relevant to gendered female development. We hypothesize that the asymmetrical distribution among girls and women of problematic eating practices may be related to the gendering of both their social environments and their self-constructed identities.

UNDERSTANDING GENDER

The study of issues related to female and male development has been infused with a multitude of terms, many of which overlap or are otherwise confusing. We focus our discussion on the following terms that are defined below: sex, gender, gender stereotypes, gender roles, gender typing, gendered identity (or gendered self), and gender schema. Some terms that are popularized in both the lay and professional realms, such as femininity and masculinity, are examples of the broader category of gender stereotypes.

Sex and Gender

The concepts of sex and gender have been used interchangeably in both the lay literature and in professional exchange. The term *sex* is used as a biological variable, to distinguish between two groups of people (female and male) by which individuals categorize themselves and others as girls or boys, women or men (Unger, 1979). Problems arise, however, when sex is used as an independent variable to account for differences in observed behavior or personal outcomes. The popular reference to the "opposite sex" is an example of the dichotomy that results from the belief that women and men are very different kinds of people. The concept of *gender* encompasses a broader range of influences on development and refers to the accumulated meanings and expectations associated with being female or male within a particular culture or subculture. Gender is used here to refer to a complex belief system about the two sexes that includes attitudes, perceptions, behaviors, and interpersonal interactions (Deaux, 1984, 1985). From this perspective, the traits that people attribute to themselves and others as women or men are not "true" characteristics, but rather are constructed from cultural understandings and beliefs about gender (Bem, 1993; Hare-Mustin & Marecek, 1988).

Gender Stereotypes

From these socially constructed understandings, cultures develop *gender stereotypes* that frame concepts of self and others and guide many aspects of behavior. Gender stereotypes are generalized beliefs about the characteristics of females or males that are intended to apply to all persons within each of these two groups (Worell, 1989a). Some of these stereotypes may be applicable across groups (e.g., the belief that women smile more frequently than men) but are seldom useful when understanding a particular person. Gender stereotypes are activated in interpersonal situations and function to influence behavior in accordance with the beliefs that individuals hold. Thus, gender stereotypes are prescriptive as well as descriptive; they imply directives about what people should do (Fiske & Stevens, 1993).

Prevailing Stereotypes. The research on gender stereotypes indicates that a wide range of information that people carry around with them is organized by gender. This gendered information includes beliefs about personality traits, occupations, physical appearance, interpersonal relationships, attitudes, interests, and abilities (Ashmore, Del-Boca, & Wohlers, 1986; Bem, 1974; Deaux & Lewis, 1984; Spence & Helmreich, 1978). To the extent that gender stereotypes are polarized as opposites they prescribe very different positions for women and men. Western culture's stereotype of femininity frames women with a socioemotional–body image cluster that characterizes them as warm, nurturing, emotionally expressive, passive, weak, dependent, attractive, shapely, concerned about appearance, and disinterested in math, science, and business. In contrast, the stereotype of masculinity for men is framed by a competence–autonomy cluster that characterizes them as assertive, competitive, independent, dominant, competent, unemotional, decisive, strong, and effective in the role of leader. The prescriptions that accompany these stereotypes suggest that women should be "feminine," which means taking care of others and attending to their own appearance. In comparison, men should be "masculine," which means taking risks, assuming the lead, and achieving success in the workplace. Implicit in these polarized stereotypes is the assignment of power and influence to men and the exclusion of competence and self-assertion from women. This discrepancy in gender expectations has important consequences for the course of development across the life span.

Alternative Stereotypes.   It should be recognized, however, that particular subcultures within the dominant society may hold gender stereotypes that vary in substantive ways from the majority views (Binion, 1990; Landrine, Klonoff, & Brown-Collins, 1992). Women of color are influenced by their within-group norms in their attributions about self and others. For example, African American women's gender stereotypes about self and social roles have been reported to be less polarized with respect to self-descriptions of masculinity and femininity, but more traditional in terms of family role expectations (Binion, 1990; Fleming, 1989). However, these women develop within a dominant society that influences their norms and expectations, and enculturation into this majority culture also influences their expectations and evaluations of self (Harris, 1994; Pumariega, 1986; Thompson, 1992). When working with individuals who belong to ethnic minorities and other subcultures it is essential to understand their particular gender stereotypes and expectations (Reid & Kelly, 1994; Root, 1990).

Implications of Stereotyping.   For both women and men, there are personal risk factors for adhering to these stereotypes as well as for violating them. As we discuss in this chapter, women who adopt a passive, self-critical, and "helpless" role may avoid interpersonal conflict but are at risk for experiences of anxiety and depression. In the face of ambiguity or negative social feedback such persons are likely to respond with rumination and self-blame (Nolen-Hoeksema, 1987). As a result, they are likely to try to "fix the self" rather than to "fix the situation." Girls and women who allow themselves to be defined and validated by their bodies and physical appearance may enjoy their attractiveness, or they may become obsessed with managing the size of their bodies and the presentation of their physical selves. When confronted with stress or indecision such individuals may resort to excessive dieting or bingeing as a means of reassurance. Moreover, girls who accept the expectation that they be popular and sociable may find that their problems in meeting such expectations lead to social anxiety, loneliness, and isolation.

On the other hand, those who violate gender prescriptions may be subjected to negative evaluation by others (Crawford, 1988; Nieva & Gutek, 1980). In particular, women who fail to meet cultural prescriptions for attractiveness and sociability (e.g., by looking pretty and smiling often) may experience sanctions for being insufficiently feminine (Fiske & Stevens, 1993).

At a broader level, *gender roles* represent stereotyped lifestyle activities that tend to be segregated by sex. Thus, in most cultures women are expected to care for households and children and to organize social activities, and men are expected to be the "heads of the household," the major wage-earners, and the defenders of the country in times of war. Gender roles are associated with attributions of femininity and masculinity, such that women who enter traditionally gendered occupations such as law or engineering may be expected by others to act and dress in a more masculine manner than do women who care for households and children. There is evident confusion between role assignments to life activities or occupations, on the one hand, and personality characteristics frequently associated with masculinity and femininity, on the other.

The association of masculinity and femininity with lifestyle activities has been problematic for those who conduct research on gender. Issues of construct validity and measurement confound the application of gender stereotypes to broader sets of behavior. In particular, the concepts of masculinity and femininity appear to have considerable limitations for empirical research (Cook, 1985; Morawski, 1987; Spence, 1993; Worell, 1978). First, concepts of masculinity and femininity are multidimensional, in that they contain a range of attributes that vary across measures and individuals. Typical measures of these attributes, such as the Bem Sex Role Inventory (BSRI; Bem, 1974) or the Personality Attributes Questionnaire (PAQ; Spence, Helmreich, & Stapp, 1975), tap only a limited aspect of gender: selected self-reported personality traits. It is unrealistic to presume that simple measures of personality traits can predict complex behavior patterns or individual well-being across all situations. Second, it has been shown that assessments of masculinity and femininity across traits, activities, home–career decisions, and beliefs are generally uncorrelated (Orlofsky & O'Heron, 1987; Spence & Helmreich, 1980). In the face of the broad reach of gender stereotypes and roles, simple measures of trait femininity are not likely to bear the weight of explaining the complex behavior patterns involved in developmental concerns such as depression or disordered eating (Lancelot & Kaslow, 1994; Timko, Striegel-Moore, Silberstein, & Rodin, 1987). Furthermore, even trait measures of femininity such as the BSRI contain multiple components of stereotypic female expectations that may have differential consequences for subsequent behavior.

Gender Beyond Stereotypes

Considering the pervasive effects of gender stereotypes and gendering in U.S. culture, the question may be asked, how do these processes filter down to the development of the individual child?

Gender Identity.   In the second year of life, gender identity begins to develop as each child constructs a concept of the self as female or male. For females, the development of the *gendered identity* involves addressing such issues as who they are and who they want to be as girls and women. Girls also consider how their behavior and appearance compare with those of their peers, their parents, their cultural images, their ideals. Other issues to evaluate include the feminine attributes that the girl possesses and how her interests, goals, and ambitions fit with what she wants to be as a woman. Behaviors are then modeled and matched to the extent that these ideals match cultural steotypes for girls and women. Thus, the female gendered identity encompasses all aspects of the self as a girl or woman. For each individual, this identity may be constructed with unique combinations of culturally gendered behavior patterns, beliefs, and goals.

Gender Schemata. In contrast to simple stereotypes, gender schemata are multidimensional and encompass the range of an individual's knowledge and beliefs about gender-related traits, behaviors, occupations, interests, and roles (Bem, 1981). As children develop and mature, they accumulate increasingly complex and interrelated gender schemata that guide their behavior in terms of their constructed selves and their relationships with others (Golombok & Fivush, 1994; Martin & Halverson, 1981). Individuals with highly developed gender schemata are primed to interpret their worlds in gender-polarized ways (Bem, 1993). In some areas, at least, such persons are therefore likely to function in more sex-typed ways than those with less highly developed gender schemata.

Understanding both the gendered identity and the broader gender schemata of individuals may be helpful in determining their personal expectations and internalized acceptance of social prescriptions about stereotyped behaviors in particular contexts. Although the cognitive component of the gendered identity can be thought of as a type of self-schema or set of beliefs about the self, there are affective and behavioral components of gender identity as well. Thus, it may be useful to maintain separate boundaries for these two concepts. Further, stereotypes about the self are not necessarily correlated with stereotypes about others, and these two types of gendering may relate differentially to behavior. Indeed, people tend to stereotype others more stringently than they stereotype themselves (Spence & Sawin, 1985). Perhaps if each concept is measured separately, behavior observed in real-life situations can be predicted more efficiently.

Gendered environments are those in which gender stereotypes are salient and functional; these can include environments maintained by parents, peers, education, media, or the workplace. Similarly, the reinforcement by parents, peers, and teachers of stereotyped behavior in girls and boys is referred to as *gendering,* and the overt result of this socialization is referred to as *gender-typed* behavior. There is a continuing interaction between gendered environments and gender-typed behavior that functions to reinforce cultural stereotypes and to strengthen gendered patterns of behavior. There is evidence that individuals are capable of adjusting their gender-typed behaviors in order to influence self-presentation in gendered environments. Thus, women may act in a more feminine manner if they expect approval and reinforcement for doing so. In this manner, gender stereotypes can function as self-fulfilling prophecies by confirming expectations of both self and others about gendered behaviors (Towson, Zanna, & MacDonald, 1989). Gendered environments can become oppressive for women when their expectations are *androcentric,* or framed within masculine images and values. Examples of cultural androcentrism include common language forms that are sex-specific rather than inclusive (as in the words *chairman* and *craftsman*), as well as pervasive media promotion of the youthful and scantily attired female body.

The task for social scientists extends beyond the individual, however; a broader issue concerns the ways in which gender remains a central organizing factor in human society. To help address this question, we turn to theoretical accounts of gender development.

THEORIES OF GENDER DEVELOPMENT

Research on gender correlates of ability and behavior suggests that there are more variations within the sexes than between them. Although some personality variables covary modestly with sex (Feingold, 1994; Helgeson, 1994), it is hypothesized that women and men are generally more alike than different from one another on a range of assessments (Hyde, 1994; Hyde & Linn, 1986). To test this hypothesis, researchers have pooled the results from many different studies on gender differences by means of meta-analysis for each variable under consideration. Variables that have been believed to differentiate between women and men include, for example, helping behavior, verbal ability, mathematical and spatial skills, sexuality, and aggression. When large numbers of studies are considered together in a meta-analysis, effect sizes for gender are generally low or insignificant except for a few isolated variables (Hyde, 1994). Of course, individual studies may show significant gender effects when situational variables are engineered to produce them. For example, men are more likely than women to demonstrate helping behavior (as the "hero") in situations that are dangerous or public, but in situations where there is no surveillance these gender effects disappear (Eagly & Crowley, 1986). Thus, situations can be constructed to accentuate or minimize the effects of gender through control of stimuli, instructions, and settings.

Theories of gender development, however, propose to explain gender polarization, or how and why the two sexes differ in personal characteristics, social power, and developmental outcomes. Three major approaches to conceptualizing gender include biological, psychological, and social–structural theories. We consider each of these briefly in terms of their primary focus related to gender polarization.

The Biological View: Predetermination?

From a biological perspective, girls and boys develop in different ways because their genes, hormones, or physical attributes diverge. Two representative conceptions are those of sociobiology and gender intensification.

The *sociobiological* approach proposes that the two sexes are genetically primed toward divergent goals (Wilson, 1975). According to Darwinian principles of evolution, male aggression and dominance in interpersonal encounters has been essential to the survival of the species. Likewise, women's attention to their physical attractiveness and their caretaking behaviors with others ensure that they will be selected as desirable mates and successful as nurturant mothers. This view of female–male relations functions to objectify women's bodies as a commodity to be bartered in exchange for safety and protection. In support of this sociobiological hypothesis, Buss (1989) concluded that across a range of respondents from 37 cultures, women preferred men who would be good providers and men sought women who were physically attractive.

The sociobiological view has sparked considerable debate and controversy (cf. Tobach & Rosoff, 1978). In particular, its adoption implies that traditional gender roles, as well as asymmetries in social power, are both desirable and inevitable. Accordingly, women's greater concern with and attention to their physical appearance, as well as sexual initiation, aggression, and dominance by males, are both appropriate and "natural." In our view, a major limitation of this approach is its neglect of sociohistorical factors that may modify gender expectations and the rules for female–male engagement. As women and men renegotiate their social and economic positions, revised expectations may result in new norms and alternative contingencies for interpersonal transactions.

Gender Intensification Theory (Hill & Lynch, 1983) represents a link between biological and psychological perspectives. Accordingly, the internal and external changes that take place during puberty serve as gender markers to both self and others. These changes in physical functioning and appearance mobilize the adolescent and the parent–peer environment toward increased gender typing (Peterson & Taylor, 1980; Simmons, Blyth, & McKinney, 1983). For the adolescent girl, entrance into puberty is accompanied by hormonal changes that stimulate menarche, breast development, and increments in body fat (Boxer, Levinson, & Peterson, 1989; Buchanan, Eccles, & Becker, 1992; Golub, 1983). The experience of these dramatic changes in body function and appearance engages the young girl in a reevaluation of the female self. This emerging image sets the stage for new modes of self-presentation that may either enhance or deny her gender-related attributes (Worell, 1989).

In conjunction with these biological variables, gender intensification theory incorporates a psychological socialization approach. In her attempts to fashion her female self, the developing adolescent requires images and models borrowed from her family, friends, and the broader culture. In this way the behavioral consequences of biological changes are modified by the gendering of her environment and are influenced by changes in cultural norms and ideals with respect to women. For parents and peers, the changing image of the adolescent girl signals her status as an emerging woman and refocuses attention on both her appearance and behavior. Parents increase their awareness of their responsibilities to raise a marriageable daughter and, in recent times, one who can be economically self-sufficient. Male peers perceive the postpubertal girl as a viable target for sexual advances, because the male gender role incorporates sexual initiation as a male prerogative. Moreover, because boys enter puberty approximately 2 years later than do girls, these males are likely to be older than the girls to whom they direct their attentions, with more dominance privileges based on age as well as on male status. Female peers begin to evaluate their friends in terms of their popularity (Bush & Simmons, 1987), and this evaluation is in turn influenced by girls' appearance and attractiveness to boys. These socializing influences each have their particular effects on the adolescent's emerging gender identity and may contribute separately or in conjunction to shape her subsequent adaptation to the gendered female role.

Although the original formulation of gender intensification theory targeted adolescence as a primary source of increased gendering, it seems reasonable to assume that other periods in the life cycle may stimulate a renewed interest in the gendered self. In a study comparing gender-role attitudes from the 7th to the 12th grade, Urberg (1979) found 12th graders were characterized by more stereotyped attitudes than were those in the earlier grades. For example, males of this age admired submissive and dependent females to a greater extent than did either the females of the same age or children in earlier grades. As adolescents approach the independence of adulthood issues related to mate selection may become more salient, and this may lead to a reevaluation of desirable gender roles. Other periods involving change in status may also intensify awareness of the gendered self: Examples include the transition from singleness to marriage (or to other kinds of coupling), the reverse transition back to singleness following breakup or divorce, and the transition from childlessness to parenthood. In view of the sparse research attention to these topics with respect to issues related to eating, we do not further consider these periods of gender development.

Gender intensification theory has received mixed support. The theory predicts that sex differences should increase at puberty and should be tied to pubertal timing. In a comprehensive review, Hill and Lynch (1983) reported increased sex differences in six areas deemed critical to the theory, including selected aspects of academic achievement, self-esteem, and sociability. However, not all measures on all variables showed these effects. Further, pubertal timing was not considered and the data were not gathered across time periods within groups, as they are in longitudinal designs. In a subsequent review of the stability of gender-role attributes during the adolescent years, Worell (1989b) concluded that gender-role attitudes did not peak at early adolescence, but rather were found to be reliably, and surprisingly, consistent across grades. As noted earlier, however, the move toward more traditional attitudes in late adolescence does provide some support for gender salience.

As for pubertal timing, a recent longitudinal study by Galambos, Almeida, and Peterson (1990) reported increased sex differences from Grades 6 to 8 on measures of masculinity and attitudes toward women, with boys' self-reports becoming more dominant and assertive and less egalitarian in comparison with girls. However, these results were uncorrelated with pubertal timing, which casts doubt on a biological explanation for the sex differences that did emerge. The literature on pubertal timing is inconsistent with respect to gender intensification. In view of the multiple issues related to conceptualization and measurement of the effects of puberty (Brooks-Gunn, Peterson, & Eichorn, 1985), we do not pursue this topic further. We prefer to conclude that most documented gender polarization in adolescence may be attributable to parent, peer, and teacher expectations that are socioculturally engendered as society prepares its young for their assigned life tasks (Katz, 1986).

Psychological Approaches

In contrast to biological predeterminism, psychological theories propose, in general, that gender develops through the socializing functions of the culture and that young women and men are thus channeled into separate life spheres. Across theories, three major processes have been emphasized: the visible organization of established social roles that define "normal" behavior, thereby providing gender-polarized models for children to imitate; differential expectations, rewards, and sanctions for gender-stereotyped behaviors, which channel children into divergent life pathways; and individual integration of these multiple influences into a gendered self based on the level of cognitive development and personal experiences. Conceptions of the nature of this gendered self tend to vary across different theories. Two such theories are considered here as examples.

According to *social learning theory* (Bandura, 1977, 1986), children (and adults) pattern their behavior to conform to the messages that they receive from the social environment. These messages may be modeled by the physical and verbal behavior of others or by social responses to the person's own behavior. From these diverse images and reactions, individuals gradually construct a gendered self that reflects a merger of the multiple influences impinging on them. The theory provides for a continual reconstruction of the gendered self through exposure to alternative social images, new information, and revised consequences.

Social-learning-theory hypotheses about the effects of verbal, pictorial, and behavioral models on children's gendered behavior are well supported by research (Bandura, 1986; Bussey & Bandura, 1984; Perry & Bussey, 1979). Children learn about what is regarded as culturally appropriate for each sex through observation of the relative frequencies of women's and mens' visible social behaviors and role enactments. From these observations and their outcomes they form concepts of what is acceptable for themselves as girls or boys. It follows, then, that behavioral scientists should attend to family and community models that influence the messages that children integrate into their self-images. These observations also provide a reminder that as children develop in an androcentric culture that depicts women as subordinate to men, many young girls will continue to integrate this "natural" disadvantage into their self-identity.

Bandura's (1977, 1986) elegant theory of modeling has had an extensive influence on our attention to the effects of the media on children's behavior. His research on vicarious reinforcement has been useful in conceptualizing how imitation of high-status models can lead individuals to withhold self-reward even when it is available. For example, daughters' self-reported dieting behavior has been related to their mother's dieting patterns (Attie & Brooks-Gunn, 1987). Certainly this theory is well-positioned to integrate women's adherence to the "culture of thinness" into its explanatory model. The theory is limited, however, by its failure to address the inequality between women and men in the structure of society, which presents very different models and opportunities to young women and men. Beyond the observation that gendered roles are self-perpetuating in each new generation, the theory does not help behavioral scientists to understand why women as a group are at risk for devaluation and disadvantage.

According to *object relations theory* (Chodorow, 1978), which represents a more intrapsychic orientation, the gendered self develops very early in the first few years and becomes relatively stabilized throughout life. Because of the asymmetrical assignment of parenting to women, girls and boys develop different trajectories in life. Girls and women remain connected and attached to the mother or female caregiver, thus reproducing a stable and internalized "self-in-relation" personality formation. During adolescence this connection may prove problematic for girls as they struggle to separate themselves psychically from the mother. Boys, on the other hand, separate early: To be masculine, they must learn to be "not feminine." Therefore, boys distance themselves emotionally from the mother as well as from others, developing an autonomous personality that is also stable over time. The theory assumes a core personality with regard to the gendered self that positions women as essentially more caring and socially responsible than men. In our opinion, research does not support the stable affective and cognitive sex differences proposed by this theory (Bohan, 1993; Crawford, 1989; Worell, 1988). The theory further assumes that the differences are within people, rather than enacted and maintained by the environment. That is, the gender polarization of the learning environment is located as a reality within individuals. Rather than hypothesize how a universal "mothering" factor shapes the psyche of all girls, it seems more relevant to determine the conditions under which some girls and women internalize the external dictates of a gendered society.

Social–Structural Theories

In contrast to socialization approaches that focus on the individual, several theories start with the structure of the culture within which children develop. Such theories posit that the gendered self begins with a polarized culture in which role assignment and the resources that accompany these roles are unequally distributed by sex. Thus, girls and boys who are born into a gender-polarized society tend to be channeled into separate pathways. The attitudes and behavioral skills that they develop are fashioned by the social structure that dichotomizes these roles (Eagly, 1987). A basic assumption in these theories is the androcentric or male-centered organization of most cultures, which provides the background for the development of personal gendering.

Gender schema theory (Bem, 1981, 1993) focuses on the cognitive processing of gender-linked information from the environment. On the basis of growing up in an androcentric environment, children tend to assimilate the gender-polarized images of society into their self-concept. Children thus become gender-typed not by the extent to which their behavior is masculine or feminine, but to the degree that they categorize the world in gender-stereotyped ways. Bem (1993) viewed the gender-polarized environment as the background against which individuals evaluate and classify new experiences. According to Bem, "in imposing a gender-based classification on reality, children evaluate different ways of behaving in terms of the cultural definitions of gender appropriateness and reject any way of behaving that does not match their sex" (pp. 125–126).

Support for this theory is evidenced by data that gender-typed persons are more likely to notice and recall gender-polarized, as opposed to neutral, material (Frable & Bem, 1985). In this manner, the disposition of the gender-schematic person to construct the world in dichotomous terms promotes a self-fulfilling outcome in which the environment does indeed appear to be organized by separate female and male activities.

Gender schema theory may be more useful in understanding the integration of the gendered self than the more limited constructs of masculinity and femininity. We see at least two critical challenges for the theory; first, to account for the specific learning mechanisms by which individuals internalize societal norms; and second, how to assess an individual's gender schema in ways that make it possible to intervene early to modify the schema's negative effects.

Feminist theory offers a second approach based on social structure (Brabeck & Brown, in press; Worell & Remer, 1992). Like Bem's (1993) gender-polarization approach, feminist theory begins with the assumption of an androcentric social structure that relegates women to a position subordinate to that of men. The contribution of feminist theory with respect to our discussion is twofold. First, feminist theory locates privilege and the power of decision making and resource allocation to one dominant group, White males. Behavior and achievement expectations are based on the White male as the norm. From this norm flows the assumption of male dominance in domestic and employment settings, and especially in the definitions of what it means to be feminine and masculine. Thus, the hierarchical structure of privilege frames masculine behavior in terms of authority, competence, and leadership; women are defined in terms of their relationships to men and also as nurturant, compliant, and socially motivated to meet the needs of others.

The consequences of this gendered arrangement are to institutionalize and normalize male dominance and to legislate to females the subordinate role of pleasing and serving the needs of others at the expense of their own achievement. This pattern is apparent as early as the third to sixth grades, as was demonstrated in an interview study with gifted girls. It was found that these girls were caught between wanting to be pleasing to others and wanting to excel. They were most concerned with not hurting the feelings of others with their academic achievements, with being modest and not boasting, and with being beautiful and attractive (Bell, 1989).

The second factor contributed by feminist theory is the elaboration of women's position as devalued and limited to those activities that members of the dominant group find undesirable for themselves, such as homemaking and child care. In support of this hypothesis, studies have shown that in heterosexual dual-earner families women still do the bulk of homemaking and child-care activities (Blumstein & Schwartz, 1983; Crosby & Jaskar, 1993). Moreover, these findings hold true even when the wife earns as much as or more than her spouse (Steil, 1994).

As proposed by feminist theory, these two factors are likely to have disadvantageous implications for the developing adolescent girl as well as for the adult woman. First, girls and women are likely to view these asymmetrical arrangements as natural and therefore tend to internalize such norms as their own. Second, by internalizing norms of lower social power and relative incompetence, many girls and women become prone toward critical self-evaluation and attributions of blame to the self, both of which may be components of depression. Healthy development of positive self-evaluation as women may become more difficult for such girls. The highly gendered female self thus incorporates some attributes related to low self-esteem, ineffectiveness, and lack of control, which creates negative outcomes that will not serve the girl well in future situations. Indeed, one study reported evidence of comorbidity among anxiety, depression, and eating disorders in adolescent girls (Lewinsohn, Hops, Roberts, Seeley, & Andrews, 1993), although the direction of causality was not confirmed.

For women of color or minority status, these gender images may differ. Feminist theory posits that differences among women that are derived from factors such as ethnicity, sexuality, or socioeconomic status may be greater than those between the sexes themselves. Understanding the dynamics of problems in living such as depression or self-defeating eating practices requires a cognizance of the actual life conditions of each individual.

Although the full scope of feminist theory has yet to be supported, many findings reported in the literature are consistent with its position. The data are too numerous to be reviewed here; they include research on both external and internalized factors that limit opportunities for girls and women in economic and employment spheres (Eccles & Hoffman, 1984); place the burden of household management and child care on girls and women (Blumstein & Schwartz, 1983; Gilbert, 1985; Nyquist, Sliven, Spence, & Helmreich, 1985); pose greater threats of sexual abuse and family violence to young girls and women (Strauss, Gelles, & Steinmetz, 1980); and encourage the development of cognitive patterns in girls and women that are detrimental to feelings of competence, control, and self-efficacy (Dweck, 1986). For example, these socialized cognitive patterns include self-defeating attributions of success and failure (Dweck, Davidson, Nelson, & Enna, 1978), lower expectations for academic and occupational success, and less confidence in their abilities during childhood and adolescence (Dweck, 1986; Eccles, 1994). To the extent that the developing adolescent girl has internalized the cultural prescription that women be incompetent at challenging tasks, she may be reluctant to leave the safety of female-stereotyped roles and behaviors. Her achievement strivings, then, may focus on female-typed activities, including the mandate to be physically attractive and pleasing to others.

Summary

In considering the range of theories presented here, it can be seen that two separate camps emerge: Some theories are concerned with individual development and some with development within a gender-oriented society. It is our position that any useful theory for understanding women's development (as compared to that of men) must take two factors into consideration: first, the context within which people are enculturated and from which they derive their sense of who they are, and second, the mechanisms whereby some individuals are channeled into more gender-polarized directions than others. Perhaps an amalgamation of social learning with gender schema and feminist theories would present a useful contribution to the dialogue. This is a task yet to be accomplished.

A DEVELOPMENTAL RISK FOR GIRLS AND WOMEN: THE CASE OF SEXUAL COERCION AND SEXUAL ABUSE

In an androcentric environment, girls and women are vulnerable to external events that present a threat to their sense of safety, autonomy, self-confidence, and development of effective coping skills. Of all the gendering processes and events discussed earlier, few are as clearly polarized by sex as the evidence of sexual abuse and sexual coercion experienced by girls and women. No other gendered events are as traumatic or potentially damaging to healthy development and personal well-being. Sexual coercion and abuse of girls and women occurs both in the United States and internationally at rates that make them normative in most societies (Koss, Heise, & Russo, 1994; Rozee, 1993; Russell, 1984). How might sexual abuse or coercion in early and later adolescence lead to deficits or excesses in responses to the body and on attempts to establish control over one's physical presentation and personal space? We consider the cognitive and affective sequelae of sexual abuse for girls and women, and we explore the possible relationships between sexual abuse in childhood and adolescence and problematic eating patterns.

Sexual Abuse and Problematic Eating

Clinicians who work with women and female adolescents who have problematic eating patterns have been struck by the number of these clients who also have histories of sexual abuse (Connors & Morse, 1993; Wheeler & Schmitz, 1992). Both sexual abuse and problematic eating patterns are so common among girls and women in U.S. society that clinicians and researchers have wondered whether the two are related in any meaningful way (Calum & Slade, 1989; Finn, Hartman, Leon, & Lawson, 1986). Empirical studies examining the relationship between the two phenomena have produced equivocal results (Beckman & Burns, 1990; Connors & Morse, 1993). Some researchers have concluded that there is a clear link (Calum & Slade, 1989; Hall, Tice, Beresford, Wooley, & Hall, 1989; Root & Fallon, 1988; Sloan & Leichner, 1986), whereas others have found less support for such a relationship (Beckman & Burns, 1990; Finn et al., 1986; Oppenheimer, Howells, Palmer, & Chaloner, 1985).

Research reports of a connection between eating patterns and a history of sexual abuse have been generally uncontrolled or are anecdotal case studies (Connors & Morse, 1993; Pope & Hudson, 1992). The conclusion that there is such a relationship is based on finding that within the populations studied a high percentage of women with eating disorders also have histories of sexual abuse. These findings may be deceptive, however, owing to the high rate of occurrence of both phenomena. Estimates of the prevalence of childhood or adolescent sexual abuse among females in the general population range from approximately 27% to 51% (Finkelhor, 1986; Pope & Hudson, 1992; Russell, 1984). The prevalence of sexual abuse histories among adult women with all eating disorders is reported to be between 30% and 50% (Waller, 1992). Thus, the rate of sexual abuse reported in studies of disordered eating is very similar to the range of rates reported in the general population (Pope & Hudson, 1992). Controlled studies, on the other hand, usually find no significantly greater prevalence of childhood sexual abuse among eating-disordered patients than among their control groups (Connors & Morse, 1993; Pope & Hudson, 1992).

Research to date has not adequately accounted for the complexity of the issues involved in understanding and measuring the impact of sexual abuse; nor have investigators given adequate attention to the many specific factors intrinsic to sexual abuse. These factors include age at the time of victimization, the severity of the abuse, the relationship of the abuser to the victim, and the response of others if they learn of the abuse. To understand the role of sexual abuse in the development of disordered eating practices, it is not sufficient simply to determine the presence or absence of a sexual abuse history. Thus, the question of a link between disordered eating and sexual abuse remains unsettled (Kearney-Cooke & Striegel-Moore, 1994).

Although existing empirical studies offer limited support for a causal connection, it appears that development of an eating disorder may be one possible response to trauma (Thompson, 1992), and specifically to the trauma of sexual abuse. Many women do associate their eating disorders with their experiences of sexual abuse and understand this to be the way that they have coped with the trauma and its sequelae (Connors & Morse, 1993). Connors and Morse give these examples from their own clinical experience: "[O]ne anorexic patient quite consciously began to starve herself in order to be unappealing to her sexually abusive brother, and another patient developed anorexia after being forced to perform oral sex during a rape. Other patients have reported binge eating with large weight gains that they found reassuring in assuaging their feelings of vulnerability following sexual predation" (p. 9).

Several theories have emerged to explain the association between sexual abuse and disordered eating. As seen in the example just presented, a common explanation focuses on the desire of the person who has experienced the abuse to make her body unattractive or nonsexual. She accomplishes her goal either by "skeletizing" herself in the hope of being disgusting to the perpetrator or by gaining large amounts of weight in order to lose any sense of sexuality or sexual attractiveness (Hall et al., 1989; Sloan & Leichner, 1986; Waller, 1992). A related explanation is that the person who experienced the abuse comes to perceive the body as a source of shame and therefore loses weight in order to "get rid of the body" (Kearney-Cooke & Striegel-Moore, 1994). Similarly, another link is seen in the feelings of self-hatred, disgust, and guilt that are often experienced by sexual abuse victims and which may lead to self-destructive behavior such as self-defeating eating patterns (Oppenheimer et al., 1985; Waller, 1992).

Issues of control are accepted by many as central to and underlying the development of eating disorders (Kearney-Cooke & Striegel-Moore, 1994). Loss of control and feelings of powerlessness are experienced by victims of sexual abuse at the time of the assault and, frequently, later through flashbacks, nightmares, and panic attacks. The persistent feelings of lack of control and powerlessness may be alleviated by the sense of control experienced through ritualized, overcontrolled eating behavior.

In sum, sexual abuse of females is a common experience in American society. The possibility of its occurrence must be taken into account when considering factors that influence the development of disorders that are more prevalent among females than males. The feelings of powerlessness and lack of control as well as the focus on the female body that accompany the trauma of sexual abuse can be seen as an intensification of the contemporary female experience. Even in modern Western culture women still have relatively little power and limited control over many aspects of their lives, and are valued disproportionately for their sexual qualities.

SUMMARY AND CONCLUSIONS

From the standpoint of feminist theory we have considered two sources of developmental risk for the growing girl: the structure of the gendered environment in which she develops and her consequent experiences of gendered socialization for womanhood. To the extent that girls are exposed to the multitude of factors that contribute to a gendered environment, they are likely to be gender-schematic in their thinking and to incorporate a gendered identity in selected aspects of their development.

Moreover, when aspects of the environment are androcentric some girls and women incorporate images of ideal womanhood that are developmentally detrimental to them. As we have discussed, several aspects of the stereotyped female identity contribute in negative ways to the establishment of autonomy, competence, and an independent sense of self. Those aspects of gendered social roles that define womanhood in terms that devalue women may encourage lowered self-confidence and continual dependency on others for approval. During developmental periods of change or uncertainty for girls and women with respect to their gender roles and gender identity (e.g., during adolescence, at college entry, or following divorce), these developmental paths contribute to stress and distress. Culturally prevalent experiences of sexual coercion and abuse add further stress to the lives of many young women. When coping skills are gendered (e.g., when they include self-blame and self-criticism for trauma or perceived failure), attempts to change the self are likely to dominate over strategies for effective action. The result of such action may be to perpetuate chronic feelings of incompetence and lack of control that habituate the individual to striving for continual revision of the physical or social self.

REFERENCES

Ashmore, R. D., DelBoca, F. K., & Wohlers, A. J, (1986). Gender stereotypes. In R. D. Ashmore & F. K. DelBoca (Eds.), *The social psychology of female-male relations: A critical analysis of central concepts* (pp. 69–119). New York: Academic Press.

Attie, I., & Brooks-Gunn, J. (1987). Weight concerns as chronic stressors in women. In R. C. Barnett & G. K. Baruch (Eds.), *Gender and stress* (pp. 218–254). New York: The Free Press.

Bandura, A. (1977). *Social learning theory.* Englewood Cliffs, NJ: Prentice-Hall.

Bandura, A. (1986). *Social foundations of thought and action.* Englewood Cliffs, NJ: Prentice-Hall.

Beckman, K. A., & Burns, G. L. (1990). Relation of sexual abuse and bulimia in college women. *International Journal of Eating Disorders, 9,* 487–492.

Bell, L. A. (1989). Something's wrong here and it's not me: Challenging the dilemmas that block girls' success. *Journal for the Education of the Gifted, 12,* 118–130.

Bem, S. L. (1974). The measurement of psychological androgyny. *Journal of Consulting and Clinical Psychology, 47,* 155–162.

Bem, S. L. (1981). Gender schema theory: A cognitive account of sex-typing. *Psychological Review, 88,* 354–364.

Bem, S. L (1993). *The lenses of gender: Transforming the debate on sexual inequality.* New Haven, CT: Yale University Press.

Binion, V. J. (1990). Psychological androgyny: A Black female perspective. *Sex Roles, 22,* 487–507.

Blumstein, P., & Schwartz, P. (1983). *American couples: Money, work, and sex.* New York: Morrow.

Bohan, J. S. (1993). Regarding gender: Essentialism, constructionism, and feminist psychology. *Psychology of Women Quarterly, 17,* 9–22.

Boxer, A., Levinson, R. A., & Peterson, A. C. (1989). Adolescent sexuality. In J. Worell & F. Danner (Eds.), *The adolescent as decision-maker: Applications to development and education* (pp. 209–245). New York: Academic Press.

Brabeck, M., & Brown, L. (in press). Feminist theory. In J. Worell & N. Johnson (Eds.), *Feminist visions: New directions in education and practice.* Washington, DC: American Psychological Association.

Brooks-Gunn, J., Peterson, A., & Eichorn, D. (1985). The study of maturational timing effects in adolescence. *Journal of Youth and Adolescence, 14,* 149–161.

Buchanan, C. M., Eccles, J. S., & Becker, J. B. (1992). Are adolescents the victims of raging hormones: Evidence for activational effects of hormones on moods and behavior at adolescence. *Psychological Bulletin, 111,* 62–107.

Bush, D. M., & Simmons, R. G. (1987). Gender and coping with entry into early adolescence. In R. L. Barnett & G. K. Baruch (Eds.), *Gender and stress* (pp. 185–217). New York: The Free Press.

Buss, D. (1989). Sex differences in human mate preference: Evolutionary hypotheses tested in 37 cultures. *Behavioral and Brain Sciences, 12,* 1–49.

Bussey, K., & Bandura, A. (1984). Influence of gender constancy and social power on sex-linked modeling. *Journal of Personality and social Psychology, 47,* 1292–1302.

Calum, R. M., & Slade, P. D. (1989). Sexual experience and eating problems in female undergraduates. *International Journal of Eating Disorders, 8,* 391–397.

Chodorow, N. (1978). *Reproduction of mothering: Psychoanalysis and the sociology of gender.* Berkeley: University of California Press.

Connors, M. E., & Morse, W. (1993). Sexual abuse and eating disorders: A review. *International Journal of Eating Disorders, 13,* 1–11.

Cook, E. P. (1985). *Psychological Androgyny.* New York: Pergamon.

Crawford, M. (1988). Gender, age, and the social evaluation of assertion. *Behavior Modification, 12,* 459–464.

Crawford, M. (1989). Agreeing to differ: Feminist epistemologies and women's ways of knowing. In M. Crawford & M. Gentry (Eds.), *Gender and thought* (pp. 128–145). New York: Springer-Verlag.

Crosby, F. J., & Jaskar, K. L. (1993). Women and men at home and at work: Realities and illusions. In S. Oskamp & M. Costanzo (Eds.), *Gender issues in contemporary society* (pp. 143–172). Newbury Park, CA: Sage.

Deaux, K. (1984). From individual differences to social categories: A decade's research on gender. *American Psychologist, 39,* 105–106.

Deaux, K. (1985). Sex and gender. *Annual Review of Psychology, 36,* 49–82.

Deaux, K., & Lewis, L. L. (1984). Structure of gender stereotypes: Interrelationships among components and gender label. *Journal of Personality and Social Psychology, 46,* 991–1004.

Dweck, C. S. (1986). Motivational processes affecting learning. *American Psychologist, 10,* 1040–1048.

Dweck, D., Davidson, W., Nelson, S., & Enna, B. (1978). Sex differences in learned helplessness: II. The contingencies of evaluative feedback in the classroom; and III. An experimental analysis. *Developmental Psychology, 14,* 268–276.

Eagly, A. H. (1987). *Sex differences in social behavior: A social role interpretation.* Ithaca, NY: Cornell University Press.

Eagly, A. H., & Crowley, M. (1986). Gender and helping behavior: A meta-analytic review of the social psychological literature. *Psychological Bulletin, 100,* 283–308.

Eccles, J. S. (1994). Understanding women's educational and occupational choices: Applying the Eccles et al. model of achievement-related choices. *Psychology of Women Quarterly, 18,* 585–610.

Eccles, J. S., & Hoffman, L. W. (1984). Sex roles, socialization, and occupational behavior. In H. W. Stevenson & A. E. Siegel (Eds.), *Child development research and social policy* (Vol. 1, pp. 367–420). Chicago: University of Chicago Press.

Feingold, A. (1994). Gender differences in personality: A meta-analysis. *Psychological Bulletin, 116,* 429–456.

Finkelhor, D. (1986). *A sourcebook on child sexual abuse.* Beverly Hills, CA: Sage.

Finn, S. E., Hartman, M., Leon, G. R., & Lawson, L. (1986). Eating disorders and sexual abuse: Lack of confirmation for a clinical hypothesis. *International Journal of Eating Disorders, 5,* 1051–1060.

Fiske, S. T., & Stevens, L. E. (1993). What's so special about sex? Gender stereotyping and discrimination. In S. Oscamp & M. Costanzo (Eds.), *Gender issues in contemporary society* (pp. 173–196). Newbury Park, CA: Sage.

Fleming, J. (1989). *The impact of college environments on black students.* San Francisco: Jossey-Bass.

Frable, D. E. S., & Bem, S. L. (1985). If you're gender schematic, all members of the opposite sex look alike. *Journal of Personality and Social Psychology, 49,* 459–468.

Galambos, N. L., Almeida, D. M., & Peterson, A. C. (1990). Masculinity, femininity, and sex role attitudes in early adolescence: Exploring gender intensification. *Child Development, 61,* 1905–1914.

Gilbert, L. A. (1985). *Men in dual-career families: Current realities and future prospects.* Hillsdale, NJ: Lawrence Erlbaum Associates.

Golombok, S., & Fivush, R. (1994). *Gender development.* Cambridge, England: Cambridge University Press.

Golub, S. (1983). Menarche, the beginning of menstrual life. *Women and Health, 8,* 17–36.

Hall, R. C., Tice, L., Beresford, T. P., Wooley, R. N., & Hall, A. K. (1989). Sexual abuse inpatients with anorexia nervosa and bulimia. *Psychosomatics, 30,* 73–79.

Hare-Mustin, R. T., & Marecek, J. (1988). The meaning of difference: Gender theory, post-modernism, and psychology. *American Psychologist, 43,* 455–464.

Harris, S. M. (1994). Racial differences in predictors of college womens' body image attitudes. *Women and Health, 21,* 89–104.

Helgeson, V. S. (1994). Relation of agency and communion to well-being: Evidence and potential explanations. *Psychological Bulletin, 116,* 412–428.

Hill, J. P., & Lynch, M. E. (1983). The intensification of gender-related role expectations during early adolescence. In J. Brooks-Gunn & A. Peterson (Eds.), *Girls at puberty: Biological and psychological perspectives* (pp. 201–230). New York: Plenum.

Hyde, J. S. (1994). Can meta-analysis make feminist transformations in psychology? In J. Worell & C. Etaugh (Eds.), *Transformations: Reconceptualizing theory and research with women. Psychology of Women Quarterly, 18,* 451–462.

Hyde, J. S., & Linn, M. E. (1986). *The psychology of gender: Advances through meta-analysis.* Baltimore: Johns Hopkins University Press.

Katz, P. (1986). Gender identity: Development and consequences. In R. D. Ashmore & F. K. DelBoca (Eds.), *The social psychology of female–male relations* (pp. 21–67). Orlando, FL: Academic Press.

Kearney-Cooke, A., & Striegel-Moore, R. H. (1994). Treatment of child sexual abuse in anorexia nervosa and bulimia nervosa: A feminist psychodynamic approach. *International Journal of Eating Disorders, 15,* 305–319.

Koss, M. P., Heise, L., & Russo, N. F. (1994). The global health burden of rape. *Psychology of Women Quarterly, 18,* 585–610.

Lancelot, C., & Kaslow, N. J. (1994). Sex role orientation and disordered eating in women: A review. *Clinical Psychology Review, 14,* 139–157.

Landrine, H., Klonoff, E. A., & Brown-Collins, A. (1992). Cultural diversity and methodology in feminist psychology: Critique, proposal, and empirical example. *Psychology of Women Quarterly, 16,* 145–164.

Lewinsohn, P. M., Hops, H., Roberts, R. E., Seeley, J. R., & Andrews, J. A. (1993). Adolescent psychopathology: I. Prevalence and incidence of depression and other DSM-III-R disorders in high school students. *Journal of Abnormal Psychology, 102,* 133–144.

Martin, C. L., & Halverson, C. (1981). A schematic processing model of sex typing and stereotyping in children. *Child Development, 52,* 1119–1134.

Morawski, J. G. (1987). The troubled quest for masculinity, femininity, and androgyny. In P. Shaver & C. Hendricks (Eds.), *Sex and gender: Review of personality and social psychology* (Vol. 7, pp. 44–69). Beverly Hills, CA: Sage.

Nieva, V. F., & Gutek, B. A. (1980). Sex effects on evaluation. *Academy of Management Review, 5,* 267–276.

Nolen-Hoeksema, S. (1987). Sex differences in unipolar depression: Evidence and theory. *Psychological Bulletin, 101,* 259–282.

Nyquist, L., Sliven, K., Spence, J. T., & Helmreich, R. T. (1985). Household responsibilities in middle-class couples: The contribution of demographic and personality variables. *Sex Roles, 12,* 15–34.

Oppenheimer, R., Howells, E., Palmer, R. L., & Chaloner, D. A. (1985). Adverse sexual experience in childhood and clinical eating disorders: A preliminary description. *Journal of Psychiatric Research, 19,* 357–361.

Orlofsky, J., & O'Heron, C. A. (1987). Stereotypic and nonstereotypic sex-role traits and behavior orientation: Implications for personal adjustment. *Journal of Personality and Social Psychology, 52,* 1034–1052.

Perry, D. G., & Bussey, K. (1979). The social learning of sex differences: Imitation is alive and well. *Journal of Personality and Social Psychology, 17,* 1699–1712.

Peterson, A. C., & Taylor, C. (1980). Biological change and psychological adaptation. In J. Adelson (Ed.), *Handbook of adolescent psychology* (pp. 117–155). New York: Wiley.

Pope, H. G., & Hudson, J. I. (1992). Is childhood sexual abuse a risk factor for bulimia nervosa? *American Journal of Psychiatry, 149,* 455–463.

Pumariega, A. J. (1986). Acculturation and eating attitudes in adolescent girls: A comparative and correlational study. *Journal of the American Academy of Child Psychiatry, 25,* 276–279.

Reid, P. T., & Kelly, E. (1994). Research on women of color: From ignorance to awareness. *Psychology of Women Quarterly, 18,* 477–486.

Root, M. P. (1990). Disordered eating in women of color. *Sex Roles, 22,* 525–536.

Root, M. P., & Fallon, P. (1988). The incidence of victimization experiences in a bulimic sample. *Journal of Interpersonal Violence, 3,* 161–173.

Rozee, P. D. (1993). Forbidden or forgiven? Rape in cross-cultural perspectives. *Psychology of Women Quarterly, 17,* 409–514.

Russell, D. (1984). *Sexual exploitation: Rape, child sexual abuse, and workplace harassment.* Beverly Hills, CA: Sage.

Simmons, R. G., Blyth, D. A., & McKinney, K. L. (1983). The social and psychological effects of puberty on white females. In J. Brooks-Gunn & A. C. Peterson (Eds.), *Girls at puberty: Biological and psychosocial perspectives* (pp. 229–272). New York: Plenum.

Sloan, G., & Leichner, P. (1986). Is there a relationship between sexual abuse or incest and eating disorders? *Canadian Journal of Psychiatry, 31,* 656–660.

Spence, J. T. (1993). Gender-related traits and gender ideology: Evidence for a multifactorial theory. *Journal of Personality and Social Psychology, 64,* 624–635.

Spence, J. T., & Helmreich, R. L. (1978). *Masculinity and femininity: Their psychological dimensions, correlates, and antecedents.* Austin: University of Texas Press.

Spence, J. T., & Helmreich, R. L. (1980). Masculine instrumentality and feminine expressivity: their relationship with sex-role attitudes and behavior. *Psychology of Women Quarterly, 5,* 147–163.

Spence, J. T., Helmreich, R. L., & Stapp, J. (1975). Rating of self and peers on sex-role attributes and their relations to conceptions of self-esteem and masculinity and femininity. *Journal of Personality and Social Psychology, 32,* 29–39.

Spence, J. T., & Sawin, L. L. (1985). Images of masculinity and femininity. In V. E. O'Leary, R. K. Unger, & B. S. Wallston (Eds.), *Women, gender, and social psychology* (pp. 35–66). Hillsdale, NJ: Lawrence Erlbaum Associates.

Steil, J. (1994). Equality and entitlement in marriage: Benefits and barriers. In M. Lerner & G. Mikula (Eds.), *Entitlement and the affectional bonds.* New York: Plenum.

Strauss, M. A., Gelles, R. J., & Steinmetz, S. K. (1980). *Behind closed doors: Violence in the American family.* New York: Doubleday.

Thompson, B. W. (1992). "A way outa no way": Eating problems among African-American, Latina, and White women. *Gender and Society, 6,* 546–561.

Timko, C., Striegel-Moore, R. H., Silberstein, L. R., & Rodin, J. (1987). Femininity/masculinity and disordered eating in women: Are they related? *International Journal of Eating Disorders, 6,* 701–712.

Tobach, E., & Rosoff, B. (Eds.) (1978). *Genes and gender.* New York: Gordian Press.

Towson, S. M. J., Zanna, M. P., & MacDonald, G. (1989). Self-fulfilling prophecies: Sex role stereotypes as expectations for behavior. In R. K. Unger (Ed.), *Representations: Social constructions of gender* (pp. 97–108). Amityville, NY: Haywood.

Unger, R. K. (1979). Toward a redefinition of sex and gender. *American Psychologist, 14,* 1085–1094.

Urberg, K. A. (1979). Sex role conceptualizations in adolescents and adults. *Developmental Psychology, 15,* 90–92.

Waller, G. (1992). Sexual abuse and bulimic symptoms in eating disorders: Do family interaction and self-esteem explain the links? *International Journal of Eating Disorders, 12,* 235–240.

Wheeler, J., & Schmitz, C. D. (1992). Prior sexual abuse in women with eating disorders. *College Student Journal, 26,* 323-329.

Wilson, E. O. (1975). *Sociobiology: The new synthesis.* Cambridge, MA: The Belnap Press of Harvard University Press.

Worell, J. (1978). Sex roles and psychological well-being: Perspectives on methodology. *Journal of Consulting and Clinical Psychology, 46,* 777–791.

Worell, J. (1988). Women's satisfaction in close relationships. *Clinical Psychology Review, 8,* 477–498.

Worell, J. (1989a). Images of women in psychology. In M. Paludi & G. Steuernagel (Eds.), *Foundations for a feminist restructuring of the academy* (pp. 185–224). New York: Harrington Park Press.

Worell, J. (1989b). Sex roles in transition. In J. Worell & F. Danner (Eds.), *The adolescent as decision-maker: Applications to development and education* (pp. 245–289). New York: Academic Press.

Worell, J., & Remer, P. (1992). *Feminist perspectives in therapy: An empowerment model for women.* Chichester, England: Wiley.

7

Attachment, Organization, and the Coherence of Individual Development

Russell A. Isabella

Questions regarding the coherence of individual development across the life span have long been a motivating force in developmental psychology. For example, as the young child undergoes the changes inherent in movement through subsequent stages of development, are there important ways in which he or she remains unchanged? If so, is such continuity a function of nurture, such that optimal experiences early in life may be expected to insure a lifetime of benefits? Conversely, do nonoptimal early experiences sentence a person to lifelong disappointment and despair? And what might "optimal" and "nonoptimal" early experiences look like?

In this chapter such questions are considered by applying an organizational perspective of infant development to a discussion of the link between attachment theory and a body of research that has devised a valid measure of socioemotional functioning during infancy, explained individual differences on this measure in terms of specific antecedent experiences, and linked these same differences between infants to meaningful aspects of development beyond the infancy period. The first section of the chapter is devoted to a summary of attachment theory, with particular attention to the theory's explanation of the development of attachment relationships and, to a lesser degree, the importance of these relationships to subsequent development. Next, an overview is presented of an organizational perspective of infant development (Sroufe, 1979, 1990; Sroufe & Waters, 1977) that is consistent with attachment theory but that also provides greater depth in its explanation of the processes by which infant development proceeds in a social context. The third section of the chapter consists of a review of empirical studies of the developmental origins of attachment. Finally, an integration of the ideas and findings presented in the previous sections of the chapter is provided.

ATTACHMENT THEORY[1]

A Brief Overview

An *attachment* is a discriminating and specific affectional tie that is formed between one person or animal and another. The behavioral marker of an attachment relationship is a striving to achieve and maintain proximity to the specific attachment object. Although attachments may occur at all ages, the first such relationship develops during the first year of life between the infant and primary caregiver, typically the mother.

Two of the major issues addressed by attachment theorists concern the reasons for attachment relationships and the mechanisms by which they develop. Although this chapter is concerned primarily with the latter issue, full consideration of the theory requires attention to its position regarding the purposes served by human attachment relationships. At a general level, attachment theory describes the development of the infant–mother relationship as a species-characteristic phenomenon that promotes the protection, survival, and perceived security of the infant who, although helpless in terms of assuring its own survival, is nevertheless endowed from birth with a repertoire of instinctive behaviors (e.g., sucking, clinging, gazing, crying) that are believed to contribute to the development of attachments (Bowlby, 1969). Reciprocally, adults are predisposed to respond to these *attachment behaviors* by initiating and maintaining closeness to the infant and providing necessary care, thereby promoting the infant's safety and survival.

The theoretical position regarding the process by which attachment relationships develop recognizes that the very young infant's attachment behaviors are independently and indiscriminantly exhibited. Over time, however, these behaviors become organized in more complex ways and, perhaps more important, infants become more discriminating about the person or persons toward whom they prefer to direct these behaviors. In fact, it is only when the infant's attachment behaviors are integrated into a coherent behavioral–motivational system and organized around a particular figure or figures who provide care, comfort, and safety that the term *attachment* is properly applied (Bretherton, 1987). A somewhat detailed accounting of this process has been provided by attachment theorists, who delineate four phases through which the

---

[1]For more detailed accounts of attachment theory, refer to Bowlby (1969), Ainsworth (1979), and Bretherton (1987).

development of attachments proceeds (Ainsworth, Blehar, Waters, & Wall, 1978; Bowlby, 1969). Three of these phases are relevant to the infancy period and are outlined briefly (see Bowlby and Ainsworth et al. for more detailed accounts).

In the *initial preattachment phase* (birth–12 weeks), the young infant exhibits species-characteristic behaviors (e.g., visual orientation toward people, reaching, smiling) likely to evoke proximity to, and caretaking from, adults, but the infant does not effectively discriminate among these adults. The hallmark of the second phase, that of *attachment-in-the-making* (12 weeks–6 months), is the infant's ability to discriminate between familiar and unfamiliar figures. Also during this period, the infant typically demonstrates a preference for a particular figure, typically the mother, by being more likely to direct attachment behaviors toward this person and appearing more content when this person is the one responding to those behaviors. During the third phase, the phase of *clear-cut attachment* (7 months–3 years), the child becomes much more active in promoting and maintaining proximity to and contact with the preferred attachment figure, also becoming more active in exploring the environment. Perhaps most important, however, is that the behavior of the infant becomes organized on a goal-corrected basis (Bowlby, 1969), which is to say that the infant's behaviors toward the attachment figure may now be viewed as directed by specific plans for the purpose of accomplishing particular attachment-oriented goals. For example, whereas the younger infant might cry when frightened and the caregiver might respond by picking up and comforting the infant, the infant in Phase 3 might respond to fear by crawling toward the attachment figure and clambering up into his or her lap with the specific intention of seeking comfort. The onset of such goal-directed attachment behaviors (typically at 6–9 months) may be viewed as an appropriate criterion for the onset of attachment.

Three Central Propositions

Having provided a brief overview of some general notions of attachment theory, three specific theoretical propositions related to the development of attachment relationships are now considered. An understanding of these propositions can shed further light on the overview just presented, and also provides necessary groundwork for considerations of the research to be reviewed concerning the interactional origins of attachment. Additionally, these propositions are directly relevant to questions regarding the coherence of individual development.

On the basis of Ainsworth's early empirical demonstrations of variation in attachment quality across mother–infant pairs (Ainsworth et al., 1978), it became necessary for the theory to explain why attachment relationships differ from one dyad to another. Accordingly, the first proposition to be considered here holds that attachment relationships develop in the context of, and are thus directly influenced by, interactions between primary caregiver and infant during the first year of life. Individual infant–caregiver pairs are thus expected to develop attachments that are distinctive in that they are based on the idiosyncratic patterns of behavioral exchange that have evolved within the dyad over time (Ainsworth et al., 1978; Sroufe & Waters, 1977). It is on the basis of this very proposition of the theory that researchers have devoted their efforts to identifying the interactional antecedents of attachment.

The second proposition maintains that in the course of development over the first year and in the context of interactions with the caregiver, the infant eventually comes to represent the attachment relationship in the form of an internal working model. This representational model is comprised of two components: a notion of the acceptability of self in the eyes of the attachment figure, and a complementary notion of the accessibility and emotional supportiveness of that figure (Bowlby, 1969; Bretherton, 1987; Main, Kaplan, & Cassidy, 1985; Sroufe & Fleeson, 1986). In addition, it is expected that once the infant is capable of the representation necessary to form an internal model of the relationship, its choice of behaviors in interaction with the caregiver will be guided by this model, as discussed earlier in the description of Phase 3. It is based on this proposition that the Strange Situation, a laboratory procedure designed to activate the infant's attachment–behavioral system, is expected to provide a window on the infant–caregiver relationship via the infant's behavioral organization in the context of the heightened-attachment experience (Ainsworth et al., 1978). In other words, if the infant's cumulative experiences of interaction with the caregiver indeed form the basis of its relationship with this person, and if the infant's behavior is in fact guided by some internal representation of this relationship, then the nature of these behaviors in the Strange Situation should reveal something meaningful about the relationship.

The third proposition from attachment theory holds that as the child grows older and moves into a broader social context, its model of its relationship with the initial attachment figure will be transformed into a generalized model of self in relation to all others. Furthermore, this generalized (and modifiable) representational model is expected to influence subsequent development through its impact on the individual's selection of, behaviors in, and interpretations of interactions with others. It is on the basis of this proposition that researchers have attempted to determine the extent to which the quality of the infant's attachment to the initial caregiver is predictive of its socioemotional functioning throughout later childhood. In other words, if the infant's Strange Situation behavior and thus the measured quality of its relationship with the initial attachment figure are guided by a representational model of that relationship, and if a generalized version of that same model influences development beyond infancy, then the quality of attachment during infancy should be predictive of later functioning. Attachment theory's treatment of the development of attachment has been quite useful in providing information regarding the general stages through which attachment development occurs. This information has in turn served researchers well in terms of their planning of the timing of their attempts to observe interactions for the purpose of identifying the interactional origins of attachment. As the review to follow demonstrates, moreover, behavioral scientists have learned a great deal about associations between interaction and attachment. However, it is also true that attention to more detailed accounts of infant development in attempting to interpret the findings of these works might lead to greater understanding of the complexities involved in the process (Isabella, 1995).

INFANT DEVELOPMENT:
AN ORGANIZATIONAL PERSPECTIVE

Overview

It is consistent with attachment theory to consider infant development from an organizational perspective (Sroufe, 1979; Sroufe & Waters, 1977). This perspective holds that any meaningful analysis of development must occur at the level of patterns, relationships, and the meanings of behaviors as defined by their context (Sroufe, 1990). Additionally, this perspective maintains that development should be viewed in terms of the individual's "inner *organization* of attitudes, feelings, expectations, and meanings, which arises itself from an *organized* caregiving matrix, and which has *organizational* significance for ongoing adaptation and experience" (Sroufe, 1990, p. 281). Accordingly, development is perceived as being organized and is characterized in terms of increasing organization. As development proceeds, children increasingly select and structure their own experiences. A hierarchical integration occurs whereby early behaviors are organized with other behaviors into more complex forms, and development is directed toward increasing flexibility and organization (Sroufe, 1990). It should come as no surprise that this perspective has proved useful in guiding researchers' attempts to identify constructs and develop corresponding measures appropriate for empirical examination of the coherence of individual development (cf. Sroufe, Egeland, & Kreutzer, 1990).

What is most compelling about this approach to understanding not only infant development but also the development of attachments is its assumption that the development of the individual's organization grows out of an organized context that resides in the infant–caregiver dyadic system (Sander, 1975). Where this perspective departs from attachment theory, however, is in providing a more detailed delineation of infant development in a dyadic context, which, in this author's opinion and in line with Sroufe (1990), might contribute significantly to interpretations of findings from research on the interactional origins of attachment and thus shed further light on the understanding of the coherence of development.

Four Stages of Infant Development

Four stages of infant development across the first year of life have been identified (Sander, 1975; Sroufe, 1979, 1990). In the *basic regulation phase* (birth–3 months), what is most important for the infant is the extent to which the caregiver's interventions are coordinated with the infant's basic physiological processes (e.g., sleep, feeding, elimination, and postural maintenance). The manner in which the dyad negotiates the infant's needs for physiological regulation is believed to play a significant role in shaping future psychological regulation, as will eventually be characterized by coordinated sequences of behavioral interactions. From the perspective of attachment theory, then, it may be suggested that in the process of reacting to the infant's species-characteristic behaviors and thus providing safety and comfort, the caregiver is also serving the function of helping the infant to establish some degree of regularity and control (i.e., organization) over basic biological processes and is setting the stage for the more highly organized, complex forms of dyadic exchange that will eventually occur.

From 4 to 6 months, during the stage of *coordinated interaction sequences,* marked changes in the infant's social capacities are evident. Infants spend more time awake and alert; they smile, coo, and in other ways communicate a variety of spontaneous affective states; they demonstrate voluntary control over motor systems and have also achieved a level of basic state regulation. As a function of these developments and, presumably, on the basis of what has transpired during the previous stage, the hallmark of this period is the emergence of coordinated interactional exchanges between infant and caregiver (cf. Brazelton, Koslowski, & Main, 1974). It must be emphasized, however, that both the coordination and reciprocity characteristics of interactions during this stage are occasioned largely by the caregiver's responsiveness to the infant's behaviors (Sander, 1975; Sroufe, 1990). That is, the caregiver is capable of making adjustments to fit the infant's actions, whereas the infant, although capable of participating in interactional sequences started and kept on track by the caregiver, can neither initiate nor maintain such coordinated sequences autonomously.

During the third stage (7–9 months), that of the *initiatory infant* (Sroufe, 1990), the infant is seen as making dramatic advances in its ability to actively and creatively coordinate, initiate, and maintain reciprocal exchanges with the attachment figure. Also during this period and partly as a function of its increasing motor abilities, the infant spends more time in exploration of its environment. The developmental milestone of this stage appears to be the infant's burgeoning ability to internally represent its world. This is evidenced by its anticipation of the caregiver's behavior in the course of familiar interactional exchanges, the emergence of object constancy, the rise in negative reactions to strangers, and in specific affects such as anger, surprise, and fear (cf. Sroufe, 1990). Of further importance is the fact that the infant–mother system undergoes a qualitative change during this stage: "a relationship exists where once there was organized interaction" (Sroufe, 1990, p. 286). That infants older than 7 months react adversely to a break in this relationship, whereas younger infants do not (Heinicke & Westheimer, 1966, cited in Sroufe, 1990; Schaffer & Callender, 1959), suggests that the older infants have begun internalizing the organized caregiver context. As Sroufe stated, "The organized caregiver matrix has begun to become part of a core of emerging inner organization" (p. 287), with the infant's intentionality and goal-directedness aimed at maintaining the known organization. This perspective is thus in line with attachment theory in suggesting that the infant–mother relationship may be thought to have developed once the infant's behaviors become integrated into a coherent behavioral–motivational system organized around a specific attachment figure (Bretherton, 1987).

The final stage of development during the first year (10–12 months) is referred to by Sroufe (1990) as that of *specific attachment–dyadic emotional regulation* and by Sander (1975) as a time of *focalization*. It is during this period that the infant's advancing motor and cognitive skills lead it to become more active in organizing its behaviors around the attachment figure. Thus, for example, as the infant becomes a more active explorer of its surroundings, it also becomes more likely to rely on the attachment figure as a haven of safety from which exploratory forays may be centered. As such the infant's behaviors become more complex, organized, and goal-directed and its expectations become more specific, all of which are suggestive of advances in inner organization. In Sroufe's words, "From a history of coordinated interaction—first orchestrated by the caregiver but ultimately including the intentional signals of need and desire by the infant—the infant learns that when the caregiver is available, organized behavior may be maintained, or re-achieved if lost" (p. 288). This is of course in line with the suggestion put forth by the attachment theorists that by the end of the first year, the nature of the infant's organization of attachment behavior around the caregiver is revealing of the internal working model of the infant–caregiver attachment relationship that has developed.

In the preceding discussion, the course of infant development across the first year has been considered in terms of both attachment theory and an organizational perspective. The following section consists of a review of the research on the interactional origins of attachment.

ATTACHMENT ANTECEDENTS RESEARCH

Researchers' attempts to identify the origins of infant–caregiver attachment have been guided by the identification, within attachment theory, of infant–caregiver interaction as the context within which relationships are shaped. As such, most of this work, and all of the studies considered here, have been directed toward identifying variations in caregivers' interactive behaviors that are predictive of distinctive patterns of infant–caregiver attachment. In more general terms, researchers have attempted to determine whether very early experiences (interactions) are predictive of later developmental outcomes (attachment).

This work could not have been carried out without Ainsworth's development of a standardized procedure for measuring attachment (Ainsworth & Wittig, 1969) or, more specifically, for assessing the quality of the infant–caregiver relationship. A brief summary of this procedure follows, which should contribute to an understanding of the empirical review and also serve to demonstrate the translation from a conceptual to an empirical level (see the second proposition outlined earlier) that is so central to developmental research in general and to questions concerning the coherence of development specifically.

The Strange Situation

The Strange Situation (Ainsworth & Wittig, 1969) is a standardized laboratory procedure designed for infants between 12 and 18 months of age. It involves the infant, its mother, and an unfamiliar female adult (i.e., the stranger) in a series of seven 3-minute episodes designed to gradually increase the amount of attachment-relevant stress experienced by the infant. After the infant and mother have been introduced into an unfamiliar room, the stranger enters the room, eventually approaches the infant and attempts to interact with the infant. Additionally, the mother twice departs from and then returns to the room, first leaving the infant with the stranger and then leaving it alone in the unfamiliar room.

In line with attachment theory as already summarized, an assumption inherent in the development and use of the Strange Situation is that under heightened stress the infant will organize its behavior around the caregiver in a manner consistent with its internalized model of their relationship. In other words, the infant is not expected to behave in a random fashion in this setting. Rather, given the attachment-relevant stress assumed to occur in this situation, the infant is expected to behave in accordance with its experience-based expectations regarding the caregiver's availability and his or her willingness and ability to meet its specific attachment-oriented needs. Accordingly, a system has been developed for classifying the quality of the infant–caregiver relationship on the basis of the infant's behavioral organization (Ainsworth et al., 1978) and in terms of four aspects of infant behavior during two reunion episodes. These include the extent to which the infant seeks proximity or contact with the caregiver, strives to maintain contact with the caregiver, directs angry or resistant behaviors toward the caregiver, and ignores or otherwise avoids the caregiver's bids for interaction.

Three general patterns of attachment have been identified on the basis of reliably observed differences in infants' organization of the four behavior categories considered. One of these is a pattern of secure attachment, and the other two represent different manifestations of insecure attachment relationships.[2]

Three Patterns of Attachment

In the Strange Situation, infants with *secure* attachment relationships exhibit a marked ability to use the caregiver (in this case the mother) as a secure base for exploration. These infants explore their environment in the comfort of the mother's presence and, when not distressed, greet the caregiver in an unambiguously positive manner upon her return from brief separations. When distressed, securely attached infants are likely to initiate, maintain, and derive comfort from proximity and contact with the mother. This comfort, in turn, allows the securely attached infant to return to exploration. *Insecure–avoidant* infants are characterized by their tendency to ignore the mother's return to the room or to actively avoid her attempts to reestablish contact, proximity, or interaction during the reunion episodes of the Strange Situation. Such avoidance may take the form of ignoring the mother altogether despite her attempts to gain the infant's attention, averting its gaze from her, or beginning to approach and then markedly turning away from her. Finally, *insecure–resistant* infants are conspicuous for their tendency to direct substantial levels of negative behavior toward the mother during the reunion episodes of the Strange Situation. Such negativity is typi-

---

[2]A fourth pattern, "disorganized–disoriented," has been identified recently (Main & Solomon, 1986). Given that there are no published works in which the interactional origins of the disorganized–disoriented attachment pattern have been examined, this new attachment category is not addressed in this chapter.

cally expressed as anger directed toward the mother and is often mixed with an apparent desire to reestablish proximity to her. Thus, inse-cure–resistant infants often give the impression of being quite ambiva-lent; for example, they may seek proximity to the mother and then push her away or exhibit some similarly negative behavior once contact has been established.

Evidence for the validity of these distinctions comes from research that has examined the developmental consequences of attachment as guided by the third proposition of attachment theory outlined earlier. A fairly consistent set of findings reveals that infants classified as inse-curely attached generally look less competent as they grow older. Such infants have been found as toddlers and preschoolers to be less em-pathic, less compliant, less cooperative, less emotionally healthy, and less competent with peers; they also exhibit more negative affect and less self-control than their securely attached agemates (e.g., Erickson, Sroufe, & Egeland, 1985; Jacobson & Wille, 1986; LaFreniere & Sroufe, 1985; Londerville & Main, 1981; Main & Weston, 1981; Sroufe, 1983; Sroufe et al., 1990). Additionally, as 5- and 6-year-olds, infants who had been insecurely attached have been found to be at greater risk for developing behavior problems (Arend, Gove, & Sroufe, 1979) and less emotionally healthy and less competent with their peers (Sroufe et al., 1990) than their securely attached counterparts.

Interactional Origins of Attachment: Findings

Given the identification of distinct patterns of attachment that have also been linked to important aspects of development beyond infancy (i.e., that have been revealed as an element of coherence), it is not surprising that researchers have concerned themselves with questions regarding the interactional origins of attachment. In this review 20 reports are considered in which maternal interactive behavior was observed, at-tachment quality was assessed, and relations between the two were examined. It is important to note that although there are important methodological differences among these studies, consideration of how these differences might influence the findings from these works is beyond the scope of this chapter. These methodological differences are nevertheless summarized in Table 7.1.

Another issue that is relevant to the current analysis is that infant age at time of observation differs across studies. It is this writer's suggestion that whereas the theory-based goal of antecedents research to date has been to link caregiver behavior to subsequent attachment quality with little or no attention to the infant's developmental level, understanding of these works will be enhanced by such considerations. Presentation of findings from these works is thus organized around the four stages of infant development as provided by an organizational perspective; across-stage patterns of findings are also presented. Additionally, in my interpretation of these findings I consider them first as they are considered most typically—as a whole—and then discuss them in light of the infants' developmental levels.

Basic Regulation Stage.   Fourteen of the 20 studies examined maternal interactive behavior during infants' first 3 months of life. A general finding from these works was that mothers of young "future secure" infants, who would eventually develop secure attachments, were more sensitive and responsive in their interactions than were mothers of "future insecure" infants, who would develop insecure relationships (Ainsworth et al., 1978; Isabella, 1993; Isabella & Belsky, 1991). Additionally, mothers of future insecure infants were observed to be more averse to physical contact (Ainsworth et al., 1978) than were mothers of future secure infants. Similar findings are seen in three studies in which only "very secure" dyads were compared to insecure dyads. Mothers of very secure infants were found to be more sensitive (Goldberg, Perrotta, Minde, & Corter, 1986; Isabella, Belsky, & von Eye, 1989), more accepting (Goldberg et al, 1986), more responsive to infant initiations, and less abrupt (Blehar, Lieberman, & Ainsworth, 1977) than mothers of future insecure infants.

A number of these studies also reported distinctions between secure, insecure–avoidant, and insecure–resistant dyads. Mothers of infants who would later develop resistant attachments were observed to be more unresponsive to infant cries (Belsky, Rovine, & Taylor, 1984), more inappropriate in responding to infant distress (Miyake, Chen, & Campos, 1985), and more insensitive (Grossmann, Grossmann, Spangler, Suess, & Unzer, 1985) than mothers of future secure infants. Additionally, mothers of future resistant infants were more insensitive and rejecting (Isabella, 1993) and also more underinvolved (Isabella & Belsky, 1991) than were mothers of either future secure or future avoidant infants. Finally, during the developmental stage of basic regulation, mothers of infants who would later develop avoidant attachments were found to be more unresponsive to infant distress during feedings (Egeland & Farber, 1984), more verbally intrusive or unresponsive (Isabella & Belsky, 1991), and more contingently responsive (which may be indicative of intrusiveness; Lewis & Feiring, 1989) than were mothers of either future secure or future resistant infants.

Coordinated Interaction Sequences Stage.   Only eight studies observed interaction during the period of coordinated interaction sequences (4–6 months). Once again, mothers of future secure infants were more sensitive and responsive than mothers of insecure infants (Grossmann et al., 1985; Isabella, 1993). Similar findings were reported for a study involving only the mothers of boys; in addition, mothers of secure

TABLE 7.1
Summary of Antecedent Studies and Their Identifying Methodological Features

Reference [Sample Size]	Age and Type of Interaction Observed	No. of Observations At Each Age	Length of Observation	Where Observed	Source of Coded Data			Level of Data Analyzed		
					NA	DO	VT	Disc	Qual	Subj
Ainsworth et al., 1978 [n =23]	3, 6, 9, 12 wks; Crying, Contact	1	4 hrs	Home	x			x		x
	39, 42, 24, 48 wks; Crying, Contact, and Compliance	1	4 hrs	Home	x			x		x
Belsky et al., 1984 [n = 60]	1, 3, 9 months; Naturalistic	1	45 min	Home		x		x		
Blehar et al., 1977 [n = 23]	6, 9, 12, 15 wks; Face to face	1	4 hrs	Home	x			x	x	
Egeland & Farber, 1984 [n = 189]	3 months; Feeding	1	?	Home		x		x		x
	6 months; Feeding	2	?	Home		x		x		x
	6 months; Play	1	?	?		x				x
Goldberg et al., 1986 [n = 56]	6 wks; 3, 6, 9 months; Seminaturalistic	1	1.5–2 hrs	Home		x		x		x
Grossman et al., 1985 [n =49]	2, 6 months; Naturalistic	1	2 hrs	Home	x					x
	10 months; Naturalistic	1	2 hrs	Home	x			x		x

Reference [Sample Size]	Age and Type of Interaction Observed	No. of Observations At Each Age	Length of Observation	Where Observed	Source of Coded Data			Level of Data Analyzed		
					NA	DO	VT	Disc	Qual	Subj
Isabella, 1993 [n = 32]	1, 4, 9 months; Naturalistic	2–3	30 min	Home	x		x			x
Isabella & Belsky, 1991 [n = 153]	3, 9 months; Naturalistic	1	45 min	Home		x		x	x	
Isabella et al., 1989 [n = 30]	1, 3, 9 months; Naturalistic	1	45 min	Home		x		x	x	
Kiser et al., 1986 [n = 63]	6 months; Face to face	1	9 min	Lab		x		x	x	
Lewis & Feiring, 1989 [n = 174]	3 months; Naturalistic	1	2 hrs	Home		x		x	x	
Lyons-Ruth et al., 1987 [n = 56]	12 months; Seminaturalistic	1	40 min	Home			x	x		x
Malatesta et al., 1989 [n = 58]	2.5, 5, 7.5 months; Face to face	1	7 min	Lab			x	x	x	
Mangelsdorf et al., 1990 [n = 75]	9 months; Seminaturalistic	1	60–75 min	Home		x		x		x
Maslin & Bates, 1983 [n = 74]	6 months; Naturalistic	2	3 hrs	Home		x		x		

(continued)

TABLE 7.1 (continued)

Reference [Sample Size]	Age and Type of Interaction Observed	No. of Observations At Each Age	Length of Observation	Where Observed	Source of Coded Data			Level of Data Analyzed		
					NA	DO	VT	Disc	Qual	Subj
Miyake et al., 1985 [n = 29]	1, 3 months; Seminaturalistic	1	2 hrs	Home		x		x		
	7.5 months; Unstructured free play	1	10 min	Lab		x		x	x	
Pederson et al., 1990 [n = 40]	12 months; Seminaturalistic	2	2 hrs	Home		x				x
Smith & Pederson, 1988 [n = 48]	12 months; Seminaturalistic	1	3 min	Lab			x	x	x	
Tracy & Ainsworth, 1981 [n = 23]	3-week intervals from 3–48 weeks; Affectionate	1	4 hrs	Home	x			x		
Wille, 1988 [n = 54]	6 months; Seminaturalistic	1	15 min	Lab			x		x	

Note. NA = narrative account; DO = direct observation; VT= videotape; Disc. = Discrete behaviors (i.e., frequency counts of specifically defined maternal behaviors); Qual. = Qualitative codes (i.e., frequency counts of specifically defined behaviors where coders made judgments regarding the meaning of the behavior observed; e.g., "mother encouraging further interaction"); Subj. = Subjective measures—typically rating scales for which the coders made ratings based on their appraisals of the meaning of maternal behavior in the context of the interactions observed (e.g., "sensitivity," "appropriateness of response"); ? = unclear from published report. Finally, Seminaturalistic = interactions structured but not fully scripted.

infant boys were found to be more cooperative (Egeland & Farber, 1984). Mothers of very secure infants were also more sensitive, cooperative, accepting, and available than mothers of future insecure infants (Goldberg et al., 1986). Regarding differences among the three attachment groups, mothers of future resistant infants were reported to exhibit less affectionate contact and to be less willing to engage in closeness than mothers of either future secure or future avoidant infants (Wille, 1988). No significant findings have been reported to distinguish dyads who eventually develop avoidant attachments on the basis of maternal behaviors observed between 4 and 6 months of age.

Initiatory Infant Stage. Eight antecedents studies observed interactions during the period of the initiatory infant (7–9 months). Mothers of infants who would later develop secure attachments were more sensitive and responsive (i.e., synchronous) in their interactions than were mothers of future insecure infants (Isabella & Belsky, 1991). Mothers of future insecure infants were, in turn, more rejecting (Isabella, 1993) and more contingently responsive in reacting to their infants' facial expressions (Malatesta, Culver, Tesman, & Shepard, 1989) than were mothers of future secure infants. In line with these findings, Goldberg et al. (1986) reported that mothers of very secure infants once again were more sensitive, cooperative, accepting, and available than mothers of future insecure infants. It is of interest to note, however, that two studies failed to reveal an association between attachment quality and maternal sensitivity as observed when infants were 9 months of age (Isabella, 1993; Mangelsdorf, Gunnar, Kestenbaum, Lang, & Andreas, 1990).

With regard to distinctions among the three attachment groups, mothers of future resistant infants were less responsive to infant distress and vocalization (Belsky et al., 1984), and more intrusive (Miyake et al., 1985) than mothers of future secure infants. Additionally, mothers of future resistant infants were less involved with their infants than mothers of either future secure or future avoidant infants (Isabella & Belsky, 1991). Mothers of insecure–avoidant infants were distinguished by being more rejecting of their infants than were mothers of secure infants (Isabella, 1993). They were also reported to exhibit higher levels of reciprocal interaction and involvement (Belsky et al., 1984) and to be more verbally intrusive and unresponsive (Isabella & Belsky, 1991) than were mothers of either future secure or future resistant infants.

Specific Attachment Stage. Six studies report on associations between attachment quality and interactions observed during the stage of specific attachment (10–12 months). In general, mothers of secure infants were more sensitive (Ainsworth, Bell, & Stayton, 1971; Pederson et al., 1990), cooperative, available, accepting (Ainsworth et al., 1971), and responsive to infant cries (Ainsworth et al., 1978) than were mothers of insecure infants. Of interest is that Grossmann et al. (1985) failed to find a relation between attachment quality and maternal sensitivity observed when infants were 10 months of age.

During the fourth stage of infant development, only one finding distinguished insecure–resistant dyads from others: mothers in this group were observed to respond least appropriately and most insufficiently to their infants' behaviors when compared to mothers of secure and insecure–avoidant infants (Smith & Pederson, 1988). Mothers belonging to insecure–avoidant dyads were reported to be more rejecting (Ainsworth et al., 1971), more abrupt and interfering in their physical handling of their infants (Ainsworth et al., 1978), and more intrusive in responding to their infants' behaviors (Smith & Pederson, 1988) than were mothers of either secure or insecure resistant infants.

Findings Across Stages.   It is somewhat surprising given the longitudinal nature and developmental focus of most of these studies that in only two cases have findings been reported regarding relations between patterns of maternal behavior over time and quality of infant–mother attachment. It is also of interest that these two studies report converging results. Malatesta et al. (1989) reported that mothers of infants who developed insecure relationships were observed to exhibit a higher degree of variability in their expressions of negative affect over the course of the first year. Isabella (1993) reported that mothers of insecure–avoidant infants became more rejecting from 1 to 9 months whereas mothers of insecure–resistant infants became less rejecting from 1 to 9 months, and that these patterns of change in maternal rejection were significantly different between these insecure groups.

Interactional Origins of Attachment: Interpretation

The general function of this review of the attachment antecedents literature is to shed light on questions of whether and how early interactional experiences are related to the subsequent development of attachment. Given the apparent evidence of such an association, the interpretation focuses more exclusively on the processes that might account for this observed link between interaction and attachment.

Overviews of the findings summarized here typically focus on consistencies across studies. As such, mothers of secure 1-year-olds are often characterized as sensitive, appropriately responsive, and affectionate in their interactions with their infants. Conversely, mothers of insecure 1-year-olds are typically characterized as insensitive, unresponsive, and rejecting. Where attention is paid to distinctions between the insecure groups, mothers of resistant infants are characterized as underinvolved and inconsistent; mothers of avoidant infants are characterized as rejecting and intrusive.

Assuming that these findings are indeed consistent across studies, the general conclusions drawn from them are both warranted and appropriate. However, further attention to the potential importance of infant developmental level may serve as a basis for even greater understanding. Developmentally based interpretation of the set of findings may be guided by two meaningful questions. First, is the effect on attachment development of a certain interactional experience dependent on the timing of that experience? Second and relatedly, how do patterns of interaction over time influence the development of attachment? It should be noted in addressing these questions that because they have not guided the relevant research to date, answers attempted on the basis of the findings summarized here are to be viewed as speculative.

Timing of Interactional Experience.   That sensitivity and responsiveness foster security whereas insensitivity and unresponsiveness breed insecurity is a consistent finding across the first 6 months of life. Interactions observed during the second half of the first year, however, are not as likely to lead to these results. In fact, Ainsworth (Ainsworth et al., 1978) is the only researcher to report an association between maternal sensitivity and attachment security when sensitivity was observed late in the first year (fourth quarter), the measurement involved traditional considerations of the meaning of maternal behaviors in the context of ongoing interactions (i.e., subjective evaluations), and all secure dyads were included in the analysis. Three studies using a similar approach have failed to replicate this finding (Grossmann et al., 1985, 10 months; Isabella, 1993, 9 months; Mangelsdorf et al., 1990, 9 months).

There are at least three ways to interpret this combination of results. First, it is possible that the role played by caregiver sensitivity in the development of secure attachments is most significant during the earliest stages of infant development. As such, although differences in sensitivity may be observable during the latter part of the first year, these may not be related to attachment in any meaningful way. A second possibility is that as the infant's behaviors come more under its own control and are guided to a greater degree by plans, goals, and expectations regarding the relationship with the caregiver, the infant is less likely to behave in ways, at least under usual circumstances, that allow for observation of meaningful differences in caregiver sensitivity. This would explain why Ainsworth, given her lengthy and frequent observations of interaction, would have been in the best position to capture differences between caregivers that might be very subtle or rarely exhibited. Still a third possibility is that by the end of the first year there are in fact very few differences among caregivers in terms of their sensitivity toward infants. This suggests that all caregivers move toward a "middle ground" and thus cannot be distinguished on the basis of this construct. Although it is difficult to believe that this is the case, only future attempts to address this question directly can afford opportunities for answering the question with any authority. And regardless of which explanation (if any) proves most meaningful, an important conclusion to be drawn from these works is that there are a multiplicity of ways in which the route from sensitivity to attachment security may be negotiated. More specifically, although the pathway from sensitivity to security has been consistently and reliably observed, it appears to be a rather wide one within which a great deal of variation may exist regarding timing and developmental level, specific caregiver behaviors, and consistency and inconsistency over time.

Perhaps a more striking suggestion to come from the reviewed works concerns maternal rejection, typically defined as a combination of physically interfering behaviors and expressions of negative affect. A number of studies have revealed that infants who develop insecure–avoidant attachment relationships have mothers who exhibit high levels of rejection during the latter part of the first year (Ainsworth et al., 1978; Isabella, 1993). Additional support for this association comes from findings (not reviewed here) that report that maltreating mothers are more likely to be rejecting (cf. Crittenden, 1981) and that maltreated infants are more likely to exhibit the avoidant manifestation of insecurity (e.g., Egeland & Sroufe, 1981). In all cases, experiences of maternal rejection were documented in samples of infants averaging 9 months of age or older. In my own work, however, in addition to finding this link between rejection at 9 months and insecure–avoidant attachment, I found that infants who developed insecure–resistant relationships with their mothers had experienced high levels of maternal rejection at 1 month, but not later (Isabella, 1993). This led me to propose that the effects on the infant of the experience of maternal rejection may differ as a function of the infant's developmental level at the time of this experience.

From an organizational perspective, resistant attachments were fostered by high levels of rejection during the developmental period (1 month) when infants require some coordination of their states and caregivers' interventions in order to achieve homeostatic regulation (Pipp, 1990; Sander, 1975; Sroufe, 1990). This might lead to incorporation in the infant's internal working model of persistent sensorimotor codings of the unreliability of homeostatic regulation (Pipp & Harmon, 1987; Sander, 1975). Insecure–avoidant relationships, on the other hand, were fostered by high levels of rejection experienced during (but not before) the developmental period (9 months) when relatively competent infants exhibit burgeoning capacities for expressing emotions, anticipating partner's behaviors (Sroufe, 1990), and knowing and acting on behalf of their own intentions. Rejection experienced by this older infant might thus lead to conflict as the caregiver's behaviors would be in more direct opposition to the infant's intentions. This is in line with Main's findings that insecure–avoidant infants direct conspicuously high levels of angry, aggressive, and uncooperative behaviors toward their mothers in settings less stressful than the Strange Situation (George & Main, 1980; Main, 1981). It should also be recognized that this interpretation incorporates several notions from an organizational perspective of development. First, it is suggested that the same form of treatment—caregiver rejection—may be interpreted differently and thus may have differential consequences at different ages. Second, this interpretation suggests that whereas both forms of insecurity may be fostered by the same form of caregiver behavior, there are multiple pathways to this infant outcome: Early experiences of rejection, late experiences of rejection, and various forms of inconsistency in caregiver expression of negative affect have all been reported as predictive of insecure attachment.

It is of course likely that there are alternative, plausible interpretations of these specific findings. Nevertheless, the emphasis here is on the recommendation that attention to developmental level, in the course of understanding the interactional origins of attachment, should guide subsequent inquiry in this area. It has not been common to inquire whether the same caregiver behavior might have strikingly different consequences for an infant depending on the timing, duration, or consistency of its experience of that behavior; nor has it been common to inquire whether seemingly equivalent infant outcomes might be fostered by a variety of interaction histories. The examples cited here serve to highlight the potential significance of making such questions routine.

Patterns of Interaction Over Time.   In a sense, the general question to be considered here is whether caregivers are consistent in their interactions with their infants over the first year, and whether any inconsistencies that might be noted are of significance to an understanding of the interactional origins of attachment. When the group of findings is considered across developmental stages, only one consistent finding emerges: Mothers of insecure–resistant infants appear to be underinvolved at all ages of measurement (e.g., Isabella & Belsky, 1991; Wille, 1988). It is more difficult, however, to present a coherent picture of patterns of caregiver sensitivity over time. As noted earlier, whereas researchers have been quite successful in their attempts to link sensitivity measured early in the first year to attachment quality at 1 year of age, the same has not been true for attempts to link attachment quality to sensitivity measured later in the first year. This general trend allows for the possibility that there are patterns of change in caregiver sensitivity that can be identified and linked to attachment quality. In my own work (Isabella, 1993), for example, mothers of insecure–resistant infants were very insensitive at 1 month, but by 9 months were indistinguishable from mothers of secure infants. Although I cannot say with any certainty that this is a meaningful element of the interactional origins of resistance, I do feel it important to urge that such trends be examined in the future.

A final consideration regarding patterns of interactional change over time concerns mothers' negative affect. In my own work (Isabella, 1993), mothers of insecure–resistant infants were most rejecting at 1 month and became less rejecting over the course of the first year. Conversely, mothers of insecure–avoidant infants were no more (significantly) rejecting than mothers of secure infants at 1 month, but they became increasingly rejecting over the course of the first year and were most rejecting by 9 months. When this set of findings is combined with Malatesta et al.'s (1989) discovery that mothers of insecure infants were more variable than mothers of secure infants in their expression of negative affect over the course of the first year, it appears that there is good reason to identify this as an important focus of future work. In both studies, insecure attachment relationships were fostered by mothers who exhibited marked inconsistencies in their expression of negative affect toward their infants. Is it the inconsistency that is most important? Or is it perhaps a question of the infant's developmental level at the time when this particular aspect of caregiver behavior reaches its highest level of expression? Although the questions cannot be answered at this time, it is apparent that in addition to supposing that caregivers' expressions of negative affect are likely to contribute to insensitivity and thus to foster insecurity, attachment researchers should be prepared to measure and assess the effects of specific patterns of change over time in these expressions. Once again, questions regarding potential differences in the interpretation of similar behaviors and concerning multiple pathways to similar outcomes are relevant here.

CONCLUSION

In closing this chapter, it is useful to come back to some of the questions raised at the outset concerning the coherence of individual development over time. First, is early experience related to later development? Attachment research provides compelling support for this notion. Attachment antecedents studies reveal consistently that specific patterns of interaction experienced during the first year are systematically related to attachment quality at 1 year. Furthermore, research on the consequences of attachment (presented in this chapter only as evidence for the validity of the Strange Situation procedure) reveals a systematic association between attachment quality at 1 year and socioemotional functioning throughout the preschool and early childhood years.

A second important question is whether optimal early experiences are predictive of positive outcomes and, conversely, whether nonoptimal early events are predictive of negative outcomes. Here, again, a good portion of the data from attachment research provides support for this assumption. The antecedents works are most striking in this regard, with early interactions (deemed optimal by virtue of an understanding of infant development) consistently linked with outcomes of secure attachment (also viewed as optimal). Conversely, interactions deemed nonoptimal are consistently linked with the nonoptimal outcome of insecure attachment. Where consequences of attachment have been examined, however, the picture revealed is a good deal more complicated. In general, the optimal (i.e., secure) pattern of attachment at 1 year that has been fostered by optimal patterns of interaction is predictive of positive socioemotional functioning for children between the ages of 2 and 7 years. The reverse pattern of nonoptimal early experiences and outcomes predicting nonoptimal later functioning is also commonly observed. However, the research in this area also reports on portions of the samples for whom the anticipated early-to-later predictions do not hold: Nonoptimal functioning in childhood is sometimes predated by optimal early experiences, and optimal functioning is sometimes predated by nonoptimal early experiences. In these cases, what researchers have discovered is that the impact of early experiences appears to have been modified by more recent experiences and events (e.g., Sroufe et al., 1990). This collection of findings thus suggests, in line with the work of Bowlby (1973), that development at any point is always a product of both developmental history and current circumstances, with early experiences incorporated into new patterns of adaptation (Sroufe et al., 1990). It is further suggested that early experiences are never lost: They "may again become manifest in certain contexts, in the face of further environmental change, or in the face of certain critical developmental issues" (p. 1364). In other words, early experiences do not cast in stone a specific developmental trajectory: There is always the potential for change as guided by changes in the immediate environment and experiences of the individual. Nevertheless, the effects of early experience, although they potentially can be overcome, can never be erased.

A third question of interest concerns the nature of early optimal versus nonoptimal experience. Based exclusively on the attachment antecedents literature, a general answer to this question is as follows: Early experiences are optimal when characterized by interactions in which caregivers are consistently sensitive, appropriately responsive, and affectionate. Early experiences are nonoptimal when characterized by interactions in which caregivers are insensitive, unresponsive, unaffectionate, rejecting, or inconsistent. When the same findings that lead to these conclusions are considered from an organizational perspective, however, a more complex picture emerges. For example, even the characterizations of optimal experiences given earlier allow for a good deal of variation. Any number of behaviors might be considered "optimal"; these may vary from one caregiver to another, from one infant to another, or even over time. The same is true of nonoptimal experiences, which, in addition, appear to encompass an even wider array of caregiver behaviors. Thus, although it is possible to define optimal and nonoptimal early experiences, it must also be recognized that current definitions lack in their specificity and complexity.

In conclusion, two final points are warranted. First, the evidence presented here for the coherence of individual development serves to highlight the sensibility and importance of efforts to provide early optimal experiences for all infants. Such early experiences should provide a strong and positive foundation for subsequent development, and this apparent reality should not be diminished by the possibility that such a positive foundation might be overridden, even temporarily, by subsequent experiences. In addition, the demonstrated potential for developmental change during childhood suggests that there is every reason to intervene in the lives of children for the sake of improving their environments and thus their experiences. Finally, I suggest that an organizational perspective of development is useful not only in interpreting research findings, but perhaps more importantly as a guide in the development of measures needed for the study of questions concerning the coherence of development. This is evident in the development and implementation of the Strange Situation, as well as in the attachment consequences research reviewed only briefly in this chapter. Although a detailed accounting of the measures employed in these studies is beyond the scope of the current work, the reader is directed to the relevant reports cited.

REFERENCES

Ainsworth, M. D. S. (1979). Attachment as related to mother–infant interaction. In J. Rosenblatt, R. Hinde, C. Beer, & M. Bushel (Eds.), *Advances in the study of mother–infant interaction* (Vol. 9., pp. 1–51). New York: Academic Press.

Ainsworth, M. D. S., Bell, S. M., & Stayton, D. J. (1971). Individual differences in strange situation behavior of one-year-olds. In H. R. Schaffer (Ed.), *The origins of human social relations* (pp. 17–57). New York: Academic Press.

Ainsworth, M. D. S., Blehar, M. C., Waters, E., & Wall, S. (1978). *Patterns of attachment.* Hillsdale, NJ: Lawrence Erlbaum Associates.

Ainsworth, M. D. S., & Wittig, B. A. (1969). Attachment and exploratory behavior of one-year-olds in a strange situation. In B. M. Foss (Ed.), *Determinants of infant behavior* (Vol. 4, pp. 113–136). London: Methuen.

Arend, R., Gove, F. L., & Sroufe, L. A. (1979). Continuity of individual adaptation from infancy to kindergarten: A predictive study of ego resiliency and curiosity in preschoolers. *Child Development, 50,* 950–959.

Belsky, J., Rovine, M., & Taylor, D. G. (1984). The Pennsylvania Infant and Family Development Project: III. The origins of individual differences in infant–mother attachment: Maternal and infant contributions. *Child Development, 55,* 718–728.

Blehar, M. C., Lieberman, A. F., & Ainsworth, M. D. S. (1977). Early face-to-face interaction and its relation to later infant–mother attachment. *Child Development, 48,* 182–194.

Bowlby, J. (1969). *Attachment and loss: Vol. 1. Attachment.* New York: Basic Books.

Bowlby, J. (1973). *Attachment and loss: Vol. 2. Separation.* New York: Basic Books.

Brazelton, T. B., Koslowski, B., & Main, M. (1974). The origins of reciprocity: The early mother–infant interaction. In M. Lewis & L. A. Rosenblum (Eds.), *The effect of the infant on its caregiver* (pp. 49–76). New York: Wiley.

Bretherton, I. (1987). New perspectives on attachment relations: Security, communication, and internal working models. In J. D. Osofsky (Ed.), *Handbook of infant development* (pp. 1061–1100). New York: Wiley.

Crittenden, P. M. (1981). Abusing, neglecting, problematic, and adequate dyads: Differentiating by patterns of interaction. *Merrill-Palmer Quarterly, 27,* 201–218.

Egeland, B., & Farber, E. A. (1984). Infant–mother attachment: Factors related to its development and changes over time. *Child Development, 55,* 753–771.

Egeland, B., & Sroufe, L. A. (1981). Attachment and early maltreatment. *Child Development, 52,* 44–52.

Erickson, M. F., Sroufe, L. A., & Egeland, B. (1985). The relationship between quality of attachment and behavior problems in preschool in a high-risk sample. In I. Bretherton & E. Waters (Eds.), Growing points in attachment theory and research. *Monographs of the Society for Research in Child Development, 50*(1–2, Serial No. 209), 147–166.

George, C., & Main, M. (1980). Abused children: Their rejection of peers and caregivers. In T. M. Field, S. Goldberg, D. Stern, & A. M. Sostek (Eds.), *High-risk infants and children: Adult and peer interaction* (pp. 293–312). New York: Academic Press.

Goldberg, S., Perrotta, M., Minde, K., & Corter, C. (1986). Maternal behavior and attachment in low-birth-weight twins and singletons. *Child Development, 57,* 34–46.

Grossmann, K., Grossmann, K. E., Spangler, G., Suess, G., & Unzner, L. (1985). Maternal sensitivity and newborns' orientation responses as related to quality of attachment in northern Germany. In I. Bretherton & E. Waters (Eds.), Growing points of attachment theory and research. *Monographs of the Society for Research in Child Development, 50*(1–2, Serial No. 209), 233–256.

Heinicke, C., & Westheimer, I. (1966). *Brief separations.* New York: International Universities Press.

Isabella, R. A. (1993). Origins of attachment: Maternal interactive behavior across the first year. *Child Development, 64,* 605–621.

Isabella, R. A. (1995). The origins of infant–mother attachment: Maternal behavior and infant development. In R. Vasta (Ed.), *Annals of child development* (Vol. 10, pp. 57–81). London: Jessica Kingsley.

Isabella, R. A., & Belsky, J. (1991). Interactional synchrony and the origins of infant–mother attachment: A replication study. *Child Development, 62,* 373–384.

Isabella, R. A., Belsky, J., & von Eye, A. (1989). The origins of infant-mother attachment: An examination of interactional synchrony during the infant's first year. *Developmental Psychology, 25,* 12–21.

Jacobson, J. L., & Wille, D. E. (1986). The influence of attachment pattern on developmental changes in peer interaction from the toddler to the preschool period. *Child Development, 57,* 338–347.

Kiser, L., Bates, J., Maslin, C., & Bayles, K. (1986). Mother–infant play at six months as a predictor of attachment security at thirteen months. *Journal of the American Academy of Child Psychiatry, 25,* 68–75.

LaFreniere, P., & Sroufe, L. A. (1985). Profiles of peer competence in the preschool: Interrelation between measures, influence of social ecology, and relation to attachment history. *Developmental Psychology, 21,* 56–68.

Lewis, M., & Feiring, C. (1989). Infant, mother, and mother–infant interaction behavior and subsequent attachment. *Child Development, 60,* 831–837.

Londerville, S., & Main, M. (1981). Security of attachment, compliance, and maternal training methods in the second year of life. *Developmental Psychology, 17,* 289–299.

Lyons-Ruth, K., Connell, D. B., Zoll, D., & Stahl, J. (1987). Infants at social risk: Relations among infant maltreatment, maternal behavior, and infant attachment behavior. *Developmental Psychology, 23,* 223–232.

Main, M. (1981). Avoidance in the service of attachment: A working paper. In K. Immelman, G. Barlow, L. Petrinovich, & M. Main (Eds.), *Behavioral development* (pp. 651–693). Cambridge, England: Cambridge University Press.

Main, M., Kaplan, N., & Cassidy, J. (1985). Security in infancy, childhood, and adulthood: A move to the level of representation. In I. Bretherton & E. Waters (Eds.), Growing points in attachment theory and research. *Monographs of the Society for Research in Child Development, 50*(1–2, Serial No. 209), 66–104.

Main, M., & Solomon, J. (1986). Discovery of an insecure disorganized/disoriented attachment pattern: Procedures, findings and implications for the classification of behavior. In T. B. Brazelton & M. Yogman (Eds.), *Affective development in infancy* (pp. 95–124). Norwood, NJ: Ablex.

Main, M., & Weston, D. R. (1981). The quality of the toddler's relationship to mother and to father: Related to conflict behavior and the readiness to establish new relationships. *Child Development, 52,* 932–940.

Malatesta, C. Z., Culver, C., Tesman, J. R., & Shepard, B. (1989). The development of emotion expression during the first two years of life. *Monographs of the Society for Research in Child Development, 54*(1–2, Serial No. 219).

Mangelsdorf, S., Gunnar, M., Kestenbaum, R., Lang, S., & Andreas, D. (1990). Infant proneness-to-distress temperament, maternal personality, and mother–infant attachment: Associations and goodness of fit. *Child Development, 61,* 820–831.

Maslin, C. A., & Bates, J. E. (1983, April). *Precursors of anxious and secure attachments: A multivariate model at age 6 months.* Paper presented at the biennial meeting of the Society for Research in Child Development, Detroit, MI.

Miyake, K., Chen, S., & Campos, J. (1985). Infant temperament, mother's mode of interaction, and attachment in Japan: An interim report. In I. Bretherton & E. Waters (Eds.), Growing points of attachment theory and research. *Monographs of the Society for Research in Child Development, 50*(1–2, Serial No. 209), 276–297.

Pederson, D. R., Moran, G., Sitko, C., Campbell, K., Ghesquire, K., & Acton, H. (1990). Maternal sensitivity and the security of infant–mother attachment: A Q-sort study. *Child Development, 61,* 1974–1983.

Pipp, S. (1990). Sensorimotor and representational internal working models of self, other, and relationship: Mechanisms of connection and separation. In D. Cicchetti & M. Beeghly (Eds.), *The self in transition: Infancy to childhood* (pp. 243–264). Chicago: University of Chicago Press.

Pipp, S., & Harmon, R. J. (1987). Attachment as regulation: A commentary. *Child Development, 58,* 648–652.

Sander, L. W. (1975). Infant and caretaking environment: Investigation and conceptualization of adaptive behavior in systems of increasing complexity. In E. J. Anthony (Ed.), *Explorations in child psychiatry* (pp. 129–165). New York: Plenum.

Schaffer, H., & Callender, M. (1959). Psychologic effects of hospitalization in infancy. *Pediatrics, 21,* 528–539.

Smith, P. B., & Pederson, D. R. (1988). Maternal sensitivity and patterns of infant–mother attachment. *Child Development, 59,* 1097–1101.

Sroufe, L. A. (1979). The coherence of individual development. *American Psychologist, 34,* 834–841.

Sroufe, L. A. (1983). Infant–caregiver attachment and patterns of adaptation in preschool: The roots of maladaptation and competence. In M. Perlmutter (Ed.), *Minnesota symposia on child psychology* (Vol. 16, pp. 41–81). Hillsdale, NJ: Lawrence Erlbaum Associates.

Sroufe, L. A. (1990). An organizational perspective on the self. In D. Cicchetti & M. Beeghly (Eds.), *The self in transition: Infancy to childhood* (pp. 281–307). Chicago: University of Chicago Press.

Sroufe, L. A., Egeland, B., & Kreutzer, T. (1990). The fate of early experience following developmental change: Longitudinal approaches to individual adaptation in childhood. *Child Development, 61,* 1363–1373.

Sroufe, L. A., & Fleeson, J. (1986). Attachment and the construction of relationships. In W. Hartup & Z. Rubin (Eds.), *Relationships and development* (pp. 51–71). Hillsdale, NJ: Lawrence Erlbaum Associates.

Sroufe, L. A., & Waters, E. (1977). Attachment as an organizational construct. *Child Development, 48,* 1184–1199.

Tracy, R. L., & Ainsworth, M. D. S. (1981). Maternal affectionate behavior and infant–mother attachment patterns. *Child Development, 52,* 1341–1343.

Wille, D. E. (1988, April). *Attachment: The effects of prematurity and mother–infant interaction.* Paper presented at the International Conference on Infant Studies, Washington, DC.

8

The Implications of Developmental Research for Eating Disorders

Linda Smolak
Ruth Striegel-Moore

The focus of this volume is on developmental psychopathology models of eating problems and their implications for research, treatment, and prevention. Developmental psychopathology approaches have been used to study a wide range of disorders including both internalizing and externalizing disorders (Cicchetti & Toth, 1991). Although these studies invariably contain references to developmental psychology's theory and research, the typical focus is on developmental studies of children and adolescents with problems. While the current volume does indeed contain such approaches (see part III), the preceding five chapters have been much more concerned with normal development. Indeed, several of these chapters barely mention eating disorders per se. Why include such work in a book about eating problems?

The major rationale comes from the history of the field of eating disorders. Even the early theorizing concerning eating disorders, especially anorexia nervosa (AN), emphasized developmental factors (Bruch, 1973; Crisp, 1980; Lasegue, 1873). Etiological models have typically included factors such as adjustment to puberty, separation–individuation processes, and gender-role development. However, the bulk of such theorizing has been based on retrospective report and analysis of a relatively small group of severely eating-disordered individuals, that is, adult patients with severe, chronic eating disorders.

These clinically based models have made and will continue to make crucial contributions to our understanding of eating problems. As Smolak (chapter 2, this volume) has noted, retrospective data are particularly useful in examining AN and bulimia nervosa (BN), whose low incidence rates make prospective research extremely costly. However, retrospective data do have their limitations. For example, available information is probably more limited than in studies examining current influences. Also, the possibility always exists of memory biases (schematic distortions), whether the reporting agent is the client or a family member. Although precautions can be taken to reduce such biases, they are still a concern, and verification from nonretrospective studies is still required.

Furthermore, clinical populations may differ from other women with eating disorders (Striegel-Moore & Marcus, 1995). They are more likely to be White, at least middle-class, and already adults. They may be more likely to suffer from other disorders such as depression or personality disorders. Symptom expression may be different (e.g., more salient to observers) for these chronic clinical clients than for women who are not part of this population. By examining only clinical samples, then, researchers are not likely to see the full variety of paths that can lead to the varying forms of eating problems.

More subtly and perhaps more important, clinicians may introduce their own professional biases into their research. They may, for example, tend to overestimate the importance of a particular developmental status or event because their clients consider it important. Discussions of puberty may illustrate this tendency. Eating disorders theorists have sometimes suggested that it is puberty per se (e.g., the fat gain or the sexual maturation) that triggers eating disorders. However, as all girls experience puberty and only a minority develop eating disorders, it is clear that those who do not adjust well must have a special vulnerability. Such vulnerability has often been assumed to be intraindividual, that is, an indicator of individual pathology.

A developmental psychologist, on the other hand, might locate the vulnerability in the context of development. Brooks-Gunn and Warren's (1985) work with ballet dancers exemplifies this approach, as does Richards, Boxer, Petersen, and Albrecht's (1990) study of girls in two different communities. Both projects demonstrate the impact of the girls' environments on eating attitudes and behaviors as well as on puberty and other adolescent developmental tasks. Thus, the bias of developmental psychologists differs from that of clinical psychologists. They work from different models, including different assumptions as to what causes behavior. These differences in "lenses" lead to different questions and, hence, to different answers.

Recent findings in anatomy provide a dramatic example of how new approaches can lead to entirely new sets of questions. Because pathologists have been dissecting the human body since the Renaissance, it had long been believed that all structures (muscles, connective tissues, bones, etc.) have been discovered and documented. However, in February 1995 a small structure was found that connects the neck muscles to the dura mater. This structure may play a role in some tension headaches and may suggest some new treatments for them. It was discovered because the people performing the autopsy used a nonstandard cut to section the head (*New York Times*, February 19, 1995, p. 12). Sometimes radical changes in approach can bring exciting new insights. We believe that developmental psychology's theories and methods can do this for the field of eating disorders.

WHY DEVELOPMENTAL PSYCHOPATHOLOGY?

Developmental approaches are often useful in understanding the etiology of pathology. However, for several reasons they are especially well suited to the study of eating disorders. First, several eating disorder symptoms appear to represent the extreme end of a continuum that is at least partially grounded in normal functioning and behavior (Polivy & Herman, 1987). This points to a relationship between normal and abnormal development (see Rosen, chapter 1, this volume).

Second, the diagnosis of AN or BN is approximately 9 to 10 times more likely to be given to women than to men (American Psychiatric Association, 1994). Diagnoses of Eating Disorders–Not Otherwise Specified (EDNOS) and Binge Eating Disorder (BED) also appear to be somewhat more common among women. Given that there does not appear to be an inherent biological difference between men and women that can explain this gender difference, there must be something about female development that is potentially problematic. We argue, consistent with Worell and Todd (chapter 6, this volume), that this factor is contextual rather than intraindividual. Such emphasis on contextual issues is consistent with a developmental model (see Rosen, chapter 1, this volume).

Third, eating disorders, especially AN and BN, show fairly distinct developmental trends. Onset typically occurs during a fairly restricted period of adolescence or early adulthood (see Smolak & Levine, chapter 9, this volume). This suggests that there may be particular developmental risk factors that may be either intraindividual or contextual.

Continua of Attitudes and Behaviors

Both the attitudes and behaviors listed among the symptoms of eating disorders are commonly seen in non-eating-disordered, nonclinical populations. These include fear of fat, the tying of weight and shape to self-esteem, and binge eating. Indeed, one reason that it has been necessary to define a threshold level at which binge eating is considered symptomatic of BN is the frequent acknowledgment of binge eating by U.S. women (Striegel-Moore & Marcus, 1995). There are also behaviors and attitudes associated with BN and AN that are not part of the official diagnostic criteria, such as dieting and body dissatisfaction, that are very common in the general female population.

Dieting is virtually a normative behavior among White U.S. female adolescents and adults (Rodin, Silberstein, & Striegel-Moore, 1985). Indeed, a substantial minority of elementary school girls, perhaps as many as 40%, have tried dieting (Gustafson-Larson & Terry, 1992; Smolak & Levine, 1994b). In one survey, over one half of eighth-grade girls indicated that they had dieted during the previous year (American School Health Association, 1989). By high school, 40% to 60% of girls are dieting on any given day (Rosen & Gross, 1987; Wadden, Brown, Foster, & Linowitz, 1991).

Of course, self-reported dieting can range from skipping a candy bar at one lunch to eating fewer than 500 kcal daily for several weeks. Clearly, some of the children and adolescents (and even adults) who claim to be dieting are not significantly restricting calories (Nichter & Vuckovic, 1994). However, these children have apparently learned that there is some value to being thinner (although they may not be able to articulate what that advantage is) and that dieting is a means to achieving a slimmer body. Furthermore, some of these girls truly are dieting and others eventually will.

Dieting is a common precursor to all of the eating disorders. Atkins and Silber (1993), for example, reported that all 21 of the children with AN in their study had dieted. Early dieting predicts BED (Yankovski, 1993) as well as BN (Mitchell, Hatsukami, Eckert, & Pyle, 1985). There are a number of theories explaining the link between dieting and eating problems, most notably Polivy and Herman's (1985, 1987) restrained eating model. Thus, one common starting point, dieting, may initiate different paths to BED, BN, AN, or nonpathological eating.

Calorie restricton by eating-disordered dieters probably differs only quantitatively from that seen in "normative" dieters. However, other aspects of attempts at weight loss or maintenance may be qualitatively different. For example, purging behavior is relatively rare among individuals who do not have BN, although it is sufficiently common that the authors of recent editions of th *Diagnostic and Statistical Manual of Mental Disorders* (III–R and IV) felt it necessary to define a threshold. More dramatically, persons with AN may develop unusual eating patterns (e.g., food rituals) that may be sequelae of severe starvation (Keys, Brozek, Henschel, Mickelsen, & Taylor, 1950), and which are not commonly seen in the general population.

Body dissatisfaction also occurs in both normal and eating-disordered women. The relationship of body dissatisfaction to body esteem, fear of fat, and other weight and shape concerns has not been fully delineated in part because definitions and measures of body dissatisfaction vary widely across studies (Thompson, Penner, & Altabe, 1990). Nonetheless, it is clear that at least some of these concerns are common among girls by the fifth grade. Gustafson-Larson and Terry (1992), for example, reported that almost one half of the girls in their survey wished that they were thinner and that about one third were "very often" worried about being fat. Even among elementary school children, both overall body esteem and specific aspects of weight and shape satisfaction are associated with dieting (Smolak & Levine, 1994b).

Body dissatisfaction is even more common among adolescent and adult females, however (Rodin et al., 1985; Rosen & Gross, 1987). It is clear that girls and women are well aware that society expects women to be attractive (more so than it does men; Bem, 1993; Worell & Todd, chapter 6, this volume; but see Hamermesh & Biddle, 1994). Indeed, some have argued that concern about attractiveness ought to be considered a part of the feminine gender role (Timko, Striegel-Moore, Silberstein, & Rodin, 1987). Whether body dissatisfaction or poor body esteem translates to poor self-esteem among children (Mendelson & White, 1985) or among non-eating-disordered adults (Silberstein, Striegel-Moore, Timko, Rodin, 1988) is less clear. The interweaving of body esteem and self-esteem among individuals with BN and among subthreshold clients may set them apart from most other women. Indeed, the *DSM–IV* (1994) criteria for eating disorders reflect a shift away from emphasizing body dissatisfaction to emphasizing overvaluation of shape and weight, a shift that was made to ensure the distinction between clinical and nonclinical concerns (Fairburn & Garner, 1988; Garfinkel et al., 1992). Nevertheless, body esteem problems themselves are not unique to women with eating problems.

Thus, for binge eating, dieting, and the various elements of body dissatisfaction, we see a continuum ranging from no problems (there are women who are satisfied with their bodies and who never diet) to "normative" states to pathological conditions. This suggests the possibility that for at least some eating-disordered women, these behaviors and attitudes begin in the normative range. In some cases, stressors ranging from sexual abuse to cumulative normative developmental tasks move women from normative status to eating disorders (Connors, chapter 12, this volume; Smolak & Levine, 1994a, chapter 9, this volume; Striegel-Moore, 1993). In other cases the behavior itself, especially perhaps dieting, may start a cycle of weight gain and increasingly dramatic weight control methods that culminates in BN or BED (Heatherton & Polivy, 1992; Polivy & Herman, 1985). In still others there may be a consolidation of attitudes and behaviors concerning the body, attractiveness, and weight control into a thinness schema (see Smolak, chapter 2, this volume) or perhaps even a "superwoman" constellation. Such schemata include acute sensitivity to societal cues, a high need for social approval, and the integration of attractiveness into self-definitions. These characteristics, in turn, cause the woman to place a premium on thinness (given its societal value), which may set the stage for the use of extreme methods to obtain the perfect body (Levine & Smolak, 1992; Steiner-Adair, 1986; Striegel-Moore, Silberstein, & Rodin, 1993). These and other potential pathways from normal to abnormal eating attitudes and behaviors require empirical verification. The point here is that there is substantial reason to argue that the hypothesized pathways exist.

What distinguishes one point on the continuum from others is not the only question, however, the other core issue concerns the reasons that these behaviors and attitudes might occur on continua in the first place. What is it about dieting, body dissatisfaction, and so on that "links" well-functioning women to those suffering from eating disorders? We argue that the construction of the female gender role is one possible answer to this question.

Gender Differences

Gender differences in the eating disorders are substantial: AN, BN, EDNOS, and to a lesser extent BED are all considerably more common in women than in men (American Psychiatric Association, 1994). Few other psychiatric disorders show such large gender differences. The conclusion is almost obvious that women must have some special vulnerability to these disorders. The real question is the nature of that vulnerability.

Several possibilities have been postulated. Some have proposed that adoption of masculine or feminine sex roles might be the issue (Lancelot & Kaslow, 1994). Others have suggested that women's special interest in relationships (and need for nurturance) makes them more vulnerable to the disapproval of others (Steiner-Adair, 1986, but see Berndt & Hestenes, chapter 4, this volume). Still others suggest that societal messages concerning the importance of thinness to women's success is important (Levine & Smolak, chapter 10, this volume).

To varying degrees, all of these arguments place the female gender role at the center of their etiological model. There can be little doubt that girls and women receive different messages than do boys and men about appropriate attitudes, characteristics, and behaviors (Bem, 1993; Orenstein, 1994; Sadker & Sadker, 1994; Tavris, 1992; Worell & Todd, chapter 6, this volume). Women are more likely to be judged in terms of attractiveness (both for dating and for job advancement), are supposed to eat less in front of other people, and are expected to be more concerned about the maintenance of relationships (Rodin et al., 1985; Striegel-Moore, 1993; Worell & Todd, chapter 6, this volume). Girls are relatively silenced (in terms of assertively expressing opinions, desires, etc.) by middle school and may find attractiveness one of the few available pathways to success (Brown & Gilligan, 1992; Johnson, 1995; Orenstein, 1994; Sadker & Sadker, 1993; Wolf, 1991).

The decision to try to be attractive is not, then, by definition a pathological one. Every day our society reinforces that decision through advertisements for makeup, weight control programs, exercise machines, and even plastic surgery, including liposuction (Bordo, 1993; Kilbourne, 1994). Certainly these techniques and procedures carry risk. For example, breast enhancement surgery is associated with a number of complications. Nevertheless, when these risks were first documented and publicized many women protested the government's efforts to regulate and perhaps prohibit the surgery. Why would women take such risks? Because they know the importance of attractiveness to their social and career success. This is also a primary reason that girls and women diet and engage in other potentially dangerous weight management behaviors.

Developmental psychologists have been investigating gender role development for a long time (e.g., Maccoby, 1966; Maccoby & Jacklin, 1974). More recent work on gender schema development (Bem, 1993; Liben & Signorella, 1987, 1993) has particularly led researchers to focus on how children receive and then reconstruct societal messages concerning gender. This approach raises issues not only about society's construction of gender (Bem, 1993; Bordo, 1993; Worell & Todd, chapter 6, this volume) but also on how interventions might be designed to alter sexist schemata and their negative effects (Bigler & Liben, 1992). Developmental models and research should play a core role in our efforts to disentangle the relationship between gender roles and eating problems.

Developmental Trends

As is true of most psychiatric disorders, AN can develop at any time during the life course. However, it is extremely rare in children and in women over 40. The average age of onset is 17 years, and this mean may actually represent bimodal peaks at 14 and 18 years (American Psychiatric Association, 1994; Thelen, Lawrence, & Powell, 1992). Few disorders are as clearly linked to a particular life stage as AN is to adolescence.

The onset of BN, too, is linked to a limited period of the life span. The vast majority of cases begin during late adolescence or early adulthood before age 25 (Woodside & Garfinkel, 1992). The diagnosis is virtually unheard of in prepubertal children (Thelen et al., 1992). The developmental demands of the transition to adulthood appear to present special risks for the development of BN (and related EDNOS; see Smolak & Levine, chapter 9, this volume).

Many theorists and researchers have noted and capitalized on these developmental trends (e.g., Smolak & Levine, chapter 9, this volume; Wooley & Wooley, 1985). Indeed, when developmental psychologists have investigated eating problems, they have often focused on the adolescent period and its transitions (e.g., Attie & Brooks-Gunn, 1989; Graber, Brooks-Gunn, Paikoff, & Warren, 1994; Smolak & Levine, 1993; Smolak, Levine, & Gralen, 1993). Models of developmental transitions as well as developmental data concerning puberty, separation–individuation, and other developmental tasks of adolescence can help to guide researchers investigating the reasons that this is a particular risk period (Smolak & Levine, chapter 9, this volume).

Initial data regarding BED suggest a different developmental pattern, however. Some of these individuals with this disorder struggle with overeating from an early age, perhaps in part as an attempt to gain a sense of safety or security and to comfort themselves (Thompson, 1994). Often, patients with BED find it difficult to recall when they began to binge; rather, they describe how they had their "hand in the cookie jar" as early as they can remember. About half of individuals with BED recall that their binge eating was not preceded by dieting (Wilson, Nonas, & Rosenblum, 1993). Whether the age of onset of binge eating in this group differs from the age of onset in those whose binge eating was preceded by a period of restrictive weight control efforts remains to be explored (Striegel-Moore, 1993). Developmental research concerning self-development (Ewell, Smith, Karmel, & Hart, chapter 5, this volume), attachment (Isabella, chapter 7, this volume) and social support (Berndt & Hestenes, chapter 4, this volume) may all be helpful in identifying contexts in which children might begin to view food rather than people as sources of strength and support.

The different types of developmental patterns seen in AN, BN, and BED raise the question of symptom change over the course of development. Do symptoms emerge suddenly or are they the culmination of a gradual process? Some women report beginning to binge eat following an episode of abuse (Thompson, 1994). On the other hand, for some women binge eating follows an extended period of repeated calorie-restrictive dieting (Heatherton & Polivy, 1992). For these women there appears to be a gradual buildup to the disordered eating pattern. There are also some women who begin binge eating occasionally but then the binge eating escalates in terms of frequency; it may also eventually be accompanied by purging. The triggers of such shifts is an issue for developmentally oriented research.

SOME THEMES FROM DEVELOPMENTAL PSYCHOLOGY

Clearly, models from developmental psychology and developmental psychopathology can be immensely helpful in our efforts to delineate etiological models of eating disorders and to design the research to evaluate those models. The chapters by developmental psychologists in this volume provide a wealth of specific and useful information about developmental behavioral genetics, self, social support systems, attachment, and gender roles. Taken together, the chapters provide five major themes for researchers and theorists who wish to integrate a developmental approach into their work on eating disorders (see also Smolak & Levine, 1994a).

Development as a Lifelong Process

Developmental psychologists have come to believe that all phases of development are potentially periods of important change (Hetherington & Baltes, 1988). This means several things. First, no one period of development has primacy over the others. Thus, although infancy may produce the foundations for many individual characteristics and behavioral patterns, those foundations are not immutable. More important, they do not guarantee a particular outcome to development, even in a very general way (Rosen, chapter 1, this volume). An insecure infant–mother attachment, for example, does not doom a child to psychopathology or even poor adjustment (Smolak & Levine, 1994a). There is, then, considerable plasticity in development. Ultimately, outcomes are shaped by the ongoing processes of development, including interactions with the environment (Isabella, chapter 7, this volume). This life-span perspective also implies that there are both quantitative and qualitative changes in development (or, at least that such changes are possible; Hetherington & Baltes, 1988). This in turn implies that there are periods of transition when there is special vulnerability to stress (Rosen, chapter 1, this volume; Smolak & Levine, 1994a; Smolak & Levine, chapter 9, this volume).

Evidence. The developmental chapters in this volume provide several compelling examples of this life-span perspective. Ewell et al. (chapter 5, this volume) provide evidence of qualitative shifts in theories of self from childhood to adolescence. In early childhood, theories of self are relatively unorganized; during elementary school, they are typically based on social comparisons. By adolescence, however, acceptance into a social network becomes the guiding principle for theories of self. As Ewell et al. note, for many adolescent girls attractiveness in general and thinness in particular provide a path for social acceptance and, hence, for self-definition.

What might initiate such a path? Is it rooted in the girl's earlier theory of self based on social comparison? Or do changes in social support and social relationships (see Berndt & Hestenes, chapter 4, this volume), contribute to an entire redefinition of the self? Or could adolescent gender role demands (see Worell & Todd, chapter 6, this volume) lead a girl toward this path? These and other factors, as well as their interactions, may well produce an outcome qualitatively different from the one that would have been predicted on the basis of the social comparison theories alone. In addition, it is not clear that girls who select attractiveness as a path to success in adolescence necessarily "stick with it" as they move into adulthood. Again, no trajectory of development is irretrievable, because previous development is never the sole determinant of current or future functioning (Isabella, chapter 7, this volume).

Why might paths change? As Isabella points out in his work on attachment (chapter 7, this volume), developmental processes, in this case the nature of mother–infant interaction, may change or have differential effects at varying ages. He demonstrates that even within the infancy period, the effects of maternal sensitivity or rejection on attachment may differ depending on timing. This is an important finding because eating disorders theorists who have discussed attachment as an etiological factor have frequently assumed that mother–infant interaction patterns are stable over (and, by implication, beyond) infancy, such that one can talk about a "rejecting" mother. As Isabella's work shows, although this is true for some mothers it is not true for all. One might hypothesize, for example, that women who suffer from depression when their children are infants might also recover while the children are still babies. How would such a recovery affect mother–infant interaction and attachment status (Smolak & Levine, 1994a)?

Furthermore, it is important to note that the relationship between parents and children is a transactional one (Rosen, chapter 1, this volume). A given parent may find certain child developmental stages to be more challenging than other stages. For example, Chatoor (1989) described mothers who enjoy the early infancy of their children but who react very negatively to the emerging autonomy of the older infant. Other parents might display the opposite pattern, preferring a child who can do some things for herself. Again, then, a parent is not necessarily permanently "good" or "poor" in providing adequate developmental support to the child. Even a biologically influenced characteristic is not necessarily fixed early in development. Rende (chapter 3, this volume) notes that some genes can be "turned on" during development and that the expression of a genetic characteristic may change during development. Most important, he explains the probabilistic effect of genes on psychopathology, including eating disorders. Such a model is important not only for categories of disorders but also for precursors. For example, high childhood body mass is one often-cited etiological precursor of eating problems (Zerbe, 1993). Body shape and weight, including obesity, are typically considered to have a significant genetic component (Brownell & Rodin, 1994; Meyer & Stunkard, 1993). However, this genetic component may be differentially expressed under varying environmental circumstances. Although genetics may contribute to a tendency to gain weight easily, an individual's particular weight does not simply reflect that genetic predisposition (Meyer & Stunkard, 1993). This may be one reason that childhood body mass index is only moderately predictive of adult body mass index (Guo, Roche, Chumlea, Gardner, & Siervogel, 1994) and may also explain why predictive power increases with age (because the adolescent's environment is likely to be more similar to an adult's than is the child's).

Implications. Why emphasize that developmental processes are ongoing and that no one period determines later development? The reason is that the tendency to focus on one period of development as either deterministic (as is often the case with theories discussing infancy) or as particularly crucial (as with the emphasis on adolescence) can create a variety of problems.

First, the focus on adolescence, which is understandable given the demographics noted earlier, has led us to underestimate the importance of the childhood developmental patterns that help define the meaning of adolescence. For example, the individual's interpretation of pubertal changes is probably more crucial than the changes themselves (see Smolak & Levine, chapter 9, this volume). Many factors, including media (Levine & Smolak, chapter 10, this volume), self-schema (Ewell et al., chapter 5, this volume), gender roles (Worell & Todd, chapter 6, this volume), and history of abuse (Connors, chapter 12, this volume; Worell & Todd, chapter 6, this volume), probably contribute to an individual's interpretation of pubertal changes. Beliefs and attitudes developed during childhood can certainly be expected to influence which of these factors are primary and which are ignored (Smolak & Levine, 1994b). Future research needs to move away from merely examining pubertal (or other adolescent task) status and toward understanding the factors (including those based in childhood) that contribute to the development of adolescent eating patterns.

Second, an emphasis on infancy tends to lead to a vilification (or glorification) of the primary caregiver. For research and clinical practice, this means mothers. Fathers, siblings, and other sources of social support (or nonsupport) have therefore frequently been neglected (Maine, 1991). However, it is not clear that the effects of poor mothering are independent of the fathering that the child receives (Chatoor, 1989; Phares, 1992). Similarly, extrafamilial support, even beyond infancy, may mediate the effects of inadequate parenting (Garmezy, 1983). Limited research does indeed suggest that nonmaternal social influences, including paternal pressures, teasing by friends and family, and peer emphasis on dieting, all have an impact on eating attitudes and behaviors (Fabian & Thompson, 1989; Levine, Smolak, & Hayden, 1994; Levine, Smolak, Moodey, Shuman, & Hessen, 1994; Proffitt & Smolak, 1995).

Third, the natural history of eating disorders is poorly described at this time. This is at least partially attributable to our tendency to focus less on developmental process than on current status. Exceptions to this tendency are typically focused on specific events such as sexual abuse. More attempts need to be made to determine why some people develop eating problems following such events (or following certain parent–child interaction patterns, e.g.), and some do not (Connors, chapter 12, this volume; Smolak & Levine, 1994a). Developmental models tend to be more process-oriented and can help us to move in this direction.

Checking Assumptions of Theories

Eating disorders theorists and researchers often base their work on developmental concepts. Object relations theorists, for example, commonly hold that women are more invested in relationships than men are (Worell & Todd, chapter 6, this volume). This, in turn, is viewed as making women potentially more vulnerable to the social-support shifts of developmental transitions (such as adolescence). There are also arguments that adolescence is in and of itself an unusually stressful life period. Some personality characteristics (e.g., concerns about social acceptance) are defined as part of temperament and hence are seen as genetic in nature. There is also discussion of genetic predispositions toward obesity, substance abuse, depression, and eating disorders.

Developmental data do not address all of these questions, and the chapters included in this volume do not encompass all of the available research concerning these issues. Nevertheless, the chapters contain enough information to draw at least one conclusion: Some of the assumptions routinely found in theories of eating disorders (and therefore in prevention and treatment approaches) are not well supported by the developmental data.

The assumption that men and women are fundamentally different in their "care" versus "justice" and their "relatedness" versus "autonomy" orientations (Chodorow, 1978; Gilligan, 1982) is an interesting case in point. This perspective is often adopted in part to explain the overwhelming gender difference in eating disorders. In other words, there is a reasonable attempt to explain one gender difference by looking at another gender difference. Yet the data suggest that when differences in relatedness exist, they are not typically of the pervasive type suggested by object relations theories (and their adaptations; see Berndt & Hestenes, chapter 4, this volume; Ewell et al., chapter 5, this volume; Worell & Todd, chapter 6, this volume). For example, although adolescent girls' friendships are more intimate than boys', both boys' and girls' friendships increase in intimacy during adolescence (Berndt & Hestenes, chapter 4, this volume). Furthermore, although boys may have less social support, social support is equally important to boys and girls

(Berndt & Hestenes, chapter 4, this volume). Self-development, with the exception of body esteem issues, looks remarkably similar for boys and girls (Ewell et al., chapter 5, this volume). Thus, while there are some differences, they are not as extensive as some eating disorders theorists may have assumed (see also Tavris, 1992; Worell & Todd, chapter 6, this volume).

The argument that women's development may not be as different from men's as some have assumed does not negate the possibility that eating-disordered women define themselves too heavily in terms of relationships. Instead, it raises the question of how these women move into that path. Perhaps this is merely one form of feminine development currently available, albeit one particularly favored by society. Alternatively, it may represent a pathological form of development. In any case, it is premature to assume that all (or most) women follow this pattern. Furthermore, it raises the question of whether the gendered vulnerability lies within individual development or in societal definitions of womanhood and opportunities for women (Bem, 1993; Worell & Todd, chapter 6, this volume).

Context Is Crucial

Most developmental psychologists argue that developmental outcomes represent a transaction between the organism and the environment (Rosen, chapter 1, this volume; cf. Scarr, 1992). In this model the person and environment are viewed as reciprocal influences. However, there are different types or levels of environment (Bronfenbrenner, 1989); these range from the microsystem of immediate influences on daily life, such as parents and peers, to the macrosystem of general societal or cultural norms, laws, and beliefs, including sexism and racism.

This complex model suggests that context is crucial in understanding development (Rosen, chapter 1, this volume). (Feminist psychologists also emphasize context: See, e.g., Striegel-Moore, 1994.) It is inappropriate to look only at personality characteristics, cognitions, individual events, and the like. All such factors, as well as their impact, are only understandable when context is taken into account. What constitutes a risk factor in one setting may not in another.

Important examples come from Worell and Todd's work on gender role development (chapter 6, this volume), as well as Rende's work on developmental behavioral genetics (chapter 3, this volume). Worell and Todd note that "there is a continuing interaction between gendered environments and gender-typed behavior that functions to reinforce cultural stereotypes and to strengthen gendered patterns of behavior" (p. 140). For example, a woman may act more feminine in those situations that reward femininity. Some therapy and research situations may (inadvertently) encourage the expression of certain gender-role behaviors. College women, for example, might see it as socially expected to endorse masculine characteristics (assertiveness, etc.) on a sex-role inventory. On the other hand, women in general may view therapy as a situation in which they are expected to be helpless and passive, at least initially. These conflicting contextual demands may partially explain the confusion in the literature concerning the relation between gender-role orientation and eating problems (Lancelot & Kaslow, 1994).

Rende (chapter 3, this volume) specifies a probabilistic model of genetic effects. Although his examples refer to pathology, such effects have also long been documented for individual characteristics that may contribute to eating disorders. As noted previously, despite its genetic component obesity may only develop under certain environmental conditions. Certainly the degree of obesity is influenced by the environment. Similarly, temperament and personality are likely to be shaped by the environment, including within-family differences in interactions with different children (Plomin, 1990). A difficult infant may be at some risk of growing into a difficult or even disordered child or adult. However, in a flexible, understanding environment such risk is considerably reduced (Chess & Thomas, 1984; Werner & Smith, 1982). Thus, descriptions of predisposing temperamental or personality characteristics are more precise and accurate if they include a description of the environmental contexts most likely to exacerbate or ameliorate the characteristic.

It is worth noting here that context is often stable for extended periods of time. Most Americans are raised by the same parents (or at least by one of the same parents) throughout their childhoods. They may attend the same school for several years and even have the same friends. The more stable the environment, the more stable individual characteristics are likely to be (Atchley, 1989). However, changes in environment (including societal demands) may produce changes in functioning or intensify personality strengths or weaknesses. This is one reason that developmental transitions are often periods of risk (see Smolak & Levine, chapter 9, this volume).

Protective Factors

Developmental psychopathology models suggest that there is a relationship between normal development and psychopathology (Rosen, chapter 1, this volume; Smolak & Levine, 1994a). Psychopathology is viewed as a path that diverges from normal development (or perhaps runs parallel to it). All of the developmental chapters in this volume endorse this principle. Self-development, for example, may be derailed as early as the infant attachment phase (see Isabella, chapter 7, this volume) or as late as adolescence, when the need for group acceptance increases (Ewell et al., chapter 6, this volume). This principle shifts some of the focus to factors that maintain normal development and it encourages psychologists to look at protective as well as risk factors (Garmezy & Masten, 1991). This, in turn, implies that girls and women who develop eating disorders are not necessarily disordered from birth or even from an early age. This argument is consistent with data suggesting that not all adolescents with eating disorders have had childhood eating problems (Marchi & Cohen, 1990) and that many girls who develop AN and BN have been of normal weight, done well in school, and gotten along adequately with friends and family prior to the onset of their symptoms.

The principle of a relationship between normal and pathological development also fits with the argument that there is at least a partial continuum between normative attitudes and behaviors and eating disorders (see preceding discussion). Many women diet but few become bulimic or anorexic. There is even a group of women and girls who have subthreshold eating disorders but who will, as best as is known, never develop full-blown AN or BN (Striegel-Moore & Marcus, 1995).

What protects these latter groups of women? The developmental literature offers a variety of specific possibilities. For example, high public self-consciousness, which is related both to depressive affect (Rosenberg, 1979) and to eating disorders (Striegel-Moore et al., 1993), is associated with high parental emphasis on achievement (Klonsky, Dutton, & Liebel, 1990; see Ewell et al., chapter 5, this volume, for a discussion). Thus, parents who are supportive rather than pressuring may have children who can face the increased achievement demands of adolescence (Smolak & Levine, chapter 9, this volume) more adequately. This is generally consistent with findings that continued close (but not too close) relationships with parents might benefit adolescents (see Berndt & Hestenes, chapter 4, this volume). Whether certain types of social support are more protective than others remains an issue for future research.

Special Methodological Issues

Working with children and adolescents adds new demands to research (see Smolak, chapter 2, this volume). One such demand is the development of new measures. Several of the developmental chapters in this volume contain discussions of specific measures of children's development. In all of the chapters, of course, research is cited that can serve as a source of additional information about assessment. In addition, Rende (chapter 3, this volume) provides fairly detailed information about the types of statistical analyses that are appropriate in developmental behavioral genetics studies.

This information is valuable for those of us wishing to conduct research in the specified areas. In addition, such measures and techniques may serve as prototypes for the development of more psychometrically sound and theoretically meaningful measures of eating attitudes and behaviors for use with children. They can, for example, help us to decide when to use forced-choice questions, how detailed a Likert scale can effectively be for a particular age level, and the appropriate level of wording complexity.

The information in the developmental chapters can also be helpful in addressing molar change in developmental structures. One of the great challenges of prospective longitudinal research is to find measures that adequately represent qualitatively different forms of a behavior (Rosen, chapter 1, this volume; Smolak & Levine, 1994a). Consider, for example, the concept of the "superwoman." Several theorists have suggested that this characteristic (or role) is a risk factor for the development of eating problems (Levine & Smolak, 1992; Smolak & Levine, chapter 9, this volume; Steiner-Adair, 1986; Timko et al., 1987). As typically defined, however, the "superwoman" is an adolescent or an adult. What does she look like in childhood? What element(s) are critical to the development of this characteristic and identifiable during the developmental period? Possibilities include social approval, multiple roles, achievement orientation, low self-esteem coupled with perfectionism, or some early combination of these (Proffitt & Smolak, 1995). Developmental research on self, gender roles, and achievement can be used to help frame these questions and design the studies that can address them.

Linking qualitatively different structures across periods of development can be difficult. Even if a group is initially relatively homogeneous for a characteristic, not all of them necessarily follow the same developmental paths to identical outcomes. For example, some securely attached infants develop psychopathologies whereas some insecurely attached infants do not (see Smolak & Levine, 1994a, for a discussion). Thus, the task facing psychologists is to chart not simply the relationship between two developmentally distinct states but the evolving pathways from one or more states to their particular outcomes. This endeavor requires not only longitudinal data but special analytic methods (Smolak, chapter 2, this volume). Most important, it requires theory that can in many cases already be found in the developmental literature.

CONCLUSIONS

Etiological models of the eating disorders have been predominantly based on the experiences and rememberances of women seen in clinical practices. Such models have made crucial contributions to the understanding of eating disorders, but they are limited by both their referent sample and their theoretical perspectives. Developmental psychopathology offers a new approach to studying eating disorders, encouraging greater emphasis on developmental process, protective factors, and childhood precursors.

As its name implies, developmental psychopathology has its roots in developmental psychology. As a discipline that is heavily (although by no means exclusively) focused on children and adolescents, developmental psychology has much to offer in terms of theory and research techniques. As the chapters in this volume have already demonstrated, there is a wealth of information on a variety of characteristics and experiences that have long been assumed to play some role in the development of eating problems. This information can be helpful—and, indeed, may be necessary—in formulating more specific hypotheses concerning these factors and in designing research to assess their contributions to eating problems.

Developmental psychopathology also holds the potential to facilitate primary prevention. By understanding childhood precursors, it prepares us to design prevention programs that focus on ameliorating weaknesses and encouraging strengths. It also provides information about the concerns of children and adolescents as well as about their ability to comprehend certain material. This can help us gear our programs to the interests and levels of our audience.

REFERENCES

American Psychiatric Association. (1987). *Diagnostic and statistical manual of mental disorders* (3rd ed., rev.). Washington, DC: Author.

American Psychiatric Association. (1994). *Diagnostic and statistical manual of mental disorders* (4th ed.). Washington, DC: Author.

American School Health Association, Association for the Advancement of Health Education, & Society for Public Health Education, Inc. (1989). *The national adolescent student health survey: A report on the health of America's youth.* Oakland, CA: Third Party Publishing.

Atchley, R. (1989). A continuity theory of normal aging. *The Gerontologist, 29,* 183–190.

Atkins, D., & Silber, T. (1993). Clinical spectrum of anorexia nervosa in children. *Journal of Developmental and Behavioral Pediatrics, 14,* 211–216.

Attie, I., & Brooks-Gunn, J. (1989). Development of eating problems in adolescent girls: A longitudinal study. *Developmental Psychology, 25,* 70–79.

Bem, S. (1993). *The lenses of gender.* New Haven, CT: Yale University Press.

Bigler, R., & Liben, L. (1992). Cognitive mechanisms in children's gender stereotyping: Theoretical and educational implications of a cognitive-based intervention. *Child Development, 63,* 1351–1363.

Bordo, S. (1993). *Unbearable weight: Feminism, Western culture, and the body.* Berkeley: University of California Press.

Bronfenbrenner, U. (1989). Ecological systems theory. In R. Vasta (Ed.), *Annals of child psychology* (Vol. 6, pp. 187–251). Greenwich, CT: JAI.

Brooks-Gunn, J., & Warren, M. (1985). Effects of delayed menarche in different contexts: Dance and nondance students. *Journal of Youth and Adolescence, 14,* 285–300.

Brown, L., & Gilligan, C. (1992). *Meeting at the crossroads*. Cambridge, MA: Harvard University Press.

Brownell, K., & Rodin, J. (1994). The dieting maelstrom: Is it possible and advisable to lose weight? *American Psychologist, 49,* 781–791.

Bruch, H. (1973). *Eating disorders: Obesity, anorexia nervosa, and the person within.* New York: Basic Books.

Chatoor, I. (1989). Infantile anorexia nervosa: A developmental disorder of separation and individuation. *Journal of the American Academy of Psychoanalysis, 17,* 43–64.

Chess, S., & Thomas, A. (1984). *Origins and evolution of behavior disorders.* New York: Brunner/Mazel.

Chodorow, N. (1978). *The reproduction of mothering: Psychoanalysis and the sociology of gender.* Berkeley: University of California Press.

Cicchetti, D., & Toth, S. (Eds.). (1991). *Rochester Symposium on Developmental Psychopathology: Vol. 2. Internalizing and externalizing expressions of dysfunction.* Hillsdale, NJ: Lawrence Erlbaum Associates.

Crisp, A. H. (1980). *Anorexia nervosa: Let me be.* New York: Grune & Stratton.

Fabian, L., & Thompson, J. K. (1989). Body image and eating in young females. *International Journal of Eating Disorders, 8,* 63–74.

Fairburn, C., & Garner, D. (1988). Diagnostic criteria for anorexia nervosa and bulimia nervosa: The importance of attitudes to weight and shape. In D. Garner & P. Garfinkel (Eds.), *Diagnostic issues in anorexia nervosa and bulimia nervosa* (pp. 36–55). New York: Brunner/Mazel.

Garfinkel, P., Goldbloom, D., Davis, R., Olmstead, M., Garner, D., & Halmi, K. (1992). Body dissatisfaction in bulimia nervosa: Relationship to weight and shape concerns and psychological functioning. *International Journal of Eating Disorders, 11,* 321–325.

Garmezy, N. (1983). Stressors of childhood. In N. Garmezy & M. Rutter (Eds.), *Stress, coping, and development in children* (pp. 43–84). New York: McGraw-Hill.

Garmezy, N., & Masten, A. (1991). The protective role of competence indicators in children at risk. In E. M. Cummings, A. Greene, & K. Karraker (Eds.), *Life-span developmental psychology: Perspectives on stress and coping* (pp. 151–174). Hillsdale, NJ: Lawrence Erlbaum Associates.

Gilligan, C. (1982). *In a different voice.* Cambridge, MA: Harvard University Press.

Graber, J., Brooks-Gunn, J., Paikoff, R., & Warren, M. (1994). Prediction of eating problems: An eight year study of adolescent girls. *Developmental Psychology, 30,* 823–834.

Guo, S., Roche, A., Chumlea, W., Gardner, J., & Siervogel, R. (1994). The predictive value of childhood body mass index values for overweight at age 35 y. *American Journal of Clinical Nutrition, 59,* 810–819.

Gustafson-Larson, A., & Terry, R. (1992). Weight-related behaviors and concerns of fourth-grade children. *Journal of the American Dietetic Association, 92,* 818–822.

Hamermesh, D., & Biddle, J. (1994). Beauty and the labor market. *American Economic Review, 84,* 1174–1194.

Heatherton, T., & Polivy, J. (1992). Chronic dieting and eating disorders: A spiral model. In J. Crowther, D. Tennenbaum, S. Hobfoll, & M. Stephens (Eds.), *The etiology of bulimia nervosa: The individual and familial context* (pp. 133–156). Washington, DC: Hemisphere.

Hetherington, E. M., & Baltes, P. (1988). Child psychology and life-span development. In E. Hetherington, R. Lerner, & M. Perlmutter (Eds.), *Child development in life-span perspective* (pp. 1–20). Hillsdale, NJ: Lawrence Erlbaum Associates.

Johnson, E. (1995, March). *Supporting young women's voices: Factors related to voice across six relationships.* Paper presented at the biennial meeting of the Society for Research in Child Development, Indianapolis, IN.

Keys, A., Brozek, J., Henschel, A., Mickelsen, O., & Taylor, H. (1950). *The biology of human starvation.* Minneapolis: University of Minnesota Press.

Kilbourne, J. (1994). Still killing us softly: Advertising and the obsession with thinness. In P. Fallon, M., Katzman, & S. Wooley (Eds.), *Feminist perspectives on eating disorders* (pp. 395–418). New York: Guilford.

Klonsky, B., Dutton, D., & Liebel, C. (1990). Developmental antecedents of private self-consciousness, public self-consciousness and social anxiety. *Genetic, Social, and General Psychology Monographs, 116,* 273–297.

Lancelot, C., & Kaslow, N. (1994). Sex role orientation and disordered eating in women: A review. *Clinical Psychology Review, 14,* 139–157.

Lasegue, C. (1873, September 30). On hysterical anorexia. *Medical Times and Gazette,* 265–466, 367–369.

Levine, M. P., & Smolak, L. (1992). Toward a model of the developmental psychopathology of eating disorders: The example of early adolescence. In J. Crowther, D. Tennenbaum, S. Hobfoll, & M. Stephens (Eds.), *The etiology of bulimia nervosa: The individual and familial context* (pp. 59–80). Washington, DC: Hemisphere.

Levine, M. P., Smolak, L., & Hayden, H. (1994). The relation of sociocultural factors to eating attitudes and behaviors among middle school girls. *Journal of Early Adolescence, 14,* 471–490.

Levine, M. P., Smolak, L., Moodey, A., Shuman, M., & Hessen, L. (1994). Normative developmental challenges and dieting and eating disturbances in middle school girls. *International Journal of Eating Disorders, 15,* 11–20.

Liben, L., & Signorella, M. (Eds.). (1987). *Children's gender schemata.* San Francisco: Jossey-Bass.

Liben, L., & Signorella, M. (1993). Gender-schematic processing in children: The role of initial interpretations of stimuli. *Developmental Psychology, 29,* 141–149.

Maccoby, E. (Ed.). (1966). *The development of sex differences.* Stanford, CA: Stanford University Press.

Maccoby, E., & Jacklin, C. (1974). *The psychology of sex differences.* Stanford, CA: Stanford University Press.

Maine, M. (1991). *Father hunger.* Carlsbad, CA: Gruze.

Marchi, M., & Cohen, P. (1990). Early childhood eating behavior and adolescent eating disorders. *Journal of the American Academy of Child and Adolescent Psychiatry, 29,* 112–117.

Mendelson, B., & White, D. (1985). Development of self body-esteem in overweight youngsters. *Developmental Psychology, 21,* 90–96.

Meyer, J., & Stunkard, A. (1993). Genetics and human obesity. In A. Stunkard & T. Wadden (Eds.), *Obesity: Theory and therapy* (pp. 137–150). New York: Raven.

Mitchell, J., Hatsukami, D., Eckert, E., & Pyle, R. (1985). Characteristics of 275 patients with bulimia. *American Journal of Psychiatry, 142,* 482–485.

New York Times (1995, February 19). p. 12.

Nichter, M., & Vuckovic, N. (1994). Fat talk: Body image among adolescent girls. In N. Sault (Ed.), *Many mirrors: Body image and social relations* (pp. 109–131). New Brunswick, NJ: Rutgers University Press.

Orenstein, P. (1994). *Schoolgirls.* New York: Doubleday.

Phares, V. (1992). Where's poppa? The relative lack of attention to the role of fathers in child and adolescent psychopathology. *American Psychologist, 47,* 656–664.

Plomin, R. (1990). *Nature and nurture: An introduction to human behavioral genetics.* Pacific Grove, CA: Brooks/Cole.

Polivy, J., & Herman, C. P. (1985). Dieting and bingeing: A causal analysis. *American Psychologist, 40,* 193–201.

Polivy, J., & Herman, C. P. (1987). Diagnosis and treatment of normal eating. *Journal of Consulting and Clinical Psychology, 55,* 635–644.

Proffitt, J., & Smolak, L. (1995, March). *Gender roles and body esteem in elementary school girls.* Poster presented at the biennial meeting of the Society for Research in Child Development, Indianapolis, IN.

Richards, M., Boxer, A., Petersen, A., & Albrecht, R. (1990). Relation of weight to body image in pubertal girls and boys from two communities. *Developmental Psychology, 26,* 313–321.

Rodin, J., Silberstein, L., & Striegel-Moore, R. (1985). Women and weight: A normative discontent. In T. Sonderegger (Ed.), *Nebraska Symposium on Motivation: Vol. 32. Psychology and gender* (pp. 267–308). Lincoln: University of Nebraska Press.

Rosen, J., & Gross, J. (1987). Prevalence of weight reducing and weight gaining in adolescent girls and boys. *Health Psychology, 6,* 131–147.

Rosenberg, M. (1979). *Conceiving the self.* New York: Basic Books.

Sadker, M., & Sadker, D. (1994). *Failing at fairness: How America's schools cheat girls.* New York: Scribner's.

Scarr, S. (1992). Developmental theories for the 1990s: Development and individual differences. *Child Development, 63,* 1–19.

Silberstein, L., Striegel-Moore, R., Timko, C., & Rodin, J. (1988). Behavioral and psychological implications of body dissatisfaction: Do men and women differ? *Sex Roles, 19,* 219–232.

Smolak, L., & Levine, M. P. (1993). Separation-individuation difficulties and the distinction between bulimia nervosa and anorexia nervosa in college women. *International Journal of Eating Disorders, 14,* 33–41.

Smolak, L., & Levine, M. P. (1994a). Critical issues in the developmental psychopathology of eating disorders. In L. Alexander & D. Lumsden (Eds.), *Understanding eating disorders* (pp. 37–60). Washington, DC: Taylor & Francis.

Smolak, L., & Levine, M. P. (1994b). Toward an empirical basis for primary prevention of eating problems with elementary school children. *Eating Disorders: The Journal of Treatment and Prevention, 2,* 293–307.

Smolak, L., Levine, M. P., & Gralen, S. (1993). The impact of puberty and dating on eating problems among middle school girls. *Journal of Youth and Adolescence, 22,* 355–368.

Steiner-Adair, C. (1986). The body politic: Normal female development and the development of eating disorders. *Journal of the American Academy of Psychoanalysis, 14,* 95–114.

Striegel-Moore, R. (1993). Etiology of binge eating: A developmental perspective. In C. Fairburn & G. T. Wilson (Eds.), *Binge eating: Nature, assessment, and treatment* (pp. 144–172). New York: Guilford.

Striegel-Moore, R. (1994). A feminist agenda for psychological research on eating disorders. In P. Fallon, M. Katzman, & S. Wooley (Eds.), *Feminist perspectives on eating disorders* (pp. 438–454). New York: Guilford.

Striegel-Moore, R., & Marcus, M. (1995). Eating disorders in women: Current issues and debates. In A. Stanton & S. Gallant (Eds.), *Women's health* (pp. 445–490). Washington, DC: American Psychological Association.

Striegel-Moore, R., Silberstein, L., & Rodin, J. (1993). The social self in bulimia nervosa: Public self-consciousness, social anxiety, and perceived fraudulence. *Journal of Abnormal Psychology, 102,* 297–303.

Tavris, C. (1992). *The mismeasure of woman.* New York: Simon & Schuster.

Thelen, M., Lawrence, C., & Powell, A. (1992). Body image, weight control, and eating disorders among children. In J. Crowther, D. Tennenbaum, S. Hobfoll, & M. Stephens (Eds.), *The etiology of bulimia nervosa: The individual and familial context* (pp. 81–102). Washington, DC: Hemisphere.

Thompson, B. (1994). *A hunger so wide and so deep.* Minneapolis: University of Minnesota Press.

Thompson, J. K., Penner, L., & Altabe, M. (1990). Procedures, problems, and progress in the assessment of body images. In T. Cash & T. Pruzinsky (Eds.), *Body images: Developmental, deviance, and change* (pp. 21–50). New York: Guilford.

Timko, C., Striegel-Moore, R., Silberstein, L., & Rodin, J. (1987). Femininity/masculinity and disordered eating in women: How are they related? *International Journal of Eating Disorders, 6,* 701–712.

Wadden, T., Brown, G., Foster, G., & Linowitz, J. (1991). Salience of weight-related worries in adolescent males and females. *International Journal of Eating Disorders, 10,* 407–414.

Werner, E., & Smith, R. (1982). *Vulnerable but invincible: A study of resilient children.* New York: McGraw-Hill.

Wilson, G. T., Nonas, C. A., & Rosenblum, G. D. (1993). Assessment of binge eating in obese patients. *International Journal of Eating Disorders, 13,* 25–33.

Wolf, N. (1991). *The beauty myth.* New York: Morrow.

Woodside, D. B., & Garfinkel, P. (1992). Age of onset in eating disorders. *International Journal of Eating Disorders, 12,* 31–36.

Wooley, S., & Wooley, O. W. (1985). Intensive outpatient and residential treatment for bulima. In D. Garner & P. Garfinkel (Eds.), *Handbook of psychotherapy for anorexia nervosa and bulimia* (pp. 391–430). New York: Guilford.

Yankovski, S. (1993). Binge eating disorder: Current knowledge and future directions. *Obesity Research, 1,* 306–318.

Yuker, H., & Allison, D. (1994). Obesity: Sociocultural perspectives. In L. Alexander-Mott & D. B. Lumsden (Eds.), *Understanding eating disorders: Anorexia nervosa, bulimia nervosa, and obesity* (pp. 243–270). Washington, DC: Taylor & Francis.

Zerbe, K. (1993). *The body betrayed.* Washington, DC: American Psychiatric Press.

III

DEVELOPMENTAL ISSUES AND EATING DISORDERS

9

Adolescent Transitions and the Development of Eating Problems

Linda Smolak
Michael P. Levine

Eating disorders most commonly begin sometime during adolescence, rather than in childhood or adulthood. Bulimia nervosa (BN) is virtually unheard of prior to adolescence (Gislason, 1988) and the vast majority of women clinically diagnosed with BN have symptom onset before age 25 (Woodside & Garfinkel, 1992). Similarly, in clinical samples the modal age of onset of binge eating is 18; it is rarely seen in children (Streigel-Moore, 1993). Anorexia nervosa (AN) does occur in prepubertal children (Gislason, 1988) but it increases dramatically after puberty, with the majority of cases beginning before age 25 (Halmi, Casper, Eckert, Goldberg, & Davis, 1979; Woodside & Garfinkel, 1992).

Early adolescence and late adolescence may constitute special risk periods for the development of eating disorders (Halmi et al., 1979; Wooley & Wooley, 1985). This suggests that adaptation to the events or developmental changes commonly associated with these transitions can take the form of eating disorders. The increase in associated eating problems, such as body dissatisfaction and dieting during early adolescence, bolsters this impression (Gralen, Levine, Smolak, & Murnen, 1990; Koff & Rierdan, 1991; Richards, Casper, & Larson, 1990).

The focus of this chapter is on the early and late adolescence transitions. The study of developmental transitions represents an important component of the developmental psychopathology approach (Smolak & Levine, 1994a). Indeed, the way in which adolescents organize experiences during these transitions may be especially important in predicting future adaptation (Cicchetti & Schneider-Rosen, 1986). Developmental transitions may be viewed as times of special risk because they involve changes in molar (core or underlying) structures and in normative challenges and stressors (in addition to any non-normative stressors that might appear). In a sense, they represent "crossroads" (Brown &

207

Gilligan, 1992) of development, points at which a variety of developmental paths might be followed.

This chapter is divided into four major sections. In the first we explore the meaning of developmental transitions. In the second we examine the early adolescent transition, and in the third we discuss the late adolescent transition. These transitions are considered separately because they may differ in their relations to BN and to AN (Smolak & Levine, 1993). Furthermore, age of onset may provide clues to the etiology of these disorders (Woodside & Garfinkel, 1992). In the last section we consider the implications of developmental transitions for prevention, research, and theory concerning eating problems.

THE MEANING OF DEVELOPMENTAL TRANSITIONS

Historically, developmental psychologists spent little time discussing how children moved from one stage to the next and instead focused on describing stages of development. In the 1970s, however, theorists working in adult development began to emphasize the ways in which developmental changes occurred (e.g., Levinson, 1978). This has led to greater interest in developmental *transitions,* the periods between the end of one stage and the beginning of another. These transitions involve substantial reorganizations in personality, cognitive, and relationship structures, as well as changes in social roles and cultural expectations. The reorganizations are gradual and represent qualitative shifts in the structures. Thus, after a transitional period there are new relations among behaviors, beliefs, concepts, and attitudes. Generally, such changes represent healthy adaptations to the demands of the new life stage. Nonetheless, these transitional periods are of great interest to developmental psychopathologists because the person may lack the stable internal mechanisms or social support necessary for coping with the inherent challenges and with any concomitant non-normative stressors. If this is the case, changes in attitudes, emotions, and relationships may be a step toward developmental deviation.

Interest in developmental transitions is more than a simple extension of stressor–appraisal–coping models. By emphasizing normative change, the transitions model focuses on the way in which adaptive coping facilitates development. The stressors in these situations, unlike those frequently studied in the stressor–coping models, are both expected and socially sanctioned and defined. Although they may have negative aspects, the stressors are generally viewed as positive. Consider, for example, the stress of moving into a career path, which is one of the tasks of the late adolescence transition. Certainly from both a societal and an individual perspective this is a positive move toward adult functioning. Developmental psychopathologists seek to determine the circumstances under which this generally positive stressor (developmental task) leads to a problematic adaptation (such as an eating disorder) rather than to a positive one.

The study of developmental transitions also reinforces the principle that no one stage in the life span takes precedence over the others. It moves us away from viewing infancy and early childhood as the critically important period in development, by reminding us that development can change to a more or less normal path, temporarily or chronically, at various points in the life span (Smolak & Levine, 1994a). Thus, for example, more than half of all eating-disordered clients have no history of clinically significant childhood eating problems (Marchi & Cohen, 1990). This suggests that eating behaviors only become problematic when a reorganization occurs that ties them to attractiveness, success, control, and self-worth.

Cytrynbaum's Model of Midlife Transition

The midlife transition has received considerable attention from developmental psychologists (Smolak, 1993). Cytrynbaum et al. (1980) provided a detailed model of the transition itself that may prove useful in understanding three critical questions about the early and late adolescent transitions and their relationships to eating problems. First, are some people particularly vulnerable during the transition? Second, do some people face more difficult transitions than others? Third, what might lead to pathological versus nonpathological outcomes from a transition?

Cytrynbaum's model is outlined in Table 9.1. We consider only the model's applicability to the development of eating problems during the early and late adolescence transitions and expand the application in the sections examining each transition. There is no reason to believe that the structure of either the midlife or the adolescent transitions is unique. Thus, a general model of transition is probably applicable to all of them.

Cytrynbaum's model assumes that previous development, consolidated as a set of predispositions, influences but does not determine how a transition is negotiated. Predispositions include two elements: personality characteristics and the nature of surrounding social systems. The dimension of personality includes all elements of self. In terms of eating disorders, issues such as identity development, investment in thinness as part of self-definition, and interoceptive awareness (both of emotions and of physical states) may all create either risk factors or protective factors for the girl approaching adolescence or adulthood. Availability of social support as an adolescent enters middle school or moves away to college may either buffer or intensify the stresses of the adolescent transitions.

TABLE 9.1

A Schematic Overview of Major Personality and Social Systems Parameters and Processes During the Midlife Transition

Predispositions	Developmental Processes			Outcomes
	Precipitators or Triggers	**Developmental Tasks**	**Developmental Processes**	
Personality Differences in personality (ego strength, narcissism, coping strategies, defenses, etc.) which predispose individuals to respond differentially to the midlife transition	**Individual:** Encounter death anxiety; shift in time orientation.	Accept death and mortality.	Destructuring	**Adaptive** Acceptance of mortality; achieve a sense of individuation and coherent identity; integration of creative and destructive forces; attain a sense of community; integrate masculine, feminine, and related emergent components of personality; reinvest narcissism in self.
Interacts with ⟷	**Stressful or Unanticipated Life Events:** Biological changes; illness or death of parents, spouse, friends; life-threatening illness.	Accept biological limitations and risks. Restructure self-concept and sexual identity	Reassessment →	Able to cope with developmental tasks for the second half of life.
Systems Extent to which primary systems (couples, family, work organization) can adapt and support individual member's engagement with midlife tasks as assessed by system's flexibility, communication, boundary management, leadership, role differentiation, culture and myths; vary by social class, racial, ethnic background, etc.	**Social System:** Reduction in parental imperative; work organization or professional culture signals limitations on mobility and rewards or pressures to retire.	Reorientation to work, creativity, and achievement Reassess primary relationships.	Reintegration and restructuring → Behavioral and role change →	**Maladaptive** Failure to establish sexual bimodality which integrates male and female components of personality; failure to transfer narcissism; inability to accept mortality and associated losses. Casualties of one's own developmental potential expresses in midlife-related symptoms (depression, anxiety, decreased appetite for food and sex, poor concentration, fear of homosexuality, alcoholism, psychosomatic disorders) or in vulnerabilities and predispositions to distress and maladaptive symptoms as older adults.

Note. From Cytrynbaum, S., et al. (1980). Midlife development: A personality and social systems perspective. In L. Poon (Ed.), *Aging in the 1980s*, p. 465. Copyright © 1980 by the American Psychological Association. Reprinted by permission of the APA.

There are three components to the actual transitions. First, the transition must be triggered. Triggers are internal or external events or changes that initiate the questioning of existing psychological structures. Internal triggers include psychological and physical changes; external triggers may relate to role expectations, for example. Internal and external forces may also combine, as when there is a social reaction to a physical change such as puberty. Age is generally not a trigger in and of itself, rather, it is simply a marker. Indeed, the important triggers are not perfectly correlated with age. This is exemplified in findings that pubertal status is a better indicator of body dissatisfaction and dieting than is age or grade (Gralen et al., 1990; Levine, Smolak, Moodey, Shuman, & Hessen, 1994).

The second component is the developmental tasks, which may be conceptualized as the demands of the particular life stage. Three points are noteworthy. First, the presence of these tasks makes it clear that important changes do occur after infancy. Second, these tasks are normative. For example, adjusting to pubertal changes is one of the early adolescent tasks. All healthy people go through puberty: It is not a stressor in the sense that the death of a parent or serious illness might be. Nonetheless, as Cytrynbaum's model indicates, such tasks do require adaptation.

Third, the fact that these tasks are normative does not mean that they are the same for all people. The timing of the tasks is one variable: For example, girls who mature early may begin adult behaviors such as smoking, drinking, and dieting sooner than do girls who mature on time or late (Stattin & Magnusson, 1990). Gender almost certainly colors interpretations of puberty: Maturation moves girls away from their ideal body type whereas it moves boys closer to the preferred male body type. Race also affects identity development insofar as assimilation into the majority culture (still largely a requirement for career success) means denying part of one's own culture (Thompson, 1994). These tasks, then, are socially constructed inasmuch as their meaning and importance is determined by society. This, in turn, implies that gender, race, sexual orientation, and other factors that influence social acceptability affect the meaning of, and ease of adaptation to, these tasks.

The developmental processes themselves constitute the steps within a transition. First there is a *destructuring* or breaking down of existing psychological and social structures. The person gradually realizes that existing patterns of interaction and personal coping do not meet the demands of the new stage's developmental tasks. Destructuring is analagous to Piaget's equilibration process, in which a moderately novel event puts cognitive structures into disequilibrium, thus requiring adaptation by the child. Destructuring often occurs subconsciously, taking the form of discomfort or dissatisfaction.

This discomfort leads to the second process, reassessment. As in Levinson's (1978) model, Cytrynbaum et al. (1980) suggested that the individual questions the value and validity of relationships, goals, and personal characteristics. Brown and Gilligan (1992) captured some of the complexity of this reassessment as it takes place during early adolescence. They described how young girls struggle to balance what they see as the growing societal demand to be nice, cooperative women versus their own desires, dislikes, and needs, including the need to express themselves. These girls talk about their beliefs that their younger behaviors were rude or inappropriate and about how they have now changed their goals and want to be less vocal and more polite. This struggle may lead girls to lose contact with their own feelings and hence may be related to the interoceptive awareness problems commonly seen in women with eating disorders.

After examining one's self and one's life, reintegration and restructuring can occur. As Levinson (1978) demonstrated for the middle-age transition among men, such restructuring may range from minor adjustments to complete departures from previous functioning. Some people are unable to form effective new structures and make a negative adjustment (see Table 9.1). Although many people move through adolescence with little difficulty, a minority find the prospect of adulthood too daunting (Offer, Ostruv, & Howard, 1984). This can be attributed in part to the inadequacy of the self-system, social networks, and coping mechanisms that existed prior to the transition. For example, an adolescent girl whose family members have difficulty accepting her maturation and who fight to keep her enmeshed in their network may find eating behaviors to be an effective way of exerting control over her own body and of at least partially separating herself from her family (Smolak & Levine, 1993; Strober & Humphrey, 1987).

Finally, there are behavioral and role changes. These can be adaptive or maladaptive. We have presented a model (Levine & Smolak, 1992; see Fig. 9.1) that outlines how the tasks and demands of early adolescence might result in a continuum of outcomes ranging from positive adaptation to relatively minor eating problems (such as normative body dissatisfaction) to subthreshold problems and eating disorders. The model demonstrates that there are different paths of development through a transition. The healthiness of the path depends on mediators such as personality structures and the simultaneity of stressors.

EARLY ADOLESCENCE TRANSITION

The early adolescence transition represents the change from being a child to being an adolescent. Because it includes puberty, the transition can cover a fairly wide age range. Typically, however, it is defined as

FIG. 9.1. Developmental model of nonpathological dieting and eating problems. Adapted from Levine & Smolak, 1992 by permission.

ably a more difficult transition for girls than for boys. Girls experience greater drops in self-esteem, particularly in body esteem (Abramowitz, Petersen, & Schulenberg, 1984); the sex difference in depression emerges (Hirsch & Rapkin, 1987); girls' interest in taking leadership roles declines.

Nonetheless, many girls do navigate the transition successfully. This raises the specific forms of the general questions posed earlier: First, are girls more vulnerable than boys during this transition? Second, do some girls face especially difficult transitions and, if so, what exactly constitutes such a transition? Third, why do some girls develop serious psychopathology, particularly eating disorders? That is, what mediators or predispositions create such an outcome?

The components of the early adolescence transition are outlined in Table 9.2, with special emphasis on how the outcome of this transition might include eating disorders. Thus, Table 9.2 represents an integration of Cytrynbaum et al.'s (1980) model and our own model (Levine & Smolak, 1992; Smolak & Levine, 1994a).

TABLE 9.2
Paths to Eating Problems During the Early Adolescent Transition

Predispositions	Precipitators or Triggers	Developmental Tasks	Mediators	Outcomes
Individual Personality	*Individual*	Adjusting to adult physical (reproductive, body size, strength) features	Simultaneity of task demands	*Most Adaptive* In the absence of individual predispositions, tasks may be positively interpreted → body satisfaction, positive self-esteem, mature interpersonal relationships, achievements motive
Thinness schema Perfectionism Need for social approval Body dissatisfaction Dieting Self-esteem ↑	Awareness of ending childhood: puberty, school changes, parent relationship changes	Begin heterosocial relations	Timing of puberty	
Interacts with →	*Stressful or Unanticipated Life Events*	Begin realistic career exploration ("tracking" toward high school)		*Moderate* With presence of thinness schema and nonsimultaneous tasks, simple dieting, without notable pathology. With thinness schema, simultaneous events → disturbed eating with dieting and reduced slef-esteem, due to body dissatisfaction
Systems	Sexual abuse or harassment	Assess relationship with family vs. peers		
Family enmeshment Family hostility Peer pressure Teasing Family attitudes and behaviors concerning weight & shape	*Social Systems* ↑→ Peer interaction ↑→ Parental support and influence ↑↑ Teacher support ↑↑ Pressure from coaches, teachers ↑ Exposure to media messages	Gender role intensification		*Least adaptive* Presence of thinness schema and three simultaneous, especially early, tasks → sub-threshold eating disorders Presence of several personality predispositions and three simultaneous tasks → eating disorder

Predispositions

Even in elementary school, some of the behaviors, attitudes, and beliefs that may lead a girl to emerge from the early adolescence transition with eating problems may be in place. These include personality predispositions such as perfectionism and low self-esteem (Brown & Gilligan, 1992). Girls' strong investment in social relationships may also render them vulnerable as they move into a setting (middle school) where such relationships change dramatically (Brown & Gilligan, 1992; Eccles & Midgley, 1990). Attitudes about the importance of thinness and about weight management behavior may also be risk factors (Killen, Taylor et al., 1994; Smolak & Levine, 1994b).

Although we cannot examine all of these potential predispositions in detail, some discussion is possible. Perfectionism has long been linked to adult eating problems (Garner, Olmstead, & Polivy, 1983). Indeed, the original image of the anorexic was that of "the best little girl in the world" (Levenkron, 1978). Perfectionism may be linked to eating problems through the "superwoman" role (Levine & Smolak, 1992; Steiner-Adair, 1986). Brown and Gilligan (1992) documented the existence of perfectionism among some elementary school girls. These girls want to always be pretty, be nice, do well in school, and please others. Such unrealistic goals may set the stage for a loss of self-esteem as it becomes clear to the girls that they are falling short of their own ideal. These goals may also be driven by a need for social approval, which has been associated with eating problems in adults. This pattern may be especially insidious for girls who adopt White middle-class ideals when their race or ethnicity guarantees that they will never find full acceptance, even if they do become thin, earn good grades, and so forth (Brown & Gilligan, 1992; Thompson, 1994).

In terms of behavioral predispositions, research has established repeated dieting, especially with weight fluctuations, as a risk factor for AN, BN, and their subthreshold variants (Brownell & Rodin, 1994; Lowe, 1993; Polivy & Herman, 1993). Early onset of dieting behavior is associated with increased risk (Tobin, Johnson, Steinberg, Staats, & Dennis, 1991). Dieting children and adolescents tend to be heavier than nondieters, but they are usually not obese or even overweight by medical standards (Emmons, 1994; Smolak & Levine, 1994b). The risk created by dieting, then, is not solely attributable to real weight problems. It is possible that the risk is due to dieting itself, which can lead to metabolic slowing requiring more extreme methods to lose weight and maintain weight loss (Garner & Wooley, 1991). As the body struggles to escape starvation, binge eating may develop (Striegel-Moore, 1993). Given this possible path toward the development of eating problems, it is worrisome that up to 40% of elementary school girls report trying to lose weight (Gustafson-Larson & Terry, 1992; Smolak & Levine, 1994b).

In addition, research suggests that young children know that it is undesirable to be fat (Yuker & Allison, 1994). Not all elementary school children believe that thinness is important to attractiveness (Smolak & Levine, 1994b), but those girls who do may be especially susceptible to the peer and media pressure that is part of the early adolescent world, and hence to the development of eating problems (Levine, Smolak, & Hayden, 1994; Levine, Smolak, Moodey, et al., 1994).

Triggers

As is true at other developmental transitions, there are many possible triggers of the early adolescence transition. There are changes in peer and family relationships, academic demands, and social role expectations (e.g., gender role intensification) that render childhood cognitive, personality, and social structures inadequate. All of these changes might be viewed as marking the gradual ending of childhood. Puberty is probably the most salient indicator, both to the child and to others. Thus, puberty itself requires adaptation by both the girl and her social networks. Among the events that the girl must accept are substantial weight and fat gain (relative to muscle mass), reproductive maturity, and an adult body that may evoke increases in sexual harassment. Changes in the social network include shifts in the parent–child relationship. For example, mother–daughter conflict as well as daughters' resistance to paternal conversational interruptions increase (Hill, 1988). Such changes may make the daughter feel distant from her family, especially if, as is true for many individuals with AN, conflict and disobedience are unacceptable in the family (Strober & Humphrey, 1987).

It is noteworthy that the hormonal changes associated with puberty have few substantial direct effects on behavior (Richards, Abell, & Petersen, 1993). When hormonal effects are documented, they tend to be either fairly small (Brooks-Gunn & Warren, 1989) or mediated by other factors (Richards et al., 1993). Furthermore, puberty's effects are not the same in all cultures (Orenstein, 1994; Rodriguez-Tome, Bariaud, Zardi, Delmas, & Szlagyi, 1993). This implies that many of the behavioral effects associated with puberty are attributable to the social construction of puberty rather than to the biological processes per se. Puberty is a biopsychosocial event, not just a biological shift.

The social meaning of puberty in the United States has several implications for the development of eating disorders. More than anything else, puberty indicates to others than a child is becoming an adult. In general, achieving adult female status is at best an ambivalent event, whereas the attainment of adult male status is generally positive. Thus, as girls go through puberty they find themselves moving away from the ideal body shape for women; their options for careers, sports, and other types of opportunities becoming more rather than less restricted; and the value of their strengths (e.g., in relationships) diminishing (Brown & Gilligan, 1992; Sadker & Sadker, 1994).

One thing becomes increasingly clear to girls as they move into the early adolescence transition: Attractiveness is an important component of female success. This is true academically, socially, and in terms of career and some athletics (Yuker & Allison, 1994). Small wonder, then, that as girls go through puberty they work harder and harder at their appearance. Given that puberty means that most girls no longer have the long-legged, slender, lean prepubescent body that White middle-class society deems beautiful, it should not be surprising that eating problems begin to increase substantially at puberty.

Findings relating puberty to eating problems are summarized in Table 9.3. It is clear that as White American girls go through puberty they become more dissatisfied with their weight and, to a lesser extent, with their shape (they are generally pleased about breast development). They are also more likely than same-aged prepubertal girls to diet and to worry about their weight.

Findings about the timing of puberty are more ambiguous. Girls who are "off time," especially those who mature early, are more dissatisfied with their bodies, partially because early maturers weigh more than their prepubertal peers (see Table 9.3). Whether the greater weight or dissatisfaction of early maturers persists once all girls have completed puberty is not clear.

Developmental Tasks and Adaptation

Transitions present multiple challenges in the form of developmental tasks. Table 9.2 lists some of the tasks of early adolescence, which within the White, middle-class American culture are a normative part of the healthy movement toward adulthood. Indeed, variants of the tasks occur in most cultures because of, for example, the universal expectation that adults contribute to society in terms of work and procreation.

How might something so positive contribute to the development of eating problems? The eating problems represent an adaptation to the transition's demands (see Table 9.2). This idea is central to the developmental psychopathology model (Smolak & Levine, 1994a; Sroufe, 1989) as well as to many feminist models of eating problems (Bordo, 1993; Striegel-Moore, 1994). A girl who decides to diet may not be making an unreasonable decision, even if that dieting eventually endangers her life and well-being.

Different paths may lead to problematic adaptation. For some girls, predispositions are critical in their appraisal of the early adolescent tasks. Girls who are very invested in thinness, for example, may be appalled at the fat that maturation brings. The fat gain may be espe-

TABLE 9.3
Studies Relating Puberty to Eating Problems/Disorders

Author, Date	Sample	Puberty Measure	Findings
Alsaker, 1992	1,109 girls and 1,256 boys in Norway in Grades 6 through 9 (cross-sectional)	Students rated a measure of timing of global pubertal development (computed pubertal timing; CPT). Also rated their relative timing to their same-sex classmates (Perceived Pubertal Timing; PPT).	No relationship between CPT and body dissatisfaction for the girls. Among 8th-grade boys, early maturers were more satisfied with their bodies. PPT was related to body dissatisfaction among 6th-grade girls; among 8th-grade girls, the girls who perceived themselves as on-time showed greater body dissatisfaction. Among 7th- and 8th-grade boys, self-perceived late maturers had poorer body image.
Atkins & Silber, 1993	21 female childhood anorexics (9–12 years at diagnosis)	Tanner Stages (breast & pubic hair); menarcheal status	For 10 of the girls, onset of AN coincided with early, but normal, puberty
Attie & Brooks-Gunn, 1989	193 7th through 10th grade, private school, White girls and their mothers. Retested 2 years later.	Classified as early, late, or on-time maturers based on time of menarche, Tanner breast stage, and Tanner pubic hair stage at Time 1. Girls were also asked about their own perceptions of their pubertal timing.	In the longitudinal analysis, actual timing was not related to EAT-26 scores. In the concurrent analyses, the combination of actual and perceived timing and body fat was related to EAT scores at Time 1 and Time 2.
Blyth, Simmons, & Zakin, 1985	210 White girls, tested in 6th, retested in 7th grades	Self-report time of menarches	Earlier developers were more dissatisfied with their weight in 7th grade.
Brooks-Gunn, Attie, Burrow, Rosso, & Warren, 1989	Study 1: 424 girls aged 14–18, 287 nonathletes, 72 competitive swimmers, 64 students from national ballet schools. Almost all White and high SES. Study 2: 238 girls, mostly White, in Grades 7–10 at Time 1 testing. Retested 2 years later. 193 were nonathletes; 45 were dancers.	Timing based on self-reported menarcheal age. Tanner Stage based on self-report menarche and Tanner Breast Development Scale.	Late-maturing dancers had more positive body image and dieted less than on-time maturing dancers. Physical development (pubertal stage + weight/height) was significantly related to EAT-26 scores for the nonathletes only in the Time 1 Concurrent Analysis. In the longitudinal analysis, physical development (at Time 1) was not related to Time 2 EAT-26 scores.

Author, Date	Sample	Puberty Measure	Findings
Brooks-Gunn & Warren, 1985	276 private school girls and 69 dance school girls, aged 14–17.	Menarcheal age.	On-time dancers were heavier, had higher pathology, BN, and higher perfectionism scores and poorer body image than late-maturing dancers. More dancers were late maturers.
Cattarin & Thompson, 1994	210 10–15-year-old girls, 87 of whom were retested after 3 years.	Pubertal Development Scale; Age at menarche	Time 1 maturational status did not predict Time 2 teasing, body image, eating disturbance, or global psychological functioning.
Crockett & Petersen, 1987	Longitudinal sample (253 boys & girls) beginning in 6th grade and ending in 8th	Pubertal Development Scale	In Grades 7 and 8, more mature girls were less satisfied with their weight.
Dorn, Crockett, & Petersen, 1988	253 girls and boys followed from 6th through 8th grade. No information on race.	The Pubertal Development Scale (PDS; Petersen, Crockett, Richards, & Boxer, 1988).	In the 7th and 8th grades, girls who were more advanced in pubertal development were more dissatisfied with their weight. No multivariate effects for boys.
Dornbusch et al., 1984	6,768 12–17-year-olds (45% female), examined as part of the U.S. National Health Examination Survey between 1966 and 1970.	A composite based on Tanner breast and pubic hair development scales.	Within social class, as maturity level increased for girls, the desire to be thinner increased. The majority of girls who were postpubertal wanted to be thinner.
Fabian & Thompson, 1989	61 pre- and 60 postmenarcheal girls, aged 10–15	Self-reported menarcheal history.	Postmenarcheal girls were both heavier and higher on Drive for Thinness than age-matched premenarcheal girls.

(continued)

TABLE 9.3 (continued)

Author, Date	Sample	Puberty Measure	Findings
Graber, Brooks-Gunn, Paikoff, & Warren, 1994	116 girls tested initially at 7th, 8th, or 9th grade and then again in 9th, 10th, or 11th grade and then again between ages 21 and 23. Private school, predominantly White	Self-reported age at menarche.	Early maturers were more likely, as young adults, to be "chronically" at risk for eating problems (EAT-26 score ≥ 20 at all three times of testing). However, this effect appears to be due to higher body fat among the early maturers rather than to early puberty per se.
Gralen, Levine, Smolak, & Murnen, 1990	121 6th-, 116 8th-, 144 9th-, and 73 10th-grade girls, almost all White	Self-reported menarcheal status (yes/no). Used only in 6th- and 8th-grade regressions.	Menarcheal status was related to dieting and EAT-factor-2 (Bulimia) scores for the 6th graders only.
Gross & Duke, 1980	National Health Examination Survey of 3,196 girls aged 12–17	Tanner Scales	Early-maturing girls were more dissatisfied with their weight.
Killen et al., 1992	939 6th- and 7th-grade girls. 49.6% White; 22.8% Latina; 19.7% Asian; 3.2% Pacific-Islander; 3.6% Black; 2.6% Native American; 7.5% other.	Self-ratings of breast and pubic hair development (Tanner Stages) summarized as one measure: The Sexual Maturity Index (SMI).	More advanced pubertal development was associated with more symptoms of eating problems/disorders.
Killen, Hayward, et al., 1994	839 6th- and 7th-grade girls	Tanner Breast and Pubic Hair Developmental Scales	Girls with bulimic symptoms were more developmentally mature than asymptomatic girls.
Killen, Taylor, et al., 1994	3-year study of 939 6th- & 7th grade girls	Sexual Maturity Index (SMI) based on Tanner Breast and Pubic Hair Development Stages.	SMI was not related to the likelihood of developing symptoms over the 3-year period.
Koff, 1993	146 girls followed from 6th through 9th grade	Early (menarche before Fall of Grade 7) vs. nonearly maturing based on self-reports of age at menarche.	Early puberty was associated with higher body weight and greater BMI. The early maturers had higher scores on EDI Subscales for Drive for Thinness, Body Dissatisfaction, and Ineffectiveness in 6th grade and for the first two in 9th grade. Early maturers showed higher BES Weight Concern scores in 6th and 9th grades.

Author, Date	Sample	Puberty Measure	Findings
Koff & Rierdan, 1993	209 White, public school, ≥ middle-class, 6th-grade girls participating in a longitudinal study	Self-report timing of menarche. Self-ratings of Tanner breast development.	More advanced pubertal status was associated with higher scores on EDI subscales for Drive for Thinness, Body Dissatisfaction, BN, and Ineffectiveness as well as with dissatisfaction as evidenced in the Body Esteem Scale's subscales for Weight Concerns and Physical Condition. More advanced girls were more likely to rate themselves as "overweight" and to want to lose weight than the premenarcheal girls. No group differences on dieting.
Leon, Fulkerson, Perry, & Cudeck, 1993	937 7th- through 10th-grade girls	Puberty Development Scale.	Pubertal development was not a substantial influence on current risk for eating problems.
Leon, Fulkerson, Perry, & Early-Zaid, 1995	843 girls in Grades 7–10 at Year 1; followed for 3 consecutive years	Pubertal Development Scale.	Year 1 pubertal level did not predict Year 3 eating disorders.
Levine, Smolak, Moodey, Shuman, & Hessen, 1994	382 White, public school, 6th–8th-grade girls (cross-sectional)	Self-reported age at menarche.	Girls who had begun menstruating during the past year had higher weight management scores than girls who had not yet begun. Girls who began menstruating and dating in the same year had higher weight management scores.
Rodriguez-Tome et al., 1993	73 boys and 84 girls, French, aged 11–16	Tanner Breast, Pubic, and Genital Scales; Menarcheal status	Sense of body attractiveness increased for boys, but not girls, with pubertal advancement.
Simmons, Blyth, & McKinney, 1983	151 White girls, followed from 6th to 10th grades	Presence vs. absence of menstruation; relative onset of menstruation.	Early maturing girls were more concerned about their weight and figure at 9th and 10th grade and were actually heavier than later maturers.
Smolak, Levine, & Gralen, 1993	79 public school, White girls; surveyed in 6th and 8th grades	Self-reported age at menarche.	Early, on-time, vs. late menstruation was not related to body dissatisfaction, ChEAT, or Weight Management scores as measured in the 8th grade. Girls who were early in menstruating and who began dieting early showed higher body dissatisfaction and higher ChEAT scores.

(continued)

TABLE 9.3 (continued)

Author, Date	Sample	Puberty Measure	Findings
Stattin & Magnusson, 1990	Longitudinal data from 509 Swedish girls first tested as 3rd graders. A subsample was tested in 6th grade. Pubertal data were collected in 1970, when the girls were about 14 (8th grade). Retested in 9th grade. Subjects were contacted again at age 25.	Self-report of menarcheal age, validated by skeletal maturity in a subsample, divided into four timing groups.	There were no differences in overall concerns with appearance. Early maturers were more likely to report themselves overweight in the 8th grade than were later maturers. In adolescence, there was a significant correlation between weight and pubertal timing, but by adulthood this relationship had washed out.
Striegel-Moore, Schreiber, Pike, Wilfley, & Rodin, 1995	311 Black and 302 White 9–10-year-old girls	A 5-point scale (1 = prepubescent) based on pubic hair and areolar development as well as menstrual status.	With BMI (which was correlated with pubertal status) controlled, pubertal status was not a significant predictor of Drive for Thinness.
Tobin, Richards, Boxer, & Petersen, 1983	70 pre- and postmenarcheal 7th-grade girls and 52 pre- and postpubertal boys	Pubertal Development Scale	Curvilinear relationship between pubertal status and perceived attractiveness and body image such that both early and late maturing girls saw themselves as less attractive and were more dissatisfied with their bodies. Early maturers were especially negative. Early maturing boys had positive body images.
Zakin, Blyth, & Simmons, 1984	Pre- and postmenarcheal 12–13-year-olds	Age at menarche, recorded by nurse.	Early developers were more dissatisfied with their weight but not with their figures.

cially difficult for the girl who has been restraining her eating to control her weight during childhood and who now finds her efforts inadequate. Girls' appraisal of the developmental tasks is also affected by their sociocultural context. Teasing about weight, for example, increases the risk of eating problems (Fabian & Thompson, 1989; Levine, Smolak, Moodey, et al., 1994). We have demonstrated that some middle school girls live in a "culture of dieting" in which their mothers and friends diet and worry about weight and the girls read the teen magazines that send the broader culture's slenderness message. Such girls tend to have higher Eating Attributes Test scores, to diet more frequently, and to express greater body dissatisfaction (Levine, Smolak, & Hayden, 1994). These girls may be developing a thinness schema, similar to those hypothesized to occur in restrained eaters and eating-disordered patients (Markus, Hamill, & Sentis, 1987; Vitousek & Hollon, 1990). This schema includes information about the importance of thinness to attractiveness, the importance of attractiveness to social and career success, the dangers of fat, methods of becoming thin, and the relevance of attractiveness to one's own self-esteem. The thinness schema is hypothesized to lead to selective processing of information that supports the girl's assessment of thinness and its importance.

Predispositions may affect a girl's appraisal of, and hence adaptation to, developmental tasks. Also, not all girls face the same types of tasks. Based on the work of Simmons and Blyth (1987), we have proposed that cumulative normative developmental stressors increase the likelihood of eating problems. Specifically, disordered eating attitudes and behaviors may be fostered when simultaneous weight gains, changes in female–male relationships, and threats to achievement are filtered through the thinness schema (Levine & Smolak, 1992; Smolak & Levine, 1994a). Events are considered to be simultaneous when they occur within the same year. If either weight gains or heterosocial changes occur alone, the outcome is likely to be an intensification of weight and shape concern and the development of nonpathological dieting. In early adolescence, weight gains can be related to pubertal development and heterosocial changes to the onset of dating, both of which have been shown to contribute to increased body dissatisfaction and dieting (Gralen et al., 1990; Levine & Smolak, 1992; Levine, Smolak, Moodey, et al., 1994). If these challenges occur simultaneously and the thinness schema is severe, the risk of subthreshold eating disturbances rises. If there are also threats to one's sense of achievement, such as the new demands of middle school (Eccles & Midgley, 1990), and if the girls' self-definition emphasizes success in multiple roles in order to gain external approval (the "superwoman complex"; Steiner-Adair, 1986), the risk of frank eating disorders increases. Without the thinness ideal or the superwoman complex, the simultaneous stressors are likely to result in a different disorder (e.g., depression; Ge, Lorenz, Conger, Elder, &

Simons, 1994), adjustment problems (Simmons, Burgeson, Carlton-Ford, & Blyth, 1987), or successful coping.

We have presented longitudinal evidence suggesting that simultaneity of the normative tasks is more influential than the relative timing (early vs. late) in the development of eating problems (Smolak, Levine, & Gralen, 1993). Not surprisingly, girls who have been both early and simultaneous in the onset of dating and puberty (and who concurrently enter middle school) are particularly likely to develop problematic attitudes and behaviors. These girls experience the dual stress of being "off time" (Smolak, 1993) and of having to cope with multiple changes.

LATE ADOLESCENCE TRANSITION

During the early adolescence transition increasingly mature behavior is expected, but so is the daily financial, emotional, and social support of the teenager's family. The late adolescence transition marks the movement from adolescence into adulthood. At the end of this transition the individual is expected to be independent from the family of origin, although not isolated from it, and capable of contributing to and participating in society as a full-fledged member. Thus, responsibilities for family, work, and community involvement, along with rights to decide one's own lifestyle, schedule, residence, and so on are gained during this transition. For some people, both the responsibilities and the rights are frightening or at best ambivalently welcomed. This, then, raises the possibility of maladaptive outcomes, including eating disorders.

The late adolescence transition is similar to other life transitions in terms of process and components. Again, then, we can adapt Cytrynbaum et al.'s (1980) model, integrating it with our own model, to explain how eating problems might develop.

Predispositions

The predispositions relevant to the development of eating problems at the early adolescence transition are probably also important here. For example, women who have a history of repeated dieting, especially if it started early, and who view attractiveness and thinness as an important part of self are almost certainly at greater risk (Lowe, 1993; Striegel-Moore & Marcus, 1995; Timko, Striegel-Moore, Silberstein, & Rodin, 1987; Tobin et al., 1991). These women may be at greater risk during the late adolescence transition than they were during the earlier transition because these attitudes and behaviors have become more consolidated than they were previously.

In addition, women who are socially anxious and who need substantial social approval may be at special risk during this transition (Striegel-Moore, Silberstein, & Rodin, 1993). Such women seem particularly likely to endorse and to try to achieve the superwoman image (Steiner-Adair, 1986; Striegel-Moore, 1993). These women, who are likely to be high in public self-consciousness (Ewell, Smith, Karmel, & Hart, chapter 5, this volume; Striegel-Moore et al., 1993), may also be unusually sensitive to media and societal messages about thinness because they are extremely aware of the importance of first impressions and of a "great package." This sensitivity leads them to believe that slimness is important to all aspects of the superwoman role: family (especially marriage), career, and looks. High public self-consciousness may also contribute to a tendency to be guided more by external than by internal cues related to eating (Lowe, 1993).

We hypothesize that women who adopt multiple roles primarily for social approval are the women at risk for adopting superwoman attitudes and hence eating problems. These are likely to be women with low self-esteem. (We are not arguing that multiple roles in general are dangerous for women: Research indicates that multiple roles are typically health-enhancing for women; McBride, 1990.)

Predispositions are not limited to personality dimensions. Social context is also relevant. Although family influences are neither straightforward nor independent of personality, it is evident that family dysfunction is common among individuals with AN and BN. The enmeshment and hostility (sometimes covert, sometimes overt) commonly found in these families (Strober & Humphrey, 1987) may well make the separation–individuation process, which is integral to independent functioning, difficult if not impossible to negotiate.

Triggers

The triggers for this transition are probably not as universally defined as those for the early adolescent transition. Given that definitions of adulthood vary across racial, ethnic, and social class lines even within the United States, it is not surprising that no one event marks the end of adolescence and the beginning of the transition to adulthood (Smolak, 1993). For some young women, pregnancy, even as a teenager, might mark adult status. For others, it might be finding a job or marrying. However, for a slight majority of American women, including those most at risk for developing eating problems, the event marking the end of adolescence is finishing high school and starting college.

As is true of any trigger, leaving home for college results in a number of changes and challenges. Changes in social milieu may mean that standards of attractiveness change or intensify. Going to college almost certainly results in reduced social support, at least temporarily, as neither friends nor family are readily available. Dating and sexual pressures may be different. For example, rates of virginity typically drop during the college years (Michael, 1994). Academic and career pressures typically intensify, and faculty support may be less available than it was in high school. Financial concerns may appear, increasing the young woman's concern about career success. Thus, the young woman starting college needs to evaluate the adequacy of her social and personal structures to cope with the emerging demands of adulthood. This reassessment is likely to lead to changes in self, cognitive, and social structures.

Developmental Tasks

Research has established that most of the work in establishing an independent identity is completed during college rather than during high school (Marcia, 1980; Waterman, 1982). Most college students spend at least part of their college years in a state of moratorium. During moratorium one actively explores options for values and beliefs concerning politics, religion, career, and, at least for women, family and gender roles. Thus, during moratorium, which is so psychologically stressful that it is considered impossible for it to be a permanent status (Marcia, 1980), the young adult has no stable, well-defined sense of self. This type of flux is what makes transitions risky.

Separation–individuation is part of the process of establishing an identity. Individuation involves increased responsibility for self, whereas separation refers to decreased emotional and instrumental dependency on parents. The separation–individuation process is lifelong but has a "peak" crisis in late adolescence. It is especially important that the process evolve without excessive guilt or anxiety about the separation from parents (Lapsley, Rice, & Shadid, 1989).

Separation may be particularly difficult for some women for at least two reasons. First, many women may be more reluctant, and even socially less permitted, to separate from their family of origin. Research across the life span shows women to be more connected to their parents than men are (Smolak, 1993). Some feminist authors (e.g., Gilligan, 1982) have suggested that women are raised to value connection over independence. Yet, increasingly, society is sending women a mixed message about connection and independence. Unlike women of the recent past (whose images are still commonplace on cable television), today's women are supposed to have careers that enable them to be financially independent of their spouses. Thus, women's interest and skills in interpersonal relationships seem devalued. However, the need for connection in the form of establishing a family is not eliminated. Instead, women are somehow supposed to put families first and maintain brilliant careers. This superwoman model is presented without irony by the media. Those young women who have long tried to please everyone (Brown & Gilligan, 1992) may try to adopt this role without recognition of its inherent conflicts (Steiner-Adair, 1986). Eventually, however, these conflicts take their toll, perhaps in the form of eating disorders.

Second, some families are unable to support the separation–individuation process. Sometimes the problem is family enmeshment, a situation in which no member is permitted to have an individual identity. When enmeshment is combined with emotional hostility and coldness or with an uneasy overprotectiveness, it is difficult to escape the family. Given the enmeshment and hostility commonly found in families of eating-disordered clients (Strober & Humphrey, 1987), it is not surprising that many of them face particular difficulty with the separation–individuation process (Friedlander & Siegel, 1990; Smolak & Levine, 1993).

As they complete this stage of the separation–individuation process, some women may face an additional challenge. Autonomy from parents should facilitate the development of a serious intimate relationship. Those women who especially value relationships and who fail to establish such intimacy may find their newly emerging identity threatened (Striegel-Moore, 1993). This, then, may be an example of the type of heterosocial (perhaps heterosexual) threat described in our model (Fig. 9.1).

Adaptation

The possible adaptation patterns for late adolescence are similiar to those outlined for early adolescence. Some women come to this transition with a thinness schema (Markus et al., 1987; Vitousek & Hollon, 1990). Some college women also subscribe to the superwomen ideal and have high needs for social approval and success in multiple roles, including attractiveness (Striegel-Moore et al., 1993; Timko et al., 1987). If such women encounter simultaneously a weight gain (or a new standard at college that makes their current weight unacceptable), new heterosocial–sexual pressures, and new threats to their career (academic success), our model predicts that they may develop eating problems. The problems are likely to be subthreshold if the woman does not have the superwoman personality pattern, but may include frank eating disorders if this or another pathological personality constellation (Johnson & Wonderlich, 1992) is in place.

CONCLUSIONS

Throughout life there are fairly distinct periods in which psychological structures change significantly in response to new internal and external demands. These transitions facilitate developmental advances because the resultant structures tend to be more flexible and able to deal with more complex problems.

The transitions themselves, however, are periods of considerable instability. Extant social, cognitive, and personality (including self-) structures are deconstructed and reorganized. This means that the individual has limited resources on which to rely while moving through the transition.

Transitions, then, are periods of great opportunity but also of great risk. Adaptations may be positive or negative. Research with middle-aged males supports this idea of differential adaptation (Levinson, 1978), which suggests that there are multiple pathways through and out of these transitions.

Throughout this chapter we have suggested factors that might affect the process and outcome of negotiating the early and late adolescence transitions. In general, there is little empirical evidence to directly substantiate (or invalidate) these paths. For example, despite the many studies of puberty and eating problems, the process by which girls differentially evaluate the changes in their bodies remains poorly understood. There is a need for longitudinal research that follows girls from elementary school and the beginnings of dieting and body dissatisfaction through the adolescent transitions (Smolak, chapter 2, this volume). Only this type of data can elucidate what intensifies and consolidates those early concerns for some girls such that the demands of adolescence can only be faced by developing eating problems.

In addition, we have raised the general issue of the ambiguous value of adulthood for American girls. Women's skills and even their normal body shapes are devalued in today's society. Unlike boys, girls experience a drop in self-esteem and an increase in emotional problems as they approach adulthood. Although many people have offered hypotheses about why and how this happens, more research is needed to identify the sources of the messages about the value of womanhood, the characteristics that make some girls particularly vulnerable to these messages (especially to messages concerning thinness and the superwoman role), and ways of eliminating or at least diminishing the effects of such messages.

The role of predispositions, including attitudes and behaviors related to eating, highlights the importance of beginning prevention programs before the early adolescence transition. Elementary school prevention programs may be able to prevent consolidation of the thinness schema. They may also be useful in preventing acceptance of the superwoman role. Finally, they can teach children about the normality of body fat and the futility and danger of dieting to get below normal weight.

However, only a minority of girls are likely to receive elementary school intervention programs. Furthermore, predispositions influence but do not determine developmental pathways. The models presented in this chapter suggest that girls who experience simultaneous and perhaps off-time developmental tasks are at special risk. These girls might be targeted for prevention programs. It is also possible to work to reeducate adolescents about dieting, superwoman ideals, and so on (Killen, chapter 13, this volume; Shisslak, Crago, Estes, & Gray, chapter 14, this volume).

Developmental psychopathology models emphasize the importance of transitions as well as recognition of multiple pathways of development (Smolak & Levine, 1994a). These pathways may, at various points throughout life, move girls and women toward or away from eating disorders. By examining the paths through and out of the adolescent transitions, psychologists may make important strides in understanding and preventing the development of eating problems.

REFERENCES

Abramowitz, R., Petersen, A., & Schulenberg, J. (1984). Changes in self-image during early adolescence. In D. Offer, E. Ostrov, & K. Howard (Eds.), *Patterns of adolescent self-image* (pp. 19–28). San Francisco: Jossey-Bass.

Alsaker, F. (1992). Pubertal timing, overweight, and psychological adjustment. *Journal of Early Adolescence, 12,* 396–419.

Atkins, D., & Silber, T. (1993). Clinical spectrum of anorexia nervosa in children. *Developmental and Behavioral Pediatrics, 14,* 211–216.

Attie, I., & Brooks-Gunn, J. (1989). Development of eating problems in adolescent girls: A longitudinal study. *Developmental Psychology, 25,* 70–79.

Blyth, D., Simmons, R., & Zakin, D. (1985). Satisfaction with body image for early adolescent females: The impact of pubertal timing within different school environments. *Journal of Youth and Adolescence, 14,* 207–227.

Bordo, S. (1993). *Unbearable weight: Feminism, Western culture, and the body.* Berkeley: University of California Press.

Brooks-Gunn, J., Attie, I., Burrow, C., Rosso, J., & Warren, M. (1989). The impact of puberty on body and eating concerns in athletic and nonathletic contexts. *Journal of Early Adolescence, 9,* 269–290.

Brooks-Gunn, J., & Warren, M . (1985). Effects of delayed menarche in different contexts: Dance and nondance students. *Journal of Youth and Adolescence, 14,* 285–300.

Brooks-Gunn, J., & Warren, M. (1989). Biological contributions to affective expression in young adolescent girls. *Child Development, 60,* 372–385.

Brown, L., & Gilligan, C. (1992). *Meeting at the crossroads.* Cambridge, MA: Harvard University Press.

Brownell, K., & Rodin, J. (1994). The dieting maelstrom: Is it possible and advisable to lose weight? *American Psychologist, 49,* 781–791.

Cattarin, J., & Thompson, J. K. (1994). A three-year longitudinal study of body image, eating disturbance, and general psychological functioning in adolescent females. *Eating Disorders: The Journal of Treatment and Prevention, 2,* 114–125.

Cicchetti, D., & Schneider-Rosen, K. (1986). An organizational approach to childhood depression. In M. Rutter, C. Izard, & P. Read (Eds.), *Depression in young people: Developmental and clinical perspectives* (pp. 71–134). New York: Guilford.

Crockett, L., & Petersen, A. (1987). Pubertal status and psychosocial development: Findings from the Early Adolescence Study. In R. Lerner & T. Foch (Eds.), *Biological-psychosocial interactions in early adolescence: A life-span perspective* (pp. 173–188). Hillsdale, NJ: Lawrence Erlbaum Associates.

Cytrynbaum, S., Blum, L., Patrick, R., Stein, J, Wadner, D., & Wilk, C. (1980). Midlife development: A personality and social systems perspective. In L. Poon (Ed.), *Aging in the 1980s* (pp. 463–474). Washington, DC: American Psychological Association.

Dorn, L., Crockett, L., & Petersen, A. (1988). The relations of pubertal status to intrapersonal changes in young adolescents. *Journal of Early Adolescence, 8,* 405–419.

Dornbusch, S., Carlsmith, J., Duncan, P., Gross, R., Martin, J., Ritter, P., & Siegel-Gorelik, B. (1984). Sexual maturation, social class, and the desire to be thin among adolescent females. *Journal of Developmental and Behavioral Pediatrics, 5,* 308–314.

Eccles, J., & Midgley, C. (1990). Changes in academic motivation and self-perception during early adolescence. In R. Montemayor, G. Adams, & T. Gullota (Eds.), *From childhood to adolescence: A transitional period?* (pp. 134–155). Newbury Park, CA: Sage.

Emmons, L. (1994). Predisposing factors differentiating adolescent dieters and nondieters. *Journal of the American Dietetic Association, 94,* 725–731.

Fabian, L., & Thompson, K. (1989). Body image and eating disturbance in young females. *International Journal of Eating Disorders, 9,* 63–74.

Friedlander, M., & Siegel, S. (1990). Separation–individuation difficulties and cognitive–behavior indicators of eating disorders among college women. *Journal of Counseling Psychology, 37,* 74–78.

Garner, D., Olmstead, M., & Polivy, J. (1983). Development and validation of a multidimensional eating disorder inventory for anorexia nervosa and bulimia. *International Journal of Eating Disorders, 2,* 15–34.

Garner, D., & Wooley, S. (1991). Confronting the failure of behavioral and dietary treatments for obesity. *Clinical Psychology Review, 11,* 729–780.

Ge, X., Lorenz, F., Conger, R., Elder, G., & Simons, R. (1994). Trajectories of stressful life events and depressive symptoms during adolescence. *Developmental Psychology, 30,* 467–483.

Gilligan, C. (1982). *In a different voice.* Cambridge, MA: Harvard University Press.

Gislason, I. L. (1988). Eating disorders in childhood. In B. Blinder, B. Chaitin, & R. Goldstein (Eds.), *The eating disorders: Medical and psychological bases of diagnosis and treatment* (pp. 285–293). New York: PMA.

Graber, J., Brooks-Gunn, J., Paikoff, R., & Warren, M. (1994). Prediction of eating problems: An eight year study of adolescent girls. *Developmental Psychology, 30,* 823–834.

Gralen, S., Levine, M. P., Smolak, L., & Murnen, S. (1990). Dieting and disordered eating during early and middle adolescence: Do the influences remain the same? *International Journal of Eating Disorders, 9,* 501–512.

Gross, R., & Duke, P. (1980). The effect of early versus late physical maturation on adolescent behavior. *Pediatric Clinics of North America, 27,* 71–77.

Gustafson-Larson, A. M., & Terry, R. D. (1992). Weight-related behaviors and concerns of fourth-grade children. *Journal of the American Dietetic Association, 92,* 818–822.

Halmi, K., Casper, R., Eckert, E., Goldberg, S., & Davis, J. (1979). Unique features associated with age of onset of anorexia nervosa. *Psychiatry Research, 1,* 209–215.

Hill, J. (1988). Adapting to menarche: Familial control and conflict. In M. Gunnar & W. A. Collins (Eds.), *Development during the transition to adolescence* (pp. 43–78). Hillsdale, NJ: Lawrence Erlbaum Associates.

Hirsch, B., & Rapkin, B. (1987). The transition to junior high school: A longitudinal study of self-esteem, psychological symptomatology, school life, and social support. *Child Development, 58,* 1235–1243.

Johnson, C., & Wonderlich, S. (1992). Personality characteristics as a risk factor in the development of eating disorders. In J. Crowther, D. Tennenbaum, S. Hobfoll, & M. Stephens (Eds.), *The etiology of bulimia nervosa: The individual and familial context* (pp. 179–196). Washington, DC: Hemisphere.

Killen, J., Hayward, C., Litt, I., Hammer, L., Wilson, D., Miner, B., Taylor, C., Varady, A., & Shisslak, C. (1992). Is puberty a risk factor for eating disorders? *American Journal of Diseases of Children, 146,* 323–325.

Killen, J., Hayward, C., Wilson, D., Taylor, C., Hammer, L., Litt, I., Simmonds, B., & Haydel, F. (1994). Factors associated with eating disorder symptoms in a community sample of 6th and 7th grade girls. *International Journal of Eating Disorders, 15,* 357–367.

Killen, J., Taylor, C., Hayward, C., Wilson, D., Hammer, L., Robinson, T., Litt, I., Simmonds, B., Haydel, F., Varady, A., & Kraemer, H. (1994). The pursuit of thinness and the onset of eating disorder symptoms in a community sample of adolescent girls: A three year prospective analysis. *International Journal of Eating Disorders, 16,* 227–238.

Koff, E. (1993, March). *Impact of early pubertal timing for eating disturbance in early and mid-adolescent girls.* Paper presented at the meeting of the Society for Research in Child Development, New Orleans, LA.

Koff, E., & Rierdan, J. (1991). Perceptions of weight and attitudes toward eating in early adolescent girls. *Journal of Adolescent Health, 12,* 307–312.

Koff, E., & Rierdan, J. (1993). Advanced pubertal development and eating disturbance in early adolescent girls. *Journal of Adolescent Health, 14,* 433–439.

Lapsley, D., Rice, K., & Shadid, G. (1989). Psychological separation and adjustment to college. *Journal of Counseling Psychology, 36,* 286–294.

Leon, G., Fulkerson, J., Perry, C., & Cudeck, R. (1993). Personality and behavioral vulnerabilities associated with risk status for eating disorders in adolescent girls. *Journal of Abnormal Psychology, 102,* 438–444.

Leon, G., Fulkerson, J., Perry, C., & Early-Zald, M. (1995). Prospective analysis of personality and behavioral vulnerabilities and gender influences in the later development of disorder eating. *Journal of Abnormal Psychology, 104,* 140–149.

Levenkron, S. (1978). *The best little girl in the world.* Chicago: Contemporary Books.

Levine, M. P., & Smolak, L. (1992). Toward a model of the developmental psychopathology of eating disorders: The example of early adolescence. In J. Crowther, D. Tennenbaum, S. Hobfoll, & M. Stephens (Eds.), *The etiology of bulimia nervosa: The individual and familial context* (pp. 59–80). Washington, DC: Hemisphere.

Levine, M. P., Smolak, L., & Hayden, H. (1994). The relation of sociocultural factors to eating attitudes and behaviors among middle school girls. *Journal of Early Adolescence, 14,* 471–490.

Levine, M. P., Smolak, L., Moodey, A., Shuman, M., & Hessen, L. (1994). Normative developmental challenges and dieting and eating disturbances in middle school girls. *International Journal of Eating Disorders, 15,* 11–20.

Levinson, D. (1978). *The seasons of a man's life.* New York: Knopf.

Lowe, M. (1993). The effects of dieting on eating behavior: A three factor model. *Psychological Bulletin, 114,* 100–121.

Marchi, M., & Cohen, P. (1990). Early childhood eating behavior and adolescent eating disorders. *Journal of the American Academy of Child and Adolescent Psychiatry, 29,* 112–117.

Marcia, J. (1980). Identity in adolescence. In J. Adelson (Ed.), *Handbook of adolescent psychology* (pp. 159–187). New York: Wiley.

Markus, H., Hamill, R., & Sentis, K. (1987). Thinking fat: Self-schemas for body weight and the processing of weight relevant information. *Journal of Applied Social Psychology, 17,* 50–71.

McBride, A. (1990). Mental health effects of women's multiple roles. *American Psychologist, 45,* 381–384.

Michael, R. (1994). *Sex in America: A definitive survey.* Boston: Little, Brown.

Offer, D., Ostruv, E., & Howard, K. (1984). The self-image of normal adolescents. In D. Offer, E. Ostruv, & K. Howard (Eds.), *Patterns of adolescent self-image* (pp. 5–18). San Francisco: Jossey-Bass.

Orenstein, P. (1994). *School girls: Young women, self-esteem, and the confidence gap.* New York: Doubleday.

Polivy, J., & Herman, C. P. (1993). Etiology of binge eating: Psychological mechanisms. In C. Fairburn & G. T. Wilson (Eds.), *Binge eating: Nature, assessment, and treatment* (pp. 173–205). New York: Guilford.

Richards, M., Abell, S., & Petersen, A. (1993). Biological development. In P. Tolan & B. Cohler (Eds.), *Handbook of clinical research and practice with adolescents* (pp. 21–44). New York: Wiley.

Richards, M., Casper, R., & Larson, R. (1990). Weight and eating concerns among pre- and young adolescent boys and girls. *Journal of Adolescent Health Care, 11,* 203–209.

Rodriguez-Tome, H., Bariaud, F., Zardi, M., Delmas, C., & Szlagyi, P. (1993). The effects of pubertal changes on body image and relations with peers of the opposite sex in adolescence. *Journal of Adolescence, 16,* 421–438.

Sadker, M., & Sadker, D. (1994). *Failing at fairness: How America's schools cheat girls.* New York: Scribner's.

Simmons, R., & Blyth, D. (1987). *Moving into adolescence: The impact of pubertal change and school context.* Hawthorne, NJ: Aldine.

Simmons, R., Blyth, D., & McKinney, K. (1983). The social and psychological effects of puberty on white females. In J. Brooks-Gunn & A. Petersen (Eds.), *Girls at puberty: Biological and psychosocial perspectives* (pp. 229–272). New York: Plenum.

Simmons, R., Burgeson, R., Carlton-Ford, S., & Blyth, D. (1987). The impact of cumulative change in early adolescence. *Child Development, 58,* 1220–1234.

Smolak, L. (1993). *Adult development.* Englewood Cliffs, NJ: Prentice-Hall.

Smolak, L., & Levine, M. P. (1993). Separation–individuation difficulties and the distinction between bulimia nervosa and anorexia nervosa in college women. *International Journal of Eating Disorders, 14,* 33–41.

Smolak, L., & Levine, M. P. (1994a). Critical issues in the developmental psychopathology of eating disorders. In L. Alexander & D. B. Lumsden (Eds.), *Understanding eating disorders* (pp. 37–60). Washington, DC: Taylor & Francis.

Smolak, L., & Levine, M. P. (1994b). Toward an empirical basis for primary prevention of eating problems with elementary school children. *Eating Disorders: The Journal of Treatment and Prevention, 2,* 293–307.

Smolak, L., Levine, M. P., & Gralen, S. (1993). The impact of puberty and dating on eating problems among middle school girls. *Journal of Youth & Adolescence, 22,* 355–368.

Sroufe, A. (1989). Pathways to adaptation and maladaptation: Psychopathology as developmental deviation. In D. Cicchetti (Ed.), *Rochester Symposium on Developmental Psychopathology: Vol. 1. The emergence of a discipline* (pp. 13–40). Hillsdale, NJ: Lawrence Erlbaum Associates.

Stattin, H., & Magnusson, D. (1990). *Pubertal maturation in female development.* Hillsdale, NJ: Lawrence Erlbaum Associates.

Steiner-Adair, C. (1986). The body politic: Normal female adolescent development and the development of eating disorders. *Journal of the American Academy of Psychoanalysis, 14,* 95–114.

Striegel-Moore, R. (1993). Etiology of binge eating: A developmental perspective. In C. Fairburn & G. T. Wilson (Eds.), *Binge eating: Nature, assessment, and treatment* (pp. 144–172). New York: Guilford.

Striegel-Moore, R. (1994). Toward a feminist agenda in the psychological research on eating disorders. In P. Fallon, M. Katzman, & S. Wooley (Eds.), *Eating disorders: Feminist perspectives* (pp. 438–454). New York: Guilford.

Striegel-Moore, R., & Marcus, M. (1995). Eating disorders in women: Current issues and debates. In A. Stanton & S. Gallant (Eds.), *Women's health* (pp. 454–490). Washington, DC: American Psychological Association.

Striegel-Moore, R., Schreiber, G., Pike, K., Wilfley, D., & Rodin, J. (1995). Drive for thinness in black and white preadolescent girls. *International Journal of Eating Disorders, 18,* 59–69.

Striegel-Moore, R., Silberstein, L., & Rodin, J. (1993). The social self in bulimia nervosa: Public self-consciousness, social anxiety, and perceived fraudulence. *Journal of Abnormal Psychology, 102,* 297–303.

Strober, M., & Humphrey, L. (1987). Familial contributions to the etiology and course of anorexia nervosa and bulimia. *Journal of Consulting and Clinical Psychology, 55,* 654–659.

Thompson, B. (1994). *A hunger so wide and so deep.* Minneapolis: University of Minnesota Press.

Timko, C., Striegel-Moore, R., Silberstein, L., & Rodin, J. (1987). Femininity/masculinity and disordered eating in women: How are they related? *International Journal of Eating Disorders, 6,* 701–712.

Tobin, D., Johnson, C., Steinberg, S., Staats, M., & Dennis, A. (1991). Multifactorial assessment of bulimia nervosa. *Journal of Abnormal Psychology, 100,* 14–21.

Tobin-Richards, M., Boxer, A., & Petersen, A. (1983). The psychological significance of pubertal change: Sex differences in perceptions of self during early adolescence. In J. Brooks-Gunn & A. Petersen (Eds.), *Girls at puberty: Biological and psychosocial perspectives* (pp. 127–154). New York: Plenum.

Vitousek, K., & Hollon, S. (1990). The investigation of schema content and processing of eating disorders. *Cognitive Therapy and Research, 14,* 191–214.

Waterman, A. (1982). Identity development from adolescence to adulthood: An extension of theory and a review of research. *Developmental Psychology, 18,* 341–358.

Woodside, D. B., & Garfinkel, P. (1992). Age of onset in eating disorders. *International Journal of Eating Disorders, 12,* 31–36.

Wooley, S., & Wooley, O. W. (1985). Intensive outpatient and residential treatment for bulimia. In D. Garner & P. Garfinkel (Eds.), *Handbook of psychotherapy for anorexia nervosa and bulimia* (pp. 391–430). New York: Guilford.

Yuker, H., & Allison, D. (1994). Obesity: Sociocultural perspectives. In L. Alexander & D. B. Lumsden (Eds.), *Understanding eating disorders* (pp. 243–270). Washington, DC: Taylor & Francis.

Zakin, D., Blyth, D., & Simmons, R. (1984). Physical attractiveness as a mediator of the impact of early pubertal changes of girls. *Journal of Youth and Adolescence, 13,* 439–450.

10

Media as a Context for the Development of Disordered Eating

Michael P. Levine
Linda Smolak

Dissatisfaction and envy constitute important ingredients in the business of selling transformation. . . . Being "self made" has given way to being "made over." Inspiring the work of the makeover are typifications of unobtainable/unsustainable beauty found in the fantasy of airbrushed, body sculpted models of cover girl perfection.

—Nichter & Nichter (1991, pp. 249–250)

That myths can persist despite conflicting evidence is illustrated by the robustness of the belief that television and other mass media have sizable impacts on the public's thoughts, feelings, and action even though most empirical studies indicate small to negligible effects. The general acceptance of the myth of sizable media impacts is understandable because it seems commonsensical and serves the needs of media friends and foes alike.

—McGuire (1986, p. 174)

In a recent study adolescent girls described the "ideal girl" as being 5'7", 100 pounds, size 5, with long blonde hair and blue eyes (Nichter & Nichter, 1991). The girls related this ideal to the "model look" found in teen magazines. This type of comment, heard in the context of critical analyses of sociocultural factors (Bordo, 1993; Kilbourne, 1994; Wolf, 1991), focuses attention on the role of mass media in the cultivation of unrealistic standards of beauty, body dissatisfaction, and disordered eating.

Ideally, this chapter would contain an outline of several prominent theories concerning mass media as a "context" in which disordered eating flourishes, a review of data bearing on these theories, and a critical evaluation of the theories and data. Unfortunately, this attractive scheme is undermined by a lack of clear and testable theory, and by limited empirical research. Many multidimensional models of disordered eating (e.g., Garfinkel & Garner, 1982) subsume mass media under the heading of "sociocultural (risk) factors" without a great deal of attention to mechanisms of influence. In more elaborate analyses media are construed as instruments of propaganda in the service of patriarchy and big business (Bordo, 1993; Wolf, 1991). Whatever theoretical consensus exists appears to revolve around two points. First, mass media both promote and reflect body shapes, styles of clothing, and other images that symbolize ("embody") complex themes of gender, race, class, beauty, identity, desire, success, and self-control in postindustrial societies (Bordo, 1993; Gordon, 1990; Kilbourne, 1994; Nichter & Nichter, 1991; Stice, 1994). Second, mass media are part of a sociocultural network—including families, peers, schools, athletics, business, and health care professionals—which generates and legitimizes a host of interlocking effects, primarily in females, that combine with various moderators (e.g., low self-esteem or a genetic propensity to obesity) to produce the continuum of eating disorders (Stice, 1994). Some of the proposed negative effects are listed in Table 10.1.

Given the status of current theory and research and the many complicated effects being proposed, we analyze the relation between mass media and disordered eating by addressing some ostensibly simple questions (after Harris, 1994):

1. What reason is there to suspect that media help provide a "context" in which the components and syndromes of disordered eating flourish?
2. Do content analyses support arguments about the nature and extent of messages that might contribute to disordered eating?
3. To what extent are females between the ages of 9 and 25, the population at risk for eating disorders, exposed to those mass media containing toxic messages?
4. What is the status of the evidence from correlational and experimental studies examining the impact of mass media or media images on that population?
5. Which theories within the field of mass communication, developmental psychology, and social psychology might guide theory and research toward an understanding of media effects?
6. What are the specific implications of current work on mass media for research on the etiology of eating disorders?

The "mass media" are publicly supported institutions and forms of communication that generate messages designed for a very large, very

TABLE 10.1
A Sample of the Proposed Negative Effects of Mass Media in Relation to
Eating Disorders

- Promotion of the importance (i.e., the reality) of image as substance
- Advocacy of individuality while restricting standards of physical beauty to a narrow range
- Creation of slenderness as the "gold standard" for a narrow range of ideal body shapes, which in turn creates widespread anxiety, self-consciousness, and dissatisfaction about body weight and body shape
- Glorification of slenderness as a testament to beauty, fitness, and feminine morality
- Promotion of slenderness as the path to social, sexual, and occupational success for women
- Open abhorrence of fat and fat women
- Emphasis on the possibility, desirability, and safety of personal transformation through fashion and dieting
- Establishment of gender roles based on impossible expectations
- Simultaneous dramatization and obfuscation of the issues of indulgence and self-control

heterogeneous, and essentially anonymous audience (Gerbner, Gross, Morgan, & Signorielli, 1994; Harris, 1994). The messages serve many purposes, including entertainment, education, government, and, of course, engagement of huge groups of people so that advertisers can sell them products. Children, adolescents, and adults interact with a wide variety of mass media, including television, music delivered by compact discs and radio, and telecommunications available through personal computers. In fact, books and articles about eating disorders in and of themselves constitute a form of mass media that may be contributing to proliferation of those disorders (Gordon, 1990; Murray, Touyz, & Beumont, 1990). In this chapter we focus on television and fashion magazines because they traffic in potentially powerful visual images, they are sustained by advertising, and they have been the target of considerable criticism by advocates of a sociocultural perspective in understanding eating disorders.

WHY STUDY MEDIA EFFECTS?

There are at least four provocative reasons to suspect that mass media play a role in the development and reinforcement of attitudes, goals, and practices that contribute to the continuum of disordered eating. First, it is quite common for patients with anorexia nervosa (AN) or bulimia nervosa (BN) to recall that models in fashion magazines have been a source of motivation and guidance in their quest for slenderness and self-control (see, e.g., Levine, 1987). Second, the epidemic prevalence among postpubertal females of drive for thinness, fear of fat, body dissatisfaction, and unhealthy weight management practices suggests the operation of mechanisms capable of reaching large numbers of people (Gordon, 1990; Polivy & Herman, 1987). Television in particular is one plausible source of social influence on the significant minority of American girls ages 8 through 11 who, despite not being overweight, worry about being "fat" or report having dieted (Smolak & Levine, 1994b). Third, analyses of historical changes in direct and indirect media messages about the importance of slenderness in the definition of ideal femininity during the 20th century reveal a strong positive correlation between periods of message intensification following women's political activism (e.g., during the 1920s and in the 1970s and 1980s) and an increased incidence of eating disorders (e.g., Garner, Garfinkel, Schwartz, & Thompson, 1980; Silverstein, Perdue, Peterson, & Kelly, 1986).

Finally, it is clear that marketing of images other than slenderness to populations other than girls and women can contribute to the spread of unhealthy behaviors other than calorie-restrictive dieting. Prime-time television programs, as well as the majority of commercials presented during network programming aimed at children, directly and indirectly promote foods high in calories and low in nutritional value (Liebert & Sprafkin, 1988; Story & Faulkner, 1990). As predicted by media influence theory, increased levels of television viewing are positively correlated with levels of obesity, between-meal snacking, consumption of nonnutritious foods, and children's attempts to influence what foods their parents purchase (Dietz, 1990; Jeffrey, McLellarn, & Fox, 1982; Story, 1990; but see Robinson et al., 1993). Goldberg, Gorn, and Gibson (1978, reviewed in Liebert & Sprafkin, 1988) showed that children exposed to commercials for sugared snacks and cereals were more likely than children who saw high-quality public service announcements for nutritious foods to choose sweet snacks when given a chance.

Research on television viewing and poor nutrition highlights the power of media to influence health. Compelling evidence for the power of *specific images* is found in studies demonstrating that media exposure influences initiation of tobacco use by adolescents. For example, Pierce et al. (1991) examined the efforts of the R.J. Reynolds Company to market Camel cigarettes via a multimedia campaign featuring cartoon camels. The greatest recognition of this advertising campaign occurred among 12- and 13-year-olds. The percentage of people who named Camel as the most advertised brand decreased appreciably over the teenage years and into early adulthood, whereas those naming Marlboro increased with age over adolescence. These trends are mirrored in brand preference. For those ages 12 through 17, 24.5% of the males and 21.7%

of the females preferred to purchase Camels, whereas the figures for those ages 18 through 24 were 12.7% for males and 5.5% for females (Pierce et al., 1991). Subsequent research by Pierce, Lee, and Gilpin (1994) focused on the intense advertising campaigns directed at "modern" women by Philip Morris (maker of Virginia Slims) and other companies from 1967 through 1974. During that period, initiation rates for 11- to 17-year-old girls rose dramatically as follows: 12-year-olds, 110%; 13-year-olds, 55%; 14-year-olds, 70%; 15-year-olds, 75%; 16-year-olds, 55%; and 17-year-olds, 35%. In that same period there was only a slight increase or no change for 12- to 17-year-old boys or among women 18 or older.

CONTENT ANALYSES

The Glorification of Slenderness

Models Appearing in Magazines. There is ample evidence that the prototypical female model appearing in fashion layouts and advertisements in women's magazines during the past 20 to 25 years is young (under 30 years old), tall, long-legged, and very slender. For example, by our count the 106 pages of the April 1994 issue of *Teen* magazine contain full-body or face plus part-body images of approximately 95 girls or women. None is the least bit heavy, only two are African Americans, and only two could be construed as having moderately substantial waists or hips. Silverstein, Peterson, and Perdue (1986) measured the curvaceousness of models appearing in *Ladies Home Journal* and *Vogue* from 1901 through 1980. The curvaceousness of these models declined sharply during the period between 1910 and 1930, rose again between 1930 and 1950, and then declined sharply during the 1960s to a steady low level at the end of that decade and throughout the 1970s.

Magazine Articles. Silverstein and colleagues also compared the number of articles dealing with body shape, dieting, and food or cooking that appeared in the 1980 issues of the four most widely circulated American women's magazines—*Family Circle, Ladies Home Journal, Redbook,* and *Woman's Day*—versus the four most widely circulated men's magazines—*Field and Stream, Playboy, Popular Mechanics,* and *Sports Illustrated* (Silverstein, Perdue, et al., 1986). The 48 issues of the women's magazines contained 63 ads for diet foods, 96 ads and articles about the body, 1,179 food ads, and 228 food articles, as compared with 1, 12, 15, and 10 in the men's magazines, respectively.

In a similar type of content analysis, Andersen and DiDomenico (1992) found that the 10 magazines read most by women in the fall of

1987 had 56 diet ads or articles and 20 muscle-building or "toning" ads or articles, as compared with the 5 and 17, respectively, for magazines read most by males. Thus, as predicted by a dose–response conception of media effects in relation to the gender difference in prevalence of eating disorders, there were 11 times as many diet ads or articles in magazines read predominantly by young women. This finding was replicated by Nemeroff, Stein, Diehl, and Smilack (1994) in their content analysis of articles appearing in half of the issues of *Good Housekeeping* and *Ladies Home Journal* ("traditional" women's magazines), *Cosmopolitan* and *Glamour* (fashion), and *New Woman* and *Ms.* (modern) published each year during 1980 to 1991 inclusive. Nemeroff et al. (1994) found that, although the number of fitness articles per 6-month period was similar for men's and women's magazines (3.28 and 4.77, respectively), in the women's magazines there were 13 times as many weight-loss articles and nearly 6 times as many articles on beauty.

Two studies have examined recent historical changes in the content of women's magazines. Building on data reported by Garner et al. (1980), Wiseman, Gray, Mosimann, and Ahrens (1992) demonstrated a significant increase over the 1959 to 1988 period in the number of diet, exercise, and diet and exercise articles in six women's magazines. It is noteworthy that the absolute number of diet and exercise articles is not large; for example, diet articles increased from approximately 0.5% of the total articles in the 1959 magazines to a peak of approximately 1.8% in 1981. Although the number of diet articles declined somewhat after 1981, there was an increase in articles that discussed diet and exercise together. Wiseman et al. (1992) interpreted this latter trend as arising from a cultural redefinition of approved methods of achieving weight loss and slenderness. However, this inference about exercise and its role in sustaining the glorification of slenderness is not supported by Nemeroff et al.'s (1994) finding that weight-loss articles, including those featuring exercise as a weight management technique, declined significantly between 1980 and 1991, especially in the fashion and modern magazines. The mean decrease was not dramatic (11.83 per 6-month period in the first 6 years vs. 9.53 in the second 6 years), but, coupled with a significant increase over time in health articles in the traditional and modern women's magazines, it may reflect an encouraging shift toward a healthier perspective (Nemeroff et al., 1994).

Television. Research has consistently demonstrated that the vast majority of female characters are thinner than the average American woman (Gonzalez-Lavin & Smolak, 1995; Kaufman, 1980; Silverstein, Perdue, et al., 1986). Fewer than 10% of women in television shows and commercials are overweight. Although overweight men are rarely seen in commercials, they are 2 to 5 times more common than overweight women as television characters (Kaufman, 1980; Silverstein, Perdue, et al., 1986). Gonzalez-Lavin and Smolak (1995) found that these effects appear to be even more pronounced on the television shows favored by middle school girls. Fully 94% of the female characters on these shows were below average in weight, and the median rating of body shape for the girls' favorite characters was 2.75 on a scale in which 4.5 represented the "average woman." Thus, as is the case for magazines, the range of female body shapes presented in magazines and on television is skewed toward slenderness in a manner that severely distorts the actual diversity of female shapes and symbolically obliterates fat women (Jasper, 1993).

Beauty and Success

Magazines. In addition to glorifying slenderness and weight loss, mass media may contribute to the development of eating disorders by emphasizing the importance of beauty and external appearance for girls and women over the substance of education, coping skills, assertion, and so forth (Jasper, 1993; Stice, 1994). For example, relative to portrayals of men, magazine advertisements are more likely to feature a woman's full body and to show her lying down or bending, rather than standing tall (Matlin, 1993). Several recent content analyses have shown that 45% to 52% of articles in teen fashion magazines such as *Sassy* and *Seventeen* focus on appearance, and only one third or less of the articles are devoted to identity and self-development issues (Evans, Rutberg, Sather, & Turner, 1991; Peirce, 1990).

Television. There is good reason to believe that television advertisements also frequently emphasize the importance of beauty for women (Bretl & Cantor, 1988; Matlin, 1993). Downs and Harrison (1985) studied all of the commercials (nearly 4,300) aired between 8:00 a.m. and 10:00 p.m. on the three major networks during a week in the spring of 1982. "Some form of attractiveness message was observed in one out of every 3.8 commercials" (p. 13), and 1 in 11 commercials contained "a direct message that beauty is good, important, valuable and so on" (p. 16). Although girls age 16 to 18 believe that commercials with "beauty messages" are less effective than commercials with other types of messages, these girls remember more about the beauty commercials (Tan, 1979). Ogletree, Williams, Raffeld, Mason, and Fricke (1990) found that even among the commercials supporting Saturday morning cartoons, 14% concerned the enhancement of physical appearance. Of these, 91% had a female voice-over and 86% were clearly intended for female consumers. In addition, more male than female characters were found in food commercials, whereas the reverse was true for appearance-related commercials.

EXPOSURE TO MEDIA

Magazines

There is no doubt that women's magazines (e.g., *Vogue, Glamour*) and magazines that target teenage girls (e.g., *Teen, Seventeen*) are readily available in many homes, libraries, bookstores, and offices. Here are some sample 1993 subscription figures (Winklepleck, Restum, & Strange, 1993): *Glamour,* 2,012,305; *Ladies Home Journal,* 5,001,739; *Seventeen,* 1,815,521. The scope of this distribution can be appreciated by comparing it to the 1,400 paid subscribers for the *International Journal of Eating Disorders.*

Subscription figures aside, it is surprisingly difficult to determine how often and how intently older children, adolescents, and young women "read" these magazines. Results from several convenience samples suggest that many college women frequently read women's magazines as a leisure activity (Richins, 1991; Then, 1992). Moreover, it appears that they do (sometimes against their better judgment) compare their own bodies to those of the models in order to inspire themselves toward self-improvement or to assure themselves that their own bodies are not all that bad.

In the fall of 1989, Teenage Research Unlimited (TRU) was commissioned by *Seventeen* magazine to survey a nationwide sample of 1,034 girls ages 12 to 19. TRU (1989) reported that 40% of the girls read *Seventeen,* and the figures for *Teen, Young Miss,* and *Sassy* were 32%, 30%, and over 20%, respectively. Overall, 83% of the girls in that age range reported spending an average of 4.3 hours reading magazines for pleasure or for school in the previous week.

However, the findings of TRU's survey are contradicted by Larson, Kubey, and Colletti's (1989) study of media choices by children ages 11 through 14. An activity sampling methodology revealed that during the school year these adolescents also spent approximately 1 to 4 hours per week reading nonschool material. However, most of that was the Bible, *Reader's Digest,* or a variety of fiction, not magazines such as *Seventeen.* In addition, Larson et al. found that for young adolescents, at least, reading magazines was not nearly as important and engaging an activity as watching TV or listening to music.

On the other hand, three recent studies support TRU's (1989) conclusions that a vast majority of White girls ages 12 to 19 read fashion or self-improvement magazines and that a sizable percentage read them frequently (Desmond, Price, Gray, & O'Connell, 1986; Evans, 1989; Levine, Smolak, & Hayden, 1994). For example, Levine et al. (1994) found that approximately 42% of the middle school girls in their sample both read fashion magazines frequently and reported that this medium was at least a "moderately important" source of information about beauty and fitness. In addition, 13% reported a high degree of interest in emulating the models shown in the magazines.

Television

Virtually every American household has at least one TV (Liebert & Sprafkin, 1988). In the average American household the TV is on, whether or not anyone is actually watching, for over 7 hours per day (Harris, 1994). Over the course of a typical year, children and adolescents spend more time watching television than any other activity except sleeping. This means, among other things, that the average person in the United States sees over 35,000 commercials per year.

According to Liebert and Sprafkin (1988), television viewing increases steadily from age 2 (approximately 1.5 hours per day) to age 4 (approximately 2.5 hours per day), levels off until age 8, and then increases steadily to around 4 hours per day at ages 11 to 12. At this age 95% of what is watched is intended for adults (Harris, 1994). Interestingly, in comparison with younger children and adolescents, children ages 10 to 12 spend the most time attending directly to the TV when it is on (Huston, Watkins, & Kunkel, 1989). There is a slight but steady decrease in viewing to around 3.5 hours per day at ages 15 to 16, perhaps as adolescents become more interested in music and peers and less interested in watching TV with the family (Harris, 1994; Larson et al., 1989; Liebert & Sprafkin, 1988). The typical adult still watches 2 to 3 hours per day (Harris, 1994; Liebert & Sprafkin, 1988).

Implications

Although much more research is needed, three of four studies suggest that at least 50% of adolescent girls regularly read magazines such as *Seventeen* or *Vogue*. There is also some evidence that middle school and younger high school girls (ages 11–15) read magazines more frequently than do older adolescents, and that they express greater interest in the magazines' messages about beauty, style, and fitness. Three associated facts are potentially relevant for understanding (and preventing) negative effects of media. First, this high level of involvement with one type of medium occurs at approximately the same ages as do peak levels of exposure and attentiveness to another medium, TV, which also emphasizes the importance of appearance and slenderness for females. Second, this peak in magazine reading occurs not too long after social comparison begins to be used for purposes of self-evaluation (Ruble, 1983). Third, this also coincides with the period during which girls' self-perceptions of physical attractiveness (and self-esteem in general) is in full decline (see, e.g., Abramowitz, Petersen, & Schulenberg, 1984). In this regard it is noteworthy that approximately one third of the ninth-grade girls (ages 14 to 15) in Desmond et al.'s (1986) study reported that television was a leading source of information about weight control. The level of exposure to fashion magazines in children ages (say) 9 to 11 is unknown, but there is no doubt that they watch a lot of television.

MEDIA EXPOSURE, BODY IMAGE, AND DISORDERED EATING

Many theorists have contended (or assumed) that the media's constant and salient equating of slenderness with beauty and success has a powerful and adverse effect on the ideal body shape and resultant body satisfaction of most, if not all, young girls and women (Garner, Rockert, Olmsted, Johnson, & Coscina, 1985; Jasper, 1993; Kilbourne, 1994; Nichter & Nichter, 1991; Wolf, 1991). Research has shown that body image is indeed sensitive to manipulation by images and symbols (Haimovitz, Lansky, & O'Reilly, 1993) and that some people are characteristically predisposed to compare their physical appearance to that of other people (Thompson, Heinberg, & Tantleff, 1991). In addition, Martin and Kennedy (1993, 1994a, 1994b) used both self-report questionnaire items and a projective story-telling test to demonstrate that a clear majority of the 4th-, 8th-, and 12th-grade females in their sample thought about self-comparison and self-enhancement in association with reading magazines and looking at models. As was the case for the women in Then's (1992) study of Stanford students, a clear majority of the girls in each grade also associated negative self-evaluation with the process of reading magazines, noticing how pretty the models are, and thinking about or comparing oneself to the models. However, demonstrating that a significant number of girls and women attend to and compare themselves unfavorably with models in ads is one thing; demonstrating that media help to create negative body image, drive for thinness, and disordered eating is another matter entirely.

Correlational Studies

Content analyses such as those by Andersen and DiDomenico (1992) and by Silverstein, Perdue, et al. (1986) seem to assume a positive linear correlation between the amount of exposure to media glorification of slenderness and the level of disordered eating. The evidence for this proposition is limited, but more recent and more rigorous analyses do provide support for the hypothesized relationship.

Abramson and Valene's (1991) study of a small sample of women attending an American college indicated that frequency of media exposure was not significantly correlated with bulimic behavior, dietary restraint scores, or attitudes about fat. Similarly, insofar as Edwards-

Hewitt and Gray (1993) reported no statistics involving their measure of hours of TV per week watched by their college sample, we assume that it was uncorrelated with the various measures of dietary restraint and eating problems. On the other hand, Martin and Kennedy (1993) found that for their sample of 4th-, 8th-, and 12th-grade girls, a two-item measure of the tendency to compare self with advertising models was negatively correlated to a moderate degree ($r = -.48$) with self-reported physical attractiveness.

In the most sophisticated cross-sectional study to date, Stice, Schu-pak-Neuberg, Shaw, and Stein (1994) applied structural equation modeling to test their hypothesis that high(er) levels of media exposure promote disordered eating directly, as well as through two indirect paths involving internalization of the thin ideal body shape. Nearly 240 women attending Arizona State University (mean age = 20) completed a battery of questionnaires, including the Eating Attitudes Test and a measure both of how many magazines they had "looked at" in the past month and of the number of hours of "comedy, drama, and game shows" that they had watched. Although the univariate correlation between media exposure and eating disorder symptomology was only +.25, within the path analysis the direct and indirect relationships between the two variables accounted for 43.5% of the variance in the latter. The existence of a direct connection implies the operation of social learning variables (e.g., modeling of dieting behavior and incentives for it) unrelated to assimilation of the slender ideal of beauty. Interestingly, the only indirect path to emerge (within the limits automatically imposed by the set of variables chosen) suggested the following chain of mediating associations: media exposure leading to endorsement of the stereotypical feminine gender role, leading to internalization of a slender ideal body shape, leading to body dissatisfaction, leading to eating disorder symptoms. Thus, this study points to a strong relationship between media exposure and eating disorder symptomatology. It also suggests the existence of several possible mediators, none of which involve the *direct* assimilation of slenderness as a personal standard of beauty.

Given the great involvement of girls ages 11 through 14 with magazines and television, it is highly likely that there is also a significant correlation between their interpretation (and use) of those media, on the one hand, and negative body image and disordered eating, on the other. Recently, our group conducted two large-scale survey studies of middle school girls that confirm this association. In the first (Levine et al., 1994) stepwise multiple regressions controlling for age revealed that the extent to which the girls reported magazine advertisements and articles as influencing their ideal shape and how to obtain it (e.g., through diet and exercise) was highly correlated with measures of weight management behavior (25% of the variance explained), disordered eating (35%), and investment in thinness (41%). In the second study (Gonzalez-Lavin

& Smolak, 1995) self-reported number of hours of TV watched was unrelated to either dieting or disordered eating, but girls who watched 8 or more hours per week reported significantly greater body dissatisfaction than did those girls who watched less. Moreover, the linear combination of how much girls thought their conceptions of beauty and of shape management were influenced by TV and perceived peer investment in dieting accounted for moderate proportions of the variance in disordered eating (22%), weight management behavior (30%), and body dissatisfaction (11%).

In the Levine et al. (1994) study, girls with high scores on the magazine influence measure and on measures of peer and family investment in thinness and dieting had very high scores on the measure of disordered eating. This finding, coupled with the regression data from Gonzalez-Lavin and Smolak (1995), suggests that some middle school girls find and place themselves in a "subculture of dieting" reflecting the intersection of consistent messages from family, peers, and media (Levine et al., 1994). This possibility is particularly intriguing in light of the finding that girls ages 13 to 15 who have greater weight and eating concerns also report more daily dysphoric affect, lower levels of psychological arousal and self-esteem, and less time spent in social activities with friends (Richards, Casper, & Larson, 1990). This might well predispose these girls to more media exposure, more negative comparison of self with models in the magazines, increased dissatisfaction, and so on.

Experimental Studies With Eating Disordered Participants

It is tempting to conclude that our research and that of Martin and Kennedy (1993) and Stice et al. (1994) confirm that some young girls and young women who look to media for guidance about beauty encounter a glorification of slenderness and dietary restraint that in turn stimulates body dissatisfaction, a drive for thinness, and potentially unhealthy weight management behavior. However, this type of correlational study cannot rule out the distinct possibility that girls (or women) with a high drive for thinness find it useful to consult fashion magazines or other media for guidance in constructing an ideal shape, for weight loss advice, or for personal inspiration (see Smolak, chapter 2, this volume, for a discussion of what longitudinal designs can and cannot do for efforts to establish direction of effects). Consequently, a number of investigators have conducted controlled experiments to examine the *immediate* impact of media portrayals of slender beauty on conceptions of beauty and on evaluations of one's own shape.

Waller, Hamilton, and Shaw (1992) studied the effects of exposure to 20 photographs of female bodies as shown in fashion magazines versus exposure to 20 neutral images (e.g., beautiful homes) on the visual body size estimations of 11 women with AN, 13 women with BN, and 40 comparison women. Relative to the effect of the neutral condition, exposure to photographs of fashion models resulted in a significant increase in body size overestimation by the eating-disordered groups, whereas there was no difference between the two conditions for the comparison group. Following only 6 to 7 minutes of exposure to slides of slender models, women with eating disorders increased their body size overestimation an average of 25%. This effect occurs only in response to "whole-body" pictures of the models, not to "head-only" pictures (Waller et al., 1994, cited in Shaw & Waller, 1995). In a subsequent study Sumner, Waller, Killick, and Elstein (1993) found that early in pregnancy women overestimated only their stomach size after seeing the slender models, whereas later in pregnancy they overestimated the size of their entire body. Both of these studies indicate that media images of slenderness do not immediately precipitate body shape distortion, but instead exacerbate it in those who have an unstable body image or who are already anxious about some aspect(s) of body shape (Shaw & Waller, 1995).

However, an oft-cited study by Irving (1990) provides only slight support for this vulnerability model. Consistent with Waller's studies, Irving found that increasing levels of bulimic symptoms in college women were strongly associated with an increased perception of pressure to be thin, and that the most pressure was seen as coming from media, followed by peers, and then family. Yet bulimic participants did not respond differentially to slides of slender or heavy models in comparison to a no-slide condition. In fact, across all levels of bulimic symptomatology, exposure to slides of thin models had no effect whatsoever on self-esteem or weight satisfaction *relative to the no-exposure condition.* Moreover, in contradiction to their previous studies, Waller et al. (1994, cited in Shaw & Waller, 1995) also found that watching 6 to 7 minutes of televised images of "ideal women's bodies" produced no immediate effect on the body images of eating-disordered or non-eating-disordered women.

Experimental Studies With Nonclinical Samples

Then (1992) found that 68% of a small sample of undergraduate and graduate women at Stanford University said they felt worse about their own looks after reading women's magazines. Similarly, approximately 70% of a small sample of women attending the University of Massachusetts reported that at least half the time they compared themselves to the models they saw in clothing ads (Richins, 1991). Roughly 33% agreed that ads for clothing made them feel dissatisfied with their looks, and nearly 50% agreed that they had wished that they looked more like the models in personal care and cosmetics advertisements.

According to social comparison theory, people are motivated both to evaluate and to improve their own opinions, abilities, and looks (Festinger, 1954, as reviewed and extended by Wood, 1989; see also Martin & Kennedy, 1994b). When objective standards are unavailable, as in the case of beauty, people tend to compare themselves either with similar others or with social "comparisons that impinge on the individual, whether or not he or she has 'selected' them" (Wood, 1989, p. 233).

The important issue of when a person selects someone similar (e.g., a peer), as opposed to someone dissimilar (e.g., an older, elite fashion model), for comparison and self-evaluation is poorly understood. Based on Wood's (1989) extensive review of the literature, it appears that when a previously familiar dimension is being evaluated in a new context, people may "consult" a wider range of comparison individuals who are similar on a variety of unrelated dimensions. For example, White middle school girls who are beginning to evaluate their attractiveness in the context of boy–girl interactions may look to and be influenced by fashion models who are young, White, and apparently interested successfully in boys and fashion. Such comparison with "extreme positives" may facilitate long-term self-improvement through attention to learning cues or through inspiration (Martin & Kennedy, 1994b). However, in a yet another twist within what is clearly a tricky area of theory and research, when the dimension in question (e.g., slenderness) is very relevant to the person and when immediate self-enhancement (ego protection) is the goal, there seems to be a preference in favor of downward rather than upward comparisons (Wood, 1989).

We were able to locate eight controlled studies (reporting a total of 11 experiments) that have examined whether exposure to pictures of attractive women raises the standards of attractiveness and also lowers the self-perceptions of non-eating-disordered girls and women (a table summarizing these studies is available on request from the authors). Six experiments reported in Kenrick and Gutierres (1980), Martin and Kennedy (1993), and Richins (1991) are consistent in demonstrating that exposure to pictures of an attractive woman raises the viewer's standards for judging other women whose pictures are rated a short time later. However, in four single-experiment studies that included female participants ranging from 4th grade to college, viewing pictures of slender models had no significant effect on peresonal ratings of weight and figure satisfaction, attractiveness, or body size (Irving, 1990; Martin & Kennedy, 1993; Myers & Biocca, 1992; Waller et al., 1992). Furthermore, in the three studies (comprising four experiments) that did demonstrate such an effect on self-ratings for college students, the effects were either very small (Richins, 1991, Experiment 1; Stice & Shaw, 1994); limited to the comparison between the effects of thin versus average-size models (with no effect for thin model vs. a no-model control; Stice & Shaw, 1994); or confined to decreased ratings of overall appearance *but not of satisfaction with body or figure* (Cash, Cash, & Butters, 1983; Richins, 1991, Experiment 2). Collectively, this literature provides little support for the commonly expressed belief that perusal of the photographs of slender models accompanying articles and advertisements in fashion magazines makes girls and women *immediately* feel worse about their own bodies and their own attractiveness in general. However, the impact of these pictures on girls and women who actually *choose* to read the magazines for various reasons related to social comparison (e.g., self-evaluation) has not yet been studied. In this regard, Shaw and Waller (1995) offered some preliminary evidence that media images of slenderness have the greatest effect on those adolescent girls (and not adult women) whose personality predisposes them to make social comparisons. Finally, it remains a distinct possibility that media exposure increases the risk for disordered eating because repeated exposure promotes internalization of standards of beauty and attitudes about slenderness and fat that are unrelated to immediate perceptions and feelings about one's body shape (Stice, 1994; Stice et al., 1994). To test this hypothesis, laboratory experiments in the tradition of social comparison theory need to be discarded in favor of longitudinal designs (see Smolak, chapter 2, this volume).

POTENTIALLY USEFUL THEORIES FROM THE FIELD OF MASS COMMUNICATIONS

Based on the preceding review of the literature, it is possible that theorists have grossly overestimated the impact of media as primary contributors to body image, weight management behavior, and disordered eating. It is also possible that much more research needs to be done in accordance with models that have guided the study of media influences within the field of mass communication. Two potentially useful approaches are cultivation theory, which emphasizes the cumulative and insidious effects of content (and omissions), and uses and gratifications theory, which focuses on the interaction between content and the viewer's motives and contexts.

Cultivation Theory

This model, developed by Gerbner and colleagues (1994), begins with the assumption that "television is the source of the most broadly shared images and messages in history. It is the mainstream of the common symbolic environment into which our children are born and in which we all live out our lives" (Gerbner et al., 1994, p. 17; see also Signorielli & Morgan, 1990). The constant repetition of certain forms and themes (values), as well as the constant omission of certain types of people, actions, and stories, powerfully influences and homogenizes viewers' conceptions of social reality. Most people in the eating disorders field are familiar with cognitive social learning theory and its emphasis on modeling of attitudes and behavior and on provision of vicarious incentives. According to cultivation theory, however, the effect of heavy use of television, magazines, and other mass media is to gradually establish and reinforce a preference for certain beliefs about the nature of reality (Gerbner et al., 1994; Potter, 1991).

Thus, the focus of cultivation research has been the ways in which individual differences in the amount of television watching (heavy vs. light viewing) contribute to differential assimilation of television's "lessons" about social and physical reality. This approach has been fruitful in understanding several phenomena, including one related to disordered eating, namely gender stereotyping (see, e.g., reviews in Signorielli & Morgan, 1990). For example, a longitudinal study by Morgan (1982; cited in Van Ezra, 1990) found that adolescent girls, but not boys, who were heavy viewers had higher sexism scores a year later; significantly, there was no indication that initial sex-typing led to heavier viewing a year later. Just the reverse was true for boys. Interestingly, it was found that those girls who were otherwise least likely to have traditional views reflected the greatest impact of heavier TV viewing, which illustrates the mainstreaming effect of media exposure.

It is not surprising, given both the complexity of the cognitive processes involved in cultivation and the tremendous variability across television programs and viewers, that this theory has been subjected to important empirical and theoretical criticism (Harris, 1994; Potter, 1991; Van Ezra, 1990). Nevertheless, we recommend its application to research on media and disordered eating. Advocates of a sociocultural perspective in the understanding and prevention of eating disorders, ourselves included, proceed from a number of assumptions. First magazines and other media grossly distort the diversity of human body shapes and weight, associating slenderness with beauty, success, and femininity (see Table 10.1). Second, repeated exposure year after year to these images and lessons leads readers and viewers to overestimate both the actual prevalence and the value of those shapes, as well as the mutability of the human body. Third, those who endorse these cognitive–emotional "distortions" are more likely to have a negative body image and to engage in unhealthy weight and shape management practices. Finally, media have a particularly insidious effect when they are construed as mere diversions, when portrayals (e.g., of women's bodies) are accepted uncritically as realistic, and when there are few alternatives to, and multiple sources of reinforcement for, media standards (Bordo, 1993; Harris, 1994; Kilbourne, 1994; Levine et al., 1994; Stice, 1994). Research reviewed earlier leaves little doubt that the first proposition is true, but aside from a study with middle school girls that is currently under way in our laboratory, we know of no studies that have explicitly and carefully tested the second and third propositions. These propositions are considered gospel by most eating disorders theorists concerned with prevention; thus, there is a real need for research based on the cultivation model.

Such research will sooner or later need to acknowledge not only the multiple steps involved in the cultivation of attitudes and behavior (Potter, 1991), but also the role of developmental factors. Van Ezra (1990) noted cultivation theory's assumption that because heavy users are less selective and more automatic in their engagement with media, they experience (and possibly encode) more redundancy in content. If this is the case, Van Ezra argued, young children should be particularly susceptible to the effects of heavy viewing because they have a limited knowledge base, limited access to competing information, and a greater tendency to perceive the content of TV as "realistic." Nevertheless, some research has shown adolescents to be more vulnerable to heavy viewing. This suggests an important role for the cognitive capacity to extract social beliefs from repetitive information (Van Ezra, 1990), or perhaps for the increasing tendency in adolescence to look outside of the family for the information necessary to "fit in" with peers (see Berndt & Hestenes, chapter 4, this volume).

Uses and Gratifications Theory

Cultivation theory focuses on the ways in which artists, programmers, and advertisers use media to mechanically constrict and influence the symbolic environment of "the audience." In contrast, uses and gratifications theory emphasizes the role of individuals within the audience in making choices about when to watch, what to watch, how long to pay attention (e.g., to an advertisement), the context of viewing, and how to use the information communicated (Rubin, 1994). Media content is important (and at times may be very important), but the effects of content are determined by, at a minimum, what the "user" hopes to obtain from a particular medium, schematic predispositions in information processing, and the consequences of assimilating and putting into practice the information extracted (Rubin, 1994).

As discussed previously, there is some evidence that young adolescent girls who look to fashion magazines and television for guidance about fashion, beauty, and weight management show a strong tendency to report greater and less healthy concerns with weight and shape (Gonzalez-Lavin & Smolak, 1995; Levine et al., 1994). In another recent study we found preliminary support for the existence of subgroups of non-obese elementary school girls who have either a dieting history, a belief that slenderness is an important component of attractiveness, or both (Smolak & Levine, 1994b). In chapter 9 of this volume we review theory and research demonstrating that the pubertal transition is an important phenomenon for understanding the emergence of negative body image, unhealthy weight management practices, and disordered eating in adolescent girls. Seen from the perspective of uses and gratifications theory, these three findings point directly to the need for longitudinal research to assess the interplay between (a) childhood schema and motives in regard to weight and shape, (b) pubertal development, and (c) orientation toward and use of media such as television and magazines prior to and during puberty (Levine et al., 1994; Smolak & Levine, 1994a). At the very least, research on media use by girls and women and its effects on them needs to acknowledge, as social comparison theory has done for some time (Martin & Kennedy, 1993; Wood, 1989), the role of different motives for involvement.

CONCLUSIONS AND IMPLICATIONS

School-based curricula for the prevention of eating disorders tend to include at least one lesson on understanding and resisting media pressure for slenderness, for self-consciousness about weight and shape, and for weight management behavior (see Killen, chapter 13, this volume; Shisslak, Crago, Estes, & Gray, chapter 14, this volume). Such lessons are predicated on successful approaches to preventing initiation of substance use by young adolescents (Dryfoos, 1990) and on the unquestioned assumption that media such as magazines and television contribute to and reinforce unhealthy messages about weight, shape, gender, and so forth. Programs for the primary prevention of eating disorders have been notably unsuccessful in changing the attitudes and behaviors of adolescents, even when such programs are implemented and evaluated by experts in prevention (Killen et al., 1993; Rosen, 1989). Interestingly, such failures are typically not attributed to faulty assumptions or inadequate knowledge about the paths to disordered eating; if anything, they are seen as reflecting the monstrous impact of monolithic sociocultural factors such as media.

With respect to media effects, our review of the literature suggests three conclusions. First, the contention that media play a role in the development and consolidation of negative body image and other factors contributing to disordered eating is supported by (a) research on the role of media in the initiation and maintenance of other unhealthy behavior in children and adolescents, (b) content analyses of various magazine and televised "messages" that glorify slenderness and weight loss, and (c) preliminary data indicating that fashion magazines and television are psychologically significant in the lives of two at-risk groups: young adolescents and young women attending college.

Second, data from experimental studies in general provide precious little evidence that exposure to the aforementioned content immediately increases body dissatisfaction in females who are not already processing that content in terms of well-established weight and shape concerns. For those girls and women who do bring such a predisposition (schema) to their use of media, exposure to slender models and weight-loss messages is very likely to exacerbate their conflicts and problems. At present the nature of that schema remains a tantalizing mystery (Smolak & Levine, 1994a, 1994b). Furthermore, there is currently no research that examines the role of media or of other sociocultural factors in the development of such a predisposition in children or adolescents.

Third, there is a great deal of theorizing and media criticism available, but far too little systematic research.

These conclusions do not demolish the argument that media portrayals of feminine beauty and success are an important aspect of the contexts in which unhealthy weight and shape concerns and disordered eating develop. Nor do these conclusions contradict research indicating that prevention efforts are facilitated by changes in media messages (Rice & Atkin, 1994) and by efforts to teach females and males how to think critically about media (Brown, 1991; Nichter & Nichter, 1991). The material reviewed does, however, constitute a plea for basic research grounded in clear and testable hypotheses about media influence (see, e.g., Stice et al., 1994) *and* in the wealth of experience provided by paradigms and problems in both mass communication and developmental psychology (Bryant & Zillmann, 1994; Harris, 1994; Smolak & Levine, 1994a; Van Ezra, 1990). As Striegel-Moore (personal communication, November 23, 1994) noted, at some point in its development this line of theory and research will need to confront the question of how media exposure contributes to obesity in some instances and eating disorders in others.

The image of the desirable women is posed as the model of success. She is a painfully familiar sight, appearing before us in the mass media and reflected in the expectations of others. There are few women who have not negotiated some relationship with her.

—Tolman & Debold (1994, p. 302)

REFERENCES

Abramowitz, R. H., Petersen, A., & Schulenberg, J. E. (1984). Changes in self-image during early adolescence. In D. Offer, E. Ostrov, & K. I. Howard (Eds.), *Patterns of adolescent self-image* (pp. 19–28). San Francisco: Jossey-Bass.

Abramson, E., & Valene, P. (1991). Media use, dietary restraint, bulimia, and attitudes toward obesity: A preliminary study. *British Review of Bulimia and Anorexia Nervosa, 5,* 73–76.

Andersen, A. E., & DiDomenico, L. (1992). Diet vs. shape content of popular male and female magazines: A dose–response relationship to the incidence of eating disorders. *International Journal of Eating Disorders, 11,* 283–287.

Bordo, S. (1993). *Unbearable weight: Feminism, Western culture, and the body.* Berkeley: University of California Press.

Bretl, D. J., & Cantor, J. (1988). The portrayal of men and women in U.S. television commercials: A recent content analysis and trend over 15 years. *Sex Roles, 18,* 595–608.

Brown, J. A. (1991). *Television "critical viewing skills" education: Major media literacy projects in the United States and selected countries.* Hillsdale, NJ: Lawrence Erlbaum Associates.

Bryant, J., & Zillmann, D. (Eds.). (1994). *Media effects: Advances in theory and research.* Hillsdale, NJ: Lawrence Erlbaum Associates.

Cash, T. F., Cash, D. W., & Butters, J. W. (1983). "Mirror, mirror, on the wall...?": Contrast effects and self-evaluations of physical attractiveness. *Personality and Social Psychology Bulletin, 9,* 351–358.

Desmond, S. M., Price, J. H., Gray, N., & O'Connell, J. K. (1986). The etiology of adolescents' perceptions of their weight. *Journal of Youth and Adolescence, 15,* 461–474.

Dietz, W. H. (1990). You are what you eat—What you eat is what you are. *Journal of Adolescent Health Care, 11,* 76–81.

Downs, A. C., & Harrison, S. K. (1985). Embarrassing age spots or just plain ugly? Physical attractiveness stereotyping as an instrument of sexism on American television commercials. *Sex Roles, 13,* 9–19.

Dryfoos, J. G. (1990). *Adolescents at risk: Prevalence and prevention.* New York: Oxford University Press.

Edwards-Hewitt, T., & Gray, J. (1993). The prevalence of disordered eating attitudes and behaviors in Black-American and White-American college women: Ethnic, regional, class, and media differences. *Eating Disorders Review, 1,* 41–54.

Evans, E. D. (1989, April). *Adolescent females' utilization and perception of contemporary teen magazines.* Paper presented at the meeting of the Society for Research in Child Development, Kansas City, MO.

Evans, E. D., Rutberg, J., Sather, C., & Turner, C. (1991). Content analyses of contemporary teen magazines for adolescent females. *Youth & Society, 23,* 99–120.

Garfinkel, P. E., & Garner, D. M. (1982). *Anorexia nervosa: A multidimensional approach.* New York: Brunner/Mazel.

Garner, D. M., Garfinkel, P. E., Schwartz, D., & Thompson, M. (1980). Cultural expectations of thinness in women. *Psychological Reports, 47,* 483–491.

Garner, D. M., Rockert, W., Olmsted, M. P., Johnson, C. G., & Coscina., D. V. (1985). Psychoeducational principles in the treatment of bulimia and anorexia nervosa. In D. M. Garner & P. E. Garfinkel (Eds.), *Handbook of psychotherapy for anorexia nervosa and bulimia* (pp. 513–572). New York: Guilford.

Gerbner, G., Gross, L., Morgan, M., & Signorielli, N. (1994). Growing up with television: The cultivation perspective. In J. Bryant & D. Zillmann (Eds.), *Media effects: Advances in theory and research* (pp. 17–41). Hillsdale, NJ: Lawrence Erlbaum Associates.

Gonzalez-Lavin, A., & Smolak, L. (1995, March). *Relationships between televison and eating problems in middle school girls.* Paper presented at the meeting of the Society for Research in Child Development, Indianapolis, IN.

Gordon, R. A. (1990). *Anorexia and bulimia: Anatomy of a social epidemic.* Cambridge, MA: Basil Blackwell.

Haimovitz, D., Lansky, L. M., & O'Reilly, P. (1993). Fluctuations in body satisfaction across situations. *International Journal of Eating Disorders, 13,* 77–84.

Harris, R. J. (1994). *A cognitive psychology of mass communication* (2nd ed.). Hillsdale, NJ: Lawrence Erlbaum Associates.

Huston, A. C., Watkins, B. A., & Kunkel, D. (1989). Public policy and children's television. *American Psychologist, 44,* 424–433.

Irving, L. M. (1990). Mirror images: Effects of the standard of beauty on the self- and body-esteem of women exhibiting varying levels of bulimic symptoms. *Journal of Social and Clinical Psychology, 9,* 230–242.

Jasper, K. (1993). Monitoring and responding to media messages. *Eating Disorders, 1,* 109–114.

Jeffrey, D. B., McLellarn, R. W., & Fox, D. T. (1982). The development of children's eating habits: The role of television commercials. *Health Education Quarterly, 9,* 174–189.

Kaufman, L. (1980). Prime-time nutrition. *Journal of Communication, 30,* 37–46.

Kenrick, D. T., & Gutierres, S. E. (1980). Contrast effects and judgments of physical attractiveness: When beauty becomes a social problem. *Journal of Personality and Social Psychology, 38,* 131–140.

Kilbourne, J. (1994). Still killing us softly: Advertising and the obsession with thinness. In P. Fallon, M. A. Katzman, & S. C. Wooley (Eds.), *Feminist perspectives on eating disorders* (pp. 395–418). New York: Guilford.

Killen, J. D., Taylor, C., Hammer, L., Litt, I., Wilson, D., Rich, T., Hayward, C., Simmonds, B., Kraemer, H., & Varady, A. (1993). An attempt to modify unhealthful eating attitudes and weight regulation practices of young adolescent girls. *International Journal of Eating Disorders, 13,* 369–384.

Larson, R., Kubey, R., & Colletti, J. (1989). Changing channels: Early adolescent media choices and shifting investments in family and friends. *Journal of Youth and Adolescence, 18,* 583–599.

Levine, M. P. (1987). *Student eating disorders: Anorexia nervosa and bulimia.* Washington, DC: National Education Association.

Levine, M. P., Smolak, L., & Hayden, H. (1994). The relation of sociocultural factors to eating attitudes and behaviors among middle school girls. *Journal of Early Adolescence, 14,* 472–491.

Liebert, R. M., & Sprafkin, J. (1988). *The early window: Effects of television on children and youth* (3rd ed.). New York: Pergamon.

Martin, M. C., & Kennedy, P. F. (1993). Advertising and social comparison: Consequences for female preadolescents and adolescents. *Psychology & Marketing, 10,* 513–530.

Martin, M. C., & Kennedy, P. F. (1994a). The measurement of social comparison to advertising models: A gender gap revealed. In J. A. Costa (Ed.), *Gender issues in consumer behavior* (pp. 104–124). Thousand Oaks, CA: Sage.

Martin, M. C., & Kennedy, P. F. (1994b). Social comparison and the beauty of advertising models: The role of motives for comparison. *Advances in Consumer Research, 21,* 365–371.

Matlin, M. W. (1993). *The psychology of women* (2nd ed.). Fort Worth, TX: Harcourt Brace Jovanovich.

McGuire, W. J. (1986). The myth of massive media impact: Savagings and salvagings. In G. Comstock (Ed.), *Public communication and behavior* (Vol. 1, pp. 173–254). New York: Academic Press.

Murray, S., Touyz, S., & Beumont, P. (1990). Knowledge about eating disorders in the community. *International Journal of Eating Disorders, 9,* 87–93.

Myers, P. N., Jr., & Biocca, F. A. (1992). The elastic body image: The effect of television advertising and programming on body image distortion in young women. *Journal of Communication, 42,* 108–133.

Nemeroff, C. J., Stein, R. I., Diehl, N. S., & Smilack, K. M. (1994). From the Cleavers to the Clintons: Role choices and body orientation as reflected in magazine article content. *International Journal of Eating Disorders, 16*, 167–176.

Nichter, M., & Nichter, M. (1991). Hype and weight. *Medical Anthropology, 13*, 249–284.

Ogletree, S. M., Williams, S. W., Raffeld, P., Mason, B., & Fricke, K. (1990). Female attractiveness and eating disorders: Do children's television commercials play a role? *Sex Roles, 22*, 791–797.

Peirce, K. (1990). A feminist theoretical perspective on the socialization of teenage girls through *Seventeen* magazine. *Sex Roles, 23*, 491–500.

Pierce, J. P., Gilpin, E., Burns, D. M., Whalen, E., Rosbrook, B., Shopland, D., & Johnson, M. (1991). Does tobacco advertising target young people to start smoking? Evidence from California. *Journal of the American Medical Association, 266*, 3154–3158.

Pierce, J. P., Lee, L., & Gilpin, E. A. (1994). Smoking initiation by adolescent girls, 1944 through 1988: An association with targeted advertising. *Journal of the American Medical Association, 271*, 608–611.

Polivy, J., & Herman, C. P. (1987). Diagnosis and treatment of normal eating. *Journal of Consulting and Clinical Psychology, 55*, 635–644.

Potter, W. J. (1991). Examining cultivation from a psychological perspective. *Communication Research, 18*, 77–102.

Rice, R. E., & Atkin, C. (1994). Principles of successful public communication campaigns. In J. Bryant & D. Zillmann (Eds.), *Media effects: Advances in theory and research* (pp. 365–387). Hillsdale, NJ: Lawrence Erlbaum Associates.

Richards, M. H., Casper, R. C., & Larson, R. (1990). Weight and eating concerns among pre- and young adolescent boys and girls. *Journal of Adolescent Health Care, 11*, 203–209.

Richins, M. L. (1991). Social comparison and idealized images of advertising. *Journal of Consumer Research, 18*, 71–83.

Robinson, T. N., Hammer, L. D., Killen, J. D., Kraemer, H. C., Wilson, D. M., Hayward, C., & Taylor, C. B. (1993). Does television viewing increase obesity and reduce physical activity? Cross-sectional and longitudinal analyses among adolescent girls. *Pediatrics, 91*, 273–280.

Rosen, J. C. (1989, April–June). Prevention of eating disorders. *Newsletter of the National Anorexic Aid Society, 12*, 1–3.

Rubin, A. M. (1994). Media uses and effects: A uses-and-gratifications perspective. In J. Bryant & D. Zillmann (Eds.), *Media effects: Advances in theory and research* (pp. 417–436). Hillsdale, NJ: Lawrence Erlbaum Associates.

Ruble, D. N. (1983). The development of social–comparison processes and their role in achievement-related self-socialization. In E. T. Higgins, D. N. Ruble, & W. W. Hartup (Eds.), *Social cognition and social development: A sociocultural perspective* (pp. 134–157). Cambridge, England: Cambridge University Press.

Shaw, J., & Waller, G. (1995). The media's impact on body image: Implications for prevention and treatment. *Eating Disorders: The Journal of Treatment & Prevention, 3*, 115–123.

Signorielli, N., & Morgan, M. (Eds.). (1990). *Cultivation analysis: New directions in media effects research.* Newbury Park, CA: Sage.

Silverstein, B., Perdue, L., Peterson, B., & Kelly, E. (1986). The role of mass media in promoting a thin standard of bodily attractiveness for women. *Sex Roles, 14*, 519–532.

Silverstein, B., Peterson, B., & Perdue, L. (1986). Some correlates of the thin standard of bodily attractiveness for women. *International Journal of Eating Disorders, 5*, 895–905.

Smolak, L., & Levine, M. P. (1994a). Critical issues in the developmental psychopathology of eating disorders. In L. Alexander & D. B. Lumsden (Eds.), *Understanding eating disorders* (pp. 37–60). Washington, DC: Taylor & Francis.

Smolak, L., & Levine, M. P. (1994b). Toward an empirical basis for primary prevention of eating disorders with elementary school children. *Eating Disorders: The Journal of Treatment & Prevention, 2,* 293–307.

Stice, E. (1994). Review of the evidence for a sociocultural model of bulimia nervosa and an exploration of the mechanisms of action. *Clinical Psychology Review, 14,* 1–29.

Stice, E., Schupak-Neuberg, E., Shaw, H. E., & Stein, R. I. (1994). Relation of media exposure to eating disorder symptomatology: An examination of mediating mechanisms. *Journal of Abnormal Psychology, 103,* 836–840.

Stice, E., & Shaw, H. E. (1994). Adverse effects of the media portrayed thin-ideal on women and linkages to bulimic symptomatology. *Journal of Social and Clinical Psychology, 13,* 288–308.

Story, M. (1990). Study group report on the impact of television on adolescent nutritional status. *Journal of Adolescent Health Care, 11,* 82–85.

Story, M., & Faulkner, P. (1990). The prime time diet: A content analysis on eating behavior and food messages in television program content and commercials. *American Journal of Public Health, 80,* 738–740.

Sumner, A., Waller, G., Killick, S., & Elstein, M. (1993). Body image distortion in pregnancy: A pilot study of the effects of media images. *Journal of Reproductive and Infant Psychology, 11,* 203–208.

Tan, A. S. (1979). TV beauty ads and role expectations of adolescent female viewers. *Journalism Quarterly, 56,* 283–288.

Teenage Research Unlimited. (1989, Fall). *Seventeen research.* (Available from TRU, 601 Skokie Boulevard, Northbrook, IL 60062.)

Then, D. (1992, August). *Women's magazines: Messages they convey about looks, men and careers.* Paper presented at the annual convention of the American Psychological Association, Washington, DC.

Thompson, J. K., Heinberg, L., & Tantleff, S. (1991). The physical appearance comparison scale. *Behavior Therapist, 14,* 174.

Tolman, D. L., & Debold, E. (1994). Conflicts of body and image: Female adolescents, desire, and the no-body body. In P. Fallon, M. A. Katzman, & S. C. Wooley (Eds.), *Feminist perspectives on eating disorders* (pp. 301–317). New York: Guilford.

Van Ezra, J. (1990). *Television and child development.* Hillsdale, NJ: Lawrence Erlbaum Associates.

Waller, G., Hamilton, K., & Shaw, J. (1992). Media influences on body size estimation in eating disordered and comparison subjects. *British Review of Bulimia and Anorexia Nervosa, 6,* 81–87.

Winklepleck, J., Restum, E. J., & Strange, B. (Eds.). (1993). *Gale directory of publications and broadcast media* (125th ed., Vols. 1 & 2). Detroit, MI: Gale Research.

Wiseman, C., Gray, J., Mosimann, J., & Ahrens, A. (1992). Cultural expectations of thinness in women: An update. *International Journal of Eating Disorders, 11,* 85–89.

Wolf, N. (1991). *The beauty myth: How images of beauty are used against women.* New York: William Morrow.

Wood, J. W. (1989). Theory and research concerning social comparisons of personal attributes. *Psychological Bulletin, 106,* 231–248.

11

The Role of Race in the Development of Eating Disorders

Ruth Striegel-Moore
Linda Smolak

In both the professional literature and the mass media, eating disorders are portrayed as a problem that affects almost exclusively White women. The belief that race is a major risk factor for the development of eating disorders derives from at least three sources. First, early case descriptions of anorexia nervosa (AN) were based on European or, later, American cases of White girls or women (Brumberg, 1988). Early formulations of AN emphasized the cultural (Western) and class (bourgeois) context of the disorder. Second, cross-cultural studies comparing women in Western societies with women in non-Western cultures found significantly greater prevalence rates of eating disorders in Western industrialized countries (e.g., Pate, Pumariega, Hester, & Garner, 1992). Finally, racial differences have been reported for a number of variables (e.g., body dissatisfaction and fear of fat; Abrams, Allen, & Gray, 1993) that have been hypothesized to contribute to the development of eating disorders.

More recently, however, evidence has been accumulating that challenges the view of eating disorders as an exclusively White phenomenon. For example, a growing number of case studies have been published describing AN or bulimia nervosa (BN) in Black patients (for reviews see Hsu, 1987; Root, 1990). Furthermore, researchers (e.g., Yanovski, 1993) investigating eating disorder symptoms among obese populations have found significant rates of disordered eating in Black women who are overweight.

In this chapter we aim to accomplish three things. First, we describe the data concerning the prevalence of eating disorder symptoms and syndromes in Black women. This review shows that eating problems are not limited to White women. However, it also demonstrates that patterns of eating problems are not identical across American cultures or

259

subcultures. The former finding leads to our second goal, which is to illustrate how the dominant "White model of eating disorders" limits researchers' understanding of the etiology of eating disorders. Here we hope to show that scholarship focusing on Black women serves to increase the understanding of eating problems not only in this racial group but in women of all races (Brown, Powell, & Earls, 1989).

Our third goal is to consider how a culture might protect itself against some eating problems while fostering others. Thus, we offer hypotheses as to why rates and patterns of eating disorders differ between Black and White females. It is worth emphasizing that part of this discussion will focus on what is protective within Black culture. This issue of protective factors has been largely overlooked in the extant eating disorders literature (Smolak & Striegel-Moore, chapter 8, this volume).

Ideally, this chapter would consider the issues of prevalence, etiology, and protective factors for women of all races and ethnicities. Unfortunately it is beyond the scope of this chapter to do so. We have therefore limited our focus to the non-White American group about which there is the largest amount of empirical evidence, namely Black American women.[1] While information about Black and White women may be helpful in understanding eating disorders and eating problems in all women, it is not sufficient to answer all questions. There are substantive differences between the groups considered "minorities" in the United States. For example, Latina adolescents do not show the same patterns of self-esteem development that Black teenage girls do (Orenstein, 1994). Furthermore, data suggest that Asian girls in both the U.S. and Britain may be more susceptible to eating problems than are Black girls (compare, e.g., Hill & Bhatti, 1995, and Killen et al., 1994, to Chandler, Abood, Lee, Cleveland, & Daly, 1994, and Childress, Brewerton, Hodges, & Jarrell, 1993). Thus, it should not be assumed that what is true for Black women is also automatically true for Latina, Asian, or Native American women.

Data on Black women are also limited in terms of the socioeconomic status represented, much as is true of the data concerning White women. For example, in one of the largest surveys of eating problems among Black women, the *Essence* survey, the mean household income was $41,150, and 22% of the women earned over $60,000. In the same year only 8% of the general population of Black women earned over $60,000 (Pumariega, Gustavson, Gustavson, Motes, & Ayers, 1994). The always problematic overrepresentation of the middle and upper-middle classes in eating disorder research may be an even more serious flaw when

---

[1]There is considerable debate about the most appropriate term to use when referring to Black American women. Although many authors choose the term *African American women*, not all Black women in the U.S. have African ancestry (e.g., Caribbean Blacks). We utilize the term Black women throughout the remainder of the chapter as a convenient way of describing Black women who reside in the U.S.

trying to understand the etiology of eating problems among Black women, who are in general underrepresented in the middle class.

SYMPTOMS AND SYNDROMES OF EATING DISORDERS IN BLACK WOMEN

To date, no empirical data are available to answer conclusively whether Black women are at differential risk when compared to White women for developing an eating disorder. So far, with the exception of AN, prevalence rates for eating disorders among women in the U.S. are based on nonrepresentative samples. A majority of studies in the eating disorders field have been conducted at tertiary treatment centers and therefore have included mostly women who have requested treatment for their eating disorders. Judging from the racial composition of participants in studies of AN or BN, these eating disorders are indeed rare among Black women. Fairburn and Beglin (1990) have provided a compelling argument for the need to use representative, community-based samples when seeking to estimate incidence or prevalence of an eating disorder. Clinic-based research participants are representative neither of women in the general population nor of women with an eating disorder (for a review, see Striegel-Moore & Marcus, 1995). For example, experts estimate that only 10% of women with an eating disorder request treatment specifically for their eating disorder (Fairburn, 1995). Due to racial differences in health care utilization, it is likely that Black women may be underrepresented in clinic-based samples, compared to White women. As we propose later in this chapter, the fact that our empirical knowledge rests almost exclusively on data obtained from clinic-based samples has had profound implications for theoretical formulations of eating disorders.

Prevalence Rates of Eating Disorders Among Black Women

Prevalence of AN.   The Epidemiological Catchment Area (ECA) study (Robins & Regier, 1991) reported rates for the point prevalence and lifetime prevalence of AN. The ECA study involved a representative sample of the U.S. population of adult men and women. AN was found to be exceedingly rare (occuring in less than 0.5% of the sample), and no racial comparisons of prevalence rates of AN have been reported. In a population-based study (Walters & Kendler, 1994) of 2,163 same-sex twins, only White women were included. The lifetime prevalence rate in this study was also 0.5%, again suggesting that AN is very rare. Racial comparisons of prevalence rates for AN clearly require large samples.

Prevalence of BN and of Bulimic Symptoms. We are not aware of any study of the incidence or prevalence of BN that involves a representative sample of adolescent or adult women in the U.S. However, a study of female college students reported significantly lower prevalence rates for BN among Black students compared to White students (Gray, Ford, & Kelly, 1987).

A few studies have provided information about the prevalence of specific behavioral symptoms of BN, including binge eating, vomiting, and abuse of purgatives. Moreover, several investigators have published data based on standardized scales of eating disorder symptoms such as the Bulimia subscales of the Eating Disorder Inventory (EDI; Garner & Olmsted, 1984) or the Eating Attitudes Test (EAT; Garner, Olmsted, Bohr, & Garfinkel, 1982). These preliminary studies suggest that recurrent binge eating may be as common among Black women as it is among White women. For example, a study of high school girls (Rosen, Silberg, & Gross, 1988) and a study of adult women (Wilfley, Schreiber, Pike, Rodin, & Striegel-Moore, in press) found no racial differences on the EDI Bulimia subscale. Similarly, Black female college students did not differ from White students on the Bulimia subscale of the EAT-26, a measure of dysfunctional food-and weight-related attitudes and behaviors (Wing, Adams-Campbell, Marcus, & Janney, 1993). A survey of stratified sample adults living in north central Florida found comparable lifetime prevalence rates among Black and White women for binge eating and for vomiting or use of diuretics for weight control (Warheit, Langer, Zimmerman, & Biafora, 1993). Similarly, surveys of high school students (Bennett, Spoth, & Borgen, 1991), of college students (Gray et al., 1987), and of adult women (Striegel-Moore, Wilfley, Caldwell, Needham, & Brownell, in press) reported comparable point prevalence rates of binge eating in Black and White females.

Indeed, several studies suggest greater rates of binge eating in Black girls or young women than in White females. For example, a recent study of 1,610 girls in grades 4–8 found that binge eating was reported by 11.4% of Black girls as compared to 5.4% of White girls, a difference that was statistically significant (Childress et al., 1993). In a study of college students, Black women scored significantly higher on the Bulimia subscale of the EDI than did White women (Chandler et al., 1994).

On the other hand, at least two studies have reported lower rates of binge eating in Black college women than in White college women (Abrams et al., 1993; Edwards-Hewitt & Gray, 1993). In the Abrams et al. study, for example, 68% of the White college women reported having engaged in binge eating at some time, whereas only 42% of the Black women did. Similarly, 21% of the White women reported binge eating at least once a week, compared to 11% of the Black women.

Two studies reported that the use of purgatives as a means of purging (as opposed to vomiting) was favored to a greater extent among Black women than among White women. For example, a survey of high school students found that compared to White girls (7%), Black girls reported significantly higher rates of laxative use (18%) and use of diuretics (11% vs. 7%), but lower rates of vomiting (11% vs. 16%; Langer, Warheit, & Zimmerman, 1991). Similarly, a survey of *Essence* magazine readers (who are predominantly Black) likewise found that use of laxatives to control weight (16.5%) was more common than vomiting (3.5%; Pumariega et al., 1994).

These various studies suggest that some behavioral symptoms of eating disorders are more common among Black women than had previously been recognized. Perhaps these results reflect secular trends; in other words, Black women may be "catching up" with White women in terms of disordered eating. Another intriguing possibility is that Black women do not differ from White women at the level of behavioral symptoms, but that when strict diagnostic criteria are applied Black women fall outside of these categories because they have fewer or milder symptoms than do White women. Regarding the prevalence data of binge eating, we speculate that Black women may be more likely to develop binge eating disorder (BED), a syndrome described later, rather than BN.

Prevalence of BED.   The field trial studies conducted to determine the need for a new diagnostic entity, BED, found that non-White patients (most of whom were African Americans) enrolled in weight-loss programs were just as likely to meet criteria for BED (22%) as were White patients (29%; Spitzer et al., 1992; Spitzer et al., 1993). In an ongoing treatment trial for obese binge eaters, requests by Black women to be included in the treatment were found to be proportionate to the percentage of Black residents (14%) in the geographic area of the clinic conducting the trial (Marcus, 1993). Similarly, a study of obese patients found comparable rates of BED in Black and in White women (Yanovski, Nelson, Dubbert, & Spitzer, 1993).

Prevalence of Eating Disorders not Otherwise Specified (EDNOS). Several recent studies have shown that a majority of women requesting treatment for eating disorder symptoms do not meet diagnostic criteria for AN, BN, or BED. Many of these women are suffering from subthreshold eating disorders; that is, they meet some but not all of the diagnostic criteria for AN or BN. As described in the Introduction, it is important to study these subthreshold eating disorders because such research may answer questions regarding the natural course of eating disorders and their etiology and may also provide useful data for efforts to prevent eating disorders. Moreover, this group of individuals represents a large portion of the caseloads at clinics, which suggests a need for a better understanding of the nature of EDNOS and of how these individuals might be best helped (Shisslak, Crago, & Estes, 1995; Striegel-Moore & Marcus, 1995). Research has yet to examine the extent to which Black women are likely to be represented among EDNOS cases, or what particular types of subthreshold syndromes they might have.

Racial Differences: Fact or Artifact? As described earlier, most studies of eating disorders have been conducted using clinic-based samples. Such studies have had an important, if not definitive, impact on the classification of eating disorders. Given the almost complete absence of research on Black women with disordered eating, it is unclear whether the current nosology is suitable for capturing and diagnosing disordered eating in Black women. Keeping in mind the limitations of the current data, it appears at present that AN and BN are rare among Black women, that BED occurs at rates comparable to those observed among White women, and that nothing is known about EDNOS in Black women.

There are several possible explanations for these preliminary findings. One is that Black women may indeed be less likely than White women to develop AN or BN. If this is the case, race is a relevant factor in the development of AN and BN, with being White representing a major risk factor for these disorders. If this is the case, a logical next step in efforts to understand this differential risk is to examine racial differences in variables (e.g., body image and gender roles) thought to be involved in the development of an eating disorder. Alternatively, it is possible that Black women are as likely as White women to develop AN or BN, but that their underrepresentation in clinic-based samples results in inaccurate estimates of their vulnerability to these disorders. Finally, racial differences in prevalence rates for the major eating disorders may reflect racial differences in the clinical presentation of eating disorders, with Black women being more likely than White women to express their eating disorder in the form of BED or EDNOS rather than of BN or AN. In other words, Black women may share with White women risk factors for developing an eating disorder, but the "symptom choice" (Brumberg, 1988) may differ depending on race.

ETIOLOGICAL MODELS OF EATING DISORDERS

Every major theory of psychopathology has been applied to eating disorders, ranging from primarily biological explanations (e.g., Blundell & Hill, 1993) to purely cultural explanations (Bordo, 1993). An attempt to evaluate these theories from an empirical perspective is severely hampered by the lack of data from Black women. There are two theoretical models of the etiology of eating disorders for which we found sufficiently empirical data to begin to address the question of race as a risk factor for an eating disorder. These are the restraint model and the interpersonal vulnerability model. Neither is likely to explain fully the etiology of eating disorders; rather, it is reasonable to assume that etiological variables from these models need to be combined into a cumulative model (Pike, 1995), along with additional variables from other theoretical models. For heuristic purposes, however, we present these models separately. Such an approach may render race-related differences more salient.

The Restraint Model

The restraint model proposes a developmental sequence beginning with the internalization of Western culture's unrealistically thin beauty ideal and progressing to body image dissatisfaction, cognitive and behavioral restraint, and, in the case of BN and BED, to binge eating (Polivy & Herman, 1993; Stice, 1994; Striegel-Moore, 1993).[2] Women are thought to be disproportionately more vulnerable to developing binge eating because pursuit of beauty is an essential feature of the female gender role stereotype (Rodin, Silberstein, & Striegel-Moore, 1985). In this model several key variables are hypothesized to contribute the development of eating disorders.

The Thin Beauty Ideal. An extensive literature has documented the fact that in Western cultures the ideal female form has become increasingly thin over the past few decades (Garner, Garfinkel, Schwartz, & Thompson, 1980). Several studies have examined the question of whether the beauty ideal for Black women differs from the ideal upheld for White women. This research has produced mixed results. Some studies support a racial difference, with Black adolescent girls (Kemper, Sargent, Drane, Valois, & Hussey, 1994; Wilson, Sargent, & Diaz, 1994) or Black adult women (Powell & Kahn, 1995; Rucker & Cash, 1992) reporting a larger ideal body size than do White females. Other studies have found that when asked to select body silhouettes to represent the ideal self, the ideal for health, or the ideal for female attractiveness, Black women choose body shapes as thin as those chosen by White women (Callan, Mayo, & Michel, 1993; Singh, 1994). A look at the popular media illustrates that many Black female stars in the music,

---

[2]We recognize that body image dissatisfaction holds a dual status in the eating disorders literature, being considered both a risk factor for and a symptom of an eating disorder. Similarly, dieting is considered a risk factor (e.g., Polivy & Herman, 1985; Striegel-Moore et al., 1986) and may be a symptom of AN or BN. Operational definitions of body image dissatisfaction and dieting as clinical symptoms are not yet available. In other words, it is unclear what degree of body dissatisfaction is needed to warrant recognition as a clinical symptom for an eating disorder. For the purpose of illustrating pathways to an eating disorder, we chose to discuss body dissatisfaction and dieting as risk factors.

film, and fashion industries are just as thin as their White counterparts (cf. Pumariega et al., 1994). The thin beauty ideal for women may be becoming the ideal across various racial and ethnic groups.

Degree of Overweight.   Within White culture, the more overweight a girl or woman is, the greater the discrepancy between the cultural beauty norm and her actual body shape or size. Not surprisingly, adiposity is highly correlated with weight dissatisfaction (Striegel-Moore et al., 1995; Wilfley et al., in press). Moreover, overweight women are more likely than women of normal weight to be the subject of social pressure in the form of teasing, criticism, or discrimination (Crandall, 1994).

Research has consistently shown that Black women tend to be heavier than White women. Several national health surveys in the U.S. have reported that Black women are three times more likely than White women to be obese (Burke et al., 1992; National Center for Health Statistics, 1991; National Heart, Lung, and Blood Institute Research Group, 1992). Moreover, over a 10-year period rates of obesity appear to have increased to a greater degree among Black women than among White women (Williamson, 1993). This racial difference in the rate of overweight and obesity cannot be explained on the basis of socioeconomic status alone; rather, risk for obesity appears to be determined by multiple factors, ranging from genetic factors to cultural variables (Kumanyika, 1987, 1994).

Fairburn (1994) found that childhood or adolescent obesity is a specific constitutional risk factor for BN. A history of obesity is common in women with BED (Smith, Marcus & Eldredge, 1995). Obese binge eaters have been reported to recall earlier ages of onset of obesity than do nonbingeing obese individuals (deZwaan, Nutzinger, & Schoenbeck, 1992; Spitzer et al., 1992, 1993). Whether obesity represents a risk factor for eating disorders among Black women remains to be determined.

Social Pressure to Be Thin.   Studies of White women have shown consistently that overweight or obese girls and women experience frequent social pressure in the form of weight-related teasing, criticism, and even discrimination (Rothblum, 1992). Several studies have found that Black girls and women reportedly experience less social pressure to conform to the thin ideal than do their White counterparts (Childress et al., 1993; Powell & Kahn, 1995; Striegel-Moore et al., in press). For example, Black schoolchildren are reportedly less likely to feel that they "look fat to others" (Childress et al., 1993). Another study found that Black adolescent girls were more likely than White adolescent girls to report that their friends and family viewed them as thin, even though the two groups did not differ on a measure of current body size (Kemper et al., 1994). A study of 162 adult Black women and 162 White women (matched as to age, educational level, and income) found that the Black women reported significantly less parental criticism of their weight and fewer incidents of weight-related discrimination than did the White women (Striegel-Moore et al., 1995). Importantly, these differences remained when controlling for group differences in adiposity. On a related note, in a sample of obese Black women attending a weight-loss program, most women reported an absence of social pressure to become thin (Kumanyika, Wilson, & Guilford-Davenport, 1993).

In an anthropological study in which Black girls participated in focus groups, many Black girls described obsession with thinness as a distinctly "White" problem (Parker, Nichter, Nichter, Vuckovic, Sims, & Ritenbaugh, 1995). These girls talked about the importance in Black culture of "having attitude," which means that one should develop pride in one's body regardless of its physical appearance. The girls further emphasized the importance of "making the most" of one's physical features. The narratives of these girls made it clear that physical appearance is important in Black culture, but that the person is not enslaved by a given ideal appearance. Rather, women are encouraged to emphasize their assets through careful grooming and creative and individualized choice of clothing. This cultural norm may serve a protective function against White culture's "tyranny of slenderness."

It is interesting to note, however, that when social pressure to be thin is experienced, it appears to be just as strongly related to body dissatisfaction (Wilfley et al., in press) or to drive for thinness in Black as in White females (Striegel-Moore et al., 1995). Hence, when Black girls or women experience weight-related social pressure, they are likely to want to be thinner, to attempt to lose weight, or both.

Body Image Disturbances. Of all of the etiological variables delineated in the restraint model, body image dissatisfaction has been studied the most. The importance of body image dissatisfaction as a central variable in the causal sequence that leads to eating disorders has been supported in studies that compare women with eating disorders to normal controls, and in prospective studies that link body image concerns with the worsening of behavioral symptoms of eating disorders. White women with eating disorders have consistently been found to differ from normal controls on three related yet distinct body image variables: They aspire to a thinner body ideal, report greater weight dissatisfaction, and attribute greater importance to weight as central to their identity (Cooper & Fairburn, 1993; Garfinkel et al., 1992; Slade, 1994). A 2-year prospective study of White girls found that body image dissatisfaction in early adolescence predicted increased scores on the EAT-26 (Attie & Brooks-Gunn, 1989).

We have reviewed evidence that suggests that Black women tend to be heavier than White women and yet appear to experience less social pressure about weight. At the same weight levels, Black women appear to be less likely than White women to perceive themselves as overweight (e.g., Wilfley et al., in press). The question of dissatisfaction in Black women is a key issue in developing an understanding of their risk of eating disorders. Several studies have shown comparable levels of body image dissatisfaction in Black and White women (Pumariega et al., 1994; Rosen et al., 1988; Wilfley et al., in press). However, when differences in adiposity are controlled for, White women report greater weight dissatisfaction than do Black women. For example, Wilfley et al. grouped subjects based on body mass index quintiles and obtained significant racial differences as follows: Black women and White women in the first quintile (i.e., at the lowest weight) reported similar scores on the Body Dissatisfaction scale of the EDI. In each of the remaining quintile groups, however, White women reported greater body dissatisfaction than did Black women. These results are consistent with other studies reporting greater acceptance of overweight among Black women compared to White women (Kemper et al., 1994; Kumanyika et al., 1993) and among Black men compared to White men (Powell & Kahn, 1995).

Several studies suggest that Black girls or women are more satisfied with their weight than are their White counterparts, even when the researchers make no effort at controlling for racial differences in adiposity (Chandler et al., 1994; Harris, 1995; Powell & Kahn, 1995). By the same token, Black children have been found to be less likely than White children to fear becoming fat, a result that is particularly remarkable in light of the consistent reports of significant prevalence of obesity among Black adolescent and adult women (Childress et al., 1993).

In White women, body image dissatisfaction appears to peak during adolescence and to remain high during adulthood (Rosen et al., 1988; Shore & Porter, 1990; Smolak & Levine, 1994a; Story et al., 1991). In contrast, body image dissatisfaction may follow a different developmental course in Black women. Preliminary data from a prospective study of 2,000 Black and White girls suggest that for Black girls, body dissatisfaction peaks in early adolescence and then declines with age (Schreiber, personal communication).

Finally, body image dissatisfaction may hold different meanings for White and Black women. Black women's body dissatisfaction may be more realistic and less pathological (Abrams et al., 1993; Strauss, Levy, & Kreipe, 1994). There are several indicators of this. As noted earlier, Black women who are dissatisfied with their bodies are more likely to actually be overweight. They are also less obsessive about their bodies; that is, they would "like" to lose weight but do not see weight loss as crucial or important to their self-definitions. Black women are also less likely to want to lose weight for a reason other than appearance or health. White women, for example, associate weight loss with self-control whereas Black girls and women do not (Abrams et al., 1993; Parker et al., 1995; Strauss et al., 1994).

Dietary Restraint.   Dietary restraint is seen as the final link in the progression from internalizing the cultural beauty ideals to binge eating. Dieting is thought to result in cognitive and physiological changes that promote binge eating (for a review see Polivy & Herman, 1985). With compelling consistency, an extensive literature documents the concurrent association of dieting and binge eating in both nonclinical and clinical samples and in both Black and White samples (for reviews see Lowe, 1993; Polivy & Herman, 1985; Striegel-Moore, Silberstein, & Rodin, 1986; Striegel-Moore, 1993; see also Abrams et al., 1993).

Several studies support the role of dieting as a key variable in the development of eating disorders. A majority of patients with AN (Hsu, 1990) and BN (Mitchell, Hatsukami, Pyle, & Eckert, 1986) recall a history of dieting prior to the onset of binge eating. In a sample of obese binge eaters, frequency of binge eating and the number of prior weight losses of at least 10 lb (4.5 kg) were highly correlated (Marcus et al., 1990). Prospective studies found that over the course of 1 year "excessive dieters" were significantly more likely than "normal dieters" or nondieters to meet criteria for BN (King, 1991; Patton, Johnson-Sabine, Wood, Mann, & Wakeling, 1990). Weight-reducing efforts in female adolescents were significantly associated with bulimic status 2 years later (Marchi & Cohen, 1990).

Whether Black women are as likely as White women to engage in weight-control efforts in response to weight dissatisfaction is unclear. Depending on the questions asked or instrument used, racial differences do or do not emerge (Parker et al., 1995; Strauss et al., 1994). Black girls scored significantly higher than White girls on the Drive for Thinness scale of the EDI, a measure of the key motivational variable underlying dieting (Striegel-Moore et al., in press). In contrast, studies of adult women utilizing the Restraint scale have reported significantly lower scores for Black women compared to White women (Klem, Klesges, Bene, & Mellon, 1990; Wing et al., 1993). Similarly, at comparable levels of age and body mass index Black women score lower than White women on the dieting subscale of the EAT (Chandler et al., 1994). At present, it is impossible to ascertain whether these conflicting results represent measurement (and, perhaps, conceptual) differences in studies or a cohort shift among younger versus older Black females in weight-control effects.

Rather than using standardized scales, several studies have utilized one or a few single items to determine prevalence rates of dieting to control weight. These results have also been inconsistent. Some studies have reported that Black children or women are less likely to engage in dieting to lose weight than are White females (Childress et al., 1993; Emmons, 1992; Langer, Warheit, & Zimmerman, 1991; Story et al., 1991; Rucker & Cash, 1992; Warheit et al., 1993) whereas other studies have found no racial differences on rates of dieting efforts (Bennett et al., 1991; Gray et al., 1987; Williamson, Serdula, Anda, Levy, & Byers, 1992). In conclusion, the literature of dieting among Black women offers conflicting findings. In part this may be attributable to differences in methodology and sampling strategies. For example, definitions of dieting are crucial in determining prevalence rates of dieting (e.g., Nichter & Vuckovic, 1994; Schreiber et al., in press). Furthermore, Black girls may respond to survey questions in ways that they think White researchers expect. Black girls are very aware of White norms concerning dieting and the use of "fat talk" (Nichter & Vuckovic, 1994) and so may say that they are dieting to appear to be in conformity with the dominant White culture (Parker et al., 1995).

In sum, Black women differ from White women on rates of obesity, a variable that has been strongly implicated as a risk factor for eating disorders. As is true for White women, adiposity in Black women is linked with weight dissatisfaction and with a desire to be thinner. However, Black women appear to be subjected to less social pressure toward thinness than are White women, and this greater social acceptance of overweight and normal weight in the Black community may serve as an important protective factor against the development of eating disorders. A mixed picture emerges from our review of body image dissatisfaction and dieting. Because only two studies (Abrams et al., 1987; Gray et al., 1987) have reported data on the co-occurrence of both dieting and binge eating in the same Black women, we can only speculate about the link between dieting and binge eating in this population. Thus, the extent to which the full set of restraint model risk factors predicts BED in Black women still needs to be tested.

Limitations of the Restraint Model. Two major challenges to the validity of the restraint model of eating disorders include the fact that despite the pervasive prevalence of dieting efforts few women actually develop a clinical eating disorder (for reviews see Beebe, 1994; Striegel-Moore et al., 1986; Striegel-Moore, 1993), and the observation that in a considerable number of obese binge eaters binge eating has preceded the onset of dieting (Wilson, Nonas, & Rosenblum, 1993). Several alternatives to the restraint model have emphasized the role of emotions in causing or precipitating binge eating: for example, describing binge eating as an attempt to escape awareness of unpleasant emotional states (e.g., Heatherton & Baumeister, 1991), or in response to specific stressors (for reviews see Cattanach & Rodin, 1988; Greeno & Wing, 1994). Striegel-Moore (1993) proposed an interpersonal vulnerability model of eating disorders, thereby describing another potential pathway to binge eating, BED, and BN.

The Interpersonal Vulnerability Model

In essence, the interpersonal vulnerability model proposes a sequence from inadequate interactions between the primary caregiver and the child, to insecure attachment, to heightened vulnerability regarding stressful events and identity concerns, to overeating as a way of self-soothing or stress management. The particular vulnerability for eating disorders derives from our culture's definition of feminine identity in terms of an emphasis on interpersonal orientation and on internalizing distress. Consistent with this model, at its core an eating disorder is a disturbance of the self. The main domains of the self implicated in this model are the self as it relates to others (social self) and self-evaluation (self-esteem; Polivy & Herman, 1993; Striegel-Moore, 1993; Striegel-Moore, Silberstein, & Rodin, 1993). Women who struggle to maintain a positive sense of self may be particularly preoccupied with how others perceive them and may focus on their appearance as a tangible domain in which to construct a salient and adequate self. Although the full model encompasses a wide range of variables such as attachment style, parental psychopathology, and social self-concerns, we focus only on those variables for which data concerning Black women are available.

Identity Development. Based on data collected from White women, it appears that eating-disordered women are more likely to have encountered family experiences or life events that can interfere with developing secure child-to-parent attachment. Examples include prolonged parent–child separation, divorce, parental psychopathology, parental underinvolvement, and child physical or sexual abuse (Andrews, Valentine, & Valentine, 1995; Boumann & Yates, 1994; Fairburn, 1994; Kendler et al., 1991, 1995; Holden, 1991; Kassett et al., 1989; Strober, Lampert, Morrell, Burroughs, & Jacobs, 1990). These adverse childhood experiences may establish a foundation that makes it difficult to develop a stable, positive sense of self. Adolescence complicates the self-deficits that characterize a person who has been unable to form secure attachments.

Black children are significantly more likely to grow up in single-parent households. However, because of the greater reliance on the extended kinship network observed in Black families, the impact on attachment of separation from a parent or of divorce may not be the same for Black children as for White children (Taylor, Chatters, Tucker, & Lewis, 1990). Indeed, the Black extended family may serve as a buffer against a wide range of stressors including poverty and racial prejudice (Harrison, Wilson, Pine, Chan, et al., 1990). Racial differences in each culture's understanding of and response to particular adverse events need to be taken into consideration when examining the contribution of these nonspecific factors to the development of eating disorders (see Connors, chapter 12, this volume).

Stressful Life Events. Interpersonal theory postulates that the risk for psychopathology among insecurely attached individuals derives from an inability to regulate affective experiences, particularly when exposed to stress. Several studies have reported a link between stressful life events and the onset of eating disorders. Strober (1984) found that the magnitude of life stress experienced by patients with AN or BN 18 months prior to the onset of their disorder was 2.5 times greater than that of a normative sample of female adolescents. Furthermore, the degree of life stress was significantly correlated with the severity of binge eating. Levine and Smolak (1992; Smolak, Levine, & Gralen, 1993) found that girls whose transition to middle school coincided with other stressors (e.g., onset of dating, onset of menarche) were significantly more likely to have elevated scores on the EAT-26 (Garner et al., 1982) than were girls for whom the school transition was not accompanied by other stressors. Interestingly, initial research suggests that interpersonal stressors may be particularly likely to result in binge eating (Strober, 1984).

In general, Black individuals are more likely than their White counterparts to experience poverty, substandard housing, discrimination in the workforce, and traumatic life events. This greater exposure to stressful life conditions has been implicated in the differences in health and emotional well-being of Black compared to White individuals (for a review see Anderson, 1991). Black adolescents encounter significantly more stressful life events than do their White peers (Newcomb, Huba, & Butler, 1981). As has been observed among White individuals, the amount of stress experienced is predictive of the development of psychopathology. For example, a longitudinal study of 2,787 adolescent Black girls found that the number of stressful life events was significantly corelated with the degree of psychiatric impairment 1 year later (Brown, Powell, & Earls, 1989).

Sexual abuse, particularly childhood sexual abuse, has received considerable attention as a potential risk factor for the development of eating disorders and of obesity (for reviews see Connors & Morse, 1993; Pope & Hudson, 1992; Felitti, 1993). Based on current empirical evidence it appears that childhood abuse is a "general" risk factor for eating disorders (e.g., Welch & Fairburn, 1994), raising the risk for eating disorders to levels comparable to the risk for other major psychiatric problems. Nevertheless, Kearney-Cooke and Striegel-Moore (1994) cautioned that it may be premature to conclude that sexual abuse does not play a "specific," unique role in the etiology of eating disorders. For example, to date sexual abuse has been studied as a single risk factor rather than in more complex, multi-risk-factor model designs. Moreover, we are unaware of any research of the role of sexual trauma in the development of disordered eating in Black women (see Thompson, 1994, for case studies).

Limitations of the Interpersonal Vulnerability Model.   Although the interpersonal vulnerability model "rings true" from our clinical experience with women with eating disorders, the model cannot fully explain the "choice of the symptoms." Specifically, the underlying mechanisms that lead to eating disorders rather than to other forms of psychopathology require further definition and empirical exploration (see Connors, chapter 12, this volume). Furthermore, the processes that lead to an insecure attachment style in adulthood or to an overinvestment in relationships are poorly understood (Ewell, Smith, Karmel, & Hart, chapter 5, this volume; Isabella, chapter 7, this volume; Smolak & Striegel-Moore, chapter 8, this volume).

DEVELOPMENTAL ISSUES

The preceding discussion has indicated that in general, weight concerns and eating problems may differ between Black and White girls and women. However, as is always the case with group differences there is considerable overlap in the problems. Thus, there is no eating disorder or problem to which either Black or White women are immune. Furthermore, there is some evidence to suggest that Black women, perhaps particularly those in the middle class, may be gradually joining the majority in terms of weight concerns (e.g., Pumariega et al., 1994; Root, 1990). Nonetheless, the limited data tend to indicate that Black women are more likely to be overweight and even obese; that Black women may binge eat and possibly purge at rates at least equal to and perhaps higher than those of White women; that Black adolescent girls and women appear to have more positive body images, including more body esteem and less body dissatisfaction; and that AN appears to be even more rare among Black than among White girls. Thus, in generating hypotheses concerning cultural factors in the etiology of eating problems, we can suggest that some components of Black culture may create vulnerabilities to some forms of eating problems (obesity, binge eating) while other elements may be protective against other aspects of eating problems (body dissatisfaction, AN).

Developmental research on Black children and adolescents continues to be fairly limited (Spencer & Markstrom-Adams, 1990). Hence, we cannot offer data on all possible risk and protective factors. Instead, we focus on three factors which may be relevant to the differential rate and pattern of eating problems among Black women: adiposity, gender roles, and identity.

Adiposity

As was noted earlier, Black women are three times more likely than White women to be obese (National Center for Health Statistics, 1991; National Heart, Lung, and Blood Institute Research Group, 1992). Since obesity does tend to run in families (Epstein, 1993), children of Black women are at greater risk for becoming obese. Furthermore, by early adulthood (a peak period for the development of BN), Black women are about 2.5 times more likely than White women to be obese (Williamson, 1993). Even among nonobese samples, Black girls and women are likely to have higher body mass indices (indicating more body fat) than are White girls and women (Abrams et al., 1993; Chandler et al., 1994).

In addition, Black girls are more likely to be enter puberty earlier than White girls (NGHS; Richards, Abell, & Peterson, 1993). Early maturation is frequently, although not invariably, associated with heavier weights that continue into adulthood (Richards, Abell, & Peterson, 1993; but see, e.g., Stattin & Magnusson, 1990). Interestingly, greater chronicity of eating problems has been associated with early puberty when the timing is associated with greater body mass index (Graber et al., 1994). In other words, the pubertal timing effects actually reflected the effects of heavier weights.

What might this mean for eating problems among Black women? It is possible that Black women's greater adiposity makes it more difficult for them to achieve the White American body ideal. Following the restraint model, efforts to diet might ultimately lead to binge eating and, perhaps, to purging. Phrased differently, it may be the case that of the women who subscribe to the White ideal body shape (although there may be fewer of these among Black women than among White women), Black women are at greater risk for developing bulimic behaviors because it is more difficult for them to lose weight. Thus, the rate of bulimic behaviors among Black dieters may be higher than among White dieters. This is an issue for future research.

Gender Roles

Numerous theorists have suggested that gender roles may contribute to the etiology of eating problems (Bordo, 1993; Lancelot & Kaslow, 1994; Smolak & Striegel-Moore, chapter 8, this volume; Worell & Todd, chapter 6, this volume). These theoretical positions and their associated studies have sometimes implicated traditional gender roles, sometimes the patriarchal society more generally, and sometimes the newly described "superwoman" role (see Smolak & Levine, chapter 9, this volume). In any case it is difficult to claim that gender is irrelevant to the development of eating problems given the tremendous preponderance of women among diagnosed cases of BN, AN, and EDNOS. At least among Whites, women also show higher rates of eating-related problems such as body dissatisfaction and dieting, which actually begin in elementary school (Smolak & Levine, 1994b; Striegel-Moore et al., 1986).

Nevertheless, despite higher body mass indices, Black girls and women often show less body dissatisfaction than do White girls and women (Abrams et al., 1993; Chandler et al., 1994; Striegel-Moore et al., 1995). Gender roles may offer one possible explanation for this. Black children apparently are not as gender stereotyped in their beliefs as White children are (Bardwell, Cochran, & Walker, 1986). There may be several reasons for this. First, until very recently Black women have been employed at much higher rates than White women (Council of Economic Advisors, 1987). Second, Black children are much more likely to be raised in single-parent homes or in predominantly female multigenerational homes that are not marked by traditional gender roles (Harrison et al., 1990). Third, Black women have a long history of achievement relative to White women because slavery and its aftermath often denied Black men access to the type of economic security enjoyed by White men (Giddings, 1984).

With less traditionally defined gender roles, Black women may not routinely feel the strain of superwomen roles. They may not, for example, feel the need to prove that they can be something other than wives or mothers in the manner that White daughters of full-time homemakers have done, nor may they feel the anxiety related to "superpassing" (i.e., achieving professional success) their mothers (Wooley & Wooley, 1985). Alternatively, Black women's gender identities may not be as heavily related to attractiveness as White women's are. Consistent with this argument, Black mothers (Parker et al., 1995) do not seem to encourage their daughters to attend to their weight and shape in ways that White mothers do (e.g., Levine, Smolak, Moodey, Shuman, & Hessen, 1994; Pike & Rodin, 1991; Striegel-Moore & Kearney-Cooke, 1994). Another possibility is that Black women may be less likely than White women (see Smolak & Levine, chapter 9, this volume) to experience conflicts about establishing autonomy in early adulthood (Abrams et al., 1993). Again, these and other gender-related hypotheses are areas for future research and are particularly intriguing given the lack of clarity in researchers' understanding of the relation between gender roles and eating problems.

Identity

White Americans do not typically think about their racial identity. Instead, concerns about racial identity are typically restricted to those people who identify themselves as members of other racial or ethnic groups (Phinney, 1991). Typically these are people who do not see themselves as completely assimilated into the racial or ethnic majority. It might be assumed that self-identification as a member of a racial minority would have a negative effect on self-esteem and overall psychological functioning. Assimilation is often viewed as a prerequisite for success in society, which is by definition dominated by the majority. Indeed, this is a common argument against bilingual education. It might also be suggested that people who identify themselves as minority members are particularly sensitive to, and hence hurt by, racial discrimination.

Minority group members are well aware of racial stereotypes and negative evaluations of their group by others (Phinney, 1991). However, individuals commonly dissociate themselves from these group evaluations. Thus, contrary to theoretical perspectives, these negative images tend not to be internalized (Spencer & Markstrom-Adams, 1990). This protective mechanism probably diminishes the direct individual psychological effects of racism (although, it cannot, of course, reduce the institutionalized effects, including violence against minority members and poverty as a result of educational and job discrimination, which, in turn, create stress for minority members).

This rejection of racial stereotypes may be bolstered by acceptance of membership in the racial minority. In other words, although data are too limited to allow a definitive statement, some evidence suggests that identification with the group, including a search for understanding one's racial identity, may facilitate positive self-esteem (Phinney, 1991; Phinney & Chavira, 1992; Spencer & Markstrom-Adams, 1990). Indeed, it is interesting that across the life span, Blacks consistently demonstrate self-esteem that is at least as high as that of Whites. Thus, low ethnic identity may result in poor mechanisms for coping with prejudice and discrimination and hence may lead to pathology (Phinney & Chavira, 1992).

Why might group identification increase self-esteem? First, it may allow the individual to receive full support from the community. The Black family and community have long been havens from not only discrimination but also from violence perpetrated by Whites against Blacks (Harrison et al., 1990). Second, identification and identity search make more salient the accomplishments of the group. Blacks in the United States have survived and even prospered under overwhelming odds (Spencer & Markstrom-Adams, 1990). Their contributions are, however, frequently overlooked in standard school curricula and thus only become known to (and thereby a source of pride for) young Blacks who make an effort to learn about them. Such pride and awareness of the survival struggles of Blacks (including today's Blacks) may be one reason why the suicide rate (Weiner, 1992) is so low among American Blacks.

In the specific case of eating problems, identification with Black culture may also include accepting Black standards for attractiveness. As discussed earlier, these standards may encompass greater tolerance of more diverse body shapes, including heavy bodies. Inasmuch as there is evidence for sociocultural or familial transmission of these attitudes (Levine, Smolak, & Hayden, 1994; Levine, Smolak, Moodey, et al., 1994; Pike & Rodin, 1992), this may be a specific protective factor against eating problems. Indeed, some research suggests that Blacks who identify with White culture show more eating problems, including dietary restraint and fear of fat, than do Blacks who identify with Black culture (Abrams et al., 1993; Harris, 1995; Pumariega et al., 1994; but see Edwards-Hewitt & Gray, 1993 and Strauss et al., 1994).

CONCLUSIONS

One of the major lessons of a developmental psychopathology approach is that the context of development is crucial. Racial differences in eating problems, both in terms of symptoms and of developmental processes, provide a striking example of this principle. Although existing data do not make it possible to make definitive statements about racial differences, there can be little doubt that some exist. While a few of these differences, most notably adiposity, may be attributable to biological factors, in general they seem more attributable to cultural differences in gender roles, definitions of beauty, and social pressures to conform to a particular ideal.

It seems almost trite to say that growing up Black in America is a different experience from growing up White. Stereotypically, we think of growing up Black as negative. Yet, as the data on suicide, adolescent alcohol abuse, and eating problems demonstrate, there is apparently something protective and survival enhancing in Black culture. This seems particularly true for Black girls and women, whose gender roles, compared to those of White women, seem less shaped by an emphasis on outward appearance and more determined by pride in self and community.

Studies of eating problems among Blacks can accomplish several things. First, research can determine the extent and nature of eating problems among Blacks. Just as has been true for Whites, there is a need to ascertain the intragroup variability for Blacks and to describe the various pathways that they take to and away from eating problems. It seems especially crucial to determine whether there are cohort effects in eating problems among Black women such that today's adolescent population is at greater risk than those of the 1970s and 1980s. The effects of socioeconomic status also need to be examined.

Second, comparing the development of eating problems in Blacks versus Whites may elucidate some of the cultural factors involved.

Unfortunately, in comparisons between cultures, one culture (usually the minority one) is frequently treated as inferior (Spencer & Markstrom-Adams, 1990). In this case, however, the comparison may help to clarify what is protective for various eating problems in each culture. For example, the broader acceptance of body fat found in Black culture may be protective against AN as well as against general body dissatisfaction and dieting. However, the same tolerance may encourage obesity, which is a greater problem among Black than among White women. In the latter example, the White culture's preoccupation with body shape may have some (limited) positive effects. Thus, each culture serves to protect against some problems while possibly facilitating others.

The developmental psychopathology model also suggests that there are multiple pathways to and away from eating problems. As we have noted, current models are heavily based on clinical samples. To understand the diversity of pathways, however, it is important to study diverse populations. Hence, studying Black women may yield new information about pathways. It must be emphasized, however, that studying Black women will not answer questions about all minority women. The culture of Asian Americans, for example, may be more similar to White than to Black culture in encouraging thinness (or "smallness") and body dissatisfaction. Although minority status is certainly part of Black culture, it should be borne in mind that the two are not equivalent. It is therefore important to investigate eating problems in other minority groups, as well.

It is difficult to evaluate the meaning of racial differences for prevention. Inasmuch as they reflect cultural differences, however, it does seem advisable to continue including lessons on media and cultural messages in prevention curricula (Shisslak et al., chapter 14, this volume). The little that is known about the messages that Black parents and peers provide to adolescent girls (Parker et al., 1995), also provide a possible prototype of the message that might be conveyed to all girls.

REFERENCES

Abrams, K. K., Allen, L. R., & Gray, J. J. (1993). Disordered eating attitudes and behaviors, psychological adjustment, and ethnic identity: A comparison of black and white female college students. *International Journal of Eating Disorders, 14,* 49–57.

Allan, J. D., Mayo, K., & Michel, Y. (1993). Body size values of white and black women. *Research in Nursing and Health, 16,* 323–333.

Anderson, L. P. (1991). Acculturative stress: A theory of relevance to black Americans. *Clinical Psychological Review, 11,* 685–702.

Andrews, B., Valentine, E. R., & Valentine, J. D. (1995). Depression and eating disorders following abuse in childhood in two generations of women. *British Journal of Psychology, 34,* 37–52.

Attie, I., & Brooks-Gunn, J. (1989). Development of eating problems in adolescent girls: A longitudinal study. *Developmental Psychology, 25,* 70–79.

Bardwell, J. R., Cochran, S. W., & Walker, S. (1986). Relationship of parental education, race, and gender to sex role stereotyping in five-year-old kindergarteners. *Sex Roles, 15,* 275–281.

Beebe, D. W. (1994). Bulimia nervosa and depression: A theoretical and clinical appraisal in light of the binge–purge cycle. *British Journal of Clinical Psychology, 33,* 259–276.

Bennett, N. A. M., Spoth, R. L., & Borgen, F. H. (1991). Bulimic symptoms in high school females: Prevalence and relationship with multiple measures of psychological health. *Journal of Community Psychology, 19,* 13–28.

Blundell, J. E., & Hill, A. J. (1993). Binge eating: Psychobiological mechanisms. In C. G. Fairburn & G. T. Wilson (Eds.), *Binge eating: Nature, assessment, and treatment* (pp. 206–226). New York: Guilford.

Bordo, S. (1993). *Unbearable weight: Feminism, Western culture, and the body.* Berkeley: University of California Press.

Boumann, C. E., & Yates, W. R. (1994). Risk factors for bulimia nervosa: A controlled study of parental psychiatric illness and divorce. *Addictive Behaviors, 19,* 667–675.

Brown, L. J. P., Powell, J., & Earls, F. (1989). Stressful life events and psychiatric symptoms in black adolescent females. *Journal of Adolescent Research, 4,* 140–151.

Brumberg, J. J. (1988). *Fasting girls.* Cambridge, MA: Harvard University Press.

Burke, G. L., Savage, P. J., Manolio, T. A., Sprafka, J. M., Wagenknecht, L. E., Sidney, S., Perkins, L. L., Liu, K., & Jacobs, D. R. (1992). Correlates of obesity in young black and white women: The CARDIA study. *American Journal of Public Health, 82,* 10–14.

Cattanach, L., & Rodin, J. (1988). Psychosocial components of the stress process in bulimia. *International Journal of Eating Disorders, 7,* 75–88.

Chandler, S. B., Abood, D. A., Lee, D. T., Cleveland, M. Z., & Daly, J. A. (1994). Pathogenic eating attitudes and behaviors and body dissatisfaction differences among black and white college students. *Eating Disorders, 2,* 319–328.

Childress, A. C., Brewerton, T. D., Hodges, E. L., & Jarrell, M. P. (1993). The Kids' Eating Disorders Survey (KEDS): A study of middle school students. *Journal of the American Academy of Child and Adolescent Psychiatry, 32,* 843–850.

Connors, M. E., & Morse, W. (1993). Sexual abuse and eating disorders: A review. *International Journal of Eating Disorders, 13,* 1–12.

Cooper, P. J., & Fairburn, C. G. (1993). Confusion over the core psychopathology of bulimia nervosa. *International Journal of Eating Disorders, 13,* 385–390.

Council of Economic Advisors. (1987). *The economic report of the President.* Washington, DC: Government Printing Office.

Crandall, C. S. (1994). Prejudice against fat people: Ideology and self-interest. *Journal of Personality and Social Psychology, 66,* 882–894.

deZwaan, M., Nutzinger, D. O., & Schoenbeck, G. (1992). Binge eating in overweight women. *Comprehensive Psychiatry, 33,* 256–261.

Edwards-Hewitt, T., & Gray, J. J. (1993). *The prevalence of disordered eating attitudes and behaviors in Black-American and Caucasian-American college women: Ethnic, regional, class and media differences.* Paper presented at the Annual Meeting of the Eastern Psychological Association.

Emmons, L. (1992). Dieting and purging behavior in black and white high school students. *Journal of the American Dietetic Association, 92,* 306–312.

Fairburn, C. G. (1994, April). *Risk factors for bulimia nervosa.* Paper presented at the International Conference on Eating Disorders, New York.

Fairburn, C. G. (1995). The prevention of eating disorders. In K. D. Brownell & C. G. Fairburn (Eds.), *Eating disorders and obesity* (pp. 289–293). New York: Guilford.

Fairburn, C. G., & Beglin, S. A. (1990). Studies of the epidemiology of bulimia nervosa. *American Journal of Psychiatry, 147,* 401–408.

Felitti, V. J. (1993). Childhood sexual abuse, depression, and family dysfunction in adult obese patients: A case control study. *Journal of the Southern Medical Association, 86,* 732–736.

Garfinkel, P. E., Goldbloom, D., Davis, R., Olmsted, M. P., Garner, D. M., & Halmi, K. A. (1992). Body dissatisfaction in bulimia nervosa: Relationship to weight and shape concerns and psychological functioning. *International Journal of Eating Disorders, 11,* 151–161.

Garner, D. M., Garfinkel, P. E., Schwartz, D., & Thompson, M. (1980). Cultural expectations of thinness in women. *Psychological Reports, 47,* 183–191.

Garner, D. M., & Olmsted, M. P. (1984). *The Eating Disorder Inventory Manual.* Odessa, FL: Psychological Assessment Resources, Inc.

Garner, D. M., Olmsted, M. P., Bohr, Y., & Garfinkel, P. (1982). The Eating Attitudes Test: Psychometric features and clinical correlates. *Psychological Medicine, 12,* 871–878.

Giddings, P. (1984). *When and where I enter: The impact of black women on race and sex in America.* New York: Morrow.

Graber, J., Brooks-Gunn, J., Paikoff, R., & Warren, M., (1994). Prediction of eating problems: An eight year study of adolescent girls. *Developmental Psychology, 30,* 823–834.

Gray, J. J., Ford, K., & Kelly, L. M. (1987). The prevalence of bulimia in a black college population. *International Journal of Eating Disorders, 6,* 733–740.

Greeno, C. G., & Wing, R. R. (1994). Stress-induced eating. *Psychological Bulletin, 115,* 444–464.

Harris, S. M. (1995). Family, self, and sociocultural contributions to body-image attitudes of African-American women. *Psychology of Women Quarterly, 19,* 129–145.

Harrison, A. O., Wilson, M. N., Pine, C. J., Chan, S. Q., et al. (1990). Family ecologies of ethnic minority children. *Child Development, 61,* 347–362.

Heatherton, T. F., & Baumeister, R. Y. (1991). Binge eating as escape from self-awareness. *Psychological Bulletin, 110,* 86–108.

Hill, A. J., & Bhatti, R. (1995). Body shape perception and dieting in preadolescent British Asian Girls: Links with eating disorders. *International Journal of Eating Disorders, 17,* 175–183.

Holden, N. L. (1991). Adoption and eating disorders: A high-risk group? *British Journal of Psychiatry, 158,* 829–833.

Hsu, L. K. (1987). Are eating disorders becoming more common in blacks? *International Journal of Eating Disorders, 6,* 113–124.

Hsu, L. K. (1990). *Eating disorders.* New York: Guilford.

Kassett, J. A., Gershon, E. S., Maxwell, M. E., Guroff, J. J., Kazuba, D. M., Smith, A. L, Brandt, H. A., & Jimmerson, D. C. (1989). Psychiatric disorders in the first-degree relatives of probands with bulimia nervosa. *American Journal of Psychiatry, 146,* 1468–1471.

Kearney-Cooke, A., & Striegel-Moore, R. H. (1994). Treatment of childhood sexual abuse in anorexia nervosa and bulimia nervosa: A feminist psychodynamic approach. *International Journal of Eating Disorders, 15,* 305–319.

Kemper, K. A., Sargent, R. G., Drane, J. W., Valois, R. F., & Hussey, J. W. (1994). Black and white females' perceptions of ideal body size and social norms. *Obesity Research, 2,* 117–126.

Kendler, K. S., MacLean, C., Neale, M., Kessler, R., Heath, A., & Eaves, L. (1991). The genetic epidemiology of bulimia nervosa. *American Journal of Psychiatry, 148,* 1627–1637.

Killen, J. D., Taylor, C. B., Hayward, C., Wilson, D. M., Hammer, L. D., Robinson, T. N., Litt, I., Simmonds, B. A., Varady, A., & Kraemer, H. (1994). The pursuit of thinness and onset of eating disorder symptoms in a community sample of adolescent girls: A three year prospective analysis. *International Journal of Eating Disorders, 16,* 227–238.

King, M. B. (1991). The natural history of eating pathology in attenders to primary medical care. *International Journal of Eating Disorders, 10,* 379–387.

Klem, M., Klesges, R., Bene, C., & Mellon, M. (1990). A psychosomatic study of restraint: The impact of race, gender, weight and marital status. *Addictive Behaviors, 15,* 147–152.

Kumanyika, S. (1987). Obesity in black women. *Epidemiologic Reviews, 9,* 31–50.

Kumanyika, S. K. (1994). Obesity in minority populations: An epidemiological assessment. *Obesity Research, 2,* 166–182.

Kumanyika, S., Wilson, J. F., & Guilford-Davenport, M. (1993). Weight-related attitudes and behaviors of black women. *Journal of the American Dietetic Association, 93,* 416–422.

Lancelot, C., & Kaslow, N. (1994). Sex role orientation and disordered eating in women: A review. *Clinical Psychology Review, 14,* 139–157.

Langer, L. M., Warheit, G. J., & Zimmerman, R. S. (1991). Epidemiological study of problem eating behaviors and related attitudes in the general population. *Addictive Behaviors, 16,* 167–173.

Levine, M. P., & Smolak, L. (1992). Toward a model of the developmental psychopathology of eating disorders. In J. Crowther, D. Tennebaum, S. Hobfoll, & M. Stephens (Eds.), *The etiology of bulimia nervosa* (pp. 59–80). Washington, DC: Hemisphere.

Levine, M. P., Smolak, L., & Hayden, H. (1994). The relation of sociocultural factors to eating attitudes and behaviors among middle school girls. *Journal of Early Adolescence, 14,* 471–490.

Levine, M. P., Smolak, L., Moodey, A., Shuman, M., & Hessen, L. (1994). Normative develomental challenges and dieting and eating disturbances in middle school girls. *International Journal of Eating Disorders, 15,* 11–20.

Lowe, M. R. (1993). The effects of dieting on eating behavior: A three-factor model. *Psychological Bulletin, 114,* 100–121.

Marchi, M., & Cohen, P. (1990). Early childhood eating behaviors and adolescent eating disorders. *Journal of the American Academy of Child and Adolescent Psychiatry, 29,* 112–117.

Marcus, M. D. (1993, May). *Binge eating disorder.* Paper presented at the National Institutes of Mental Health Symposium on Eating Disorders, Chicago, IL.

Marcus, M. D., Wing, R. R., Ewing, L., Kern, E., Gooding, W., & McDermott, M. (1990). Psychiatric disorders among obese binge eaters. *International Journal of Eating Disorders, 9,* 69–77.

Mitchell, J. E., Hatsukami, D., Pyle, R. L., & Eckert, E. D. (1986). The bulimia syndrome: Cause of the illness and associated problems. *Comprehensive Psychology, 27,* 165–170.

National Center for Health Statistics. (1991). *Health, United States, 1990.* Washington, DC: U.S. Department of Health and Human Services, Public Health Service, Centers for Disease Control; DHHS (PHS) Publication No. 91–1232.

National Heart, Lung, and Blood Institute: Growth and Health Study Research Group. (1992). Obesity and cardiovascular disease risk factors in black and white girls: The NHLBI growth and health study. *American Journal of Public Health, 82,* 1613–1621.

Newcomb, M., Huba, G., & Butler, P. (1981). A multidimensional assessment of stressful life events among adolescents: Derivations and correlates. *Journal of Health and Social Behaviors, 22,* 400–414.

Nichter, M., & Vuvkovic, N. (1994). Fat talk: Body image among adolescent girls. In N. Sault (Ed.), *Many mirrors: Body image and social relations* (pp. 109–131). New Brunswick, NJ: Rutgers University Press.

Orenstein, P. (1994). *Schoolgirls: Young women, self-esteem, and the confidence gap.* New York: Doubleday.

Parker, S., Nichter, M., Nichter, M., Vuckovic, N., Sims, C., & Ritenbaugh, C. (1995). Body image and weight concerns among African American and white adolescent females: Differences that make a difference. *Human Organization, 54,* 103–114.

Pate, J. E., Pumariega, A. J., Hester, C., & Garner, D. M. (1992). Cross-cultural patterns in eating disorders: A review. *Journal of the American Academy of Child and Adolescent Psychiatry, 31,* 802–809.

Patton, G. C., Johnson-Sabine, E., Wood, K., Mann, A. H., & Wakeling, A. (1990). Abnormal eating attitudes in London school girls—a prospective epidemiological study. *Psychological Medicine, 20,* 383–394.

Phinney, J. S. (1991). Ethnic identity and self-esteem: A review and integration. *Hispanic Journal of Behavioral Sciences, 13,* 193–208.

Phinney, J. S., & Chavira, V. (1992). Ethnic identity and self-esteem: An exploratory longitudinal study. *Journal of Adolescence, 15,* 271–281.

Pike, K. M. (1995). Bulimic symptomatology in high school girls: Toward a model of cumulative risk. *Psychology of Women Quarterly, 19,* 373–396.

Pike, K. M., & Rodin, J. (1991). Mothers, daughters, and disordered eating. *Journal of Abnormal Psychology, 100,* 198–204.

Polivy, J., & Herman, C. P. (1985). Dieting and binging: A causal analysis. *American Psychologist, 40,* 193–201.

Polivy, J., & Herman, C. P. (1993). Etiology of binge eating: Psychological mechanisms. In C. G. Fairburn and G. T. Wilson (Eds.), *Binge eating: Nature, assessment, and treatment* (pp. 173–205). New York: Guilford.

Pope, H. G., & Hudson, J. I. (1992). Is childhood sexual abuse a risk factor for bulimia nervosa? *American Journal of Psychiatry, 149,* 455–463.

Powell, A. D., & Kahn, A. S. (1995). Racial differences in women's desires to be thin. *International Journal of Eating Disorders, 17,* 191–195.

Pumariega, A. J., Gustavson, C. R., Gustavson, J. C., Motes, P. S., & Ayers, S. (1994). Eating attitudes in African-American women: The *Essence* Eating Disorders Survey. *Eating Disorders: The Journal for Treatment and Prevention, 2,* 5–16.

Richards, M. H., Abell, S., & Peterson, A. C. (1993). Biological development. In P. H. Tolan & B. J. Cohler (Eds.), *Handbook of clinical research and practice with adolescents* (pp. 21–44). New York: Wiley.

Robins, L. N., & Regier, L. N. (1991). *Psychiatric disorders in America: The Epidemiologic Catchment Area study.* New York: The Free Press.

Rodin, J., Silberstein, L. R., & Striegel-Moore, R. H. (1985). Women and weight: A normative discontent. In T. B. Sonderegger (Ed.), *Nebraska Symposium on Motivation* (pp. 267–308). Lincoln: University of Nebraska Press.

Root, M. P. P. (1990). Disordered eating in women of color. *Sex Roles, 22,* 525–536.

Rosen, J. G., Silberg, N. T., & Gross, J. (1988). Eating Attitudes Test and Eating Disorder Inventory: Norms for adolescent girls and boys. *Journal of Consulting and Clinical Psychology, 56,* 305–308.

Rothblum, E. D. (1992). The stigma of women's weight: Social and economic realities. *Feminism and Psychology, 2,* 61–73.

Rucker, C. E., III, & Cash, T. F. (1992). Body images, body-size perceptions, and eating behaviors among African-American and white college women. *International Journal of Eating Disorders, 12,* 291–300.

Schreiber, G. B., Robins, M., Striegel-Moore, R. H., Obarzanek, E., Morison, J., & Wright, D. J. (in press). Weight modification efforts reported by black and white adolescents: The NHLBI Growth and Health Study (NGHS). *Pediatrics.*

Shisslak, C., Crago, M., & Estes, L. (1995). The spectrum of eating disturbances. *International Journal of Eating Disorders, 18,* 209–219.

Shore, R. A., & Porter, J. E. (1990). Normative and reliability data for 11 to 18 year olds on the Eating Disorder Inventory. *International Journal of Eating Disorders, 9,* 201–207.

Singh, D. (1994). Is thin really beautiful and good? Relationship between waist-to-hip ratio (WHR) and female attractiveness. *Personality and Individual Differences, 16,* 123–132.

Slade, P. D. (1994). What is body image? *Behavior Research and Therapy, 32,* 497–502.

Smith, D. E., Marcus, M. D., & Eldredge, K. L. (1994). Binge eating syndromes: A review of assessment and treatment with an emphasis on clinical application. *Behavior Therapy, 25,* 635–658.

Smolak, L., & Levine, M. P. (1994a). Critical issues in the developmental psychopathology of eating disorders. In L. Alexander & D. Lumsden (Eds.), *Understanding eating disorders* (pp. 37–60). Washington, DC: Taylor & Francis.

Smolak, L., & Levine, M. P. (1994b). Toward an empirical basis for primary prevention of eating problems with elementary school children. *Eating Disorders: The Journal of Treatment and Prevention, 2,* 293–307.

Smolak, L., Levine, M. P., & Gralen, S. (1993). The impact of puberty and dating on eating problems among middle school girls. *Journal of Youth and Adolescence, 22,* 355–368.

Spencer, M. B., & Markstrom-Adams, C. (1990). Identity processes among racial and ethnic minority children in America. *Child Development, 61,* 290–310.

Spitzer, R. L., Devlin, M., Walsh, B. T., Hasin, D., Wing, R., Marcus, M., Stunkard, A., Wadden, T., Yanovski, S., Agras, S., Mitchell, J., & Nonas, C. (1992). Binge eating disorder: A multisite field trial of the diagnostic criteria. *International Journal of Eating Disorders, 11,* 191–204.

Spitzer, R. L., Yanovski, S., Wadden, T., Wing, R., Marcus, M. D., Stunkard, A., Devlin, M., Mitchell, J., & Hasin, D. (1993). Binge eating disorder: Its further validation in a multisite study. *International Journal of Eating Disorders, 13,* 137–154.

Stattin, H., & Magnusson, D. (1990). *Pubertal maturation in female development.* Hillsdale, NJ: Lawrence Erlbaum Associates.

Stice, E. (1994). Review of the evidence for a sociocultural model of bulimia nervosa and an exploration of the mechanisms of action. *Clinical Psychology Review, 14,* 633–661.

Story, M., Rosenwinkel, K., Himes, J. H., Resnick, M., Harris, L. J., & Blum, R. W. (1991). Demographic and risk factors associated with chronic dieting in adolescents. *American Journal of Disorders of Childhood, 145,* 994–998.

Strauss, J., Levy, C., & Kreipe, R. (1994, April). *Body norms, satisfaction, and cultural pressures in African-American and White women.* Paper presented at the Sixth International Conference on Eating Disorders, New York.

Striegel-Moore, R. H. (1993). Etiology of binge eating: A developmental perspective. In C. G. Fairburn and G. T. Wilson (Eds.), *Binge eating: Nature, assessment, and treatment* (pp. 144–172). New York: Guilford.

Striegel-Moore, R. H., & Kearney-Cooke, A. (1994). Exploring determinants and consequences of parents' attitudes about their children's physical appearances. *International Journal of Eating Disorders, 15,* 377–385.

Striegel-Moore, R. H., & Marcus, M. D. (1995). Eating disorders in women: Current issues and debates. In A. Stanton & S. Gallant (Eds.), *Women's health* (pp. 145–187). Washington, DC: American Psychological Association.

Striegel-Moore, R. H., Schreiber, G. B., Pike, K. M., Wilfley, D. E., Schreiber, G., & Rodin J. (1995). Drive for thinness in black and white preadolescent girls. *International Journal of Eating Disorders, 18,* 59–69.

Striegel-Moore, R. H., Silberstein, L. R., & Rodin, J. (1986). Toward an understanding of risk factors for bulimia. *American Psychologist, 4,* 246–263.

Striegel-Moore, R. H., Silberstein, L. R., & Rodin, J. (1993). The social self in bulimia nervosa: Public self-consciousness, social anxiety, and perceived fraudulence. *Journal of Abnormal Psychology, 102,* 297–303.

Striegel-Moore, R. H., Wilfley, D. E., Caldwell, M. B., Needham, M. L., & Brownell, K. D. (in press). Weight related attitudes and behaviors of women who diet to lose weight: A comparison of black dieters and white dieters. *Obesity Research.*

Strober, M. (1984). Stressful life events associated with bulimia in anorexia nervosa: Empirical findings and theoretical speculations. *International Journal of Eating Disorders, 3,* 3–17.

Strober, M., Lampert, C., Morrell, W., Burroughs, J., & Jacobs, C. (1990). A controlled family study of anorexia nervosa: Evidence of familial aggregation and lack of shared transmission with affective disorders. *International Journal of Eating Disorders, 9,* 239–253.

Taylor, J. R., Chatters, L. M., Tucker, M. B., & Lewis, E. (1990). Developments in research on black families. *Journal of Marriage and the Family, 52,* 993–1014.

Thompson, B. W. (1994). *A hunger so wide and so deep: American women speak out on eating problems.* Minneapolis: University of Minnesota Press.

Walters, E., & Kendler, K. (1994). Anorexia nervosa and anorexic-like syndromes in a population-based female twin study. *American Journal of Psychiatry, 152,* 64–71.

Warheit, G. J., Langer, L. M., Zimmerman, R. S., & Biafora, F. A. (1993). Prevalence of bulimic behaviors and bulimia among a sample of the general population. *American Journal of Epidemiology, 137,* 569–576.

Weiner, I. (1992). *Psychological disturbance in adolescence.* New York: Wiley.

Welch, S. L., & Fairburn, C. G. (1992). Sexual abuse and bulimia nervosa: Three integrated case control comparisons. *American Journal of Psychiatry, 151,* 402–407.

Wilfley, D. E., Schreiber, G., Pike, K., Rodin, J., & Striegel-Moore, R. H. (in press). Similarities in eating disturbances among black and white women. *International Journal of Eating Disorders.*

Williamson, D. F. (1993). Descriptive epidemiology of body weight and weight change in U.S. adults. *Annals of Internal Medicine, 119,* 646–649.

Williamson, D. F., Serdula, M. K., Anda, R. F., Levy, A., & Byers, T. (1992). Weight loss attempts in adults: Goals, duration, and rate of weight loss. *American Journal of Public Health, 82,* 1251–1257.

Wilson, D. B., Sargent, R., & Dias, J. (1994). Racial differences in selection of ideal body size by adolescent females. *Obesity Research, 2,* 38–43.

Wilson, G. T., Nonas, C. A., & Rosenblum, G. D. (1993). Assessment of binge eating in obese patients. *International Journal of Eating Disorders, 13,* 25–33.

Wing, R. R., Adams-Campbell, L. L., Marcus, M. D., & Janney, C. A. (1993). Effect of ethnicity and geographical location on body weight, dietary restraint, and abnormal eating attitudes. *Obesity Research, 1,* 193–198.

Wooley, S., & Wooley, O. W. (1985). Intensive outpatient and residential treatment for bulimia. In D. Garner & P. Garfinkel (Eds.), *Handbook of psychotherapy for anorexia nervosa and bulimia* (pp. 391–430). New York: Guilford.

Yanovski, S. (1993). Binge eating disorder: Current knowledge and future directions. *Obesity Research, 1,* 306–318.

Yanovski, S. Z., Nelson, J. E., Dubbert, B. K., & Spitzer, R. L. (1993). Association of binge eating disorder and psychiatric comorbidity in obese subjects. *American Journal of Psychiatry, 150,* 1472–1479.

12

Developmental Vulnerabilities for Eating Disorders

Mary E. Connors

Etiological models of eating disorders over the last decade and a half (e.g., a multidimensional model, Garfinkel & Garner, 1982; a biopsychosocial model, Johnson & Connors, 1987) have been useful in identifying some possible pathways to the development of anorexia nervosa (AN) and bulimia nervosa (BN). As Striegel-Moore and colleagues have noted (Striegel-Moore, 1993; Striegel-Moore, Silberstein, & Rodin, 1986), investigations of this topic must address the overrepresentation of young women in an eating-disordered group and the reasons that this phenomenon is occurring among females now. Furthermore, as only a minority of young women develop a clinically diagnosable eating disorder, factors that differentiate the most vulnerable group must be delineated. The latter question comprises the major focus of this chapter. Literature on high-risk groups, clinical samples, and their families are drawn from in constructing a risk factor model. The fullest exploration of vulnerabilities must go beyond dividing groups into those with eating disorders and those with no eating disorders and examine pathways that might lead to some aspects of an eating disorder but not to a clinical syndrome, to diagnosable pathology other than an eating disorder, and to no pathology.

Body dissatisfaction, the perception of oneself as fat, and dieting behaviors are all extremely widespread in the female population (Connors & Johnson, 1987). They affect a heterogeneous group ranging from normal women with no life impairment to severely disabled eating-disordered patients. Since these issues distinguish between eating disorders and other types of psychopathology or no pathology, this investigation begins with a brief exploration of the sociocultural and physical factors that place a certain cohort at risk for body dissatisfaction and disturbed eating. Individual vulnerabilities are explored for the purpose of understanding who might experience these concerns most acutely and what other variables combine with body dissatisfaction to result in a clinical syndrome.

RISK FACTORS FOR BODY DISSATISFACTION
AND DISTURBED EATING

Contextual and Physical Factors

Reports on clinical samples of eating disorders have repeatedly noted that patients are predominantly young White females from middle- to upper-class backgrounds (e.g., Johnson & Connors, 1987). Selection bias in favor of these variables is not surprising in clinical samples seeking psychotherapy, but recent research confirms that it is this group that experiences the most pressure to conform to the current very slender cultural ideal. The identification of female gender as a risk factor for the development of eating disorders is so robust that many studies investigate only female populations. Eating-disordered patients are approximately 95% female (Johnson & Connors, 1987), and research has found that body dissatisfaction and restrictive eating practices are much more common among females than among males (e.g., Connors & Johnson, 1987; Striegel-Moore et al., 1986). The greater importance of physical appearance in feminine socialization has been discussed by many authors (e.g., Brownmiller, 1984). The current culture is preoccupied with the female body and idealizes a specific hyperslim version of it that is biogenetically impossible for the great majority of women to attain (Garner, Garfinkel, Schwartz, & Thompson, 1980). Research on adolescents suggests that worries about physical appearance and weight have much more salience for young women than for young men (e.g., Wadden, Brown, Foster, & Linowitz, 1991), and some authors have concluded that weight dissatisfaction among girls has become a "normative discontent" (Rodin, Silberstein, & Striegel-Moore, 1985; Striegel-Moore et al., 1986).

Youth as a risk factor is also robustly documented. Both AN and BN typically begin in adolescence, and two thirds of female high school students report trying to lose weight (Rosen, Tacy, & Howell, 1990). A summary of several large clinical and community samples of patients with BN revealed that 86% were between the ages of 15 and 30 (Johnson & Connors, 1987). Although eating disorders occur in non-White populations (e.g., Dolan, 1991), several studies have shown that White high school students, college students, and adult women exhibit greater body dissatisfaction and dieting than do African Americans (Abrams, Allen, & Gray, 1993; Gray, Ford, & Kelly, 1987; Fisher, Pastore, Schneider, Pegler, & Napolitano, 1994; Rand & Kuldau, 1990).

An inverse relationship between weight and socioeconomic status, particularly strong for women, has been documented (Goldblatt, Moore, & Stunkard, 1965); higher socioeconomic status is associated with lower desired and current body weights for 18-year-old women and men, as well as with higher levels of dieting, binge eating, and exercise for weight control (Drewnowski, Kurth, & Krahn, 1994). Lesbian women show less body dissatisfaction and vulnerability to eating disorders than do heterosexual women (Brand, Rothblum, & Solomon, 1992; Siever, 1994). Thus, young White heterosexual females from higher socioeconomic backgrounds are especially concerned with adhering to the cultural mandate for slenderness and are at greatest risk for body dissatisfaction and dieting.

Females of a particular body type seem most vulnerable. A number of studies have reported that young women with higher weights and higher levels of body fat than peers exhibit more body dissatisfaction, dieting, and eating disorder symptoms (Attie & Brooks-Gunn, 1989; Killen et al., 1994; Lacey, 1992; Nylander, 1971; Yates, 1992). Women with the greatest distribution of fat in the hips and buttocks relative to the waist and abdomen or with a larger hip diameter seem to be the most dissatisfied (Davis, Durnin, Dionne, & Gurevich, 1994; Radke-Sharpe, Whitney-Saltiel, & Rodin, 1990). Yates (1992) found that mothers of patients with BN were more likely to report a larger current body mass index than mothers of controls. Since weight is approximately 70% heritable (Stunkard, Harris, Pedersen, & McClearn, 1990), this is suggestive of a familial propensity to be heavier than peers and thus more deviant from the current ideal.

Thompson and Heinberg (1993) found that a history of having been teased about one's weight or size was a significant predictor of body dissatisfaction and eating disturbance. Lacey (1992) interviewed the mothers and sisters of a group of patients with BN, and these relatives reported that they had viewed the bulimic patient as heavier in late childhood and adolescence than other family members. Johnson and Connors (1987) found that over one half of patients with BN in large samples reported a history of overweight.

Maternal attitudes about weight seem influential: Mothers' perceived investment in their own slenderness was a predictor of dieting in middle-school-aged daughters (Levine, Smolak, Moodey, Shuman, & Hessen, 1994). Mothers of adolescent daughters with disordered eating had chronic concerns with dieting and were dieting at a younger age than were mothers of daughters with normal eating (Pike & Rodin, 1991). Parents who themselves dieted were significantly more likely to propose weight-loss methods to their children than were nondieting parents (Striegel-Moore & Kearney-Cooke, 1994).

Developmental Challenges

Some authors have focused on how the developmental tasks of adolescence and the manner in which they are negotiated might influence the development of disturbed eating attitudes and behaviors. Early menarche, which involves having to contend with a different and fatter body before one's peers do, has been cited as a risk factor in some reports

(Killen et al., 1994; Striegel-Moore et al., 1986), although other researchers suggest that timing of menarche does not seem to have predictive value longitudinally (Attie & Brooks-Gunn, 1989; Gralen, Levine, Smolak, & Murnen, 1990; Lacey, 1992; for a detailed review see also Smolak & Levine, chapter 9, this volume).

However, the stresses of adolescent transitions, including menarche, may have other implications. Levine et al. (1994) found that girls who were beginning the process of heterosexual dating at the same time that they started menstruating were at greater risk for disturbed eating. The addition of a sense of increased academic pressure and worry over school performance combined with the simultaneity of these two changes increased disordered eating significantly.

Our culture stresses achievement and success, and for young women interpersonal attractiveness is a large component of "success." Adolescence involves an intensified focus on gender, which causes greater strain on young women to conform to gender roles and to be "real women" (Galatzer-Levy & Cohler, 1993). This requires adherence to cultural norms mandating thinness so that one may be viewed as an acceptable romantic partner. Body dissatisfaction engendered by the disparity between cultural images of female beauty and adolescents' real bodies leads to dieting behaviors intended to correct the perceived deficiencies.

Dieting is a precursor to eating disorders. For eample, AN involves dieting to dangerous levels of weight loss; in addition, the deprivation of dieting often promotes binge eating (Polivy & Herman, 1983), and the onset of BN is commonly preceded by dieting (Johnson & Connors, 1987). Dieting causes stress (Rosen et al., 1990) and may place women at risk for depression (McCarthy, 1990); also, its typical ineffectiveness as a means of weight control (Bennett & Gurin, 1982; Polivy & Herman, 1983) can lead to frustration, feelings of failure, and lowered self-esteem (Johnson & Connors, 1987). Normative body dissatisfaction and dieting result in immense suffering in the female population. However, although a large cohort of adolescent and young adult women is at risk for disturbed eating due to contextual, physical, and developmental variables, most of these individuals do not go on to exhibit clinical eating disorders.

DIFFERENTIATION BETWEEN NORMAL AND ABNORMAL

High-Risk Groups

Research on psychological variables that distinguish between more symptomatic and less symptomatic groups is examined. Several authors have found negative body image and body dissatisfaction to be associated with more eating disorder symptoms in adolescence (Attie & Brooks-Gunn, 1989; Gralen et al., 1990; Johnson, Lewis, Love, Lewis, & Stuckey, 1984; Killen et al., 1994; Leon, Fulkerson, Perry, & Cudeck, 1993; Steiger, Leung, Puentes-Neuman, & Gottheil, 1992). The internalizing dimension of psychopathology, specifically depression, was an important predictor of eating pathology in later adolescence (Attie & Brooks-Gunn, 1989). Lack of interoceptive awareness (also called alexithymia) has been associated with eating pathology in adolescence (Leon et al., 1993; Killen et al., 1994). Fisher et al. (1994) found an association between disturbed eating attitudes and lower self-esteem and higher anxiety in high school students. Negative emotionality (specifically stress reactivity; Leon et al.) and feelings of inadequacy and worthlessness (Killen et al.) also predicted eating problems in adolescence.

Studies of young adults reveal similar findings. Dunn and Ondercin (1981) found that college students who scored high on a measure of compulsive eating reported more inner tension, suspiciousness, and less emotional stability than did the low scorers. Smolak and Levine (1993) found that college women with anorexic and bulimic tendencies showed more conflictual dependence (excessive guilt, mistrust, and resentment) on both parents than did controls without eating pathology. Button and Whitehouse (1981) and Thompson and Schwartz (1982) reported that college women who scored high on a measure of pathological dieting attitudes and behaviors tended to be in a period of stressful development and to have unattainable body ideals.

Steiger and colleagues (Steiger, Leung, Puentes-Newman, et al., 1992; Steiger, Leung, Ross, & Gulko, 1992) assessed high school women for the presence of eating and mood symptoms. Eating symptoms without mood problems were associated with body image concerns but not with other disturbances. Those who reported concurrent eating and mood problems also exhibited more pronounced body image concerns and more psychological disturbance, including greater impulsivity and self-criticism, than did aysmptomatic individuals or those with eating problems alone. This group with concurrent symptomatology also displayed more signs of diagnosable AN and BN on interview than did other subjects. The young women with circumscribed eating symptoms were no more likely than the asymtomatic group to show signs of a clinical disorder.

The data suggest that the normative levels of body dissatisfaction and dieting so prevalent in the current sociocultural context may be differentiated from clinically significant eating disorders on the basis of emotional disturbance. Body dissatisfaction and dieting behaviors could be viewed as spanning a continuum from slight to very intense. Individuals may have mild to moderate levels without other life impairment. Women with more symptoms of eating disorders seem to have high levels of body dissatisfaction and disturbed eating attitudes and behaviors in conjunction with other psychological problems, including greater levels of depression, feelings of ineffectiveness, alexithymia, self-criticism, impulsivity, emotional reactivity, and life impairment.

Personality Profile of Clinical Samples

The personality profile of clinically diagnosed eating-disordered patients includes the characteristics already mentioned. Patients with the restricting form of AN have high levels of depression, anxiety, and alienation (Norman & Herzog, 1983). They tend to display social isolation and sexual withdrawal, often living restricted lives primarily spent alone (Thompson & Schwartz, 1982). Patients with BN and AN with binge eating are generally less isolated but also have more difficulty than do those with restricting AN with impulsivity and substance abuse (Johnson & Connors, 1987; Holderness, Brooks-Gunn, & Warren, 1994) and frequently report depression and anxiety (Johnson & Larson, 1982). Numerous studies utilizing different measures have found that patients with AN and BN report significantly lower self-esteem than normals. The self-esteem problems include high self-expectations, self-criticism, guilt, high needs for approval from others, and interpersonal sensitivity (Connors, Johnson, & Stuckey, 1984; Garfinkel & Garner, 1982; Katzman & Wolchik, 1984).

Armstrong and Roth (1989) found that both AN and BN was marked by intense sensitivity to separations and much more evidence of anxious attachment than was seen in controls. Even mild separations induced distress and were interpreted as a sign of rejection resulting from personal inadequacies. Deficient interoceptive awareness is significantly greater in individuals with BN and AN compared to controls (Cochrane, Brewerton, Wilson, & Hodges, 1993; Garfinkel & Garner, 1982). High rates of additional Axis I diagnoses and personality disorders have been found in eating-disordered subjects (e.g., Kendler et al, 1991; Steiger, Liquornik, Chapman, & Hussain, 1991). Overall, individuals with AN and BN exhibit more disturbances in interpersonal functioning, self-esteem, and self-regulation of affective states than do normal controls.

Some aspects of this poorer functioning may be related to the distressing experience of having an eating disorder. Social isolation may increase as the disorder progresses and the individual increasingly organizes her life around ingesting or avoiding food (Thompson & Schwartz, 1982). Self-esteem might worsen with perceived failure to achieve one's ideal weight and control eating behavior, and tends to increase when treatment enables patients to achieve symptom reduction or remission (Connors et al., 1984). However, the psychological characteristics of the high-risk groups with the greatest levels of disturbed eating attitudes and behaviors suggest that emotional vulnerabilities are important predictors of eating problems. It is likely that poorer self-esteem and psychological functioning leads to as well as results from the development of eating disorders (Garfinkel & Garner, 1982; Johnson & Connors, 1987; Striegel-Moore et al., 1986).

ETIOLOGICAL FACTORS FOR PSYCHOLOGICAL DISTURBANCE IN EATING DISORDERS

A biopsychosocial perspective on the development of psychopathology suggests that a complete explanation must take into account biological variables such as inherited vulnerabilities and predispositions, the interpersonal experiences of the developing child, and the sociocultural milieu (Connors, 1994). Temperamental and familial factors that may be important in the etiology of eating disorders are reviewed, as is the role of stressful life events.

Temperament

Recent research in genetic epidemiology has suggested some degree of familial transmission of risk for AN and BN (Fichter & Noegel, 1990; Kendler et al., 1991; Strober, Lampert, Morrell, Burroughs, & Jacobs, 1990). Kendler et al. estimate that the heritability of a liability to BN is between 50% and 55%. Strober et al. propose that for AN the transmitted vulnerability may involve variations in personality traits that underlie avoidant or phobic tendencies. For all eating disorders it may be useful to explore temperamental factors or characteristic patterns of emotional reactions that develop from biological influences. Commonly agreed-upon aspects of temperament include sensitivity and intensity of reaction, emotional self-regulation, sociability, and activity (Bates, 1994).

Strober et al. (1990) relate Cloninger's (1987) model of personality dimensions to AN. This model describes three phenotypic dimensions: harm avoidance and behavioral inhibition (the intensity of response to signals of aversive stimuli and situations that convey threat or uncertainty), novelty seeking and behavioral activation (a tendency toward exhilaration or excitement in response to novel stimuli and thus exploratory activity), and reward dependence (a propensity to respond intensely to signals of reward such as social approval and to maintain such behavior once it has been conditioned). Strober et al. describe patients with AN as being low in novelty seeking, as manifested in such tendencies as stoicism, persistence, preference for the familiar, and orderliness. Patients with AN are high in harm avoidance, as seen in their emotional restraint, anxious worry, overarousal to affect-generating stimuli, and extreme caution, and are high in reward dependence as reflected in their sensitivity and hypervigilance to signs of rejection from others. Strober et al. suggest that these genotypic tendencies predispose individuals to the pathological control and avoidance mechanisms seen in patients with AN.

Cloninger's (1987) model may also be applied to BN. Some reports have emphasized impulsivity as characteristic of many patients with BN and with bulimic AN (e.g., Johnson & Connors, 1987), and authors have noted the presence of histrionic personality disorder or traits in patients with BN (e.g., Wonderlich, Swift, Slotnick, & Goodman, 1990). Patients with BN may be higher than patients with AN on the dimension of novelty seeking. Individuals higher than average in novelty seeking are described as impulsive, exploratory, fickle, quick-tempered, disorderly, and excitable (Cloninger, 1987). Like those with AN, patients with BN are probably high in reward dependence, with their sensitivity to interpersonal rejection, and high in harm avoidance, although probably not as high as is seen in AN.

Kagan and colleagues (e.g., Kagan & Snidman, 1991) reported results that also may be relevant to eating disorders. These authors have identified a temperamental characteristic known as behavioral inhibition. Inhibited children, who comprise about 10% of groups studied, are withdrawn, shy, and avoidant in response to novel situations. Their physiology differs from that of uninhibited children on measures of heart rate acceleration and pupil dilation, suggesting increased reactivity in the sympathetic nervous system. Behavioral inhibition has been related to psychological disorders in adulthood, particularly to anxiety disorders. Behavioral inhibition probably captures a domain of experience that overlaps with Cloninger's dimension of novelty seeking. The comorbidity of eating disorders and anxiety disorders noted by some authors (e.g., Kendler et al., 1991) suggests that this style may have some association with eating disorders.

Family Interaction

The families of eating-disordered patients have been studied in efforts to explore the possible impact of development within a particular family context. Family interactional styles as perceived by eating-disordered women and their parents have been researched, and a limited number of studies have utilized behavioral observations. Parental psychopathology has also been viewed as a possible contributor to the development of eating disorders.

Cohesion. A number of investigations have found differences between families of eating-disordered women and controls on the dimensions of support, helpfulness, empathy, and understanding, known collectively as Cohesion on the Family Environment Scale (Moos, 1974), a frequently used measure. Lower perceived family cohesion has been reported by patients with BN (Johnson & Flach, 1985; Kenny & Hart, 1992; Ordman & Kirschenbaum, 1986; Stern et al., 1989); by patients with restricting AN and bulimic AN (Stern et al., 1989); by mothers of adolescents with AN (Leon, Lucas, Colligan, Ferdinande, & Kamp, 1985); and by mothers of adolescent girls scoring high on a measure of eating disturbance (Attie & Brooks-Gunn, 1989). Fathers and mothers of patients with AN and BN have been perceived as lower in warmth, empathy, and emotional support (Calam, Waller, Slade, & Newton, 1990) and also in affectionate responsiveness than controls (Steiger et al., 1991).

In one study, daughters with BN reported perceiving less attention and affection from parents than did controls, expressing their sense that parents did not know them well or spend time with them, and that there were few meaningful caring exchanges in the family (Dolan, Lieberman, Evans, & Lacey, 1990). Patients with BN and bulimic AN perceived their families as lacking nurturance and empathy; members of the latter group also experienced their families as being less supportive, less involved, and more detached; patients with restricting AN, bulimic AN, and BN all saw parents as neglectful (Humphrey, 1986a, 1986b). Observations of family interactions revealed that families of patients with BN showed little affection or support in their interactions and that they could be characterized as withholding, depriving, and lacking in empathy (Humphrey, 1989).

Support for Autonomy.   Formulations of AN based on clinical samples (e.g., Bruch, 1973; Minuchin, Rosman, & Baker, 1978) have stressed that familial enmeshment, overcontrol, and lack of support for autonomy characterizes these families. Empirical studies have provided some confirmation of this hypothesis for both BN and AN, although the findings are strongest for AN. Overprotection by mothers has been perceived by patients with AN and BN (Perednia & Vandereycken, 1989), as has overprotection and control by fathers (Calam et al., 1990). High familial control has also been perceived by patients with BN and AN (Hastings & Kern, 1994; Johnson & Connors, 1987; Strober, 1981). Encouragement of self-sufficient behavior by parents has been rated as low by patients with BN (Johnson & Flach, 1985; Kenny & Hart, 1992; Ordman & Kirschenbaum, 1986); by patients with AN and bulimic AN (Johnson & Connors; Strober, 1981); and mothers of patients with AN (Leon et al., 1985). Observations of family interactions showed that parents of patients with AN were lacking in support for their daughters' autonomy and tended to ignore and negate their daughters' self-expression (Humphrey, 1989). Humphrey (1987) also observed that parents of patients with bulimic AN gave mixed messages to their daughters, juxtaposing messages of control and autonomy, but finally resorting to hostile control.

Communication and Expressiveness. Perceptions of how much emphasis a family places on open communication of feelings have been explored, with several studies suggesting that families of eating-disordered women may not encourage expressiveness. Patients with BN reported perceiving low expressiveness within the family (Hastings & Kern, 1994; Johnson & Flach, 1985; Ordman & Kirschenbaum, 1986; Shisslak, McKeon, & Crago, 1990; Stern et al., 1989), as did patients with both restricting AN and bulimic AN (Johnson & Connors, 1987; Stern et al., 1989; Strober, 1981). Mothers and fathers of the three eating-disordered groups also perceived low expressiveness (Stern et al., 1989), and similar findings were reported for mothers of adolescent females scoring high on a measure of eating disturbance (Attie & Brooks-Gunn, 1989). Patients with AN and their mothers reported poorer communication in their families compared to controls (Garfinkel et al., 1983).

Organization. The degree of familial structure or organization has been explored, with some studies finding no differences between eating disorder families and controls on this variable (e.g., Johnson & Flach, 1985). Lower family organization has been perceived by patients with BN compared with controls (Hastings & Kern, 1994), and these patients have described their families as understructured (Humphrey, 1986a). Patients with both AN and BN as well as their parents have reported perceiving more disorganization in their families compared to controls (Kog, Vertommen, & Vandereycken, 1989), as have mothers of adolescents at risk for eating disorders (Attie & Brooks-Gunn, 1989).

Conflict and Hostility. Higher levels of conflict and anger within the family have been perceived by patients with BN as compared with controls (Hastings & Kern, 1994; Humphrey, 1986b; Johnson & Flach, 1985; Ordman & Kirschenbaum, 1986; Shisslak et al., 1990; Stern et al., 1989). Similar findings have been reported for patients with AN and bulimic AN (Johnson & Connors, 1987; Stern et al., 1989; Strober, 1981. Mothers and fathers of women in all three eating-disordered groups perceived more conflict in their families compared to controls (Stern et al., 1989). The women themselves experienced their families as more blaming and rejecting than did controls (Humphrey, 1986b), and observations of family interactional styles showed that families of patients with BN were characterized by high levels of belittling and blaming (Humphrey, 1989).

Achievement Expectations. Studies in this area have not found a distinct pattern differentiating eating disorder families and control families. Some research has found no significant differences on this variable (Johnson & Flach, 1985; Ordman & Kirschenbaum, 1986), although Johnson and Connors (1987) suggested that even average achievement expectations in a family context of little emphasis on intellectual, social, or recreational activities may leave young women unprepared to achieve at the desired level. Stern et al. (1989) did find that all three eating-disordered groups rated their families as more achievement-oriented than did controls. Daughters described their families as significantly more achievement-oriented than parents did, which was opposite to the pattern displayed by controls.

Summary of Family Interaction. Data from self-report and observational studies converge to describe a problematic family environment for women with eating disorders of all subtypes. Family relationships seem characterized by a preponderance of negative interactions such as blaming, belittling, and overcontrol and by a dearth of positively toned exchanges. Parental support, empathy, and nurturance seem lacking, as does open expression of feelings. Findings concerning familial organization and achievement expectations are less robust but suggest that these areas may also be of concern.

Importance of Comorbid Depression. A few studies have reported that comorbid depression rather than eating disorders per se have been correlated with perceptions of a problematic family environment. Wonderlich and Swift (1990) found that depressed eating-disordered individuals perceived more hostility in parental relationships than did controls but that nondepressed eating-disordered women did not differ from controls on any measure of interaction. Thienemann and Steiner (1993) found a positive relationship between degree of depression and reports of a negative family environment regardless of eating disorder diagnosis. Blouin, Zuro, and Blouin (1990) reported that persons with both BN and depression perceived higher achievement expectations and control and lower support for independence and expressiveness compared to controls, but that persons suffering from BN but not from depression were close to controls in family perception. The implications of these findings are discussed in a later section.

Parental Psychopathology. The existence of parental psychopathology that may impair parenting and influence the development of eating disorders has been investigated. The evidence mentioned earlier for a degree of familial transmission of eating disorders suggests that at least some women with eating disorders were raised by mothers who may have been preoccupied with eating disorders of their own. Strober et al. (1990) reported a fivefold greater risk of eating disorder for female relatives of patients with AN compared to female relatives of patients with other (noneating) disorders. Other problems that have been studied include affective disorder, substance abuse, and general personality functioning.

Affective Disorders. A high incidence of depression has been found among first-degree relatives of eating-disordered women. Hudson and colleagues (Hudson, Laffer, & Pope, 1982; Hudson, Pope, Jonas, & Yurgelun-Todd, 1983) found that 53% of patients with BN had first-degree relatives with major affective disorder. The morbid risk factor for affective disorder in relatives was 28%, similar to that found in families of individuals with bipolar disorder. Strober and colleagues (Strober, 1981; Strober, Salkins, Burroughs, & Morrell, 1982) found prevalence rates of affective disorder in relatives of patients with bulimic AN equivalent to a morbid risk of 20%, compared to 6% in the general population.

Substance Abuse. An association between familial alcoholism and eating disorders, particularly BN, has been noted in the literature by many authors (e.g., Johnson & Connors, 1987). A recent review of the comorbidity of eating disorders and substance abuse (Holderness et al., 1994) reports on 51 studies of the topic and finds a strong link between familial alcoholism and BN. A median of 39% of bulimics sampled described family histories of alcoholism and a median of 19% reported drug or substance use disorder. Figures are also high for patients with bulimic AN (18% and 44% in two studies) and much lower for those with restricting AN.

Other Psychopathology. Strober (1981) administered the Minnesota Multiphasic Personality Inventory to parents of patients with bulimic AN and restricting AN and found that 50% of both the mothers and fathers in the bulimic group evidenced some disorder, compared to 18% of the mothers and 14% of the fathers in the restrictor group. Fathers of patients with bulimic AN showed more signs of personality disorder (hostility, impulsiveness, immaturity, and dyscontrol), whereas fathers of restrictors seemed more passive and reserved. Mothers of patients with BN evidenced more depression, emotional dissatisfaction, and hostility. Perednia and Vandereycken (1989) reported that parents of patients with both AN and BN scored higher than did controls on a measure of neuroticism and depression, with scales indicating anxiety, agoraphobia, somatization, distrust, and interpersonal sensitivity.

Parents of patients with BN were also found to differ significantly from controls on personality disorder subscales measuring histrionic, schizotypal, and obsessive–compulsive traits (Carney, Yates, & Cizadlo, 1990). Family members of patients with BN were more likely to endorse items indicating that they tended to act very emotionally when little things went wrong, that others considered them self-centered, and that they wasted time trying too hard to make things perfect. Finally, mothers of patients with BN and AN reported having experienced poor parenting while they were growing up, characterized as affectionless but highly controlling (Perednia & Vandereycken, 1989).

Stressful Life Events

A number of studies have explored the possible contribution of traumatic events, specifically child sexual abuse, to the development of eating disorders. Some authors (e.g., Root & Fallon, 1988) have argued for the importance of victimization experiences as etiological factors. Connors and Morse (1993) reviewed the literature in this area and concluded that rates of child sexual abuse were around 30% in the eating-disordered populations studied, a figure not significantly different from rates found in nonclinical populations. Most of these subjects were outpatients, and it is likely that inpatient samples would have shown higher rates. A minority of eating-disordered patients may show a relatively direct link between abusive experiences and the development of an eating disorder (e.g., drastic weight loss to discourage sexual predation). For most individuals, however, abuse is neither necessary nor sufficient for the development of eating disturbance. The importance of trauma as an etiological factor in other pathology is discussed shortly.

The family context in which abuse occurs or in which a child may be helped to recover from abuse is probably central. Smolak, Levine, and Sullins (1990) found that parental unreliability was associated with BN in sexually abused women. Hastings and Kern (1994) reported that a chaotic family environment moderated the relationship between child sexual abuse and BN; this association was found only in chaotic families.

AN ETIOLOGICAL MODEL

These descriptions suggest that a variety of interpersonal disturbances and difficulties in affective self-regulation occur in eating-disordered women and their families that are significantly different from those of controls. Early studies focusing on differences between eating-disordered patients and normal controls, and between patients with AN and BN, led researchers to postulate relatively specific types of psychopathology and familial contexts for each disorder (e.g., Humphrey, 1989; Johnson & Connors, 1987; Strober, 1981). The accumulation of data on the comorbidity of eating disorders with other Axis I and Axis II pathology suggests that questions involving etiology and differentiation among disorders are extremely complex. For example, up to 70% of patients with BN are reported to suffer from major affective disorder

(Hudson et al., 1983; Walsh, Roose, & Glassman, 1985). The percentages of eating-disordered women reporting alcohol abuse or dependency are high, with 23% as the median for those with BN and 26% as the median for those with bulimic AN (Holderness et al., 1994). Kendler et al. (1991) reported that over three fourths of the patients with BN in their sample had at least one other Axis I diagnosis, most commonly major depression, an anxiety disorder, or substance abuse.

Axis II pathology seems very common in eating disorders, with some studies reporting that from one half to three fourths of patients in their samples have a probable diagnosis of personality disorder (Levin & Hyler, 1986; Piran, Lerner, Garfinkel, Kennedy, & Brouillette, 1988; Steiger et al., 1991; Wonderlich et al., 1990). Diagnoses of borderline, obsessive compulsive, histrionic, avoidant, and dependent personality disorders are most common. Borderline personality disorder may be found in one third or more of some eating-disordered individuals (Johnson, Tobin, & Enright, 1989; Piran et al.; Wonderlich et al., 1990). Moreover, specific differences between patients with AN and BN (and also their respective families) have been slight or nonexistent in some studies (e.g., Steiger et al. 1991; Stern et al., 1989). The various studies reviewed earlier that found no perceived differences between families of individuals with eating disorders and control families except for depressed patients (Blouin et al., 1990; Wonderlich & Swift, 1990) further suggests that much of the psychopathology seen in eating-disordered patients may not be specific to the eating disorder per se.

It is likely that eating disorders result from the intersection of two domains of experience, one leading an individual to body dissatisfaction with subsequent dieting and eating disturbance, and the other predisposing to interpersonal and self-regulatory difficulties. As illustrated in Fig. 12.1, both lines of development are considered necessary for a diagnosable eating disorder (Connors & Johnson, 1987; Garner, Olmsted, Polivy, & Garfinkel, 1984; Steiger, Leung, Puentes-Newman, & Gottheil, 1992). Body dissatisfaction (resulting from the contextual, physical, and developmental factors mentioned earlier) in the absence of emotional disturbance results in normal dieting. Some of these individuals may have high levels of weight preoccupation, as body dissatisfaction increases they more closely resemble the eating-disordered group. A subclinical or at-risk group for eating disorders may consist of those with relatively high body dissatisfaction and some vulnerability for affective dysregulation under stress.

Psychological impairment without body dissatisfaction is characteristic of such diagnoses as affective disorders, anxiety disorders, and personality disorders. These individuals may struggle with low self-esteem, painful affective states, and troubled interpersonal relationships, but eating and weight issues lack salience for them. They are relatively unconflicted about eating, may be more prone to lose weight than to gain

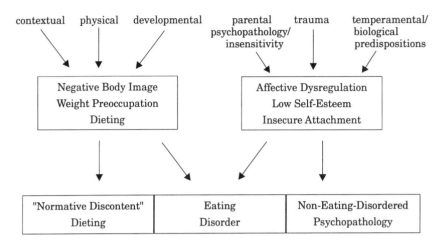

Risk Factors for Body Dissatisfaction   Risk Factors for Self-Regulatory Difficulties

contextual   physical   developmental   parental   trauma   temperamental/
                                          psychopathology/   biological
                                          insensitivity   predispositions

Negative Body Image	Affective Dysregulation
Weight Preoccupation	Low Self-Esteem
Dieting	Insecure Attachment

| "Normative Discontent" | Eating | Non-Eating-Disordered |
| Dieting | Disorder | Psychopathology |

FIG. 12.1 A two-component model of eating disorders.

when under stress, and are relatively satisfied with or unconcerned about their weight.

Individuals with high body dissatisfaction and major difficulties with affective regulation are the most likely to receive a diagnosis of AN or BN, as well as possibly other Axis I and Axis II diagnoses. Those who have few risk factors for either body dissatisfaction or affective difficulties are most likely to be free of diagnosable pathology. Individuals with moderate levels of risk for each dimension may or may not have a diagnosable eating disorder or other pathology, depending on factors such as current stress level, weight status, and social support. They might be considered to possess a vulnerability to disorder that could be expressed under conditions of sufficient stress.

Psychologists' understanding of genetic factors in eating disorders is limited at this time, and it is not yet known whether familial transmission occurs largely through affecting temperamental traits or whether other risk components such as single gene effects are operative (Strober et al., 1990). This should prove a fruitful area for further research, in that specific gene effects may be shown to link eating disorder syndromes to particular biological risk factors rather than to more general risk factors associated with a number of pathological syndromes. Temperamental predispositions toward behavioral inhibition and negative affectivity may be factors in a variety of anxiety, affective, and personality disorders. In the absence of data suggesting specific genetic effects, it is proposed that the temperamental, familial, and traumatic factors reviewed earlier predispose individuals to a range of pathological outcomes, including but not limited to those seen in AN and BN. Such temperamental factors may be particularly important in leading individuals to develop either AN or BN in the context of relatively similar environmental factors.

The family interactional styles characteristic of families with an eating-disordered member are likely seen in other types of pathology. Blouin et al. (1990) reviewed data suggesting that depressed patients commonly report that their families are conflicted, noncohesive, nonexpressive, and disorganized. Patients with anxiety disorders have described their parents as critical, frightening, angry, and controlling (Shear, Cooper, Klerman, Busch, & Shapiro, 1993) and ambivalent about individuation (Goldstein, 1982). Calam et al. (1990) noted that the tendency for families of most pathological groups is to be described as low in warmth and support and high in intrusion and control. The heterogeneity of eating-disordered patients (Johnson & Connors, 1987) and the comorbidity of AN and BN with other disorders may be more easily understood if most aspects of the interactional styles of families with eating-disordered members are viewed as general risk factors for psychological disturbance rather than as elements specifically predisposing to eating disorders. Needed research would utilize observational techniques to compare subgroups of eating-disordered patients and their families to other pathological groups, not simply normal controls, with careful screening for comorbidity to determine any specific differences.

Nonspecific Risk Factors

Two advances in research in the last decade make it possible to draw less speculative conclusions about the relationship between developmental trajectories and psychopathology. The first is evidence suggesting a strong relationship between traumatic events such as sexual and physical abuse and psychological impairment. The second body of work links insensitive parenting to later psychopathology.

Stressful Life Events. Controversy over the significance of stressful events such as child sexual abuse in the etiology of eating disorders may be resolved by viewing such trauma as a predisposing factor for a range of pathological outcomes rather than for more specific impairment. Trauma such as physical, sexual, and emotional abuse or severe neglect has been linked to interpersonal disturbances, depression, anxiety, somatization, sexual difficulties, personality disorders, and dissociation (e.g., Cortois, 1988; Herman, 1992; Putnam, 1989). Particularly severe trauma has been associated with psychological diagnoses connoting significant impairment; for instance, 67% of a sample of patients with borderline personality disorder reported a history of sexual abuse

(Herman, Perry, & van der Kolk, 1989), and 97% of a group of patients with multiple personality disorder reported serious childhood abuse of various sorts (Putnam, Guroff, Silberman, Barban, & Post, 1986). Herman (1992) has suggested that much severe psychopathology should be conceptualized as complex posttraumatic stress involving disturbances in affect regulation, self-perception, consciousness, and relationships.

Parental Sensitivity as Moderator of Experience. Insensitive parenting, characterized by rejection, intrusion, lack of attunement, and inconsistency has been associated with insecure attachment styles in infancy and childhood (Ainsworth, Blehar, Waters, & Wall, 1978; for a review see Isabella, chapter 7, this volume). Insecurely attached infants are overly avoidant or excessively clingy with caregivers (Ainsworth et al.). Insecurely attached children display more negative affect (unrelated to temperamental factors) than do secure children (Matas, Arend, & Sroufe, 1978) and are less competent and confident in interpersonal relationships (Waters, Wippman, & Sroufe, 1979). Longitudinal studies following infants through adulthood are not completed, but data from children aged 10 and 11 indicate that attachment style is significantly related to emotional health, competence, and the capacity to develop positive relationships (Elicker, Englund, & Sroufe, 1992). The emotional insensitivity of families with eating-disordered members described earlier has thus been associated in other research with insecure attachment in childhood. Further, caregivers who are depressed, disturbed, or alcoholic are particularly likely to have insecurely attached children (O'Connor, Sigman, & Brill, 1987; Radke-Yarrow, Cummings, Kuczynski, & Chapman, 1985).

Parental sensitivity may moderate the impact of traumatic events, as seen in studies linking sexual abuse and eating disorders only in chaotic families with parental unreliability (Hastings & Kern, 1994; Smolak et al., 1990). Studies of individuals who display competent and adaptive functioning despite environmental risk and adversity suggest that emotionally responsive caregiving and the presence of supportive relationships offering unconditional acceptance promote positive outcomes (Egeland, Carlson, & Sroufe, 1993; Werner, 1993). Conversely, parental lack of empathy may worsen the impact of aversive events, as when a child seeks comfort following trauma and is attacked or punished.

Parental sensitivity also interacts with temperamental variables, as seen in recent research that exposed children to arousing unfamiliar events and separations and measured cortisol secretion to assess stress level (Nachmias, 1993, in Gunnar, 1994). The behaviorally inhibited children with insecure attachment showed high cortisol levels; behaviorally uninhibited children did not, and neither did behaviorally inhibited children with secure attachment. The biological vulnerability coupled with insensitive parenting led to difficulty in adaptation, whereas highly responsive caregiving prevented untoward stress in children with a temperamental predisposition for overarousal.

Authors from a variety of perspectives have stressed the importance of parental sensitivity for appropriate self-development. Attachment theorists have described the formation of internal working models of self and other, that is, dynamic mental representations based on caregiving interactions that then mediate expectations and behavior (Bowlby, 1969). Others are viewed as trustworthy or unreliable, and the self is seen as deserving of care or not. Kohut (1971) postulated the existence of various vital developmental needs, including the need to be accepted and affirmed (mirroring needs), as well as a need to feel connected to another who is seen as strong, wise, and calm (idealizing needs). If these needs are met adequately in a responsive interpersonal milieu, a child gradually internalizes capacities to regulate self-esteem and affective states.

Sroufe (1991) described the movement from dyadic regulation of affect and arousal in the child–caregiver system to self-regulation when caregivers provide appropriately sensitive help and guidance. Krystal (1974) and Stolorow, Brandchaft, and Atwood (1987) suggested that with aid from empathic caregivers, children gradually learn to experience affects as distinguishable from bodily states and to differentiate among affects. Attuned caregivers help children to perceive affects as signals of changing self-states that can be experienced and managed. Increased cognitive skills aid in the verbal articulation of affect and in the capacity to tolerate strong emotion. In the absence of sensitive regulating others, affects may remain indistinguishable and primarily experienced somatically. Emotions may be experienced as overwhelming and dangerous states that must be avoided. The alexithymia, poor self-esteem, and affective dysregulation seen in eating-disordered populations suggests the aforementioned developmental difficulties related to insensitive parental responsiveness to affect.

The heterogeneity of eating-disordered populations and the varying degrees of comorbidity with other disorders may be explained in part by differences in parental sensitivity and traumatic events in the life histories of eating-disordered women. Such variations in developmental trajectories might be viewed on a continuum from mild to extremely severe. At the mild end of the spectrum there may be women who have experienced some parental insensitivity and unreliability but who have had some developmental needs fairly well met. These individuals may have other Axis I cormorbid disorders such as anxiety or dysthymia, but are likely to function relatively well. As parental insensitivity increases or as women are exposed to more gross trauma in the form of sexual and physical abuse, Axis II pathology is more likely. On the most severe end of the continuum, characterized by profound abuse and few ameliorative experiences, diagnoses such as borderline personality disorder and dissociative disorders are probable. Eating disorder diagnoses span the entire continuum, but there are significant differences in functioning between individuals exposed to variable levels of trauma and parental unresponsiveness.

The one third or so of eating-disordered subjects identified as having borderline personality disorder (e.g., Johnson et al., 1989) is roughly equivalent to the 30% reporting sexual abuse (Connors & Morse, 1993), and there is probably considerable overlap between these subgroups. Because trauma is associated with impairment, many of these individuals are likely to have difficulty functioning and may require some inpatient treatment. The link between traumatic experiences and dissociative disorders is particularly strong (Putnam, 1989), and some authors have found dissociative experiences in an eating-disordered sample (Demitrack, Putnam, Brewerton, Brandt, & Gold, 1990) and comorbidity of eating disorder and multiple personality disorder (Torem, 1986). This is further evidence of the heterogeneity in eating-disordered populations and of the need to attend to severe posttraumatic impairment in a subgroup of patients.

Interaction of Specific and Nonspecific Risk Factors

For young females at risk because of contextual factors, a genetic propensity toward slenderness is probably the most important protective factor in guarding against body dissatisfaction. Because of the very slim cultural ideal, it is likely that risk of body dissatisfaction decreases with more pronounced thinness. Striegel-Moore (1993) noted that being underweight seems to mediate against the initiation of dieting. Having a slender, socially desirable body and a mother who is not preoccupied with weight because she has the same acceptable figure makes a focus on dieting much less likely. These individuals are not protected against psychopathology in general, but they are unlikely to develop eating disorders.

It is possible that higher achievement expectations in the absence of structures to facilitate performance differentiate some families with eating-disordered members from other dysfunctional families (Johnson & Flach, 1985; Stern et al., 1989). The propensity toward higher weight status that often characterizes mothers and daughters in these families may lead to maternal weight concerns, critical and belittling interactions concerning weight, and a ready arena for achievement expectations to be expressed. Patients with BN have a significantly thinner body ideal than do non-eating-disordered women (Kendler et al., 1991; Williamson, Kelley, Davis, Ruggiero, & Blouin, 1985), and mothers of adolescent daughters with disordered eating have been found to want their daughters to be thinner than mothers of normal adolescents prefer and to rate their daughters' appearance very critically (Pike & Rodin, 1991). Insensitive parenting with respect to weight-related issues, which for adolescent young women are so fraught with implications for acceptability and attractiveness, may have a particularly deleterious impact.

Low self-esteem, insecurity in relationships, and difficulty in managing affects are problematic for many adolescents. Body dissatisfaction combined with affective dysregulation could easily lead to dieting behaviors more driven and intense than those exhibited by less troubled individuals. Thinness as a solution to parental criticism and relationship insecurity may be desperately sought by women with little self-worth concerning attributes besides appearance. In addition to the vulnerability to binge eating promoted by the deprivation of dieting, these young women may also be in need of self-regulating strategies. The hyperactivity and food refusal of AN or the bingeing and purging of BN provide means to escape affects through behavioral action (Connors, 1994). Further, avoiding or ingesting food offers distance from the world of relationships, which may have been experienced as predominantly negative by eating-disordered women.

It is suggested, then, that body dissatisfaction and affective dysregulation are necessary and sufficient conditions for the development of eating disorders. However, only longitudinal prospective research can determine whether this is actually the case. Further research into specific genetic factors in eating disorders and greater clarification of differences between families of eating-disordered patients and those with other pathologies is needed. If, in fact, eating disorders result from an interaction of body dissatisfaction and a more general emotional impairment, preventive efforts could target both aspects of the disorder and attempt to facilitate greater self-esteem and better affect management in high-risk groups, as well as to intervene with dieting and body image concerns.

REFERENCES

Abrams, K. K., Allen, L. R., & Gray, J. J. (1993). Disordered eating attitudes and behaviors, psychological adjustment, and ethnic identity: A comparison of black and white female college students. *International Journal of Eating Disorders, 14,* 49–57.
Ainsworth, M., Blehar, M., Waters, E., & Wall, S. (1978). *Patterns of attachment.* Hillsdale, NJ: Lawrence Erlbaum Associates.
Armstrong, J., & Roth, D. (1989). Attachment and separation difficulties in eating disorders: A preliminary investigation. *International Journal of Eating Disorders, 8,* 141–155.
Attie, I., & Brooks-Gunn, J. (1989). Development of eating problems in adolescent girls: A longitudinal study. *Developmental Psychology, 25,* 70–79.

Bates, J. (1994). Introduction. In J. Bates & T. Wachs (Eds.), *Temperament: Individual differences at the interface of biology and behavior* (pp. 1–14). Washington, DC: American Psychological Association.

Bennett, W., & Gurin, J. (1982). *The dieter's dilemma.* New York: Basic Books.

Blouin, A., Zuro, C., & Blouin, J. (1990). Family environment in bulimia nervosa: The role of depression. *International Journal of Eating Disorders, 9,* 649–658.

Bowlby, J. (1969). *Attachment and loss: Vol. 1. Attachment.* New York: Basic Books.

Brand, P., Rothblum, E., & Solomon, L. (1992). A comparison of lesbians, gay men, and heterosexuals on weight and restrained eating. *International Journal of Eating Disorders, 11,* 253–259.

Brownmiller, S. (1984). *Femininity.* New York: Simon & Schuster.

Bruch, H. (1973). *Eating disorders: Obesity, anorexia, and the person within.* New York: Basic Books.

Button, E. J., & Whitehouse, A. (1981). Subclinical anorexia nervosa. *Psychosomatic Medicine, 11,* 509–516.

Calam, R., Waller, G., Slade, P., & Newton, T. (1990). Eating disorders and perceived relationships with parents. *International Journal of Eating Disorders, 9,* 479–485.

Carney, C., Yates, W., & Cizadlo, B. (1990). A controlled family study of personality in normal-weight bulimia nervosa. *International Journal of Eating Disorders, 9,* 659–665.

Cloninger, C. R. (1987). A systematic method for clinical description and classification of personality variants. *Archives of General Psychiatry, 44,* 573–588.

Cochrane, C., Brewerton, T., Wilson, D., & Hodges, E. (1993). Alexithymia in the eating disorders. *International Journal of Eating Disorders, 14,* 219–222.

Connors, M. E. (1994). Symptom formation: An integrative self-psychological perspective. *Psychoanalytic Psychology, 11,* 509–523.

Connors, M. E., & Johnson, C. (1987). Epidemiology of bulimia and bulimic behaviors. *Addictive Behaviors, 12,* 165–179.

Connors, M. E., Johnson, C., & Stuckey, M. (1984). Treatment of bulimia with brief psychoeducational group therapy. *American Journal of Psychiatry, 141,* 1512–1516.

Connors, M. E., & Morse, W. (1993). Sexual abuse and eating disorders: A review. *International Journal of Eating Disorders, 13,* 1–11.

Cortois, C. (1988). *Healing the incest wound.* New York: Norton.

Davis, C., Durnin, J., Dionne, M., & Gurevich, M. (1994). The influence of body fat content and bone diameter measurements on body dissatisfaction in adult women. *International Journal of Eating Disorders, 15,* 257–263.

Demitrack, M., Putnam, F., Brewerton, T., Brandt, H., & Gold, P. (1990). Relation of clinical variables to dissociative phenomena in eating disorders. *American Journal of Psychiatry, 147,* 1184–1188.

Dolan, B. (1991). Cross-cultural aspects of anorexia nervosa and bulimia: A review. *International Journal of Eating Disorders, 10,* 67–78.

Dolan, B., Lieberman, S., Evans, C., & Lacey, J. H. (1990). Family features associated with normal body weight bulimia. *International Journal of Eating Disorders, 9,* 639–647.

Drewnowski, A., Kurth, C., & Krahn, D. (1994). Body weight and dieting in adolescence: Impact of socioeconomic status. *International Journal of Eating Disorders, 16,* 61–65.

Dunn, P., & Ondercin, P. (1981). Personality variables related to compulsive eating in college women. *Journal of Clinical Psychology, 37,* 43–49.

Egeland, B., Carlson, E., & Sroufe, L. A. (1993). Resilience as process. *Development and Psychopathology, 5,* 517–528.

Elicker, J., Englund, M., & Sroufe, L. A. (1992). Predicting peer competence and peer relationships in childhood from early parent–child relationships. In R. Parke & G. Ladd (Eds.), *Family–peer relationships: Modes of linkage* (pp. 77–106). Hillsdale, NJ: Lawrence Erlbaum Associates.

Fichter, M. M., & Noegel, R. (1990). Concordance for bulimia nervosa in twins. *International Journal of Eating Disorders, 9,* 255–263.

Fisher, M., Pastore, D., Schneider, M., Pegler, & Napolitano, B. (1994). Eating attitudes in urban and suburban adolescents. *International Journal of Eating Disorders, 16,* 67–74.

Galatzer-Levy, R., & Cohler, B. (1993). *The essential other: A developmental psychology of the self.* New York: Basic Books.

Garfinkel, P., & Garner, D. (1982). *Anorexia nervosa: A multidimensional approach.* New York: Brunner/Mazel.

Garfinkel, P., Garner, D., Rose, J., Darby, P, Brandes, J. S., O'Hanlon, J., & Walsh, N. (1983). A comparison of characteristics in the families of patients with anorexia nervosa and normal controls. *Psychological Medicine, 13,* 821–828.

Garner, D., Garfinkel, P., Schwartz, D., & Thompson, M. (1980). Cultural expectations of thinness in women. *Psychological Reports, 47,* 483–491.

Garner, D., Olmsted, M., Polivy, J., & Garfinkel, P. (1984). Comparison between weight-preoccupied women and anorexia nervosa. *Psychological Medicine, 46,* 255–266.

Goldblatt, P., Moore, M., & Stunkard, A. (1965). Social factors in obesity. *Journal of the American Medical Association, 192,* 1039–1044.

Goldstein, A. (1982). Agoraphobia: Treatment successes, treatment failures: Theoretical implications. In D. Chambless & A. Goldstein (Eds.), *Agoraphobia* (pp. 183–213). New York: Wiley.

Gralen, S., Levine, M., Smolak, L., & Murnen, S. (1990). Dieting and disordered eating during early and middle adolescence: Do the influences remain the same? *International Journal of Eating Disorders, 9,* 501–512.

Gray, J., Ford, K., & Kelly, L. (1987). The prevalence of bulimia in a black college population. *International Journal of Eating Disorders, 6,* 733–740.

Gunnar, M. (1994). Psychoendocrine studies of temperament and stress in early childhood: Expanding current models. In J. Bates & T. Wachs (Eds.), *Temperament: Individual differences at the interface of biology and behavior* (pp. 175–198). Washington, DC: American Psychological Association.

Hastings, T., & Kern, J. (1994). Relationships between bulimia, childhood sexual abuse, and family environment. *International Journal of Eating Disorders, 15,* 103–111.

Herman, J. (1992). *Trauma and recovery.* New York: Basic Books.

Herman, J., Perry, C., & van der Kolk, B. (1989). Childhood trauma in borderline personality disorder. *American Journal of Psychiatry, 146,* 490–495.

Holderness, C., Brooks-Gunn, J., & Warren, M. (1994). Co-morbidity of eating disorders and substance abuse: Review of the literature. *International Journal of Eating Disorders, 16,* 1–34.

Hudson, J., Laffer, P., & Pope, H. (1982). Bulimia related to affective disorder by family history and response to the dexamethasone suppression test. *American Journal of Psychiatry, 137,* 695–698.

Hudson, J., Pope, H., Jonas, J., & Yurgelun-Todd, D. (1983). Family history study of anorexia nervosa and bulimia. *British Journal of Psychiatry, 142,* 133–138.

Humphrey, L. L. (1986a). Family relations in bulimic–anorexic and nondistressed families. *International Journal of Eating Disorders, 5,* 223–232.

Humphrey, L. L. (1986b). Structural analysis of parent–child relationships in eating disorders. *Journal of Abnormal Psychology, 95,* 395–402.

Humphrey, L. L. (1987). Comparison of bulimic–anorexic and nondistressed families using structural analysis of social behavior. *Journal of the American Academy of Child and Adolescent Psychiatry, 26,* 248–255.

Humphrey, L. L. (1989). Observed family interactions among subtypes of eating disorders using structural analysis of social behavior. *Journal of Consulting and Clinical Psychology, 57,* 206–214.

Johnson, C., & Connors, M. E. (1987). *The etiology and treatment of bulimia nervosa: A biopsychosocial perspective.* New York: Basic Books.

Johnson, C., & Flach, A. (1985). Family characteristics of 105 patients with bulimia. *American Journal of Psychiatry, 142,* 1321–1324.

Johnson, C., & Larson, R. (1982). Bulimia: An analysis of moods and behavior. *Psychosomatic Medicine, 44,* 333–345.

Johnson, C., Lewis, C., Love, S., Lewis, L., & Stuckey, M. (1984). Incidence and correlates of bulimic behavior in a female high school population. *Journal of Youth and Adolescence, 13,* 15–26.

Johnson, C., Tobin, D., & Enright, A. (1989). Prevalence and clinical characteristics of borderline patients in an eating disordered population. *Journal of Clinical Psychiatry, 50,* 9–15.

Kagan, J., & Snidman, N. (1991). Temperamental factors in human development. *American Psychologist, 46,* 856–862.

Katzman, M., & Wolchik, S. (1984). Bulimia and binge eating in college women: A comparison of personality and behavioral characteristics. *Journal of Consulting and Clinical Psychology, 52,* 423–428.

Kendler, K., MacLean, C., Neale, M., Kessler, R., Heath, A., & Eaves, L. (1991). The genetic epidemiology of bulimia nervosa. *American Journal of Psychiatry, 148,* 1627–1637.

Kenny, M., & Hart, K. (1992). Relationship between parental attachment and eating disorders in an inpatient and a college sample. *Journal of Counseling Psychology, 39,* 521–526.

Killen, J., Hayward, C., Wilson, D., Taylor, C., Hammer, L., Litt, I., Simmonds, B., & Haydel, F. (1994). Factors associated with eating disorder symptoms in a community sample of 6th and 7th grade girls. *International Journal of Eating Disorders, 15,* 357–367.

Kog, E., Vertommen, H., & Vandereycken, W. (1989). Self-report studies of family interaction in eating disorder families compared to normals. In W. Vandereycken, E. Kog, & J. Vanderlinden (Eds.), *The family approach to eating disorders* (pp. 107–117). New York: PMA.

Kohut, H. (1971). *The analysis of the self.* New York: International Universities Press.

Krystal, H. (1974). The genetic development of affects and affect regression. *Annals of Psychoanalysis, 2,* 98–126.

Lacey, J. H. (1992). A comparative study of menarchal age and weight of bulimic patients and their sisters. *International Journal of Eating Disorders, 12,* 307–311.

Leon, G., Fulkerson, J., Perry, C., & Cudeck, R. (1993). Personality and behavioral vulnerabilities associated with risk status for eating disorders in adolescent girls. *Journal of Abnormal Psychology, 102,* 438–444.

Leon, G., Lucas, A., Colligan, R., Ferdinande, R., & Kamp, J. (1985). Body image, sexual attitudes, and family interaction patterns in anorexia nervosa. *Journal of Abnormal Child Psychology, 13,* 245–258.

Levin, A. P., & Hyler, S. (1986). DSM–III personality diagnosis in bulimia. *Comprehensive Psychiatry, 17,* 47–53.

Levine, M., Smolak, L., Moodey, A., Shuman, M., & Hessen, L. (1994). Normative developmental challenges and dieting and eating disorders in middle school girls. *International Journal of Eating Disorders, 15,* 11–20.

Matas, L., Arend, R., & Sroufe, L.A. (1978). Continuity of adaptation in the second year: The relationship between quality of attachment and later competence. *Child Development, 49,* 547–556.

McCarthy, M. (1990). The thin ideal, depression and eating disorders in women. *Behavioral Research and Therapy, 28,* 205–215.

Minuchin, S., Rosman, B., & Baker, L. (1978). *Psychosomatic families: Anorexia nervosa in context.* Cambridge, MA: Harvard University Press.

Moos, R. H. (1974). *Family environment scale.* New York: Consulting Psychologists Press.

Norman, D., & Herzog, D. (1983). Bulimia, anorexia nervosa, and anorexia nervosa with bulimia: A comparative analysis of MMPI profiles. *International Journal of Eating Disorders, 2,* 43–52.

Nylander, I. (1971). The feeling of being fat and dieting in a school population: Epidemiologic interview investigation. *Acta Sociomedica Scandinavica, 3,* 17–26.

O'Connor, M., Sigman, M., & Brill, N. (1987). Disorganization of attachment in relation to maternal alcohol consumption. *Journal of Consulting and Clinical Psychology, 55,* 831–836.

Ordman, A., & Kirschenbaum, D. (1986). Bulimia: Assessment of eating, psychological adjustment, and familial characteristics. *International Journal of Eating Disorders, 5,* 865–878.

Perednia, C., & Vandereycken, W. (1989). An explorative study on parenting in eating disorder families. In W. Vandereycken, E. Kog, & J. Vanderlinden (Eds.), *The family approach to eating disorders* (pp. 119–146). New York: PMA.

Pike, K. M., & Rodin, J. (1991). Mothers, daughters, and disordered eating. *Journal of Abnormal Psychology, 100,* 198–204.

Piran, N., Lerner, P., Garfinkel, P., Kennedy, S., & Brouillette, C. (1988). Personality disorders in anorexic patients. *International Journal of Eating Disorders, 7,* 589–599.

Polivy, J., & Herman, P. (1983). *Breaking the diet habit.* New York: Basic Books.

Putnam, F. (1989). *Diagnosis and treatment of multiple personality disorder.* New York: Guilford.

Putnam, F., Guroff, J., Silberman, E., Barban, L., & Post, R. (1986). The clinical phenomenology of multiple personality disorder: A review of 100 recent cases. *Journal of Clinical Psychiatry, 47,* 285–293.

Radke-Sharpe, N., Whitney-Saltiel, D., & Rodin, J. (1990). Fat distribution as a risk factor for weight and eating concerns. *International Journal of Eating Disorders, 9,* 27–36.

Radke-Yarrow, M., Cummings, E., Kuczynski, L., & Chapman, M. (1985). Patterns of attachment in two- and three-year-olds in normal families and families with parental depression. *Child Development, 56,* 884–893.

Rand, C., & Kuldau, J. (1990). The epidemiology of obesity and self-defined weight problems in the general population: Gender, race, age, and social class. *International Journal of Eating Disorders, 9,* 329–343.

Rodin, J., Silberstein, L., & Striegel-Moore, R. (1985). Women and weight: A normative discontent. In T. B. Sonderegger (Ed.), *Nebraska Symposium on Motivation: Vol. 32. Psychology and Gender* (pp. 267–308). Lincoln: University of Nebraska Press.

Root, M. P. P., & Fallon, P. (1988). The incidence of victimization experiences in a bulimic sample. *Journal of Interpersonal Violence, 3,* 161–173.

Rosen, J., Tacy, B., & Howell, D. (1990). Life stress, psychological symptoms and weight reducing behavior in adolescent girls: A prospective analysis. *International Journal of Eating Disorders, 9,* 17–26.

Shear, M., Cooper, A., Klerman, G., Busch, F., & Shapiro, T. (1993). A psychodynamic model of panic disorder. *American Journal of Psychiatry, 150,* 859–866.

Shisslak, C., McKeon, R., & Crago, M. (1990). Family dysfunction in normal weight bulimic and bulimic anorexic families. *Journal of Clinical Psychology, 46,* 185–189.

Siever, M. (1994). Sexual orientation and gender as factors in socioculturally acquired vulnerability to body dissatisfaction and eating disorders. *Journal of Consulting and Clinical Psychology, 62,* 252–260.

Smolak, L., & Levine, M. (1993). Separation–individuation difficulties and the distinction between bulimia nervosa and anorexia nervosa in college women. *International Journal of Eating Disorders, 14,* 33–41.

Smolak, L., Levine, M., & Sullins, E. (1990). Are child sexual experiences related to eating-disordered attitudes and behaviors in a college sample? *International Journal of Eating Disorders, 9,* 167–178.

Sroufe, L. A. (1991). Considering normal and abnormal together: The essence of developmental psychopathology. *Development and Psychopathology, 2,* 335–347.

Steiger, H., Leung, F., Puentes-Newman, G., & Gottheil, N. (1992). Psychosocial profiles of adolescent girls with varying degrees of eating and mood disturbances. *International Journal of Eating Disorders, 11,* 121–131.

Steiger, H., Leung, F., Ross, D., & Gulko, J. (1992). Signs of anorexia and bulimia nervosa in high school girls reporting combinations of eating and mood symptoms: Relevance of self-report to interview-based findings. *International Journal of Eating Disorders, 12,* 143–149.

Steiger, H., Liquornik, K., Chapman, J., & Hussain, N. (1991). Personality and family disturbances in eating-disorder patients: Comparison of "restrictors" and "bingers" to normal controls. *International Journal of Eating Disorders, 10,* 501–512.

Stern, S., Dixon, K., Jones, D., Lake, M., Nemzer, E., & Sansone, R. (1989). Family environment in anorexia nervosa and bulimia. *International Journal of Eating Disorders, 8,* 25–31.

Stolorow, R., Brandchaft, B., & Atwood, G. (1987). *Psychoanalytic treatment: An intersubjective approach.* Hillsdale, NJ: Analytic Press.

Striegel-Moore, R. (1993). Etiology of binge eating: A developmental perspective. In C. Fairburn & G. T. Wilson (Eds.), *Binge eating: Nature, assessment, and treatment* (pp. 144–172). New York: Guilford.

Striegel-Moore, R., & Kearney-Cooke, A. (1994). Exploring parents' attitudes and behaviors about their childrens' physical appearance. *International Journal of Eating Disorders, 15,* 377–385.

Striegel-Moore, R., Silberstein, L., & Rodin, J. (1986). Toward an understanding of risk factors for bulimia. *American Psychologist, 41,* 246–263.

Strober, M. (1981). The significance of bulimia in juvenile anorexia nervosa: An exploration of possible etiological factors. *International Journal of Eating Disorders, 1,* 28–43.

Strober, M., Lampert, C., Morrell, W., Burroughs, J., & Jacobs, C. (1990). A controlled family study of anorexia nervosa: Evidence of familial aggregation and lack of shared transmission with affective disorders. *International Journal of Eating Disorders, 9,* 239–253.

Strober, M., Salkin, B., Burroughs, J., & Morrell, W. (1982). Validity of the bulimia-restrictor distinction in anorexia nervosa. *Journal of Nervous and Mental Disease, 170,* 345–351.

Stunkard, A., Harris, J., Pedersen, N., & McClearn, G. (1990). The body-mass index of twins who have been reared apart. *The New England Journal of Medicine, 322,* 1483–1487.

Thienemann, M., & Steiner, H. (1993). Family environment of eating disordered and depressed adolescents. *International Journal of Eating Disorders, 14,* 43–48.

Thompson, J. K., & Heinberg, L. (1993). Preliminary test of two hypotheses of body image disturbance. *International Journal of Eating Disorders, 14,* 59–63.

Thompson, M., & Schwartz, D. (1982). Life adjustment of women with anorexia nervosa and anorexic-like behavior. *International Journal of Eating Disorders, 1,* 47–60.

Torem, M. (1986). Dissociative states presenting as an eating disorder. *American Journal of Clinical Hypnosis, 29,* 137–142.

Wadden, T., Brown, G., Foster, G., & Linowitz, J. (1991). Salience of weight-related worries in adolescent males and females. *International Journal of Eating Disorders, 10,* 407–414.

Walsh, B., Roose, S., & Glassman, A. (1985). Bulimia and depression. *Psychosomatic Medicine, 47,* 123–131.

Waters, E., Wippman, J., & Sroufe, L. A. (1979). Attachment, positive affect, and competence in the peer group: Two studies in construct validation. *Child Development, 50,* 821–829.

Werner, E. (1993). Risk, resilience, and recovery: Perspectives from the Kauai longitudinal study. *Development and Psychopathology, 5,* 501–515.

Williamson, D., Kelley, M., Davis, C., Ruggiero, L., & Blouin, D. (1985). Psychopathology of eating disorders: A controlled comparison of bulimic, obese, and normal subjects. *Journal of Consulting and Clinical Psychology, 53,* 161–166.

Wonderlich, S., & Swift, W. (1990). Borderline versus other personality disorders in the eating disorders. *International Journal of Eating Disorders, 9,* 629–638.

Wonderlich, S., Swift, W., Slotnick, H., & Goodman, S. (1990). DSM–III–R personality disorders in eating-disorder subtypes. *International Journal of Eating Disorders, 9,* 607–616.

Yates, W. (1992). Weight factors in normal weight bulimia nervosa: A controlled family study. *International Journal of Eating Disorders, 11,* 227–234.

IV

IMPLICATIONS FOR
TREATMENT AND PREVENTION

13

Development and Evaluation of a School-Based Eating Disorder Symptoms Prevention Program

Joel D. Killen

Eating disorders have become an important public health concern (Herzog & Copeland, 1985). As a result, organizations such as the American College of Physicians (ACP) and several groups of investigators have called for public education and early intervention to prevent the development of eating disorders and to promote healthful weight regulation practices among children and adolescents (ACP, 1986; Shisslak, Crago, & Neal, 1987; Striegel-Moore, Silberstein, & Rodin, 1986). However, at present, little if any research effort has been devoted to the promotion of healthful weight regulation practices among normal-weight children and adolescents, and very few controlled studies have examined programs designed to prevent the onset of disordered eating behaviors. This chapter describes an ongoing program of research aimed at the development and controlled evaluation of a comprehensive school-based intervention designed to prevent the development of eating disorder symptoms in a sample of young adolescent girls.

The chapter begins with a presentation of the conceptual framework for the prevention intervention. Since the bulk of work in the field of prevention research has focused on substance use and cardiovascular disease risk factors, examples from these fields are employed in order to illustrate linkages between behavior change theory and intervention practice. Next, the development of the intervention for the prevention of eating disorder symptoms is described accompanied by a presentation of results from the initial field testing of the program. The chapter concludes with a discussion of the findings and with a consideration of issues for a future research agenda.

CONCEPTUAL FRAMEWORK FOR THE INTERVENTION

The Utility of a Comprehensive Approach to Prevention

The eating disorder symptoms prevention program described in this chapter is an example of a comprehensive, multiple-factor prevention intervention. The decision to target multiple factors in a comprehensive prevention effort stems, in part, from the experience of workers in the field of substance abuse prevention. Substance abuse researchers have devoted much effort to the development and testing of prevention programs derived from diverse conceptual models. Hansen (1992) recently reviewed the substance abuse prevention research literature and identified four basic prevention models for which there is an existing database: information–values clarification, affective education, social influence resistance, and comprehensive prevention approaches. The comprehensive prevention model was judged to be generally more effective than competing models in preventing substance use. Although comprehensive interventions may include a variety of strategies, all of the comprehensive interventions for which an empirical base exists include as key components both normative information on the actual prevalence of substance use and training in decision making and social influence resistance skills. Of the comprehensive interventions reviewed, 72% achieved positive effects and none was associated with negative outcomes.

The social influence resistance model was judged the next most effective. Social influence resistance interventions are designed to equip adolescents to resist the various social environment influences that promote unhealthful behavior. Social influence resistance is the single most effective component examined in the substance abuse prevention research literature. All the comprehensive prevention programs examined by Hansen (1992) included a social influence resistance component. Of interventions based upon this model, 63% were judged to have a positive effect and 11% were rated as having produced a negative effect.

Interventions based on affective education and information–values clarification models have had far more variable results. Affective education interventions, which can include decision-making, values clarification, stress management, and self-esteem building strategies in their formats have achieved positive results in 42% of the studies examined. However, 25% were rated as having had a negative effect. Of programs geared primarily to providing information and values clarification, 30% achieved positive results but 30% were associated with negative outcomes.

Bandura's (1986) social cognitive model was selected to provide the conceptual framework for the development of a comprehensive intervention for the prevention of eating disorder symptoms. In Bandura's model, behavior develops, is altered by, and is maintained through the interplay of personal, behavioral and environmental factors. In order to develop effective prevention interventions it is important to address factors in each of these three domains of influence.

With respect to the development of eating disorder symptoms, personal factors may include an adolescent's valuation of thinness, expectations derived from observation of and experience with the positive and negative consequences of maintaining a thin body shape or gaining weight, and expectations about personal ability to achieve culturally prescribed thinness. The risk of adoption of unhealthful weight regulation practices could also be influenced by the degree to which healthful weight regulation skills are already a part of the adolescent's behavioral repertoire. In addition, from an intervention perspective, behavioral factors could include the number of coping skills available to the adolescent and the degree of mastery that the adolescent has attained in using these coping skills to combat the range of social influences promoting dieting and overconcern with weight and shape. Environmental factors may include peers and family members who, by virtue of their own endorsement of a thin shape as the cultural ideal, influence the development of an adolescent's own attitudes toward weight and shape. Also significant are the media which, in the words of one eminent clinician, convey the message "day in and day out, that one can be loved and respected only when slender" (Bruch, 1978, p. viii).

With Bandura's (1986) general framework as a guide, an intervention for the prevention of eating disorder symptoms has been developed which is designed to provide adolescent females with incentives to manage weight through the practice of healthful diet and physical activity habits, self-regulatory skills enabling them to make changes both in their own behavior and in the environmental contexts providing support for their behavior, and specific practice in using skills in order to strengthen their perceived competence in employing newly acquired behaviors effectively. The factors addressed in our intervention model are described in the following sections of this chapter.

Personal Factors: Increasing the Perceived Incentive Value of Healthful Behavior

The first goal of our eating disorder symptoms prevention program was to build students' motivation to adopt and practice healthful weight regulation skills. Incentives play a substantial role in the regulation of human conduct. The high incentive value our culture places on thinness may promote excessive dieting and other eating disorder symptoms in adolescents. Therefore, our intervention model suggests that we must reduce the incentive value associated with a thin body shape and to increase the extent to which adolescents value healthful diet and physical activity practices as tools for successfully managing their weight. An attempt has been made to create this shift by helping students to perceive the negative consequences of embracing the cultural ideal that associates beauty with extreme thinness; the immediate and longer-term positive benefits of adopting healthful weight regulation practices; the immediate as well as longer-term negative consequences of excessive dieting and disordered eating behaviors which increase risks to health and well-being; and the fact that rejection of society's standard for beauty and the practice of healthful weight regulation practices will not produce important, immediate negative effects.

Our intervention model and our experience suggest that the selection of weak or inappropriate incentives can undermine efforts to increase valuation of good health practices. The results of early research on the prevention of cigarette smoking may serve to illustrate this point. Early prevention research emphasized the harmful long-term health effects of smoking. Numerous antismoking programs were implemented in junior and senior high schools in attempts to dissuade adolescents from smoking. These programs employed a wide range of techniques including lectures, discussions, posters, and films aimed at increasing students' awareness of the harmful long-term effects. Although some researchers reported positive changes in knowledge and attitudes, most found little or no effect on students' reported smoking behavior (Andrus, 1964; Evans & Borgatta, 1970). Smoking prevention programs that emphasize long-term health effects may miss the mark because the perceived positive benefits associated with smoking may outweigh the long-term negative health effects. For example, most adolescents believe the traditional health education message that smoking is dangerous to their physical health (Johnston, O'Malley, & Bachman, 1986). Despite this knowledge, sources of social influence (i.e., peers, siblings, parents, and the mass media) may exert considerable pressure on adolescents to adopt the smoking habit.

The social cognitive model suggests that interventions must emphasize proximal outcomes that are salient to the target audience. Emphasis on immediate consequences may be particlarly critical for health behavior change among adolescents. For example, formative evaluations conducted by our research team indicate that students' interests in health issues stem primarily from concerns for personal appearance and, to a lesser extent, physical conditioning. Therefore, health behavior change interventions aimed, for example, at promoting healthful weight regulation practices may achieve behavior change objectives most effectively by emphasizing relationships between good eating and exercise practices and personal appearance and physical condition.

Behavioral Factors: Skills for Countering Environmental Influences

A second goal of our eating disorder symptoms prevention program was to equip adolescents with skills to resist the social-environmental influences that promote dieting and overconcern with weight and body shape and that ultimately may potentiate the development of disordered eating behaviors.

The social environment can profoundly affect the development and durability of health-related behaviors. For example, advertisers spend vast sums to promote the consumption of tobacco, alcohol, and fatty foods and "conveniences" that encourage a sedentary lifestyle. Research suggests that such advertising does indeed influence children's food preferences and consumption (Cantor, 1981; Jeffrey, McLellarn, & Fox, 1982).

Among adolescents, perceptions of peer behaviors probably represent the strongest social environmental influences on health behaviors. This has been demonstrated repeatedly for smoking and other substance use. For example, in the Rand report on strategies for controlling adolescent drug use it was concluded that the main influences on adoption of alcohol and other substances by adolescents are social and stem from peers, family, and society in general (Polich & Ellickson, 1984). Adolescents typically begin using alcohol in a group setting among friends or relatives. The principal factors affecting whether and when young people begin using alcohol are peer use and peer approval of alcohol coupled with the behavior and norms of influential adults. Research by the author's team strongly supports the hypothesis that social environmental factors exert profound influence on alcohol and on substance use involvement generally. In our study of patterns of alcohol and drug use in a population of 1,447 tenth graders, perceived friends' use accounted for 40% of the variance in level of substance use (Robinson et al., 1987).

Research in the field of substance use prevention suggests that interventions that equip adolescents with skills to resist the diverse social and environmental influences that promote tobacco use may prevent or delay the onset of cigarette smoking (Hansen, 1992). Methods for teaching social influence resistance skills are derived from McGuire's (1969) social inoculation theory. Inoculation theory was developed out of the rich tradition in social psychology concerned with processes of persuasion and attitude change. Earlier work on the effects of preparatory communications provided the foundation for McGuire's research (Lumsdaine & Janis, 1953). Social inoculation is viewed as analogous to immunologic inoculation (immunization). Physiological immunizations provide resistance to infections by introducing weakened, noninfectious forms of organisms to the body; this stimulates the production of antibodies to those organisms, which will be present in increased numbers if true infection eventually occurs. Social inoculation theory suggests that beliefs can be protected from persuasive appeals by pretreating persons with weak forms of those appeals. McGuire summarized data from a variety of studies investigating resistance building techniques. The findings suggest that inoculation is likely to be effective to the degree that persons are motivated to acquire a defense for beliefs and to practice defending beliefs against attack.

In smoking prevention programs based on inoculation theory adolescents are presented with a variety of inducements to smoke followed by opportunities to invent and practice overt and covert counters to these inducements. The primary training objectives are to acquaint students with the powerful social influences that may trigger smoking (e.g., advertising, peer smoking) and to provide them with the coping skills and the strong sense of self-efficacy that will enable them to resist these influences when they encounter them in the future. The findings from a number of research teams indicate that smoking prevention programs which teach adolescents to become aware of the social inducements to smoke and help them to acquire skills to counter the effects of inducements may reduce the rate at which adolescents adopt the smoking habit (Botvin & Eng, 1980; Flay et al., 1985; Leupker, Johnson, Murray, & Pechacek, 1983; Schinke, Gilchrist, & Snow, 1985; Telch, Killen, McAlister, Perry, & Maccoby, 1982).

Research conducted by our own group has demonstrated the efficacy of a prevention intervention for reducing smoking prevalence based on inoculation and social modeling principles. The intervention employs older peers as models and teachers as well as a student-centered curriculum in an attempt to counter the social influences that promote smoking in our society. Our training program consists of seven sessions conducted over a 9-month academic period in the seventh grade. Each session requires a 45-min class period. Regular classroom teachers do not attend the sessions; this encourages students to discuss openly with peer leaders issues and feelings concerning smoking and other substance use. The first three sessions are conducted during the first month of school. In the first session, students make public commitments not to become dependent on tobacco and to become acquainted with some of the social influences that encourage young people to begin smoking. In the second session, slide shows and films present promotional techniques used to encourage smoking. Peer leaders help students to identify "selling strategies" and to model a variety of responses to counter the effects of cigarette advertising. For example, covert rehearsal techniques are used to help students learn to respond to advertising depicting women smokers as liberated (i.e., "She's not really independent if she's hooked on nicotine."). During the third session, group discussions evaluate peer influences on individual behavior. With the aid of peer leaders, subjects create skits on peer pressure and perform them in front of the class. This enables students both to acquire and to practice ways to resist pressures to smoke. Remaining sessions are conducted at 2-month intervals over the academic year. These sessions repeat activities from previous classes with minor variations. In order to help maintain interest and enthusiasm, prizes (e.g., buttons, record albums, and T-shirts) are awarded for skits and slogans that demonstrate effective coping with smoking pressures. In a longitudinal evaluation of this program, statistically significant differences in smoking prevalence were found between treatment and control groups (Telch, Killen, et al., 1982). For example, at a 33-month follow-up the percentage of students in the treatment group reporting smoking in the preceding week was about 5%. In contrast, the rate was about 15% among students in the control condition.

Cigarette smoking, dieting, binge eating, and self-induced vomiting are different intervention targets. However, theory and evidence implicate sociocultural factors in the development of weight concerns and disordered eating behaviors. In particular, the mass media often promote acquisition of problem behaviors in very explicit fashion. The persuasion tactics used to encourage both smoking and dieting are relatively salient and thus are recognizable by adolescents following training. Recognition of persuasion tactics may be critical to the success of the social resistance intervention because it is the adolescents' newfound awareness of social influence processes that may trigger the use of resistance skills.

Behavioral Factors: Developing Healthful Weight Regulation Practices

A third goal of our eating disorder symptoms prevention program was to help students acquire and practice healthful weight regulation skills. The importance of adopting healthful weight regulation practices in place of dieting must be emphasized, given the potential role that excessive dieting may play in potentiating the development of eating disorder symptoms. As Polivy and Herman (1985) argued, the apparent increase in bulimia nervosa (BN) among women in recent years might be expected since the cultural forces promoting dieting as the pathway to thinness have intensified. As these authors concluded, "A dispassionate view suggests that perhaps dieting is the disorder that we should be attempting to cure" (p. 200).

Several lines of research implicate caloric restriction in the development of bulimic behaviors. For example, Coscina and Dixon (1983) compared the weight gain of rats previously deprived of food with that of nondeprived controls after the deprived group had regained to baseline weight levels. Previously deprived rats gained substantially more weight than did controls when given access to a highly palatable diet.

Significantly, weight gain was accomplished by increased food intake rather than by increased energy utilization efficiency. The results suggest that previous caloric restriction produced substantial overeating even after predeprivation body weight levels had been attained.

Polivy and Herman (1985) reviewed evidence from human studies suggesting that dieting may precede binge eating in a causal chain. A variety of clinical reports indicate that patients with BN and with the bulimic form of anorexia nervosa (AN) engage in dieting attempts prior to the emergence of bulimic symptoms. For example, Garfinkel, Moldofsky, and Garner (1980) found that dieting preceded binge eating, on average, by more than 1.5 years. Dally and colleagues (1979) reported that binge eating typically occurred about 9 months after the initiation of dieting. In another investigation, 30 of 34 patients with BN reported dieting prior to the onset of the disorder (Polivy & Herman, 1985).

A famous study by Keys and colleagues (1950) on the effects of starvation on a group of World War II conscientious objectors provides further support for the relationship between dieting and binge eating. After volunteers dieted to approximately 74% of their initial weight they were allowed access to unlimited quantities of food. Even after the men had regained the lost weight they continued to binge-eat and gorge at meals in a fashion uncharacteristic of their predeprivation eating behavior.

Although dieting appears to be pandemic in our culture, it may be possible to teach adolescents to develop healthful eating and exercise practices. A summary of previous work conducted by our research group is presented to illustrate an application of Bandura's (1986) social cognitive model in the design of prevention interventions to promote the development of healthful weight regulation skills.

The objective, with respect to the development of healthful weight regulation practices, was to reduce consumption of calories and foods high in saturated fat, cholesterol and salt; to increase levels of aerobic physical activity and consumption of complex carbohydrates; and to lower heart rate, blood pressure, body mass index, and skin fold thickness.

The intervention program consisted of 20 classroom sessions, each lasting 50 min. The first goal was to capture students' attention and to increase the perceived incentive value of adopting healthful eating and physical activity practices. A 40-min video drama was therefore developed and was shown on Day 1 of the intervention. The drama, called *CHOICES,* presented several intertwining vignettes involving adolescent and adult characters. In the context of each vignette, the characters were faced with decisions regarding the adoption of different health-related behaviors. The vignettes portrayed the costs and benefits associated with different choices. The setting of proximal and distal goals, demonstrated attainment or temporary failure to attain goals, and the resulting consequences of different personal choices were presented. The next 12 sessions coupled strategies designed to build students' motivation to adopt healthful behaviors with efforts designed to help them acquire self-regulatory skills. To build motivation, the sessions emphasized information on the important immediate effects on life quality as well as the potential long-term health consequences of adopting healthful behaviors. As previously noted, the emphasis on immediate consequences was considered of primary importance in this age group. The sessions also introduced self-regulatory skills specific for each area. These included the setting of specific, proximal change goals, methods of monitoring progress toward proximal goals, problem-solving skills, and application of self-managed incentives. Educational methods utilized within each module included discussion-oriented information sessions, slide and music–slide presentations, videotaped vignettes modeling peers learning to use skills successfully, guided role-playing simulations to aid in invention of coping strategies for managing high-risk situations, and performance-based exercises (e.g., heart rate measurement, stretching exercises, healthful snack preparation, meal planning, relaxation, and guided imagery exercises).

Sessions 14 and 15 were devoted to a competitive game. Students were divided into teams of three or four and were quizzed on information and skills introduced in the previous four modules. Points were awarded to teams responding with correct answers, and point scores were doubled for the second game session. Members of the team with the highest point total in each classroom received $5 gift certificates to a local music store. Students were made aware of the available prizes during the first educational session of the program. Prizes were selected based on results of earlier formative research into salient motivators.

The final five sessions were devoted to training in problem solving and the development of an action plan for behavior change. This module began with each student's choice of a specific long-term lifestyle change goal. Through examples drawn from the previous modules, students were led step by step through the development of a behavior change plan. Steps in planning included the specification of proximal goals leading to the ultimate long-term behavior change objective, specification of the strategies to be used in achieving proximal goals and identification of the contexts in which strategies would be implemented, specification of self-incentives for attainment of each of the proximal goals, and completion of a contract to follow the specified action plan for a specified period of time. Students were then encouraged to identify potential physical, psychological, and social–environmental barriers that might deter achievement of the specified action plan. Finally, students were introduced to problem solving as a method of overcoming barriers to successful behavior change and used this process with their own specific barriers to change.

The intervention was evaluated in a controlled trial with all 10th graders in four senior high schools (Killen et al., 1988). The results indicated that the intervention produced a beneficial impact on physical fitness, nutrition practices, and weight regulation. For example, both boys and girls in the treatment group reduced their resting heart rate compared with their control-group counterparts. The resting heart rate of boys and girls in the treatment group decreased an average of 2.3 and 4.1 beats per min, respectively. The resting heart rate of boys and girls in the control group increased an average of 0.4 beats per min. Body mass index decreased an average of 0.2 units among girls in the treatment group and increased an average of 0.1 units among girls in the control group. These results demonstrate the potential efficacy of a comprehensive intervention based on social cognitive theory to modify weight regulation behaviors in adolescents.

THE STANFORD EATING DISORDER SYMPTOMS PREVENTION PROGRAM

Primary Focus of the Intervention: Weight Concerns

The intervention described in this section was designed to prevent or reduce the development of weight concerns that may mediate the onset of eating disorder symptoms. The decision to focus on weight concerns as a primary mediating variable was based on current social learning conceptualizations that suggest that society's preoccupation with thinness may promote excessive dieting and may lead to the development of frank clinical syndromes (Garner & Garfinkel, 1980; Pike & Rodin, 1991; Striegel-Moore et al., 1986).

However, although weight concerns and attendant behaviors such as dieting may be pandemic among girls and women, comparatively few go on to develop severe, full-blown eating disorders (Strober, 1986). Evidence demonstrating a prospective linkage between culturally induced preoccupations with thinness, excessive dieting and other eating disorder symptoms has been lacking. Evidence for this linkage, which supports the focus on weight concerns, was provided by a prospective analysis conducted by Killen et al. (1994) on a sample of 887 young adolescent girls (mean age 12.4). Over a 3-year interval, 32 girls, or 3.6% of the sample, developed major eating disorder symptoms and 1.4% met all *DSM–III–R* criteria for BN. Although a number of theoretically interesting variables were included in a Cox proportional hazards analysis, only the measure of Weight Concerns was associated with the development of major eating disorder symptoms over the 3-year period ($\chi^2 = 12.3$, $p < .001$). About 12% of the girls with scores in the highest quartile of Weight Concerns developed major symptoms by age 14.5. In contrast, only about 2% of girls with scores in the lowest quartile developed major symptoms by age 14.5. Survival curves for each Weight Concerns quartile are shown in Fig. 13.1. The groups show different patterns of survival (log-rank χ^2 = 26.5, p < .001).

This finding is one of the first prospective demonstrations of a link between weight concerns and later onset of eating disorder symptoms. Given that weight and shape concerns are core features of eating disorders, there is necessarily some overlap between the independent variable and the dependent variable. However, in order for those concerns to be classified as symptomatic, it was specified that girls must manifest not only weight concerns but also recurrent binge eating, regular compensatory behaviors, and perceived loss of control. Although a relatively high proportion of adolescent girls show evidence of some level of weight or shape concerns and even occasional binge eating, few go on to develop the full clinical syndrome. In Killen et al.'s (1994) prospective analysis, girls who scored highly on the measure of weight concerns were more likely to develop eating disorder symptoms over time, even if they did not otherwise manifest disordered eating behaviors at baseline. This finding is useful inasmuch as it provides support for a focus on weight concerns as a rational target for prevention intervention.

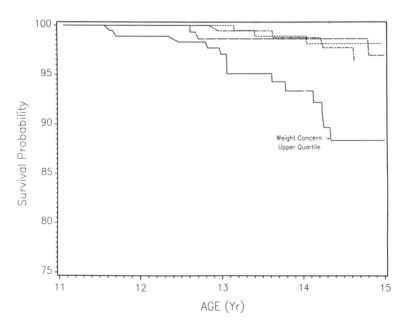

FIG. 13.1. Onset of eating disorder symptoms.

Prevention Intervention

The prevention of eating disorder symptoms consisted of 18 classroom sessions, each lasting 50 min. Sessions occurred during regularly scheduled class time. Program content was delivered via slide-show presentations in order to capture students' attention and to engage them in the intervention. Slide shows illustrated the stories of seven girls who demonstrated both healthful and unhealthful approaches to weight regulation. Text of dialogue between characters, which focused on the issues related to the lesson topic of the day, was superimposed on each slide and read by student volunteers. To enhance program credibility, models used in the slide show were similar in age, ethnicity, and socioeconomic status to girls in the target schools. Students were also given a workbook with written assignments.

In addition to specifying the multiple sources of influence on behavior, Bandura's (1986) model identifies four processes that mediate the acquisition and performance of behavior. *Attention* regulates exploration and perception and is highly influenced by factors such as salience, conspicuousness, functional value of the behavior, affective valence, and attractiveness. In our work, we find that an emphasis on the meaningful short-term consequences of behaviors rather than on more distal health outcomes improves our ability to capture and retain participants' attention. *Retention,* or memory, is influenced by the processes of symbolic coding, organization of information, and cognitive and enactive rehearsal. To increase retention of both declarative and procedural knowledge, we use approaches that couple explicit verbal instruction with visual demonstrations. *Production* is the conversion of conceptual representations into actions and is influenced by immediate intrinsic and extrinsic feedback. Thus, to increase the likelihood that students will be able to perform new behaviors successfully, they are engaged in role-playing exercises coupled with specific feedback that highlights successes and corrects performance deficits. *Motivation* is strongly influenced by external, vicarious, and internal incentives and affects the extent to which behaviors are performed. We attempt to build motivation by demonstrating the short-term positive and negative consequences of various behaviors and by teaching self-regulatory skills designed to help students achieve some degree of control over events. All four processes are emphasized in all components of the intervention for the prevention of eating disorder symptoms. These components are described in the following.

Weight gain is a normal and necessary part of pubertal growth in females. Research indicates that at each successive stage of pubertal development in females there is increasing dissatisfaction with one's body and an increasing desire to be thinner (Brooks-Gunn & Peterson,

1983). Disordered eating practices may be adopted, in part, in an attempt to combat weight gain and the changes in body shape and fat distribution associated with pubertal development (Killen et al., 1992). Therefore, lessons were developed that focused on normal growth and development processes and on ways in which obsessions with thinness may interfere with these processes. For example, students were introduced to the five Tanner stages (Marshall & Tanner, 1969); shown why weight gain is a natural and important part of human development; and shown that the healthful weight range within each Tanner stage is relatively wide. The lessons stressed that each student will pass through each of the Tanner stages at her own pace, thus making comparisons with others (i.e., same-age peers as well as popular icons) misleading.

Excessive caloric restriction is not an effective long-term weight control strategy. In an effort to persuade students that excessive caloric restriction is not an effective long-term weight control strategy, the team created lessons focusing on the physical and psychological reasons for the failure of most diets and the effects of diets on normal health and development. Students were instructed on the metabolic changes that result from dieting, how these changes influence weight loss and maintenance attempts, and how diets can cause physical problems among growing adolescents.

Third, caloric restriction may actually potentiate weight gain and difficulties with weight regulation. The curriculum also addressed the psychological effects associated with dieting. Students were shown how simple dieting techniques can lead to binge eating behaviors and can result in diet–binge cycles. Definitions were provided for BN and AN, symptoms were outlined, and the negative medical and psychological outcomes associated with these disorders were illustrated.

Fourth, adolescents can learn to counteract cultural pressures promoting dieting and a thin body ideal. This component of the intervention focused on helping students to identify effective methods for making healthful choices and resisting cultural pressures to adopt unhealthful weight regulation practices. Students were taught how to recognize social pressure to achieve excessive thinness, to evaluate the outcomes of potential choices, and to identify and use counter-arguments to resist social influence.

Fifth, adolescents can be trained to adopt more healthful nutrition practices and physical activity regimens. Five lessons addressed physical activity and healthful nutrition practices. Students were introduced to the benefits of regular aerobic activity and of choosing a diet high in fiber and complex carbohydrates. Students were also provided with facts about the deleterious effects of a sedentary lifestyle and of diets high in saturated fat and cholesterol. Students were assisted in the development, evaluation, and adoption of personalized long-term nutritional and physical activity plans.

Study Design

A total of 967 sixth- and seventh-grade girls (11–13 years of age) enrolled in four northern California middle schools (6th–8th grades) were randomized to either the intervention for the prevention of eating disorder symptoms or to the no-treatment control classes. Randomization was done within each grade and school by class. Of the 967 girls randomized, 931 actually participated in the study. Missed follow-up assessments and missing data caused the number of subjects to vary from one analysis to another. In each case, however, all subjects with the relevant data are included in each analysis.

Primary Outcome Variables

Weight Concerns Scale. One primary focus of the intervention was to prevent the development and reduce the level of weight concerns in the treatment group. The model suggests that weight concerns may mediate the development of eating disorder symptoms. By reducing weight concerns it was hoped that the onset of symptoms such as binge eating and purging would be delayed or prevented. Weight concerns were measured with a 5-item instrument designed to tap various aspects of students' preoccupation with thinness and body shape. Specifically, items designed to ascertain subjects' fear of weight gain, worry over weight and body shape, level of concern with weight, diet history, and perceived fatness were developed and included in the set of independent variables used in the analyses. The instrument is presented in Table 13.1.

Purging Behaviors. A second principal focus of the intervention was to prevent the development of eating disorder symptoms. A paper-and-pencil instrument was developed to measure the prevalence of the following forms of purging behavior for weight control: vomiting, laxative use, diuretic use, and ipecac use.

Secondary Outcome Variables

Restraint. Dietary restraint was measured using the revised Restraint scale developed by Herman, Policy, Pliner, and Threlkeld (1978).

Eating Disorder Inventory (EDI). The EDI is a 64-item instrument designed to assess a variety of psychological and behavioral charac-

TABLE 13.1
Weight Concerns

1. How much *more or less* do you feel you worry about your weight and body shape than other girls your age?

  1. I worry a lot less than other girls
  2. I worry a little less than other girls
  3. I worry about the same as other girls
  4. I worry a little more than other girls
  5. I worry a lot more than other girls

2. How afraid are you of gaining 3 pounds?

  1. Not afraid of gaining
  2. Slightly afraid of gaining
  3. Moderately afraid of gaining
  4. Very afraid of gaining
  5. Terrified of gaining

3. When was the last time you went on a diet?

  1. I've never been on a diet
  2. I was on a diet about one year ago
  3. I was on a diet about 6 months ago
  4. I was on a diet about 3 months ago
  5. I was on a diet about 1 month ago
  6. I was on a diet less than 1 month ago
  7. I'm now on a diet

4. Compared to other things in your life, how important is your weight to you?

  1. My weight is not important compared to other things in my life
  2. My weight is a little more important than some other things
  3. My weight is more important than most, but not all, things in my life
  4. My weight is the most important thing in my life

5. Do you ever feel fat?

  1. Never
  2. Rarely
  3. Sometimes
  4. Often
  5. Always

teristics common to AN and BN (Garner, Olmsted, & Polivy, 1983). The instrument consists of eight subscales. The analysis of treatment effects included subscales for drive for thinness, bulimia, and body dissatisfaction. Since drive for thinness and body dissatisfaction were highly correlated in this sample, they were combined into one variable, labeled Appearance, for analytic purposes.

Body Mass Index.   Standing height was measured to the nearest millimeter using a portable direct-reading stadiometer. Students were measured with shoes removed and the body positioned such that the heels and buttocks were against the vertical support of the stadiometer and the head aligned so that the auditory canal and the lower rim of the orbit were in a horizontal plane. Body weight was determined to the nearest 0.1 kg using digital scales with the subjects wearing light indoor clothing without shoes or coats. Body mass index was computed from the formula kg/m^2, which is generally considered to be the preferred index of relative body weight as a reflection of adiposity (Kraemer, Berkowitz, & Hammer, 1990).

Knowledge Test.   A pool of items was written to reflect the knowledge basic to understanding healthy weight regulation principles, for example, the biology of normal growth and development, how cultural factors affect attitudes about weight and nutrition, and the dangers of using laxatives, diet pills, and so forth to lose weight. Prior to inclusion in the outcome assessment battery, the items were pretested with a group of 6th- and 7th-grade students who were not participating in the intervention.

Identification of "High-Risk" Girls

One objective was to gauge the effects of the intervention both on the entire sample and on a subgroup of girls at higher risk for the development of eating disorder symptoms. In order to devise a method of identifying girls at comparatively higher risk, the BN section of the Structured Clinical Interview for *DSM–III–R* Disorders (SCID) was administered at baseline to assess the prevalence of BN (Spitzer, Williams, & Gibbon, 1987). The interviews were conducted by 10 graduate students in psychology who were trained in the use of the structured interview. Training consisted of reviewing the *DSM–III–R* diagnostic criteria, observing live interviews of eating disorder patients conducted by one of the investigators, and observing videotapes of SCID interviews. Interrater reliability was assessed by having two interviewers rate 40 study interviews. Kappa coefficients for the interview questions ranged from .66 to 1.00. Liberalized eating disorder criteria were used to assign girls to symptomatic and asymptomatic groups in the absence of established criteria for such a young age group. The case definition of BN encompassed any girl who met the following criteria: recurrent binge eating; regular use of either self-induced vomiting, laxatives, diuretics, strict dieting, or fasting in order to prevent weight gain; and either feelings of lack of control over eating during binges or persistent over-concern with weight and body shape.

Next, the validity of each of the outcome measures was examined by comparing the scores for symptomatic and asymptomatic students identified by the SCID. The measures of Restraint, Weight Concerns, Purging Behaviors, Appearance (EDI), and Bulimia (EDI) all discriminated SCID-defined cases from noncases.

Finally, signal detection analysis was employed to identify an optimally efficient indicator of high-risk status for eating disorders (Kraemer, 1992). Signal detection methods can be used to develop as many as three algorithms, each consisting of a series of simple "and/or" decision rules, one for optimal sensitivity (to rule out a disorder), one for optimal specificity (to rule out other disorders), and one for optimal efficiency (to discriminate those who do have the disorder from those who do not). In this study the focus was on the development of an optimally efficient algorithm for distinguishing those at high risk of developing an eating disorder from those at low risk. The signal detection analysis, which included all of the outcome measures, indicated that the Weight Concerns scale was the optimally efficient discriminator with sensitivity of 86% and a specificity of 63% at a cutpoint score of 57. Specifically, girls with high scores (> 57) on the Weight Concerns scale were classified as being at higher risk for developing a clinical eating disorder.

Schedule for the Assessment of Outcome Data

Because of time constraints, not all measures were collected at each assessment. Weight Concerns and Purging Behaviors were assessed at baseline and at 7, 14, and 24 months; Restraint was assessed at baseline and at 7 and 24 months; EDI score was assessed at baseline, 18 weeks, and at 14 and 24 months; Height and Weight were assessed at baseline, 18 weeks, and at 7, 14, and 24 months; Knowledge was assessed at baseline, 18 weeks, and 7 months.

Primary Outcome Analysis: Weight Concerns, Purging Behaviors

Bandura (1976) argued that the process of behavior change can be separated into induction, generalization, and maintenance phases with each phase at least partly determined by different variables. The analysis is focused on the induction phase since this represented an initial attempt to design an intervention for the prevention of disordered eating behaviors. The effects of the intervention on students' weight concerns and purging behaviors were therefore examined in the initial weeks and months following delivery of the prevention program. Data for program effects on body mass index are also presented, as one component of the intervention focused on the development of healthful nutrition and physical activity practices.

Each primary outcome variable was defined a priori as the difference between baseline and the first assessment period following the conclusion of the intervention. A nested analysis of variance was used, with Treatment, Classes Within Treatment Group, and Subjects Within Classes as sources of variance. The effect of treatment was tested with Classes Within Treatment Group providing the error mean square. However, the effect of Classes Within Treatment group is also compared to that of Subjects Within Classes to gain insight into the possibility of intraclass dependence of responses, an issue of importance for design of future studies in which randomization must be done by class rather than by individual.

Results

Dropout Analysis.   Participants with missing data in the treatment group were not different from participants with missing data in the control group on any baseline variables. Thus, there appears no significant compromise to the internal validity of the results.

Primary Analysis.   Analyses were conducted comparing students from treatment and control conditions who completed both the baseline and the 7-month follow-up assessment. Students receiving the curriculum gained significantly more knowledge than did the control students $[F(4, 25) = 40.11; p < .001]$. Mean change for girls in the treatment group was +4.5 $(SD = 4.9)$; mean change for girls in the control group was –0.0 $(SD = 3.5)$. No other comparisons were statistically significant. Girls in both treatment and control groups reported small decreases in weight concerns over the 7-month interval. The mean change for those in the treatment group was –4.9 $(SD = 20.8)$; the mean change for girls in the control group was –2.4 $(SD = 16.6)$.

High-Risk Girls.   For the sake of clarifying the nature of high- and low-risk groups, data on alcohol use, depressive symptoms, and several eating disorder symptoms variables are presented in Table 13.2. As previously noted, girls with high scores (> 57) on the Weight Concerns scale were classified as being at higher risk for developing a clinical eating disorder.

TABLE 13.2
Comparison of Students Designated High and Low Risk for Eating Disorders on the
Basis of Weight Concerns Score

	High Risk % (n)	Low Risk % (n)
Self-induced vomiting		
Never	77.6% (118)	91.5% (593)
Once or Twice	11.8 % (18)	4.9% (32)
< Monthly	2.0% (3)	1.7% (11)
≥ Monthly	8.6% (13)	1.9% (12)
Laxatives		
Never	84.9% (129)	92.9% (603)
Once or Twice	7.9% (12)	4.5% (29)
< Monthly	3.3% (5)	1.4% (9)
≥ Monthly	3.9% (6)	1.2% (8)
Diet pills		
Never	88.1% (133)	97.4% (639)
Once or Twice	6.6% (10)	0.8% (5)
< Monthly	1.3% (2)	0.4% (3)
≥ Monthly	4.0% (6)	1.4% (9)
Alcohol in last month		
Never	65.4% (100)	74.8% (487)
Few Sips	16.3% (25)	17.4% (113)
Part of one drink	7.8% (12)	3.8% (25)
2–4 drinks	4.6% (7)	2.6% (17)
5–10 drinks	4.6% (7)	0.6% (4)
11–20 drinks	0.0	0.2% (1)
20+ drinks	1.3% (2)	0.6% (4)
Depressive symptoms (CES–D)	24.2 (12.0)	16.6 (10.4)

Analyses were conducted comparing high-risk students from treatment and control conditions who attended both baseline and the initial follow-up assessment. Results are presented in Table 13.3. There was a significant gain, $F(4, 20) = 34.62$; $p = .0001$, in Knowledge for high-risk subjects who received the curriculum. Mean change for girls in the treatment group was +6.1; mean change for girls in the control group was −0.1. Weight Concerns and Purging Behaviors decreased in both the treatment and control groups between baseline and the 7-month follow-up. Although the decrease in Weight Concerns for the treatment group was approximately twice that for the control group this difference did not meet the conventional standard for statistical significance.

High-risk girls in both conditions showed increases in body mass index between baseline and the 18-week follow-up. Interestingly, the mean change for girls in the intervention group (+.2, $SD = .8$) was

TABLE 13.3
Treatment vs. Control Comparisons: All High-Risk Students Present at Both Baseline and Initial Follow-up

Variable	N	Pretreatment	18 Weeks	7 Months	Mean Change
Knowledge	C ($n = 67$)	4.9 (3.5)	4.8 (4.0)	—	-.1 (3.6)
	T ($n = 68$)	5.7 (2.9)	11.8 (5.5)*	—	6.1 (5.1)
EDI Scales					
Bulimia scale	C ($n = 64$)	0.3 (.43)	0.2 (.28)	—	-.1 (.04)
	T ($n = 66$)	0.4 (.52)	0.1 (.26)	—	-.3 (.05)
Appearance	C ($n = 61$)	1.8 (.54)	1.6 (.67)	—	-.2 (0.6)
	T ($n = 64$)	1.7 (.62)	1.2 (.67)	—	-.5 (0.8)
Restraint	C ($n = 54$)	14.5 (3.9)	—	14.4 (4.2)	-.1 (4.5)
	T ($n = 54$)	16.1 (4.3)	—	12.5 (4.9)	-3.6 (4.7)
Eating Attitudes					
Weight Concerns	C ($n = 61$)	71.5 (10.0)	—	58.6 (19.9)	-12.9 (22.8)
	T ($n = 52$)	73.1 (12.7)	—	47.8 (21.4)	-25.3 (23.0)
Purging Behaviors	C ($n = 60$)	8.7 (13.6)	—	5.8 (8.3)	-2.9 (13.6)
	T ($n = 49$)	10.3 (16.1)	—	5.7 (8.4)	-4.6 (13.7)
Body Mass Index	C ($n = 65$)	24.2 (4.5)	24.5 (4.5)	—	.3 (.04)
(kg/m^2)	T ($n = 66$)	23.1 (3.8)	23.3 (3.9)*	—	.2 (.01)

*$p < .001$.

slightly smaller and statistically significant compared to controls (+.3, $SD = .8$), $F(4, 20) = 6.65, p < .001$.

Changes in a Cohort of High-Risk Girls Present at all Assessments

Figure 13.2 illustrates patterns of change in the measure of Weight Concerns for a cohort of girls who were present at all assessments (baseline–24-month follow-up). Figure 13.3 illustrates changes in body mass index for this same group. Girls in the treatment group reported a substantial reduction in the level of Weight Concerns compared to those in the control condition. As this is a secondary analysis, statistical testing was not conducted.

CONCLUSIONS AND IMPLICATIONS

This is perhaps the first controlled study evaluating the efficacy of an intervention designed to prevent the development of unhealthful eating attitudes and weight regulation practices in young adolescent girls. The analysis based on the full sample revealed that the intervention had little, if any, impact on weight concerns and disordered eating behaviors.

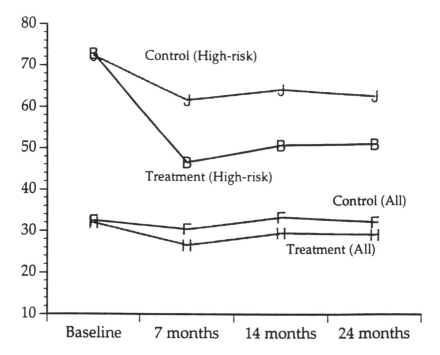

FIG. 13.2. Weight concerns for girls present at all assessments.

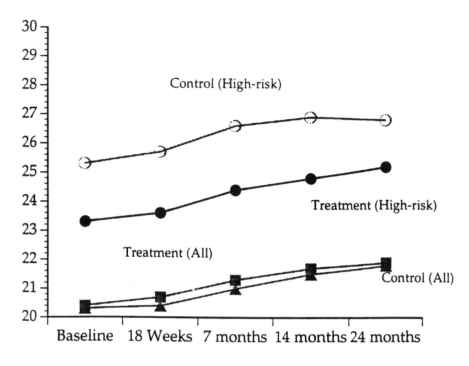

FIG 13.3. Body mass index for girls present at all assessments.

However, the intervention may have had positive effects for girls at comparatively higher risk of developing eating disorder symptoms.

The failure to establish an effect in the primary analysis may stem in large measure from the assumption that without intervention the incidence of dysfunctional eating attitudes and weight concerns is likely to increase over time. Contrary to expectations, weight concerns and frequency of disordered eating behaviors remained relatively stable over the 2 years of follow-up in both intervention and control groups. Given the self-report nature of the data, the possibility that students were more reluctant to report unfavorable attitudes or behaviors cannot be discounted. However, students in this study did report increased drug and alcohol use over time which suggests that they were not simply providing only prosocial responses.

The results of the primary analysis call into question the wisdom of providing a curriculum directed at all young adolescents, most of whom are not at risk to develop eating disorders. However, those at higher risk may benefit from prevention efforts. In order to target high-risk adolescents with prevention programs, the risk factors for developing the disorder need to be identified and must be relatively specific and sensitive.

The data from this study suggest that the measure of Weight Concerns may be useful in identifying higher-risk girls. The Weight Concerns scale, based on items assessing importance of weight, worry about weight, fear of weight gain, recency of last diet, and feeling fat, was the most efficient factor for identifying those at high risk for the development of eating disorders. Girls scoring above the cutpoint of 57 on the scale reported higher prevalences of unhealthful weight regulation practices such as self-induced vomiting, more depressive symptoms, and more frequent substance use. The measure appears useful as a screening tool but additional longitudinal studies are necessary to replicate the finding and to identify additional measures predicting future risk.

It may be reasonable to target high-risk adolescents with prevention interventions. For example, an examination of Figure 13.2 suggests that the curriculum may also have been useful in reducing weight concerns among the high-risk cohort present at all assessments. In addition, the intervention produced a very small albeit statistically significant effect on body mass index among high-risk girls. This suggests that the intervention may have produced an increase in the use of healthful eating and exercise practices among high-risk girls exposed to the intervention. However, this result should be accepted with caution because the analysis is secondary, and there may be questions about its clinical importance.

Given the findings, prevention efforts designed to modify eating attitudes and unhealthful weight regulation practices may focus more profitably on high-risk adolescents rather than on the entire population. It is likely, however, that such higher-risk adolescents may need more intensive intervention than was provided by the eating disorders prevention curriculum. For example, although the scores for Weight Concerns improved considerably among high-risk girls, the mean score for the high-risk group was still twice that of the lower-risk students. In addition, girls identified as high-risk remained substantially heavier as measured by body mass index than did lower-risk girls over the 2-year period.

The prevention intervention designed for this study was not intended as a clinical intervention for students who already manifested eating disorders or for those at high risk of developing eating disorders. It is possible that a more broad-based eating disorders prevention curriculum such as the one designed by the Stanford research team could be linked to treatment resources. For example, Shisslak et al. (1987) incorporated a consultation component into their pilot eating disorders program for high school students. Although this consultation service was publicized in the school newspaper and through announcements in the students' homerooms during the 9-week period, only six students chose the consultation and only one student returned for more than one visit. Alternatively, it may be useful to embed a more intensive intervention within a curriculum that provides important information and behavior change skills appropriate to all students, such as the cardiovascular disease prevention program described earlier (Killen et al., 1988).

The intervention was delivered to girls between 11 and 12 years of age. Younger girls were targeted in part because there is a dominant conventional wisdom that suggests that it is preferable to intervene at very early ages (Killen et al., 1988). Yet, as Fig. 13.1 appears to indicate, the greatest hazard for onset of eating disorder symptoms in girls may occur between 13 and 14 years of age. Thus, it seems very important to target girls at various ages and stages of development. Even in more developed fields of prevention research there is no evidence that interventions with younger children are more successful in achieving prevention goals than are programs designed for older adolescents. Indeed, older adolescents may benefit more from prevention education because they possess the cognitive and behavioral competencies necessary to understand and act upon health and behavior change instruction. In addition, there is no guarantee that programs designed to produce health behavior change at one point in life will protect against the return of or shift to other less healthful lifestyles in later years. Training at one period of development may well require upgrading to be effective in new and perhaps more complex psychosocial environments (Killen, 1985).

Future research should consider the inclusion of family members in prevention efforts. There is much interest in the role of family practices in the etiology and course of eating disorders because they provide the primary context for the early and influential modeling, adoption, and reinforcement of behaviors in general and for the development of specific attitudes and expectations concerning food and eating in particular. However, conclusions about the nature of the relationship between familial factors and eating disorders are speculative and the data upon which the conclusions are based are limited. Strober and Humphrey (1987), in a recent review of the research on familial contributions to the development of eating disorders, concluded that because of the cross-sectional nature of the data, "inferences regarding causation are tentative at best." Although some studies indicate that eating disorders are prevalent in families that demonstrate poorly defined family structures, disorganized communication patterns, or conflict avoidance behaviors, other studies suggest that the families of those suffering from eating disorders are distinguished more by their variability than by their similarity (Kog, Vandereycken, & Vertommen, 1985).

In sum, the results indicate that an untargeted prevention intervention is unlikely to be cost-effective, as the need for prevention is limited to a minority of the general population. On the other hand, the results also suggest that it may be possible to screen a population in order to identify an at-risk subgroup that may be successfully targeted for prevention intervention. Because an identifiable subgroup of 11- and 12-year-old at-risk girls reported higher prevalences of substance use, unhealthful weight regulation strategies, and depressive symptoms, the development and testing of unhealthful weight regulation prevention programs for such subgroups remains a worthwhile endeavor.

ACKNOWLEDGMENTS

Research support for our development of the prevention intervention was provided by Public Health Service Grant HD24779 from the National Institute of Child Health and Development.
Some of the material contained in this chapter is drawn from:

Killen, J. D., & Robinson, T. N. (1988). School-based health behavior change research: The Stanford Adolescent Heart Health Program as a model for cardiovascular disease risk reduction. In E. Rothkopf (Ed.) *Review of Research in Education, 15,* Washington, DC: AERA, pp. 171–200. Copyright 1988 by the American Educational Research Association. Adapted by permission of the publisher.
Killen, J. D., Taylor, C. B., Hammer, L. D., Litt, I., Wilson, D. M., Rich, T., Hayward, C., Simmonds, B. A., Kraemer, H., & Varady, A. (1993). An attempt to modify unhealthful eating attitudes and weight regulation practices of young adolescent girls. *International Journal of Eating Disorders, 13,* 369–384. Copyright 1994 by John Wiley & Sons, Inc.
Killen, J. D., Taylor, C. B., Hayward, C., Wilson, D. M., Haydel, K. F., Robinson, T. N., Litt, I., Simmonds, B. A., Varady, A., & Kraemer, H. (1994). The pursuit of thinness and onset of eating disorder symptoms in a community sample of adolescent girls: A three year prospective analysis. *International Journal of Eating Disorders, 16,* 227–238. Copyright 1994 by John Wiley & Sons, Inc.

REFERENCES

American College of Physicians, Health and Public Policy Committee. (1986). Eating disorders: Anorexia nervosa and bulimia. *Annals of Internal Medicine, 105,* 790–794.
Andrus, L. H. (1964). Smoking by high school students: Failure of a campaign to persuade adolescents not to smoke. *California Medicine, 101,* 246–247.
Bandura, A. (1976). Effecting change through participant modeling. In J.D. Krumboltz & C.E. Thoresen (Eds.), *Counseling methods* (pp. 248–265). New York: Rinehart & Winston.
Bandura, A. (1986). *Social foundations of thought and action.* Englewood Cliffs, NJ: Prentice-Hall.
Botvin, G., & Eng, A. (1980). A comprehensive school-based smoking prevention program. *Journal of School Health, 11,* 209–213.
Brooks-Gunn, J., & Petersen, A. (1983). *Girls at puberty.* New York: Plenum.
Bruch, H. (1978). *The golden cage.* Cambridge, MA: Harvard University Press.
Cantor, J. (1981). Modifying children's eating habits through television ads—Effects of humorous appeals in a field setting. *Journal of Broadcasting, 25,* 37–48.
Coscina, D. V., & Dixon, L. M. (1983). Body weight regulation in anorexia nervosa: Insights from an animal model. In P. L. Darby, P. E. Garfinkel, D. M. Garner, & D. V. Coscina

(Eds.), *Anorexia nervosa: Recent developments in research* (pp. 207–220). New York: Alan R. Liss.

Dally, P., Gomez, J., Issacs, A. J. (1979). *Anorexia nervosa*. London: William Heineman.

Evans, R. I., & Borgatta, E. F. (1970). An experiment in smoking dissuasion among university freshmen. *Journal of Health and Social Behavior, 11*, 30–36.

Flay, B. R., Ryan, K. B., Best, J. A., Brown, K. S., Kersell, M. W., d'Avernas, J. R., & Zanna, M. P. (1985). Are social psychological smoking prevention programs effective? The Waterloo study. *Journal of Behavioral Medicine, 8*, 37–59.

Garfinkel, P. E., Moldofsky, H., & Garner, D. M. (1980). The heterogeneity of anorexia: Bulimia as a distinct subgroup. *Archives of General Psychiatry, 37*, 1036–1040.

Garner, D. M., Olmsted, M. P., & Polivy, J. (1983). The development and validation of a multidimensional eating disorder inventory for anorexia nervosa and bulimia. *International Journal of Eating Disorders, 2*, 15–34.

Hansen, W. B. (1992). School-based substance abuse prevention: A review of the state of the art in curriculum, 1980–1990. *Health and Education Research, 7*, 403–430.

Herman, C. P., Polivy, J., Pliner, P., & Threlkeld, J. (1978). Distractibility in dieters and nondieters: An alternative view of "externality." *Journal of Personality and Social Psychology, 5*, 536–548.

Herzog, D. B., & Copeland, P. M. (1985). Eating disorders. *New England Journal of Medicine, 313*, 295–303.

Jeffrey D. B, McLellarn, R. W., & Fox, D. T. (1982). The development of children's eating habits: The role of television commercials. *Health Education Quarterly, 9*, 174–189.

Johnston L. D., O'Malley, P. M., & Bachman, J. G. (1986). *Drug use among American high school students, college students, and other young adults: National trends through 1985* (DHHS Publication No. ADM 86–1450). Rockville, MD: National Institute on Drug Abuse.

Keys, A., Brozek, J., Henschel, A., Mickelson, O., & Taylor, H. L. (1950). *The biology of human starvation* (2 vols). Minneapolis: University of Minnesota Press.

Killen, J. D. (1985). Prevention of adolescent tobacco smoking: The social pressures resistance training approach. *Journal of Child Psychiatry and Psychology, 26*, 7–15.

Killen, J. D., Hayward, C., Litt, I., Hammer, L. D., Wilson, D. M., Miner, B., Taylor, C. B., Varady, A., & Shisslak, C. (1992). Is puberty a risk factor for eating disorders? *American Journal of Diseases of Children, 146*, 323–325.

Killen, J. D., Taylor, C. B., Hayward, C., Wilson, D. M., Hammer, L. D., Robinson, T. N., Litt, I., Simmonds, B. A., Varady, A., & Kraemer, H. (1994). The pursuit of thinness and onset of eating disorder symptoms in a community sample of adolescent girls: A three year prospective analysis. *International Journal of Eating Disorders, 16*, 227–238.

Killen, J. D., Telch, M. J., Robinson, T. N., Saylor, K. E., Maccoby, N., Taylor, C. B., & Farquhar, J. W. (1988). Cardiovascular disease risk reduction for tenth graders. *Journal of the American Medical Association, 260*, 1728–1733.

Kog, E., & Vandereycken, W. (1985). Family characteristics of anorexia nervosa and bulimia: A review of the literature. *Clinical Psychology Review, 5*, 159–180.

Kog, E., Vandereycken, W., & Vertommen, H. (1985). Towards a verification of the psychosomatic family model: A pilot study of ten families with an anorexia/bulimia nervosa patient. *International Journal of Eating Disorders, 4*, 525–538.

Kraemer, H. C. (1992). *Evaluating medical tests: Objective and quantitative guidlines*. Newbury Park, CA: Sage.

Kraemer, H. C., Berkowitz, R. I. & Hammer, L. D. (1990). Methodological difficulties in studies of obesity: I. Measurement issues. *Annals of Behavioral Medicine, 12*, 112–118.

Leupker, R. V., Johnson, C. A., Murray, D. M., & Pechacek, T. F. (1983). Prevention of cigarette smoking: Three year follow-up of an education program for youth. *American Journal of Public Health, 71*, 1320–1324.

Lumsdaine, A. A., & Janis, I. L. (1953). Resistance to counter-propaganda produced by one-sided and two-sided presentations. *Public Opinion Quarterly, 17,* 311–318.

Marshall, W. A., & Tanner, J. M. (1969). Variations in the pattern of pubertal changes in girls. *Archives of Disease in Children, 44,* 291.

McGuire, W. (1964). Inducing resistance to persuasion. In L. Berkowitz (Ed.), *Advances in experimental social psychology* (pp. 191–229). New York: Academic Press.

Pike, K. M., & Rodin, J. (1991). Mothers, daughters and disordered eating. *Journal of Abnormal Psychology, 100,* 198–204.

Polich, J. M., & Ellickson, P. L. (1984). *Strategies for controlling adolescent drug use* (Report No. R-3076–CHF). Santa Monica, CA: Rand Corporation.

Polivy, J., & Herman, C. P. (1985). Dieting and binging: A causal analysis. *American Psychologist, 40,* 193–201.

Robinson, T. N., Killen, J. D., Taylor, C. B., Telch, M. J., Bryson, S., Maron, D. J., Saylor, K. E., Maccoby, N., & Farquhar, J. W. (1987). Perspectives on adolescent substance use: A defined population study. *Journal of the American Medical Association, 258,* 2072–2076.

Shisslak, C. M., Crago, M., & Neal, M. E. (1987). Prevention of eating disorders among adolescents. *Journal of Consulting and Clinical Psychology, 55,* 660–667.

Spitzer, R. L., Williams, J. B., & Gibbon, M. (1987). Structured Clinical Interview for DSM–III–R (SCID). New York: New York State Psychiatric Institute.

Striegel-Moore, R. H., Silberstein, L. R, & Rodin, J. (1986). Toward an understanding of risk factors for bulimia. *American Psychologist, 41,* 246–263.

Strober, M. (1986). Anorexia nervosa: History and psychological concepts. In K. D. Brownell & J. P. Foreyt (Eds.), *Handbook of eating disorders: Physiology, psychology and treatment of obesity, anorexia and bulimia* (pp. 231–246). New York: Basic Books.

Strober, M., & Humphrey, L. L. (1987). Familial contributions to the etiology and course of anorexia nervosa and bulimia. *Journal of Consulting and Clinical Psychology, 55,* 654–659.

Telch, M. J., Killen, J. D., McAlister, A. L., Perry, C. L., & Maccoby, N. (1982). Long-term follow-up of a pilot project on smoking prevention with adolescents. *Journal of Behavioral Medicine, 5,* 1–8.

14

Content and Method of Developmentally Appropriate Prevention Programs

Catherine M. Shisslak
Marjorie Crago
Linda S. Estes
Norma Gray

The primary goal in writing this chapter is to suggest prevention strategies for eating disorders that take into account both the salient developmental issues across the life span and research findings on putative risk factors at each developmental stage. The chapter begins with a review of existing prevention programs. The remainder of the chapter is devoted to a discussion of developmental stages; topics include important milestones, research regarding risk factors, and prevention interventions tailored to each stage of development. The discussion is focused on girls and women. This is not meant to suggest that inclusion of boys, young men, fathers, and other male figures in prevention strategies is not important. However, it was decided that female development should provide the basis for discussion of intervention strategies.

REVIEW OF CURRENT PREVENTION PROGRAMS

The importance of prevention programs for eating disorders has been emphasized by eating disorder theorists, researchers, and clinicians for some time (e.g., American College of Physicians, 1986; Crisp, 1979; Levine, 1987; Shisslak, Crago, Neal, & Swain, 1987). Various eating disorder curricula suitable for elementary, junior high, and high school students have been developed (Carney, 1986; Center for the Study of Anorexia and Bulimia, 1983; Giarrantano, 1991; Kennedy, 1990; Killen et al., 1993; Levine & Hill, 1991; Moreno & Thelen, 1993; National Eating Disorder Information Center, 1989; Paxton, 1993; Porter, Morrell, & Moriarty, 1986; Rhyne-Winkler & Hubbard, 1994; Rosen, 1989; Shisslak, Crago, & Neal, 1990). Prevention programs for college students have been designed as well (Huon, 1994b; Sesan, 1989a, 1989b). In general, these programs include some or all of the following components: signs, symptoms, and health consequences of eating disorders; treatments available for these disorders; risk factors (e.g., sociocultural emphasis on thinness in women, low self-esteem, family problems, and dieting); healthy versus unhealthy weight regulation; and enhancement of life skills (e.g., problem solving, decision making, communication, and self-affirmation).

Only a few of these eating disorder prevention programs have been evaluated, however. Porter et al. (1986) designed and evaluated a half-day program for pre- and early adolescents that consisted of specially designed art, dance, and music workshops combined with an educational film. Pre- and posttesting indicated a significant program impact, especially among children who had scored above the mean and in the anorexic direction on the pretest.

Moriarty, Shore, and Maxim (1990) evaluated the eating disorder curriculum that had been developed by Carney (1986). Pre- and posttesting of students in 10 Canadian elementary and high schools revealed that students who received the curriculum showed positive changes in knowledge and attitudes about eating disorders compared to students who had not received the curriculum. Similar results were obtained in an evaluation of a 9-week high school eating disorder curriculum designed by Shisslak et al. (1990). Shisslak and associates also included an eating disorder consultation component in the prevention program. Several students initiated consultations and several others were referred by parents or teachers.

Paxton (1993) evaluated an Australian eating disorder prevention program consisting of five classes for high school girls aimed at reducing extreme weight loss behaviors, disordered eating, and negative body image. Self-report questionnaire responses of 107 students in two schools who received the program were compared to the responses of 29 students who had not received the program. All of the students were tested prior to the program, 1 month after the program, and 1 year later. None of the variables showed an effect of the prevention program.

Moreno and Thelen (1993) examined the effectiveness of a short videotape and discussion group focused on eating disorders. An experimental group of 80 junior high school girls and a control group of 139 girls were pretested, assessed again 4 days later, and reassessed 1 month after pretesting. The results indicated that the prevention program was successful in changing the students' knowledge, attitudes, and behavioral intentions regarding dieting, weight preoccupation, and purging.

Huon (1994b) evaluated the effects of discussion groups involving 24 college women. The groups were focused on discouraging dieting and developing a more positive body image. Pre- and posttesting revealed that women who were involved in groups in which strategies for change were discussed had a more positive body image following the discussion than they did before the group began. These changes in body image were not found among the women who participated in groups that focused on barriers to change. In addition, 5 of the 12 women (42%) who participated in the strategies groups reported that they were definitely less likely to go on a diet during the next 12 months, and 7 of the women (58%) reported much less weight preoccupation after participation in the groups.

The only long-term study of an eating disorder prevention curriculum is that of Killen et al. (1993; for a detailed discussion see Killen, chapter 13, this volume). The curriculum they designed consisted of 18 lesson plans divided into three components: unhealthy weight regulation practices, healthy weight regulation practices, and development of coping skills to resist sociocultural pressures to diet. A total of 995 sixth- and seventh-grade girls in four middle schools were randomly assigned to receive either the prevention curriculum or no-treatment control classes. Evaluations were conducted before the curriculum was begun and at four intervals during the 2 years following the completion of the curriculum. The results showed a significant increase in knowledge about eating disorders in the experimental group, but there were no significant differences between the experimental and control groups in eating attitudes and weight regulation practices during the follow-up period. Based on these findings, Killen et al. suggested that it might be more cost-effective to target at-risk students for preventive interventions or, alternatively, to embed a more intensive intervention within a curriculum providing information appropriate for all students (e.g., nutrition, exercise).

The Norwegian government is currently in the process of developing a nationwide plan for the treatment and prevention of eating disorders (Gresko & Karlsen, 1994). This plan includes the education of all health care and school personnel about eating disorders. Also, instructional materials about these disorders will be integrated into the school curriculum. An outcome evaluation of the school-based prevention curriculum involving 1,000 Norwegian girls and boys in the ninth grade is now being conducted. Information on the results of this evaluation will be available within the next year or two.

To summarize the results of these evaluations of eating disorder prevention programs: Those programs that included components aimed at increasing knowledge about eating disorders were all successful in achieving this goal (Killen et al., 1993; Moreno & Thelen, 1993; Moriarty et al., 1990; Shisslak et al., 1990). Program components aimed at changing attitudes related to eating disorders were successful in some cases (Huon, 1994b; Moreno & Thelen, 1993; Moriarty et al., 1990; Porter et al., 1986) but not in others (Killen et al., 1993; Paxton, 1993; Rosen, 1989). Also, components aimed at changing behaviors or behavioral intentions were successful in some cases (Huon, 1994b; Moreno & Thelen, 1993) but not in others (Killen et al., 1993; Paxton, 1993; Rosen, 1989).

Most of the eating disorder prevention programs developed thus far have not emphasized the importance of developmental factors in relation to eating disorders. Most of the programs have been geared toward middle or high school students. However, by adolescence negative eating attitudes and behaviors appear to be widespread and strongly ingrained (Attie & Brooks-Gunn, 1992; Striegel-Moore, 1993). For this reason, we and others (e.g., Smolak & Levine, 1994b) propose that focusing prevention programs on elementary school children rather than adolescents may be more effective.

DEVELOPMENTAL ISSUES AND PREVENTION INTERVENTIONS IN PREPUBERTAL CHILDREN

In approximately 5% of anorexia nervosa (AN) cases, onset occurs before puberty (Atkins & Silber, 1993; Gowers, Crisp, Joughin, & Bhat, 1991). No cases of bulimia nervosa (BN) have been documented in prepubertal children, but BN symptoms have been reported in some prepubertal AN cases (Thelen, Lawrence, & Powell, 1992). The clinical features of prepubertal and later-onset AN are similar in boys and girls, but the proportion of boys is higher in early-onset AN, that is, approximately 25% to 30% (Fosson, Knibbs, Bryant-Waugh, & Lask, 1987; Thelen et al., 1992). Serious developmental problems can result if the onset of AN occurs before puberty, including stunted growth, decreased bone density, and delayed menarche (Russell, 1985). No consensus has been reached as to whether the prognosis for prepubertal AN is better, similar, or worse than the prognosis for AN with onset at or after puberty (Fosson et al., 1987; Thelen et al., 1992).

Although clinical cases of eating disorders are relatively rare in prepubertal children, various eating disturbances occur among children that may lead to subsequent development of eating disorders during adolescence (Marchi & Cohen, 1990). Among the risk factors for eating disorders that have been identified in children are early feeding problems, family dysfunction, perfectionism, low self-esteem, and being teased about being fat (Atkins & Silber, 1993; Fabian & Thompson, 1989; Gowers et al., 1991; Marchi & Cohen, 1990).

Prevention Strategies

Specific strategies to help prevent the development of eating disorders or risk factors for later eating disorders in prepubertal children have been suggested by various investigators, including Levine (1994), Shisslak et al. (1987), Smolak and Levine (1994a, 1994b), and Striegel-Moore (1992). Some of the strategies that have been suggested for parents and caregivers include educating expectant parents about children's eating patterns and preferences at different stages of development and emphasizing that how one responds to an infant's hunger cries is as important as what the infant is fed; teaching day-care workers to detect feeding problems in children so that they can serve as a support and referral system for early intervention; making parents aware of how their own eating behaviors and weight concerns can affect their children; educating parents to refrain from commenting on children's weight and body shape and to focus instead on health, strength, or abilities; and alerting parents and family therapists to the possibility that a child may develop eating problems in response to family conflict or to loss of a parent through separation, divorce, or death. Suggested strategies for children include teaching them acceptance of a wide range of body shapes; encouraging them to develop interests and skills that will lead to success and personal fulfillment without being based on appearance; teaching them healthy eating and exercise habits and emphasizing the negative effects of dieting; teaching ways to resist teasing about weight and being pressured to diet; and providing children with information about the facts of development to allay some of their anxieties about puberty, emphasizing that weight gain is a normal and necessary part of pubertal development.

DEVELOPMENTAL ISSUES AND PREVENTION INTERVENTIONS IN ADOLESCENTS

Petersen and Hamburg (1986) described adolescence as the second decade of life, extending from ages 11 to 20. The period of adolescence is further broken down into early, middle, and late adolescence. The timing of these stages is different for boys and girls, with girls typically entering adolescence earlier than boys. Early adolescence for girls generally encompasses the ages 11 through 13; middle adolescence, 14 through 16; and late adolescence, 17 through 20.

Developmental Challenges of Adolescence

The developmental challenges occurring in adolescence include dealing with the psychological and physical effects of puberty; moving toward increased autonomy, both psychologically and physically; developing peer relationships, including sexual relationships; internalizing values of achievement; and achieving an integrated sense of self with which to regulate mood, impulses, and self-esteem (Attie, Brooks-Gunn, & Petersen, 1990; Levine & Smolak, 1992).

Although many studies have been conducted on eating disorders in adolescence, few studies relate the development of eating disorders during this period to specific developmental issues. In this section we attempt to relate research findings on eating- and weight-related problems in early, middle, and late adolescence to developmental issues associated with the adolescent years. Suggestions for preventive interventions appropriate for each stage of adolescence are given.

Early Adolescence

Research has indicated that the majority of early adolescent girls are dissatisfied with their bodies and want to weigh less (Gralen, Levine, Smolak, & Murnen, 1990; Rosen, Silberg, & Gross, 1988; Shore & Porter, 1990). The increase in concern about eating and weight seems to occur around eighth and ninth grade (Gralen et al., 1990; Richards, Casper, & Larson, 1990). Unhealthy eating attitudes and behaviors appear to increase around the same time (Bennett, Spoth, & Borgen, 1991; Gralen et al., 1990; Leichner, Arnett, Rallo, Srikameswaran, & Vulcano, 1986; Shore & Porter, 1990), suggesting that this may be a critical age group to target for prevention. The following brief review of developmental issues suggests some specific areas to be addressed in prevention interventions for early adolescents.

Pubertal Development. Several studies have found a connection between the emergence of eating problems and the physical changes of puberty, specifically changes in body fat and body image (Attie & Brooks-Gunn, 1989, 1992; Killen et al., 1992; Killen et al., 1994; Striegel-Moore, 1993). The effects of puberty appear to be intensified by co-occurrence with other stressful changes associated with this developmental stage, such as beginning to date and entering middle school (Levine & Smolak, 1992; Levine, Smolak, Moodey, Shuman, & Hessen, 1994; Smolak, Levine, & Gralen, 1993). Early maturation may also increase risk for the development of eating problems (Striegel-Moore, 1993). Early-maturing girls tend to be shorter and heavier than peers, tend to be more dissatisfied with weight, tend to begin dating younger, may experience decreased popularity among female peers, experience more emotional distress, and have poorer self-concepts (Peskin, 1973; Simmons, Blyth, & McKinney, 1983; Striegel-Moore, 1993; Tobin-Richards, Boxer, & Petersen, 1983).

Taken together, these studies suggest that helping girls to cope with the physical, social, and emotional changes that occur with puberty is an important component of prevention. Special efforts may need to be addressed to those girls who develop younger than their peers, since these girls may be at higher risk.

Increasing Independence. It has been thought that families of eating-disordered girls contribute to feelings of ineffectiveness and poor self-esteem and do not support efforts at autonomy (Minuchin, Rosman, & Baker, 1978; Selvini-Palazzoli, 1974; Sours, 1974). A number of investigators have observed that the mothers of AN patients are overprotective and discourage separation–individuation, either overtly or covertly (Bruch, 1973; Crisp, 1980; Selvini-Palazzoli, 1974). However, research on families of eating-disordered girls has not shown any clear relationship between family functioning and eating problems (Shisslak et al., 1987).

Research does indicate that beginning in early adolescence there is a decrease in the amount of time spent with parents and a change in the level of emotional closeness to parents, as the amount of conflict between adolescents and parents increases (see Attie & Brooks-Gunn, 1992). This increase in conflict is seen especially in the mother–daughter dyad, which may have negative effects on girls because of their greater needs for emotional involvement with parents (Striegel-Moore, 1993). This decrease in closeness that begins in early adolescence, rather than lack of encouragement for autonomy, may present a risk factor for eating problems. However, Attie and Brooks-Gunn found no association between girls' perceptions of family relationships and eating problems. Nevertheless, theory and research in this area suggest at least two considerations for prevention. First, it seems that girls and their parents need help in understanding and accepting increased needs for independence. Second, teaching girls and their families conflict management skills could potentially lessen the negative impact of increasing strivings for independence on the maintenance of family relationships.

Peer Relationships. During adolescence there is an increase in involvement with peers and, for girls, an increased emphasis on intimacy, shared thoughts, and shared feelings as the basis of friendship (Petersen & Hamburg, 1986). Girls change from being largely self-centered in preadolescence to emphasizing conformity based on shared norms and expectations in early and middle adolescence (Petersen & Hamburg, 1986). This conformity may take the form of compliance with social demands and gender-role expectations in order to win the approval and esteem from others that is so important to girls (Hill & Lynch, 1983). The increased emphasis on peer involvement and conformity suggests the importance of developing prevention interventions that can be used in a group format.

Group interventions can also be used to encourage girls to develop healthy norms for eating and weight. Girls, because of their sensitivity to feedback from others, may be especially vulnerable to messages regarding acceptable standards of beauty and appearance (Steiner-Adair, 1986; Striegel-Moore, Silberstein, & Rodin, 1986). They receive these messages about the prevailing standards of beauty and about acceptable techniques for achieving these standards from peers, as well as from magazines and family (Levine, Smolak, Moodey, Shuman, & Hessen, 1994). They also receive feedback from peers concerning weight and body shape through teasing. For premenarcheal girls, frequency and effect of teasing about weight and body size have been shown to be related to body dissatisfaction, eating disturbance, low self-esteem, and depression (Fabian & Thompson, 1989; see also Levine et al., 1994). This research suggests that helping girls to cope with teasing may be an important component of prevention.

Another important aspect of peer relationships during this period concerns the development of dating relationships. The onset of dating, in conjunction with menarche and entering middle school, appears to be a risk factor for eating disturbances (Levine et al., 1994; Levine & Smolak, 1992; Smolak et al., 1993). Striegel-Moore (1993) reviewed research suggesting a relationship between interest in dating and dieting behavior in early adolescence. She also suggested the possibility that early sexual activity and resulting sexual anxieties contribute to dieting and binge eating. Thus, coping with dating and emerging sexuality also appear to be important components of prevention. (See Berndt & Hestenes, chapter 4, this volume, for further discussion of peer relationships.)

Achievement Pressures. The transition from elementary school to middle school or junior high school is a difficult one for many young adolescents. Those girls who put the most pressure on themselves to achieve may be at risk, because high achievement strivings may be associated with the perfectionism commonly reported in individuals with eating disorders (Shisslak et al., 1990). These girls in particular may need to be targeted in prevention interventions aimed at helping them to balance scholastic achievement with other areas of their lives.

Achieving an Integrated Sense of Self. Development of a sense of self includes developing self-esteem, self-control, abilities for self-soothing, and self-efficacy (Wexler, 1991). Impairments in these aspects of self-development have long been associated with eating disorders (Bruch, 1973). In terms of identity development, the self-image of girls seems to be more interpersonally oriented than that of boys, and girls seem to worry more about what other people think of them, to care more about being liked, and to try to avoid negative reactions from others (Simmons & Rosenberg, 1975; Striegel-Moore et al., 1986). The more a girl defines herself in terms of physical appearance and acceptance from others, the more at risk she may be for developing eating problems. Again, prevention interventions at this age should recognize the importance of group acceptance in the development of female identity and should help girls to explore and develop other ways of being accepted aside from appearance. (For further discussion see Ewell, Smith, Karmel, & Hart, chapter 5, this volume.)

Prevention Strategies.   Cognitively, early adolescent girls are still at a concrete operational level (Petersen & Hamburg, 1986). Therefore, prevention interventions in this age group should be geared toward providing specific information tailored to the developmental tasks at hand.

Specific areas addressed in prevention efforts should include a number of elements. First, girls need information regarding the changes that occur with puberty, such as the normal increases in body fat (Story et al., 1991). Information should be given on psychological and social components such as increased emotional arousal, relationships with boys, and problems with parents (Shisslak et al., 1987). Special attention and support may need to be given to girls maturing earlier than their peers.

Second, girls and their parents need information about normal adolescent development, including increased needs for independence. Providing girls and their families with information on conflict resolution skills could help to ease tensions during early adolescence and beyond.

Third, because peer acceptance is so important in the early and middle adolescent years, prevention efforts need to incorporate peer groups (Gibbs, 1986; Shisslak & Crago, 1994; Shisslak et al., 1987). The early establishment of peer support groups should be facilitated to help ease the transition into middle school or junior high school. Group feedback, especially using older peer facilitators, can be utilized to correct unrealistic attitudes and misperceptions regarding weight and appearance (Shisslak & Crago, 1994; Shisslak et al., 1987). Our experience with focus groups in schools has shown that girls are open and eager to talk about issues that are troubling them (Taylor, Shisslak, & Killen, 1994).

Girls also need help in learning to cope with teasing from others (Cattarin & Thompson, 1994). Group exercises utilizing role-playing techniques and assertiveness training can be used to teach girls such coping skills. These same skills can be used in helping girls deal with increased pressures regarding dating and sexuality.

Fourth, behavioral training in assertiveness and relaxation could be used to help girls learn to regulate emotions in healthy ways. Education regarding unhealthy ways of coping with emotions, including the use of food, drugs, and alcohol, should be incorporated and continued throughout the adolescent years.

Fifth, teaching problem-solving and time management skills could help girls to deal with academic pressures. Girls can also be taught about realistic goal setting and about the importance of balancing achievement and relaxation.

Sixth, girls need specific information to help them recognize and accept realistic body weights (Eisele, Hertsgaard, & Light, 1986). Story et al. (1991) recommended that prevention efforts aimed at chronic dieting need to occur prior to the ninth grade, when the incidence of this behavior seems to increase. Girls should also be given understandable information on healthy eating and exercise, the effects of food restriction and chronic dieting, and the physiological and psychological dangers of drastic weight-loss techniques (Bennett et al., 1991; Killen et al., 1986; Story et al., 1991). To make this information more concrete, girls could be given classroom assignments involving the development of healthy food and exercise plans for weight maintenance and weight loss.

Middle Adolescence

Several studies show evidence of dieting behaviors in girls aged 14 years and over (Dwyer, Feldman, & Mayer, 1967; Dwyer, Feldman, Seltzer, & Mayer, 1969; Johnson, Lewis, Love, Stuckey, & Lewis, 1983; Whitaker et al., 1989). Dieting has been associated with higher weights (Attie & Brooks-Gunn, 1989, 1992; Leichner et al., 1986), and frequent dieting in this age group has been associated with other problems such as self-induced vomiting, use of laxatives and diuretics, binge eating, feeling overweight, and poor body image (Huon, 1994a; Story et al., 1991). At least one study suggests that heavier adolescents are at higher risk for eating problems (Whitaker et al., 1989). These findings indicate that dieting, binge eating, and purging behaviors need to be addressed in prevention interventions with this age group. Heavier girls may need to be selectively targeted for intervention. The following brief review of developmental issues suggests other specific areas to be addressed in prevention interventions for middle adolescence.

Pubertal Development. Pubertal factors need not be a major focus of intervention for middle adolescent girls, because the impact of pubertal factors on eating and weight appears to decrease as girls get older (Attie & Brooks-Gunn, 1989, 1992).

Increasing Independence. Steiner-Adair (1986) addressed conflicts between cultural values of autonomy and female valuation of relationships in middle and late adolescent girls. Subjects were interviewed and assessed on two measures of dysfunctional eating, the Eating Attitudes Test and a questionnaire developed to assess food, eating, and weight concerns. Two patterns of responses emerged, which

Steiner-Adair labeled the wise woman and the superwoman. Wise-woman respondents recognized societal pressures for achievement and independence, but retained values focused on the importance of relationships. Superwoman respondents identified with an ideal described as successful and independent from others. The Superwoman ideal was associated by subjects with being tall and thin.

All of the wise-woman respondents scored in the non-eating-disordered range on the Eating Attitudes Test. Of the superwoman respondents, 11 out of 12 scored in the eating-disordered range. Steiner-Adair (1986) concluded that girls who are able to identify cultural values for women and still maintain their own, sometimes conflicting, values are less at risk for eating disorders. Those girls who most strongly identify with societal values that are in conflict with their developmental needs for connection are at greater risk for developing eating disorders. The results of this study suggest that acceptance of society's emphasis on independence may be associated with eating- and weight-related problems in girls. Prevention efforts need to recognize this and to help girls feel comfortable with their needs for connectedness with others.

Peer Relationships. Anxiety about friendships is thought to increase during middle adolescence (Petersen & Hamburg, 1986), making girls in this age group even more vulnerable to peer influences regarding weight and body shape. Supportive evidence comes from Gibbs (1986), who found correlations between dysfunctional eating attitudes and behaviors and the following: frequency of talking to peers about dieting and weight loss, and engagement in activities requiring specific weights or body types (cheerleading, modeling, dancing, weight lifting, wrestling, running, aerobics, gymnastics). These findings again emphasize the powerful potential of using peer groups for intervention and the need to encourage healthy attitudes about eating, weight, and body shape.

Achievement Pressures. According to Striegel-Moore (1993), middle adolescence is associated with intensified concerns regarding achievement. The issue of choosing a career becomes increasingly important during this time. This may be a time when the superwoman ideal comes into play. The superwoman is seen as "having it all"—successful career, husband and family, and beauty, which also includes being thin (Steiner-Adair, 1986). Striegel-Moore saw the emergence of binge eating in connection with the superwoman ideal as a means of coping with stress associated with high achievement. The amount of stress may be compounded if the individual is not meeting her achievement needs. Identification of girls who hold the superwoman ideal may be important for prevention, as these girls may be at increased risk for binge eating and other problems.

Achieving an Integrated Sense of Self. A deficit in one component of self, self-esteem, has been shown to be associated with abnormal eating attitudes in middle adolescent girls (Fisher, Pastore, Schneider, Pegler, & Napolitano, 1994; Fisher, Schneider, Pegler, & Napolitano, 1991). Problems in self-soothing and emotional regulation are suggested by research indicating that depression, anxiety, and high stress reactivity are associated with increased risk for dysfunctional eating attitudes and behaviors in middle and late adolescent girls (Bennett et al., 1991; Gross & Rosen, 1988; Leon, Fulkerson, Perry, & Cudeck, 1993). Low levels of self-efficacy have also been associated with eating disorder symptoms in this age group (Bennett et al., 1991). Although open to different interpretations, these findings suggest that helping girls to develop better affective regulation could be beneficial in promoting self-development and prevention of abnormal eating attitudes and behaviors.

Prevention Strategies. Middle adolescence is marked by an increased capacity for abstract thinking and by increased anxiety regarding social relationships (Petersen & Hamburg, 1986) and achievement (Striegel-Moore, 1993). Concerns about puberty are starting to wane for most girls, and psychological factors are becoming more important in predicting problems with eating and weight (Attie & Brooks-Gunn, 1989, 1992). Issues regarding nutrition, self-regulation, and peer relationships addressed earlier need continued attention. In addition, several new issues need to be addressed with middle adolescent girls.

First, cognitive–behavioral strategies for dealing with emotions can be introduced, taking advantage of the increased capacity for abstract thinking. Girls can be helped to see connections between emotions and use of food or substances and can explore healthy alternatives for dealing with negative affect (Shisslak et al., 1987).

Second, girls at this age can begin to question and discuss personal values, self-worth, and achievement (Shisslak et al., 1987). Girls can be given classroom exercises to help make concepts more concrete, such as listing various means other than academic or career success for maintaining self-worth. Shisslak and Crago (1994) suggested teaching girls to examine gender-role expectations and helping them to critically evaluate the negative outcomes of attempting to live up to these expectations. Images of women in the media can be used as points of departure for discussion of women's roles. Appropriate adult female role models can be used to help girls in selecting healthy lifestyles.

Third, girls' needs for continued emotional connection should be addressed and validated. Common problems between peers and between parents and teens can be discussed, and girls can be encouraged to use problem-solving skills to come up with constructive solutions.

Fourth, building on factual information regarding nutrition and weight, girls can now begin to explore the abstract issue of body image and how it relates to health and self-esteem. Exercises using photographs, drawings, and movement to enhance body image can be used to make these issues more concrete.

Late Adolescence

Dysfunctional eating attitudes and behaviors remain high through late adolescence (Huon, 1994a; Jakobovits, Halstead, Kelley, Roe, & Young, 1977). The following brief review of developmental issues suggests other specific areas to be addressed in prevention interventions for late adolescents.

Increasing Independence.   In late adolescence girls once again face transitions that challenge their needs for continued relationships in order to increase their autonomy. These transitions may include moving from high school to college or the workplace and possibly leaving home. Once again, prevention interventions need to help girls build the relational bridges that they need to make these transitions.

Peer Relationships.   Late-adolescent girls are beginning to move away from conformity and toward a level of relationship based on principled reasoning that takes into consideration the feelings of others (Gilligan, 1982). Nevertheless, the impact of peer feedback and especially of weight-related teasing remains important. This may be particularly true for obese girls (Cattarin & Thompson, 1994). Late adolescence is also a time when dating and attractiveness to the opposite sex become increasingly important, and many girls either begin considering marriage or cohabitation or feel some pressure to do so. This may be a time when helping girls to balance their needs and wants with the needs and wants of others could be important for prevention.

Achievement Pressures.   Striegel-Moore et al. (1986) discussed college as a risk factor for eating problems. College is a competitive environment in which women are pressured to achieve physically, in terms of weight, as well as academically. Some women may respond to this pressure by developing dysfunctional eating and weight regulation behaviors (see also Johnson & Connors, 1987). This suggests that prevention efforts should continue to help girls evaluate their achievement needs and expectations and learn adaptive ways of coping with pressure.

Achieving an Integrated Sense of Self.   Self-esteem seems to improve from middle to late adolescence (Wigfield, Eccles, Iver, Reuman, & Midgley, 1991). Some research suggests that those girls who continue to struggle with low self-esteem and self-consciousness may be at greater risk for eating pathology (Attie & Brooks-Gunn, 1992; Striegel-

Moore, 1993). Attie and Brooks-Gunn also found that impairments in affective regulation and problems with impulse control were associated with binge eating in late-adolescent girls. These findings suggest that individuals with low self-esteem, poor impulse control, and problems with emotional regulation may need to be selectively targeted for intervention in order to prevent eating pathology.

Prevention Strategies. In late adolescence girls display an increased capacity for discussing and evaluating abstract concepts. There is a greater ability to tolerate differences, and peers, although still representing a powerful influence, are not quite as important as in earlier years. This is a period when critical thinking skills can be encouraged and developed. Several issues can be addressed.

First, as girls in this age group prepare for another series of transitions (graduation from high school, going to college or entering the job market, marriage, potential separations from family and friends), they once again need support and validation of their needs for dependency and connection. Open discussion of these anticipated changes and of the associated feelings should be encouraged. Girls should be encouraged to explore ways of maintaining old ties and establishing new support networks. The use of adult mentors and role models (e.g., young women already in the workplace or in college) would be helpful. Girls at this age could also benefit from being peer facilitators and role models of healthy behaviors for younger girls.

Second, this is a period when, following Steiner-Adair's (1986) suggestion, important aspects of prevention may include helping girls to recognize society's values and expectations for women and encouraging discussion, criticism, and the maintenance of different values. Building on earlier prevention suggestions, girls should continue to examine other avenues for maintaining self-esteem besides work or academic achievement.

Third, by the same token girls at this age need to continue to question the associations between society's ideal body image for women, and happiness, self-esteem, and success. It is important to continue to present girls with factual information about healthy body weight, exercise, and nutrition.

DEVELOPMENTAL ISSUES AND PREVENTION
INTERVENTIONS IN YOUNG ADULTS

A number of theorists and researchers (Gilligan, 1982, 1990; Jordan, Kaplan, Miller, Stiver, & Surrey, 1991; Wooley, 1991) have discussed the potentially damaging effects on girls of growing up in a culture that emphasizes competition and autonomy, rather than connecting with others. As they progress from adolescence to adulthood, young women continue to adapt to cultural pressures and relational patterns that developed earlier in their lives. Steiner-Adair (1991) described how women with eating disorders have exceptional skills in developing relationships that appear to have connection but that are in fact emotionally vacuous. She stated that much of the work of psychotherapy with these women is to "make conscious and valid the eating-disordered women's perceptions of previous false relationships, which have blunted their hope, desire, and ability for true relationships" (p. 230).

Shisslak and Crago (1994) described how role destabilization and resulting gender-role conflict may create tremendous pressures on young women as they strive to be successful in their work at the same time that they are attempting to maintain marital and child-care roles. This conflict could lead to greater vulnerability to emotions and behaviors related to pathological eating. Silverstein, Carpman, Perlick, and Perdue (1990) found that college women who valued intellectual and professional success but who did not value being a wife or homemaker were "almost twice as likely as other women to report that they [ate] uncontrollably to the point of stuffing themselves at least once a week, or that they [tried] to control their weight using laxatives, diuretics, or intentional vomiting" (p. 692). These findings are consistent with those of Timko, Striegel-Moore, Silberstein, and Rodin (1987), which indicated that young women who considered socially desirably masculine traits as important were more likely to experience disordered eating. Another study of college women (Striegel-Moore, Silberstein, Grunberg, & Rodin, 1990) found that symptoms of disordered eating were associated more with interpersonal competitiveness than with other aspects of achievement orientation such as fear of success or a preference for difficult and challenging tasks. Taken together, these studies appear to support Timko et al.'s finding that stress for young women involves not only striving to excel in a number of roles but also having an ideal for oneself that is aggressive and individualistic.

Other concerns of young adulthood may also be risk factors. Lacey, Coker, and Birtchnell (1986) found that major changes in relationships or life circumstances, such as changes in occupation or residence, were the most frequently cited precipitant events in the development of BN in young adult women. For example, living in a college setting may have specific risks associated with it. Streigel-Moore (1992) reviewed the connections between the college environment and the development of BN. Achievement and dating pressures, eating norms, weight gain, and the "contagion effect" of dieting and binge eating were seen as potential risk factors for young adult women. In a study of first-year college students, disordered eating increased as weight dissatisfaction, levels of perceived ineffectiveness, and stress increased (Striegel-Moore, Silberstein, Frensch, & Rodin, 1989).

Another important consideration for the development of eating disorders in young adult women is the question of whether participation in sports is a risk factor. Warren, Stanton, and Blessing (1990) compared female college athletes to female nonathletes and found that none of the athletes showed similar response patterns on self-report measures to those of young women with AN or BN. They did, however, find that gymnasts were more likely to be at risk for weight preoccupation than were cross-country runners. Thus, cultural expectations may be playing a significant role in the development of risk behaviors, insofar as gymnasts are evaluated for body size and shape and runners are evaluated primarily for speed.

Some risks found in research with college students can also be applied to young adult women who have started working rather than pursuing higher education. Doubts concerning femininity and poor relations with parents have been the two major underlying factors identified (Lacey et al., 1986).

Prevention Strategies

Community- or college-based support and education groups for young women focusing on "growth in connection" issues would provide validation for emotional connections with others. This might decrease isolation and the likelihood of engaging in eating-disordered behavior, as Steiner-Adair's (1991) work suggests. Education regarding the impact of achievement and dating pressures would allow for the opportunity to discuss the stress of changing and multiple roles. The use of journaling in these groups may enhance participants' ability to reduce emotional barriers.

College educational presentations regarding high-risk behaviors and the contagion effect of dieting and binge eating found by Streigel-Moore (1992) among college women would increase awareness and help young women to provide support for each other when they saw these behaviors occurring. Educational presentations could also provide information about emotional health and stress management.

Prevention groups for women athletes could include presentations and discussions illuminating some of Warren et al.'s (1990) findings regarding high-risk behaviors, management of stress related to performance pressures, and examination of the impact of cultural norms. Desensitization to personal comments about body size by coaches, parents, and other significant people would be an important aspect of these groups. Consultation and training for coaches of women's sports could emphasize the importance of encouraging of healthy eating and weight and could highlight awareness of the impact of personal comments about body size or shape.

Consultation and training for other professionals who interact with young women and who are available to provide positive information about body image and eating issues would also be important. Physicians, clergy, teachers, dance instructors, and directors of youth groups are all in key positions to provide health-enhancing feedback to young women. Therapists treating young women should emphasize healthy connections rather than traditional separation–individuation issues (Steiner-Adair, 1991).

DEVELOPMENTAL ISSUES AND PREVENTION INTERVENTIONS IN OLDER ADULTS

Although most eating disorders begin in adolescence or young adulthood, it has been estimated that onset occurs after the age of 25 in 5% to 10% of eating disorder cases (Boast, Coker, & Wakeling, 1992; Mitchell, Hatsukami, Pyle, Eckert, & Soll, 1987). Some eating disorder cases have been reported in which onset did not occur until after menopause (Hall & Driscoll, 1993; Hsu & Zimmer, 1988). Boast et al. (1992) reviewed the case records of late-onset versus typical-onset AN patients, and Mitchell et al. (1987) reviewed the case records of late-onset versus typical-onset BN patients. In both studies there were few differences in eating problems and behaviors between the late- and typical-onset groups. There were, however, significant differences between the two groups regarding some eating disorder risk factors. For example, teasing about weight or body shape occurred much more often as a precipitating factor in the typical-onset group, as did stress arising from work or school. Family and relationship problems occurred equally often in both the late- and typical-onset groups (66% of cases). In other studies, precipitating factors for the development of eating disorders in older adults have included marital problems, death of a spouse or parent, marriage of a child, retirement, and fear of aging (Gupta, 1990; Hall & Driscoll, 1993; Price, Giannini, & Colella, 1985).

Prevention Strategies

1. Make men and women aware that weightism is a form of prejudice that is just as insidious and destructive as racism and sexism.
2. Develop support groups for women aimed at exploring the effects of role conflicts on women's physical and mental health.
3. Educate physicians about the possibility of eating disorders in older patients with weight loss, vomiting, or abnormal fear of fatness, especially if the patient has recently experienced a loss such as the illness or death of a spouse or other family member. Early intervention may prevent the development of a full-syndrome eating disorder.

4. Alert the facilitators of bereavement groups about the signs and symptoms of eating disorders and the possibility that an older adult may develop an eating disorder in response to grief and loss.
5. Present information about eating disorders in the elderly to workers in nursing and retirement homes, senior centers, and home health services.
6. Submit articles on eating disorders in adults over the age of 50 to magazines widely read by this age group, such as *Modern Maturity*.

SUMMARY

In this chapter we have emphasized the need to expand developmental models used in the creation of prevention programs for eating disorders. We believe that models that are gender-sensitive to the unique issues that girls and young women face are in order. Specifically, we support a shift away from the individuation–separation model to one that includes a relationship–differentiation orientation. We have reviewed many of the problems that girls and young women encounter in their attempts at connection with others in relation to approval within the cultural definition of beauty and success. In addition, we have provided many preventive strategies that specifically address interpersonal needs and stressors in female development. Ideally, longitudinal risk factor studies would provide a better understanding of the relation between individual vulnerability, specific stressors, and the development of eating disorders. Wierson and Forehand (1994) reviewed the important questions that longitudinal studies can best address, such as developmental changes over time, issues of behavioral continuity–discontinuity, the establishment of temporal relationships between variables, and assessment of treatment outcome.

We are currently in the first phase of such a project in which we are developing gender- and culturally sensitive risk factor assessment instruments to be used in a longitudinal study of risk factor development over a 4-year period. This will be followed by a 4-year preventive intervention for those identified as being at risk for eating disorders. In the meantime it is incumbent on psychologists to make prevention programs more relevant to the unique problems that female development encompasses.

REFERENCES

American College of Physicians. (1986). Eating disorders: Anorexia nervosa and bulimia. *Annals of Internal Medicine, 105,* 790–794.

Atkins, D. M., & Silber, T. J. (1993). Clinical spectrum of anorexia nervosa in children. *Journal of Developmental and Behavioral Pediatrics, 14,* 211–216.

Attie, I., & Brooks-Gunn, J. (1989). Development of eating problems in adolescent girls: A longitudinal study. *Developmental Psychology, 25,* 70–79.

Attie, I., & Brooks-Gunn, J. (1992). Developmental issues in the study of eating problems and disorders. In J. Crowther, D. Tennenbaum, S. Hobfoll, & M. Stephens (Eds.), *The etiology of bulimia: The individual and familial context* (pp. 37–58). Washington, DC: Taylor & Francis.

Attie, I., Brooks-Gunn, J., & Petersen, A. C. (1990). The emergence of eating problems: A developmental perspective. In M. Lewis & S. Miller (Eds.), *Handbook of developmental psychopathology* (pp. 409–420). New York: Plenum.

Bennett, N. A. M., Spoth, R. L., & Borgen, F. H. (1991). Bulimic symptoms in high school females: Prevalence and relationship with multiple measures of psychological health. *Journal of Community Psychology, 19,* 13–28.

Boast, N., Coker, E., & Wakeling, A. (1992). Anorexia nervosa of late onset. *British Journal of Psychiatry, 160,* 257–260.

Bruch, H. (1973). *Eating disorders: Obesity, anorexia nervosa, and the person within.* New York: Basic Books.

Carney, B. (1986). A preventive curriculum for anorexia nervosa and bulimia. *Canadian Association for Health, Physical Education and Recreation Journal, 52,* 10–14.

Cattarin, J. A., & Thompson, J. K. (1994). A three-year longitudinal study of body image, eating disturbance, and general psychological functioning in adolescent females. *Eating Disorders: Journal of Treatment and Prevention, 2,* 114–125.

Center for the Study of Anorexia and Bulimia. (1983). *Teaching about eating disorders: Grades 7–12.* New York: Author.

Crisp, A. H. (1979). Early recognition and prevention of anorexia nervosa. *Developmental Medicine and Child Neurology, 21,* 393–395.

Crisp, A. H. (1980). *Anorexia nervosa: Let me be.* London: Academic Press.

Dwyer, J. T., Feldman, J. J., & Mayer, J. (1967). Adolescent dieters: Who are they? *American Journal of Clinical Nutrition, 20,* 1045–1056.

Dwyer, J. T., Feldman, J. J., Seltzer, C. C., & Mayer, J. (1969). Adolescent attitudes towards weight and appearance. *Journal of Nutrition Education, 1,* 14–19.

Eisele, J., Hertsgaard, D., & Light, H. K. (1986). Factors related to eating disorders in young adolescent girls. *Adolescence, 21,* 283–290.

Fabian, L. J., & Thompson, J. K. (1989). Body image and eating disturbance in young females. *International Journal of Eating Disorders, 8,* 63–74.

Fisher, M., Pastore, D., Schneider, M., Pegler, C., & Napolitano, B. (1994). Eating attitudes in urban and suburban adolescents. *International Journal of Eating Disorders, 16,* 67–74.

Fisher, M., Schneider, M., Pegler, C., & Napolitano, B. (1991). Eating attitudes, health-risk behaviors, self-esteem, and anxiety among adolescent females in a suburban high school. *Journal of Adolescent Health, 12,* 377–384.

Fosson, A., Knibbs, J., Bryant-Waugh, R., & Lask, B. (1987). Early onset anorexia nervosa. *Archives of Disease in Childhood, 62,* 114–118.

Giarrantano, S. (1991). *Looking at body image and eating disorders: A curriculum for grades 9–12.* Santa Cruz, CA: Network.

Gibbs, R. E. (1986). Social factors in exaggerated eating behavior among high school students. *International Journal of Eating Disorders, 5,* 1103–1107.

Gilligan, C. (1982). *In a different voice: Psychological theory and women's development.* Cambridge, MA: Harvard University Press.

Gilligan, C. (1990). Teaching Shakespeare's sister: Notes from the underground of female adolescence. In C. Gilligan, N. P. Lyons, & T. J. Hanmer (Eds.), *Making connections: The relational worlds of adolescent girls at Emma Willard School* (pp. 6–29). Cambridge, MA: Harvard University Press.

Gowers, S. G., Crisp, A. H., Joughin, N., & Bhat, A. (1991). Premenarchal anorexia nervosa. *Journal of Child Psychology and Psychiatry, 32,* 515–524.

Gralen, S. J., Levine, M. P., Smolak, L., & Murnen, S. K. (1990). Dieting and disordered eating during early and middle adolescence: Do the influences remain the same? *International Journal of Eating Disorders, 9,* 501–512.

Gresko, R. B., & Karlsen, A. (1994). The Norwegian program for the primary, secondary and tertiary prevention of eating disorders. *Eating Disorders, 2,* 57–63.

Gross, J., & Rosen, J. C. (1988). Bulimia in adolescents: Prevalence and psychosocial correlates. *International Journal of Eating Disorders, 7,* 51–61.

Gupta, M. A. (1990). Fear of aging: A precipitating factor in late onset anorexia nervosa. *International Journal of Eating Disorders, 9,* 221–224.

Hall, P., & Driscoll, R. (1993). Anorexia in the elderly: An annotation. *International Journal of Eating Disorders, 14,* 497–499.

Hill, J. P., & Lynch, M. E. (1983). The intensification of gender-related role expectations during early adolescence. In J. Brooks-Gunn & A. C. Petersen (Eds.), *Girls at puberty* (pp. 201–228). New York: Plenum.

Hsu, L. K. G., & Zimmer, B. (1988). Eating disorders in old age. *International Journal of Eating Disorders, 7,* 133–138.

Huon, G. F. (1994a). Dieting, binge eating, and some of their correlates among secondary school girls. *International Journal of Eating Disorders, 15,* 159–164.

Huon, G. F. (1994b). Towards the prevention of dieting-induced disorders: Modifying negative food- and body-related attitudes. *International Journal of Eating Disorders, 16,* 395–399.

Jakobovits, C., Halstead, P., Kelley, L., Roe, D. A., & Young, C. M. (1977). Eating habits and nutrient intakes of college women over a thirty-year period. *Journal of the American Dietetic Association, 71,* 405–411.

Johnson, C., & Connors, M. E. (1987). *The etiology and treatment of bulimia nervosa.* New York: Basic Books.

Johnson, C. L., Lewis, C., Love, S., Lewis, L., & Stuckey, M. (1983). A descriptive survey of dieting and bulimic behavior in a female high school population. In *Understanding anorexia nervosa and bulimia: Report of the fourth Ross conference on medical research* (pp. 14–18). Columbus, OH: Ross Laboratories.

Jordan, J. V., Kaplan, A. G., Miller, J. B., Stiver, I. P., & Surrey, J. L. (1991). *Women's growth in connection: Writings from the Stone Center.* New York: Guilford.

Kennedy, S. H. (1990). A multifaceted program for preventing and treating eating disorders. *Hospital and Community Psychiatry, 41,* 1120–1123.

Killen, J. D., Hayward, C., Litt, I., Hammer, L. D., Wilson, D. M., Miner, B., Taylor, C. B., Varady, A., & Shisslak, C. (1992). Is puberty a risk factor for eating disorders? *American Journal of the Diseases of Children, 146,* 323–325.

Killen, J. D., Hayward, C., Wilson, D. M., Taylor, C. B., Hammer, L. D., Litt, I., Simmonds, B., & Haydel, F. (1994). Factors associated with eating disorder symptoms in a community sample of 6th and 7th grade girls. *International Journal of Eating Disorders, 15,* 357–367.

Killen, J. D., Taylor, C. B., Hammer, L. D., Litt, I., Wilson, D. M., Rich, T., Hayward, C., Simmonds, B., Kraemer, H., & Varady, A. (1993). An attempt to modify unhealthful eating attitudes and weight regulation practices of young adolescent girls. *International Journal of Eating Disorders, 13,* 369–384.

Killen, J. D., Taylor, C. B., Telch, M. J., Saylor, K. E., Maron, D. J., & Robinson, T. N. (1986). Self-induced vomiting and laxative and diuretic use among teenagers: Precursors of the binge–purge syndrome? *Journal of the American Medical Association, 255,* 1447–1449.

Lacey, J. H., Coker, S., & Birtchnell, S. A. (1986). Bulimia: Factors associated with its etiology and maintenance. *International Journal of Eating Disorders, 5,* 475–487.

Leichner, P., Arnett, J., Rallo, J. S., Srikameswaran, S., & Vulcano, B. (1986). An epidemiologic study of maladaptive eating attitudes in a Canadian school age population. *International Journal of Eating Disorders, 5,* 969–982.

Leon, G. R., Fulkerson, J. A., Perry, C. L., & Cudeck, R. (1993). Personality and behavioral vulnerabilities associated with risk status for eating disorders in adolescent girls. *Journal of Abnormal Psychology, 102,* 438–444.

Levine, M. P. (1987). *Student eating disorders: Anorexia nervosa and bulimia.* Washington, DC: National Education Association.

Levine, M. P. (1994). "Beauty myth" and the beast: What men can do and be to help prevent eating disorders. *Eating Disorders, 2,* 101–113.

Levine, M. P., & Hill, L. (1991). *A 5-day lesson plan book on eating disorders: Grades 7-12.* Columbus, OH: National Anorexia Society of Harding Hospital.

Levine, M. P., & Smolak, L. (1992). Toward a model of the developmental psychopathology of eating disorders: The example of early adolescence. In J. H. Crowther, D. L. Tennebaum, S. E. Hobfoll, & M. A. Stephens, (Eds.), *The etiology of bulimia nervosa: The individual and familial context* (pp. 59-80). Washington, DC: Hemisphere.

Levine, M. P., Smolak, L., Moodey, A. F., Shuman, M. D., & Hessen, L. D. (1994). Normative developmental challenges and dieting and eating disturbances in middle school girls. *International Journal of Eating Disorders, 15,* 11–20.

Marchi, M., & Cohen, P. (1990). Early childhood eating behaviors and adolescent eating disorders. *Journal of the American Academy of Child and Adolescent Psychiatry, 29,* 112–117.

Minuchin, S., Rosman, B. L., & Baker, L. (1978). *Psychosomatic families.* Cambridge, MA: Harvard University Press.

Mitchell, J. E., Hatsukami, D., Pyle, R. L., Eckert, E. D., & Soll, E. (1987). Late onset bulimia. *Comprehensive Psychiatry, 28,* 323–328.

Moreno, A. B., & Thelen, M. H. (1993). A preliminary prevention program for eating disorders in a junior high school population. *Journal of Youth and Adolescence, 22,* 109–124.

Moriarty, D., Shore, R., & Maxim, N. (1990). Evaluation of an eating disorders curriculum. *Evaluation and Program Planning, 13,* 407–413.

National Eating Disorder Information Center. (1989). *Teacher's resource kit: A teacher's lesson plan kit for the prevention of eating disorders.* Toronto: Author.

Paxton, S. J. (1993). A prevention program for disturbed eating and body dissatisfaction in adolescent girls: A one year follow-up. *Health Education Research, 8,* 43–51.

Peskin, H. (1973). Influence of the developmental schedule of puberty on learning and ego functioning. *Journal of Youth and Adolescence, 2,* 273–290.

Petersen, A. C., & Hamburg, B. A. (1986). Adolescence: A developmental approach to problems and psychopathology. *Behavior Therapy, 17,* 480–499.

Porter, J., Morrell, T., & Moriarty, D. (1986). Primary prevention of anorexia nervosa: Evaluation of a pilot project for early and pre-adolescents. *Canadian Association for Health, Physical Education and Recreation Journal, 52,* 21–26.

Price, W. A., Giannini, A. J., & Colella, J. (1985). Anorexia nervosa in the elderly. *Journal of the American Geriatrics Society, 33,* 213–215.

Rhyne-Winkler, M. C., & Hubbard, G. T. (1994). Eating attitudes and behavior: A school counseling program. *School Counselor, 41,* 195–198.

Richards, M. H., Casper, R. C., & Larson, R. (1990). Weight and eating concerns among pre- and young adolescent boys and girls. *Journal of Adolescent Health Care, 11,* 203–209.

Rosen, J. C. (1989, April–June). Prevention of eating disorders. *Newsletter of the National Anorexic Aid Society, 12,* 1–3.

Rosen, J. C., Silberg, N. T., & Gross, J. (1988). Eating Attitudes Test and Eating Disorders Inventory: Norms of adolescent girls and boys. *Journal of Consulting and Clinical Psychology, 56,* 305–308.

Russell, G. (1985). Premenarchal anorexia nervosa and its sequelae. *Journal of Psychiatric Research, 19,* 363–369.

Selvini-Palazzoli, M. (1974). *Self-starvation.* New York: Aronson.

Sesan, R. (1989a). Eating disorders and female athletes: A three-level intervention program. *Journal of College Student Development, 30,* 568–570.

Sesan, R. (1989b). Peer education: A creative resource for the eating disordered college student. In L. C. Whitaker & W. N. Davis (Eds.), *The bulimic college student: Evaluation, treatment and prevention* (pp. 221–240). New York: Haworth.

Shisslak, C. M., & Crago, M. (1994). Toward a new model for the prevention of eating disorders. In P. Fallon, M. A. Katzman, & S. C. Wooley (Eds.), *Feminist perspectives on eating disorders* (pp. 419–437). New York: Guilford.

Shisslak, C. M., Crago, M., & Neal, M. E. (1990). Prevention of eating disorders among adolescents. *American Journal of Health Promotion, 5,* 100–106.

Shisslak, C. M., Crago, M., Neal, M. E., & Swain, B. (1987). Primary prevention of eating disorders. *Journal of Consulting and Clinical Psychology, 55,* 660–667.

Shore, R. A., & Porter, J. E. (1990). Normative and reliability data for 11 to 18 year olds on the Eating Disorders Inventory. *International Journal of Eating Disorders, 9,* 201–207.

Silverstein, B., Carpman, S., Perlick, D., & Perdue, L. (1990). Nontraditional sex role aspirations, gender identity conflict and disordered eating among college women. *Sex Roles, 23,* 687–695.

Simmons, R. G., Blyth, D. A., & McKinney, K. L. (1983). The social and psychological effects of puberty on white females. In J. Brooks-Gunn & A. C. Petersen (Eds.), *Girls at puberty* (pp. 229–278). New York: Plenum.

Simmons, R. G., & Rosenberg, F. (1975). Sex, sex roles, and self-image. *Journal of Youth and Adolescence, 4,* 229–258.

Smolak, L., & Levine, M. P. (1994a, July–September). The role of parents in the prevention of disordered eating. *National Eating Disorders Organization Newsletter,* 1–9.

Smolak, L., & Levine, M. P. (1994b). Toward an empirical basis for primary prevention of eating problems with elementary school children. *Eating Disorders: The Journal of Treatment and Prevention, 2,* 293–307.

Smolak, L., Levine, M. P., & Gralen, S. (1993). The impact of purberty and dating on eating problems among middle school girls. *Journal of Youth and Adolescence, 22,* 355–368.

Sours, J. A. (1974). The anorexia nervosa syndrome. *International Journal of Psychoanalysis, 55,* 567–576.

Steiner-Adair, C. (1986). The body politic: Normal female adolescent development and the development of eating disorders. *Journal of the American Academy of Psychoanalysis, 14,* 95–114.

Steiner-Adair, C. (1991). New maps of development, new models of therapy: The psychology of women and the treatment of eating disorders. In C. L. Johnson (Ed.), *Psychodynamic treatment of anorexia nervosa and bulimia* (pp. 225–244). New York: Guilford.

Story, M., Rosenwinkel, K., Himes, J. H., Resnick, M., Harris, L. J., & Blum, R. W. (1991). Demographic and risk factors associated with chronic dieting in adolescents. *American Journal of Diseases of Children, 145,* 994–998.

Striegel-Moore, R. H. (1992). Prevention of bulimia nervosa: Questions and challenges. In J. H. Crowther, D. L. Tennebaum, S. E. Hobfoll, & M. A. Stephens (Eds.), *The etiology of bulimia nervosa: The individual and familial context* (pp. 203–223). Washington, DC: Hemisphere.

Striegel-Moore, R. H. (1993). Etiology of binge eating: A developmental perspective. In C. Fairburn & T. Wilson (Eds.), *Binge eating* (pp. 144–172). New York: Guilford.

Striegel-Moore, R. H., Silberstein, L. R., Frensch, P., & Rodin, J. (1989). A prospective study of disordered eating among college students. *International Journal of Eating Disorders, 8,* 499-509.

Striegel-Moore, R. H., Silberstein, L. R., Grunberg, N. E., & Rodin, J. (1990). Competing on all fronts: Achievement orientation and disordered eating. *Sex Roles, 23,* 697–702.

Striegel-Moore, R. H., Silberstein, L. R., & Rodin, J. (1986). Toward an understanding of risk factors for bulimia. *American Psychologist, 41,* 246–263.

Taylor, C. B., Shisslak, C. M., & Killen, J. D. (1994). [Development of instruments to assess risk factors for eating disorders]. Unpublished raw data.

Thelen, M. H., Lawrence, C. M., & Powell, A. L. (1992). Body image, weight control, and eating disorders among children. In J. H. Crowther, D. L. Tennebaum, S. E. Hobfoll, & M. A. Stephens (Eds.), *The etiology of bulimia nervosa: The individual and familial context* (pp. 81–101). Washington, DC: Hemisphere.

Timko, C., Striegel-Moore, R. H., Silberstein, L. R., & Rodin, J. (1987). Femininity/masculinity and disordered eating in women: How are they related? *International Journal of Eating Disorders, 6,* 701–712.

Tobin-Richards, M. H., Boxer, A. M., & Petersen, A. C. (1983). The psychological significance of pubertal change: Sex differences in perceptions of self during early adolescence. In J. Brooks-Gunn & A. C. Petersen (Eds.), *Girls at puberty* (pp. 127–154). New York: Plenum.

Warren, B. J., Stanton, A. L., & Blessing, D. L. (1990). Disordered eating patterns in competitive female athletes. *International Journal of Eating Disorders, 9,* 565–569.

Wexler, D. B. (1991). *The adolescent self.* New York: Norton.

Whitaker, A., Davies, M., Shaffer, D., Johnson, J., Abrams, S., Walsh, B. T., & Kalikow, K. (1989). The struggle to be thin: A survey of anorexic and bulimic symptoms in a nonreferred adolescent population. *Psychological Medicine, 29,* 143–163.

Wierson, M., & Forehand, R. (1994). The role of longitudinal data with child psychopathology and treatment: Preliminary comments and issues. *Journal of Consulting and Clinical Psychology, 62,* 883–886.

Wigfield, A., Eccles, J. S., Iver, D. M., Reuman, D. A., & Midgley, C. (1991). Transitions during early adolescence: Changes in children's domain-specific self-perceptions and general self-esteem across the transition to junior high school. *Developmental Psychology, 27,* 552–565.

Wooley, S. C. (1991). Uses of countertransference in the treatment of eating disorders: A gender perspective. In C. L. Johnson (Ed.), *Psychodynamic treatment of anorexia nervosa and bulimia* (pp. 245–294). New York: Guilford.

15

The Changing Context of Treatment

Kathleen M. Pike
Denise E. Wilfley

A very distressed mother leaves you a message; she needs to speak to you immediately. Her 15-year-old daughter has lost 20 pounds over the past 6 months. She will not eat with the family, has become more isolated and irritable, and, most recently, returned home early from school because she felt too light-headed to concentrate on her exam. Despite the mother's efforts, the daughter refuses to speak to anyone because she denies that she has a problem.

A young woman calls from her law firm during the middle of the day. She has just spent the last 2 hours binge eating and vomiting despite a pressing deadline at work. She realizes that this eating disorder is not going away on its own but is ashamed and afraid.

A middle-aged woman telephones your office late one night. She has been binge eating all evening. She is humiliated by her lack of control as well as her weight and is getting increasingly depressed. She says that she has tried every weight-loss program that exists. Is there anything that you can do to help?

These women have anorexia nervosa (AN), bulimia nervosa (BN), and binge eating disorder (BED), respectively. Despite differences in age and symptom patterns, there are unifying issues of normative development and developmental psychopathology that contribute to an enhanced understanding of these eating disorders. This chapter discusses the implications of such developmental issues for treatment both in terms of the significance of the age at which an individual presents for treatment and the developmental conflicts that may be involved in the etiology and maintenance of the eating disorder. Although weight pre-occupation and eating disturbances may begin during childhood (Smolak & Levine, chapter 9, this volume; Striegel-Moore, Schreiber, Pike, Wilfley, & Rodin, 1995; Striegel-Moore, Nicholson, & Tamborlane, 1992; Thelen, Lawrence, & Powell, 1992), the vast majority of individuals who develop eating disorders do not enter treatment until at least their teen years. Thus, in this chapter we discuss developmental issues that affect treatment for each of the three major eating disorders across the developmental stages of adolescence, young adulthood, and middle to later adulthood.

It should be emphasized at the outset that structuring treatment for an individual with an eating disorder is often driven by clinical experience and practical considerations, given the limited empirical database regarding treatment efficacy. Although significant advances regarding the treatment of BN have occurred within the past decade, rigorous clinical trials for AN and BED are just beginning to provide treatment outcome data that can inform general practice. Thus, the discussion and recommendations provided in this chapter reflect our own judgment as well as the cited principles and practice of experts in the field. However, such theories and applications may well be overturned by empirical findings from future research.

THE EATING DISORDERS AS A REFLECTION OF DEVELOPMENTAL CHALLENGES

The frequent onset of eating disorder symptoms during adolescence suggests that the developmental challenges of this period play a central role in the formation of AN, BN, and BED (Attie & Brooks-Gunn, 1992; Bruch, 1973, 1978; Johnson, 1991; Levine & Smolak, 1992; Pike, 1995; Steiner-Adair, 1986; Striegel-Moore, 1993). Increased rates of depression, anxiety, insecurity, and self-consciousness among adolescent girls suggest that this is a vulnerable stage of development for a wide range of individuals (Kandel & Davies, 1982; O'Malley & Bachman, 1983; Simmons & Blyth, 1987). Of particular relevance to the development of the eating disorders are the psychosocial changes as well as the physical and sexual maturation characteristic of adolescence. Whereas passage into adolescence appears to be the stage of transition associated with the highest risk for developing AN, the movement out of adolescence and into adulthood is associated with the highest rates of onset of BN and BED. However, common to all three eating disorders is the struggle to establish greater autonomy from one's family of origin, build more intimate relationships with others, integrate a changing body image, and develop a cohesive and stable sense of self in the course of this stage of development. Each of the eating disorders, with its particular pattern of symptoms, reflects a compromise solution to these challenges posed by adolescence.

For those individuals who develop AN, the eating disorder provides an all-consuming, rigid set of principles and rules that promise to simplify and organize one's life. The AN halts the normal course of development, relieving the fears and anxieties aroused at this stage of development. In contrast, individuals with BN appear to maintain the external appearance of progressing along the normative developmental course more adaptively. Whereas the all-consuming nature of AN results in public exposure of severely restricted physical development, eating behavior, and psychosocial functioning, BN tends to be a secretive solution whereby individuals can maintain a semblance of mastery over their eating, shape, and interpersonal functioning. In most cases, individuals with BN are able to proceed with educational, professional, and social obligations. However, in the course of doing so, the BN reflects the subjective, albeit secretive, dissatisfaction with one's self and self-worth. As a result, many individuals with BN describe a painful discrepancy between their public and private selves and describe feeling like imposters in the world (Striegel-Moore, Silberstein, & Rodin, 1993). Individuals with BED also often appear to manage social, educational, and work challenges of this life stage more adaptively than do individuals with AN. Also, for most BED individuals, the eating disorder is a shameful and secretive behavior. However, as is the case for AN, individuals with BED stand out because of their deviant weight status. In addition, although some individuals with BED report a lifelong history of weight problems, it appears that the physical and biological changes of adolescence are associated with the onset of this eating disorder as well.

Successful treatment of an individual with AN, BN, or BED requires that the therapist both acknowledge the adaptive function of the eating disorder and challenge the assumption that the eating disorder is the only solution to developmental challenges. In the remainder of the chapter, we discuss specific treatment implications posed by developmental issues and related treatment recommendations for each of these three eating disorders.

ANOREXIA NERVOSA

The onset of AN usually occurs in adolescence, and over 90% of the cases are female. The mean age of onset is approximately 17 years, with some evidence that there are bimodal peaks around 14 and 18 years of age (American Psychiatric Association [APA], 1994). The onset of this disorder rarely occurs before puberty or after the fourth decade of life (Devlin & Walsh, 1992). The prevalence of clinically diagnosed AN among adolescent and young adult females is approximately 1% (APA, 1994). The prevalence of AN seems to be greater in White females from middle and upper-middle socioeconomic classes; however it does occur in a wider range of socioeconomic and racial groups than was once thought. For many individuals it runs a chronic course (Hsu, 1988, 1990; Hsu, Crisp, & Harding, 1979; Ratnasuriya, Eisler, Szmukler, & Russell, 1991; Santonastaso, Pantano, Panarotto, & Silvestri, 1992).

Inpatient hospitalization for weight restoration in the initial phase of treatment of AN is fairly well established and effective (see, e.g., Agras, Barlow, Chapin, Abel, & Leitenberg, 1974; Halmi, 1983). However, such interventions are not sufficient for long-term recovery from the disorder, and although clinical descriptions of a wide variety of outpatient treatments for AN exist there is a dearth of empirical data supporting most of these approaches.

General consensus in the field holds that classical psychoanalytic techniques are not especially useful for this patient population (Bruch, 1979; Kalucy, 1978; Strober & Yager, 1985). However, there is an absence of definitive data regarding which treatments are most applicable and effective in terms of theoretical orientation, form of delivery, and intensity or length of treatment (Channon, DeSilva, Hemsley, & Perkins, 1989; Crisp et al., 1991; Hall & Crisp, 1987).

The most significant statement that can be derived from the existing data is that family therapy appears to be more effective than individual supportive treatment in cases where the age of onset of AN has been 18 years or less and the duration of illness has been less than three years (Russell, Szmukler, Dare, & Eisler, 1987). In addition, preliminary data suggest that cognitive behavioral treatment (Pike, 1994) and fluoxetine (Kaye, Weltzin, Hsu, & Bulik, 1991) may be effective in relapse prevention for AN.

Adolescence and AN

Engaging the Patient.   Typically, adolescent girls with AN are the youngest patients who present for treatment for an eating disorder. The first contact with the therapist is usually with a parent by telephone, although occasionally a pediatrician or school official initiates contact. During this phone call the therapist should get some brief information about the individual in question and outline the goals and structure for a consultation.

The first treatment challenge with an adolescent with AN is overcoming resistance. Because the majority of adolescents with AN do not seek help on their own initiative and are, in fact, opposed to treatment, some parents may be inclined to trick their daughters into attending an initial consultation. Such desperate ploys are almost certain to backfire. If parents believe that their daughter's life is in imminent danger they should take her directly to a psychiatric emergency room even if they are unable to obtain her consent. In less urgent circumstances, it is our recommendation that parents work with their daughter to get her to attend the initial consultation knowingly and willingly.

Several measures can be recommended to parents to help their adolescent daughter consent to treatment. First, parents should enlist the aid of other authority figures with whom the daughter has a positive relationship, for example, a teacher, relative, school principal, religious leader, or pediatrician. These individuals in the adolescent's community can be invaluable allies in convincing a young girl that she at least attend a consultation. If a daughter continues to resist treatment it may be helpful for her to attend a self-help or support group in the area. Depending on the format of the group, it may also be an appropriate structure for providing parents with support and information. Finally, it may be necessary for the parents to make certain privileges contingent on participation in treatment and amelioration of the eating disturbance. During this time we frequently recommend to parents the book *Surviving an Eating Disorder* (Siegel, Brisman, & Weinshel, 1988).

Because initial contact with the therapist is usually not made by the adolescent with AN, issues of alliance are immediate concerns for treatment. It is critical from the outset that the therapist establish a positive connection with the adolescent who in all likelihood feels some combination of anger, betrayal, embarrassment, and relief when she first enters the therapist's office. It is also critical that the therapist make a positive connection with the adolescent's parents. These are the people who are ultimately responsible for all decisions regarding the care of their daughter. Thus, despite any conflict or mistrust between parents and child, the therapist needs to connect with all parties concerned (Strober & Yager, 1985).

Ideally, the evaluation of an adolescent with AN includes all immediate family members. The initial consultation should begin with a clarification of all information that has been shared with the therapist in the course of scheduling the appointment. It is important that the therapy not be burdened by secretive information that anyone has disclosed to the therapist. Thus, the therapist can begin by reviewing the sequence of events that led up to the initial consultation. Next, the therapist can ask the adolescent how she feels about attending the consultation. During the course of the initial consultation it is important to have a comprehensive discussion of the adolescent's eating and weight problems with both her and her family in order to assess the current nature and severity of the problem as well as the family functioning in relation to the problem.

Generally, it is useful to obtain as much information as possible from the adolescent first and then to get additional input from family members. It is also useful to meet with the adolescent individually for part of the initial session to establish an independent connection with her, to observe any changes in her demeanor, and to ask whether there are any issues about which her parents are unaware (e.g., vomiting or laxative abuse).

The Structure of Treatment. Compared with the other eating disorders, the question of inpatient hospitalization is most frequently raised in the treatment of AN, given the potentially serious consequences of weight loss and noncompliance with outpatient treatment interventions. It must be understood by the adolescent and parents that outpatient therapy can only proceed if the patient is able to maintain her weight above a minimum level (often the convention is 70% of recommended weight for height according to the Metropolitan Life Insurance Tables) and if the patient's medical status does not require inpatient care for such complications as hypokalemia or cardiac abnormalities (Andersen, 1985; Garner & Bemis, 1985).

Having established that outpatient care is the appropriate level of intervention, it is necessary to design the structure of treatment. Given that family therapy has demonstrated efficacy for younger adolescents with a relatively short duration of the illness (Russell et al., 1987), it is recommended that family therapy be a core part of the treatment. Further delineation of the treatment plan must depend on clinical judgment, given the limited additional data available with which to inform treatment at this time. It is our recommendation that treatment for the adolescent with AN include one or two individual therapy sessions per week in addition to weekly or biweekly family therapy sessions.

The Treatment Team. Depending on the details of the case, several professionals should be part of the treatment team. First, in structuring treatment for an adolescent with AN it is important to coordinate care with a pediatrician. It is essential that the individual have a complete physical at initiation of treatment to assure that there are no medical complications that warrant immediate intervention or hospitalization. Individuals with AN should be weighed on a weekly basis during the weight-gain phase of treatment. This can be done either at the therapist's office or at the pediatrician's office (Garner, Rockert, Olmsted, Johnson, & Coscina, 1985; Garner & Bemis, 1985). Once the adolescent has restored her weight, it is appropriate for her to gradually resume the responsibility for weight monitoring.

In addition to a pediatrician, a nutritionist may be involved in the care of an adolescent girl with AN for the purpose of providing her with nutritional information and guidelines for weight gain. Finally, input from someone from the adolescent's school may be helpful in making treatment decisions. The adolescent's advisor, principal, or teacher may be helpful in deciding whether to encourage an adolescent to switch schools, attend part-time, get a home tutor, or choose some other option.

However, most adolescents have strong feelings about involving anyone from school and therefore this should be discussed first with the patient.

Family Systems and AN. A significant challenge in working with an adolescent with AN is the complex task of involving parents in treatment as allies while fostering the child's move toward greater autonomy and separation. It is important that parents be involved in treatment when the patient is an adolescent; however, developing a confidential relationship with the adolescent is also critical. The therapist should be explicit in establishing at the outset of treatment how parents will be involved, with which aspects of treatment they can be most helpful, and when confidentiality will be broken.

Parental involvement and boundary setting is especially critical in the initial phase of treatment, when normalizing eating and weight is a primary goal. The state of semistarvation is debilitating for the patient physiologically and mentally and directly compromises the psychotherapy process (Garner et al., 1985). Normalizing eating and weight with an adolescent patient affects the general functioning of the family system as well. The fears and tension that AN creates for family members can compromise their ability to work constructively with the treatment team if they are not convinced that the adolescent's eating and weight are being addressed seriously and effectively (Strober & Yager, 1985).

It is our recommendation that parents not be involved directly in monitoring their adolescent's eating or weight. We encourage patients to take responsibility to increase their intake sufficiently to effect the prescribed weight gain, and we recommend that either the primary therapist or pediatrician monitor the patient's weight weekly during weight gain. At the outset it is important that an explicit plan be established whereby the parents are notified if their daughter's weight falls below an agreed-upon minimum weight. Except when parents need to be notified of such weight loss, we encourage parents not to discuss their daughter's eating and weight with her outside of treatment sessions.

Self-Development in a Social Context. As discussed by Connors (chapter 12, this volume), problems with the development of secure attachments and successful separation and individuation are characteristic of individuals with eating disorders. These conflicts are reflected in AN, which is both an attempt to achieve power, autonomy, and independence and a retreat from developmental challenges that leaves the individual psychologically and physically immature and dependent. Lacking both a secure sense of self and well-integrated attachments, many individuals with AN describe feeling suspicious and mistrustful of others and scornful of any sign of dependency (Casper, 1982). These individuals often do not have a foundation of secure and dependent relationships established during childhood that would serve as the point of departure in adolescence. Thus, these patients become paralyzed by the normative adolescent challenges that involve increasing autonomy.

These problems with the development of a secure sense of self and with related failures in social functioning have a direct impact on treatment. First, AN provides individuals with highly elaborated self-definitions and compensates for failures in earlier self-development. The tremendous relief and organization provided by the eating disorder may account greatly for the resistance that individuals with AN express regarding the resolution of the eating disorder. Overcoming such resistance depends on helping an individual develop a secure sense of self and self-worth independent of the eating disorder. It is not sufficient for the therapist to focus on the negative ramifications of the eating disorder. Individuals with AN are typically well informed about such issues; however, in their calculation they cannot afford to resolve the eating disorder and thereby surrender their newfound sense of self.

Addressing these issues of self-development in treatment entails maintaining a dual focus. One line of intervention needs to directly challenge the rules of the eating disorder and modify attitudes and behaviors related to weight and eating. The complementary line of intervention requires a focus on developing a more complex sense of self that is independent of the eating disorder. In practice, for example, this work may begin with exploring interests prior to the onset of the eating disorder, experimenting with new activities, and redefining current relationships. Such efforts should spawn more self-reflection and an opportunity for elaborating a new self-definition.

A second and related challenge for treatment posed by a poorly developed sense of self is that such individuals have a history of problematic attachments in their relationships. As already noted, suspicion and mistrust are commonplace. The resulting effect for treatment is that patients have difficulty developing secure relationships with their therapists. Such issues become especially critical in working with adolescents with AN because these patients test their therapists to determine whether it is safe to disclose highly personal information. Moreover, as patients move toward developing a more intimate relationship with the therapist it is not unusual for parents to experience anxiety posed by the threat of their daughters' increasing autonomy. It is at this point that the therapist is likely to receive a phone call from parents inquiring about treatment. In responding to this dilemma, it is of paramount importance that the therapist maintain confidentiality and not discuss the therapy with parents unless the daughter is present. Of course, certain situations require that confidentiality be broken; however, these should be defined at the outset of treatment. It is only with time and an accumulation of experiences that the adolescent can become confident that she can develop a relationship of dependency and disclosure with the therapist. This is the prerequisite for moving toward the longer term goal of separation.

Physical and Sexual Development.   The rise of AN in the context of the emergence of puberty reflects significant challenges in the area of physical and sexual development that are problematic for the individual with AN. The development of a more mature body shape and the secondary sexual characteristics associated with adolescent development run contrary to societal ideals of beauty for women. Furthermore, the pressures of increased heterosexual contact during the course of adolescence appear to contribute to the retreat from sexual development characteristic of AN. Thus, decreased sexual interest, dyspareunia, decreased sexual attractiveness, and an impoverished sexual life are common for individuals with AN (Andersen, 1985).

Treatment for the adolescent with AN can address these issues at three levels. First, it is useful to address the discrepancy between the natural course of female development and societal ideals regarding beauty. It can be helpful to delineate the specific physical changes that are a normal and healthy part of adolescence, including the increase in fat as a percentage of body mass and the related development of more rounded hips and breasts.

At a second level, it can be useful to discuss with patients their specific thoughts and feelings about their developing sexuality and the prospect of developing sexual relationships. In this context, it may be useful to explore the possibility of a history of sexual abuse and its implications for current sexual development. However, it is our recommendation that this type of exploratory, historical work not be a major focus of treatment until a patient has been able to maintain a minimum weight and make strides in normalizing her eating.

Finally, adolescents with AN often describe feeling in control and secure as a result of staying emaciated. In such cases, it is useful to explore the fears and anxiety associated with the exaggerated needs for mastery and control. By the same token, it can also be useful to explore how this developmental retreat from physical and sexual maturation provides for such needs.

Young Adulthood and AN

Compared to working with adolescents, the process of engaging the young adult patient with AN and of structuring treatment is more variable. In addition, because young adult patients have typically had the disorder for a significant number of years, other issues become important in treatment. In particular, the halted self-development becomes more severe and complicating for treatment. The social support derived from the family and peer network also changes dramatically as an individual navigates the course of young adulthood.

Engaging the Patient.   Treatment of patients who have AN during their young adult years may be initiated by parents in the same manner that occurs most commonly with adolescent patients. In such cases we recommend following the same procedures as were described in the previous section. However, in the case of older patients it is important to note that when parents continue to take primary initiative for seeking treatment it reflects their daughter's inability to assume responsibilities appropriate to young adulthood. It is important to work toward narrowing this gap in treatment.

In addition to family members, an increasing variety of individuals may call inquiring about treatment for the young adult with AN—a concerned roommate of a college student, an office colleague, a boyfriend, or an internist. When the individual with AN is a young adult, it is our recommendation that the therapist keep such inquiries brief and direct the caller to have the individual with the eating disorder call directly. Following such procedures reduces the risk of undermining a potential relationship with the individual who has the eating disorder, should she decide to pursue treatment.

Finally, at this stage of development an increasing number of individuals with AN seek treatment on their own behalf. These individuals have reached the point in their illness where they recognize the reality of the eating disorder. For these individuals the denial commonly seen among adolescent patients has waned. For many, seeking treatment is associated with an exacerbation of the disorder or with an acute problem secondary to the eating disorder. Treatment thus begins at a different point because there is a shared understanding that a problem exists.

The Structure of Treatment.   As patients increase in age, the structure of therapy may change in that it may not be appropriate for the family to play a central role in therapy. Although empirical studies support family therapy for younger patients, there are no current data to indicate substantial benefit from family therapy for older patients. The decision whether to make family therapy central to the treatment depends on the stage of development of the individual, her degree of separation from the family, and the stage of treatment. It is our experience that it is useful to have a family session during the initial consultation phase and periodically throughout the course treatment. In general clinical practice, the core therapy for young adults with AN is individual treatment, and preliminary data suggest that a broad cognitive behavioral therapy is useful for such patients (Pike, 1994). Clinical judgment may suggest adjunctive group therapy, although such treatments have not been evaluated empirically.

As noted, treating an adult with AN typically means treating someone who has had an eating disorder for many years. As a result, patients have often been in multiple previous treatments with only limited benefit. This results in increased hopelessness and skepticism regarding treatment. It is extremely important that the therapist be well informed about the phenomenology and course of AN. In this way the therapist can anticipate the typical problems and concerns that arise in the course of treatment. In addition, such expertise enables the therapist to instill hope by providing detailed information to the patient about what needs to happen in treatment to resolve the AN.

Self-Development in a Social Context.   Given the all-consuming nature of AN, by young adulthood the eating disorder dominates an individual's self-schema so completely that frequently patients describe being fearful of giving up the eating disorder because that is all they have known for many years. The all-consuming self-schema has been in operation for many years and has governed how the individual with AN thinks and feels about herself. It has filtered her attention and has transformed how she processes new information. In fact, our clinical impression is that as the duration of the eating disorder increases, the existence of other elaborated aspects of one's self decreases.

This presents a particular challenge in therapy because if the eating disorder is resolved it creates a vacuum, leaving the patient with no alternative way to integrate new experiences. It also challenges years of decisions that were based on the rules of the eating disorder. As suggested by Padesky (1994), cognitive interventions that explicitly challenge the maladaptive eating disorder schema and promote the development of more adaptive, alternative schemata may be quite helpful in treatment.

Social Support.   Young adults with AN frequently have limited social support available from family and friends. In the normal course of development, the transition to young adulthood entails increasing separation and autonomy from the family of origin. Although parents of adolescent daughters with AN are often very involved in treatment, as the years pass their ability and desire to provide major social and financial support wanes. Parents describe feeling frustrated, hopeless, bitter, and financially depleted. They also describe "wanting to get on with their lives," which might entail retiring to a warmer climate or moving to a smaller apartment, for example. However, these same parents often report feeling guilty about such desires because of the implications for their daughter with AN, who remains very dependent on them. In treatment it is important to validate the parents' own development so that the entire family avoids becoming embroiled in the eating disorder (Siegel et al., 1988). This means helping parents and patients move forward rather than getting stuck in either a state of enmeshment or of abandonment.

Social support from peers is often very limited at this stage of development for the individual with AN. The exception to this is the less common circumstance wherein an individual has a late onset of the eating disorder, which was preceded by more adaptive social development. Typically, by adulthood these women feel increasingly isolated and out of step with their peers, who are moving out on their own, pursuing careers, dating, marrying, and having children.

Clinical practice suggests that it may be helpful for such patients to participate in group therapy for individuals with eating disorders. Such groups can be helpful in terms of addressing social and interpersonal deficits and offer in vivo opportunities for feedback from and experimentation with peers. It can also be useful to encourage patients to become involved in social organizations that would put them into contact with peers who do not have AN.

Middle to Later Adulthood and AN

The incidence of new cases of AN in the middle to later adult years is relatively low. Typically, patients who are in treatment during the middle to later adult years have a chronic and severe disorder. In addition to potentially increased morbidity associated with chronic AN, as the duration of illness increases the mortality rates for this eating disorder increase as well (Hsu, 1988, 1990).

Because patients with AN during their thirties and forties tend to have had the eating disorder since adolescence, the developmental issues raised in the preceding sections remain applicable. In terms of engaging the patient and structuring treatment, recommendations for younger adult patients are applicable. The major distinction in treating older patients with AN is in adjusting treatment goals as described in the following.

Modifying Treatment Goals.   Treatment goals for the older, chronic patient with AN may need to be modified from those goals that would have been set for the same patient if she were first presenting for treatment as an adolescent or young adult. Crisp (1980) reported that aggressive treatment for a chronic patient may actually exacerbate her condition and result in increased depression and suicidality.

Of particular importance in treating this age group with AN is the issue of pressure to make up for lost time that patients describe in their subjective experience. Given the time that has elapsed since the onset of the AN, many patients at this stage of life report feelings of failure and guilt that they have not achieved their goals in any area of their lives. Therapy can be useful to patients by assisting them in resolving these feelings and by helping them to set realistic goals for themselves. It is important to instill hope and convey to patients that they can still achieve meaningful goals by charting their unique course.

BULIMIA NERVOSA

BN usually begins in late adolescence or early adulthood, and the overwhelming majority of individuals with BN are female. Although estimates of the prevalence vary widely, rigorous epidemiological studies with strict criteria for BN generally report prevalence rates of 1% to 2% of all females (Fairburn & Beglin, 1990; Fairburn, Hay, & Welch, 1993; Kendler et al., 1991). The rate of occurrence of BN in males is approximately one tenth of that in females. It remains unclear whether BN has increased in recent years, although research suggests that a cohort shift has occurred, with females born after 1960 having a higher risk for BN than those born earlier (Bushnell, Wells, Hornblow, Oakley Browne, & Joyce, 1990; Kendler et al., 1991; Fairburn et al., 1993).

Compared to AN and BED, the empirical database regarding treatment for BN is much better established. Since BN was first described (Russell, 1979), there have been over 20 controlled treatment trials (Fairburn, 1990). Together, these studies indicate that cognitive-behavior therapy (CBT) is consistently superior to other interventions for BN, with the exception of interpersonal psychotherapy (IPT), which approaches CBT in terms of treatment efficacy (Agras, 1993; Fairburn, Agras, & Wilson, 1992; Fairburn et al., 1994).

Both CBT and IPT are short-term, focused therapies. CBT addresses attitudes and behaviors related to eating, weight, and shape. Details of manual-based CBT interventions and their application are provided by Fairburn, Marcus, and Wilson (1993), Wilson and Fairburn (1993), and Wilson and Pike (1993). The primary focus of IPT is on problem areas in current interpersonal relationships, as described by Klerman, Weissman, Rounsaville, and Chevron (1984). This type of therapy has been adapted for BN (Fairburn, 1993) and for BED (Wilfley et al., 1993).

In terms of psychopharmacological interventions, antidepressant medications may be helpful for a significant percentage of individuals in the short run. However, treatment effects tend to be more modest than those reported for IPT or CBT (Mitchell et al., 1990; Walsh, Hadigan, Devlin, Gladis, & Roose, 1991). In addition, CBT and IPT are considered to have greater long-term efficacy than psychopharmacological interventions because of the more enduring nature of change that occurs following a course of these psychotherapies (Fairburn et al., 1992). Although CBT and IPT appear to be more effective than antidepressant medication alone, these psychotherapies used in combination with antidepressant medication may result in enhanced treatment efficacy (Agras et al., 1994; Mitchell et al., 1990). This may be especially true if there is clear evidence of a coexisting affective disorder that preceded the onset of the eating disorder (Mitchell & de Zwaan, 1993). Clinical trials of CBT report full remission of the binge eating in approximately 50% to 70% of individuals and full remission of purging in 36% to 56% (Agras, Schneider, Arnow, Raeburn, & Telch, 1989; Agras et al., 1992; Fairburn et al., 1991; Wilson, Eldredge, Smith, & Niles, 1991). The results of IPT are comparable to CBT 1 year after treatment (Fairburn, Jones, Peveler, Hope, & O'Connor, 1993). Clearly these treatments are effective for a significant number of individuals. However, the data also indicate that a substantial number of individuals remain symptomatic with little or no benefit upon completion of either CBT or IPT. As discussed subsequently, it may be that the efficacy of these treatments would be enhanced by consideration of developmental issues.

Adolescence and BN

Engaging the Patient. Unlike patients with AN, adolescents with BN can and most often do try to keep their disorder a secret. Also, unlike most patients with AN, patients with BN have symptoms that they find aversive, that is, the binge eating and purging. Typically the patient seeks treatment on her own initiative and is motivated to resolve the eating disorder. This combination of facts makes engaging the patient with BN in treatment a different prospect.

It is not unusual for the therapist to be the first person whom an adolescent with BN has told about her eating disorder. In the initial phase of treatment, especially for the young adolescent patient with BN, issues of shame may be pronounced. Building a positive therapeutic alliance depends on maintaining a nonjudgmental posture on the part of the therapist. As in the case of AN, it can be useful to acknowledge the adaptive function of the BN to help relieve the patient of some of the shame associated with the eating disorder (Silberstein, Striegel-Moore, & Rodin, 1987). In addition, providing the adolescent patient with psychoeducational information regarding the normalization of weight and eating and the deleterious consequences of binge eating and purging can help orient patients to the process of recovery (Fairburn et al., 1993; Garner et al., 1985).

One of the greatest threats to engaging the adolescent with BN is that frequently these patients remain overinvested in the pursuit of thinness. Appearance is overvalued, and typically weight-loss goals are unrealistic and unsustainable. As in the case of AN, patients with BN believe that the achievement of a particular body shape and weight ideal will be associated with tremendous benefit in terms of self-worth and self-esteem. The potential incompatiblity of dieting and resolving the eating disorder needs to be addressed clearly at the outset of treatment. This is especially significant when treating an adolescent who has yet to relinquish belief in the myth that bodies are infinitely malleable and that achievement of a body ideal simply requires more effort.

The Structure of Treatment. The empirical support for CBT and IPT suggests that both therapies target important domains, and it is our recommendation that these treatments constitute the core interventions for adolescents with BN. Given that we do not have clear prognostic indicators to identify a priori who will respond better to CBT versus IPT, and because data indicate that CBT may have a more rapid effect than IPT in terms of symptom reduction for BN (Fairburn, Jones, et al., 1993), it is our recommendation that CBT be the first line of intervention.

For those individuals who do not respond to CBT it may be useful to pursue a course of IPT. It is our recommendation that these therapies be sequenced to maintain the intensity of focus of each treatment. Intensive focus may be a critical ingredient in the efficacy of these treatments, which might otherwise be diffused if the treatments were combined. If the BN is not resolved after this sequence of interventions, it may be useful to consider more long-term treatment to address developmental issues that may be compromising the patient's ability to benefit from these therapies. Also, in some cases it may be useful to pursue a more long-term treatment that addresses developmental issues even after a successful course of CBT or IPT. Once the BN is resolved, developmental experiences of loss, trauma, or family disturbances, for example, may be addressed without the confounding factor of the eating disorder. For many individuals, this is the first time in their lives that they have had the opportunity to work through these issues without having them clouded by the cycle of binge eating and purging.

In terms of structuring treatment for younger adolescents, it is important to note that studies documenting the efficacy of CBT and IPT have not included individuals younger than 18 years. Therefore, these individual treatments may need to be modified to accommodate the cognitive and interpersonal capacities of a younger patient. In addition, given the shame and secrecy that surrounds BN, group therapy may be useful in helping patients feel less isolated. Also, given the difficulties with interpersonal relationships reported by individuals with BN, group therapy offers the opportunity to develop more adaptive skills in this area.

The Treatment Team. The treatment team for adolescents with BN includes an individual therapist who may coordinate care with several other treatment providers depending on the case. First, as mentioned earlier, a family therapist may be part of the team. As in the case of AN, it is important that the adolescent with BN have a complete medical evaluation at the initiation of treatment. Although generally considered to be less dangerous than AN, medical complications in BN may develop because of the extreme dietary restriction, binge eating, and purging practices. Dental erosion and periodontal disease are not uncommon. In some cases, electrolyte imbalance and dehydration can occur and may result in serious physical complications such as cardiac arrhythmias. Rare complications include esophageal bleeding, tears, and gastric rupture (Mitchell, 1986). Those with purging BN, in comparison to those with nonpurging BN, are much more likely to have physical problems such as fluid and electrolyte disturbances.

Finally, for some adolescents with BN it may be helpful to arrange for a consultation with a nutritionist. Although CBT provides basic recommendations regarding the normalization of eating, a nutritionist may be able to provide additional support and education regarding principles of healthful eating and weight management. Also, a nutritionist may be particularly helpful for patients with concurrent medical conditions such as diabetes.

Family Systems and BN. A significant body of research documents a range of problems in the families of individuals with BN (Dolan, Lieberman, Evans, & Lacy, 1990; Humphrey, 1989; Pike & Rodin, 1991; Strober & Humphrey, 1987; Van Buren & Williamson, 1988; Wilfley, 1989). However, because of the secrecy that often surrounds BN as well as the age of the typical patient with BN, it is less common for such patients to be in family therapy. Some experts advocate family therapy for these patients; however, very little empirical data are available in support of family therapy. The only systematic study of family treatment that we are aware of suggests that family therapy alone does not appear to be particularly beneficial to this group of patients (Russell et al., 1987). However, it is important to note that family issues may be a major focus in IPT. Thus, family systems work may be conducted within the structure of individual treatment. This is especially important for patients who have significant family issues but who do not want to involve their families in treatment or who live away from families of origin.

It would be an important contribution to the field to determine the conditions under which family therapy augments treatment outcome for individuals with BN. Until such data exist, our clinical experience suggests that family systems interventions may be useful in cases where the individual with BN is a young adolescent living at home. Specifically, it will be useful to include a family evaluation as part of the initial consultation. To the extent that significant family problems are reported that may contribute to the eating disorder, adjunctive family therapy may be helpful.

Self-Development in a Social Context. Disturbances in the development of one's self in a social context have consistently been documented among individuals with BN (Herzog, Keller, Lavori, & Ott, 1987; Johnson & Connors, 1987; Norman & Herzog, 1986; Striegel-Moore, Silberstein, & Rodin, 1986). Given their problems with self-esteem and self-worth, individuals with BN appear to be especially vulnerable to social prejudices regarding weight and appearance for females in our society. In an effort to compensate for these deficits, individuals with BN strive to achieve a body shape and weight that they believe will make them feel more secure in their social world and enhance their social status (Johnson & Connors, 1987; Polivy & Herman, 1993; Striegel-Moore, 1993).

Individuals with BN are also exquisitely sensitive to cues from others and often attempt to guide their own behavior to obtain approval and prevent rejection (Schwalberg, Barlow, Alger, & Howard, 1992; Striegel-Moore et al., 1993). In addition, individuals with BN have poor coping skills (Cattanach, Malley, & Rodin, 1988; Cattanach & Rodin, 1988). As a result, they report using binge eating and purging as a means of coping with problems that they feel unable to manage otherwise.

Thus, similar to treatment goals for AN, a significant focus of therapy for BN consists of helping individuals develop a more internalized sense of self-worth independent of the eating disorder. In the case of BN this means developing a more secure sense of self that is not so dependent on pleasing others or achieving an idealized appearance. It also means developing a sense of self-efficacy that can promote more adaptive coping strategies and self-assertion.

Physical and Sexual Development. As with AN, the rise of BN during adolescence suggests that the physical and sexual developments characteristic of adolescence may pose a problem for vulnerable individuals. However, BN is different from AN in that BN alters one's physical and sexual development to a lesser extent. Despite the desire to achieve lower body weights, individuals with BN tend to be of average weight and generally continue to menstruate, albeit in some cases irregularly. As in the case of AN, it is useful to discuss the sociocultural pressures on females regarding weight and shape and to educate patients regarding physical development during adolescence and principles of weight maintenance.

In terms of sexual development, adolescents with BN tend to appear more on course. It is not unusual for these girls to date and become involved in sexual relationships. However, dissatisfaction with appearance as well as problems with intimacy appear to result in suboptimal sexual relationships for many patients with BN (Andersen, 1985). In such cases, these issues are important to address in treatment.

Young Adulthood and BN

The majority of patients with BN seek treatment as young adults and have typically had the eating disorder for approximately 7 years (e.g., Walsh et al., 1991). Given that the majority of adolescents who seek treatment for BN are on the verge of entering their twenties, the process of engaging patients and structuring treatment is essentially identical for this slightly older group. Similarly, issues of self-development and social functioning for young adult patients reflect earlier issues.

Engaging the Patient. Two distinctions warrant comment in the process of engaging an adult patient. First, it is our experience that young adult patients with BN are more able to acknowledge the futility of dieting in an effort to achieve a particular ideal body shape. Although they may be apprehensive about abandoning dieting efforts or relinquishing their overvaluation of weight and shape, they have typically had the eating disorder long enough to know that what they are doing is not moving them toward their ideal. As a result, therapists may meet less resistance to treatment efforts focused on changing attitudes and behavior.

A second point relevant to engaging young adult patients with BN is the fact that this is a very mobile group of individuals. Many of these women are single college students or young professionals who relocate with a high frequency. Treatment plans may need to be modified depending on a patient's plans and therefore this issue should be raised during the initial stage of treatment.

The Structure of Treatment. As discussed previously, we recommend that CBT and IPT be the first interventions, given their proven efficacy. The same principles of sequencing and staying focused in treatment apply for young adult patients as for adolescents. Given the limited empirical support for family therapy as a primary intervention for this group of patients, it is our recommendation that it be included in the treatment plan to complement individual therapy if current family issues would otherwise interfere with treatment. Similarly, group therapy may be a useful complement to individual therapy, particularly for patients who have difficulties with interpersonal relationships or social isolation.

Self-Development in a Social Context. The issues of self-development discussed for adolescents with BN also apply to older individuals with BN. In addition, older patients are more likely to have more chronic and severe cases of BN. Such individuals tend to report decreased levels of social support (Grissett & Norvell, 1992) and a greater degree of social and interpersonal problems (Herzog, Norman, Rigotti, & Pepose, 1986;

Herzog et al., 1987). The clinical implications are that such individuals are likely to have had significant problems in developing intimate relationships appropriate to their developmental stage of life. Again, therapy interventions that target deficits in self-development and interpersonal functioning should address important domains for the individual with BN.

Middle to Later Adulthood and BN

By later adulthood significantly fewer patients present for treatment for BN for the first time. This may be because of developmental changes (either physical or psychological) that result in a resolution of the eating disorder. Alternatively, given that there appears to be a greater risk of developing BN for females born after 1960, it may be that a cohort effect is occurring, which suggests that with time there will be more patients in treatment for BN in their middle to later adult years.

Engaging the adult patient with BN, structuring treatment, and addressing issues of self-development are essentially consistent with the discussions pertaining to adolescents and younger adults. However, decisions about long-term commitments as well as about pregnancy may also become central. Thus, in this section we highlight these issues and their implications for treatment.

Entering and Exiting Long-Term Relationships. In many cases, BN patients seeking treatment during this stage of life are struggling with making major life decisions related to choosing partners, ending long-term relationships, and childbirth (Van den Broucke & Vandereycken, 1989). Whether entering or exiting long-term relationships, it is often the case that the individual with BN has not revealed her eating disorder to her partner (Andersen, 1985). Although some patients resolve their eating disorder without divulging their secret, it is our clinical impression that disclosure to a trusted significant other is often a good prognostic indicator. As described by Van den Brouke and Vandereycken, when the eating disorder is revealed the partner often reports feeling relieved because the eating disorder seems less pernicious than other suspected problems. However, if the eating disorder is not resolved in a timely matter it may become a source of increasing conflict. In such situations marital therapy may be warranted.

Pregnancy. Significant issues are stirred up for the individual with BN in the anticipation of the developmental milestone of pregnancy and becoming a parent. In the normal course of development, pregnancy can be associated with conflicts about changes in body shape, changes in roles and status, and concerns about parenting (Franko & Walton, 1993). These issues are of paramount importance and can be especially problematic for women with BN (Johnson, 1991). Although early clinical accounts reported that bulimic symptomatology typically did not interfere with pregnancy and childbirth, more recent studies indicate that maternal and fetal health can be jeopardized. In particular, the risk of fertility problems, premature births, and low-birthweight babies increases for women with BN (Stewart, 1992). In addition, preliminary data suggest that women with BN are at greater risk for providing inadequate nutrition to their children (Fahy & Treasure, 1989; Stein & Fairburn, 1989). The broader implications of BN on general parenting skills have yet to be assessed systematically.

Several clinical implications for treating patients with BN who become pregnant warrant discussion. First, although the patient may want to keep the disorder a secret, given the medical implications, it is important that the primary therapist help the patient with BN communicate honestly with her obstetrician. Second, it is important that patients with BN be made aware of the potential ramifications of continuing to binge eat and purge while pregnant. Third, the guilt and fears associated with continuing to be symptomatic during pregnancy need to be addressed. And finally, longer term issues of becoming a parent may become an important focus of longer term therapy.

BINGE EATING DISORDER

Binge eating disorder (BED) is a newly defined eating disorder that is characterized by recurrent episodes of binge eating without the regular attempts to engage in extreme compensatory weight-control practices found in BN. About 30% of obese patients who present to university-based weight-control programs report serious problems with binge eating. In comparison, initial data suggest that in the community, approximately 2% of women meet BED criteria, and about half of those with BED are obese (Bruce & Agras, 1992; Spitzer et al., 1991; Spitzer et al., 1992). Although the prevalence of BED among obese persons in the community is uncertain, preliminary data suggest that it affects between 5% and 10% of the general population (Yanovski, 1993).

In contrast to AN and BN, preliminary data suggest that BED has a broader distribution in terms of gender, race, and age. Data suggest that among patients attending weight-loss programs BED is only slightly more common among women than among men (3:2; Spitzer et al., 1992, Spitzer et al., 1993). Moreover, Black women and White women appear to be at equal risk for BED (Marcus, 1993). The age distribution of patients with BED is also broader, with people from 20 to 70 presenting for treatment (Wilfley et al., 1993).

Although binge eating was first described by Stunkard in 1959, reseachers are still in the early stages of identifying effective treatments for BED. To date most BED patients have been treated in traditional weight-loss programs, which do not appear to lead to long-term reduction of binge eating and associated eating disorder pathology. In addition, some data suggest that BED patients may be prone to greater attrition during weight-loss treatment and to more rapid regain of lost weight than are nonbinge eaters (Yanovski, 1993).

Recent studies have examined whether treatments that focus on binge eating rather than on weight loss might be effective in treating individuals with BED. In terms of psychopharmacological treatment for BED, antidepressant medication significantly decreases binge eating during active treatment; however, relapse rates are very high and most patients return to pretreatment levels of bingeing within 4 weeks after the drug is discontinued (McCann & Agras, 1990). In contrast, and consistent with patients with BN, BED patients appear to report lasting benefit from CBT (Smith, Marcus, & Kaye, 1992; Telch, Agras, Rossiter, Wilfley, & Kenardy, 1990; Wilfley et al., 1993) and from IPT (Wilfley et al., 1993). The comparable effects of these treatments across disorders suggest that a similar mechanism may underlie the binge eating syndrome in BN and BED patients, and that similar treatments may be used with both.

Adolescence and BED

Engaging the Patient.   Very few adolescent patients present for treatment for BED. Although it is unclear why this would be, it might be hypothesized that because BED is a relatively new diagnosis, an adolescent patient population exists that has not yet presented for treatment. Alternatively, it may be that individuals who are binge eating during adolescence are more preoccupied with the associated weight gain and therefore seek treatment for weight loss at this stage in their lives. Data from older patients with BED offer tentative support for this hypothesis. Retrospective reports indicate that adult patients with BED have had chronic weight problems, that most have attempted innumerable weight-loss efforts, and that many have experienced psychosocial consequences of being overweight (Marcus, 1993; Stunkard & Wadden, 1992; Yanovski, 1993).

Thus, with the exception of discussing the role of the family in the treatment of adolescents with BED, the process of engaging patients, structuring treatment, and establishing a treatment team is discussed in the context of the adult patient with BED.

Family Systems and BED.   Family therapy has not been evaluated empirically in the treatment of BED; however, consistent with our recommendations for AN and BN, when treating an adolescent with

BED a family evaluation is essential. In addition, several common issues among adolescent patients with BED suggest that ongoing family systems work may be warranted.

First, a significant percentage of patients report very chaotic patterns in their family systems, which include but are not limited to family patterns around food. In terms of eating, patients may either describe an extreme overinvolvement in their family or an extreme lack of structure around meals and eating. Interventions that normalize eating patterns in the family and minimize the risk of promoting eating disturbances might be helpful for the adolescent with BED. By the same token, a significant number of adults with BED report that during adolescence parents often pressured them to lose weight, which almost inevitably was associated with an exacerbation of symptoms. Educating family members about eating disorders and weight problems can help to relieve some of the pressure that the individual with BED experiences.

In addition to working with the family around eating and weight problems, general problems in the family system may also warrant attention. In particular, retrospective reports of adult patients with BED suggest that disturbances in family functioning may include alcoholism and depression in a significant percentage of cases (Wilfley, 1989). To the extent that such family problems exist and are associated with increased dissatisfaction with family functioning and increased eating-disordered symptomatology, family systems work may be essential.

Self-Development in a Social Context. Retrospective reports from adult patients with BED describe the subjective experience of being neglected and overlooked in their families of origin (Wilfley, 1989). As a result, these individuals report feeling that they were cheated from getting the love and nurturing to which they felt entitled. They describe feeling that they did not have sound, positive attachments, and they continue to long for the nurturing that they never got as children.

Related empirical data are consistent with these clinical reports, suggesting that problems in self-development are characteristic of individuals with BED. In particular, it appears that obese binge eaters exhibit similar types of social self-deficits (Grilo, Wilfley, Jones, Brownell, & Rodin, 1994; Schwalberg et al., 1992) and similar levels of psychopathology as are found in BN patients (Kolotkin, Revis, Kirkley, & Janick, 1987; Marcus, Wing, & Hopkins, 1988; Marcus et al., 1990; Schwalberg et al., 1992; Wilfley, 1989; Yanovski, Nelson, Dubbert, & Spitzer, in press). Thus, to the extent that the development of a secure sense of self and the developmental task of learning to nurture oneself has been thwarted, it is critical to address this issue in treatment.

As described in the preceding section on BN, clinical reports from patients indicate that adolescents who are binge eating are excessively "other-directed." This style may be learned as a means of coping with any number of interpersonal problems, which the patient attempts to solve by becoming the caregiver for others. In addition, it appears that individuals with BED try to compensate for their shape and weight by placing an excessive focus on other's needs. These individuals describe attempting to ingratiate themselves to prevent teasing and to win friends. One of the important tasks of therapy is to assist such patients in the development of a more internally directed and secure sense of self. Therapy can also help these individuals develop more effective coping strategies in response to problems in these social systems.

Physical and Sexual Development.   As already noted, most adults with BED describe long histories of weight problems often beginning in childhood. Many of these individuals describe being "born fat," and studies of biological vulnerability for obesity suggest that these individuals may, in fact, be predisposed to obesity (Yanovski, 1993). Thus, they often report significant teasing because of the social stigma of overweight status in Western society (Stunkard & Wadden, 1992). These individuals are also likely to be more awkward physically given their size and as a result describe significant problems with body image (Cash, 1991). In the midst of adolescence, when appearance, athletic skills, and achieving high ideals are paramount, the development of BED appears to be the culmination of an often long and futile struggle to achieve a more satisfactory weight and psychosocial adaptation.

Consistent with treatment goals for AN and BN, treatment of BED needs to address body shape and weight concerns that are integral to the eating disorder. However, treatment interventions need to be modified to address the physical and psychosocial implications of the associated obesity.

Young Adulthood and BED

An increasing number of patients seek treatment for binge eating during the young adult years. Among individuals presenting for treatment, the course of BED appears to be chronic (Yanovski, 1993). Typically, these patients come to treatment after many efforts at weight loss. As a result, many are demoralized and feel like so-called treatment failures. One of the major goals of treatment is to redirect the patient's focus from weight loss to resolution of the eating disorder. Efforts to do so may be met with feelings of loss, opposition, or relief.

Engaging the Patient.   In helping patients shift their focus of treatment, it is important to get a thorough history of weight, weight cycling, and associated eating patterns, all of which should help in establishing reasonable weight goals (Brownell & Wadden, 1992). It is also helpful to provide patients with important psychoeducational information. In particular, therapists should let BED patients know that if they continue to binge eat it is unlikely that they will be successful at regulating their weight. However, therapists can also reassure patients that preliminary data do suggest that abstinence from binge eating is associated with weight loss (Agras et al., 1994; Smith et al., 1992).

Once the binge eating is stabilized, it is unclear how much weight patients will continue to lose; however, clinical reports indicate that they will most likely be better prepared to ward off further weight gain and be more successful at engaging in lifestyle activities that are compatible with weight loss and weight maintenance, such as heart-healthy eating and moderate exercise (Wilfley, Grilo, & Brownell, 1994). Patients should be explicitly encouraged to recognize that even modest weight losses (10% to 15% body weight) can produce significant health benefits, which include improving blood pressure, blood glucose control, and blood lipids and lipoproteins (Brownell & Rodin, 1994). Moreover, it is much more likely that small amounts of weight loss will be more readily maintained (Brownell & Rodin, 1994), as many who lose more than that regain all of their lost weight (Wilson, 1994).

Further encouragement to shift treatment goals from a primary focus on weight loss to a primary focus on the eating disturbance can be achieved by outlining for patients broader benefits that they can anticipate as the eating disorder is resolved. In particular, it can be emphasized that along with being in a better position to control their weight, BED patients who stop binge eating typically report feeling more in control of their eating, less preoccupied with thoughts about eating, shape, and weight, and better about themselves generally.

The Structure of Treatment.   As in the treatment of BN, the two forms of treatment that have been most studied for this patient population are CBT and IPT. These treatments have been adapted for the particular needs of adult patients with BED (Fairburn, Marcus, & Wilson, 1993; Wilfley et al., 1993; Wilfley, Grilo, & Rodin, in press).

The main adaptation for CBT is the dual focus on binge eating and weight regulation. Whereas normalization of eating for BN patients often necessitates increased eating, for BED patients clearer demarcation of mealtimes is indicated. In contrast to BN patients, for whom decreased restraint is a goal of treatment, increased restraint is a focus for BED patients. Excessive restraint is of course to be avoided, but normalization of eating and elimination of "grazing," overeating, and binge eating is necessary. As eating behavior becomes better regulated, attention to losing modest amounts of weight should be reviewed and successful techniques to help achieve those changes should be encouraged. Specifically, this entails establishing reasonable weight-loss goals, maintaining changes in eating, and establishing a moderate exercise program (Brownell & Wadden, 1992). Because the focus is on the interpersonal problems and not on the eating disorder per se, IPT for BN is easily adapted for BED.

The Treatment Team.   In addition to the primary therapist, a family therapist may be involved in the treatment team as described earlier. In addition, as is the case with AN and BN it is essential that an individual with BED have a complete physical evaluation as part of the initial assessment. Thus, depending on the age of the patient either a pediatrician or an internist should be an integral member of the treatment team. It is essential that the physician be informed about treating the combined problems of obesity and binge eating. In particular, it is important that the physician refrain from treating the obesity with recommendations of excessive dieting and weight loss, which may contradict treatment recommendations for the eating disorder. It is important to provide the physician with a clear rationale for the utility of modifying weight-loss goals so that they will be sustainable for individuals with BED. Once the binge eating is resolved, if an individual is in good control of her eating a nutritionist may be able to help a patient to achieve a safe weight loss. Finally, an exercise physiologist may be helpful to individuals with BED in developing exercise routines specifically designed for an individual's abilities and needs.

Self-Development in a Social Context.   Young adult patients with BED describe significant difficulties navigating the developmental challenges that arise at this stage of life. Although these individuals are typically able to lead productive work lives, they suffer significantly in their emotional development and interpersonal relationships. In particular, most individuals with BED report significant shame related to body shape and weight issues. Related to this shame, many of these individuals have difficulty participating in the normative social activities of dating. For those individuals who do establish lasting partnerships, many describe feeling perpetually fearful of losing their partners because of the binge eating and associated weight problems. These individuals tend to be highly conflict-avoidant and run the risk of selecting partners who replicate family-of-origin problems.

These developmental issues have several implications for therapy. First, treatment can help patients gain increased self-awareness by relating the eating disorder to these interpersonal issues. Once these links are established, active ingredients of treatment include behavioral experimentation with assertiveness and increased self-disclosure with significant others, especially around potentially conflictual situations. Furthermore, as in the case of BN, many of the individuals with BED who present for treatment at this stage of life have partners. Many of these individuals are struggling with other developmentally appropriate issues such as marriage, parenthood, and career. To the extent that the binge eating reflects problems in these domains of functioning, it is important for treatment to help patients work directly on the particular problem issues, which will thereby reduce the risk of binge eating.

Middle to Later Adulthood and BED

Despite long histories of eating and weight problems frequently dating back to childhood, it is not until middle adulthood that we see the majority of patients with BED. Most BED patients have pursued multiple weight-loss efforts in their earlier years. Moreover, although their overweight status is publicly shameful, it is often the case that the binge eating remains a secretive as well as shameful behavior in its own right.

The process of engaging the adult patient with BED and the issues of the development of a sense of self and self-worth are consistent across the age span for patients with BED. Thus, in this section we highlight three points particularly relevant to the treatment of older adult patients with BED. First, in contrast with patients who present for treatment with AN and BN, by middle adulthood most patients with BED are further along the path of developing their own marriages and families. Second, the issues of social isolation and social support have significant implications for treatment. Finally, for patients with BED the medical complications associated with obesity are likely to become increasingly significant and debilitating at this stage of life.

Family Systems and BED.   Over one fourth of patients with BED experience significant role disputes in their interpersonal relationships, and as in the case of BN, the marriage is the primary relationship in which these conflicts occur (Wilfley et al., 1993). In addition, clinical reports from adult patients with BED suggest that high rates of family psychopathology, alcohol abuse, and general family dysfunction existed in their families of origin. Taken together, adult patients with BED tend to be concerned about the stability of their marriages and express concern about their parenting skills. They express fears that they will recreate the problems that they knew and observed as children.

In addition, given the close link between BED and obesity, and given the genetic influences on body weight and shape, these parents tend to worry about their children's weight status. They describe feeling guilty for any weight problems among their children and describe feeling worried that their children will develop chronic eating disturbances similar to their own and experience similar interpersonal problems as a result.

Finally, these patients are often the primary caregivers in the family and are often caring for ill parents at this stage of their lives. This becomes especially important in psychotherapy when an individual is overinvolved in caring for an ill parent and the parent is suffering from health consequences related to obesity and BED.

Several treatment interventions may be appropriate in addressing these issues. First, to the extent that these individuals have social deficits it is important for treatment to focus on helping patients build more effective interpersonal skills. For example, this may involve assertiveness training and developing more effective conflict management and communication skills. In addition, supportive and psychoeducational parent training programs may be useful for adult BED patients who are having difficulty in their roles as parents. Furthermore, in addition to individual or group treatments, it may be helpful to consider marital or family therapy to address the broader interpersonal issues.

Physical Health Problems. The overweight status associated with BED can result in significant medical and physical problems for adult patients with BED. The patient's physical status can be associated with problems such as impaired sexual functioning and intimacy, high blood pressure, diabetes, and joint problems (Brownell & Wadden, 1992). Thus, it is often the case that weight concerns that were initially linked to concerns with appearance become linked with concerns about health. These patients express fears that their physical condition will deteriorate to the point that they are unable to take care of themselves. In addition, given that they are often the caregivers in their families, they fear that no one will be there to take care of them. The serious medical conditions associated with BED make it essential that skilled medical care is provided to an adult patient with BED. Related psychotherapy goals include advocating healthy, modest exercise goals, resolving the binge eating, and establishing heart-healthy eating patterns.

SUMMARY

Developmental issues are significant in shaping both the content and structure of treatment for patients with eating disorders. As described in this chapter, the age of the patient and the particular eating disorder affect the form and focus of treatment. In addition, the stage of development of the eating disorder is significant; the course of all of these eating disorders can be severe and protracted, and issues of chronicity have implications for treatment. These eating disorders reflect compromise solutions and failures in mastering critical developmental tasks. Thus, increasing age is often associated with an accumulation of such failures. Unifying developmental themes that influence the focus of treatment include developing an identity apart from one's family of origin, establishing more intimate relationships with others, defining a new body image, and achieving a cohesive and stable sense of self. Fundamental to the treatment of individuals with eating disorders is the process of helping patients to modify their current functioning such that they are able to establish more adaptive solutions to these developmental challenges. Thus, successful resolution of the eating disorders is associated with the development of a more secure and internally directed sense of self in the context of greater satisfaction in one's social world.

REFERENCES

Agras, W. S. (1993). Short-term psychological treatments for binge eating. In C. G. Fairburn & G. T. Wilson (Eds.), *Binge eating: Nature, assessment and treatment* (pp. 270–286). New York: Guilford.

Agras, W. S., Barlow, D. H., Chapin H. N., Abel, G. G., & Leitenberg, H. (1974). Behavior modification of anorexia nervosa. *Archives of General Psychiatry, 30,* 279–286.

Agras, W. S., Rossiter, E. M., Arnow, B., Schneider, J. A., Telch, C. F., Raeburn, S. D., Bruce, B., Perl, M., & Koran, L. M. (1992). Pharmacologic and cognitive–behavioral treatment for bulimia nervosa: A controlled comparison. *American Journal of Psychiatry, 149,* 82–87.

Agras, W. S., Schneider, J. A., Arnow, B., Raeburn, S. D., & Telch, C. F. (1989). Cognitive–behavioral and response–prevention treatments for bulimia nervosa. *Journal of Consulting and Clinical Psychology, 57,* 215–221.

Agras, W. S., Telch, C. F., Arnow, B., Eldredge, K., Wilfley, D. E., Raeburn, S. D., Henderson, J., & Marnell, M. (1994). Weight loss, cognitive–behavioral, and desipramine treatments in binge eating disorder. An additive design. *Behavior Therapy, 25,* 225–238.

American Psychiatric Association. (1994). *Diagnostic and statistical manual of mental disorders* (4th ed.). Washington, DC: Author.

Andersen, A. E. (1985). *Practical comprehensive treatment of anorexia nervosa and bulimia.* Baltimore, MD: Johns Hopkins University Press.

Attie, I., & Brooks-Gunn, J. (1992). Developmental issues in the study of eating problems and disorders. In J. Crowther, D. Tennenbaum, S. Hobfoll, & M. P. Stephens (Eds.), *The etiology of bulimia nervosa: The individual and familial context* (pp. 35–58). Washington, DC: Hemisphere.

Brownell, K. D., & Rodin, J. (1994). The dieting maelstrom: Is it possible and advisable to lose weight. *American Psychologist, 49,* 781–791.

Brownell, K. D., & Wadden, T. A. (1992). Etiology and treatment of obesity: Toward understanding a serious, prevalent, and refractory disorder. *Journal of Consulting and Clinical Psychology, 60,* 505–517.

Bruce, B., & Agras, W. S. (1992). Binge eating in females: A population based investigation. *International Journal of Eating Disorders, 12,* 365–373.

Bruch, H. (1973). *Eating disorders: Obesity, anorexia nervosa and the person within.* New York: Basic Books.

Bruch, H. (1978). *The golden cage: The enigma of anorexia nervosa.* Cambridge, MA: Harvard University Press.

Bruch, H. (1979). Island in the river: The anorexic adolescent in treatment. In S. C. Feinstein & P. L. Giovacchini (Eds.), *Adolescent psychiatry* (pp. 26–40). Chicago: University of Chicago Press.

Bushnell, J. A., Wells, J. E., Hornblow, A. R., Oakley Browne, M. A., & Joyce, P. (1990). Prevalence of three bulimia syndromes in the general population. *Psychological Medicine, 20,* 671–680.

Cash, T. F. (1991). Binge-eating and body images among the obese: A further evaluation. *Journal of Social Behavior and Personality, 6,* 367–376.

Casper, R. C. (1982). Treatment principles in anorexia nervosa. *Adolescent Psychiatry, 10,* 86–100.

Cattanach, L., Malley, R., & Rodin, J. (1988). Psychologic and physiologic reactivity to stressors in eating disordered individuals. *Psychosomatic Medicine, 50,* 591–599.

Cattanach, L., & Rodin, J. (1988). Psychosocial components of the stress process in bulimia. *International Journal of Eating Disorders, 7,* 75–88.

Channon, S., DeSilva, P., Hemsley, D., & Perkins, R. (1989). A controlled trial of cognitive–behavioral and behavioral treatment of anorexia nervosa. *Behavioral Research and Therapy, 27,* 529–535.

Crisp, A. H. (1980). *Anorexia nervosa: Let me be.* London: Academic Press.

Crisp, A. H., Norton, K., Gowers, S., Halek, C., Bowyer, C., Yeldham, D., Levett, G., & Bhat, A. (1991). A controlled study of the effect of therapies aimed at adolescent and family psychopathology in anorexia nervosa. *British Journal of Psychiatry, 159,* 325–333.

Devlin, M. J., & Walsh, B. T. (1992). Anorexia nervosa and bulimia nervosa. In P. Bjorntorp (Ed.), *Obesity* (pp. 436–444). Philadelphia: Lippincott.

Dolan, B. M., Lieberman, S., Evans, C., & Lacey, J. H. (1990). Family features associated with normal body weight bulimia. *International Journal of Eating Disorders, 9,* 639–647.

Fahy, T., & Treasure, J. (1989). Children of mothers with bulimia nervosa. *British Medical Journal, 299,* 1031.

Fairburn, C. G. (1990). Bulimia nervosa. *British Medical Journal, 300,* 485–487.

Fairburn, C. G. (1993). Interpersonal psychotherapy for bulimia nervosa. In G. L. Klerman, & M. M. Weissman (Eds.), *New applications of interpersonal psychotherapy* (pp. 353–378). Washington, DC: American Psychiatric Association.

Fairburn, C. G., Agras, W. S., & Wilson, G. T. (1992). The research on the treatment of bulimia nervosa: Practical and theoretical implications. In G. H. Anderson & S. H. Kennedy (Eds.), *The biology of feast and famine: Relevance to eating disorders* (pp. 317–340). San Diego, CA: Academic Press.

Fairburn, C. G., & Beglin, S. J. (1990). Studies of the epidemiology of bulimia nervosa. *American Journal of Psychiatry, 147,* 401–408.

Fairburn, C. G., Hay, P. J., & Welch, S. L. (1993). Binge eating and bulimia nervosa: Distribution and determinants. In C. G. Fairburn & G. T. Wilson (Eds.), *Binge eating: Nature, assessment, and treatment* (pp. 123–143). New York: Guilford.

Fairburn, C. G., Jones, R., Peveler, R. C., Carr, S. J., Soloman, R. A., O'Connor, M. E., & Hope, R. A. (1991). Three psychological treatments for bulimia nervosa: A comparative trial. *Archives of General Psychiatry, 48,* 463–469.

Fairburn, C. G., Jones, R., Peveler, R. C., Hope, R. A., & O'Connor, M. (1993). The long-term effects of interpersonal psychotherapy, behavior therapy and cognitive behavior therapy for bulimia nervosa. *Archives of General Psychiatry, 50,* 419–428.

Fairburn, C. G., Marcus, M. D., & Wilson, G. T. (1993). Cognitive behavior therapy for binge eating and bulimia nervosa: A comprehensive treatment manual. In C. G. Fairburn & G. T. Wilson (Eds.), *Binge eating: Nature, assessment, and treatment* (pp. 361–404). New York: Guilford.

Fairburn, C. G., O'Connor, M. E., Norman, P. A., Welch, S. L., Doll, H. A., & Peveler, R. C. (1994, April). *The short, medium, and long-term effects of three psychological treatments for bulimia nervosa.* Paper presented at the 6th Annual International Conference on Eating Disorders, New York.

Franko, D. L., & Walton, B. E. (1993). Pregnancy and eating disorders: A review and clinical implications. *International Journal of Eating Disorders, 13,* 41–48.

Garner, D. M., & Bemis, K. M. (1985). Cognitive therapy for anorexia nervosa. In D. M. Garner & P. E. Garfinkel (Eds.), *Handbook of psychotherapy for anorexia nervosa and bulimia* (pp. 107–146). New York: Guilford.

Garner, D. M., Rockert, W., Olmsted, M. P., Johnson, C. L., & Coscina, D. V. (1985). Psychoeducational principles in the treatment of bulimia and anorexia nervosa. In D. M. Garner & P. E. Garfinkel (Eds.), *Handbook of psychotherapy for anorexia nervosa and bulimia* (pp. 513–572). New York: Guilford.

Grilo, C. M., Wilfley, D. E., Jones, A., Brownell, K. D., & Rodin, J. (1994). The social self, body dissatisfaction, and binge eating. *Obesity Research, 2,* 24–27.

Grissett, N. I., & Norvell, N. K. (1992). Perceived social support, social skills, and quality of relationships in bulimic women. *Journal of Consulting and Clinical Psychology, 60,* 293–299.

Hall, A., & Crisp, A. H. (1987). Brief psychotherapy in the treatment of anorexia nervosa: Outcome at one year. *British Journal of Psychiatry, 151,* 185–191.

Halmi, K. A. (1983). Treatment of anorexia nervosa: A discussion. *Journal of Adolescent Health Care, 4,* 47–50.

Herzog, D. B., Keller, M. B., Lavori, P. W., & Ott, I. L. (1987). Social impairment in bulimia. *International Journal of Eating Disorders, 6,* 741–747.

Herzog, D. B., Norman, D. K., Rigotti, N. A., & Pepose, M. (1986). Frequency of bulimic behaviors and associated social maladjustment in female graduate students. *Journal of Psychiatric Research, 20,* 355–361.

Hsu, L. K. (1988). The outcome of anorexia nervosa: A reappraisal. *Psychological Medicine, 18,* 807–812.

Hsu, L. K. (1990). *Eating disorders.* New York: Guilford.

Hsu, L. K., Crisp, A. H., & Harding, B. (1979). Outcome of anorexia nervosa. *Lancet, 13,* 61–65.

Humphrey, L. L. (1989). Is there a causal link between disturbed family processes and eating disorders? In W. G. Johnson (Ed.), *Bulimia nervosa: Perspectives on clinical research and therapy* (pp. 119–135). New York: JAI.

Johnson, C. (Ed.). (1991). *The psychodynamic treatment of anorexia nervosa and bulimia.* New York: Guilford.

Johnson, C. L., & Connors, M. E. (1987). *The etiology and treatment of bulimia nervosa.* New York: Basic Books.

Kalucy, R. S. (1978). An approach to the therapy of anorexia nervosa. *Journal of Adolescence, 1,* 197–228.

Kandel, D. B., & Davies, M. (1982). Epidemiology of depressive mood in adolescents. *Archives of General Psychiatry, 39,* 1205–1212.

Kaye, W. H., Weltzin, T. E., Hsu, L., & Bulik, C. M. (1991). An open trial of fluoxetine in patients with anorexia nervosa. *Journal of Clinical Psychiatry, 52,* 464–471.

Kendler, K. S., Maclean, C., Neale, M., Kessler, R., Heath, A., & Eaves, L. (1991). The genetic epidemiology of bulimia nervosa. *American Journal of Psychiatry, 148,* 1627–1637.

Klerman, G. L., Weissman, M. M., Rounsaville, B. J., & Chevron, E. S. (1984). *Interpersonal psychotherapy of depression.* New York: Basic Books.

Kolotkin, R. L., Revis, E. S., Kirkley, B. G., & Janick, L. (1987). Binge eating in obesity: Associated MMPI characteristics. *Journal of Consulting and Clinical Psychology, 55,* 872–876.

Levine, M., & Smolak, L. (1992). Toward a model of the developmental psychopathology of eating disorders: The example of early adolescence. In J. Crowther, D. Tennenbaum, S. Hobfoll, & M. P. Stephens (Eds.), *The etiology of bulimia nervosa: The individual and familial context* (pp. 59–80). Washington, DC: Hemisphere.

Marcus, M. D. (1993). Binge eating in obesity. In C. G. Fairburn & G. T. Wilson (Eds.), *Binge eating: Nature, assessment, and treatment* (pp. 77–96). New York: Guilford.

Marcus, M. D., Wing, R. R., Ewing, L., Keern, E., Gooding, W., & McDermott, M. (1990). Psychiatric disorders among obese binge eaters. *International Journal of Eating Disorders, 9,* 69–77.

Marcus, M. D., Wing, R. R., & Hopkins, J. (1988). Obese binge eaters: Affect, cognitions, and response to behavioral weight control. *Journal of Consulting and Clinical Psychology, 56,* 433–439.

McCann, U. D., & Agras, W. S. (1990). Successful treatment of nonpurging bulimia nervosa with desipramine: A double-blind, placebo-controlled study. *American Journal of Psychiatry, 147,* 1509–1513.

Mitchell, J. E. (1986). Bulimia: Medical and physiological aspects. In K. D. Brownell, & J. P. Foreyt (Eds.), *Handbook of eating disorders* (pp. 379–388). New York: Basic Books.

Mitchell, J. E., & de Zwaan, M. (1993). Pharmacological treatments of binge eating. In C. G. Fairburn & G. T. Wilson (Eds.), *Binge eating: Nature, assessment, and treatment* (pp. 250–269. New York: Guilford.

Mitchell, J. E., Pyle, R. L., Eckert, E. D., Hatsukami, D., Pomeroy, C., & Zimmerman, R. (1990). A comparison study of antidepressant and structured group psychotherapy in the treatment of bulimia nervosa. *Archives of General Psychiatry, 47,* 149–157.

Norman, D. K., & Herzog, D. B. (1986). A 3–year outcome study of normal-weight bulimia: Assessment of psychosocial functioning and eating attitudes. *Psychiatry Research, 19,* 199–205.

O'Malley, P. M., & Bachman, J. G. (1983). Self esteem: Change and stability between ages 13 and 23. *Developmental Psychology, 19,* 257–268.

Padesky, C. S. (1994). Schema change processes in cognitive therapy. *Clinical Psychology and Psychotherapy, 1,* 267–278.

Pike, K. M. (1994, April). *Cognitive behavioral treatment in the relapse prevention of anorexia nervosa: A pilot study.* Paper presented at the 6th Annual International Conference on Eating Disorders, New York.

Pike, K. M. (1995). Family, peer, and personality variables associated with disordered eating in high school girls. *Psychology of Women Quarterly, 19,* 373–396.

Pike, K. M., & Rodin, J. (1991). Mothers, daughters, and disordered eating. *Journal of Abnormal Psychology, 100,* 198–204.

Polivy, J. M., & Herman, C. P. (1993). Etiology of binge-eating: Psychological mechanisms. In C. G. Fairburn & G. T. Wilson (Eds.), *Binge eating: Nature, assessment, and treatment* (pp. 173–205). New York: Guilford.

Ratnasuriya, R. H., Eisler, I., Szmukler, G. I., & Russell, G. F. M. (1991). Anorexia nervosa: Outcome and prognostic factors after 20 years. *British Journal of Psychiatry, 158,* 495–502.

Russell, G. (1979). Bulimia nervosa: An ominous variant of anorexia nervosa. *Psychological Medicine, 9,* 429–448.

Russell, G., Szmukler, G. I., Dare, C., & Eisler, I. (1987). An evaluation of family therapy in anorexia nervosa and bulimia nervosa. *Archives of General Psychiatry, 44,* 1047–1056.

Santonastaso, P., Pantano, M., Panarotto, L., & Silvestri, A. (1991). A follow-up study on anorexia nervosa: Clinical features and diagnostic outcome. *European Psychiatry, 6,* 177–185.

Schwalberg, M. D., Barlow, D. H., Alger, S. A., & Howard, L. J. (1992). Comparison of bulimics, obese binge eaters, social phobics, and individuals with panic disorder on comorbidity across *DSM–III–R* anxiety disorders. *Journal of Abnormal Psychology, 101,* 675–681.

Siegel, M., Brisman, J., & Weinshel, M. (1988). *Surviving an eating disorder.* New York: Harper & Row.

Silberstein, L. R., Striegel-Moore, R. H., & Rodin, J. (1987). Feeling fat: A woman's shame. In H. B. Lewis (Ed.), *The role of shame in symptom formation* (pp. 89–108). Hillsdale, NJ: Lawrence Erlbaum Associates.

Simmons, R. G., & Blyth, D. A. (1987). *Moving into adolescence: The impact of pubertal change and school context.* New York: deGruyter.

Smith, D. E., Marcus, M. D., & Kaye, W. (1992). Cognitive behavioral treatment of obese binge eaters. *International Journal of Eating Disorders, 12,* 257–262.

Spitzer, R. L., Devlin, M., Walsh, B. T., Hasin, D., Wing, R., Marcus, M., Stunkard, A. J., Wadden, T., Yanovski, S., Agras, W. S., Mitchell, J., & Nonas, C. (1991). Binge eating disorder: To be or not to be in *DSM–IV. International Journal of Eating Disorders, 10,* 627–629.

Spitzer, R. L., Devlin, M. J., Walsh, B. T., Hasin, D., Wing, R. R., Marcus, M. D., Stunkard, A., Wadden, T. A., Yanovski, S., Agras, W. S., Mitchell, J., & Nonas, C. (1992). Binge eating disorder: A multisite field trial for the diagnostic criteria. *International Journal of Eating Disorders, 11,* 191–203.

Spitzer, R. L., Yanovski, S., Wadden, T., Wing, R., Marcus, M. D., Stunkard, A., Devlin, M. J., Mitchell, J., Hasin, D., & Horne, R. L. (1993). Binge eating disorder: Its further validation in a multisite trial. *International Journal of Eating Disorders, 13,* 137–153.

Stein, A., & Fairburn, C. (1989). Children of mothers with bulimia nervosa. *British Medical Journal, 299,* 777–778.

Steiner-Adair, C. (1986). The body politic: Normal female adolescent development and the development of eating disorders. *Journal of the American Academy of Psychoanalysis, 14,* 95–114.

Stewart, D. E. (1992). Reproductive functions in eating disorders. *Annals of Medicine, 24,* 287–291.

Striegel-Moore, R. H. (1993). Etiology of binge eating: A developmental perspective. In C. G. Fairburn & G. T. Wilson (Eds.), *Binge eating: Nature, assessment, and treatment* (pp. 144–172). New York: Guilford.

Striegel-Moore, R. H., Nicholson, T. J., & Tamborlane, W. V. (1992). Prevalence of eating disorder symptoms in preadolescent and adolescent girls with IDDM. *Diabetes Care, 15,* 1361–1368.

Striegel-Moore, R. H., Schreiber, G., Pike, K. M., Wilfley, D. E., & Rodin, R. (1995). Drive for thinness in black and white preadolescent girls: The NHLBI growth and health study. *International Journal of Eating Disorders, 18,* 59–69.

Striegel-Moore, R. H., Silberstein, L. R., & Rodin, J. (1986). Toward an understanding of risk factors for bulimia. *American Psychologist, 41,* 246–263.

Striegel-Moore, R. H., Silberstein, L. R., & Rodin, J. (1993). The social self in bulimia nervosa: Public self-consciousness, social anxiety, and perceived fraudulence. *Journal of Abnormal Psychology, 102,* 297–303.

Strober, M., & Humphrey, L. L. (1987). Familial contributions to the etiology and course of anorexia nervosa and bulimia. *Journal of Consulting and Clinical Psychology, 55,* 654–659.

Strober, M., & Yager, J. (1985). A developmental perspective on the treatment of anorexia nervosa in adolescents. In D. M. Garner & P. E. Garfinkel (Eds.), *Anorexia nervosa & bulimia* (pp. 363–390). New York: Guilford.

Stunkard, A. J. (1959). Eating patterns and obesity. *Psychiatric Quarterly, 33,* 284–295.

Stunkard, A. J., & Wadden, T. A. (1992). Psychological aspects of severe obesity. *American Journal of Clinical Nutrition, 55,* 524S–532S.

Telch, C. F., Agras, W. S., Rossiter, E. M., Wilfley, D., & Kenardy, J. (1990). Group cognitive–behavioral treatment for the nonpurging bulimic: An initial evaluation. *Journal of Consulting and Clinical Psychology, 58,* 629–635.

Thelen, M. H., Lawrence, C. M., & Powell, A. L. (1992). Body image, weight control, and eating disorders among children. In J. Crowther, D. Tennenbaum, S. Hobfoll, M. P. Stephens (Eds.), *The etiology of bulimia nervosa: The individual and familial context* (pp. 81–102). Washington, DC: Hemisphere.

Van Buren, D. J., & Williamson, D. A. (1988). Marital relationships and conflict resolution skills of bulimics. *International Journal of Eating Disorders, 7,* 735–741.

Van den Broucke, S., & Vandereycken, W. (1989). Eating disorders in married patients: Theory and therapy. In W. Vandereycken, E. Kog, & J. Vanderlinden (Eds.), *The family approach to eating disorders* (pp. 333–346). New York: PMA.

Walsh, B. T., Hadigan, C. M., Devlin, M. J., Gladis, M., & Roose, S. P. (1991). Long-term outcome of antidepressant treatment for bulimia nervosa. *American Journal of Psychiatry, 148,* 1206–1212.

Wilfley, D. E. (1989). *Interpersonal analyses of bulimia: Normal-weight and obese.* Unpublished doctoral dissertation, University of Missouri, Columbia.

Wilfley, D. E., Agras, W. S., Telch, C. F., Rossiter, E. M., Schneider, J. A., Cole, A. G., Sifford, L., & Raeburn, S. D. (1993). Group cognitive–behavioral therapy and group interpersonal psychotherapy for the nonpurging bulimic: A controlled comparison. *Journal of Consulting and Clinical Psychology, 61,* 296–305.

Wilfley, D. E., Grilo, C. M., & Rodin, J. (in press). Group psychotherapy for the treatment of bulimia nervosa and binge eating disorder: Research and clinical methods. In J. Spira (Ed.), *Group psychotherapy for the medically ill.* New York: Guilford.

Wilson, G. T. (1994). Behavioral treatment of obesity: Thirty years and counting. *Advances in Behavior Research and Therapy, 16,* 31–75.

Wilson, G. T., Eldredge, K. L., Smith, D., & Niles, B. (1991). Cognitive–behavioral treatment with and without response prevention for bulimia. *Behaviour Research and Therapy, 29,* 575–583.

Wilson, G. T., & Fairburn, C. G. (1993). Cognitive treatments for eating disorders. *Journal of Consulting and Clinical Psychology, 61,* 261–269.

Wilson, G. T., & Pike, K. M. (1993). Eating disorders. In D. H. Barlow (Ed.), *The clinical handbook of psychological disorders* (2nd ed.; pp. 278–317). New York: Guilford.

Yanovski, S. Z. (1993). Binge eating disorder: Current knowledge and future directions. *Obesity Research, 1,* 305–324.

Yanovski, S. Z., Nelson, J. E., Dubbert, B. K., & Spitzer, R. L. (in press). Binge eating is associated with psychiatric co-morbidity in the obese. *American Journal of Psychiatry.*

16

Conclusions, Implications, and Future Directions

Michael Levine
Linda Smolak
Ruth Striegel-Moore

At the 1988 International Conference on Eating Disorders of the National Anorexic Aid Society, Dr. Christopher Fairburn delivered a keynote address on the epidemiology of eating disorders (Fairburn, 1988). Essentially, Fairburn criticized psychologists and psychiatrists for rushing to conduct epidemiological research (e.g., prevalence surveys) without taking the time and effort to master a number of basic principles of theory and methodology in the field of epidemiology. The deeper message was the need for eating disorders specialists to make a "developmental transition" from the first blush of defining and calling attention to an important set of psychopathologies toward a long-term commitment to painstaking research on causal models, effective treatments, and successful prevention.

This book is intended to be a "developmental" step in that direction with regard to the intersection between the clinical psychology of eating disorders and developmental psychology, developmental psychopathology, biopsychosocial psychiatry, and community psychology. As implied in several places throughout this volume (e.g., Smolak & Striegel-Moore, chapter 8, this volume), interest in developmental factors is not new to the field of eating disorders (Blinder & Chao, 1994; Crisp, 1980; Striegel-Moore, Silberstein, & Rodin, 1986). In fact, one might say that such interest has grown up alongside the burgeoning of theory and research on eating disorders that has occurred in the past 25 years. The founding mother of the discipline, Bruch (1973), offered her insights into the role of puberty and the negative effects of insensitive, intrusive mother–daughter interactions during various phases of development. Disturbances in family structures and family dynamics relevant to crucial issues of identity, self-esteem, affect regulation, and so forth have long been part of influential theories and research (Minuchin, Rosman, & Baker, 1978; Selvini-Palazzoli, 1974; Stunkard, 1959; see also Connors, chapter 12, this volume). The important multidimensional models of the 1980s (Garfinkel & Garner, 1982; Johnson & Connors, 1987) deserve recognition and continued study, in part for their attention to (a) the role of numerous developmental factors in the predisposition to and precipitation of anorexia nervosa and bulimia nervosa; and (b) to the way in which a multiple risk factor concept implies the existence of multiple developmental pathways to similar outcomes. Finally, the entry of accomplished developmental psychologist Brooks-Gunn (e.g., Attie & Brooks-Gunn, 1989, 1992; Attie, Brooks-Gunn, & Petersen, 1990; Brooks-Gunn, Attie, Burrow, Rosso, & Warren, 1989) into the field has inaugurated a new era characterized by clearer application of developmental theories and methodologies to the study of eating disorders and of related phenomena such as body image.

From the perspective of this brief and highly selective historical analysis, where is the field now, and what are some important considerations for development of theory and research? In this concluding chapter we attempt to address these daunting questions by considering two major sets of problems elucidated by the contributors to this volume. Where possible, findings are incorporated; however, the emphasis is on what remains to be studied and understood within "Fairburn's challenge" as it applies to the developmental psychopathology of eating disorders.

PROBLEM SET 1: WHERE TO FOCUS ETIOLOGICAL AND PREVENTION RESEARCH

Continuity and the Spectrum Model of Disordered Eating

Developmental psychopathology emphasizes the close relationship between normal and abnormal development. As acknowledged by various contributors to this volume (Connors, chapter 12; Killen, chapter 13; Rosen, chapter 1; Shisslak, Crago, Estes, & Gray, chapter 14; Smolak, chapter 2; Smolak & Striegel-Moore, chapter 8), there appears to be a continuum ranging from the psychological phenomena that characterize the normative development of White girls in North America and Britain during late childhood and adolescence—physical appearance as a key component of self-schema, slender ideal body image, weight and shape concerns, and weight management behaviors—through to the symptomatology of anorexia nervosa, bulimia nervosa, and eating disorers not otherwise specified (Gordon, 1990; Hill, 1993; Levine & Smolak, 1992; Polivy & Herman, 1987; Striegel-Moore et al., 1986).

From a static perspective, the continuum model encourages further cross-sectional comparisons of girls or women at different points along the continuum, such as those by Hesse-Biber (1989) and by Levine, Smolak, Moodey, Shuman, and Hessen (1994). Although such cross-sectional data need to be interpreted cautiously (Smolak, chapter 2, this volume), this type of research should help to identify both the risk factors that apply generally (e.g., parental messages about the importance of slenderness or the achievement orientation within upwardly mobile classes) and risk factors that are specific to the extremes of the continuum (e.g., simultaneity of weight gain in puberty and involvement with dating coupled with peer support for body dissatisfaction and weight loss; Levine et al., 1994). Cross-sectional analyses of the continuum might also point to protective factors such as aspects of social support from parents or peers (Berndt & Hestenes, chapter 4, this volume), coping skills, cognitive development, or temperament, which distinguish individuals with no or few weight and shape concerns from those with subthreshold or clinical eating disorders (see Rosen, chapter 1, this volume).

From a process-oriented perspective, the notion of a developmental continuum points directly to the need for longitudinal studies (Smolak, chapter 2, this volume). One useful focus of this research is the divergence of paths originating from similar intermediate points (developmental turning points?) such as a thinness schema in late childhood or negative body image and restrictive dieting in early adolescence (Attie & Brooks-Gunn, 1989; Smolak & Levine, 1994a, 1994b). Longitudinal studies of (initially) nonclinical populations have begun to appear more frequently in the literature (See Smolak & Levine, chapter 9, this volume, Table 9.3; Striegel-Moore, Silberstein, Frensch, & Rodin, 1989). We applaud this trend. Longitudinal research has its own important limitations, but the ability of this design to illuminate steps (stages) in the paths toward various types of disordered eating makes it potentially very informative about factors that will help direct the focus and timing of primary and secondary prevention (see Rutter, 1994; Smolak, chapter 2, this volume; Smolak & Levine, chapter 9, this volume; Smolak & Levine, 1994a; Smolak, Levine, & Gralen, 1993). At this time research points to dieting, weight concerns, negative body image, and being teased about one's size and weight as important foci of prevention efforts in middle school students (Attie & Brooks-Gunn, 1989; Cattarin & Thompson, 1994; Killen et al., 1993), but more work is needed to identify precursors and paths, particularly in the 9 to 13 age range. By contrast, effective programs for the prevention of cigarette smoking rely not only on guidance from the social psychology of attitude change and from cognitive social learning theories (see Killen, chapter 13, this volume), they also benefit from developmental research that outlines at least some of the paths to initiation of cigarette smoking and other drug use (see Flay, 1985, for a review).

The Conundrum of Primary Prevention

Shisslak and colleagues (chapter 14, this volume; Shisslak & Crago, 1994) have presented several helpful reviews of the scant literature on the primary prevention of eating disorders. Most of the prevention programs that have been systematically evaluated are based on the continuum notion in that they seek to head off disordered eating by promoting the following: resistance of general sociocultural pressures for thinness; healthy eating; elimination of unnecessary, calorie-restrictive dieting; and development of life skills such as problem-solving and decision-making (Killen, chapter 13, this volume; Shisslak et al., chapter 14, this volume). We find it noteworthy that, in contrast to Shisslak et al.'s optimistic conclusions, those programs for adolescents that have been *least successful* in changing attitudes and behavior are precisely those that are the *most rigorous* in their attention to theory of prevention, development of multiple lessons, individualizing of some behavior change plans, and systematic evaluation of outcome with standardized measures (Killen, chapter 13, this volume; Killen et al., 1993; Moriarty, Shore, & Maxim, 1990; Paxton, 1993; Rosen, 1989). It is hard to imagine someone better placed (by virtue of past experience, skill, and institutional resources) than Joel Killen to apply theory, practice, and research methodology from previous work on the primary prevention of substance abuse and other unhealthy behavior (see Hansen, 1992, for a review). Nevertheless, as described in Chapter 13, the Stanford group's careful outcome study of an intensive primary prevention program for middle school girls yielded very disappointing results, even in the realm of increasing knowledge (Killen et al., 1993).

This is a troubling conclusion and difficult admission for at least one of us, given that he is the author of a fairly popular continuum-based curriculum guide for the prevention of eating disorders in middle and high school students (Levine & Hill, 1991). There are, of course, various explanations for the negative results. As noted by Striegel-Moore (1992), multidimensional (multiple pathway) models of disordered eating "suggest that primary prevention needs to encompass multiple levels of intervention and, within each level, to target numerous variables" (p. 218). Prevention programs described to date have not addressed important social learning influences from parents (Desmond, Price, Gray, & O'Connell, 1986; Levine & Smolak, 1992; Smolak & Levine, 1994a). Similarly, the programs aimed at middle and high school students have not incorporated lessons sensitive either to the special cognitive and emotional roles of peers in the lives of adolescents or to the decline in perceived support from parents (Berndt & Hestenes, chapter 4, this volume; Smolak & Levine, chapter 9, this volume). Curricular prevention efforts have also been hampered by the lack of a developmental assessment instrument with which to match classroom prevention strategies to different risk groups. Finally, Piran (1995) has presented some preliminary data suggesting that feminist techniques for helping students to construct actual useful knowledge, skills, and support may be more effective than prepackaged knowledge and skills.

Another intriguing possibility is that primary prevention efforts aimed at girls and boys aged 11 to 17 are both too late and too early to have a significant impact on drive for thinness, fear of fat, the centrality of appearance for female self-definition, and so forth. It may be necessary to direct prevention efforts either toward elementary school children (Smolak & Levine, 1994b; Smolak, Levine, & Schermer, 1995; but see Killen, chapter 13, this volume) or toward older, college-aged adolescents (Huon, 1994; Shisslak et al., chapter 14, this volume). A significant minority of fourth and fifth graders may endorse questionnaire items indicative of a "dieting mentality" or dieting behavior (Gustafson-Larson & Terry, 1992; Smolak & Levine, 1994b), but it is unlikely that the vast majority of elementary school children have well-developed schema concerning thinness (Smolak & Levine, 1994b). It is also unlikely that they have either the cognitive ability or the motivation (grounded in intense objective self-awareness; Ewell, Smith, Karmel, & Hart, chapter 5, this volume) to distinguish between "my mind" and "my body" in ways that motivate rigid and sustained self-control toward self-defined weight-loss goals (Damon & Hart, 1988). This latter statement is, of course, just as speculative as it is intuitively appealing. It points to the need for research concerning the nature of "actual," "ideal," and "ought" self-representations in childhood and early adolescence as well as the emotional and motivational impact of disparities between the former and the latter two (Ewell et al., chapter 5, this volume). In addition, at the younger ages there is a better chance that the authority and social support of parents, teachers, and other adults can outweigh the influence of peers (Berndt & Hestenes, chapter 4, this volume).

College-aged adolescents and young adults are hardly immune to peer influences (including teasing and appearance concerns related to sexuality) and other pressures (e.g., media) that might contribute to or reinforce the groundwork for eating disorders (Levine & Smolak, chapter 10, this volume; Levine & Smolak, 1992; Smolak, 1993; Striegel-Moore et al., 1989). However, many individuals in the older group (aged 18 and over) will have developed the cognitive structures (formal operations) necessary to contemplate issues such as alternatives to institutionalized forms of weightism and the social construction of gender roles (Smolak, 1993). Moreover, by young adulthood many are likely to have developed the cognitive–emotional capacity to integrate such abstract questioning with negative personal memories and feelings about the "negative body image–dieting–bingeing–weight fluctuation" cycle. In other words, a significant number of college-aged women may be both "fed up" with the "normative discontent" and psychologically prepared to receive psychoeducational messages that discourage dieting and reconfigure body image in the direction of self-acceptance (Huon, 1994).

Discontinuity and Comorbidity

As appealing as the spectrum notion is, we believe that several types of data reviewed in this book constitute a call for future research to consider more carefully theory and research concerning the distinctions—the *discontinuities*—between normative weight and shape concerns and frank eating disorders. Although Killen et al. (chapter 13, this volume) define risk for eating disorders on a continuous scale labeled "Weight Concerns," the possibility of discontinuity is inherent in their conclusions about the desirability of focusing primary prevention efforts (studies, money, time) on "high-risk" female adolescents. However, in this volume it is Connors (chapter 12) whio speaks most clearly to the puzzling tension between continuity and discontinuity. We appreciate not only her thorough review of developmental vulnerabilities for eating disorders, but also her willingness to try to revise a popular multidimensional model (Johnson & Connors, 1987) in favor of a two-component model that highlights more clearly developmental variables (see Fig. 12.1, p. 299).

Connors' chapter makes an excellent case that developmental psychopathologists need to do more than incorporate a sociocultural model of risk for body dissatisfaction. They also need to acknowledge the role of deficits or limitations in self-representation, theories of self (see Ewell et al., chapter 5, this volume), self-regulation, and interpersonal regulation in distinguishing the paths leading toward serious eating disorders (see also Levine & Smolak, 1992; Polivy & Herman, 1987; Striegel-Moore, 1993). We encourage Connors to add a third major factor. Given the tremendous gender difference in risk for eating disorders (Striegel-Moore et al., 1986), and given the general differences between males and females in the meaning of body weight and shape and of weight management (Rodin, Silberstein, & Striegel-Moore, 1985), it seems likely that gender schemas (Worrell & Todd, chapter 6, this volume) influence both of the major components of disordered eating postulated by Connors' model. Smolak and Striegel-Moore (chapter 8, this volume) propose that the tight intertwining of appearance concerns, drive for thinness, and self-esteem may distinguish in a qualitative manner the self-representations and self-theories (Ewell et al., chapter 5, this volume) of females with eating disorders from those with less clinically significant body image issues and eating problems.

There are three implications (and none of them are pleasant) of Connors' model for research on etiology and for development of effective primary prevention programs. First, developmental psychopathologists need to become more familiar with the established comorbidity between eating disorders and affective disorders (Strober & Katz, 1988), anxiety disorders (Keery, 1995), substance abuse (Wilson, 1991), and personality disorders (Johnson, 1991). These associations need not imply either that such relationships are unique to eating disorders (see, e.g., Brown & Barlow's, 1992, discussion of anxiety disorders and comorbidity), or that eating disorders are really a *form fruste* of some other disorder. Having rejected such simplistic and unwarranted conclusions (see, e.g., Wilson, 1991), psychologists can proceed to confront another very difficult challenge. Specifically, there is a need for theories and research designs that enable longitudinal assessment of (a) multiple pathological outcomes and (b) underlying (molar) structures and behavioral manifestations (molecular stabilities and changes) pertaining to the "thinness schema," "gender schema," and "self-regulatory difficulties" (see Rosen, chapter 1, this volume; Smolak, chapter 2, this volume). Connors' model (and Rende's review in this volume of genetic liability for psychopathology) suggests that working with a population at risk because of trauma (e.g., sexual abuse), parental psychopathology (e.g., depression) or biological predisposition (temperament) may maximize the chance that this type of longitudinal study will be informative.

Ideally, the study period in the proposed longitudinal assessments should cover at least one significant developmental transition. This would increase the probability of exposing important intraindividual continuities and discontinuities in the emergence, maintenance, and reorganization or disorganization of the characteristics being studied (Rosen, chapter 1, this volume; Smolak & Levine, chapter 9, this volume; see also Attie & Brooks-Gunn, 1992; Smolak & Levine, 1994a). As implied in Isabella's work on maternal sensitivity and the nature of attachment at the end of the first year (chapter 7, this volume), the study of transitions might also reveal the effects of *changes* in the behavior of parents (e.g., a change from father's doting support to his pressure for academic success) on an adolescent girl's self-representations (e.g., of body image or gender schema; Smolak & Striegel-Moore, chapter 8, this volume; see also Maine, 1991). Ideally, the cohorts would be followed through both the early and late adolescent periods, given the possibility of their differential significance for anorexia nervosa and bulimia nervosa (Smolak & Levine, 1993; Smolak & Striegel-Moore, chapter 8, this volume). Recent research by Graber, Brooks-Gunn, Paikoff, and Warren (1995) has shown that such ambitious longitudinal projects are feasible and informative.

At the heart of this complex enterprise is the need for advances in assessment and theory concerning the ways in which cognitive, social, and emotional development are organized to shape qualitiative differences in the manifestations of disordered eating (and its precursors) at various stages of development (Rosen, chapter 1, this volume; Smolak, chapter 2, this volume; Smolak & Levine, 1994a). As Smolak observes, significant inferences about causality are *"always* rooted in theory and design, not in a statistical test per se" (p. 36). The distinctions offered by Ewell et al. (chapter 5, this volume, Table 5.1, p. 112) constitute an excellent first step toward applying developmental theory and methodology to the assessment of molar changes in self-understanding over the childhood and adolescent years.

The second implication concerns prevention. School-based or context-based primary prevention programs may have a slight but significant and sustained impact on negative body image, weight preoccupation, and dieting (see, e.g., Huon, 1994). As argued by Shisslak et al. (chapter 14, this volume), this effect may be enhanced by close attention to the different developmental challenges that children and adolescents face at different ages, and by use of techniques (e.g., life skills training) and teaching tools (e.g., focus groups) that increase a girl's self-esteem and assertive "voice" (see, e.g., Piran, 1995; Porter, Morrell, & Moriarty, 1986). However, it is inconceivable that health curricula or even a dedicated consultant to a ballet company or gymnastic team could do what is necessary to obviate the forces of discontinuity, for example, parental psychopathology, sexual abuse, dysfunctional family dynamics, or genetic vulnerability to affective instability. There is general agreement among several authors in this volume (Connors, chapter 12; Pike & Wilfley, chapter 15; Smolak & Levine, chapter 9) that eating disorders constitute a comprehensible adaptation to a complex combination of intrapsychic predispositions, developmental challenges, family factors, and sociocultural conceptions of femininity. If Connors' model is correct, then prevention of eating disorders will require large-scale social changes necessary for the protection and encouragement of children, the education and support of parents, an increase in respect for women, an increase in acceptance of diversity in body shape and weight, and so forth (Levine, 1994; Maine, 1991; Striegel-Moore, 1992; Wolf, 1991). We suggest that these sweeping changes may require a feminist sensibility coupled with a developmental psychology of sociopolitical activism in adulthood.

Finally, Connors' model is quite consistent with Pike and Wilfley's observations (chapter 15, this volume) about the potential value of a combination of cognitive behavioral therapy (CBT) and interpersonal psychotherapy (IPT) in the treatment of various eating disorders. CBT would address the factors contributing to and perpetuating negative body image, weight preoccupation, dieting behavior, and binge eating (see Connors, chapter 12, this volume, Fig. 12.1, p. 299), whereas IPT would address at least some aspects of self-regulatory and interpersonal deficits. The overlap is not perfect, but then neither are the two therapies consistently or completely effective (Pike & Wilfley, chapter 15, this volume). Nevertheless, there is a striking similarity between Connors' (chapter 12, this volume) emphasis on self-regulatory deficits, sometimes arising within and sustained by dysfunctional relationships, and

Pike and Wilfley's (chapter 15, this volume) call for attention, across disorders and across developmental stages, to "self in the social context." Future theory and practice needs to integrate this emphasis with a specification of the aspects of the development of self (see Ewell et al., chapter 5, this volume), including gender schema (Worrell & Todd, chapter 6, this volume), that might influence both the nature of the eating disorders and the adolescent's or adult's receptivity to different treatment approaches to "self in social context." In this regard Ewell et al. direct attention to promising research by Higgins, Vookles, and Tykocinski (1992) which suggests that anorexic symptoms in undergraduates are related to a disparity between the "actual" and "ought" self-representations, whereas bulimic symptoms are related to a disparity between "actual" and "ideal" self-representations.

PROBLEM SET 2: CAREFUL ATTENTION TO RESEARCH FINDINGS

Two of us (ML and RSM) attend quite a few so-called "eating disorder conferences." During the presentations, over lunch, and in the halls we hear a lot of material that purports to incorporate knowledge about the developmental psychology or developmental psychopathology of eating disorders. Although we have made no formal assessment of this phenomenon, Table 16.1 lists a sample of statements that are made so often and without hesitation or qualification that they have become a sort of comforting gospel, particularly among those involved in primary pre-

TABLE 16.1
Six Questionable Statements Commonly Expressed as "Gospel" in the Field of Eating Disorders

- Sexual abuse/insecure attachment in infancy/enmeshed or achievement-oriented families (pick one) *cause* eating disorders.
- Adolescent girls are at greater risk for eating disorders because they are more sensitive to interpersonal rejection and loss of social support.
- Early adolescence is a risk period for eating disorders because pubertal girls are subject to great pressures for gender-role intensification, including an emphasis on personal appearance.
- Early maturity is a risk factor for disordered eating in late adolescence and early adulthood.
- "Women's magazines" and other media present images of slender beauty which have an immediate and long-term (cumulative) negative effect on the body image of most girls and women. Therefore media glorifications of slenderness play an important role in the development of eating disorders.
- Black girls and women hardly ever develop eating disorders because their culture is more accepting of heavy women; this demonstrates that a change in culture would prevent eating disorders.

vention. The purpose of this list and of our critical evaluation of the statements is not to demonstrate our superiority because we somehow know the "real" answers. Rather, our purpose is to call attention to the contributions in this book that remind us—all of us—of the need for further research and for careful attention to the research findings available (see Smolak, chapter 2, this volume; Smolak & Striegel-Moore, chapter 8, this volume).

Factor X Causes Pathological Outcome Y. Familiarity with the basic principles of developmental psychopathology (Rosen, chapter 1, this volume; Smolak & Levine, 1994a; Sroufe, 1989) should engender immediate skepticism about the validity of this type of declaration. Such statements not only ignore the plasticity of development and the transactional nature of normal and abnormal development, they are not supported by a careful evaluation of data. For example, several contributors to this volume (Connors, chapter 1; Worrell & Todd, chapter 6; see also Connors & Morse, 1993) review data that contradict the existence of a special etiological connection between childhood sexual abuse and eating disorders. Childhood sexual abuse is better understood as a general but not sufficient risk factor for various forms of psychopathology (Browne & Finkelhor, 1986). As noted by Smolak and Striegel-Moore (chapter 8, this volume), the presence and nature of pathological long-term outcomes appears to be determined by complex interactions among this risk factor, continuities and discontinuities in various other personal characteristics (positive and negative), and contextual influences (positive and negative). This caveat in no way denies the importance of childhood sexual abuse in a significant minority of cases of disordered eating. There is little doubt that such abuse constitutes an important step in some paths toward eating disorders (Smolak, Levine, & Sullins, 1990), and when issues surrounding abuse arise during the course of therapy they are very relevant to successful treatment (Kearney-Cooke & Striegel-Moore, 1994; Wooley & Kearney-Cooke, 1986).

Similar considerations and conclusions apply in evaluating the effects of insecure attachments between parents and children (Isabella, chapter 7, this volume) and of dysfunctional family systems (Waller & Calam, 1994). Rende (chapter 3, this volume) reviews research (e.g., Kendler et al., 1991) that suggests that genetic liability contributes to a broad spectrum of eating disorders. However, it is noteworthy that Rende's review also emphasizes how quantitative behavior genetics research has consistently demonstrated that a substantial amount of individual difference in various forms of normal and abnormal behavior can be explained by nonshared environmental factors. This set of factors probably includes *within-family* variation in the behavior of adults toward, and in response to, their children (Plomin, 1990). As noted by Rosen (chapter 1, this volume) and Smolak (chapter 2, this volume), developmental psychopathology emphasizes reciprocal (and potentially discontinuous) transactions between individuals and family members or other important social influences such as coaches or dance instructors. We believe that family systems researchers and the many professionals influenced by their work have paid too little attention to the unique patterns of perceptions and responses evoked and sustained by vulnerable children and vulnerable adults as they create nonshared environments for each other.

Female Development and Sociability. The presumed "social sensitivity" of females in general, and of early adolescent girls in particular may have considerable power as a prescriptive gender stereotype (Worrell & Todd, chapter 6, this volume). Nevertheless, several contributors to this volume encourage a certain degree of skepticism about the foundation for this common, essentialist contention. Drawing on the metanalytic work of Feingold (1994), Ewell et al. (chapter 5, this volume) state that "it seems *reasonable* that adolescent girls may be more oriented toward thinking of themselves in terms of social relationships than are boys" (p. 122; italics added). Yet, the thrust of their review is how powerfully concerns about social acceptance shape the self-understanding of most adolescents, male or female. The literature review by Berndt and Hestenes (chapter 4, this volume) does not support the conclusion that girls in general and adolescent girls in particular are more likely than boys to be negatively affected by a reduction in parental support.

Challenges to the belief that girls are more socially oriented or socially sensitive than boys in no way minimizes the clinical significance of social anxiety or public self-consciousness for the etiology and treatment of eating disorders (Striegel-Moore, Silberstein, & Rodin, 1993). Similarly, this critique does not reduce the significance (for etiology or for prevention) of research that points to the potentially damaging effects on adolescent girls and women of peer or other social pressures to define themselves in terms of a pleasing physical appearance, that is, slenderness (Ewell et al., chapter 5, this volume; Levine & Smolak, chapter 10, this volume; Smolak & Striegel-Moore, chapter 8, this volume; Worrell & Todd, chapter 6, this volume). What needs to be kept in mind is that the research data raise serious doubts about the assumption that females are more "social," and thus more susceptible to social pressures, simply by virtue of being born and raised (constructed) as females (Smolak & Striegel-Moore, chapter 8, this volume; Worrell & Todd, chapter 6, this volume).

Gender-Role Intensification. Worrell and Todd (chapter 6, this volume) argue that, relative to early adolescence, the late adolescent transition is more likely to intensify awareness of the "gendered self."

Their review is cause, at the very least, for a healthy skepticism about the assumption that the increase in risk for eating disorders associated with early adolescence is directly attributable to a marked upsurge during that period of girls' concern about gender identity.

Early Maturity. Researchers and theorists have long believed that puberty, especially early puberty, plays a special role in the development of eating disorders, particularly of anorexia nervosa. Research does confirm that specific forms of body dissatisfaction and dieting do indeed increase as girls go through puberty (Smolak & Levine, chapter 9, this volume). Thus, girls who are early maturers begin dieting and engaging in other weight management behaviors sooner than their later developing peers.

What is less clear is whether these early maturing girls are permanently at greater risk for eating problems. The data linking maturational timing and later eating problems are mixed. More recent evidence suggests that the relationship may be indirect, mediated, for example, by adiposity (Graber et al., 1995), teasing (Cattarin & Thompson, 1994), or co-occurrence with normative stressors (Smolak et al., 1993). Such findings are a reminder of the flexible and transactional nature of development (Rosen, chapter 1, this volume). They also serve to caution against a long-standing tendency to pathologize normal female reproductive development and functioning (Tavris, 1992).

Effects of the Media. Many highly regarded experts on eating disorders believe that exposure to media images of slenderness constitutes one important risk factor for the spectrum of eating disorders (see, e.g., Andersen & DiDomenico, 1992; Garfinkel & Garner, 1982). The conviction that these images do much more than passively reflect dominant cultural values is seen in the fact that, as noted above, most curricula for prevention of eating disorders include lessons on analysis of and resistance to media messages (see, e.g., Killen et al., 1993; Levine & Hill, 1991; Paxton, 1993).

As demonstrated in the review by Levine and Smolak (chapter 10, this volume), there is a great deal yet to be learned about the ways in which the multitude of media images of slenderness and accompanying articles on diet, exercise, and so forth influence girls and women. For example, exposure to slender models appears to have little immediate effect on the body images of adolescent girls or college-aged women unless these individuals already have significant weight and shape concerns or frank eating disorders.

With respect to the cumulative effect of media, a study by Stice, Schupak-Neuberg, Shaw, and Stein (1994) offers some preliminary evidence for a direct connection between amount of media exposure during the previous month and scores on the Eating Attitudes Test

(EAT). Other studies reviewed by Levine and Smolak (chapter 10, this volume) point to the importance of the transaction between an adolescent girl's motives for using media and the nature of media selected. In a study just completed, Meade and Levine (1995) administered media use surveys, a measure of weightist prejudice, and the child version of the Eating Attitudes Test (ChEAT; Maloney, McGuire, Daniels, & Specker, 1989) to 355 middle school girls. The vast majority of the sample were White and from working-class and middle-class backgrounds. The multiple regression analysis (which accounted for 34.5% of the variation in ChEAT scores) yielded no significant main effect for amount of media use (or magazine use). Instead, this analysis pointed to the importance of weightist prejudice and motives for self-evaluation and self-improvement as significant predictors of disordered eating in middle school girls.

Replication and extension of this research is certainly necessary before firm conclusions are reached. Nevertheless, it appears that (a) exposure to media messages about the multidimensional importance of slenderness is indeed very likely a risk factor for disordered eating; and (b) the impact of this exposure should be conceptualized within the transactional perspective emphasized by developmental psychopathology. In this regard the work of two academic researchers in the area of marketing, Martin and Kennedy (1994a, 1994b), is highly recommended for its attention to the role of social comparison processes in the effects of media on young girls. From the transactional perspective, the context of that media use also appears to be very important. For example, Levine, Smolak, and Hayden (1994) found very high ChEAT scores in a subgroup of White middle school girls who reported both that magazine articles and advertisements greatly influenced their conception of the ideal body shape and how to get it, and that their peers and their parents were also highly "invested in" thinness.

African American Girls and Disordered Eating. Striegel-Moore and Smolak (chapter 11, this volume) carefully review the existing literature on the prevalence of eating disorders and components of disordered eating (e.g., body image concerns) in African American girls and women. Their conclusions are worth repeating, given the common belief among eating disorder professionals we know that the "African American community [sic]" contains factors that protect against eating disorders. As of this writing, (a) there are no community-based data on the prevalence of anorexia nervosa, bulimia nervosa, or eating disorders not otherwise specified for the African American community; (b) binge eating and other components of bulimia seem to be at least as common in female Black adults and college students as in White adults and students; and (c) Black women enrolled in weight-loss programs are just as likely as White women to have binge eating disorder.

Beyond these particular points, the issues concerning eating disorders become very complicated (Striegel-Moore & Smolak, chapter 8, this volume). Even though African American girls and women tend to be heavier in general than their White counterparts, they do report less direct pressure (e.g., teasing) to be slender, as well as less weight dissatisfaction, even when adiposity is statistically controlled. Nevertheless, despite a recent *Newsweek* article (Ingrassia, 1995) dramatically calling attention to the pride of Black girls versus the body dissatisfaction of White girls, evidence is very mixed for rates of dieting and for the commonly heard contention that Black adolescent girls have a more realistic and more rounded ideal body shape than do White adolescent girls. However, two things are clear. First, there is a need to develop culturally sensitive measures and techniques, including ways to overcome biases built into clinical referral and utilization systems. Second, it should be acknowledged that intragroup (including cohort) differences among Blacks and other ethnic minorities are at least as interesting as intergroup differences between Blacks and Whites.

FAIRBURN'S CHALLENGE: A FINAL WORD

As developmental psychology captures the fancy of more and more students and professionals interested in eating disorders, the following statement is sometimes heard: "Longitudinal designs will solve our problems in regard to demonstrating which phenomena cause eating disorders." Smolak (chapter 2, this volume) offers several cautions, however. First, longitudinal designs have limitations in regard to sampling and measurement. Second, various types of designs and statistical analyses are probably necessary to capture the blend of general influences, individuality, unidirectional causality, and reciprocality postulated by a developmental perspective. Third, statistical wizardry (e.g., in structural equation modeling) cannot substitute for elegance of theory and for clear relationships between data and a priori hypotheses. In general this volume makes it painfully clear that developmental psychopathology demands a great deal from its adherents. According to Rosen (chapter 1, this volume), Smolak (chapter 2, this volume; Smolak & Striegel-Moore, chapter 8, this volume), and Rende (chapter 3, this volume), methodological sophistication, a renewed interest in psychometry, a commitment to flexible theorizing, a multidisciplinary perspective, and a great deal of patience are core requirements for the "developmental psychopathology major." Nevertheless, advances in the understanding of depression (Rutter, Izard, & Read, 1986) have clearly demonstrated the exciting potential of the developmental perspective. Moreover, we believe that there is plenty of room for undergraduates, graduate students, and professionals alike to respond to Fairburn's challenge and to begin to fill in the many gaps in the current state of knowledge about the developmental psychopathology of eating disorders. At this point in our own development as researchers in the field, we do not understand how the implications of this work for the definition, treatment, and prevention of the eating disorders could be anything but enormous.

REFERENCES

Andersen, A. E., & DiDomenico, L. (1992). Diet vs. shape content of popular male and female magazines: A dose-response relationship to the incidence of eating disorders. *International Journal of Eating Disorders, 11,* 283–287.

Attie, I., & Brooks-Gunn, J. (1989). Development of eating problems in adolescent girls: A longitudinal study. *Developmental Psychology, 25,* 70–79.

Attie, I., & Brooks-Gunn, J. (1992). Developmental issues in the study of eating problems and disorders. In J. H. Crowther, D. L. Tennenbaum, S. E. Hobfoll, & M. A. P. Stephens (Eds.), *The etiology of bulimia nervosa: The individual and familial context* (pp. 35–58). Washington, DC: Hemisphere.

Attie, I., Brooks-Gunn, J., & Petersen, A. (1990). A developmental perspective on eating disorders and eating problems. In M. Lewis & S. M. Miller (Eds.), *Handbook of developmental psychopathology* (pp. 409–420). New York: Plenum.

Blinder, B. J., & Chao, K. H. (1994). Eating disorders: A historical perspective. In L. Alexander-Mott & D. B. Lumsden (Eds.), *Understanding eating disorders: Anorexia nervosa, bulimia nervosa, and obesity* (pp. 3–35). Washington, DC: Taylor & Francis.

Brooks-Gunn, J., Attie, I., Burrow, C., Rosso, J., & Warren, M. (1989). The impact of puberty on body and eating concerns in athletic and nonathletic contexts. *Journal of Early Adolescence, 9,* 269–290.

Brown, T. A., & Barlow, D. H. (1992). Comorbidity among anxiety disorders: Implications for treatment and *DSM–IV. Journal of Consulting and Clinical Psychology, 60,* 835–844.

Browne, A., & Finkelhor, D. (1986). Impact of child sexual abuse: A review of the research. *Psychological Bulletin, 99,* 66–77.

Bruch, H. (1973). *Eating disorders: Obesity, anorexia nervosa, and the person within.* New York: Basic Books.

Cattarin, J. A., & Thompson, J. K. (1994). A three-year longitudinal study of body image, eating disturbance, and general psychological functioning in adolescent females. *Eating Disorders: The Journal of Treatment & Prevention, 2,* 114–125.

Connors, M. E., & Morse, W. (1993). Sexual abuse and eating disorders: A review. *International Journal of Eating Disorders, 13,* 1–11.

Crisp, A. H. (1980). *Anorexia nervosa: Let me be.* Orlando, FL: Grune & Stratton.

Damon, W., & Hart, D. (1988). *Self-understanding in childhood and adolescence.* New York: Cambridge University Press.

Desmond, S. M., Price, J. H., Gray, N., & O'Connell, J. K. (1986). The etiology of adolescents' perceptions of their weight. *Journal of Youth and Adolescence, 15,* 461–474.

Fairburn, C. G. (1988, October). *Epidemiology: What we know and don't know.* Paper presented at the International Conference on Eating Disorders of the National Anorexic Aid Society, Columbus, OH.

Feingold, A. (1994). Gender differences in personality: A meta-analysis. *Psychological Bulletin, 116,* 429–456.

Flay, B. R. (1985). Psychosocial approaches to smoking prevention: A review of the findings. *Health Promotion, 4,* 449–488.

Garfinkel, P. E., & Garner, D. M. (1982). *Anorexia nervosa: A multidimensional perspective*. New York: Brunner/Mazel.

Gordon, R. A. (1990). *Anorexia and bulimia: Anatomy of a social epidemic*. Cambridge, MA: Blackwell.

Graber, J., Brooks-Gunn, J., Paikoff, R., & Warren, M. (1995). Prediction of eating problems: An eight year study of adolescent girls. *Developmental Psychology, 30,* 823–834.

Gustafson-Larson, A. M., & Terry, R. D. (1992). Weight-related behaviors and concerns of fourth-grade children. *Journal of the American Dietetic Association, 92,* 818–822.

Hansen, W. B. (1992). School-based substance abuse prevention: A review of the state of the art in curriculum, 1980–1990. *Health and Education Research, 7,* 403–430.

Hesse-Biber, S. (1989). Eating patterns and disorders in a college population: Are college women's eating problems a new phenomenon? *Sex Roles, 20,* 71–89.

Higgins, E. T., Vookles, J., & Tykocinski, O. (1992). Self and health: How "patterns" of self-beliefs predict types of emotional and physical problems. *Social Cognition, 10,* 125–150.

Hill, A. (1993). Pre-adolescent dieting: Implications for eating disorders. *International Review of Psychiatry, 5,* 87–100.

Huon, G. F. (1994). Towards the prevention of dieting-induced disorders: Modifying negative food- and body-related attitudes. *International Journal of Eating Disorders, 16,* 395–399.

Ingrassia, M. (1995, April 24). The body of the beholder. *Newsweek,* pp. 66–67.

Johnson, C. (1991). Treatment of eating-disordered patients with borderline and false-self/narcissistic disorders. In C. Johnson (Ed.), *Psychodynamic treatment of anorexia nervosa and bulimia* (pp. 165–193). New York: Guilford.

Johnson, C., & Connors, M. E. (1987). *The etiology and treatment of bulimia nervosa: A biopsychosocial perspective*. New York: Basic Books.

Kearney-Cooke, A., & Striegel-Moore, R. H. (1994). Treatment of child sexual abuse in anorexia nervosa and bulimia nervosa: A feminist psychodynamic aproach. *International Journal of Eating Disorders, 15,* 305–319.

Keery, H. (1995). *The comorbidity of eating disorders, anxiety disorders, and DSM–IV Cluster C personality disorders*. Unpublished honors thesis, Kenyon College, Gambier, OH.

Kendler, K., MacLean, C., Neale, M., Kessler, R., Heath, A., & Eaves, L. (1991). The genetic epidemiology of bulimia nervosa. *American Journal of Psychiatry, 148,* 1627–1637.

Killen, J. D., Taylor, C. B., Hammer, L. D., Litt, I., Wilson, D. M., Rich, T., Hayward, C., Simmonds, B., Kraemer, H., & Varady, A. (1993). An attempt to modify unhealthful eating attitudes and weight regulation practices of young girls. *International Journal of Eating Disorders, 13,* 369–384.

Levine, M. P. (1994). Beauty myth and the beast: What men can do and be to help prevent eating disorders. *Eating Disorders: The Journal of Treatment & Prevention, 2,* 101–113.

Levine, M. P., & Hill, L. (1991). *A five day lesson plan book on eating disorders: Grades 7–12*. Columbus, OH: National Eating Disorders Organization.

Levine, M. P., & Smolak, L. (1992). Toward a model of the developmental psychopathology of eating disorders: The example of early adolescence. In J. H. Crowther, D. L. Tennenbaum, S. E. Hobfoll, & M. A. P. Stephens (Eds.), *The etiology of bulimia nervosa: The individual and familial context* (pp. 59–80). Washington, DC: Hemisphere.

Levine, M. P., Smolak, L., & Hayden, H. (1994). The relation of sociocultural factors to eating attitudes and behaviors among middle school girls. *Journal of Early Adolescence, 14,* 472–491.

Levine, M. P., Smolak, L., Moodey, A., Shuman, M., & Hessen, L. (1994). Normative developmental challenges and dieting and eating disturbances in middle school girls. *International Journal of Eating Disorders, 15,* 11–20.

Maine, M. (1991). *Father hunger: Fathers, daughters and food.* Carlsbad, CA: Gurze Books.

Maloney, M., McGuire, J., Daniels, S., & Specker, B. (1989). Dieting behavior and eating attitudes in children. *Pediatrics, 84,* 482–489.

Martin, M. C., & Kennedy, P. F. (1994a). The measurement of social comparison to advertising models: A gender gap revealed. In J. A. Costa (Ed.), *Gender issues in consumer behavior* (pp. 104–124). Thousand Oaks, CA: Sage.

Martin, M. C., & Kennedy, P. F. (1994b). Social comparison and the beauty of advertising models: The role of motives for comparison. *Advances in Consumer Research, 21,* 365–371.

Meade, M., & Levine, M. P. (1995). *Relation of media use, motives for use, and weightist prejudice to eating disordered behavior in middle school girls.* Manuscript in preparation.

Minuchin, S., Rosman, B., & Baker, L. (1978). *Psychosomatic families: Anorexia nervosa in context.* Cambridge, MA: Harvard University Press.

Moriarty, D., Shore, R., & Maxim, N. (1990). Evaluation of an eating disorders curriculum. *Evaluation and Program Planning, 13,* 407–413.

Paxton, S. J. (1993). A prevention program for disturbed eating and body dissatisfaction in adolescent girls: A 1 year follow-up. *Health Education Research, 8,* 43–51.

Piran, N. (1995, January–March). What it takes for eating disorder prevention to make a difference. *Newsletter of the National Eating Disorders Organization, 18,* 1–2, 4–5, 10.

Plomin, R. (1990). *Nature and nurture: An introduction to human behavioral genetics.* Pacific Grove, CA: Brooks/Cole.

Polivy, J., & Herman, C. P. (1987). Diagnosis and treatment of normal eating. *Journal of Consulting and Clinical Psychology, 55,* 635–644.

Porter, J., Morrell, T., & Moriarty, D. (1986). Primary prevention of anorexia nervosa: Evaluation of a pilot project for early and pre-adolescents. *Canadian Association for Health, Physical Education and Recreation Journal, 52,* 21–26.

Rodin, J., Silberstein, L. R., & Striegel-Moore, R. H. (1985). Women and weight: A normative discontent. In T. B. Sonderegger (Ed.), *Nebraska Symposium on Motivation: Vol. 32. Psychology and gender* (pp. 267–307). Lincoln: University of Nebraska Press.

Rosen, J. C. (1989, April–June). Prevention of eating disorders. *Newsletter of the National Anorexic Aid Society, 12,* 1–3.

Rutter, M. (1994). Beyond longitudinal data: Causes, consequences, changes, and continuity. *Journal of Consulting and Clinical Psychology, 62,* 928–940.

Rutter, M., Izard, C. E., & Read, P. B. (Eds.). (1986). *Depression in young people: Developmental and clinical perspectives.* New York: Guilford.

Selvini-Palazzoli, M. P. (1974). *Self starvation.* London: Chaucer.

Shisslak, C. M., & Crago, M. (1994). Toward a new model for the prevention of eating disorders. In P. Fallon, M. Katzman, & S. Wooley (Eds.), *Feminist perspectives on eating disorders* (pp. 419–437). New York: Guilford.

Smolak, L. (1993). *Adult development.* Englewood Cliffs, NJ: Prentice-Hall.

Smolak, L., & Levine, M. P. (1993). Separation–individuation difficulties and the distinction between bulimia nervosa and anorexia nervosa in college women. *International Journal of Eating Disorders, 14,* 33–41.

Smolak, L., & Levine, M. P. (1994a). Critical issues in the developmental psychopathology of eating disorders. In L. Alexander-Mott & D. B. Lumsden (Eds.), *Understanding eating disorders: Anorexia nervosa, bulimia nervosa, and obesity* (pp 37–60). Washington, DC: Taylor & Francis.

Smolak, L., & Levine, M. P. (1994b). Toward an empirical basis for primary prevention of eating problems with elementary school children. *Eating Disorders: The Journal of Treatment & Prevention, 2,* 293–307.

Smolak, L., Levine, M. P., & Gralen, S. (1993). The impact of puberty and dating on eating problems among middle school girls. *Journal of Youth and Adolescence, 22,* 355–368.

Smolak, L., Levine, M. P., & Schermer, F. (1995). *Evaluation of a curriculum for promotion of healthy eating and positive body image in 4th and 5th grade boys and girls.* Manuscript in preparation.

Smolak, L., Levine, M. P., & Sullins, E. (1990). Are child sexual experiences related to eating disordered attitudes and behaviors in a college sample? *International Journal of Eating Disorders, 9,* 167–178.

Sroufe, L. A. (1989). Pathways to adaptation and maladaptation: Psychopathology as developmental deviation. In D. Cicchetti (Ed.), *Rochester Symposium on Developmental Psychopathology: Vol 1. The emergence of a discipline* (pp. 13–40). Hillsdale, NJ: Lawrence Erlbaum Associates.

Stice, E., Schupak-Neuberg, E., Shaw, H. E., & Stein, R. I. (1994). Relation of media exposure to eating disorder symptomatology: An examination of mediating mechanisms. *Journal of Abnormal Psychology, 103,* 836–840.

Striegel-Moore, R. H. (1992). Prevention of bulimia nervosa: Questions and challenges. In J. H. Crowther, D. L. Tennenbaum, S. E. Hobfoll, & M. A. P. Stephens (Eds.), *The etiology of bulimia nervosa: The individual and familial context* (pp. 203–223). Washington, DC: Hemisphere.

Striegel-Moore, R. H. (1993). Etiology of binge eating: A developmental perspective. In C. G. Fairburn & G. T. Wilson (Eds.), *Binge eating: Nature, assessment, and treatment* (pp. 144–172). New York: Guilford.

Striegel-Moore, R. H., Silberstein, L. R., Frensch, P., & Rodin, J. (1989). A prospective study of disordered eating among college students. *International Journal of Eating Disorders, 8,* 499–509

Striegel-Moore, R. H., Silberstein, L. R., & Rodin, J. (1986). Toward an understanding of risk factors for bulimia. *American Psychologist, 41,* 246–263.

Striegel-Moore, R. H., Silberstein, L. R., & Rodin, J. (1993). The social self in bulimia nervosa: Public self-consciousness, social anxiety, and perceived fraudulence. *Journal of Abnormal Psychology, 102,* 297–303.

Strober, M., & Katz, J. L. (1988). Depression in the eating disorders: A review and analysis of descriptive, family, and biological findings. In D. M. Garner & P. E. Garfinkel (Eds.), *Diagnostic issues in anorexia nervosa and bulimia nervosa* (pp. 80–111). New York: Brunner/Mazel.

Stunkard, A. J. (1959). Eating patterns and obesity. *Psychiatry Quarterly, 33,* 284–295.

Tavris, C. (1992). *The mismeasure of woman.* New York: Simon & Schuster.

Waller, G., & Calam, R. (1994). Parenting and family factors in eating problems. In L. Alexander-Mott & D. B. Lumsden (Eds.), *Understanding eating disorders: Anorexia nervosa, bulimia nervosa, and obesity* (pp. 61–76). Washington, DC: Taylor & Francis.

Wilson, G. T. (1991). The addiction model of eating disorders: A critical analysis. *Advances in Behavior Research & Therapy, 13,* 27–72.

Wolf, N. (1991). *The beauty myth: How images of beauty are used against women.* New York: Morrow.

Wooley, S. C., & Kearney-Cooke, A. (1986). Intensive treatment of bulimia and body-image disturbance. In K. D. Brownell & J. P. Foreyt (Eds.), *Handbook of eating disorders: Physiology, psychology, and treatment of obesity, anorexia, and bulimia* (pp. 476–502). New York: Basic Books.

Author Index

Cohen, P., 197, *201,* 209, *231,* 269, *281,* 344, *361*
Cohen, S., 77, 79, 80, 83, 91, *103*
Cohler, B., 288, *306*
Cohn, L., 48, *53*
Coker, E., 357, *359*
Coker, S., 355, 356, *361*
Cole, A. G., 377, 384, 385, 388, 390, *397*
Colella, J., 357, *361*
Colletti, J., 242, 243, *255*
Colligan, R., 293, *307*
Collins, A., 20, *26*
Collins, M., 35, 36, 48, *53*
Colman, A. M., 123, *130*
Compas, B., 34, 37, 42, *54*
Conger, R., 223, *230*
Conneally, P., 63, *75*
Connell, D. B., 169, *180*
Connors, M. E., 3, *27,* 149, 150, *153,* 272, *279,* 285, 286, 287, 288, 290, 291, 292, 293, 294, 295, 296, 297, 298, 300, 303, 304, *305, 307,* 353, *360,* 381, *394,* 400, 404, 408, *413, 414*
Cook, E. P., 139, *153*
Cooper, A., 300, *308*
Cooper, C. R., 86, *104*
Cooper, P. J., 267, *279*
Copeland, P. M., 313, *338*
Cornblatt, B., 71, *75*
Corter, C., 167, 168, 171, *179*
Cortois, C., 300, *305*
Coscina, D. V., 244, *254,* 319, *337,* 370, 378, *394*
Cox, D., 62, *75*
Crago, M., 263, *283,* 294, *308,* 313, 335, *339,* 341, 342, 343, 345, 347, 348, 349, 352, 355, *362,* 402, *415*
Crandall, C. S., 266, *279*
Crawford, M., 138, 146, *153*
Crisp, A. H., 19, *25, 26,* 183, *200,* 341, 344, 347, *359, 360,* 368, 376, *393, 394,* 399, *413*
Crittenden, P. M., 174, *179*
Crockett, L., 219, *230*
Cronkite, R. C., 98, *103*
Crosby, F. J., 147, *153*
Crowley, M., 141, *153*
Crowther, J. H., 3, *25*
Cudeck, R., 221, *231,* 289, *307,* 352, *361*
Culver, C., 169, 171, 172, 176, *180*
Cummings, E. M., 16, *26,* 301, *308*
Cytrynbaum, S., 209, 212, 213, 224, *230*

D

Dally, P., 320, *338*

Daly, J. A., 260, 262, 268, 269, 274, 275, *279*
Damon, W., 16, 18, *25,* 110, 111, 115, 119, 120, 121, 129, *130, 131,* 403, *413*
Daniels, S., 35, 48, *53,* 411, *415*
D'Aquili, E., 20, *29*
Darby, P., 294, *306*
Dare, C., 368, 370, 380, *395*
d'Avernas, J. R., 318, *338*
Davidson, W., 148, *153*
Davies, B., 81, *103*
Davies, M., 350, *363,* 366, *394*
Davis, C., 287, 303, *305, 310*
Davis, J., 207, *230*
Davis, R., 187, *200,* 267, *280*
Deaux, K., 136, 137, *153*
Debold, E., 253, *257*
DeFries, J. C., 65, 66, 72, *75*
DelBoca, F. K., 137, *152*
Delmas, C., 216, 221, *232*
Dembo, M. H., 90, *104*
Demitrack, M., 303, *305*
Dennett, D. C., 114, *130*
Dennis, A., 215, 224, *233*
DeRosier, M. E., 90, *103*
DeSilva, P., 368, *393*
Desmond, S. M., 242, 244, *254,* 402, *413*
Devlin, M. J., 263, 266, *283,* 367, 377, 382, 384, *393, 396, 397*
deZwaan, M., 266, *279,* 378, *395*
Dias, J., 265, *284*
DiDomenico, L., 239, 244, *254,* 410, *413*
Diehl, N. S., 240, *256*
Dietz, W. H., 238, *254*
Dionne, M., 287, *305*
Dixon, K., 293, 294, 295, 298, 303, *309*
Dixon, L. M., 319, *337*
Dodds, M., 63, *76*
Dohrenwend, B. P., 86, *103*
Dolan, B., 286, 293, *305,* 380, *393*
Doll, H. A., 377, *393*
Dornbusch, S. M., 19, *25*
Downs, A. C., 241, *254*
Drane, J. W., 265, 267, 268, *280*
Drewnowski, A., 286, *305*
Driscoll, R., 357, *360*
Dryfoos, J. G., 252, *254*
Dubbert, B. K., 263, *284,* 386, *397*
DuBois, D. L., 82, 93, 94, 95, 96, 97, 98, *103, 104*
Dubow, E. F., 82, 93, 96, 97, *103*
Dudleston, K., 63, *76*
Duke, P., 220, *230*
Duncan, P. D., *25,* 219, *230*
Dunn, J., 117, *130*
Dunn, P., 289, *305*

Subject Index